Anomie, Strain and Subcultural Theories of Crime

The Library of Essays in Theoretical Criminology

Series Editor: Stuart Henry

Titles in the Series:

Anomie, Strain and Subcultural Theories of Crime

Edited by

Robert Agnew
Emory University, USA

and

Joanne M. Kaufman
University at Albany, SUNY, New York, USA

ASHGATE

Published by
Ashgate Publishing Limited
Wey Court East
Union Road
Farnham
Surrey GU9 7PT
England

Ashgate Publishing Company
Suite 420
101 Cherry Street
Burlington, VT 05401-4405
USA

www.ashgate.com

British Library Cataloguing in Publication Data
Anomie, strain and subcultural theories of crime. -- (The
   library of essays in theoretical criminology)
   1. Crime–Sociological aspects.
   I. Series II. Agnew, Robert, 1953- III. Kaufman, Joanne M.
   364.2-dc22

Library of Congress Control Number: 2010921159

ISBN 9780754629122

Mixed Sources
Product group from well-managed
forests and other controlled sources
www.fsc.org Cert no. SGS-COC-2482
© 1996 Forest Stewardship Council
FSC

Printed and bound in Great Britain by
TJ International Ltd, Padstow, Cornwall

Contents

PART IV   THE DEVELOPMENT OF SUBCULTURAL THEORY

PART V   CONTEMPORARY SUBCULTURAL THEORIES

PART VI   THE DEVELOPMENT OF ANOMIE THEORY

PART VII INSTITUTIONAL-ANOMIE THEORY

Acknowledgements

The editor and publishers wish to thank the following for permission to use copyright material.

American Society of Criminology for the essays: Robert Agnew (1992), 'Foundation for a General Strain Theory of Crime and Delinquency', *Criminology*, **30**, pp. 47–87; Thomas J. Bernard (1990), 'Angry Aggression among the "Truly Disadvantaged"', *Criminology*, **28**, pp. 73–96; Jody Miller (1998), 'Up It Up: Gender and the Accomplishment of Street Robbery', *Criminology*, **36**, pp. 37–65; Eric P. Baumer and Regan Gustafson (2007), 'Social Organization and Instrumental Crime: Assessing the Empirical Validity of Classic and Contemporary Anomie Theories', *Criminology*, **45**, pp. 617–63.

American Sociological Association for the essay: Albert K. Cohen (1965), 'The Sociology of the Deviant Act: Anomie Theory and Beyond', *American Sociological Review*, **30**, pp. 5–14.

Elijah Anderson for the essay: Elijah Anderson (1994), 'The Code of the Streets', *Atlantic Monthly*, **273**, pp. 81–94.

Jock Young for the essay: Jock Young (2010), 'Sub-Cultural Theory: Virtues and Vices'. From http://www.malcolmread.co.uk/JockYoung/

Steven F. Messner, Helmut Thome and Richard Rosenfeld for the essay: Steven F. Messner, Helmut Thome and Richard Rosenfeld (2008), 'Institutions, Anomie, and Violent Crime: Clarifying and Elaborating Institutional-Anomie Theory', *International Journal of Conflict and Violence*, **2**, pp. 163–81.

Sage Publications Inc. for the essays: Thomas J. Bernard (1984), 'Control Criticisms of Strain Theories: An Assessment of Theoretical and Empirical Adequacy', *Journal of Research in Crime and Delinquency*, **21**, pp. 353–72. Copyright © 1984 Sage Publications Inc.; Lisa Broidy and Robert Agnew (1997), 'Gender and Crime: A General Strain Theory Perspective', *Journal of Research in Crime and Delinquency*, **34**, pp. 275–306. Copyright © 1997 Sage Publications, Inc.; Robert Agnew (2001), 'Building on the Foundation of General Strain Theory: Specifying the Types of Strain Most Likely to Lead to Crime and Delinquency', *Journal of Research in Crime and Delinquency*, **38**, pp. 319–61. Copyright © 2001 Sage Publications, Inc.; David J. Bordua (1961), 'Delinquent Subcultures: Sociological Interpretations of Gang Delinquency', *Annals of the American Academy of Political and Social Science*, **338**, pp. 119–36. Copyright © 1961 Sage Publications, Inc.

Simon and Schuster, Inc. for the essay: Emile Durkheim (1951 [1897]), 'Anomic Suicide', in *Suicide*, trans. John A. Spaulding and George Simpson, New York: Free Press, pp. 246–58.

Social Justice for the essay: Nikos Passas (2000), 'Global Anomie, Dysnomie, and Economic Crime: Hidden Consequences of Neoliberalism and Globalization in Russia and Around the World', *Social Justice*, **27**, pp. 16–44. Copyright © 2000 Social Justice. All rights reserved.

Springer for the essay: David F. Greenberg (1977), 'Delinquency and the Age Structure of Society', *Contemporary Crises*, **1**, pp. 189–223. Copyright © 1997 Elsevier Scientific Publishing Co.

Taylor & Francis for the essay: Steven F. Messner (1988), 'Merton's "Social Structure and Anomie": The Road Not Taken', *Deviant Behavior*, **9**, pp. 33–53. Copyright © 1988 Hemisphere Publishing Corporation.

The University of North Carolina Press for the essay: Steven F. Messner and Richard Rosenfeld (1997), 'Political Restraint of the Market and Levels of Criminal Homicide: A Cross-National Application of Institutional-Anomie Theory', *Social Forces*, **75**, pp. 1393–416. Copyright © 1997 The University of North Carolina Press.

Series Preface

Because of its pervasive nature in our mass mediated culture, many believe they are experts in understanding the reasons why offenders violate the law. Parents and schools come high on the public's list of who to blame for crime. Not far behind are governments and legal systems that are believed to be ineffective at deterring offenders – too many legal protections and too few serious sentences. Some learn how to behave inappropriately as children, while others are said to choose crime because of its apparent high reward/low cost opportunity structure. Yet others hang out with the wrong crowd, or live in the wrong neighborhood, or work for the wrong corporation, and may get their kicks from disobeying rules in the company of like-minded others. A few are seen as evil, insane or just plain stupid. While such popular representations of the causes of crime contain glimpses of the criminological reality, understanding why people commit crime is a much more complex matter. Indeed, for this reason the quest to establish the causes of crime has been one of the most elusive searches confronting humankind.

Since the mid-19th century, following the advent of Charles Darwin's *The Origin of Species*, those who sought scientific knowledge to understand crime abandoned philosophical speculation and economic reductionism. In its place they founded the multifaceted interdisciplinary field of criminology. Unlike criminal law and legal theory that explored the logic of prohibitions against offensive behavior, and in contrast to criminal justice that examined the nature and extent of societies' responses to crime through systems of courts, police and penology, criminology's central focus is the systematic examination of the nature, extent and causes of crime. Criminological theory as a subset of criminology, comprises the cluster of explanation seeking to identify the causes or etiology of crime. This *Library of Essays in Theoretical Criminology* is designed to capture the range and depth of the key theoretical perspectives on crime causation.

While there are numerous criminological theories, most can be clustered into 10 or 12 theoretical perspectives. Moreover, each of these broad theoretical frameworks is, itself, rooted in a major academic discipline. The most predominant disciplines influencing criminological theory include: economics, anthropology, biology, psychology, geography, sociology, politics, history, philosophy, as well as the more recent multi-disciplinary fields such as gender studies, critical race studies and postmodernist social theory.

Criminological theories are rarely discrete. Although they often emphasize a particular disciplinary field, they also draw on aspects of other disciplines to strengthen their explanatory power. Indeed, since 1989 a major development in criminological theory has been the emergence of explicitly integrative theoretical approaches (See Gregg Barak, *Integrative Criminology*; Ashgate, 1998). Integrative/interdisciplinary approaches bring together several theories into a comprehensive explanation, usually to address different levels of analysis; these range from the micro-individual and relational approaches common in biology and psychology, to the meso-level institutional explanations that feature in sociological analysis, to the macro-level geographical, political, cultural and historical approaches that deal with societal and global structures and patterns. Recent developments in criminological theory have seen an acceleration of this trend compared with that of single disciplinary explanations of crime (See Stuart Henry and Scott Lukas, *Recent Developments in Criminological Theory*; Ashgate, 2009).

Although there are now over 20 English-language criminological theory textbooks and numerous edited compilations, there is a need to make available to an international audience a series of books that brings together the best of the available theoretical contributions. The advantage of doing this as a series, rather than a single volume, is that the editors are able to mine the field for the most relevant essays that have influenced the present state of knowledge. Each contribution to the series thus contains many chapters, each on a different aspect of the same theoretical approach to crime causation.

In creating this series I have selected outstanding criminologists whose own theories are discussed as part of the literature and I have asked each of them to select a set of the best journal essays to represent the various facets of their theoretical framework. In doing so, I believe that you will receive the best selection of essays available together with an insightful and comparative overview placing each essay in the context of the history of ideas that comprises our search to better understand and explain crime and those who commit it.

STUART HENRY
Series Editor
School of Public Affairs
San Diego State University, USA

Introduction

This volume focuses on three related, but distinct theoretical perspectives in criminology: anomie, strain and subcultural theories. Anomie theories state that crime results from normlessness or a lack of social regulation. The dominant version of the theory states that some societies place much emphasis on the pursuit of certain goals such as monetary success, but little emphasis on the norms regulating goal achievement. As a result, individuals attempt to achieve their goals in the most expedient manner possible, which for some is through crime. This anomie is said to be partly rooted in structural strain, with the inability to achieve cultural goals through legitimate channels reducing the commitment to norms regulating goal achievement.

Strain theories focus on the individual reaction to stressful conditions and events. The early versions of this theory focus on the inability of individuals to achieve monetary success through legitimate channels. More recent versions focus on a range of strains or stressors, such as child abuse, financial problems and racial discrimination. These events and conditions lead to negative emotions, including anger and frustration, which in turn create pressure for corrective action. Crime is one possible response. Crime may allow individuals to reduce or escape from strain (for example theft, running away), seek revenge (for example assault, vandalism) or alleviate negative emotions (for example illicit drug use).

Subcultural theories state that crime stems from membership in groups that hold values and beliefs conducive to crime. These groups may be organized along friendship, neighbourhood, age, gender, class, race/ethnic and/or regional lines. The origin of these groups is usually explained in terms of strain theory, with criminal subcultures emerging as individuals attempt collectively to exploit illicit opportunities for goal achievement, reduce their strain though adopting alternatives goals and values, or express 'resistance' to those who create strain.

These theoretical perspectives were first formulated in criminology by Durkheim (1951 [1897]), Merton (1938; Chapter 2 this volume), Cohen (1955) and Cloward and Ohlin (1960). This volume opens with classic selections by these theorists. The volume then presents a set of essays dealing with strain, subcultural and anomie theories, with two sections on each theory. The first section focuses on the development of the theory and the second on the major contemporary statement(s) of the theory.

The Origins of Anomie, Strain and Subcultural Theory: Classic Statements

Emile Durkheim (1951 [1897]) provided the first modern statement of anomie and strain theory in his classic book: *Suicide: A Study in Sociology*, written at a time when Western societies had recently gone through rapid social change from agrarian communities to modern industrial societies. This volume opens with a selection from that book, describing the nature and sources of anomic suicide. Durkheim (Chapter 1) begins by stating that 'No living being can be happy or even exist unless his needs are sufficiently proportioned to his means' (p. 3).

When individuals lack the means to satisfy their needs or goals, the result is 'constantly renewed torture' (or strain). Durkheim then argues that it is necessary for society to set limits on the goals of individuals, since individuals are incapable of limiting their own goals. Without some limits on aspirations, individuals pursue unlimited or ever-escalating goals. And the misery that results from their inability to achieve such goals may eventually result in suicide. A key function of 'healthy' societies, then, is to limit or regulate the goals that individuals pursue, such that individuals have a reasonable chance of achieving them. But some societies lose their ability to regulate individual goals (and we have the state of anomie or normlessness). This occurs during periods of rapid economic change, including both economic crises and rapid increases in prosperity. Further, Durkheim argues that anomie has become a chronic state in the 'sphere of trade and industry', where economic activity is now largely free of all regulation. As he states, 'greed is aroused without knowing where to find ultimate foothold. Nothing can calm it, since its goal is far beyond all it can attain' (p. 13).

This selection from Durkheim introduces the key elements of both strain and anomie theory (see Agnew, 1997a; Bernard *et al.*, 2009; Cullen and Agnew, 2006). Strain for Durkheim involves unlimited goals and the consequent inability of individuals to achieve their goals, with a focus on economic goals. Strain manifests itself in a range of negative emotions (in the words of Durkheim, 'anger and all the emotions customarily associated with disappointment' (1951, p. 284)). And individuals may cope with such strain through crime and deviance, with Durkheim focusing on suicide. The source of strain for Durkheim is a type of anomie or normlessness, namely the inability of society effectively to regulate or set limits on individual goals. So the absence of regulation by society leads to strain at the individual level.

These arguments of Durkheim have not had a large impact in American criminology, but have had more resonance among European criminologists. Empirically, researchers have not measured strain in terms of the pursuit of unlimited goals (see Agnew, 1997a), although some have explored the impact of rapid social change on crime (for example Bernard *et al.*, 2009; Cao, 2007; Dicristina, 2004; Liu, 2005; Pridemore and Sang-Weon, 2007). Nevertheless, Durkheim's work provided the foundation for those theories of strain and anomie that are now dominant in criminology – beginning with Merton's theory formulated in the mid-twentieth century in Depression-era America.

Robert Merton introduced his version of strain and anomie theory in the 1938 essay reproduced as Chapter 2 in this volume; one of the most widely cited essays in criminology. Merton begins his classic essay by stating that societies differ in the relative emphasis they place on goals and the legitimate means for achieving goals. In some societies, equal emphasis is placed on goals and means. In other societies, much emphasis is placed on goal achievement, but little on the legitimate means that individuals are supposed to follow in pursuing their goals. Such societies reflect the view that 'it's not how you play the game, but whether you win or lose'. In these societies, individuals attempt to achieve their goals in the most expedient way possible, which for some is crime. So, while Durkheim's theory focuses on the failure of societies adequately to regulate goals, Merton's theory of anomie focuses on the failure of societies adequately to regulate the process of goal achievement. Merton's theory of anomie was neglected for a long while, but has recently experienced a major revival – as reflected in the essays in Parts VI and VII (see also the overviews in Agnew, 1997a; Bernard *et al.*, 2009; Cullen and Agnew, 2006).

While the first part of Merton's essay focuses on explaining why some societies have higher rates of crime than others, the second part addresses the question of why some groups within a society commit crimes at higher rates than others. Here Merton develops his version of strain theory. He argues that in the USA everyone – poor as well as rich – is encouraged to strive for the cultural goal of monetary success. But poor individuals often lack the means to achieve such success through legitimate channels, such as getting a good education and then a good job. This creates much frustration and such individuals may cope in a variety of ways, some of which involve crime. For example, individuals may attempt to achieve the goal of monetary success through illegitimate means, such as theft, prostitution and drug-selling. So for Merton, strain results from the presence rather than the absence of society; or at least from the presence of a certain kind of society with a certain set of cultural emphases. This kind of society, epitomized by twentieth-century America and its promotion of the American Dream, encourages individuals to pursue lofty material goals, but prevents or at least limits some individuals from achieving such goals though legitimate channels. Merton also notes that the strain these individuals experience may reduce their commitment to legitimate means, thereby increasing the level of anomie in the larger society. Merton's strain theory is a leading theory of crime in its own right, and it is the direct inspiration for subsequent versions of strain theory – with Albert Cohen (1955) developing the first major revision of Merton's theory. Cohen's theory became known as subcultural strain theory, since he discussed collective rather than individual adaptations to structural strain.

Cohen was a student of Merton and of Edwin Sutherland, who developed differential association theory (a version of social learning theory). This theory states that individuals engage in crime because they associate with others who teach beliefs favourable to crime (Sutherland *et al.*, 1992). Cohen wondered why some individuals held beliefs favourable to delinquency, and he drew on Merton's strain theory to provide an answer. In doing so, he helped develop subcultural theory. In his classic book on *Delinquent Boys* (1955), Cohen argued that delinquent gangs arise as a collective response to a particular type of strain: the inability to achieve middle-class status. Lower-class juveniles, like everyone else, are said to desire such status, which includes not only monetary success but also the respect and admiration of others. However, such boys have trouble achieving middle-class status through legitimate channels, not least because they are judged by middle-class standards of educational success. In particular, they find they lack the skills and habits necessary for success in school, which results in status frustration. If a sufficient number of lower-class boys are in regular interaction with one another, they may develop a collective solution to their status frustration. This solution involves the creation of an alternative status system in which they can successfully compete. Their hostility towards the middle-class people who frustrate them, among other things, leads them to develop an oppositional status system that values everything the middle-class condemns. So, for example, high status is accorded to those boys who show skill in theft, fighting and vandalism. (Chapter 10 by Bordua provides a more detailed overview of Cohen's theory.)

Cohen's use of strain theory to explain the development of criminal subcultures is at the heart of subcultural theory. Individuals face strains involving the inability to achieve monetary success or the broader goal of middle-class status. If conditions are right, these individuals develop a collective solution to their strains, with this solution sometimes taking the form of a criminal subculture. Cohen initially argued that the members of criminal subcultures unconditionally approve of crimes such as theft and violence. He later backed away from this extreme position and, drawing on the work of criminologists such as Sykes and Matza (1957), argued that the members of these subcultures more often justify or excuse their criminal acts (Cohen and Short, 1958).

Richard Cloward and Lloyd Ohlin (1960) elaborated on Cohen in their text on *Delinquency and Opportunity*. Like Cohen, Cloward and Ohlin argued that strains, particularly shared strains that are viewed as unjust and attributed to the larger social system, often lead individuals to form or join criminal subcultures. And these subcultures are a method for coping with strains; for example, the subcultures may focus on the pursuit of monetary success through illegitimate channels. Cloward and Ohlin went on to state that there are different types of criminal subcultures, some focused on theft, some on violence and some on drug use. And they discussed the factors that influence the development of these different types of subcultures, with a focus on neighbourhood characteristics. (See Chapter 10 for further information.) The types of subcultures described by Cloward and Ohlin are rarely found in pure form. For example, one rarely if ever finds a criminal subculture that engages only in violence. Members of criminal subcultures typically engage in a range of criminal acts. Nevertheless, subcultures do differ from one another in certain ways, with some focusing on particular types of crime, such as white-collar crime (Agnew, 2000).

In Chapter 3, Cloward does not discuss the development of criminal subcultures, but does make a critical point regarding the relationship between strain and such subcultures. Merton argued that strained individuals *may* turn to crime and he briefly discussed those factors that influence whether they turn to crime. But Cloward argues that Merton neglected a key factor: the availability of *illegitimate* means. In particular, Cloward argues that whether strained individuals turn to crime is strongly influenced by their exposure to criminal subcultures. These subcultures provide the means to engage in crime; in particular, they teach the skills necessary for certain types of crime, present beliefs that justify or excuse crime, and provide opportunities to engage in crime. Strained individuals exposed to such subcultures are therefore much more likely to engage in crime. Cloward discusses certain of the factors that influence exposure to criminal subcultures, factors such as class position and neighbourhood characteristics.

Cohen elaborates on these ideas in Chapter 4. He argues that the way in which individuals interpret and react to the strains they experience is heavily influenced by the experience of others – particularly those 'reference others' with whom they compare themselves. For example, individuals look to others in their reference group when setting their goals, determining how successful they are in achieving their goals and deciding whether crime is an appropriate strategy for achieving their goals. While these others may not necessarily constitute a criminal subculture, Cohen notes the important role that such subcultures play in the process leading from strain to crime. In sum, Cohen and Cloward and Ohlin extended Merton's strain theory in fundamental ways. Most notably, they linked strain and differential association theories, arguing that criminal subcultures frequently emerge as a collective response to shared strains, particularly the inability to achieve monetary and status goals. Further, these subcultures play a key role in the interpretation of and reaction to strains. These ideas are discussed further in Parts IV and V on subcultural theory.

The Development of Strain Theory

The strain theories of Merton, Cohen, and Cloward and Ohlin were perhaps the leading explanations of crime during the 1950s and 1960s. Such theories provided a compelling explanation for what, at the time, was believed to be the strong concentration of crime among lower-class individuals (a belief based partly on arrest data). Further, policy-makers drew heavily on these theories when designing the 'War on Poverty', one of the largest planned programmes of social change in the history of the USA (Lloyd Ohlin was a consultant to the programme, drawn in by Robert Kennedy who had read *Delinquency and Opportunity*). The War on Poverty programme was designed to reduce a range of social problems, including crime, by making it easier for individuals to achieve monetary success through legitimate channels (Empey *et al.*, 1999). Many of the programmes that were part of the War on Poverty have since been dismantled, but a few remain, such as Job Corps and Project Headstart – a preschool enrichment programme.

Strain theory, however, came under heavy attack in the late 1960s and was on the verge of being abandoned by the early 1980s. Several major criticisms were made against the theory. Most notably, self-report studies suggested that the relationship between social class and crime was weak or non-existent, contrary to the claims of strain theory (see Agnew, 2009 for an overview). Also, a series of studies found that conventional crime was highest *not* among those who desired a lot but expected a little (as strain theory would predict), but among those with both low aspirations and low expectations (Agnew, 2000; Kornhauser, 1978). Further, control theorists argued that strain is not a variable since all individuals desire more than they possess (see, for example, Hirschi, 1969; Kornhauser, 1978). Since strain is not a variable, it cannot explain variation in crime.

Thomas Bernard reviews these and other criticisms of strain theory in Chapter 5. And he finds these criticisms unconvincing (also see Agnew, Chapter 7 this volume; Burton and Cullen, 1992). Subsequent research has tended to support the arguments of Bernard. For example, Bernard states that the early self-report studies of the relationship between class and delinquency are flawed because they fail to sample the very poor and they focus on minor forms of delinquency. More recent self-report studies that correct for these problems usually find that very poor juveniles are more involved in serious delinquency (see Agnew, 2009). Also, Bernard is critical of how certain researchers measured the inability to achieve monetary goals. More recent studies, employing better measures of monetary strain, have found that such strain is related to crime (for example Agnew *et al.*, 1996, 2008; Baron, 2004; Baumer and Gustafson, Chapter 18 this volume; Cernkovich *et al.*, 2000; Hagan and McCarthy, 1997; Kubrin *et al.*, 2009). In particular, individuals who are dissatisfied with their financial situation or who are experiencing serious financial problems are more likely to engage in crime. There is therefore some reason to believe that the attacks on strain theory were misguided.

At the same time, these attacks did prompt a number of revisions and extensions in the early strain theories (for example Agnew, 2000; Bernard, Chapter 12 this volume; Elliott *et al.*, 1979; Passas and Agnew, 1997). Chapter 6 by David Greenberg represents one of the best. Like many of the revisions, Greenberg substantially expands the focus of the early strain theories – arguing that strain may involve the inability to achieve a number of different goals, not simply monetary success or middle-class status. Greenberg wants to explain why adolescents – especially adolescent males – have higher rates of offending than other groups. In doing so, he argues that adolescents pursue a variety of goals, including popularity with peers, money (which facilitates the achievement of popularity), autonomy and the achievement of masculine status. Certain recent research suggests that inability to achieve autonomy and masculinity goals does contribute to crime, although the relationship between monetary goals, popularity goals and *adolescent* offending is more complex (see, for example, Agnew and Brezina, 1997; Anderson, 1999; McCarthy and Hagan, 2004; Messerschmidt, 1993; Piquero and Brezina, 2001; Wright *et al.*, 2001). To illustrate, the achievement of monetary goals may reduce strain on the one hand, but provide adolescents with the freedom and means to engage in delinquent acts such as drug use on the other. Greenberg also discusses certain of the factors that influence the response to strain, with a focus on the costs of crime. And he examines why adolescents in contemporary societies often have difficulty achieving the goals he lists, with his analysis drawing heavily on critical criminology.

Greenberg's theory and other revisions substantially expanded the scope of the early strain theories, pointing to both new types of strain and additional factors influencing the effect of strain on crime. In doing so, these revisions set the stage for Robert Agnew's general strain theory of crime, now the dominant version of strain theory.

General Strain Theory

Chapter 7 by Robert Agnew presents the first complete statement of general strain theory (GST). Agnew drew on prior versions of strain theory and a range of other literatures to substantially expand the scope of strain theory. GST focuses on three major categories of strain. Drawing on prior strain theories, it examines the inability of individuals to achieve positively valued goals, including monetary, status, autonomy and other goals. Drawing on the stress literature, it examines the loss of positively valued things or persons (for example romantic break-up, death of a loved one) and the presentation of negative stimuli (for example bullying, bad school experiences, criminal victimization).

GST more fully describes the reasons why such strain may lead to crime. Most notably, it states that strains lead to negative emotions such as frustration, depression and anger. These emotions create pressure for corrective action, and crime is one possible response. Crime may reduce strain (for example theft, running away from abusive parents), allow one to obtain revenge against the source of strain or related targets (for example assault) or alleviate negative emotions (for example illicit drug use). Anger is said to be a key emotion because it energizes the individual for action, lowers inhibitions and creates a desire for revenge. Finally, GST presents the most comprehensive list of those factors that influence or condition the effect of strains on crime. These factors include coping skills and resources, social support, social control, beliefs regarding crime and association with delinquent friends.

GST has stimulated much research on the links between strain and crime. Data suggest that the strains identified in the theory are associated with crime.[1] There is some evidence that

---

[1] See, for example, Agnew and White (1992), Bao *et al.* (2004), Baron (2004), Froggio and Agnew (2007), Hoffman and Su (1997), Moon *et al.* (2008), Paternoster and Mazerolle (1994), Piquero and Sealock (2000) and Sigfusdottir *et al.* (2004).

these strains lead to a variety of negative emotions, particularly anger.[2] There is also some evidence that negative emotions, particularly situationally based emotions, partly mediate the effect of strains on crime.[3] The research on those factors said to condition the effect of strains on crime, however, has produced mixed results.[4] GST was originally developed to explain why some individuals are more likely than others to engage in crime. The theory has since been extended to explain group differences in crime, including age (Agnew, 1997b), community (Agnew, 1999) and race differences (Kaufman *et al.*, 2008). Chapter 8 by Lisa Broidy and Robert Agnew applies GST to gender and crime. Males are said to be more likely to engage in crime because they more often experience strains conducive to crime, react to such strains with rage and possess those factors that increase the likelihood of a criminal response to strain (for example they more often associate with delinquent peers). Broidy and Agnew also explain why some females engage in crime – for example, they note that certain strains – such as sexual assault and interpersonal network stressors – are especially relevant to female offending. This essay has simulated much research on gender, strain and crime.[5]

Chapter 9 by Robert Agnew presents a major extension of GST. Agnew notes that some strains seem to increase crime, while others do not. This of course poses a major problem for strain theory, and in Chapter 9 Agnew identifies the characteristics of those strains most likely to cause crime. In brief, such strains are high in magnitude, are seen as unjust or unfair, are associated with low social control and create some pressure or incentive for crime. This essay has also stimulated some research.[6]

In sum, GST has become one of the leading social psychological theories of crime. Future researchers are likely to better measure strain and the emotional reaction to strain, examine a broader range of deviant responses to strain (for example suicide, purging behaviours) and continue to explore those factors said to condition the effect of strain on crime and apply GST to the explanation of group differences in offending.

The Development of Subcultural Theory

Strain may lead directly to crime or may contribute to the development of criminal subcultures, which lead to crime. The most distinguishing characteristic of these subcultures is that the members hold values and beliefs conducive to crime. There has been much research on these subcultures, particularly in the USA and England.[7] Such research has examined the origins of

---

[2] See, for example, Bao *et al.* (2004), Brezina (1996), Broidy (2001), Mazerolle and Piquero (1997) and Piquero and Sealock (2000).

[3] See, for example, Bao *et al.* (2004), Broidy (2001), Jang and Johnson (2003), Mazerolle and Piquero (1997, 1998), Mazerolle *et al.* (2003) and Tittle *et al.* (2008).

[4] See, for example, Agnew and White (1992), Jang and Johnson (2003, 2005), Mazerolle and Maahs (2000), Mazerolle and Piquero (1997), Paternoster and Mazerolle (1994) and Tittle *et al.* (2008).

[5] See, for example, Baron (2007), Eitle (2002), Hay (2003), Hoffman and Su (1997), Jang (2007), Jang and Johnson (2005), Mazerolle (1998), Piquero and Sealock (2004) and Sharp *et al.* (2001).

[6] See, for example, Baron (2004), Froggio and Agnew (2007), Hay and Evans (2006), Jang and Johnson (2005), Moon *et al.* (2009) and Sigfusdottir *et al.* (2008).

[7] For overviews, see Agnew (2000), Bernard *et al.* (2009), Brake (1985), Brownfield (1996), Cullen and Agnew (2006), Messerschmidt (1993), Tanner (1978) and Williams (2007).

these subcultures, with strain explanations being dominant. Most commonly, these subcultures are said to represent an attempt to cope with shared strains, particularly the inability to achieve monetary or status goals. The research on subcultures has also devoted much attention to the composition of subcultures. These subcultures are usually said to exist among lower-class individuals, particularly adolescent males, since the monetary, status and other problems that contribute to subcultural formation are often most acute here. Criminal subcultures, however, have been located in a wide range of groups, including middle-class adolescents, Southerners in the USA, certain immigrant groups, executives in certain corporations and a range of race and ethnic groups.

Further, researchers have devoted much attention to the nature of these subcultures, particularly the values and beliefs they possess. There has been some debate here over whether the members of subcultures unconditionally approve of crime or hold beliefs that simply justify or excuse crime. The most common view is that crimes are justified or excused, although certain minor crimes – such as drug use and gambling – may be unconditionally approved. Also, there has been some debate over the extent to which subcultures are organized around particular types of crime, such as theft or drug use, or are more general. Most criminal subcultures seem to possess beliefs conducive to a range of crimes, although some are focused on particular crimes. Finally, researchers have devoted much attention to the impact of subcultures on individuals, particularly the ways in which subcultures contribute to crime. Subcultures are said to foster crime by teaching beliefs favourable to crime, differentially reinforcing crime, providing models for crime, teaching the special skills and techniques necessary to engage in certain crimes (for example white-collar crime, drug-selling), providing opportunities to engage in crime and reducing concern about the consequences of crime.

It is impossible adequately to describe the extensive research on criminal subcultures in a few chapters, but the two essays in this section provide excellent overviews. Chapter 10 by David Bordua discusses the origin of subcultural research in the USA, with a focus on delinquent subcultures. Bordua describes the seminal contributions of Cohen and of Cloward and Ohlin, as well as those by Thrasher (1927) and Miller (1958). And Bordua discusses certain of the debates regarding the origin and nature of subcultures, many of which continue today. The work described in Bordua provided the foundation for subsequent work on criminal subcultures, much of which is described and critiqued in Chapter 11 by Jock Young.

The essay by Young, in particular, provides an excellent overview of the English work on subcultural theory. Although Cohen and Cloward and Ohlin developed subcultural theory in the USA, work on the theory also flourished in England. Many excellent works on subcultural theory and on particular deviant and criminal subcultures were produced, such as those by Downes (1966), S. Cohen (1972), Willis (1977) and Brake (1985). Chapter 11 begins by describing the core assumptions of subcultural theory – all centred on the idea that subcultures develop in response to problems faced by their members. Young then describes the major works on deviant and criminal subcultures, noting the ways in which the theory evolved. Most notably, subcultural theory in England took a Marxist turn, with subcultures often being portrayed as a method of expressing resistance to class and race/ethnic oppression. Finally, Young discusses recent developments in subcultural theory, including the role of the mass media in fostering values conducive to crime in what is an emergent 'cultural criminology' (see also Ferrell *et al.*, 2008).

Contemporary Subcultural Theories

There has been a recent resurgence in subcultural theory in the USA, with most work attempting to explain the higher rates of violence in poor, inner-city communities. This work was stimulated partly by the growth in very poor, largely African-American inner-city communities in recent decades (Wilson, 1987) and partly by the sharp increase in violence that occurred in such communities from the mid-1980s to early 1990s (Agnew, 2009). While such violence is usually explained in terms of social disorganization theory, several researchers have explicitly or implicitly argued that the strains characterizing such communities have contributed to the development of violent subcultures (for example Bourgois, 2003; MacLeod, 1995; Sullivan, 1989).

Chapter 12 by Thomas Bernard represents one of the most sophisticated attempts to apply subcultural theory to the explanation of inner-city violence. Bernard traces the development of violent subcultures in such communities to the strains associated with urban life, low social position and racial and ethnic discrimination; strains exacerbated by the social isolation of poor, inner-city communities. These strains, however, do not lead to values that directly approve of violence. Rather, they lead to the development of subcultures that foster what Bernard calls 'angry aggression'. These subcultures, in particular, encourage individuals to blame their problems on others, to experience intense anger in response to these problems and to cope with this anger through violence. Bernard's ideas are compatible with the research on anger and aggression, but they have not yet been empirically tested. Many of his ideas, however, have informed general strain theory.

Chapter 13 by Elijah Anderson is less theoretical and more descriptive in nature. In particular Anderson describes those values conducive to violence in a poor inner-city community. These values, part of the 'code of the street', are said to exert an especially powerful effect on adolescent and young adult males. Among other things, they encourage individuals to be especially sensitive to slights and provocation and to respond to them in a violent manner. And while Anderson does not draw explicitly on strain theory to explain the origin of the code of the street, he traces the code to several strains prevalent in poor, inner-city, African-American communities. Such strains include the inability to achieve respect through conventional channels, the failure of the police to respond when disputes arise and the general tensions associated with poverty. Anderson provides perhaps the best description of a contemporary subculture of violence, and research suggests that individuals who adopt the code of the street are more likely to engage in violence (Brezina *et al.*, 2004; Mullins, 2006; Stewart and Simons, 2006; Wilkinson, 2003). Research, however, suggests that blacks are no more likely than whites to adopt the code. The code seems to be more common among those who live in disadvantaged communities, poor individuals, males, those who associate with violent peers and those who experience certain types of strain – such as harsh discipline, criminal victimization and limited opportunities for success (Agnew, 2000; Cullen and Agnew, 2006).

Most of the work on subcultures and violence has focused on males. Males are said to be more likely to be a part of violent subcultures, a fact that helps explain their higher rates of violence. In fact, some accounts state that a key component of violent subcultures is a particular conception of masculinity – one stressing such things as toughness and dominance. And violence is said to be a 'resource' for accomplishing masculinity, particularly when conventional resources are unavailable (Messerschmidt, 1993). But as Jody Miller points out in Chapter 14, females also engage in violence and it is critical to explain such violence. Miller's essay is based on interviews with male and female robbers in a poor urban area, and examines the similarities and differences between female and male robberies. While female violence often involves an effort to resist victimization, this is not the case with the female robbers in her sample. These females often commit robberies for many of the same reasons as males, such as a desire to obtain money and increase their status. At the same time, gender – including gendered norms and values – does structure the nature of robberies committed by males and females. Miller's essay reminds those working in the subcultural and other traditions to attend to the gendered nature of crime and to be sensitive to the similarities and differences in the causes of crime across gender.

The Development of Anomie Theory

Merton's 1938 article on 'Social Structure and Anomie' (Chapter 2) contained both an anomie theory, designed to explain societal differences in crime, and a strain theory, designed to explain differences in crime within a society (see also Merton, 1964, 1968). Strain theory attracted much attention, but anomie theory was neglected for many years. This began to change in the 1980s, with several researchers calling for new attention to be paid to Merton's anomie theory (for example Bernard, 1987; Cullen, 1984; Rosenfeld, 1989). Chapter 15 by Steven Messner clearly distinguishes between Merton's strain and anomie theories, argues that these theories are independent and encourages researchers to focus on and test Merton's anomie theory.

The work of Messner and others led to the further development of anomie theory and the application of this theory to issues such as organizational deviance and corporate crime (see, for example, Cohen, 1995; Passas, 1990; Vaughan, 1983, 1996, 1997). Vaughan (1996, 1997), for example, drew on anomie theory in an attempt to understand and explain NASA's role in the *Challenger* disaster. The rediscovery of anomie theory continued with two edited volumes in the mid-1990s that brought together important theoretical and empirical pieces: *The Legacy of Anomie Theory* (Adler and Laufer, 1995) and *The Future of Anomie Theory* (Passas and Agnew, 1997). More recently, several researchers have tested anomie theory at the macro-level within a single country or across countries, with qualified support (Baumer and Gustafson, Chapter 18 this volume; Cao, 2007; Gill, 1999; Stephens, 1994; Zhao, 2008). And certain others have explored the micro-level implications of anomie theory (see Konty, 2005; Menard, 1995).

Chapter 16 by Nikos Passas provides an excellent illustration of the application of anomie theory, with Passas drawing on the theory to explain transnational crime. In particular, Passas explores the ways in which neoliberalism and globalization have contributed to anomie, dysnomie and economic forms of crime. Passas contends that globalization and neoliberal economic policies have led to increases in relative deprivation and the loss of the traditional safety nets in various countries around the globe. These effects, in turn, have contributed to increases in crime, especially economic crime. A case study of Russia illustrates these points. Passas provides a timely and critical application and extension of Merton's anomie theory, and his work has led other scholars to examine both transnational crime and crime in the former Soviet-bloc countries (see Bennett, 2004; Karstedt, 2003; Sheptycki *et al.*, 2005; Siegel *et al.*, 2003; Zhang and Chin, 2002).

Several researchers continue to develop and apply Merton's anomie theory (see Baumer, 2007; Featherstone and Deflem, 2003; Heckert and Heckert, 2004; Marwah and Deflem, 2006; Murphy and Robinson, 2008). Thus, a theory that was largely neglected for over 40 years is now the subject of much attention.

Institutional-Anomie Theory

The most influential extension of Merton's anomie theory is Messner and Rosenfeld's (2007) institutional-anomie theory (IAT). Chapter 17 presents an overview of the theory and a key cross-national test of it. Like Merton (Chapter 2 this volume), Steven Messner and Richard Rosenfeld focus on explaining why the USA has a high rate of serious crime. Drawing heavily on Merton, they argue that this high crime rate is partly due to the fact that the cultural system in the USA encourages everyone to place great emphasis on material success but little emphasis on the legitimate means to achieve such success. They refer to this exaggerated emphasis on material success as the 'American Dream', and they build on Merton by more fully describing the origins of the Dream and its components.

Messner and Rosenfeld move beyond Merton by arguing that the cultural emphasis on monetary success is paralleled by an institutional structure that is dominated by the economy and economic concerns. That is, the other major institutions in the society, including the family, educational system and political system, are said to be subservient to the economy. This institutional imbalance of power also helps explain the high crime rate in the USA. The dominance of the economy weakens other institutions, making it more difficult for them effectively to socialize and control individuals. In particular, non-economic institutions must accommodate themselves to the requirements of the economy (for example parents must often work long hours, neglecting their families). Non-economic roles are devalued (for example homemakers and teachers have less status than business people). And economic norms penetrate non-economic institutions (for example schools are organized in a competitive manner, with students competing with one another for rewards).

Chapter 17 also presents a cross-national test of the theory. Messner and Rosenfeld roughly index the dominance of the economy by examining the extent to which countries have social policies that protect individuals from the vicissitudes of the economic market (for example generous welfare policies). They argue that societies with such policies should have lower rates of crime. A cross-national test with data from 40 nations supports this hypothesis. Additional research, some based on cross-national data and some on data from areas within a country, has also provided support for the theory,[8] although not all studies have been fully supportive.[9]

The majority of the empirical research on IAT focuses on the institutional imbalance of power, with researchers attempting to measure the extent to which the economy dominates other institutions. Chapter 18 by Eric Baumer and Regan Gustafson describes one of the few studies to examine both the cultural and institutional aspects of IAT – as well as Merton's

---

[8]   See Chamlin and Cochran (1995), Cullen *et al.* (2004), Hannon and DeFronzo (1998), Karstedt and Farrall (2006), Maume and Lee (2003), Pratt and Godsey (2003), Savolainen (2000) and Stucky (2003).

[9]   See Batton and Jensen (2002), Jensen (2002), Kim and Pridemore (2005a, 2005b), Piquero and Piquero (1998) and Schoepfer and Piquero (2006).

anomie theory. Most notably, Baumer and Gustafson measure the extent to which people place great stress on economic success, but little on the legitimate means for obtaining such success. Baumer and Gustafson's study provides support for aspects of both IAT and Merton's anomie theory, and they call on researchers to integrate both theories.

Chapter 19 by Steven Messner, Helmut Thome and Richard Rosenfeld summarizes the research on IAT, more fully describes certain of the core concepts in theory, extends the theory in important ways and discusses directions for further research. This essay appeared in a special issue of the *International Journal of Conflict and Violence* focused on anomie (see Bjerregaard and Cochran, 2008; Frerichs *et al.*, 2008; Stults and Baumer, 2008). Others have also suggested revisions and extensions in IAT (for example Bernburg, 2002; Chamlin and Cochran, 2007; Messner, 2003). IAT, in sum, has become the dominant version of anomie theory and one of the leading macro-theories of crime in general, distinguished by its focus on both the cultural and institutional arrangements in societies and communities.

Summary

Anomie, strain and subcultural theories have evolved a good deal from their initial statements by Durkheim and Merton. The leading contemporary strain theory, general strain theory, points to a much broader range of strains conducive to crime, more fully describes why these strains cause crime and provides the most complete list of factors that condition the effect of strains on crime. Further, this theory has been used to explain not only individual and class differences in crime, but also gender, race/ethnic, community and age differences. The recent work on subcultural theory focuses on a range of criminal subcultures, provides more nuanced descriptions of these subcultures and their origins, and better describes the varied mechanisms by which these subcultures contribute to individual offending. Finally, the dominant version of anomie theory, institutional anomie theory, better describes those value orientations that encourage the unrestrained pursuit of monetary success, accounts for the development of these values and devotes special attention to those institutional arrangements that promote crime.

In an interesting twist, however, the continued development of strain, anomie and subcultural theories has been accompanied by their increased divergence. Strain, anomie and/or subcultural theories were closely linked in the work of Durkheim, Merton, Cohen, and Cloward and Ohlin. In Durkheim, for example, anomie at the societal level contributed to strain at the individual level. In Merton, strain at the institutional level contributed to anomie. In Cohen and in Cloward and Ohlin, shared strains led to the development of criminal subcultures. Recent work, however, has often ignored these links. Certain examinations of criminal subcultures, particularly in the USA, fail to explicitly draw on Cohen and Cloward and Ohlin (although such work implicitly traces such subcultures to strains of various types). Institutional anomie theory devotes little attention to the ways in which the American Dream and the institutional imbalance of power create strain at the individual level. Likewise, general strain theory devotes little attention to the ways in which structural and cultural features of the larger society contribute to strain. As these theories continue to develop it is hoped that the links between them will be rediscovered and strengthened.

References

Adler, Freda and Laufer, William S. (eds) (1995), *The Legacy of Anomie Theory*, New Brunswick, NJ: Transaction.

Agnew, Robert (1997a), 'The Nature and Determinants of Strain: Another Look at Durkheim and Merton', in N. Passas and R. Agnew (eds), *The Future of Anomie Theory*, Boston: Northeastern University Press, pp. 27–51.

Agnew, Robert (1997b), 'Stability and Change in Crime over the Life Course: A Strain Theory Explanation', in T. Thornberry (ed.), *Developmental Theories of Crime and Delinquency*, New Brunswick, NJ: Transaction, pp. 101–32.

Agnew, Robert (1999), 'A General Strain Theory of Community Differences in Crime Rates', *Journal of Research in Crime and Delinquency*, **36**(2), pp. 123–55.

Agnew, Robert (2000), 'Sources of Criminality: Strain and Subcultural Theories', in J. F. Sheley (ed.), *Criminology: A Contemporary Handbook*, Belmont, CA: Wadsworth, pp. 349–71.

Agnew, Robert (2009), *Juvenile Delinquency: Causes and Control*, New York: Oxford University Press.

Agnew, Robert and Brezina, Timothy (1997), 'Relational Problems with Peers, Gender, and Delinquency', *Youth and Society*, **29**, pp. 84–111.

Agnew, Robert and White, Helen Raskin (1992), 'An Empirical Test of General Strain Theory', *Criminology*, **30**(4), pp. 475–99.

Agnew, Robert, Cullen, Francis T., Burton, Velmer S., Evans, T. David and Dunaway, Gregg R. (1996), 'A New Test of Classic Strain Theory', *Justice Quarterly*, **13**, pp. 681–704.

Agnew, Robert, Matthews, Shelley Keith, Bucher, Jacob, Welcher, Adria N. and Keyes, Corey (2008), 'Socioeconomic Status, Economic Problems, and Delinquency', *Youth & Society*, **40**, pp. 59–181.

Anderson, Elijah (1999), *Code of the Street*, New York: W.W. Norton.

Bao, W.N., Haas, A. and Pi, Y. (2004), 'Life Strain, Negative Emotions, and Delinquency: An Empirical Test of General Strain Theory in the People's Republic of China', *International Journal of Offender Therapy and Comparative Criminology*, **48**(3), pp. 281–97.

Baron, Stephen W. (2004), 'General Strain, Street Youth and Crime: A Test of Agnew's Revised Theory', *Criminology*, **42**(2), pp. 457–84.

Baron, Stephen W. (2007), 'Street Youth, Gender, Financial Strain, and Crime: Exploring Broidy and Agnew's Extension to General Strain Theory', *Deviant Behavior*, **28**(3), pp. 273–302.

Batton, Candice and Jensen, Gary (2002), 'Decommodification and Homicide Rates in the 20th-Century United States', *Homicide Studies*, **6**, pp. 6–38.

Baumer, Eric P. (2007), 'Untangling Research Puzzles in Merton's Multilevel Anomie Theory', *Theoretical Criminology*, **11**, pp. 63–93.

Bennett, Richard R. (2004), 'Comparative Criminology and Criminal Justice Research: The State of our Knowledge', *Justice Quarterly*, **21**(1), pp. 1–21.

Bernard, Thomas J. (1987), 'Testing Structural Strain Theories', *Journal of Research in Crime and Delinquency*, **24**(4), pp. 262–80.

Bernard, Thomas J., Snipes, Jeffrey B. and Gerould, Alexander L. (2009), *Vold's Theoretical Criminology*, New York: Oxford University Press.

Bernburg, Jon Gunnar (2002), 'Anomie, Social Change and Crime: A Theoretical Examination of Institutional-Anomie Theory', *British Journal of Criminology*, **42**(4), pp. 729–42.

Bjerregaard, Beth and Cochran, John K. (2008), 'Want Amid Plenty: Developing and Testing a Cross-National Measure of Anomie', *International Journal of Conflict and Violence*, **2**(2), pp. 182–93.

Bourgois, Philippe (2003), *In Search of Respect*, Cambridge: Cambridge University Press.

Brake, Michael (1985), *Comparative Youth Culture: The Sociology of Youth Cultures and Youth Subcultures in America, Britain, and Canada*, London: Routledge.

Brezina, Timothy (1996), 'Adapting to Strain: An Examination of Delinquent Coping Responses', *Criminology*, **34**(1), pp. 39–60.

Brezina, Timothy, Agnew, Robert, Cullen, Francis T. and Wright, John Paul (2004), 'The Code of the Street', *Youth Violence and Juvenile Justice*, **2**, pp. 303–28.

Broidy, Lisa M. (2001), 'A Test of General Strain Theory', *Criminology*, **39**(1), pp. 9–36.

Brownfield, David (1996), 'Subcultural Theories of Crime and Delinquency', in J. Hagan, A. R. Gillis and D. Brownfield (eds), *Criminological Controversies*, Boulder, CO: Westview, pp. 99–123.

Burton, Velmer S., Jr and Cullen, Francis T. (1992), 'The Empirical Status of Strain Theory', *Journal of Crime and Justice*, **15**, pp. 1–30.

Cao, Liqun (2007), 'Returning to Normality: Anomie and Crime in China', *International Journal of Offender Therapy and Comparative Criminology*, **51**(1), pp. 40–51.

Cernkovich, Stephen A., Giordano, Peggy C. and Rudolph, Jennifer L. (2000), 'Race, Crime, and the American Dream', *Journal of Research in Crime and Delinquency*, **37**, pp. 131–70.

Chamlin, Mitchell B. and Cochran, John K. (1995), 'Assessing Messner and Rosenfeld's Institutional Anomie Theory: A Partial Test', *Criminology*, **33**(3), pp. 411–29.

Chamlin, Mitchell B. and Cochran, John K. (2007), 'An Evaluation of the Assumptions that Underlie Institutional Anomie Theory', *Theoretical Criminology*, **11**, pp. 39–61.

Cloward, Richard A. and Ohlin, Lloyd E. (1960), *Delinquency and Opportunity*, New York: Free Press.

Cohen, Albert K. (1955), *Delinquent Boys*, New York: Free Press.

Cohen, Albert K. and Short, James F., Jr (1958), 'Research in Delinquent Subcultures', *Journal of Social Issues*, **14**, pp. 20–37.

Cohen, Deborah Vidaver (1995), 'Ethics and Crime in Business Firms: Organizational Culture and the Impact of Anomie', in F. Adler and W.S. Laufer (eds), *The Legacy of Anomie Theory*, New Brunswick, NJ: Transaction, pp. 183–206.

Cohen, Stanley (1972), *Folk Devils and Moral Panics*, London: Routledge.

Cullen, Francis T. (1984), *Rethinking Crime and Deviance Theory: The Emergence of a Structuring Tradition*, Totowa, NJ: Rowman and Allanheld.

Cullen, Francis T. and Agnew, Robert (2006), *Criminological Theory: Past to Present*, New York: Oxford University Press.

Cullen, John B., Parboteeah, K. Praveen and Hoegl, Martin (2004), 'Cross-National Differences in Managers' Willingness to Justify Ethically Suspect Behaviors: A Test of Institutional Anomie Theory', *Academy of Management Journal*, **47**(3), pp. 411–21.

Dicristina, Bruce (2004), 'Durkheim's Theory of Homicide and the Confusion of the Empirical Literature', *Theoretical Criminology*, **8**, pp. 57–91.

Downes, David (1966), *The Delinquent Solution*, London: Routledge & Kegan Paul.

Durkheim, Emile (1951 [1897]), *Suicide: A Study in Sociology*, New York: Free Press.

Eitle, David J. (2002), 'Exploring a Source of Deviance-Producing Strain for Females: Perceived Discrimination and General Strain Theory', *Journal of Criminal Justice*, **30**(5), pp. 429–42.

Elliott, Delbert S., Ageton, Suzanne S. and Canter, Rachel (1979), 'An Integrated Theoretical Perspective on Delinquent Behavior', *Journal of Research in Crime and Delinquency*, **25**, pp. 214–41.

Empey, LaMar T., Stafford, Mark and Hay, Carter H. (1999), *American Delinquency: Its Meaning and Construction*, Belmont, CA: Wadsworth.

Featherstone, Richard and Deflem, Mathieu (2003), 'Anomie and Strain: Context and Consequences of Merton's Two Theories', *Sociological Inquiry*, **73**(4), pp. 471–89.

Ferrell, Jeff, Hayward, Keith and Young, Jock (2008), *Cultural Criminology*, Los Angeles: Sage.

Frerichs, Sabine, Münch, Richard and Sander, Monika (2008), 'Anomic Crime in Post-Welfarist Societies: Cult of the Individual, Integration Patterns, and Rates of Violent Crime', *International Journal of Conflict and Violence*, **2**(2), pp. 194–214.

Froggio, Giacinto and Agnew, Robert (2007), 'The Relationship between Crime and "Objective" versus "Subjective" Strains', *Journal of Criminal Justice*, **35**(1), pp. 81–87.

Gill, Anthony (1999), 'Government Regulation, Social Anomie and Protestant Growth in Latin America: A Cross-National Analysis', *Rationality and Society*, **11**(3), pp. 287–316.

Hagan, John and McCarthy, Bill (1997), *Mean Streets*, New York: Cambridge University Press.

Hannon, Lance and DeFronzo, James (1998), 'The Truly Disadvantaged, Public Assistance, and Crime', *Social Problems*, **45**, pp. 383–92.

Hay, Carter (2003), 'Family Strain, Gender, and Delinquency', *Sociological Perspectives*, **46**(1), pp. 107–35.

Hay, Carter and Evans, Michelle M. (2006), 'Violent Victimization and Involvement in Delinquency: Examining Predictions from General Strain Theory', *Journal of Criminal Justice*, **34**(3), pp. 261–74.

Heckert, Alex and Heckert, Druann Maria (2004), 'Using an Integrated Typology of Deviance to Expand Merton's Anomie Theory', *Criminal Justice Studies: A Critical Journal of Crime, Law and Society*, **17**(1), pp. 75–90.

Hirschi, Travis (1969), *Causes of Delinquency*, Berkeley: University of California Press.

Hoffman, John P. and Su, Susan S. (1997), 'Conditional Effects of Stress on Delinquency and Drug Use: A Strain Theory Assessment of Sex Differences', *Journal of Research in Crime and Delinquency*, **34**(1), pp. 46–78.

Jang, Sung Joon (2007), 'Gender Differences in Strain, Negative Emotions, and Coping Behaviors: A General Strain Theory Approach', *Justice Quarterly*, **24**(3), pp. 523–53.

Jang, Sung Joon and Johnson, Byron R. (2003), 'Strain, Negative Emotions, and Deviant Coping among African Americans: A Test of General Strain Theory', *Journal of Quantitative Criminology*, **19**(1), pp. 79–105.

Jang, Sung Joon and Johnson, Byron R. (2005), 'Gender, Religiosity, and Reactions to Strain among African Americans', *Sociological Quarterly*, **46**(2), pp. 323–57.

Jensen, Gary (2002), 'Institutional Anomie and Societal Variations in Crime: A Critical Appraisal', *International Journal of Sociology and Social Policy*, **22**(7–8), pp. 45–74.

Karstedt, Susanne (2003), 'Legacies of a Culture of Inequality: The Janus Face of Crime in Post-Communist Countries', *Crime, Law, and Social Change*, **40**(2–3), pp. 295–320.

Karstedt, Susanne and Farrall, Stephen (2006), 'The Moral Economy of Everyday: Crime Markets, Consumers & Citizens', *British Journal of Criminology*, **46**(6), pp. 1011–36.

Kaufman, Joanne M., Rebellon, Cesar J., Thaxton, Sherod and Agnew, Robert (2008), 'A General Strain Theory of Racial Differences in Criminal Offending', *Australian and New Zealand Journal of Criminology*, **41**(3), pp. 421–37.

Kim, Sang-Weon, and Pridemore, William Alex (2005a), 'Poverty, Socioeconomic Change, Institutional Anomie, and Homicide', *Social Science Quarterly*, **86**(supplement), pp. 1377–98.

Kim, Sang-Weon and Pridemore, William Alex (2005b), 'Social Change, Institutional Anomie and Serious Property Crime in Transitional Russia', *British Journal of Criminology*, **45**(1), pp. 81–97.

Konty, Mark (2005), 'Microanomie: The Cognitive Foundations of the Relationship between *Anomie* and Deviance', *Criminology*, **43**, pp. 107–32.

Kornhauser, Ruth Rosner (1978), *Social Sources of Delinquency*, Chicago: University of Chicago Press.

Kubrin, Charis E., Stucky, Thomas D. and Krohn, Marvin D. (2009) *Researching Theories of Crime and Deviance*, New York: Oxford University Press.

Liu, Jianhong (2005), 'Crime Patterns during the Market Transition in China', *British Journal of Criminology*, **45**, pp. 613–33.

McCarthy, Bill and Hagan, John (2004), 'Money Changes Everything: The Personal Income of Adolescents and their Tendency toward Delinquency', *Criminologie*, **37**, pp. 123–49.

MacLeod, Jay (1995), *Ain't No Makin' It*, Boulder, CO: Westview.

Marwah, Sanjah and Deflem, Mathieu (2006), 'Revisiting Merton: Continuities in the Theory of Anomie-and-Opportunity Structures', in M. Deflem (ed.), *Sociological Theory and Criminological Research: Views from Europe and the United States*, Boston: Elsevier, pp. 57–76.

Maume, Michael O. and Lee, Matthew R. (2003), 'Social Institutions and Violence: A Sub-National Test of Institutional Anomie Theory', *Criminology*, **41**(4), pp. 1137–72.

Mazerolle, Paul (1998), 'Gender, General Strain, and Delinquency: Empirical Examination', *Justice Quarterly*, **15**(1), pp. 65–91.

Mazerolle, Paul and Maahs, Jeff (2000), 'General Strain and Delinquency: An Alternative Examination of Conditioning Influences', *Justice Quarterly*, **17**(4), pp. 753–78.

Mazerolle, Paul and Piquero, Alex (1997), 'Violent Responses to Strain: An Examination of Conditioning Influences', *Violence and Victims*, **12**(4), pp. 323–43.

Mazerolle, Paul and Piquero, Alex (1998), 'Linking Exposure to Strain with Anger: An Investigation of Deviant Adaptations', *Journal of Criminal Justice*, **26**(3), pp. 195–211.

Mazerolle, Paul, Piquero, Alex R. and Capowich, George E. (2003), 'Examining the Links between Strain, Situational and Dispositional Anger, and Crime: Further Specifying and Testing General Strain Theory', *Youth & Society*, **35**(2), pp. 131–57.

Menard, Scott (1995), 'A Developmental Test of Mertonian Anomie Theory', *Journal of Research in Crime and Delinquency*, **32**(2), pp. 136–74.

Merton, Robert K. (1964), 'Anomie, Anomia, and Social Interaction', in M. Clinard (ed.), *Anomie and Deviant Behavior*, New York: Free Press, pp. 213–42.

Merton, Robert K. (1968), *Social Theory and Social Structure*, New York: Free Press.

Merton, Robert K. (1995), 'Opportunity Structure: The Emergence, Diffusion, and Differentiation of a Sociological concept', in F. Adler and W.S. Laufer (eds), *The Legacy of Anomie Theory*, New Brunswick, NJ: Transaction, pp. 3–78.

Messerschmidt, James W. (1993), *Masculinities and Crime*, Lanham, MD: Rowman and Littlefield.

Messner, Steven F. (2003), 'An Institutional-Anomie Theory of Crime: Continuities and Elaborations in the Study of Social Structure and Anomie', *Cologne Journal of Sociology and Social Psychology*, **43**, pp. 93–109.

Messner, Steven F. and Rosenfeld, Richard (2007), *Crime and the American Dream* (4th edn), Belmont, CA: Wadsworth/Thomson Learning.

Miller, Walter B. (1958), 'Lower-Class Culture as a Generating Milieu of Gang Delinquency', *Journal of Social Issues*, **14**, pp. 5–19.

Moon, Byongook, Blurton, David and McClusky, John D. (2008), 'General Strain Theory and Delinquency: Focusing on the Influences of Key Strain Characteristics on Delinquency', *Crime & Delinquency*, **54**(4), pp. 582613.

Moon, Byongook, Hays, Kraig and Blurton, David (2009), 'General Strain Theory, Key Strains, and Deviance', *Journal of Criminal Justice*, **37**(1), pp. 98–106.

Mullins, Christopher W. (2006), *Holding Your Square: Masculinities, Streetlife, and Violence*, Portland, OR: Willan.

Murphy, Daniel S. and Robinson, Mathew B. (2008), 'The Maximizer: Clarifying Merton's Theories of Anomie and Strain', *Theoretical Criminology*, **12**(4), pp. 501–21.

Passas, Nikos (1990), 'Anomie and Corporate Deviance', *Contemporary Crises*, **14**, pp. 157–78.

Passas, Nikos and Agnew, Robert (eds) (1997), *The Future of Anomie Theory*, Boston: Northeastern University Press.

Paternoster, Raymond and Mazerolle, Paul (1994), 'General Strain Theory and Delinquency: A Replication and Extension', *Journal of Research in Crime and Delinquency*, **31**(3), pp. 235–63.

Piquero, Alex R. and Brezina, Timothy. (2001), 'Testing Moffitt's Account of Adolescence-Limited Delinquency', *Criminology*, **39**, pp. 353–70.

Piquero, Alex and Piquero, Nicole Leeper (1998), 'On Testing Institutional Anomie Theory with Varying Specifications', *Studies on Crime and Crime Prevention*, 7, pp. 61–84.

Piquero, Nicole Leeper and Sealock, Miriam D. (2000), 'Generalizing General Strain Theory: An Examination of an Offending Population', *Justice Quarterly*, 17(3), pp. 449–84.

Piquero, Nicole Leeper and Sealock, Miriam D. (2004), 'Gender and General Strain Theory: A Preliminary Test of Broidy and Agnew's Gender/GST Hypotheses', *Justice Quarterly*, 21(1), pp. 125–58.

Pratt, Travis C. and Godsey, Timothy W. (2003), 'Social Support, Inequality, and Homicide: A Cross-National Test of an Integrated Theoretical Model', *Criminology*, 41, pp. 611–43.

Pridemore, William Alex and Sang-Weon, Kim (2007), 'Socioeconomic Change and Homicide in a Transitional Society', *Sociological Quarterly*, 48, pp. 229–51.

Rosenfeld, Richard (1989), 'Robert Merton's Contributions to the Sociology of Deviance', *Sociological Inquiry*, 59, pp. 453–66.

Savolainen, Jukka (2000), 'Inequality, Welfare State, and Homicide: Further Support for the Institutional Anomie Theory', *Criminology*, 38(4), pp. 1021–42.

Schoepfer, Andre, and Piquero, Nicole Leeper (2006), 'Exploring White-Collar Crime and the American Dream: A Partial Test of Institutional Anomie Theory', *Journal of Criminal Justice*, 34(3), pp. 227–35.

Sharp, Susan F., Terling-Watt, Toni L., Atkins, Leslie A., Gilliam, Jay Trace and Sanders, Anna (2001), 'Purging Behavior in a Sample of College Females: A Research Note on General Strain Theory and Female Deviance', *Deviant Behavior*, 22(2), pp. 171–88.

Sheptycki, J.W.E., Wardak, Ali and Hardie-Bick, James (eds) (2005), *Transnational and Comparative Criminology*, Portland, OR: Cavendish.

Siegel, Dina, van de Bunt, H.G. and Zaitch, Damían (eds) (2003), *Global Organized Crime: Trends and Developments*, Norwell, MA: Kluwer Academic.

Sigfusdottir, Inga-Dora, Farkas, George and Silver, Eric (2004), 'The Role of Depressed Mood and Anger in the Relationship between Family Conflict and Delinquent Behavior', *Journal of Youth and Adolescence*, 33(6), pp. 509–22.

Sigfusdottir, Inga Dora, Asgeirsdottir, Bryndis Bjork, Gudjonsson, Gisli H. and Sigurdsson, Jon Fridrik (2008), 'A Model of Sexual Abuse's Effects on Suicidal Behavior and Delinquency: The Role of Emotions as Mediating Factors', *Journal of Youth and Adolescence*, 33(6), pp. 699–712.

Stephens, Gene (1994), 'The Global Crime Wave: And What We Can Do About It', *The Futurist*, 28(4), pp. 22–28.

Stewart, Eric A. and Simons, Ronald L. (2006), 'Structure and Culture in African American Adolescent Violence: A Partial Test of the "Code of the Street" Thesis', *Justice Quarterly*, 23, pp. 1–33.

Stucky, Thomas D. (2003), 'Local Politics and Violent Crime in U.S. Cities', *Criminology*, 41, pp. 1101–35.

Stults, Brian J. and Baumer, Eric P. (2008), 'Assessing the Relevance of Anomie Theory for Explaining Spatial Variation in Lethal Criminal Violence: An Aggregate-Level Analysis of Homicide within the United States', *International Journal of Conflict and Violence*, 2(2), pp. 215–47.

Sullivan, Mercer L. (1989), *Getting Paid*, Ithaca, NY: Cornell University Press.

Sutherland, Edwin H., Cressey, Donald R. and Luckenbill, David F. (1992), *Principles of Criminology*, Dix Hills, NY: General Hall.

Sykes, Gresham M. and Matza, David (1957), 'Techniques of Neutralization: A Theory of Delinquency', *American Sociological Review*, 22, pp. 664–70.

Tanner, Julian (1978), 'New Directions for Subcultural Theory', *Youth & Society*, 9, pp. 343–72.

Thrasher, Frederic M. (1927), *The Gang*, Chicago: University of Chicago Press.

Tittle, Charles R., Broidy, Lisa M. and Gertz, Marc G. (2008), 'Strain, Crime, and Contingencies', *Justice Quarterly*, 25(2), pp. 283–312.

Vaughan, Diane (1983), *Controlling Unlawful Organizational Behavior*, Chicago: University of Chicago Press.

Vaughan, Diane (1996), *The Challenger Launch Decision: Risky Technology, Culture, and Deviance at NASA*, Chicago: University of Chicago Press.

Vaughan, Diane (1997), 'Anomie Theory and Organizations', in N. Passas and R. Agnew (eds), *The Future of Anomie Theory*, Boston: Northeastern University Press, pp. 95–123.

Wilkinson, Deanna L. (2003), *Guns, Violence, and Identity among African American and Latino Youth*, New York: LFB Scholarly Publishing.

Williams, J. Patrick (2007), 'Youth-Subcultural Studies: Sociological Traditions and Core Concepts', *Sociology Compass*, **1/2**, pp. 572–93.

Willis, Paul (1977), *Learning to Labor: How Working-Class Kids Get Working Class Jobs*, New York: Columbia University Press.

Wilson, William Julius (1987), *The Truly Disadvantaged*, Chicago: University of Chicago Press.

Wright, John P., Cullen, Francis T., Agnew, Robert S. and Brezina, Timothy (2001), 'The Root of all Evil? An Exploratory Study of Money and Delinquent Involvement', *Justice Quarterly*, **18**, pp. 239–68.

Zhang, Sheldon and Chin, Ko-Lin (2002), 'Enter the Dragon: Inside Chinese Human Smuggling Organizations', *Criminology*, **40**(4), pp. 737–68.

Zhao, Linda Shuo (2008), 'Anomie Theory and Crime in a Transitional China', *International Criminal Justice Review*, **18**(2), pp. 137–57.

Part I
The Origins of Strain, Anomie and Subcultural Theory: Classic Statements

[1]

Anomic Suicide

Emile Durkheim

II

No living being can be happy or even exist unless his needs are sufficiently proportioned to his means. In other words, if his needs require more than can be granted, or even merely something of a different sort, they will be under continual friction and can only function painfully. Movements incapable of production without pain tend not to be reproduced. Unsatisfied tendencies atrophy, and as the impulse to live is merely the result of all the rest, it is bound to weaken as the others relax.

In the animal, at least in a normal condition, this equilibrium is established with automatic spontaneity because the animal depends on purely material conditions. All the organism needs is that the supplies of substance and energy constantly employed in the vital process should be periodically renewed by equivalent quantities; that replacement be equivalent to use. When the void created by existence in its own resources is filled, the animal, satisfied, asks nothing further. Its power of reflection is not sufficiently developed to imagine other ends than those implicit in its physical nature. On the other hand,

* Translated by John A. Spaulding and George Simpson

as the work demanded of each organ itself depends on the general state of vital energy and the needs of organic equilibrium, use is regulated in turn by replacement and the balance is automatic. The limits of one are those of the other; both are fundamental to the constitution of the existence in question, which cannot exceed them.

This is not the case with man, because most of his needs are not dependent on his body or not to the same degree. Strictly speaking, we may consider that the quantity of material supplies necessary to the physical maintenance of a human life is subject to computation, though this be less exact than in the preceding case and a wider margin left for the free combinations of the will; for beyond the indispensable minimum which satisfies nature when instinctive, a more awakened reflection suggests better conditions, seemingly desirable ends craving fulfillment. Such appetites, however, admittedly sooner or later reach a limit which they cannot pass. But how determine the quantity of well-being, comfort or luxury legitimately to be craved by a human being? Nothing appears in man's organic nor in his psychological constitution which sets a limit to such tendencies. The functioning of individual life does not require them to cease at one point rather than at another; the proof being that they have constantly increased since the beginnings of history, receiving more and more complete satisfaction, yet with no weakening of average health. Above all, how establish their proper variation with different conditions of life, occupations, relative importance of services, etc.? In no society are they equally satisfied in the different stages of the social hierarchy. Yet human nature is substantially the same among all men, in its essential qualities. It is not human nature which can assign the variable limits necessary to our needs. They are thus unlimited so far as they depend on the individual alone. Irrespective of any external regulatory force, our capacity for feeling is in itself an insatiable and bottomless abyss.

But if nothing external can restrain this capacity, it can only be a source of torment to itself. Unlimited desires are insatiable by definition and insatiability is rightly considered a sign of morbidity. Being unlimited, they constantly and infinitely surpass the means at their command; they cannot be quenched. Inextinguishable thirst is constantly renewed torture. It has been claimed, indeed, that human activity naturally aspires beyond assignable limits and sets itself unattainable goals. But how can such an undetermined state be any more reconciled with the conditions of mental life than with the demands of physical life? All man's pleasure in acting, moving and exerting himself implies the sense that his efforts are not in vain and that by walking he has advanced. However, one does not advance when one walks toward no goal, or—which is the same thing —when his goal is infinity. Since the distance between us and it is always the same, whatever road we take, we might as well have made the motions without progress from the spot. Even our glances behind and our feeling of pride at the distance covered can cause only deceptive satisfaction, since the remaining distance is not proportionately reduced. To pursue a goal which is by definition unattainable is to condemn oneself to a state of perpetual unhappiness. Of course, man may hope contrary to all reason, and hope has its pleasures even when unreasonable. It may sustain him for a time; but it cannot survive the repeated disappointments of experience indefinitely. What more can the future offer him than the past, since he can never reach a tenable condition nor even approach the glimpsed ideal? Thus, the more one has, the more one wants, since satisfactions received only stimulate instead of filling needs. Shall action as such be considered agreeable? First, only on condition of blindness to its uselessness. Secondly, for this pleasure to be felt and to temper and half veil the accompanying painful unrest, such unending motion must at least always be easy and unhampered. If it is interfered with only restlessness is left, with the lack of ease which it, itself, entails. But it would be a miracle if no insurmountable obstacle were never encountered. Our thread of life on these conditions is pretty thin, breakable at any instant.

To achieve any other result, the passions first must be limited. Only then can they be harmonized with the faculties and satisfied. But since the individual has no way of limiting them, this must be done by some force exterior to him. A regulative force must play the same role for moral needs which the organism plays for physical needs. This means that the force can only be moral. The awakening of conscience interrupted the state of equilibrium of the animal's dormant existence; only conscience, therefore, can furnish the means to re-establish it. Physical restraint would be ineffective; hearts cannot be touched by physio-chemical forces. So far as the appetites are not automatically restrained by physiological mechanisms, they can be halted only by a limit that they recognize as just. Men would never consent to restrict their desires if they felt justified in passing the assigned limit. But, for reasons given above, they cannot assign themselves this law of justice. So they must receive it from an authority which they respect, to which they yield spontaneously. Either directly and as a whole, or through the agency of one of its organs, society alone can play this moderating role; for it is the only moral power superior to the individual, the authority of which he accepts. It alone has the power necessary to stipulate law and to set the point beyond which the passions must not go. Finally, it alone can estimate the reward to be prospectively offered to every class of human functionary, in the name of the common interest.

As a matter of fact, at every moment of history there is a dim perception, in the moral consciousness of societies, of the respective value of different social services, the relative reward due to each, and the consequent degree of comfort appropriate on the average to workers in each occupation. The different functions are graded in public opinion and a certain coefficient of well-being assigned to each, according to its place in the hierarchy. According to accepted ideas, for example, a certain way of living is considered the upper limit to which a workman may aspire in his efforts to improve his existence, and there is another limit below which he is not willingly permitted to fall unless he has seriously bemeaned himself. Both differ for city and country workers, for the domestic servant and the day-laborer, for the business clerk and the official, etc. Likewise the man of wealth is reproved if he lives the life of a poor man, but also if he seeks the refinements of luxury overmuch. Economists may protest in vain; public feeling will always be scandalized if an individual spends too much wealth for wholly superfluous use, and it even seems that this severity relaxes only in times of moral disturbance.[10] A genuine regimen exists, therefore, although not always legally formulated, which fixes with relative precision the maximum degree of ease of living to which each social class may legitimately aspire. However, there is nothing immutable about such

---

[10] Actually, this is a purely moral reprobation and can hardly be judicially implemented. We do not consider any reestablishment of sumptuary laws desirable or even possible.

a scale. It changes with the increase or decrease of collective revenue and the changes occurring in the moral ideas of society. Thus what appears luxury to one period no longer does so to another; and the well-being which for long periods was granted to a class only by exception and supererogation, finally appears strictly necessary and equitable.

Under this pressure, each in his sphere vaguely realizes the extreme limit set to his ambitions and aspires to nothing beyond. At least if he respects regulations and is docile to collective authority, that is, has a wholesome moral constitution, he feels that it is not well to ask more. Thus, an end and goal are set to the passions. Truly, there is nothing rigid nor absolute about such determination. The economic ideal assigned each class of citizens is itself confined to certain limits, within which the desires have free range. But it is not infinite. This relative limitation and the moderation it involves, make men contented with their lot while stimulating them moderately to improve it; and this average contentment causes the feeling of calm, active happiness, the pleasure in existing and living which characterizes health for societies as well as for individuals. Each person is then at least, generally speaking, in harmony with his condition, and desires only what he may legitimately hope for as the normal reward of his activity. Besides, this does not condemn man to a sort of immobility. He may seek to give beauty to his life; but his attempts in this direction may fail without causing him to despair. For, loving what he has and not fixing his desire solely on what he lacks, his wishes and hopes may fail of what he has happened to aspire to, without his being wholly destitute. He has the essentials. The equilibrium of his happiness is secure because it is defined, and a few mishaps cannot disconcert him.

But it would be of little use for everyone to recognize the justice of the hierarchy of functions established by public opinion, if he did not also consider the distribution of these functions just. The workman is not in harmony with his social position if he is not convinced that he has his desserts. If he feels justified in occupying another, what he has would not satisfy him. So it is not enough for the average level of needs for each social condition to be regulated by public opinion, but another, more precise rule, must fix the way in which these conditions are open to individuals. There is no society in which such regulation does not exist. It varies with times and places. Once it regarded birth as the almost exclusive principle of social classification; today it recognizes no other inherent inequality than hereditary fortune and merit. But in all these various forms its object is unchanged. It is also only possible, everywhere, as a restriction upon individuals imposed by superior authority, that is, by collective authority. For it can be established only by requiring of one or another group of men, usually of all, sacrifices and concessions in the name of the public interest.

Some, to be sure, have thought that this moral pressure would become unnecessary if men's economic circumstances were only no longer determined by heredity. If inheritance were abolished, the argument runs, if everyone began life with equal resources and if the competitive struggle were fought out on a basis of perfect equality, no one could think its results unjust. Each would instinctively feel that things are as they should be.

Truly, the nearer this ideal equality were approached, the less social restraint will be necessary. But it is only a matter of degree. One sort of heredity will always exist, that of natural talent. Intelligence, taste, scientific, artistic, literary or industrial ability, courage and manual dexterity are gifts received by each of us at birth, as the heir to wealth receives his capital or as the nobleman formerly received his title and function. A moral discipline will therefore still be required to make those less favored by nature accept the lesser advantages which they owe to the chance of birth. Shall it be demanded that all have an equal share and that no advantage be given those more useful and deserving? But then there would have to be a discipline far stronger to make these accept a treatment merely equal to that of the mediocre and incapable.

But like the one first mentioned, this discipline can be useful only if considered just by the peoples subject to it. When it is maintained only by custom and force, peace and harmony are illusory; the spirit of unrest and discontent are latent; appetites superficially restrained are ready to revolt. This happened in Rome and Greece when the faiths underlying the old organization of the patricians and plebeians were shaken, and in our modern societies when aristocratic prejudices began to lose their old ascendancy. But this state of upheaval is exceptional; it occurs only when society is passing through some abnormal crisis. In normal conditions the collective order is regarded as just by the great majority of persons. Therefore, when we say that an authority is necessary to impose this order on individuals, we certainly do not mean that violence is the only means of establishing it. Since this regulation is meant to restrain individual passions, it must come from a power which dominates individuals; but this power must also be obeyed through respect, not fear.

It is not true, then, that human activity can be released from all restraint. Nothing in the world can enjoy such a privilege. All existence being a part of the universe is relative to the remainder; its nature and method of manifestation accordingly depend not only on itself but on other beings, who consequently restrain and regulate it. Here there are only differences of degree and form between the mineral realm and the thinking person. Man's characteristic privilege is that the bond he accepts is not physical but moral; that is, social. He is governed not by a material environment brutally imposed on him, but by a conscience superior to his own, the superiority of which he feels. Because the greater, better part of his existence transcends the body, he escapes the body's yoke, but is subject to that of society.

But when society is disturbed by some painful crisis or by beneficent but abrupt transitions, it is momentarily incapable of exercising this influence; thence come the sudden rises in the curve of suicides which we have pointed out above.

In the case of economic disasters, indeed, something like a declassification occurs which suddenly casts certain individuals into a lower state than their previous one. Then they must reduce their requirements, restrain their needs, learn greater self-control. All the advantages of social influence are lost so far as they are concerned; their moral education has to be recommenced. But society cannot adjust them instantaneously to this new life and teach them to practice the increased self-repression to which they are unaccustomed. So they are not adjusted to the condition forced on them, and its very prospect is intolerable; hence the suffering which detaches them from a reduced existence even before they have made trial of it.

It is the same if the source of the crisis is an abrupt growth of power and wealth. Then, truly, as the conditions of life are changed, the standard according to which needs were regulated can no longer remain the same; for it varies with social resources, since it largely determines the share of each class of producers. The scale is upset; but a new scale cannot be immediately improvised. Time is required for the public conscience to reclassify men and things. So long as the social forces thus freed have not regained equilibrium, their respective values are unknown and so all regulation is lacking for a time. The limits are unknown between the possible and the impossible, what is just and what is unjust, legitimate claims and hopes and those which are immoderate. Consequently, there is no restraint upon aspirations. If the disturbance is profound, it affects even the principles controlling the distribution of men among various occupations. Since the relations between various parts of society are necessarily modified, the ideas expressing these relations must change. Some particular class especially favored by the crisis is no longer resigned to its former lot, and, on the other hand, the example of its greater good fortune arouses all sorts of jealousy below and about it. Appetites, not being controlled by a public opinion become disoriented, no longer recognize the limits proper to them. Besides, they are at the same time seized by a sort of natural erethism simply by the greater intensity of public life. With increased prosperity desires increase. At the very moment when traditional rules have lost their authority, the richer prize offered these appetites stimulates them and makes them more exigent and impatient of control. The state of de-regulation or anomy is thus further heightened by passions being less disciplined, precisely when they need more disciplining.

But then their very demands make fulfillment impossible. Overweening ambition always exceeds the results obtained, great as they may be, since there is no warning to pause here. Nothing gives satisfaction and all this agitation is uninterruptedly maintained without appeasement. Above all, since this race for an unattainable goal can give no other pleasure but that of the race itself, if it is one, once it is interrupted the participants are left empty-handed. At the same time the struggle grows more violent and painful, both from being less controlled and because competition is greater. All classes contend among themselves because no established classification any longer exists. Effort grows, just when it becomes less productive. How could the desire to live not be weakened under such conditions?

This explanation is confirmed by the remarkable immunity of poor countries. Poverty protects against suicide because it is a restraint in itself. No matter how one acts, desires have to depend upon resources to some extent; actual possessions are partly the criterion of those aspired to. So the less one has the less he is tempted to extend the range of his needs indefinitely. Lack of power, compelling moderation, accustoms men to it, while nothing excites envy if no one has superfluity. Wealth, on the other hand, by the power it bestows, deceives us into believing that we depend on ourselves only. Reducing the resistance we encounter from objects, it suggests the possibility of unlimited success against them. The less limited one feels, the more intolerable all limitation appears. Not without reason, therefore, have so many religions dwelt on the advantages and moral value of poverty. It is actually the best school for teaching self-restraint. Forcing us to constant self-discipline, it prepares us to accept collective discipline with equanimity, while wealth, exalting the individual, may always arouse the spirit of rebellion which is the very source of immorality. This, of course, is no reason why humanity should not improve its material condition. But though the moral danger involved in every growth of prosperity is not irremediable, it should not be forgotten.

III

If anomy never appeared except, as in the above instances, in intermittent spurts and acute crisis, it might cause the social suicide-rate to vary from time to time, but it would not be a regular, constant factor. In one sphere of social life, however—the sphere of trade and industry—it is actually in a chronic state.

For a whole century, economic progress has mainly consisted in freeing industrial relations from all regulation. Until very recently, it was the function of a whole system of moral forces to exert this discipline. First, the influence of religion was felt alike by workers and masters, the poor and the rich. It consoled the former and taught them contentment with their lot by informing them of the providential nature of the social order, that the share of each class was assigned by God himself, and by holding out the hope for just compensation in a world to come in return for the inequalities of this world. It governed the latter, recalling that worldly interests are not man's entire lot, that they must be subordinate to other and higher interests, and that they should therefore not be pursued without rule or measure. Temporal power, in turn, restrained the scope of economic functions by its supremacy over them and by the relatively subordinate role it assigned them. Finally, within the business world proper, the occupational groups by regulating salaries, the price of products and production itself, indirectly fixed the average level of income on which needs are partially based by the very force of circumstances. However, we do not mean to propose this organization as a model. Clearly it would be inadequate to existing societies without great changes. What we stress is its existence, the fact of its useful influence, and that nothing today has come to take its place.

Actually, religion has lost most of its power. And government, instead of regulating economic life, has become its tool and servant. The most opposite schools, orthodox economists and extreme socialists, unite to reduce government to the role of a more or less passive intermediary among the various social functions. The former wish to make it simply the guardian of individual contracts; the latter leave it the task of doing the collective bookkeeping, that is, of recording the demands of consumers, transmitting them to producers, inventorying the total revenue and distributing it according to a fixed formula. But both refuse it any power to subordinate other social organs to itself and to make them converge toward one dominant aim. On both sides nations are declared to have the single or chief purpose of achieving industrial prosperity; such is the implication of the dogma of economic materialism, the basis of both apparently opposed systems. And as these theories merely express the state of opinion, industry, instead of being still regarded as a means to an end transcending itself, has become the supreme end of individuals and societies alike. Thereupon the appetites thus excited have become freed of any limiting authority. By sanctifying them, so to speak, this apotheosis of well-being has placed them above all human law. Their restraint seems like a sort of sacrilege. For this reason, even the purely utilitarian regulation of them exercised by the industrial world itself through the medium of occupational groups has been unable to persist. Ultimately, this liberation of desires has been made worse by the very development of industry and the almost infinite extension of the market. So long as the producer could gain his profits only in his immediate neighborhood, the restricted amount of possible gain could not much overexcite ambition. Now that he may assume to have almost the entire world as his customer, how could passions accept their former confinement in the face of such limitless prospects?

Such is the source of the excitement predominating in this part of society, and which has thence extended to the other parts. There, the state of crisis and anomy is constant and, so to speak, normal. From top to bottom of the ladder, greed is aroused without knowing where to find ultimate foothold. Nothing can calm it, since its goal is far beyond all it can attain. Reality seems valueless by comparison with the dreams of fevered imaginations; reality is therefore abandoned, but so too is possibility abandoned when it in turn becomes reality. A thirst arises for novelties, unfamiliar pleasures, nameless sensations, all of which lose their savor once known. Henceforth one has no strength to endure the least reverse. The whole fever subsides and the sterility of all the tumult is apparent, and it is seen that all these new sensations in their infinite quantity cannot form a solid foundation of happiness to support one during days of trial. The wise man, knowing how to enjoy achieved results without having constantly to replace them with others, finds in them an attachment to life in the hour of difficulty. But the man who has always pinned all his hopes on the future and lived with his eyes fixed upon it, has nothing in the past as a comfort against the present's afflictions, for the past was nothing to him but a series of hastily experienced stages. What blinded him to himself was his expectation always to find further on the happiness he had so far missed. Now he is stopped in his tracks; from now on nothing remains behind or ahead of him to fix his gaze upon. Weariness alone, moreover, is enough to bring disillusionment, for he cannot in the end escape the futility of an endless pursuit.

We may even wonder if this moral state is not principally what makes economic catastrophes of our day so fertile in suicides. In societies where a man is subjected to a healthy discipline, he submits more readily to the blows of chance. The necessary effort for sustaining a little more discomfort costs him relatively little, since he is used to discomfort and constraint. But when every constraint is hateful in itself, how can closer constraint not seem intolerable? There is no tendency to resignation in the feverish impatience of men's lives. When there is no other aim but to outstrip constantly the point arrived at, how painful to be thrown back! Now this very lack of organization characterizing our economic condition throws the door wide to every sort of adventure. Since imagination is hungry for novelty, and ungoverned, it gropes at random. Setbacks necessarily increase with risks and thus crises multiply, just when they are becoming more destructive.

Yet these dispositions are so inbred that society has grown to accept them and is accustomed to think them normal. It is everlastingly repeated that it is man's nature to be eternally dissatisfied, constantly to advance, without relief or rest, toward an indefinite goal. The longing for infinity is daily represented as a mark of moral distinction, whereas it can only appear within unregulated consciences which elevate to a rule the lack of rule from which they suffer. The doctrine of the most ruthless and swift progress has become an article of faith. But other theories appear parallel with those praising the advantages of instability, which, generalizing the situation that gives them birth, declare life evil, claim that it is richer in grief than in pleasure and that it attracts men only by false claims. Since this disorder is greatest in the economic world, it has most victims there.

Industrial and commercial functions are really among the occupations which furnish the greatest number of suicides (see Table XXIV, p. 258). Almost on a level with the liberal professions, they sometimes surpass them; they are especially more afflicted than agriculture, where the old regulative forces still make their appearance felt most and where the fever of business has least penetrated. Here is best recalled what was once the general constitution of the economic order. And the divergence would be yet greater if, among the suicides of industry, employers were distinguished from workmen, for the former are probably most stricken by the state of anomy. The enormous rate of those with independent means (720 per million) sufficiently shows that the possessors of most comfort suffer most. Everything that enforces subordination attenuates the effects of this state. At least the horizon of the lower classes is limited by those above them, and for this same reason their desires are more modest. Those who have only empty space above them are almost inevitably lost in it, if no force restrains them.

TABLE XXIV—Suicides per Million Persons of Different Occupations

	Trade	Transportation	Industry	Agricul-ture	Liberal *Professions
France (1878–87) †	440	.....	340	240	300
Switzerland (1876)	664	1,514	577	304	558
Italy (1866–76)	277	152.6	80.4	26.7	618 ‡
Prussia (1883–90)	754	.....	456	315	832
Bavaria (1884–91)	465	.....	369	153	454
Belgium (1886–90)	421	.....	160	160	100
Wurttemberg (1873–78)	273	.....	190	206	...
Saxony (1878)		341.59 §		71.17	...

* When statistics distinguish several different sorts of liberal occupations, we show as a specimen the one in which the suicide-rate is highest.
† From 1826 to 1880 economic functions seem less affected (see *Compte-rendu* of 1880); but were occupational statistics very accurate?
‡ This figure is reached only by men of letters.
§ Figure represents Trade, Transportation and Industry combined for Saxony. Ed.

Anomy, therefore, is a regular and specific factor in suicide in our modern societies; one of the springs from which the annual contingent feeds. So we have here a new type to distinguish from the others. It differs from them in its dependence, not on the way in which individuals are attached to society, but on how it regulates them. Egoistic suicide results from man's no longer finding a basis for existence in life; altruistic suicide, because this basis for existence appears to man situated beyond life itself. The third sort of suicide, the existence of which has just been shown, results from man's activity's lacking regulation and his consequent sufferings. By virtue of its origin we shall assign this last variety the name of *anomic suicide*.

[2]

SOCIAL STRUCTURE AND ANOMIE

ROBERT K. MERTON
Harvard University

THERE persists a notable tendency in sociological theory to attribute the malfunctioning of social structure primarily to those of man's imperious biological drives which are not adequately restrained by social control. In this view, the social order is solely a device for "impulse management" and the "social processing" of tensions. These impulses which break through social control, be it noted, are held to be biologically derived. Nonconformity is assumed to be rooted in original nature.[1] Conformity is by implication the result of an utilitarian calculus or unreasoned conditioning. This point of view, whatever its other deficiences, clearly begs one question. It provides no basis for determining the nonbiological conditions which induce deviations from prescribed patterns of conduct. In this paper, it will be suggested that certain phases of social structure generate the circumstances in which infringement of social codes constitutes a "normal" response.[2]

The conceptual scheme to be outlined is designed to provide a coherent, systematic approach to the study of socio-cultural sources of deviate behavior. Our primary aim lies in discovering how some social structures *exert a definite pressure* upon certain persons in the society to engage in nonconformist rather than conformist conduct. The many ramifications of the scheme cannot all be discussed; the problems mentioned outnumber those explicitly treated.

Among the elements of social and cultural structure, two are important for our purposes. These are analytically separable although they merge imperceptibly in concrete situations. The first consists of culturally defined goals, purposes, and interests. It comprises a frame of aspirational reference. These goals are more or less integrated and involve varying degrees of prestige and sentiment. They constitute a basic, but not the exclusive, component of what Linton aptly has called "designs for group living." Some of these cultural aspirations are related to the original drives of man, but they are not determined by them. The second phase of the social

---

[1] E.g., Ernest Jones, *Social Aspects of Psychoanalysis*, 28, London, 1924. If the Freudian notion is a variety of the "original sin" dogma, then the interpretation advanced in this paper may be called the doctrine of "socially derived sin."

[2] "Normal" in the sense of a culturally oriented, if not approved, response. This statement does not deny the relevance of biological and personality differences which may be significantly involved in the *incidence* of deviate conduct. Our focus of interest is the social and cultural matrix; hence we abstract from other factors. It is in this sense, I take it, that James S. Plant speaks of the "normal reaction of normal people to abnormal conditions." See his *Personality and the Cultural Pattern*, 248, New York, 1937.

SOCIAL STRUCTURE AND ANOMIE   673

structure defines, regulates, and controls the acceptable modes of achieving these goals. Every social group invariably couples its scale of desired ends with moral or institutional regulation of permissible and required procedures for attaining these ends. These regulatory norms and moral imperatives do not necessarily coincide with technical or efficiency norms. Many procedures which from the standpoint of *particular individuals* would be most efficient in securing desired values, e.g., illicit oil-stock schemes, theft, fraud, are ruled out of the institutional area of permitted conduct. The choice of expedients is limited by the institutional norms.

To say that these two elements, culture goals and institutional norms, operate jointly is not to say that the ranges of alternative behaviors and aims bear some constant relation to one another. The emphasis upon certain goals may vary independently of the degree of emphasis upon institutional means. There may develop a disproportionate, at times, a virtually exclusive, stress upon the value of specific goals, involving relatively slight concern with the institutionally appropriate modes of attaining these goals. The limiting case in this direction is reached when the range of alternative procedures is limited only by technical rather than institutional considerations. Any and all devices which promise attainment of the all important goal would be permitted in this hypothetical polar case.[3] This constitutes one type of cultural malintegration. A second polar type is found in groups where activities originally conceived as instrumental are transmuted into ends in themselves. The original purposes are forgotten and ritualistic adherence to institutionally prescribed conduct becomes virtually obsessive.[4] Stability is largely ensured while change is flouted. The range of alternative behaviors is severely limited. There develops a tradition-bound, sacred society characterized by neophobia. The occupational psychosis of the bureaucrat may be cited as a case in point. Finally, there are the intermediate types of groups where a balance between culture goals and institu-

---

[3] Contemporary American culture has been said to tend in this direction. See André Siegfried, *America Comes of Age*, 26–37, New York, 1927. The alleged extreme(?) emphasis on the goals of monetary success and material prosperity leads to dominant concern with technological and social instruments designed to produce the desired result, inasmuch as institutional controls become of secondary importance. In such a situation, innovation flourishes as the *range of means* employed is broadened. In a sense, then, there occurs the paradoxical emergence of "materialists" from an "idealistic" orientation. Cf. Durkheim's analysis of the cultural conditions which predispose toward crime and innovation, both of which are aimed toward efficiency, not moral norms. Durkheim was one of the first to see that "contrairement aux idées courantes le criminel n'apparait plus comme un être radicalement insociable, comme une sorte d'element parasitaire, de corps étranger et inassimilable, introduit au sein de la société; c'est un agent régulier de la vie sociale." See *Les Règles de la Méthode Sociologique*, 86–89, Paris, 1927.

[4] Such ritualism may be associated with a mythology which rationalizes these actions so that they appear to retain their status as means, but the dominant pressure is in the direction of strict ritualistic conformity, irrespective of such rationalizations. In this sense, ritual has proceeded farthest when such rationalizations are not even called forth.

tional means is maintained. These are the significantly integrated and relatively stable, though changing, groups.

An effective equilibrium between the two phases of the social structure is maintained as long as satisfactions accrue to individuals who conform to both constraints, viz., satisfactions from the achievement of the goals and satisfactions emerging directly from the institutionally canalized modes of striving to attain these ends. Success, in such equilibrated cases, is twofold. Success is reckoned in terms of the product and in terms of the process, in terms of the outcome and in terms of activities. Continuing satisfactions must derive from sheer *participation* in a competitive order as well as from eclipsing one's competitors if the order itself is to be sustained. The occasional sacrifices involved in institutionalized conduct must be compensated by socialized rewards. The distribution of statuses and roles through competition must be so organized that positive incentives for conformity to roles and adherence to status obligations are provided *for every position* within the distributive order. Aberrant conduct, therefore, may be viewed as a symptom of dissociation between culturally defined aspirations and socially structured means.

Of the types of groups which result from the independent variation of the two phases of the social structure, we shall be primarily concerned with the first, namely, that involving a disproportionate accent on goals. This statement must be recast in a proper perspective. In no group is there an absence of regulatory codes governing conduct, yet groups do vary in the degree to which these folkways, mores, and institutional controls are effectively integrated with the more diffuse goals which are part of the culture matrix. Emotional convictions may cluster about the complex of socially acclaimed ends, meanwhile shifting their support from the culturally defined implementation of these ends. As we shall see, certain aspects of the social structure may generate countermores and antisocial behavior precisely because of differential emphases on goals and regulations. In the extreme case, the latter may be so vitiated by the goal-emphasis that the range of behavior is limited only by considerations of technical expediency. The sole significant question then becomes, which available means is most efficient in netting the socially approved value?[5] The technically most feasible procedure, whether legitimate or not, is preferred to the institutionally prescribed conduct. As this process continues, the integration of the society becomes tenuous and anomie ensues.

---

[5] In this connection, one may see the relevance of Elton Mayo's paraphrase of the title of Tawney's well known book. "Actually the problem *is not that of the sickness of an acquisitive society; it is that of the acquisitiveness of a sick society.*" *Human Problems of an Industrial Civilization*, 153, New York, 1933. Mayo deals with the process through which wealth comes to be a symbol of social achievement. He sees this as arising from a state of anomie. We are considering the unintegrated monetary-success goal as an element in producing anomie. A complete analysis would involve both phases of this system of interdependent variables.

SOCIAL STRUCTURE AND ANOMIE   675

Thus, in competitive athletics, when the aim of victory is shorn of its institutional trappings and success in contests becomes construed as "winning the game" rather than "winning through circumscribed modes of activity," a premium is implicitly set upon the use of illegitimate but technically efficient means. The star of the opposing football team is surreptitiously slugged; the wrestler furtively incapacitates his opponent through ingenious but illicit techniques; university alumni covertly subsidize "students" whose talents are largely confined to the athletic field. The emphasis on the goal has so attenuated the satisfactions deriving from sheer participation in the competitive activity that these satisfactions are virtually confined to a successful outcome. Through the same process, tension generated by the desire to win in a poker game is relieved by successfully dealing oneself four aces, or, when the cult of success has become completely dominant, by sagaciously shuffling the cards in a game of solitaire. The faint twinge of uneasiness in the last instance and the surreptious nature of public delicts indicate clearly that the institutional rules of the game *are known* to those who evade them, but that the emotional supports of these rules are largely vitiated by cultural exaggeration of the success-goal.[6] They are microcosmic images of the social macrocosm.

Of course, this process is not restricted to the realm of sport. The process whereby exaltation of the end generates a *literal demoralization*, i.e., a deinstitutionalization, of the means is one which characterizes many[7] groups in which the two phases of the social structure are not highly integrated. The extreme emphasis upon the accumulation of wealth as a symbol of success[8] in our own society militates against the completely effective control of institutionally regulated modes of acquiring a fortune.[9] Fraud, corruption, vice, crime, in short, the entire catalogue of proscribed

---

[6] It is unlikely that interiorized norms are completely eliminated. Whatever residuum persists will induce personality tensions and conflict. The process involves a certain degree of ambivalence. A manifest rejection of the institutional norms is coupled with some latent retention of their emotional correlates. "Guilt feelings," "sense of sin," "pangs of conscience" are obvious manifestations of this unrelieved tension; symbolic adherence to the nominally repudiated values or rationalizations constitute a more subtle variety of tensional release.

[7] "Many," and not all, unintegrated groups, for the reason already mentioned. In groups where the primary emphasis shifts to institutional means, i.e., when the range of alternatives is very limited, the outcome is a type of ritualism rather than anomie.

[8] Money has several peculiarities which render it particularly apt to become a symbol of prestige divorced from institutional controls. As Simmel emphasized, money is highly abstract and impersonal. However acquired, through fraud or institutionally, it can be used to purchase the same goods and services. The anonymity of metropolitan culture, in conjunction with this peculiarity of money, permits wealth, the sources of which may be unknown to the community in which the plutocrat lives, to serve as a symbol of status.

[9] The emphasis upon wealth as a success-symbol is possibly reflected in the use of the term "fortune" to refer to a stock of accumulated wealth. This meaning becomes common in the late sixteenth century (Spenser and Shakespeare). A similar usage of the Latin *fortuna* comes into prominence during the first century B.C. Both these periods were marked by the rise to prestige and power of the "bourgeoisie."

676 AMERICAN SOCIOLOGICAL REVIEW

behavior, becomes increasingly common when the emphasis on the *cultur-ally induced* success-goal becomes divorced from a coordinated institutional emphasis. This observation is of crucial theoretical importance in examining the doctrine that antisocial behavior most frequently derives from bio-logical drives breaking through the restraints imposed by society. The difference is one between a strictly utilitarian interpretation which con-ceives man's ends as random and an analysis which finds these ends deriv-ing from the basic values of the culture.[10]

Our analysis can scarcely stop at this juncture. We must turn to other aspects of the social structure if we are to deal with the social genesis of the varying rates and types of deviate behavior characteristic of different so-cieties. Thus far, we have sketched three ideal types of social orders con-stituted by distinctive patterns of relations between culture ends and means. Turning from these types of *culture patterning*, we find five logically possible, alternative modes of adjustment or adaptation *by individuals* within the culture-bearing society or group.[11] These are schematically presented in the following table, where $(+)$ signifies "acceptance," $(-)$ signifies "elimination" and $(\pm)$ signifies "rejection and substitution of new goals and standards."

	Culture Goals	Institutionalized Means
I. Conformity	+	+
II. Innovation	+	−
III. Ritualism	−	+
IV. Retreatism	−	−
V. Rebellion[12]	±	±

Our discussion of the relation between these alternative responses and other phases of the social structure must be prefaced by the observation that persons may shift from one alternative to another as they engage in different social activities. These categories refer to role adjustments in specific situations, not to personality *in toto*. To treat the development of this process in various spheres of conduct would introduce a complexity unmanageable within the confines of this paper. For this reason, we shall be concerned primarily with economic activity in the broad sense, "the

[10] See Kingsley Davis, "Mental Hygiene and the Class Structure," *Psychiatry*, 1928, I, esp. 62–63; Talcott Parsons, *The Structure of Social Action*, 59–60, New York, 1937.

[11] This is a level intermediate between the two planes distinguished by Edward Sapir; namely, culture patterns and personal habit systems. See his "Contribution of Psychiatry to an Understanding of Behavior in Society," *Amer. J. Sociol.*, 1937, 42:862–70.

[12] This fifth alternative is on a plane clearly different from that of the others. It represents a *transitional* response which seeks to *institutionalize* new procedures oriented toward revamped cultural goals shared by the members of the society. It thus involves efforts to *change* the existing structure rather than to perform accommodative actions *within* this structure, and introduces additional problems with which we are not at the moment concerned.

SOCIAL STRUCTURE AND ANOMIE   677

production, exchange, distribution and consumption of goods and services" in our competitive society, wherein wealth has taken on a highly
symbolic cast. Our task is to search out some of the factors which exert
pressure upon individuals to engage in certain of these logically possible
alternative responses. This choice, as we shall see, is far from random.

In every society, Adaptation I (conformity to both culture goals and
means) is the most common and widely diffused. Were this not so, the
stability and continuity of the society could not be maintained. The mesh
of expectancies which constitutes every social order is sustained by the
modal behavior of its members falling within the first category. Conventional role behavior oriented toward the basic values of the group is the
rule rather than the exception. It is this fact alone which permits us to
speak of a human aggregate as comprising a group or society.

Conversely, Adaptation IV (rejection of goals and means) is the least
common. Persons who "adjust" (or maladjust) in this fashion are, strictly
speaking, *in* the society but not *of* it. Sociologically, these constitute the
true "aliens." Not sharing the common frame of orientation, they can be
included within the societal population merely in a fictional sense. In this
category are *some* of the activities of psychotics, psychoneurotics, chronic
autists, pariahs, outcasts, vagrants, vagabonds, tramps, chronic drunkards
and drug addicts.[13] These have relinquished, in certain spheres of activity,
the culturally defined goals, involving complete aim-inhibition in the polar
case, and their adjustments are not in accord with institutional norms.
This is not to say that in some cases the source of their behavioral adjustments is not in part the very social structure which they have in effect
repudiated nor that their very existence within a social area does not
constitute a problem for the socialized population.

This mode of "adjustment" occurs, as far as structural sources are concerned, when both the culture goals and institutionalized procedures have
been assimilated thoroughly by the individual and imbued with affect and
high positive value, but where those institutionalized procedures which
promise a measure of successful attainment of the goals are not available
to the individual. In such instances, there results a twofold mental conflict
insofar as the moral obligation for adopting institutional means conflicts
with the pressure to resort to illegitimate means (which may attain the goal)
and inasmuch as the individual is shut off from means which are both legitimate *and* effective. The competitive order is maintained, but the frustrated
and handicapped individual who cannot cope with this order drops out.

---

[13] Obviously, this is an elliptical statement. These individuals may maintain some orientation to the values of their particular differentiated groupings within the larger society or, in
part, of the conventional society itself. Insofar as they do so, their conduct cannot be classified
in the "passive rejection" category (IV). Nels Anderson's description of the behavior and attitudes of the bum, for example, can readily be recast in terms of our analytical scheme. See
The Hobo, 93–98, *et passim*, Chicago, 1923.

AMERICAN SOCIOLOGICAL REVIEW

Defeatism, quietism and resignation are manifested in escape mechanisms which ultimately lead the individual to "escape" from the requirements of the society. It is an expedient which arises from continued failure to attain the goal by legitimate measures and from an inability to adopt the illegitimate route because of internalized prohibitions and institutionalized compulsives, *during which process the supreme value of the success-goal has as yet not been renounced.* The conflict is resolved by eliminating *both* precipitating elements, the goals and means. The escape is complete, the conflict is eliminated and the individual is a socialized.

Be it noted that where frustration derives from the inaccessibility of effective institutional means for attaining economic or any other type of highly valued "success," that Adaptations II, III and V (innovation, ritualism and rebellion) are also possible. The result will be determined by the particular personality, and thus, the *particular* cultural background, involved. Inadequate socialization will result in the innovation response whereby the conflict and frustration are eliminated by relinquishing the institutional means and retaining the success-aspiration; an extreme assimilation of institutional demands will lead to ritualism wherein the goal is dropped as beyond one's reach but conformity to the mores persists; and rebellion occurs when emancipation from the reigning standards, due to frustration or to marginalist perspectives, leads to the attempt to introduce a "new social order."

Our major concern is with the illegitimacy adjustment. This involves the use of conventionally proscribed but frequently effective means of attaining at least the simulacrum of culturally defined success,—wealth, power, and the like. As we have seen, this adjustment occurs when the individual has assimilated the cultural emphasis on success without equally internalizing the morally prescribed norms governing means for its attainment. The question arises, Which phases of our social structure predispose toward this mode of adjustment? We may examine a concrete instance, effectively analyzed by Lohman,[14] which provides a clue to the answer. Lohman has shown that specialized areas of vice in the near north side of Chicago constitute a "normal" response to a situation where the cultural emphasis upon pecuniary success has been absorbed, but where there is little access to conventional and legitimate means for attaining such success. The conventional occupational opportunities of persons in this area are almost completely limited to manual labor. Given our cultural stigmatization of manual labor, and its correlate, the prestige of white collar work, it is clear that the result is a strain toward innovational practices. The limitation of opportunity to unskilled labor and the resultant low income

---

[14] Joseph D. Lohman, "The Participant Observer in Community Studies," *Amer. Sociol. Rev.*, 1937, 2:890–98.

SOCIAL STRUCTURE AND ANOMIE   679

can not compete *in terms of conventional standards of achievement* with the high income from organized vice.

For our purposes, this situation involves two important features. First, such antisocial behavior is in a sense "called forth" by certain conventional values of the culture *and* by the class structure involving differential access to the approved opportunities for legitimate, prestige-bearing pursuit of the culture goals. The lack of high integration between the means-and-end elements of the cultural pattern and the particular class structure combine to favor a heightened frequency of antisocial conduct in such groups. The second consideration is of equal significance. Recourse to the first of the alternative responses, legitimate effort, is limited by the fact that actual advance toward desired success-symbols through conventional channels is, despite our persisting open-class ideology,[15] relatively rare and difficult for those handicapped by little formal education and few economic resources. The dominant pressure of group standards of success is, therefore, on the gradual attenuation of legitimate, but by and large ineffective, strivings and the increasing use of illegitimate, but more or less effective, expedients of vice and crime. The cultural demands made on persons in this situation are incompatible. On the one hand, they are asked to orient their conduct toward the prospect of accumulating wealth and on the other, they are largely denied effective opportunities to do so institutionally. The consequences of such structural inconsistency are psychopathological personality, and/or antisocial conduct, and/or revolutionary activities. The equilibrium between culturally designated means and ends becomes highly unstable with the progressive emphasis on attaining the prestige-laden ends by any means whatsoever. Within this context, Capone represents the triumph of amoral intelligence over morally prescribed "failure," when the channels of vertical mobility are closed or narrowed[16]

---

[15] The shifting historical role of this ideology is a profitable subject for exploration. The "office-boy-to-president" stereotype was once in approximate accord with the facts. Such vertical mobility was probably more common then than now, when the class structure is more rigid. (See the following note.) The ideology largely persists, however, possibly because it still performs a useful function for maintaining the *status quo*. For insofar as it is accepted by the "masses," it constitutes a useful sop for those who might rebel against the entire structure, were this consoling hope removed. This ideology now serves to lessen the probability of Adaptation V. In short, the role of this notion has changed from that of an approximately valid empirical theorem to that of an ideology, in Mannheim's sense.

[16] There is a growing body of evidence, though none of it is clearly conclusive, to the effect that our class structure is becoming rigidified and that vertical mobility is declining. Taussig and Joslyn found that American business leaders are being *increasingly* recruited from the upper ranks of our society. The Lynds have also found a "diminished chance to get ahead" for the working classes in Middletown. Manifestly, these objective changes are not alone significant; the individual's subjective evaluation of the situation is a major determinant of the response. The extent to which this change in opportunity for social mobility has been recognized by the least advantaged classes is still conjectural, although the Lynds present some suggestive materials. The writer suggests that a case in point is the increasing frequency of cartoons which observe in a tragi-comic vein that "my old man says everybody can't be Presi-

in a society which places a high premium on economic affluence and social ascent for all *its members.*[17]

This last qualification is of primary importance. It suggests that other phases of the social structure besides the extreme emphasis on pecuniary success, must be considered if we are to understand the social sources of antisocial behavior. A high frequency of deviate behavior is not generated simply by "lack of opportunity" or by this exaggerated pecuniary emphasis. A comparatively rigidified class structure, a feudalistic or caste order, may limit such opportunities far beyond the point which obtains in our society today. It is only when a system of cultural values extols, virtually above all else, certain *common* symbols of success *for the population at large* while its social structure rigorously restricts or completely eliminates access to approved modes of acquiring these symbols *for a considerable part of the same population*, that antisocial behavior ensues on a considerable scale. In other words, our egalitarian ideology denies by implication the existence of noncompeting groups and individuals in the pursuit of pecuniary success. The same body of success-symbols is held to be desirable for all. These goals are held to *transcend class lines*, not to be bounded by them, yet the actual social organization is such that there exist class differentials in the accessibility of these *common* success-symbols. Frustration and thwarted aspiration lead to the search for avenues of escape from a culturally induced intolerable situation; or unrelieved ambition may eventuate in illicit attempts to acquire the dominant values.[18] The American stress on pecuniary success and ambitiousness for all thus invites exaggerated anxieties, hostilities, neuroses and antisocial behavior.

This theoretical analysis may go far toward explaining the varying correlations between crime and poverty.[19] Poverty is not an isolated variable.

---

dent. He says if ya can get three days a week steady on W.P.A. work ya ain't doin' so bad either." See F. W. Taussig and C. S. Joslyn, *American Business Leaders*, New York, 1932; R. S. and H. M. Lynd, *Middletown in Transition*, 67 ff., chap. 12, New York, 1937.

[17] The role of the Negro in this respect is of considerable theoretical interest. Certain elements of the Negro population have assimilated the dominant caste's values of pecuniary success and social advancement, but they also recognize that social ascent is at present restricted to their own caste almost exclusively. The pressures upon the Negro which would otherwise derive from the structural inconsistencies we have noticed are hence not identical with those upon lower class whites. See Kingsley Davis, *op. cit.*, 63; John Dollard, *Caste and Class in a Southern Town*, 66 ff., New Haven, 1936; Donald Young, *American Minority Peoples*, 581, New York, 1932.

[18] The psychical coordinates of these processes have been partly established by the experimental evidence concerning *Anspruchsniveaus* and levels of performance. See Kurt Lewin, *Vorsatz, Wille und Bedurfnis*, Berlin, 1926; N. F. Hoppe, "Erfolg und Misserfolg," *Psychol. Forschung*, 1930, 14:1–63; Jerome D. Frank, "Individual Differences in Certain Aspects of the Level of Aspiration," *Amer. J. Psychol.*, 1935, 47:119–28.

[19] Standard criminology texts summarize the data in this field. Our scheme of analysis may serve to resolve some of the theoretical contradictions which P. A. Sorokin indicates. For example, "not everywhere nor always do the poor show a greater proportion of crime . . . many poorer countries have had less crime than the richer countries . . . The [economic] improve-

SOCIAL STRUCTURE AND ANOMIE   681

It is one in a complex of interdependent social and cultural variables. When viewed in such a context, it represents quite different states of affairs. Poverty as such, and consequent limitation of opportunity, are not sufficient to induce a conspicuously high rate of criminal behavior. Even the often mentioned "poverty in the midst of plenty" will not necessarily lead to this result. Only insofar as poverty and associated disadvantages in competition for the culture values approved for *all* members of the society is linked with the assimilation of a cultural emphasis on monetary accumulation as a symbol of success is antisocial conduct a "normal" outcome. Thus, poverty is less highly correlated with crime in southeastern Europe than in the United States. The possibilities of vertical mobility in these European areas would seem to be fewer than in this country, so that neither poverty *per se* nor its association with limited opportunity is sufficient to account for the varying correlations. It is only when the full configuration is considered, poverty, limited opportunity and a commonly shared system of success symbols, that we can explain the higher association between poverty and crime in our society than in others where rigidified class structure is coupled with *differential class symbols of achievement*.

In societies such as our own, then, the pressure of prestige-bearing success tends to eliminate the effective social constraint over means employed to this end. "The-end-justifies-the-means" doctrine becomes a guiding tenet for action when the cultural structure unduly exalts the end and the social organization unduly limits possible recourse to approved means. Otherwise put, this notion and associated behavior reflect a lack of cultural coordination. In international relations, the effects of this lack of integration are notoriously apparent. An emphasis upon national power is not readily coordinated with an inept organization of legitimate, i.e., internationally defined and accepted, means for attaining this goal. The result is a tendency toward the abrogation of international law, treaties become scraps of paper, "undeclared warefare" serves as a technical evasion, the bombing of civilian populations is rationalized,[20] just as the same societal situation induces the same sway of illegitimacy among individuals.

The social order we have described necessarily produces this "strain toward dissolution." The pressure of such an order is upon outdoing one's competitors. The choice of means within the ambit of institutional control will persist as long as the sentiments supporting a competitive system, i.e., deriving from the possibility of outranking competitors and hence en-

---

ment in the second half of the nineteenth century, and the beginning of the twentieth, has not been followed by a decrease of crime." See his *Contemporary Sociological Theories*, 560–61, New York, 1928. The crucial point is, however, that poverty has varying social significance in different social structures, as we shall see. Hence, one would not expect a linear correlation betweem crime and poverty.

[20] See M. W. Royse, *Aerial Bombardment and the International Regulation of War*, New York, 1928.

joying the favorable response of others, are distributed throughout the entire system of activities and are not confined merely to the final result. A stable social structure demands a balanced distribution of affect among its various segments. When there occurs a shift of emphasis from the satisfactions deriving from competition itself to almost exclusive concern with successful competition, the resultant stress leads to the breakdown of the regulatory structure.[21] With the resulting attenuation of the institutional imperatives, there occurs an approximation of the situation erroneously held by utilitarians to be typical of society generally wherein calculations of advantage and fear of punishment are the sole regulating agencies. In such situations, as Hobbes observed, force and fraud come to constitute the sole virtues in view of their relative efficiency in attaining goals,— which were for him, of course, not culturally derived.

It should be apparent that the foregoing discussion is not pitched on a moralistic plane. Whatever the sentiments of the writer or reader concerning the ethical desirability of coordinating the means-and-goals phases of the social structure, one must agree that lack of such coordination leads to anomie. Insofar as one of the most general functions of social organization is to provide a basis for calculability and regularity of behavior, it is increasingly limited in effectiveness as these elements of the structure become dissociated. At the extreme, predictability virtually disappears and what may be properly termed cultural chaos or anomie intervenes.

This statement, being brief, is also incomplete. It has not included an exhaustive treatment of the various structural elements which predispose toward one rather than another of the alternative responses open to individuals; it has neglected, but not denied the relevance of, the factors determining the specific incidence of these responses; it has not enumerated the various concrete responses which are constituted by combinations of specific values of the analytical variables; it has omitted, or included only by implication, any consideration of the social functions performed by illicit responses; it has not tested the full explanatory power of the analytical scheme by examining a large number of group variations in the frequency of deviate and conformist behavior; it has not adequately dealt with rebellious conduct which seeks to refashion the social framework radically; it has not examined the relevance of cultural conflict for an analysis of culture-goal and institutional-means malintegration. It is suggested that these and related problems may be profitably analyzed by this scheme.

---

[21] Since our primary concern is with the socio-cultural aspects of this problem, the psychological correlates have been only implicitly considered. See Karen Horney, *The Neurotic Personality of Our Time*, New York, 1937, for a psychological discussion of this process.

[3]

ILLEGITIMATE MEANS, ANOMIE, AND DEVIANT BEHAVIOR

RICHARD A. CLOWARD

New York School of Social Work, Columbia University

The theory of anomie has undergone two major phases of development, as exemplified by the work of Durkheim and Merton. In this paper a third phase is outlined. As currently stated, the theory focusses on pressures toward deviant behavior arising from discrepancies between cultural goals and approved modes of access to them. It focusses, in short, upon variations in the availability of legitimate means. One may also inquire, however, about variations in access to success-goals by illegitimate means. The latter emphasis may be detected in the work of Shaw, McKay, Sutherland, and others in the "cultural transmission" and "differential association" tradition. By taking into account differentials in access to success-goals both by legitimate and by illegitimate means, the theory of anomie may be extended to include seemingly unrelated theories of deviant behavior now contained in the traditional literature of criminology.

THIS paper[1] represents an attempt to consolidate two major sociological traditions of thought about the problem of deviant behavior. The first, exemplified by the work of Emile Durkheim and Robert K. Merton, may be called the anomie tradition.[2] The second, illustrated principally by the studies of Clifford R. Shaw, Henry D. McKay, and Edwin H. Sutherland, may be called the "cultural transmission" and "differential association" tradition.[3] Despite some reciprocal borrowing of ideas, these intellectual traditions developed more or less independently. By seeking to consolidate them, a more adequate theory of deviant behavior may be constructed.

DIFFERENTIALS IN AVAILABILITY OF LEGITIMATE MEANS: THE THEORY OF ANOMIE

The theory of anomie has undergone two major phases of development. Durkheim first used the concept to explain deviant

---

[1] This paper is based on research conducted in a penal setting. For a more detailed statement see Richard A. Cloward, *Social Control and Anomie: A Study of a Prison Community* (to be published by The Free Press).

[2] See especially Emile Durkheim, *Suicide*, translated by J. A. Spaulding and George Simpson, Glencoe, Ill.: Free Press, 1951; and Robert K. Merton, *Social Theory and Social Structure*, Glencoe, Ill.: Free Press, 1957, Chapters 4 and 5.

[3] See especially the following: Clifford R. Shaw, *The Jack-Roller*, Chicago: The University of Chicago Press, 1930; Clifford R. Shaw, *The Natural History of a Delinquent Career*, Chicago: The University of Chicago Press, 1931; Clifford R. Shaw *et al.*, *Delinquency Areas*, Chicago: The University of Chicago Press, 1940; Clifford R. Shaw and Henry D. McKay, *Juvenile Delinquency and Urban Areas*, Chicago: The University of Chicago Press, 1942; Edwin H. Sutherland, editor, *The Professional Thief*, Chicago: The University of Chicago Press, 1937; Edwin H. Sutherland, *Principles of Criminology*, 4th edition, Philadelphia: Lippincott, 1947; Edwin H. Sutherland, *White Collar Crime*, New York: Dryden, 1949.

ILLEGITIMATE MEANS, ANOMIE, AND DEVIANT BEHAVIOR   165

behavior. He focussed on the way in which various social conditions lead to "overweening ambition," and how, in turn, unlimited aspirations ultimately produce a breakdown in regulatory norms. Robert K. Merton has systematized and extended the theory, directing attention to patterns of disjunction between culturally prescribed goals and socially organized access to them by *legitimate* means. In this paper, a third phase is outlined. An additional variable is incorporated in the developing scheme of anomie, namely, the concept of *differentials in access to success-goals by illegitimate means*.[4]

Phase I: Unlimited Aspirations and the Breakdown of Regulatory Norms. In Durkheim's work, a basic distinction is made between "physical needs" and "moral needs." The importance of this distinction was heightened for Durkheim because he viewed physical needs as being regulated automatically by features of man's organic structure. Nothing in the organic structure, however, is capable of regulating social desires; as Durkheim put it, man's "capacity for feeling is in itself an insatiable and bottomless abyss." [5] If man is to function without "friction," "the passions must first be limited. . . . But since the individual has no way of limiting them, this must be done by some force exterior to him." Durkheim viewed the collective order as the external regulating force which defined and ordered the goals to which men should orient their behavior. If the collective order is disrupted or disturbed, however, men's aspirations may then rise, exceeding all possibilities of fulfillment. Under these conditions, "de-regulation or anomy" ensues: "At the very moment when traditional rules have lost their author-

ity, the richer prize offered these appetites stimulates them and makes them more exigent and impatient of control. The state of de-regulation or anomy is thus further heightened by passions being less disciplined precisely when they need more disciplining." Finally, pressures toward deviant behavior were said to develop when man's aspirations no longer matched the possibilities of fulfillment.

Durkheim therefore turned to the question of *when* the regulatory functions of the collective order break down. Several such states were identified, including sudden depression, sudden prosperity, and rapid technological change. His object was to show how, under these conditions, men are led to aspire to goals extremely difficult if not impossible to attain. As Durkheim saw it, sudden depression results in deviant behavior because "something like a declassification occurs which suddenly casts certain individuals into a lower state than their previous one. Then they must reduce their requirements, restrain their needs, learn greater self-control. . . . But society cannot adjust them instantaneously to this new life and teach them to practice the increased self-repression to which they are unaccustomed. So they are not adjusted to the condition forced on them, and its very prospect is intolerable; hence the suffering which detaches them from a reduced existence even before they have made trial of it." Prosperity, according to Durkheim, could have much the same effect as depression, particularly if upward changes in economic conditions are abrupt. The very abruptness of these changes presumably heightens aspirations beyond possibility of fulfillment, and this too puts a strain on the regulatory apparatus of the society.

According to Durkheim, "the sphere of trade and industry . . . is actually in a chronic state [of anomie]." Rapid technological developments and the existence of vast, unexploited markets excite the imagination with the seemingly limitless possibilities for the accumulation of wealth. As Durkheim said of the producer of goods, "now that he may assume to have almost the entire world as his customer, how could passions accept their former confinement in the face of such limitless prospects"? Continuing,

---

[4] "Illegitimate means" are those proscribed by the mores. The concept therefore includes "illegal means" as a special case but is not coterminous with illegal behavior, which refers only to the violation of legal norms. In several parts of this paper, I refer to particular forms of deviant behavior which entail violation of the law and there use the more restricted term, "illegal means." But the more general concept of illegitimate means is needed to cover the wider gamut of deviant behavior and to relate the theories under review here to the evolving theory of "legitimacy" in sociology.

[5] All of the excerpts in this section are from Durkheim, *op. cit.*, pp. 247–257.

Durkheim states that "such is the source of excitement predominating in this part of society. . . . Here the state of crisis and anomie [are] constant and, so to speak, normal. From top to bottom of the ladder, greed is aroused without knowing where to find ultimate foothold. Nothing can calm it, since its goal is far beyond all it can attain."

In developing the theory, Durkheim characterized goals in the industrial society, and specified the way in which unlimited aspirations are induced. He spoke of "dispositions . . . so inbred that society has grown to accept them and is accustomed to think them normal," and he portrayed these "inbred dispositions": "It is everlastingly repeated that it is man's nature to be eternally dissatisfied, constantly to advance, without relief or rest, toward an indefinite goal. The longing for infinity is daily represented as a mark of moral distinction. . . ." And it was precisely these pressures to strive for "infinite" or "receding" goals, in Durkheim's view, that generate a breakdown in regulatory norms, for "when there is no other aim but to outstrip constantly the point arrived at, how painful to be thrown back!"

Phase II: Disjunction Between Cultural Goals and Socially Structured Opportunity. Durkheim's description of the emergence of "overweening ambition" and the subsequent breakdown of regulatory norms constitutes one of the links between his work and the later development of the theory by Robert K. Merton. In his classic essay, "Social Structure and Anomie," Merton suggests that goals and norms may vary independently of each other, and that this sometimes leads to malintegrated states. In his view, two polar types of disjunction may occur: "There may develop a very heavy, at times a virtually exclusive, stress upon the value of particular goals, involving comparatively little concern with the institutionally prescribed means of striving toward these goals. . . . This constitutes one type of malintegrated culture." [6] On the other hand, "A second polar type is found where activities originally conceived as instrumental are transmuted into self-contained practices, lacking further

objectives. . . . Sheer conformity becomes a central value." Merton notes that "between these extreme types are societies which maintain a rough balance between emphases upon cultural goals and institutionalized practices, and these constitute the integrated and relatively stable, though changing societies."

Having identified patterns of disjunction between goals and norms, Merton is enabled to define anomie more precisely: "Anomie [may be] conceived as a breakdown in the cultural structure, occurring particularly when there is an acute disjunction between cultural norms and goals and the socially structured capacities of members of the group to act in accord with them."

Of the two kinds of malintegrated societies, Merton is primarily interested in the one in which "there is an exceptionally strong emphasis upon specific goals without a corresponding emphasis upon institutional procedures." He states that attenuation between goals and norms, leading to anomie or "normlessness," comes about because men in such societies internalize an emphasis on common success-goals under conditions of varying access to them. The essence of this hypothesis is captured in the following excerpt: "It is only when a system of cultural values extols, virtually above all else, certain *common* success-goals for the population at large while the social structure rigorously restricts or completely closes access to approved modes of reaching these goals *for a considerable part of the same population,* that deviant behavior ensues on a large scale." The focus, in short, is on the way in which the social structure puts a strain upon the cultural structure. Here one may point to diverse structural differentials in access to culturally approved goals by legitimate means, for example, differentials of age, sex, ethnic status, and social class. Pressures for anomie or normlessness vary from one social position to another, depending on the nature of these differentials.

In summary, Merton extends the theory of anomie in two principal ways. He explicitly identifies types of anomic or malintegrated societies by focussing upon the relationship between cultural goals and norms. And, by directing attention to patterned differentials in the access to success-goals by legitimate means, he shows how the social structure

---

[6] For this excerpt and those which follow immediately, see Merton, *op. cit.,* pp. 131–194.

exerts a strain upon the cultural structure, leading in turn to anomie or normlessness.

Phase III: The Concept of Illegitimate Means. Once processes generating differentials in pressures are identified, there is then the question of how these pressures are resolved, or how men respond to them. In this connection, Merton enumerates five basic categories of behavior or role adaptations which are likely to emerge: conformity, innovation, ritualism, retreatism, and rebellion. These adaptations differ depending on the individual's acceptance or rejection of cultural goals, and depending on his adherence to or violation of institutional norms. Furthermore, Merton sees the distribution of these adaptations principally as the consequence of two variables: the relative extent of pressure, and values, particularly "internalized prohibitions," governing the use of various illegitimate means.

It is a familiar sociological idea that values serve to order the choices of deviant (as well as conforming) adaptations which develop under conditions of stress. Comparative studies of ethnic groups, for example, have shown that some tend to engage in distinctive forms of deviance; thus Jews exhibit low rates of alcoholism and alcoholic psychoses.[7] Various investigators have suggested that the emphasis on rationality, fear of expressing aggression, and other alleged components of the "Jewish" value system constrain modes of deviance which involve "loss of control" over behavior.[8] In contrast, the Irish show a much higher rate of alcoholic deviance because, it has been argued, their cultural emphasis on masculinity encourages

the excessive use of alcohol under conditions of strain.[9]

Merton suggests that differing rates of ritualistic and innovating behavior in the middle and lower classes result from differential emphases in socialization. The "rule-oriented" accent in middle-class socialization presumably disposes persons to handle stress by engaging in ritualistic rather than innovating behavior. The lower-class person, contrastingly, having internalized less stringent norms, can violate conventions with less guilt and anxiety.[10] Values, in other words, exercise a canalizing influence, limiting the choice of deviant adaptations for persons variously distributed throughout the social system.

Apart from both socially patterned pressures, which give rise to deviance, and from values, which determine choices of adaptations, a further variable should be taken into account: namely, *differentials in availability of illegitimate means.* For example, the notion that innovating behavior may result from unfulfilled aspirations and imperfect socialization with respect to conventional norms implies that illegitimate means are freely available—as if the individual, having decided that "you can't make it legitimately," then simply turns to illegitimate means which are readily at hand whatever his position in the social structure. However, these means may not be available. As noted above, the anomie theory assumes that conventional means are differentially distributed, that some individuals, because of their social position, enjoy certain advantages which are denied to others. Note, for example, variations in the degree to which members of various classes are fully exposed to and thus acquire the values, education, and skills which facilitate upward mobility. It should not be startling, therefore, to find similar variations in the availability of illegitimate means.

Several sociologists have alluded to such variations without explicitly incorporating this variable in a theory of deviant behavior. Sutherland, for example, writes that "an inclination to steal is not a sufficient explanation of the genesis of the professional

---

[7] See, e.g., Seldon D. Bacon, "Social Settings Conducive to Alcoholism—A Sociological Approach to a Medical Problem," *Journal of the American Medical Association,* 16 (May, 1957), pp. 177–181; Robert F. Bales, "Cultural Differences in Rates of Alcoholism," *Quarterly Journal of Studies on Alcohol,* 16 (March, 1946), pp. 480–499; Jerome H. Skolnick, "A Study of the Relation of Ethnic Background to Arrests for Inebriety," *Quarterly Journal of Studies on Alcohol,* 15 (December, 1954), pp. 451–474.

[8] See Isidor T. Thorner, "Ascetic Protestantism and Alcoholism," *Psychiatry,* 16 (May, 1953), pp. 167–176; and Nathan Glazer, "Why Jews Stay Sober," *Commentary,* 13 (February, 1952), pp. 181–186.

[9] See Bales, *op. cit.*
[10] Merton, *op. cit.,* p. 151.

thief." [11] Moreover, "the person must be appreciated by the professional thieves. He must be appraised as having an adequate equipment of wits, front, talking-ability, honesty, reliability, nerve and determination." In short, "a person can be a professional thief only if he is recognized and received as such by other professional thieves." But recognition is not freely accorded: "Selection and tutelage are the two necessary elements in the process of acquiring recognition as a professional thief. . . . A person cannot acquire recognition as a professional thief until he has had tutelage in professional theft, *and tutelage is given only to a few persons selected from the total population.*" Furthermore, the aspirant is judged by high standards of performance, for only "a very small percentage of those who start on this process ever reach the stage of professional theft." The burden of these remarks—dealing with the processes of selection, induction, and assumption of full status in the criminal group—is that motivations or pressures toward deviance do not fully account for deviant behavior. The "self-made" thief—lacking knowledge of the ways of securing immunity from prosecution and similar techniques of defense—"would quickly land in prison." Sutherland is in effect pointing to differentials in access to the role of professional thief. Although the criteria of selection are not altogether clear from his analysis, definite evaluative standards do appear to exist; depending on their content, certain categories of individuals would be placed at a disadvantage and others would be favored.

The availability of illegitimate means, then, is controlled by various criteria in the same manner that has long been ascribed to conventional means. Both systems of opportunity are (1) limited, rather than infinitely available, and (2) differentially available depending on the location of persons in the social structure.

When we employ the term "means," whether legitimate or illegitimate, at least two things are implied: first, that there are appropriate learning environments for the acquisition of the values and skills associ-

ated with the performance of a particular role; and second, that the individual has opportunities to discharge the role once he has been prepared. The term subsumes, therefore, both *learning structures* and *opportunity structures.*

A case in point is recruitment and preparation for careers in the rackets. There are fertile criminal learning environments for the young in neighborhoods where the rackets flourish as stable, indigenous institutions. Because these environments afford integration of offenders of different ages, the young are exposed to "differential associations" which facilitate the acquisition of criminal values and skills. Yet preparation for the role may not insure that the individual will ever discharge it. For one thing, more youngsters may be recruited into these patterns of differential association than can possibly be absorbed, following their "training," by the adult criminal structure. There may be a surplus of contenders for these elite positions, leading in turn to the necessity for criteria and mechanisms of selection. Hence a certain proportion of those who aspire may not be permitted to engage in the behavior for which they have been prepared.

This illustration is similar in every respect, save for the route followed, to the case of those who seek careers in the sphere of legitimate business. Here, again, is the initial problem of securing access to appropriate learning environments, such as colleges and post-graduate school of business. Having acquired the values and skills needed for a business career, graduates then face the problem of whether or not they can successfully discharge the roles for which they have been prepared. Formal training itself is not sufficient for occupational success, for many forces intervene to determine who shall succeed and fail in the competitive world of business and industry—as throughout the entire conventional occupational structure.

This distinction between learning structures and opportunity structures was suggested some years ago by Sutherland. In 1944, he circulated an unpublished paper which briefly discusses the proposition that "criminal behavior is partially a function of opportunities to commit specific classes of crimes, such as embezzlement, bank burglary,

---

[11] For this excerpt and those which follow immediately, see Sutherland, *The Professional Thief,* pp. 211–213.

ILLEGITIMATE MEANS, ANOMIE, AND DEVIANT BEHAVIOR   169

or illicit heterosexual intercourse." [12] He did not, however, take up the problem of differentials in opportunity as a concept to be systematically incorporated in a theory of deviant behavior. Instead, he held that "opportunity" is a necessary but not sufficient explanation of the commission of criminal acts, "since some persons who have opportunities to embezzle, become intoxicated, engage in illicit heterosexual intercourse or to commit other crimes do not do so." He also noted that the differential association theory did not constitute a full explanation of criminal activity, for, notwithstanding differential association, "it is axiomatic that persons who commit a specific crime must have the opportunity to commit that crime." He therefore concluded that "while opportunity may be partially a function of association with criminal patterns and of the specialized techniques thus acquired, *it is not determined entirely in that manner,* and consequently differential association is not the sufficient cause of criminal behavior." (emphasis not in original)

In Sutherland's statements, two meanings are attributed to the term "opportunity." As suggested above, it may be useful to separate these for analytical purposes. In the first sense, Sutherland appears to be saying that opportunity consists in part of learning structures. The principal components of his theory of differential association are that "criminal behavior is learned," and, furthermore, that "criminal behavior is learned in interaction with other persons in a process of communication." But he also uses the term to describe situations conducive to carrying out criminal roles. Thus, for Sutherland, the commission of a criminal act would seem to depend upon the existence of two conditions: differential associations favoring the acquisition of criminal values and skills, and conditions encouraging participation in criminal activity.

This distinction heightens the importance of identifying and questioning the common assumption that illegitimate means are freely available. We can now ask (1) whether there

are socially structured differentials in access to illegitimate learning environments, and (2) whether there are differentials limiting the fulfillment of illegitimate roles. If differentials exist and can be identified, we may then inquire about their consequences for the behavior of persons in different parts of the social structure. Before pursuing this question, however, we turn to a fuller discussion of the theoretical tradition established by Shaw, McKay, and Sutherland.

DIFFERENTIALS IN AVAILABILITY OF ILLEGITI-
MATE MEANS: THE SUBCULTURE
TRADITION

The concept of differentials in availability of illegitimate means is implicit in one of the major streams of American criminological theory. In this tradition, attention is focussed on the processes by which persons are recruited into criminal learning environments and ultimately inducted into criminal roles. The problems here are to account for the acquisition of criminal roles and to describe the social organization of criminal activities. When the theoretical propositions contained in this tradition are reanalyzed, it becomes clear that one underlying conception is that of variations in access to success-goals by illegitimate means. Furthermore, this implicit concept may be shown to be one of the bases upon which the tradition was constructed.

In their studies of the ecology of deviant behavior in the urban environment, Shaw and McKay found that delinquency and crime tended to be confined to delimited areas and, furthermore, that such behavior persisted despite demographic changes in these areas. Hence they came to speak of "criminal tradition," of the "cultural transmission" of criminal values.[13] As a result of their observations of slum life, they concluded that *particular importance must be assigned to the integration of different age-levels of offenders.* Thus:

> Stealing in the neighborhood was a common practice among the children and approved by the parents. Whenever the boys got together they talked about robbing and made more plans for stealing. I hardly knew any boys who

---

[12] For this excerpt and those which follow immediately, see Albert Cohen, Alfred Lindesmith and Karl Schuessler, editors, *The Sutherland Papers,* Bloomington: Indiana University Press, 1956, pp. 31–35.

[13] See especially *Delinquency Areas,* Chapter 16.

did not go robbing. The little fellows went in for petty stealing, breaking into freight cars, and stealing junk. The older guys did big jobs like stick-up, burglary, and stealing autos. The little fellows admired the "big shots" and longed for the day when they could get into the big racket. Fellows who had "done time" were the big shots and looked up to and gave the little fellow tips on how to get by and pull off big jobs.[14]

In other words, access to criminal roles depends upon stable associations with others from whom the necessary values and skills may be learned. Shaw and McKay were describing deviant learning structures—that is, alternative routes by which people seek access to the goals which society holds to be worthwhile. They might also have pointed out that, in areas where such learning structures are unavailable, it is probably difficult for many individuals to secure access to stable criminal careers, even though motivated to do so.[15]

The concept of illegitimate means and the socially structured conditions of access to them were not explicitly recognized in the work of Shaw and McKay because, probably, they were disposed to view slum areas as "disorganized." Although they consistently referred to illegitimate activities as being organized, they nevertheless often depicted high-rate delinquency areas as disorganized because the values transmitted were criminal rather than conventional. Hence their work includes statements which we now perceive to be internally inconsistent, such as the following:

> This community situation [in which Sidney was reared] was not only disorganized and thus ineffective as a unit of control, but it was characterized by a high rate of juvenile delinquency and adult crime, not to mention

the widespread political corruption which had long existed in the area. Various forms of stealing and many organized delinquent and criminal gangs were prevalent in the area. These groups exercised a powerful influence and tended to create a community spirit which not only tolerated but actually fostered delinquent and criminal practices.[16]

Sutherland was among the first to perceive that the concept of social disorganization tended to obscure the stable patterns of interaction among carriers of criminal values. Like Shaw and McKay, he had been influenced by the observation that lower-class areas were organized in terms of both conventional and criminal values, but he was also impressed that these alternative value systems were supported by patterned systems of social relations. He expressly recognized that crime, far from being a random, unorganized activity, was typically an intricate and stable system of human arrangements. He therefore rejected the concept of "social disorganization" and substituted the concept of "differential group organization."

> The third concept, social disorganization, was borrowed from Shaw and McKay. I had used it but had not been satisfied with it because the organization of the delinquent group, which is often very complex, is social disorganization only from an ethical or some other particularistic point of view. At the suggestion of Albert K. Cohen, this concept has been changed to differential group organization, with organization for criminal activities on one side and organization against criminal activities on the other.[17]

Having freed observation of the urban slum from conventional evaluations, Sutherland was able to focus more clearly on the way in which its social structure constitutes a "learning environment" for the acquisition of deviant values and skills. In the development of the theory of "differential association" and "differential group organization," he came close to stating explicitly the concept of differentials in access to illegitimate means. But Sutherland was essentially interested in learning processes, and thus he did not ask how such access varies in different parts of the social structure, nor did he inquire about

---

[14] Shaw, *The Jack-Roller*, p. 54.

[15] We are referring here, and throughout the paper, to stable criminal roles to which persons may orient themselves on a carreer basis, as in the case of racketeers, professional thieves, and the like. The point is that access to stable roles depends in the first instance upon the availability of learning structures. As Frank Tannenbaum says, "it must be insisted on that unless there were older criminals in the neighborhood who provided a moral judgement in favor of the delinquent and to whom the delinquents could look for commendation, the careers of the younger ones could not develop at all." *Crime and the Community*, New York: Ginn, 1938, p. 60.

[16] Shaw, *The Natural History of a Delinquent Career*, p. 229.

[17] Cohen, Lindesmith and Schuessler, *op. cit.*, p.21.

ILLEGITIMATE MEANS, ANOMIE, AND DEVIANT BEHAVIOR   171

the consequences for behavior of variations in the accessibility of these means.[18]

William F. Whyte, in his classic study of an urban slum, advanced the empirical description of the structure and organization of illegitimate means a step beyond that of Sutherland. Like Sutherland, Whyte rejected the earlier view of the slum as disorganized:

> It is customary for the sociologist to study the slum district in terms of "social disorganization" and to neglect to see that an area such as Cornerville has a complex and well-established organization of its own. . . . I found that in every group there was a hierarchical structure of social relations binding the individuals to one another and that the groups were also related hierarchically to one another. Where the group was formally organized into a political club, this was immediately apparent, but for informal groups it was no less true.[19]

Whyte's contribution to our understanding of the organization of illegitimate means in the slum consists primarily in showing that

---

[18] It is interesting to note that the concept of differentials in access to *legitimate* means did not attain explicit recognition in Sutherland's work, nor in the work of many others in the "subculture" tradition. This attests to the independent development of the two traditions being discussed. Thus the ninth proposition in the differential association theory is stated as follows:

> (9) *Though criminal behavior is an expression of general needs and values, it is not explained by those general needs and values since noncriminal behavior is an expression of the same needs and values.* Thieves generally steal in order to secure money, but likewise honest laborers work in order to secure money. The attempts by many scholars to explain criminal behavior by general drives and values, such as the happiness principle, striving for social status, the money motive, or frustration, have been and must continue to be futile since they explain lawful behavior as completely as they explain criminal behavior.

Of course, it is perfectly true that "striving for status," the "money motive" and similar modes of socially approved goal-oriented behavior do not as such account for both deviant and conformist behavior. But if goal-oriented behavior occurs under conditions of socially structured obstacles to fulfillment by legitimate means, the resulting pressures might then lead to deviance. In other words, Sutherland appears to assume that the distribution of access to success-goals by legitimate means is uniform rather than variable, irrespective of location in the social structure. See his *Principles of Criminology*, 4th edition, pp. 7–8.

[19] William F. Whyte, *Street Corner Society*, (original edition, 1943). Chicago: The University of Chicago Press, 1955, p. viii.

individuals who participate in stable illicit enterprise do not constitute a separate or isolated segment of the community. Rather, these persons are closely integrated with the occupants of conventional roles. In describing the relationship between racketeers and politicians, for example, he notes that "the rackets and political organizations extend from the bottom to the top of Cornerville society, mesh with one another, and integrate a large part of the life of the district. They provide a general framework for the understanding of the actions of both 'little guys' and 'big shots.' "[20] Whyte's view of the slum differs somewhat from that conveyed by the term "differential group organization." He does not emphasize the idea that the slum is composed of two different systems, conventional and deviant, but rather the way in which the occupants of these various roles are integrated in a single, stable structure which organizes and patterns the life of the community.

The description of the organization of illegitimate means in slums is further developed by Solomon Kobrin in his article, "The Conflict of Values in Delinquency Areas."[21] Kobrin suggests that urban slum areas vary in the degree to which the carriers of deviant and conventional values are integrated with one another. Hence he points the way to the development of a "typology of delinquency areas based on variations in the relationship between these two systems," depicting the "polar types" on such a continuum. The first type resembles the integrated areas described in preceding paragraphs. Here, claims Kobrin, there is not merely structural integration between carriers of the two value systems, but reciprocal participation by each in the value system of the other. Thus:

> Leaders of [illegal] enterprises frequently maintain membership in such conventional institutions of their local communities as churches, fraternal and mutual benefit societies and political parties. . . . Within this framework the influence of each of the two value systems is reciprocal, the leaders of illegal enterprise participating in the primary orientation of the conventional elements in

---

[20] *Ibid.*, p. xviii.

[21] *American Sociological Review*, 16 (October, 1951), pp. 657–658, which includes the excerpts which follow immediately.

the population, and the latter, through their participation in a local power structure sustained in large part by illicit activity, participating perforce in the alternate, criminal value system.

Kobrin also notes that in some urban slums there is a tendency for the relationships between carriers of deviant and conventional values to break down. Such areas constitute the second polar type. Because of disorganizing forces such as "drastic change in the class, ethnic, or racial characteristics of its population," Kobrin suggests that "the bearers of the conventional culture and its value system are without the customary institutional machinery and therefore in effect partially demobilized with reference to the diffusion of their value system." At the same time, the criminal "value system remains implicit" since this type of area is "characterized principally by the absence of systematic and organized adult activity in violation of the law, despite the fact that many adults in these areas commit violations." Since both value systems remain implicit, the possibilities for effective integration are precluded.

The importance of these observations may be seen if we ask how accessibility of illegal means varies with the relative integration of conventional and criminal values from one type of area to another. In this connection, Kobrin points out that the "integrated" area apparently constitutes a "training ground" for the acquisition of criminal values and skills.

> The stable position of illicit enterprise in the adult society of the community is reflected in the character of delinquent conduct on the part of children. While delinquency in all high rate areas is intrinsically disorderly in that it is unrelated to official programs for the education of the young, in the [integrated community] boys may more or less realistically recognize the potentialities for personal progress in local society through access to delinquency. In a general way, therefore, delinquent activity in these areas constitutes a training ground for the acquisition of skill in the use of violence, concealment of offense, evasion of detection and arrest, and the purchase of immunity from punishment. Those who come to excel in these respects are frequently noted and valued by adult leaders in the rackets who are confronted, as are the leaders of all income-producing enterprises, with problems of the recruitment of competent personnel.

With respect to the contrasting or "unintegrated area," Kobrin makes no mention of the extent to which learning structures and opportunities for criminal careers are available. Yet his portrayal of such areas as lacking in the articulation of either conventional or criminal values suggests that the appropriate learning structures—principally the integration of offenders of different age levels—are not available. Furthermore, his depiction of adult violative activity as "unorganized" suggests that the illegal opportunity structure is severely limited. Even if youngsters were able to secure adequate preparation for criminal roles, the problem would appear to be that the social structure of such neighborhoods provides few opportunities for stable, criminal careers. For Kobrin's analysis—as well as those of Whyte and others before him—leads to the conclusion that illegal opportunity structures tend to emerge in lower-class areas only when stable patterns of accommodation and integration arise between the carriers of conventional and deviant values. Where these values remain unorganized and implicit, or where their carriers are in open conflict, opportunities for stable criminal role performance are more or less limited.[22]

Other factors may be cited which affect access to criminal roles. For example, there is a good deal of anecdotal evidence which reveals that access to the upper echelons of organized racketeering is controlled, at least in part, by ethnicity. Some ethnic groups are found disproportionately in the upper

---

[22] The excellent work by Albert K. Cohen has been omitted from this discussion because it is dealt with in a second article, "Types of Delinquent Subcultures," prepared jointly with Lloyd E. Ohlin (mimeographed, December, 1958, New York School of Social Work, Columbia University). It may be noted that although Cohen does not explicitly affirm continuity with either the Durkheim-Merton or the Shaw-McKay-Sutherland traditions, we believe that he clearly belongs in the former. He does not deal with what appears to be the essence of the Shaw-McKay-Sutherland tradition, namely, the crucial social functions performed by the integration of offenders of differing age-levels and the integration of adult carriers of criminal and conventional values. Rather, he is concerned primarily with the way in which discrepancies between status aspirations and possibilities for achievement generate pressures for delinquent behavior. The latter notion is a central feature in the anomie tradition.

ILLEGITIMATE MEANS, ANOMIE, AND DEVIANT BEHAVIOR   173

ranks and others disproportionately in the lower. From an historical perspective, as Bell has shown, this realm has been successively dominated by Irish, East-European Jews, and more recently, by Italians.[23] Various other ethnic groups have been virtually excluded or at least relegated to lower-echelon positions. Despite the fact that many rackets (especially "policy") have flourished in predominantly Negro neighborhoods, there have been but one or two Negroes who have been known to rise to the top in syndicated crime. As in the conventional world, Negroes are relegated to the more menial tasks. Moreover, access to elite positions in the rackets may be governed in part by kinship criteria, for various accounts of the blood relations among top racketeers indicate that nepotism is the general rule.[24] It has also been noted that kinship criteria sometimes govern access to stable criminal roles, as in the case of the pickpocket.[25] And there are, of course, deep-rooted sex differentials in access to illegal means. Although women are often employed in criminal vocations—for example, thiévery, confidence games, and extortion—and must be employed in others—such as prostitution—nevertheless females are excluded from many criminal activities.[26]

Of the various criteria governing access to illegitimate means, class differentials may be among the most important. The differentials noted in the preceding paragraph—age, sex, ethnicity, kinship, and the like—all pertain to criminal activity historically associated with the lower class. Most middle- or upper-class persons—even when interested in following "lower-class" criminal careers—would no doubt have difficulty in fulfilling this ambition because of inappropriate preparation. The prerequisite attitudes and skills are more easily acquired if the individual is a member of the lower class; most middle- and upper-class persons could not easily unlearn their own class culture in order to learn a new one. By the same token, access to many "white collar" criminal roles is closed to lower-class persons. Some occupations afford abundant opportunities to engage in illegitimate activity; others offer virtually none. The businessman, for example, not only has at his disposal the means to do so, but, as some studies have shown, he is under persistent pressure to employ illegitimate means, if only to maintain a competitive advantage in the market place. But for those in many other occupations, white collar modes of criminal activity are simply not an alternative.[27]

SOME IMPLICATIONS OF A CONSOLIDATED APPROACH TO DEVIANT BEHAVIOR

It is now possible to consolidate the two sociological traditions described above. Our analysis makes it clear that these traditions are oriented to different aspects of the same problem: differentials in access to opportunity. One tradition focusses on legitimate opportunity, the other on illegitimate. By incorporating the concept of differentials in access to *illegitimate* means, the theory of anomie may be extended to include seemingly unrelated studies and theories of deviant behavior which form a part of the literature of American criminology. In this final section, we try to show how a consolidated approach might advance the understanding of both rates and types of deviant conduct.

[23] Daniel Bell, "Crime as an American Way of Life," *The Antioch Review* (Summer, 1953), pp. 131–154.

[24] For a discussion of kinship relationships among top racketeers, see Stanley Frank, "The Rap Gangsters Fear Most," *The Saturday Evening Post* (August 9, 1958), pp. 26ff. This article is based on a review of the files of the United States Immigration and Naturalization Service.

[25] See David W. Maurer, *Whiz Mob: A Correlation of the Technical Argot of Pickpockets with Their Behavior Pattern,* Publication of the American Dialect Society, No. 24, 1955.

[26] For a discussion of racial, nationality, and sex differentials governing access to a stable criminal role, see *ibid.,* Chapter 6.

[27] Training in conventional, specialized occupational skills is often a prerequisite for the commission of white collar crimes, since the individual must have these skills in hand before he can secure a position entailing "trust." As Cressey says, "it may be observed that persons trained to carry on the routine duties of a position of trust have at the same time been trained in whatever skills are necessary for the violation of that position, and the technical skill necessary to trust violation is simply the technical skill necessary to holding the position in the first place." (Donald R. Cressey, *Other People's Money,* Glencoe, Ill.: Free Press, 1953, pp. 81–82.) Thus skills required in certain crimes need not be learned in association with criminals; they can be acquired through conventional learning.

The discussion centers on the conditions of access to *both* systems of means, legitimate and illegitimate.

The Distribution of Criminal Behavior. One problem which has plagued the criminologist is the absence of adequate data on social differentials in criminal activity. Many have held that the highest crime rates are to be found in the lower social strata. Others have suggested that rates in the middle and upper classes may be much higher than is ordinarily thought. The question of the social distribution of crime remains problematic.

In the absence of adequate data, the theorist has sometimes attacked this problem by assessing the extent of pressures toward normative departures in various parts of the social structure. For example, Merton remarks that his "primary aim is to discover how some social structures exert a definite pressure upon certain persons in the society to engage in non-conforming rather than conforming conduct."[28] Having identified structural features which might be expected to generate deviance, Merton suggests the presence of a correlation between "pressures toward deviation" and "rate of deviance."

> But whatever the differential rates of deviant behavior in the several social strata, and we know from many sources that the official crime statistics uniformly showing higher rates in the lower strata are far from complete or reliable, *it appears from our analysis that the greater pressures toward deviation are exerted upon the lower strata.* . . . Of those located in the lower reaches of the social structure, the culture makes incompatible demands. On the one hand they are asked to orient their behavior toward the prospect of large wealth . . . and on the other, they are largely denied effective opportunities to do so institutionally. *The consequence of this structural inconsistency is a high rate of deviant behavior.*[29]

Because of the paucity and unreliability of existing criminal statistics, there is as yet no way of knowing whether or not Merton's hypothesis is correct. Until comparative studies of crime rates are available the hypothesized correlation cannot be tested.

From a theoretical perspective, however, questions may be raised about this correlation. Would we expect, to raise the principal query, the correlation to be fixed or to vary depending on the distribution of access to illegitimate means? The three possibilities are (1) that access is distributed uniformly throughout the class structure, (2) that access varies inversely with class position, and (3) that access varies directly with class position. Specification of these possibilities permits a more precise statement of the conditions under which crime rates would be expected to vary.

If access to illegitimate means is *uniformly distributed* throughout the class structure, then the proposed correlation would probably hold—higher rates of innovating behavior would be expected in the lower class than elsewhere. Lower-class persons apparently experience greater pressures toward deviance and are less restrained by internalized prohibitions from employing illegitimate means. Assuming uniform access to such means, it would therefore be reasonable to predict higher rates of innovating behavior in the lower social strata.

If access to illegitmate means varies *inversely* with class position, then the correlation would not only hold, but might even be strengthened. For pressures toward deviance, including socialization that does not altogether discourage the use of illegitimate means, would coincide with the availability of such means.

Finally, if access varies *directly* with class position, comparative rates of illegitimate activity become difficult to forecast. The higher the class position, the less the pressure to employ illegitimate means; furthermore, internalized prohibitions are apparently more effective in higher positions. If, at the same time, opportunities to use illegitimate methods are more abundant, then these factors would be in opposition. Until the precise effects of these several variables can be more adequately measured, rates cannot be safely forecast.

The concept of differentials in availability of illegitimate means may also help to clarify questions about varying crime rates among ethnic, age, religious, and sex groups, and other social divisions. This concept, then, can be systematically employed in the effort to further our understanding of the distribution

[28] Merton, *op. cit.*, p. 132.
[29] *Ibid.*, pp. 144–145.

of illegitimate behavior in the social structure.

Modes of Adaptation: The Case of Retreatism. By taking into account the conditions of access to legitimate *and* illegitimate means, we can further specify the circumstances under which various modes of deviant behavior arise. This may be illustrated by the case of retreatism.[30]

As defined by Merton, retreatist adaptations include such categories of behavior as alcoholism, drug addiction, and psychotic withdrawal. These adaptations entail "escape" from the frustrations of unfulfilled aspirations by withdrawal from conventional social relationships. The processes leading to retreatism are described by Merton as follows: "[Retreatism] arises from continued failure to near the goal by legitimate measures and from an inability to use the illegitimate route because of internalized prohibitions, *this process occurring while the supreme value of the success-goal has not yet been renounced.* The conflict is resolved by abandoning *both* precipitating elements, the goals and means. The escape is complete, the conflict is eliminated and the individual is asocialized."[31]

In this view, a crucial element encouraging retreatism is internalized constraint concerning the use of illegitimate means. But this element need not be present. Merton apparently assumed that such prohibitions are essential because, in their absence, the logic of his scheme would compel him to predict that innovating behavior would result. But the assumption that the individual uninhibited in the use of illegitimate means becomes an innovator presupposes that successful innovation is only a matter of motivation. Once the concept of differentials in access to illegitimate means is introduced, however, it becomes clear that retreatism is possible even in the absence of internalized prohibitions. For we may now ask how individuals respond when they fail in the use of *both* legitimate

and illegitimate means. If illegitimate means are unavailable, if efforts at innovation fail, then retreatist adaptations may still be the consequence, and the "escape" mechanisms chosen by the defeated individual may perhaps be all the more deviant because of his "double failure."

This does not mean that retreatist adaptations cannot arise precisely as Merton suggests: namely, that the conversion from conformity to retreatism takes place in one step, without intervening adaptations. But this is only one route to retreatism. The conversion may at times entail intervening stages and intervening adaptations, particularly of an innovating type. This possibility helps to account for the fact that certain categories of individuals cited as retreatists —for example, hobos—often show extensive histories of arrests and convictions for various illegal acts. It also helps to explain retreatist adaptations among individuals who have not necessarily internalized strong restraints on the use of illegitimate means. In short, retreatist adaptations may arise with considerable frequency among those who are failures in both worlds, conventional and illegitimate alike.[32]

Future research on retreatist behavior might well examine the interval between conformity and retreatism. To what extent does the individual entertain the possibility of resorting to illegitimate means, and to what extent does he actually seek to mobilize such means? If the individual turns to innovating devices, the question of whether or not he becomes a retreatist may then depend upon the relative accessibility of illegitimate means. For although the frustrated conformist seeks a solution to status discontent by adopting such methods, there is the further problem of whether or not he possesses ap-

---

[30] Retreatist behavior is but one of many types of deviant adaptations which might be re-analyzed in terms of this consolidated theoretical approach. In subsequent papers, being prepared jointly with Lloyd E. Ohlin, other cases of deviant behavior— e.g., collective disturbances in prisons and subcultural adaptations among juvenile delinquents— will be examined. In this connection, see footnote 22.

[31] Merton, *op. cit.*, pp. 153–154.

[32] The processes of "double failure" being specified here may be of value in re-analyzing the correlation between alcoholism and petty crime. Investigation of the *careers* of petty criminals who are alcoholic may reveal that after being actively oriented toward stable criminal careers they then lost out in the competitive struggle. See, e.g., Irwin Deutscher, "The Petty Offender: A Sociological Alien," *The Journal of Criminal Law, Criminology and Police Science,* 44 (January-February, 1954), pp. 592– 595; Albert D. Ullman *et al.,* "Some Social Characteristics of Misdemeanants," *The Journal of Criminal Law, Criminology and Police Science,* 48 (May-June, 1957), pp. 44–53.

propriate skills and has opportunities for their use. We suggest therefore that data be gathered on preliminary responses to status discontent—and on the individual's perceptions of the efficacy of employing illegitimate means, the content of his skills, and the objective situation of illegitimate opportunity available to him.

Respecification of the processes leading to retreatism may also help to resolve difficulties entailed in ascertaining rates of retreatism in different parts of the social structure. Although Merton does not indicate explicitly where this adaptation might be expected to arise, he specifies some of the social conditions which encourage high rates of retreatism. Thus the latter is apt to mark the behavior of downwardly mobile persons, who experience a sudden breakdown in established social relations, and such individuals as the retired, who have lost major social roles.[33]

The long-standing difficulties in forecasting differential rates of retreatism may perhaps be attributed to the assumption that retreatists have fully internalized values prohibiting the use of illegitimate means. That this prohibition especially characterizes socialization in the middle and upper classes probably calls for the prediction that retreatism occurs primarily in those classes—and that the hobohemias, "drug cultures," and the ranks of the alcoholics are populated primarily by individuals from the upper reaches of society. It would appear from

---

[33] Merton, *op. cit.*, pp. 188–189.

various accounts of hobohemia and skid row, however, that many of these persons are the products of slum life, and, furthermore, that their behavior is not necessarily controlled by values which preclude resort to illegitimate means. But once it is recognized that retreatism may arise in response to limitations on both systems of means, the difficulty of locating this adaptation is lessened, if not resolved. Thus retreatist behavior may vary with the particular process by which it is generated. The process described by Merton may be somewhat more characteristic of higher positions in the social structure where rule-oriented socialization is typical, while in the lower strata retreatism may tend more often to be the consequence of unsuccessful attempts at innovation.

SUMMARY

This paper attempts to identify and to define the concept of differential opportunity structures. It has been suggested that this concept helps to extend the developing theory of social structure and anomie. Furthermore, by linking propositions regarding the accessibility of *both* legitimate and illegitimate opportunity structures, a basis is provided for consolidating various major traditions of sociological thought on nonconformity. The concept of differential systems of opportunity and of variations in access to them, it is hoped, will suggest new possibilities for research on the relationship between social structure and deviant behavior.

[4]

THE SOCIOLOGY OF THE DEVIANT ACT: ANOMIE THEORY AND BEYOND *

ALBERT K. COHEN

University of Connecticut

Merton's "Social Structure and Anomie" is a large step toward a general theory of deviant behavior. Among the tasks that remain are: further clarification of the ways in which alter's experience and adaptations affect ego's strain and choice of solutions; fuller incorporation of the recognition that deviant behavior develops in the course of an interaction process; exploring ways of conceptualizing this interaction process; and integration of anomie theory with Meadian role theory.

MY concern in this paper is to move toward a general theory of deviant behavior. Taking "Social Structure and Anomie"[1] as a point of departure, I shall note some of the imperfections and gaps in the theory as originally stated, how some of these have been rectified, some theoretical openings for further exploration, and some problems of relating anomie theory to other traditions in the sociology of deviance. It is not important, for my purposes, how broadly or narrowly Merton himself conceived the range of applicability of his anomie theory. Whatever the intention or vision of the author of a theory, it is the task of a discipline to explore the implications of a theoretical insight, in all directions.

Many of the points I shall make are, indeed, to be found in Merton's work. In many instances, however, they either appear as leads, suggestions, or *obiter dicta,* and are left undeveloped, or they appear in some other context and no effort is made systematically to link them with anomie theory.[2]

THE ANOMIE THEORY OF DEVIANT BEHAVIOR

Merton's theory has the reputation of being the pre-eminently *sociological* theory of deviant behavior. Its concern is to account for the distribution of deviant behavior among the positions in a social system and for differences in the distribution and rates of deviant behavior among systems. It tries to account for these things as functions of system properties—*i.e.,* the ways in which

* A revised version of a paper read at the annual meeting of the American Sociological Association, August, 1963.

[1] Robert K. Merton, "Social Structure and Anomie," *American Sociological Review,* 3 (October, 1938), pp. 672–682, *Social Theory and Social Structure,* Glencoe, Ill: The Free Press, 1957, Chs. 4 and 5, and "Conformity, Deviation, and Opportunity-Structures," *American Sociological Review,* 24 (April, 1959), pp. 177–189; Richard A. Cloward, "Illegitimate Means, Anomie, and Deviant Behavior," *American Sociological Review,* 24 (April, 1959), pp. 164–176; and Robert Dubin, "Deviant Behavior and Social Structure: Continuities in Social Theory," *American Sociological Review,* 24 (April, 1959), pp. 147–164.

[2] I am not here concerned with empirical applications and tests of anomie theory, on which there is now a large literature. In view of the sustained interest in anomie theory, its enormous influence, and its numerous applications, however, it is worth noting and wondering at the relatively slow and fitful growth of the substantive theory itself. It is of some interest also that, with respect to both substantive theory and its applications, there has been little follow-up of Merton's own leads relative to the implications of anomie theory for intersocietal differences in deviant behavior. Almost all of the work has been on variations in deviance within American society.

cultural goals and opportunities for realizing them within the limits of the institutional norms are distributed. The emphasis, in short, is on certain aspects of the culture (goals and norms) and of the social structure (opportunities, or access to means). The theory *is*, then, radically sociological. And yet, as far as the formal and explicit structure of Merton's first formulation is concerned, it is, in certain respects, atomistic and individualistic. Within the framework of goals, norms, and opportunities, the process of deviance was conceptualized as though each individual—or better, role incumbent— were in a box by himself. He has internalized goals and normative, regulatory rules; he assesses the opportunity structure; he experiences strain; and he selects one or another mode of adaptation. The bearing of others' experience—their strains, their conformity and deviance, their success and failure—on ego's strain and consequent adaptations is comparatively neglected.

Consider first the concept of strain itself. It is a function of the degree of disjunction between goals and means, or of the sufficiency of means to the attainment of goals. But how imperious must the goals be, how uncertain their attainment, how incomplete their fulfillment, to generate strain? The relation between goals as components of that abstraction, culture, and the concrete goals of concrete role incumbents, is by no means clear and simple. One thing that is clear is that the level of goal attainment that will seem just and reasonable to concrete actors, and therefore the sufficiency of available means, will be relative to the attainments of others who serve as reference objects. Level of aspiration is not a fixed quantum, taken from the culture and swallowed whole, to lodge unchanged within our psyches. The sense of proportionality between effort and reward is not determined by the objective returns of effort alone. From the standpoint of the role sector whose rates of deviance are in question, the mapping of reference group orientations, the availability *to others* of access to means, and the actual distribution of rewards are aspects of the social structure important for the determination of strain.[3]

Once we take explicit cognizance of these processes of comparison, a number of other problems unfold themselves. For example, others, whom we define as legitimate objects of comparison, may be more successful than we are by adhering to legitimate means. They not only do better than we do, but they do so "fair and square." On the other hand, they may do as well as we or even better by cutting corners, cheating, using illegitimate means. Do these two different situations have different consequences for the sense of strain, for attitudes toward oneself, for subsequent adaptations? In general, what strains does deviance on the part of others create for the virtuous? In the most obvious case ego is the direct victim of alter's deviance. Or ego's interests may be adversely but indirectly affected by the chicanery of a competitor—unfair trade practices in business, unethical advertising in medicine, cheating in examinations when the instructor grades on a curve. But there is a less obvious case, the one which, according to Ranulf,[4] gives rise to disinterested moral indignation. The dedicated pursuit of culturally approved goals, the eschewing of interdicted but tantalizing goals, the adherence to normatively sanctioned means—these imply a certain self-restraint, effort, discipline, inhibition. What is the effect of the spectacle of others who, though their activities do not manifestly damage our own interests, are morally undisciplined, who give themselves up to idleness, self-indulgence, or forbidden vices? What effect does the propinquity of the wicked have on the peace of mind of the virtuous?

In several ways, the virtuous can make capital out of this situation, can convert a situation with a potential for strain to a source of satisfaction. One can become even more virtuous letting his reputation hinge on his righteousness, *building his self out of invidious comparison to the morally weak*. Since others' wickedness sets off the jewel of one's own virtue, and one's claim to virtue is at the core of his public identity, one may

---

[3] See, for example, how Henry and Short explicitly incorporate reference group theory and rela-

tive deprivation into their theory of suicide. Andrew Henry and James F. Short, Jr., *Suicide and Homicide*, Glencoe, Ill.: The Free Press, 1954, pp. 56–59.

[4] Svend Ranulf, *Moral Indignation and Middle-Class Psychology: A Sociological Study*, Copenhagen: Levin and Munksgaard, 1938.

actually develop a stake in the existence of deviant others, and be threatened should they pretend to moral excellence. In short, another's virtue may become a source of strain! One may also join with others in righteous puritanical wrath to mete out punishment to the deviants, not so much to stamp out their deviant behavior, as to reaffirm the central importance of conformity as the basis for judging men and to reassure himself and others of his attachment to goodness. One may even make a virtue of tolerance and indulgence of others' moral deficiencies, thereby implicitly calling attention to one's own special strength of character. If the weakness of others is only human, then there is something more than human about one's own strength. On the other hand, one might join the profligate.

What I have said here is relevant to social control, but my concern at present is not with social control but with some of the ways in which deviance of others may aggravate or lighten the burdens of conformity and hence the strain that is so central to anomie theory.

The student of Merton will recognize that some of these points are suggested or even developed at some length here and there in Merton's own writing. Merton is, of course, one of the chief architects of reference group theory, and in his chapter on "Continuities in the Theory of Reference Groups and Social Structure," he has a section entitled "Nonconformity as a Type of Reference Group Behavior." [5] There he recognizes the problems that one actor's deviance creates for others, and he explicitly calls attention to Ranulf's treatment of disinterested moral indignation as a way of dealing with this problem.[6] In "Continuities in the Theory of Social Structure and Anomie," he describes how the deviance of some increases the others' vulnerability to deviance.[7] In short, my characterization of the earliest version of "Social Structure and Anomie" as "atomistic and individualistic" would be a gross misrepresentation if it were applied to the total corpus of Merton's writing on deviance. He has not, however, developed the role of

comparison processes in the determination of strain or considered it explicitly in the context of anomie theory. And in general, Merton does not identify the complexities and subtleties of the concept strain as a problem area in their own right.

Finally, in connection with the concept strain, attention should be called to Smelser's treatment of the subject in his *Theory of Collective Behavior*.[8] Although Smelser does not deal with this as it bears on a theory of deviance, it is important here for two reasons. First, it is, to my knowledge, the only attempt in the literature to generate a systematic classification of types of strain, of which Merton's disjunction between goals and means is only one. The second reason is Smelser's emphasis that to account for collective behavior, one must *start with* strain, but one's theory must also specify a hierarchy of constraints, each of which further narrows the range of possible responses to strain, and the last of which rules out all alternatives but collective behavior. If the "value-added" method is sound for a theory of collective behavior, it may also be useful for a theory of deviance, starting from the concept strain, and constructed on the same model.

Now, *given strain*, what will a person do about it? In general, Merton's chief concern has been with the structural factors that account for variations in strain. On the matter of choice of solution, as on other matters, he has some perceptive observations,[9] but it has remained for others to develop these systematically. In particular, in the original version of his theory each person seems to work out his solution by himself, as though it did not matter what other people were doing. Perhaps Merton assumed such intervening variables as deviant role models, without going into the mechanics of them. But it is one thing to assume that such variables are operating; it is quite another to treat them explicitly in a way that is integrated with the more general theory. Those who continue the anomie tradition, however—most notably Merton's student, Clo-

---

[5] *Social Theory and Social Structure, op. cit.*, pp. 357–368.

[6] *Ibid.*, pp. 361–362.

[7] *Ibid.*, pp. 179–181.

[8] Neil J. Smelser, *Theory of Collective Behavior*, New York: The Free Press of Glencoe, 1963, esp. Ch. 3.

[9] *Social Theory and Social Structure, op. cit.*, p. 151.

ward—have done much to fill this gap. Cloward, with Ohlin,[10] has accomplished this in large part by linking anomie theory with another and older theoretical tradition, associated with Sutherland, Shaw and McKay, and Kobrin—the "cultural transmission" and "differential association" tradition of the "Chicago school." Cloward and Ohlin also link anomie theory to a more recent theoretical development, the general theory of subcultures, and especially the aspect of the theory that is concerned with the emergence and development of new subcultural forms.[11] What these other theories have in common is an insistence that deviant as well as nondeviant action is typically not contrived within the solitary individual psyche, but is part of a collaborative *social* activity, in which the things that other people say and do give meaning, value, and effect to one's own behavior.

The incorporation of this recognition into anomie theory is the principal signficance of Cloward's notion of illegitimate opportunity structures. These opportunity structures are going social concerns in the individual's milieu, which provide opportunities to learn and to perform deviant actions and lend moral support to the deviant when he breaks with conventional norms and goals.

This is the explicit link with the cultural transmission—differential association tradition. The argument is carried a step farther with the recognition that, even in the absence of an already established deviant culture and social organization, a number of individuals with like problems and in effective communication with one another may join together to do what no one can do alone. They may provide one another with reference objects, collectively contrive a subculture to replace or neutralize the conventional culture, and support and shield one another in their deviance. This is the explicit link to the newer theory of subcultures.[12]

There is one more step in this direction that has not been so explicitly taken. Those who join hands in deviant enterprises need not be people with like problems, nor need their deviance be of the same sort. Within the framework of anomie theory, we may think of these people as individuals with quite variant problems or strains which lend themselves to a common solution, but a common solution in which each participates in different ways. I have in mind the brothel keeper and the crooked policeman, the black marketeer and his customer, the desperate student and the term paper merchant, the bookie and the wire services. These do not necessarily constitute solidary collectivities, like delinquent gangs, but they are structures of action with a division of labor through which each, by his deviance, serves the interests of the others. Theirs is an "organic solidarity," in contrast to the "mechanical solidarity" of Cloward and Ohlin's gangs. Some of Merton's own writing on functionalism—for example, his discussion of the exchange of services involved in political corruption—is extremely relevant here, but it is not explicitly integrated into his anomie theory.[13]

THE ASSUMPTION OF DISCONTINUITY

To say that anomie theory suffers from the assumption of discontinuity is to imply that it treats the deviant act as though it were an abrupt change of state, a leap from a state of strain or anomie to a state of deviance. Although this overstates the weakness in Merton's theory the expression, "the assumption of discontinuity," does have the heuristic value of drawing attention to an important difference in emphasis between anomie theory and other traditions in American sociology, and to the direction of movement in anomie theory itself. Human action, deviant or otherwise, is something that typically develops and grows in a tentative, groping, advancing, backtracking, sounding-out process. People taste and feel their way along. They begin an act and do not complete it. They start doing one thing and end up by doing another. They extricate themselves from progressive involvement or become

---

[10] Cloward, *op. cit.*, and Richard A. Cloward and Lloyd E. Ohlin, *Delinquency and Opportunity, A Theory of Delinquent Gangs*, Glencoe, Ill.: The Free Press, 1960.

[11] *Ibid.*

[12] Albert K. Cohen, *Delinquent Boys, The Culture of the Gang*, Glencoe, Ill.: The Free Press, Ch. 3, and Merton, *Social Theory and Social Structure*, *op cit.*, p. 179.

[13] *Social Theory and Social Structure, op. cit.*, pp. 71–82.

THE SOCIOLOGY OF THE DEVIANT 9

further involved to the point of commitment. These processes of progressive involvement and disinvolvement are important enough to deserve explicit recognition and treatment in their own right. They are themselves subject to normative regulation and structural constraint in complex ways about which we have much to learn. Until recently, however, the dominant bias in American sociology has been toward formulating theory in terms of variables that describe initial states, on the one hand, and outcomes, on the other, rather than in terms of processes whereby acts and complex structures of action are built, elaborated, and transformed. Notable exceptions are interaction process analysis,[14] the brand of action theory represented by Herbert Blumer,[15] and the descriptions of deviance by Talcott Parsons[16] and by Howard Becker.[17] Anomie theory has taken increasing cognizance of such processes. Cloward and Merton both point out, for example, that behavior may move through "patterned sequences of deviant roles" and from "one type of adaptation to another."[18] But this hardly does justice to the microsociology of the deviant act. It suggests a series of discontinuous leaps from one deviant state to another almost as much as it does the kind of process I have in mind.

RESPONSES TO DEVIANCE

Very closely related to the foregoing point is the conception of the development of the act as a feedback, or, in more traditional language, interaction process. The history of a deviant act is a history of an interaction process. The antecedents of the act are an unfolding sequence of acts contributed by a

set of actors. A makes a move, possibly in a deviant direction; B responds; A responds to B's responses, etc. In the course of this interaction, movement in a deviant direction may become more explicit, elaborated, definitive—or it may not. Although the act may be socially ascribed to only one of them, both ego and alter help to shape it. The starting point of anomie theory was the question, "*Given* the social structure, or ego's milieu, what will ego do?" The milieu was taken as more-or-less given, an independent variable whose value is fixed, and ego's behavior as an adaptation, or perhaps a series of adaptations, to that milieu. Anomie theory has come increasingly to recognize the effects of deviance upon the very variables that determine deviance. But if we are interested in a general theory of deviant behavior we must explore much more systematically ways of conceptualizing the *interaction* between deviance and milieu.[19] I suggest the following such lines of exploration.

If ego's behavior can be conceptualized in terms of acceptance and rejection of goals and means, the same can be done with alter's responses. Responses to deviance can no more be left normatively unregulated than deviance itself. Whose business it is to intervene, at what point, and what he may or may not do is defined by a normatively established division of labor. In short, for any given role—parent, priest, psychiatrist, neighbor, policeman, judge—the norms prescribe, with varying degrees of definiteness, *what* they are supposed to do and *how* they are supposed to do it when other persons, in specified roles, misbehave. The culture prescribes goals and regulates the choice of means. Members of ego's role set can stray from cultural prescriptions in all the ways that ego can. They may overemphasize the goals and neglect the normative restrictions, they may adhere ritualistically to the normatively approved means and neglect the goals, and so forth. I have spelled out the five possibilities on alter's side more fully elsewhere.[20] The theoretical value of apply-

[14] Robert F. Bales, *Interaction Process Analysis: A Method for the Study of Small Groups,* Cambridge: Addison-Wesley, 1950.

[15] Herbert Blumer, "Society as Symbolic Interaction," in Arnold M. Rose (ed.), *Human Behavior and Social Processes,* Boston: Houghton, Mifflin, 1962, pp. 179–192.

[16] Talcott Parsons, *The Social System,* Glencoe, Ill.: The Free Press, 1951, Ch. 7.

[17] Howard S. Becker, *Outsiders: Studies in the Sociology of Deviance,* New York: The Free Press of Glencoe, 1963, esp. Ch. 2.

[18] Merton, *Social Theory and Social Structure, op. cit.,* p. 152; Cloward, *op. cit.,* p. 175; Cloward and Ohlin, *op. cit.,* pp. 179–184; Merton, "Conformity, Deviation, and Opportunity-Structures," *op. cit.,* p. 188.

[19] Dubin, *op. cit.,* esp. p. 151, and Merton's remarks on "typology of responses to deviant behavior," in his "Conformity, Deviation, and Opportunity-Structures," *op. cit.,* pp. 185–186.

[20] Albert K. Cohen, "The Study of Social Disorganization and Deviant Behavior," in Robert K.

ing Merton's modes of adaptation to responses to deviant acts is not fully clear; yet it seems worthy of exploration for at least two reasons.

First, *one* determinant of ego's response to alter's attempts at control, and of the responses of third parties whom ego or alter might call to their aid, is certainly the perceived legitimacy of alter's behavior. Whether ego yields or resists, plays the part of the good loser or the abused victim, takes his medicine or is driven to aggravated deviance, depends in part on whether alter has the right to do what he does, whether the response is proportional to the offense, and so on.

Normative rules also regulate the deviant's response to the intervention of control agents. How the control agent responds to the deviant, after the first confrontation, depends on his perception of the legitimacy of the deviant's response *to him,* and not only on the nature of the original deviant act. For example, this perceived legitimacy plays an important part in police dispositions of cases coming to their attention.

This approach also directs attention to strain in alter's role, the adequacy of *his* resources relative to the responsibilities with which he is charged by virtue of his role, and the illegitimate opportunities available to *him.* A familiar example would be the normative restrictions on the means police may consider effective to do the job with which they are charged, and variations in the availability to them of various illegitimate means to the same end.

The disjunction between goals and means and the choice of adaptations depend on the opportunity structure. The opportunity structure consists in or is the result of the actions of other people. These in turn are in part reactions to ego's behavior and may undergo change in response to that behavior. The development of ego's action can, therefore, be conceptualized as a series of responses, on the part of ego, to a series of changes in the opportunity structure resulting from ego's actions. More specifically, alter's responses may open up, close off, or leave unaffected legitimate opportunities for

ego, and they may do the same to illegitimate opportunities. The following simplified table reduces the possibilities to four.

RESPONSES OF THE OPPORTUNITY STRUCTURE
TO EGO'S DEVIANCE

	Legitimate Opportunities	Illegitimate Opportunities
Open up	I	II
Close off	III	IV

I. *Open up legitimate opportunities.* Special efforts may be made to find employment opportunities for delinquents and criminals. On an individual basis this has long been one of the chief tasks of probation officers. On a mass basis it has become more and more prominent in community-wide efforts to reduce delinquency rates.

Black markets may sometimes be reduced by making more of the product available in the legal market or by reducing the pressure on the legal supply through rationing.

Several years ago the Indiana University faculty had a high rate of violation of campus parking regulations, in part because of the disjunction between the demand for parking spaces and the supply. The virtuous left early for work and hunted wearily for legitimate parking spaces. The contemptuous parked anywhere and sneered at tickets. One response to this situation was to create new parking lots and to expand old ones. Since the new parking spaces were available to all, and not only to the former violators, this provides a clear instance where the virtuous—or perhaps the timid—as well as the deviants themselves are the beneficiaries of deviance.[21]

II. *Open up illegitimate opportunities.* Alter, instead of fighting ego, may facilitate his deviance by joining him in some sort of collusive illicit arrangement from which both profit. The racketeer and the law enforcement officer, the convict and the guard, the highway speeder and the traffic policeman, may arrive at an understanding to reduce the cost of deviance.

Alter, whether he be a discouraged parent, a law enforcement official, or a dean of stu-

Merton, Leonard Broom, and Leonard S. Cottrell, Jr. (eds.), *Sociology Today*, New York: Basic Books, 1959, pp. 464–465.

[21] William J. Chambliss, *The Deterrent Influence of Punishment: A Study of the Violation of Parking Regulations*, M.A. thesis (sociology), Indiana University, 1960.

dents, may simply give up efforts systematically to enforce a rule and limit himself to sporadic, token gestures.

An important element in Cloward and Ohlin's theory of delinquent subcultures is that those who run the criminal syndicates are ever alert for promising employees, and that a certain number of those who demonstrate proficiency in the more juvenile forms of crime will be given jobs in the criminal organization.

III. *Closing off legitimate opportunities.* The example that comes most readily to mind is what Tannenbaum calls the "dramatization of evil." [22] A deviant act, if undetected or ignored, might not be repeated. On the other hand, others might react to it by publicly defining the actor as a delinquent, a fallen woman, a criminal. These definitions ascribe to him a social role, change his public image, and activate a set of appropriate responses. These responses may include exclusion from avenues of legitimate opportunity formerly open to him, and thus enhance the relative attractiveness of the illegitimate.

IV. *Closing off illegitimate opportunities.* This is what we usually think of first when we think about "social control." It includes increasing surveillance, locking the door, increasing the certainty and severity of punishment, cutting off access to necessary supplies, knocking out the fix. These measures may or may not achieve the intended effect. On the one hand, they make deviance more difficult. On the other hand, they may stimulate the deviant, or the deviant coalition, to ingenuity in devising new means to circumvent the new restrictions.

The table is a way of conceptualizing alter's actions. The same alter might respond simultaneously in different cells of the table, as may different alters, and these responses might reinforce or counteract one another. Responses might fall in different cells at different stages of the interaction process. In any case, as soon as we conceive of the opportunity structure as a dependent as well as an independent variable, this way of thinking suggests itself as a logical extension of the anomie schema.

Parsons' paradigm of social control is in his opinion applicable not only to deviance, but also to therapy and rehabilitative processes in general. According to this paradigm, the key elements in alter's behavior are support, permissiveness, denial of reciprocity, and rewards, judiciously balanced, and strategically timed and geared to the development of ego's behavior.[23] To exploit the possibilities of this and other paradigms of control, one must define more precisely these categories of alter's behavior, develop relevant ways of coding ego's responses to alter's responses, and investigate both theoretically and empirically the structure of extended interaction processes conceptualized in these terms.

Finally, the interaction process may be analyzed from the standpoint of its consequences for stability or change in the normative structure itself. Every act of deviance can be thought of as a pressure on the normative structure, a test of its limits, an exploration of its meaning, a challenge to its validity. Responses to deviance may reaffirm or shore up the normative structure; they may be ritual dramatizations of the seriousness with which the community takes violations of its norms. Or deviance may prompt re-examination of the boundaries of the normatively permissible, resulting in either explicit reformulation of the rule or implicit changes in its meaning, so that the deviant becomes redefined as nondeviant, or the nondeviant as deviant. Thus deviance may be reduced or increased by changes in the norms.[24] These processes go on within the household, courts of law, administrative agencies, and legislative chambers, but also in the mass media, the streets, and the other forums in which "public opinion" is shaped. Although these processes may be punctuated by dramatic, definitive events, like the passage of a new law or the promulgation of a new set of regulations on allowable income tax deductions, the pressure of deviance on the normative structure and the responses of the normative structure to deviance constitute continuing, uninterrupted, interaction processes. One goal of deviance

---

[22] Frank Tannenbaum, *Crime and the Community*, New York: Ginn, 1938, Ch. 7.

[23] *Op. cit.,* pp. 297–325.

[24] Theodore M. Mills, "Equilibrium and the Processes of Deviance and Control," *American Sociological Review*, 24 (October, 1959), pp. 671–679.

theory is to determine under what conditions feedback circuits promote change and
under what conditions they inhibit change
in the normative structure.

In this connection, one of Merton's most
perceptive and fruitful distinctions is that
between the "nonconformist" and other types
of deviant.[25] Whereas the criminal and others typically *violate* the norms in pursuit of
their own ends, but in no sense seek to
change those norms (though such change
might very well be an unanticipated consequence of their cumulative deviance), the
nonconformist's objective is precisely to
change the normative system itself. This
distinction suggests, in turn, the concept of
the "test case" (which need not be limited
to the context of legal norms and the formal
judicial system)—*i.e.*, the act openly committed, with the intention of forcing a clarification or redefinition of the norms. What
we must not overlook, however, is that *any*
deviant act, whatever its intention, may, in
a sense, function as a test case.

DEVIANCE AND SOCIAL IDENTITY

There is another piece of unfinished business before anomie theory, and that is to
establish a more complete and successful
union with role theory and theory of the
self. The starting point of Merton's theory
is the means-ends schema. His *dramatis per-
sonae* are cultural goals, institutional norms,
and the situation of action, consisting of
means and conditions. The disjunction between goals and means provides the motive
force behind action. Deviance is an effort to
reduce this disjunction and re-establish an
equilibrium between goals and means. It issues from tension; it is an attempt to reduce
tension. Roles figure in this theory as a locational grid. They are the positions in the
social structure among which goals, norms
and means are distributed, where such disjunctions are located and such adaptations
carried out.

Another starting point for a theory of
deviant behavior grows out of the social
theory of George Herbert Mead. This start-

ing point is the actor engaged in an ongoing process of finding, building, testing,
validating, and expressing a self. The self
is linked to roles, but not primarily in a
locational sense. Roles enter, in a very integral and dynamic way, into the very structure of the self. They are part of the
categorical system of a society, the socially
recognized and meaningful categories of persons. They are the kinds of people it is
possible to be in that society. The self is
constructed of these possibilities, or some
organization of these possibilities. One es-
tablishes a self by successfully claiming
membership in such categories.[26]

To validate such a claim one must know
the social meaning of membership in such
roles: the criteria by which they are assigned, the qualities or behavior that function as signs of membership, the characteristics that measure adequacy in the roles.
These meanings must be learned. To some
degree, this learning may be accomplished
before one has identified or even toyed with
the roles. Such learning Merton has called
anticipatory socialization. To some degree,
however, it continues even after one has become more or less committed to a role, in
the process of presenting one's self, experiencing and reading the feedback, and cor-
recting one's notion of what it is to be
that kind of person. An actor learns that
the behavior signifying membership in a
particular role includes the kinds of clothes
he wears, his posture and gait, his likes and
dislikes, what he talks about and the opinions he expresses—everything that goes into
what we call the style of life. Such aspects
of behavior are difficult to conceptualize as
either goals or means; in terms of their
relation to the role, at least, their function
is better described as expressive or symbolic. But the same can be said even of the
goals one pursues and the means one employs; they too may communicate and confirm an identity.

Now, *given* a role, and *given* the orientations to goals and to means that have been

[25] Merton, *Social Theory and Social Structure,
op. cit.,* pp. 360–368; Robert K. Merton and Robert
A. Nisbet, *Contemporary Social Problems,* New
York: Harcourt, Brace, 1961, pp. 725–728.

[26] George Herbert Mead, *Mind, Self, and Society,* Chicago: University of Chicago Press, 1934;
Erving Goffman, *The Presentation of Self in Everyday Life,* New York: Doubleday Anchor, 1959, and
*Stigma, Notes on the Management of Spoiled Iden-
tity,* Englewood Cliffs: Prentice-Hall, 1963.

THE SOCIOLOGY OF THE DEVIANT 13

assumed because they are part of the social definition of that role, there may be a disjunction between goals and means. Much of what we call deviant behavior arises as a way of dealing with this disjunction. As anomie theory has been formally stated, this is where it seems to apply. But much deviant behavior cannot readily be formulated in these terms at all. Some of it, for example, is directly expressive of the roles. A tough and bellicose posture, the use of obscene language, participation in illicit sexual activity, the immoderate consumption of alcohol, the deliberate flouting of legality and authority, a generalized disrespect for the sacred symbols of the "square" world, a taste for marijuana, even suicide—all of these may have the primary function of affirming, in the language of gesture and deed, that one is a certain kind of person. The message-symbol relationship, or that of claim and evidence, seems to fit this behavior better than the ends-means relationship.

Sexual seduction, for example, may be thought of as illicit means to the achievement of a goal. The point is, however, that the seduction need not be an adaptation to the insufficiency of other means, a response to disjunction. One may cultivate the art of seduction because this sort of expertise is directly significant of a coveted role. Indeed, the very value and meaning of the prize are conferred by the means employed. One could, of course, say that the expertise is itself the goal, but then it is still a goal that expresses and testifies to a role. Finally, one could say that the goal of the act is to validate the role, and all these kinds of behavior are means to this end. I think this statement is plausible and can be defended. If it *is* the intent of anomie theory, then the language of tension reduction does not seem to fit very well. The relation I have in mind, between deviant act and social role, is like the relation between pipe and elbow patches and the professorial role. Like the professor's behavior, it is not necessarily a *pis aller*, a means that one has hit on after others have failed. It commends itself, it is gratifying, because it seems so right—not in a moral sense, but in the sense that it fits so well with the image one would like to have of oneself.

One important implication of this view

is that it shifts the focus of theory and research from the disjunction and its resolution to the process of progressive involvement in, commitment to, and movement among social roles, and the processes whereby one learns the behavior that is significant of the roles. One may, like the child acquiring his sex identity, come to accept and identify with a role before he is quite clear what it means to be that sort of person, how one goes about being one. But once one has established the identity, he has an interest in learning these things and making use of that learning. Thus Howard Becker's dance band musicians arrive at that estate by various routes. For many of them, however, it is only as this identity is crystallizing that they fully learn what being a musician means within the world of musicians. They discover, so to speak, what they are, and what they are turns out to be highly unconventional people.[27] We seek roles for various reasons, some of them having little to do with tension reduction, and having found the role, come into unanticipated legacies of deviant behavior.

The same processes operate in movement in the other direction, toward restoration to conformity. They are most dramatically illustrated in religious conversion. As the sinner is born again, with a new identity fashioned out of new roles, whole bundles of behavior, not all of them deviant, are cast aside, and new bundles are picked up. Relatively little may be learned by examining, one at a time, the items these bundles contain, the sense in which they constitute means to ends, and their adequacy to their respective goals. The decisive event is the transformation of self and social identity. At that moment a wholesale transformation of behavior is determined.

Anomie theory is, perhaps, concerned with *one* structural source of deviance, while the ideas just presented are concerned with another. Neither one need be more faithful to reality than the other, and the defense of one need not be a challenge to the other. But those who are interested in the development of a general theory of deviance can hardly let matters stand at that. Is it possible to make any general statements about the kinds of deviance that may be attrib-

[27] Howard S. Becker, *op. cit.*, Ch. 5.

uted to anomie and the kinds that may be attributed to role validation through behavior culturally significant of membership in the role? Or may two instances of *any* sort of deviant behavior, identical in their manifest or "phenotypic" content, differ in their sources or "genotypic" structure?

Ultimately, however we must investigate the possible ways in which the two kinds or sources of deviance interact or interpenetrate. For example, does role symbolism function as a structural constraint on the choice of means, and instrumental or means-ends considerations as a structural constraint on the choice of expressive symbolism? Does behavior that originates as a characteristic adaptation to the anomie associated with a particular role, come in time to signify membership in that role and thereby to exercise a secondary or even independent attraction or repulsion, depending on one's orientation toward the role itself? Finally, is it possible that in any instance of deviant behavior, or, for that matter, *any* behavior, both processes are intertwined in ways that cannot be adequately described in terms of presently available modes of conceptualization? I suggest that we must bring the two schemes into more direct and explicit confrontation and try to evolve a formulation that will fuse and harness the power of both.

Part II
The Development
of Strain Theory

[5]

CONTROL CRITICISMS OF STRAIN THEORIES: AN ASSESSMENT OF THEORETICAL AND EMPIRICAL ADEQUACY

THOMAS J. BERNARD

Strain theories have been subjected to a number of theoretical and empirical criticisms, resulting in a decline in strain-oriented research. A review of those criticisms finds that theoretical objections are largely self-contradictory, and empirical studies that focus on seriously delinquent populations provide considerable support. Separate causal processes may be at work in basically nondelinquent but somewhat "wild" youths.

Strain theories argue that crime and delinquency are the product of social forces driving individuals to do things they otherwise would not do.[1] Once the dominant theories in criminology, strain theories are now under attack from all sides. In particular, they are under attack from those favoring control theories, where crime and delinquency are viewed as the result of the weakness of social restraints, so that individuals are free to do what they want.[2] To a considerable extent, these criticisms have been accepted in the field of criminology as valid, and research based on strain theories has diminished and that based on control theories has expanded.[3]

At least some of these criticisms seem inconsistent and contradictory. For example, Nettler (1978: 233, 237) states that strain theories are untestable, but Kornhauser (1978: 180) claims that the theories are disconfirmed by empirical evidence. Strain theories have repeatedly been criticized for describing "grim" delinquents and for forgetting that delinquency can be "fun" (Bordua, 1961: 136; Nettler, 1978: 232; Empey, 1982: 257). Yet strain theories were designed to explain lower-class urban gang delinquency, and virtually all available research paints a "grim," not a "fun," picture of those delinquents (Yablonsky, 1962; Short and Strodtbeck, 1965). In contrast, Empey (1982: 249-250) cites the data on how grim gang delinquency is, and criticizes strain theories

354   JOURNAL OF RESEARCH IN CRIME AND DELINQUENCY

for their "almost romantic" picture of gang life. Kornhauser (1978: 46-50) argues that striving for monetary success is a natural human drive, and is not culturally induced. But she also argues that delinquents are not strained despite limited opportunities, because they do not aspire to anything higher (pp. 167-180). She rejects the argument that they have lowered their aspirations in response to limited opportunities, but does not indicate how they came to be in this inhuman (according to her theory) state. After examining the strain theories of Cohen (1955) and Cloward and Ohlin (1960), Kornhauser (1978: 150-162) concludes that they do not realy locate the source of delinquency in strain anyway. Rather, the real source is in the "perfect socialization" of the delinquent subcultures. Nettler (1968: 233-234), in contrast, concludes that the "real" source of delinquency in the same theories is lack of control. These examples of contradictory and inconsistent criticisms indicate that there is considerable confusion about strain theories at the present time. This article reviews some of the major criticisms that control theorists have raised about strain theories in order to assess their theoretical and empirical adequacy.

IS STRAIN A VARIABLE OR A CONSTANT?

Control theorists argue that strain is not culturally induced, as Merton argued, but that it is a function of natural human appetites and drives, as described by Durkheim. Therefore, control theorists argue that it is relatively evenly distributed throughout the social structure and not concentrated in the lower classes, (Kornhauser, 1978: 141). Kornhauser (1978: 169), for example, states that: "People hardly need to be instructed by culture to want more comfort, greater economic security, the esteem of their fellows, and greater control over their lives." Kornhauser (1978: 146-147) agrees that in societies where there is no upward mobility, such as feudal societies, there is no strain because no one expects any more than they have. She implies that the natural human drives for acquisition are repressed by the culture of such societies, and those drives are freed from control in the processes of industrialization.

Those who study the transition from feudalism to industrialism find the opposite of Kornhauser's argument. Zehr points out that "one of the first tasks of early industry . . . was to teach workers to continue working beyond what was required simply to maintain previous standards of living" (Zehr, 1981: 138). Marx (1906: 290-304) documented the extent of these efforts, and how resistant peasants were to working more than three or four days per week. Weber (1958) argued that the drive to accumulate wealth in modern capitalist societies originated in the dynamic but bleak discipline of Calvinism. Although there are disagreements between Marx and Weber on this question, both describe the drive to accumulate wealth as culturally induced, so that Durkheim may have mistaken a condition in his own society with one characteristic of humans generally.

The basic point, however, is whether strain is uniformly distributed across social classes, or whether it is concentrated in the lower classes. Kornhauser (1978: 169) states that "as long as there are more and less, those who have less will want more." She argues that they will

> compare a millionaire with a strong need to make his second million fast to a struggling clerk with a strong need to find a few thousand dollars for a down paymnent on a house. Whose need is greater? Who is more strained? [Kornhauser, 1978: 47]

Kornhauser's argument assumes that different types of natural needs have the same intensity or strength. Others who agree that human needs are natural describe different needs as having different degrees of intensity. Maslow (1943), like Durkheim, argued that "man is a perpetually wanting animal." However, he argued that there is a hierarchy of needs, beginning with the physiological needs for food, air, sleep, and so on. Once those needs are satisfied, humans turn to safety needs, then to needs for love, then to needs for self-esteem, and finally to needs for self-actualization. According to Maslow, the lower needs on the hierarchy are stronger because when unfulfilled, they dominate the organism and displace any attention to the higher needs. The needs of a millionaire to make his second million would appear fairly high on this hierarchy, probably as an esteem need. This need, according to Maslow's theory, would be weaker than the lower needs to provide for the physical and safety needs of oneself and one's loved ones.

In the context of Maslow's theory, compare the needs of Kornhauser's millionaire with the needs of Liebow's (1967) street corner men, whom Kornhauser (1968: 19) describes as follows:

> In each instance the men enter the roles of breadwinner, husband, and friend with goals they share with the rest of society. They would like to hold down steady jobs with decent pay and some social standing. When they marry, they hope to remain with their wives and support their children. In friendship they intend to show their constancy in reciprocal exchange and in generosity when aid must be unequal. In each instance they fail. At bottom all their failures rest on their job failure. The only jobs

available to these unskilled, relatively uneducated men do not pay a living wage, lead nowhere, provide only intermittent employment, are often back-breaking, and are almost always menial and despised. Their estimate of the worth of these jobs is identical to society's.

These men fulfill their physiological needs irregularly and through the generosity of others; their safety needs are largely unmet because they live in exposed positions in dangerous areas; their needs for love are thwarted when they are driven from their families and friends by job failure; their self-esteem is decimated by the menial and despised jobs they are forced to take and often are unable to hold; and they have no real possibilities for self-actualization. According to Maslow's theory, their needs, although natural and not culturally induced, are greater than the needs of a millionaire to make his second million. Given that the means to fulfill those needs are almost totally blocked, these men experience a higher level of strain than the millionaire, even if the means available to the millionaire to fulfill his needs are comparably blocked.

Strain, defined as the gap between needs and the means to fulfill those needs, in fact varies substantially among different groups in society. Consider the strain of author Joan Didion (1968: 142-143), who at nineteen faced her first real crisis:

> I had not been elected to Phi Beta Kappa. This failure could scarcely have been more predictable or less ambiguous (I simply did not have the grades), but I was unnerved by it . . . . I lost the conviction that lights would always turn green for me, the pleasant certainty that those rather passive virtues which had won me approval as a child automatically guaranteed me not only Phi Beta Kappa keys but happiness, honor, and the love of a good man; lost a certain touching faith in the totem power of good manners, clean hair, and proven competence on the Stanford-Binet scale.

This was apparently the first time in Didion's life that a gap had arisen between her needs and the means to fulfill those needs, and she was taken aback by the experience. Compare her experience with the experience of the 19-year-old unemployed, illiterate, unskilled, black youth who resides in the same ghetto—and looks forward to the same future—as Liebow's street corner men. Liebow (1967: 210-211) describes him as having experienced a lifetime of failing to meet his needs, so that he has "the smell of failure all around him." These two cases are presented as extreme examples to illustrate the range of variation of strain within our society. Whether needs are viewed as natural or culturally induced, strain must be considered a variable, and not a constant.

STRAIN THEORIES AND CULTURAL VALUES

Kornhauser raises several criticisms against strain theories that concern the concepts and mechanisms they propose as the explanation of delinquency. These criticisms are based on her argument that strain (as well as cultural deviance) theories use the term "culture" to refer to everything social. In fact, Kornhauser (1978: 1-15) argues, the term should be limited to a design for moral order passed down as a valued heritage. Thus, she denies what Merton's theory asserts—that American "culture" values monetary success more than it values honesty and hard work (Kornhauser, 1978: 162-165). She argues that the accumulation of money is interpreted in our culture as an indication of moral virtue, and poverty is interpreted as an indication of its absence. Merton's concept of "cultural imbalance" should not be interpreted in terms of too great an emphasis on goals at the expense of the institutional means, but rather in terms of the failure of society to provide "a sufficient variety of values whose achievement carries public recognition." The poor are said to be morally excluded from society because those things that publicly symbolize moral worth in their view, as well as in the view of others in the society, are simply not available to them. In contrast, she points to awards, such as "Heroine Mother of the Year" and "Hero of Production" given in the Soviet Union, that are available to all even if they fail to achieve monetary success.

One problem with Kornhauser's criticism is that she previously maintained that drive for monetary success is not culturally-induced, but is a natural inborn human drive. Thus she argues apparently that cultures should attempt to provide valued goals for those who cannot satisfy their natural inborn drives to accumulate wealth—a "sop" to the poor to divert their attention from their failure. On the other hand, it is interesting that her interpretation of "cultural imbalance" is very similar to what Cohen describes as the "problem of adjustment" faced by delinquent youth in schools. According to Cohen, schools do not provide any means by which these youths can legitimately achieve status. What she apparently denies, although she does not make it explicit, is that such a problem can have any relationship to crime and delinquency other than to reduce the effectiveness of controls. Kornhauser's interpretation of "cultural imbalance" functions as a source of strain if one argues that, as a result of the problem, people are driven to do things they do not want, rather than freed to do what they want.

Kornhauser (1978: 150-162) also criticizes both Cohen's and Cloward and Ohlin's theories for arguing that delinquent subcultures value delinquent behaviors. Such an argument, she maintains, eliminates the need for strain as a cause of delinquency, and is not supported by empirical studies that find that delinquents support conventional values. A problem with Kornhauser's criticism is that it is based on her restricted and precise definition of the term "culture," despite the fact that she criticizes Cohen and Cloward and Ohlin for using much broader definitions. That leads her to some rather ludicrous distortions of their arguments about cultures.[4] To a considerable extent, the term "culture," as it is used in both those theories, is comparable to what Liebow (1967:213) called the "shadow culture" of street corner men. Among those men, values are not passed from father to son as a valued heritage, but both father and son experience the same failures, both generate public fictions to defend against those failures, and both provide mutual support to the other in maintaining those fictions. It is those fictions, according to Liebow, that have been interpreted by sociologists as "lower-class culture." Liebow (1967: 223) concludes that: "What appears as a dynamic, self-sustaining cultural process is, in part at least, a relatively simple piece of social machinery which turns out, in a rather mechanical fashion, independently produced look-alikes."

Kornhauser cites Liebow's study favorably in order to disconfirm "cultural deviance" theories, but she fails to acknowledge that the argument Liebow makes is identical in structure to the argument made by Cohen. Liebow presents a strain theory that has cultural deviance as a secondary source of behavior. He describes part of the process as cultural, but argues that the major part is essentially a strain process similar to that described by Cohen: Each man independently confronts the socially structured strains of guaranteed failure, each generates similar "solutions" to this problem, and each then validates the other's solutions by redefining necessity as virtue. Liebow (1967: 224) argues that the strain element in this process is "of much greater importance for the possibilities of change," and makes as his primary recommendation that "the Negro man, along with everyone else, must be given the skills to earn a living and an opportunity to put these skills to work."[5] This theory is incompatible with control theories, because it describes men who are driven to do things they do not want, rather than freed to do what they want.

Cohen's delinquent boys are also driven to do what they would rather not do. Like Liebow's street corner men, they violate their own values when they commit delinquencies. Cohen and Short (1958: 20-37) later stated: "The notion that the delinquent boy has internalized the respectable value system, is therefore profoundly ambivalent about his delinquent behavior, and must contend continuously with the claims of the respectable value system is one of the central propositions of

Delinquent Boys." They went on to describe the culture of the gang as basically a "technique of neutralization." Despite Cohen's statement, studies showing that delinquents adhere to the dominant values of the culture continue to be cited as disconfirming his theory (Empey, 1982: 250; Hirschi, 1969: 223).

Kornhauser's criticism boils down to a terminological debate— whether the term "culture" should be used to describe group supports that have a separate causal impact on behavior, even though the behavior itself is primarily (or at least originally) generated by confrontation with socially structured situations.[6] Even if Kornhauser's restricted definition of culture as a valued heritage is accepted, that would not attack the strain elements of Cohen's theory, because those elements argue that the behaviors originate in the socially structured situation, not in the "culture" that develops around the behaviors to support them. Kornhauser's inability to appreciate the strain elements of Cohen's theory is derived from her excessively rigid definition of the term "culture," so that Cohen's use of that term blinds her to virtually all other aspects of his theory. Cohen's theory does in fact describe the "culture of the gang" as having a separate causal impact on the behavior of delinquent boys, whereas Kornhauser eliminates as a separate cause of behavior the type of group supports Cohen describes. But Cohen's argument here is virtually identical to Liebow's, who also describes group supports as having a separate causal impact on behavior. To argue that such group supports can have no influence on behaviors, especially among adolescents, seems an extreme position that would be difficult to defend.

DO THE DATA SUPPORT STRAIN THEORIES?

Kornhauser (1978: 167-180) argues that empirical studies measuring the gap between aspirations and expectations have failed to demonstrate that there is any relationship between higher levels of strain and increased delinquency. These studies find that delinquency is associated with low expectations, as strain theories predict, but with low rather than high aspirations. Kornhauser argues that such youths are not strained, but instead are uncontrolled since they have little to lose by committing delinquencies.

When closely examined, however, the studies cited by Kornhauser offer substantial support for strain theories, and little or no support for control theories. Kornhauser cites a study by Martin Gold (1963: 151-173), who interviewed repeated delinquents and nondelinquents in Flint, Michigan, and found that delinquents express low, not high,

360   JOURNAL OF RESEARCH IN CRIME AND DELINQUENCY

aspirations. Gold was testing both strain and control models in this study, and concluded that these data supported the strain rather than control position. Gold found that future jobs were important to both the boys and their parents, and both believed in "the America dream," agreeing that "all boys have an equal chance of getting jobs they want." Thus both were prepared to blame the boy himself, rather than factors external to him, if he failed to get a good job. At the same time, delinquent boys were doing poorly in school, and both they and their parents recognized that this probably would mean that they would be unable to get a good job. When asked "What job would you like to have when you take a job," delinquents responded by naming jobs that were less prestigious than the jobs named by nondelinquents. However, when asked to rate a variety of jobs "on how good you think it is generally," they ranked jobs in the same way as nondelinquents. Thus, they "aspired" to jobs they themselves saw as less desirable. Gold (1963: 167) acknowledged that if these aspirations represented "real preferences in jobs," it would suggest a weakening of controls, not strain, as the explanation of the boys' delinquency. But he argued that an alternate interpetation was more consistent with the entire picture—that the findings represented "defensive aspirational downgradings" that occurred because the discrepancies between occupational aspirations and expectations "were too threatening to boys to be maintained." Gold (1963: 172) concluded that "the crucial point to be made here is that repeated delinquents are more vulnerable to feelings of personal failure, whether their school achievements lead to low aspirations or not."

Kornhauser (1978: 174) rejected Gold's interpretation of his data with the following comment:

> There is no way of disproving such a speculation, but there is no reason to believe it either. In any case, if children respond to low grades by lowering their aspirations, they no longer experience strain, whether or not they ever did.

This comment ignores the fact that Gold was testing both strain and control models, and that he concludes that there are more reasons to believe a strain interpretation than there are to believe a control interpretation, given all of his findings. In addition, Kornhauser's comment that boys with lowered aspirations would not be strained is contrary to common sense, and would need to be supported by data before it could be accepted. Kornhauser (1978: 145) acknowledges that "it seems that most children bring their aspirations and expectations into reasonably close alignment, probably because they are oriented to reality . . . . " Aspirations therefore might be conceptualized as the best possible expectations, given the general situation in which one finds oneself. Kornhauser's argument assumes that all those who achieve these "best possible expectations" will be equally satisfied. But for youths at the bottom of the social scale, it is possible that these "best possible expectations" would be quite unsatisfying. Liebow, for example, describes the extreme dissatisfaction of youths who look forward to the lives of street corner men, but Kornhauser did not integrate that into her theory.

Kornhauser also cites a study by Liska (1971: 99-107) who reinterpreted four studies generally thought to support strain theories and argued that they provided more support for control theories because they demonstrate that delinquency is associated with low, not with high, aspirations. However, Liska's interpretation of these studies is highly questionable. The first of the four studies was by Clark and Wenninger (1963: 49-59), but those researchers did not measure aspirations. Instead, they presented youths with thirty questions designed to test whether they adhered to general "middle" or "lower" class values, and asked whether they thought they could achieve those values through legal means. Clark and Wenninger (1963: 57) found that "regardless of the goals juveniles desire to reach, and the importance attached to them, the extent of illegal behavior is more highly related to the chances they perceive themselves having of reaching these goals without resorting to illegal means." Liska interpreted this as meaning that aspirations are unrelated to delinquency. Clark and Wenninger, however, interpreted this finding as supporting strain theories, because "an inverse relationship exists between perceived chances of achieving goals without employing illegal means and illegal behavior rates."

Liska's interpretation is erroneous because the questions were designed to measure value orientations, not aspirations. Those questions, which Clark and Wenninger reproduce in their article, refer to adherence to the institutionalized means (hard work, honesty, etc.) and not to the goal of success. Clark and Wenninger found that those who adhere to middle-class values were less delinquent, and those who adhere to lower-class values were more delinquent, which they interpreted as supporting cultural deviance theories. This study failed to provide any support for control theories, and in fact contradicted one of control theory's basic contentions as it found that the extent to which middle-class goals were desired "is apparently not a very significant feature in the relationship."

The second study Liska reinterpreted was by Short (1964: 98-127), who tested Cloward and Ohlin's theory in a study of lower-class gang boys, lower-class nongang boys, and middle-class boys in Chicago. Liska considered only Short's data on educational aspirations. Short

362   JOURNAL OF RESEARCH IN CRIME AND DELINQUENCY

found the highest delinquency rates among boys who perceived educational opportunities to be closed, but among those boys, those with low aspirations had higher delinquency rates than those with high aspirations. Short (1964: 115), like Liska, suggested that a control theory explanation might be appropriate for this finding. But this finding does not contradict Cloward and Ohlin's theory. Cloward and Ohlin (1960: 96) argued that delinquent boys seek monetary success, not higher education. Education is one of the "approved means" for achieving monetary success, but Cloward and Ohlin argued that delinquent boys seek to achieve monetary success through "unapproved means." Thus, Cloward and Ohlin's theory does not predict that delinquents will aspire to higher education.

More important in Short's study was his examination of occupational aspirations, which Liska ignored. Short found that all boys expressed high aspirations, and that groups with larger gaps between occupational aspirations and expectations had higher official delinquency rates. Although his data showed some unexpected variations in the levels of aspiration, Short et al. (1965: 56-67) argued later that all levels of aspiration were high enough to support strain theories. Short et al. (1965: 63-66) found that perceptions of blocked legitimate opportunities are strongly related to delinquency, and that perceptions of illegitimate opportunities are also related to delinquency, but less strongly. That finding is consistent with Cloward and Ohlin's theory, which suggests that illegitimate options intervene only after legitimate options have been assessed and found wanting. An additional point can be made, however. Short measured occupational aspirations by rating their preferred jobs on a "prestige scale," yet Cloward and Ohlin argued that delinquent boys seek monetary success without seeking an increase in social status. Thus, the theory does not necessarily predict that delinquent boys will seek increasingly prestigious jobs. Despite this point, Short's data are strongly and consistently supportive of strain theories.

The third study Liska reinterpreted is by Spergel (1964), who interviewed delinquent, nondelinquent, and drug-addicted boys in three urban neighborhoods. As with Short's study, Liska limited his consideration to Spergel's data on educational—not occupational—aspirations. Spergel's discussion of that subject was very brief, and it played no role in his argument.[7] He concentrated instead on success goals and opportunities, where he presented strong and consistently supportive data for strain theories. Spergel's data are particularly relevant for Cloward and Ohlin's theory because he asked not only about desired and expected jobs, but also about desired and expected earnings. As with the Short study, delinquents reported somewhat lower occupational aspirations than nondelinquents (Spergel, 1964: 96). However, in all three communities, delinquents aspired to higher incomes than nondelinquents or drug addicts, and also aspired to the greatest increases in incomes over what their parents earned (Spergel, 1964: tables 4 and 11). But in two of the three communities, they expected to earn less than the other groups, and also expected to earn less than their parents (Spergel, 1964: tables 4 and 13). Thus, the gap between aspirations and expectations, when measured in monetary terms, was greatest for the delinquent groups in these two communities. The exception was Racketville, where delinquents aspired to and expected to achieve high paying jobs as racketeers. Spergel (1964: 122-123) argued that delinquents in Racketville were not strained, because they had the greatest access to both legal and illegal opportunities. Rather, he explained their delinquency in terms of the norms of the community and the presence of illegal opportunities, both of which concepts were derived from Cloward and Ohlin's theory.[8]

The final study that Liska reinterpreted was by Reiss and Rhodes (1961: 720-732), who conducted a self-report survey among junior and senior high school students in Nashville, Tennesee. Reiss and Rhodes did not ask about either expectations or aspirations, so Liska took his data from a table comparing delinquency rates with the occupational status of the father and with the "average" social status of all students in the school the boy attended. The data demonstrated that both had a strong effect on delinquency rates, with the status structure of the school having a greater effect. Thus, boys whose fathers had low status jobs but who attended schools with mostly high status students had relatively low delinquency rates, whereas boys in the opposite situation had relatively high delinquency rates. Liska (1971: 103) derived his data by assuming that expectations are positively related to parental social class, and aspirations are positively related to the social class of peers. It is highly questionable to derive data on aspirations and expectations on the basis of such assumptions.

Reiss and Rhodes (1963: 135-149) did ask one question that concerned "status deprivation" as hypothesized in Cohen's theory— "Would you say that most of the students in your school have better clothes and a better house to live in than you have?" A greater percentage of delinquents responded affirmatively to this question than did any age, sex, race, or class group, and the question had a small but statistically significant relationship with delinquency. Given the limited nature of the question asked, this should be interpreted as providing a minimal level of support for strain theories.

364   JOURNAL OF RESEARCH IN CRIME AND DELINQUENCY

Kornhauser also cited Hirschi's (1969: 170-184) survey of junior and senior high school students in Contra Costa County, California, which found that delinquency is associated with both low aspirations and low expectations. However, Hirschi measured aspirations to higher education and to high status occupations, neither of which, as pointed out above, is a part of Cloward and Ohlin's theory.

Hirschi (1969: 180-182) found strong and consistent support for Cloward and Ohlin's arguments about "crass materialism," as measured by agreement with the statement: "The only reason to have a job is for money." Hirschi then argued that Cloward and Ohlin's theory would predict that boys agreeing with that statement would disagree with two additional statements: "You should not expect too much out of life" and "An easy life is a happy life." He stated that control theory would predict agreement with the same two statements, and found support in his data for the control theory position. Hirschi concluded therefore: "Cloward and Ohlin's hypothesis may be said to be, as judged by the present data, false."

But the first of the two additional questions asks about expectations, not aspirations, and both strain and control theories predict that delinquents have low expectations. Thus, Cloward and Ohlin's theory, like Hirschi's, would predict disagreement with the statement. It is difficult to understand how Cloward and Ohlin's theory would predict disagreement with the second statement. Disagreement with that statement implies a general agreement with the statement "A hard life is a happy life." That can only be interpreted as adherence to the Protestant work ethic, which would be characteristic of Hirschi's controlled boys, but not of Cloward and Ohlin's delinquent boys. In contrast, agreement with the statement "An easy life is a happy life" can easily be interpreted in terms of the "fast cars, fancy clothes, and swell dames" that Cloward and Ohlin argue are the focus of attention for delinquent boys. Thus, Hirschi's conclusion about Cloward and Ohlin's theory is not supported by his data.

An even more substantial objection can be raised in arguing that Hirschi's data contradict strain theories—his data included all social classes. As Hirschi (1969: 182, ftn. 28) admitted in a footnote, Cloward and Ohlin's theory is not intended to explain delinquency across social classes—rather, it is intended to explain a very small group of lower-class, urban, gang delinquents. When this group is mixed in with the very large group of essentially nondelinquent youth who filled out the questionnaire, any special characteristics that they might have would simply disappear.

This point is illustrated by the fact that in the same survey, Hirschi (1969: 66-75) found no relationship between social class and delinquency. Kornhauser later gave several reasons for such findings in self-report surveys, including that "the delinquents of classic delinquency theory are metropolitan slum dwellers; they are by definition absent in rural areas and small towns and cities"; that self-report surveys use "weak indices of delinquency," including a great deal of "nonchargeable trivia," and that occupation is a weak indicator of economic level. Kornhauser (1978: 88-100) concludes that "in the aggregate, the results of all studies together suggest that there is a valid, nonnegligible relation between SES and extreme delinquency in large, heterogeneous communities." Kornhauser failed to acknowledge, however, that these problems would also explain why the same self-report surveys fail to find any relationship between delinquency and strain.

Hirschi's survey clearly illustrates these problems. The major city in Contra Costa County is Richmond, whose population is under 80,000 (Webster's New Collegiate Dictionary, 1980: 1472). The types of gangs described in Cohen's and Cloward and Ohlin's theories are not normally found in such small cities. Hirschi (1969: 54) used an extremely weak index of delinquency, designed to provide variation among an essentially nondelinquent population.[9] To the extent that serious delinquents were present in his population, Hirschi lost most of the data on them due to nonresponse. Hirschi (1969: 42) mentions that 64% of the Negro boys and 46% of the non-Negro boys who failed to complete the questionnaires had official police records. Because of that nonresponse, only about 180 out of the 436 boys in the original sample who were "reported" in police records as having committed three or more offenses actually completed the questionnaires (computed from Hirschi, 1969: table 2). Hirschi's nonresponse rate increased monotonically with the seriousness of delinquency involvement, so that it probably was even greater for the much smaller group who had five or more arrests (as opposed to "reported offenses"), who Wolfgang et al. (1972) found accounted for more than 50% of all juvenile arrests. Data on those boys were then aggregated with data on over 2300 basically nondelinquent boys. Yet it is the behavior of those boys that strain theories attempt to explain.[10]

Hirschi (1969: 41-46) argued that if serious delinquents were included in his sample, the relations that appeared would be even stronger. That argument is true only if the same causal processes are at work in seriously delinquent youth as in basically nondelinquent but somewhat "wild" youth.[11] Serious delinquency, however, does not appear to have a

366   JOURNAL OF RESEARCH IN CRIME AND DELINQUENCY

linear relationship with social class. Rather, as Kornhauser (1978: 88-100) points out, it is relatively concentrated in a "bump" on the bottom of the social structure, while nonserious, "wild" delinquency is relatively evenly distributed throughout the social structure.[12] It is possible that the same causal processes are at work in that "bump" as in the rest of the social structure, but such an assumption should not be made without empirical support. In fact, the studies reviewed above all concentrate on the small "bump" of most seriously delinquent youth and all tend to support strain rather than control theories. This suggests that two separate causal processes may be at work.[13] For basically nondelinquent but somewhat "wild" youth, delinquency is "natural" behavior that is "fun" and needs no other explanation. Variations in the incidence of this delinquency are then explained primarily by the variations in the strength of the social controls. For seriously delinquent youth, however, delinquency is neither "natural" nor "fun." Rather, it is a "grim" situation in which youths are driven to do things they would rather not do.

IMPLICATIONS FOR STRAIN THEORIES

The data on serious gang delinquency virtually demand a strain-type explanation, as they describe individuals who are driven to do what they would rather not do, rather than individuals who are having fun doing what they want. Whether the specific strain theories of Merton, Cohen, and Cloward and Ohlin are adequate is another question. In view of the empirical studies reviewed above, some suggestions can be made about those theories.

Merton's theory is frequently criticized for the role it assigns to culture, which is said to supply the goals, institutionalized means, and egalitarian ideology. This view has been criticized in a variety of ways, including the control theory argument that the goal of success is natural and not cultural (see also Lemert, 1964: 57-97). The role of culture can be reduced or eliminated in Merton's theory if strain is defined in terms of the structural elements of inequality and mobility. In unequal, but generally mobile societies, those who occupy the lower-socioeconomic strata and who also lack upward mobility would be strained, regardless of whether success goals are assumed to be natural or culturally prescribed. This group would include primarily those with low social abilities, an implication that is consistent with most of the research on delinquents and criminals (see Nettler, 1984: 209-218).[14]

This argument is not that different from Merton's original formulation of his theory, where he focused more directly on lack of vertical mobility in a stratified society (Merton, 1938: 672-682). The major difference is that this argument rejects the Durkheimian view of the "biological meritocracy"—that people who are at the appropriate social level, given their abilities, will be satisfied (Taylor et al., 1973: 81-87). It would argue that those who fail to achieve at least some degree of monetary success are strained, even if they see their failure as personal and not social. This definition of strain is consistent with the definition that Gold (1966) used in his study. Gold found that delinquent boys believed that all had an equal chance to achieve high status jobs. They therefore blamed themselves, not society, for their own looming failure. In contrast, most researchers base their definition of strain on Cloward and Ohlin's (1960: 113-121) view that delinquents are strained because of a sense of injustice. Thus, the researchers look for perceptions of blocked opportunity as evidence of strain, rather than perceptions of personal failure.

Cohen's theory of gang delinquency is often interpreted as a future-oriented theory (e.g., Empey, 1982: 234-238). However, it focuses primarily on the present problem of the lack of status in school, rather than on the future achievement of middle class status. Studies show that present problems in school are strongly related to delinquency (Elliott and Voss, 1974; Frease, 1973; Polk and Schafer, 1972) and Gold (1966) has argued convincingly that delinquent boys are more afflicted with feelings of personal failure. These indicate support for the argument Cohen makes. The theory should be interpreted primarily as a structural theory, however, in which the gang is basically a group of "independently produced look-alikes," and the group supports for criminal behavior are secondary.

Cloward and Ohlin's theory, in contrast, is more fully a future-oriented theory. Research testing the theory should focus on the aspired and expected levels of monetary earnings, as the question was phrased by Spergel, and not on aspired and expected levels of occupational or educational achievement, because those do not enter into the theory. Cloward and Ohlin's agrument that gang boys have strong social abilities and that strain arises from a sense of injustice is inconsistent with the data and should be discarded. Again, this argument is necessary only if one adheres to the Durkheimian view of a "biological meritocracy."

In the above formulations, the three major strain theories are primarily structural theories, with the cultural elements reduced or eliminated. The theories are consistent with each other in these forms, although the theoretical linkages among them could be developed further. For example, in unequal, but generally mobile societies, those without mobility lack status among their peers; concentration on achievement of money objectives to the exclusion of increased status levels may in part be a reaction formation against the denial of mobility, and so on.

All three of these theories are also linked to explanations of the form that the criminal behavior takes. Merton (1968) proposed a typology of adaptations to strain, Cohen and Short (1958) speculated about the origins of different types of gang subcultures, and Cloward and Ohlin (1960) presented a more formal and systematic theory about the types of gang behaviors. However, in each case, it seems best to discard these typologies, and to shift to arguments about group process for the explanation of specific forms of behavior. This is consistent with Cohen's (1965) recommendations about Merton's theory, with which Merton (1964) agreed, and with Short's and Strodbeck (1965) research on Cloward and Ohlin's theory.

CONCLUSION

Empirical studies that focus on representative samples of juvenile populations must employ weak measures of delinquency and relatively broad definitions of social class in order to achieve variation within the population. Seriously delinquent youth are a statistically insignificant group within such populations, and information about them cannot be derived from such studies. These studies have failed to find a relationship between delinquency and strain for the same reasons that they have failed to find a relationship between delinquency and social class. These studies have generally supported control theories, but such support should be interpreted primarily in terms of explaining the variation between underconformity and overconformity (i.e., "wild" youth and "square" youth) in a basically nondelinquent population.

Strain theories, in contrast, focus on explaining the behavior of a small group of seriously delinquent youth, primarily urban male gang delinquents. Studies that have focused specifically on these youth find support for strain theories rather than control theories. This suggests that separate causal processes may be at work in seriously delinquent youth. Those separate causal processes are primarily structural forces driving individuals to do things they would not otherwise do.

Paul Rock (1980: 290-303) described criminology as "a number of fitful leaps from one partially examined thesis to another." This situation arises because criminology receives infusions of theory and research from a variety of different academic disciplines, and criminologists tend to close off old areas of research as new ones open up, rather than to fully explore each area. Strain theories seem to be one such area that has been prematurely closed off. C. Wright Mills (1959) argued that the calling of the sociological imagination is to link the personal troubles of individuals to the broader characterisitics of the social structure. Strain theories respond to that calling, and in that sense are emininently sociological. They deserve a resurgence of interest in criminology.

NOTES

1. The major strain theories are found in Merton (1968: 185-214), Cohen (1955), and Cloward and Ohlin (1960).

2. The major control theory is found in Hirschi (1969).

3. For example, the 1982 Annual Meeting of the American Society of Criminology contained five sessions devoted to various aspects of control theories, but none devoted to strain theories.

4. Compare, for example, Kornhauser's (1978: 153-154) overwrought portrayal of Cohen's view of working-class culture with Cohen's (1955: 94-97) moderate and cautious description.

5. Nettler (1978: 225) comments that "what is stressed as causal is best recognized by the policy prescriptions, if any, that these many authors offer." Thus, Lieblow's policy prescriptions remove any doubt that his is a strain theory.

6. Kornhauser (1978: 61) cites Suttles' (1968) argument as an alternate interpretation to cultural deviance theories. Suttles argues that there are "shared behavioral expectations" that are neither approved nor valued. Suttles' argument suggests that these shared expectations have a separate causal impact on behavior, but Kornhauser does not deal with the theoretical implications of that fact.

7. See Spergel (1964: 37-38). I was unable to reconstruct Liska'a data from Spergel's discussion of educational aspirations.

8. Kornhauser (1978: 177-178) raised a number of other objections to Spergel's work, claiming it did not demonstrate support for strain theories. However, her criticisms arose from the fact that delinquents in Racketville were not strained, or the fact that responses from drug addicts were inconsistent.

9. Hirschi's index (1969: 62-64) contained six relatively minor offenses, the most serious being stealing an item worth more than $50. He used a "recency index" for most of his results, in which respondants were given one point for each of the six offenses they reported committing in the last year, regardless of the number of times they reported committing it. His data aggregate those reporting two or more of these minor offenses into the most serious category. Kornhauser (1978: 97) specifically comments on the weakness of Hirschi's measure.

10. Other studies reporting that delinquents have lowered aspirations have similarly been afflicted with an absence of seriously delinquent youth. Rankin (1980: 420-434), for example, surveyed suburban areas around Detroit with practically no black population whatsoever. Johnson (1979: 105-108) included only 58 underclass youths in his survey of 734 high school sophomores, only 4 of whom were black. He also used extremely broad criteria for the "underclass," which for example, would include a youth whose father is

370   JOURNAL OF RESEARCH IN CRIME AND DELINQUENCY

employed as construction worker, machine operator, truck driver, assembly line worker, journeyman, carpenter, electrician, plumber, jeweler, foreman of a work gang, factory inspector, or owner of a small store or small company, as long as the father had been unemployed any time during the last three years, or was ill, disabled, retired, or working part-time, and the mother was a housewife. These studies should be interpreted as finding that, among basically nondelinquent youth, youths with lower aspirations are "wilder" than youths with higher aspirations.

11. Toby (1959) raised the same point in his review of F. Ivan Nye's earlier control theory.

12. See also Gold (1966: 27-46), Gordon (1967: 927-944), Hewett (1970: 77), Clelland and Carter (1980: 319-336), Elliott and Ageton (1981: 95-110). Several studies that claim to focus on the very small group at the bottom of the social structure report no differences in crime rates. However, these studies actually employ very broad cirteria for inclusion in that group. For example, Berger and Simon (1974: 146-161) claim to test the "tangle of pathology" hypothesis in lower-class black families. However, their data are based on a sample whose characteristics "closely match the demographic characteristics of the 14-to 18-year old population of the state (of Illinois)," and they include approximately 20% of that sample in the "Low SES" group (percentage computed from Table 1). Johnson (1979: 99-100) found no differences in crime rates between "underclass" and "working class," but see note 10 above for his very broad definition of "underclass." Hindelang et al. (1981: 181-198) also found no class differences, but based their conclusion on a comparison between 402 "Low SES" and 444 "High SES" white males, where the criteria for the "Low SES" group was similar to Johnson's (1979).

13. Matza (1964) suggests a similar argument. He presents a control theory of "drift" to explain minor delinquency, but suggests that serious delinquency may be explained by the more traditional sociological and psychological theories.

14. Nettler (1984) maintains that these studies disconfirm strain theories, but under the present interpretation, strain theories are supported by them.

REFERENCES

Berger, A. S. and W. Simon
    1974 "Black families and the Moynihan report: a research evaluation." Social Problems 22: 146-161.
Bordua, D. J.
    1961 "Delinquent subculture." Annals of the Amer. Society of Pol. and Social Sci. 338 (November): 119-136.
Clark, J. P. and E. P. Wenninger
    1963 "Goal orientation and illegal behavior among juveniles." Social Forces 42 (October): 49-59.
Clelland, D. and J. Carter
    1980 "The new myth of class and crime." Criminology 18: 319-336.
Cloward, R. A. and L. E. Ohlin
    1960 Delinquency and Opportunity. New York: Free Press.
Cohen, A. K.
    1955 Delinquent Boys. New York: Free Press.
    1965 "The sociology of the deviant act." Amer. Soc. Rev. 30: 5-14.

Bernard / THEORETICAL AND EMPIRICAL ADEQUACY   371

Cohen, A. K. and J. F. Short, Jr.
 1958 "Research in delinquent subcultures." J. of Social Issues 14: 20-37.
Didion, J.
 1968 Slouching Towards Bethlehem. New York: Simon & Schuster.
Elliott, D. S. and S. Ageton
 1981 "Reconciling race and class differences in self-reported and official estimates of delinquency." Amer. Soc. Rev. 45: 95-110.
Elliott, D. S. and H. L. Voss
 1974 Delinquency and Dropout. Lexington, MA: D. C. Heath.
Empey, L. T.
 1982 American Delinquency. Homewood, IL: Dorsey.
Frease, D. D.
 1973 "Delinquency, social class, and the schools." Sociology and Social Research 57: 443-459.
Gold, M.
 1963 Status Forces in Delinquent Boys. Ann Arbor, MI: Institute for Social Research.
 1966 "Undetected delinquent behavior." J. of Research in Crime and Delinquency 3: 27-46.
Gordon, R. A.
 1967 "Issues in the ecological study of delinquency." Amer. Soc. Rev. 32: 927-944.
Hewett, J. P.
 1970 Social Stratification and Deviant Behavior. New York: Random House.
Hindelang, M. J., T. Hirschi, and J. G. Weis
 1981 Measuring Delinquency. Beverly Hills, CA: Sage.
Hirschi, T.
 1969 Causes of Delinquency. Berkeley: Univ. of California Press.
Johnson, R. E.
 1979 Juvenile Delinquency and Its Origins. Cambridge: Cambridge Univ. Press.
Kornhauser, R. R.
 1978 Social Sources of Delinquency. Chicago: Univ. of Chicago Press.
Lemert, E. M.
 1964 "Social structure, social control and deviation," in M. B. Clinard (ed.) Anomie and Deviant Behavior. New York: Free Press.
Liebow, E.
 1967 Tally's Corner. Boston: Little, Brown.
Liska, A. E.
 1971 "Aspirations, expectations, and delinquency." Soc. Q. 12 (Winter): 99-107.
Marx, Karl
 1906 Capital—A Critique of Political Economy. New York: Modern Library.
Maslow, A. H.
 1943 "A theory of human motivation." Psych. Rev. 50: 370-396.
Matza, D.
 1964 Delinquency and Drift. New York: John Wiley.
Merton, R. K.
 1938 "Social structure and anomie." Amer. Soc. Rev. 3: 672-682.
 1964 "Anomie, anomia, and social interaction," in M. B. Clinard (ed.) Anomie and Deviant Behavior. New York: Free Press.
 1968 Social Theory and Social Structure. New York: Free Press.

Mills, C. W.
   1959   The Sociological Imagination. New York: Oxford Univ. Press.
Nettler, G.
   1978   Explaining Crime. New York: McGraw-Hill.
   1984   Explaining Crime. New York: McGraw-Hill.
Polk, K. and W. E. Schafer (eds.)
   1972   Schools and Delinquency. Englewood Cliffs, NJ: Prentice-Hall.
Rankin, J. H.
   1980   "School factors and delinquency." Sociology and Social Research 64: 420-434.
Reiss, A. J., Jr., and A. L. Rhodes
   1961   "The distribution of juvenile delinquency in the social class structure." Amer.
          Soc. Rev. 26 (October): 720-732.
   1963   "Status deprivation and delinquent behavior." Soc. Q. 4: 135-149.
Rock, P.
   1980   "Has a deviance a future?" in H. M. Blalock (ed.) Sociological Theory and
          Research. New York: Free Press.
Short, J. F., Jr.
   1964   "Gang delinquency and anomie," in M. B. Clinard (ed.) Anomie and Deviant
          Behavior. New York: Free Press.
Short, J. F., Jr., and F. L. Strodtbeck
   1965   Group Process and Gang Delinquency. Chicago: Univ. of Chicago Press.
Short, J. F., Jr., R. Rivers, and R. A. Tennyson
   1965   "Perceived opportunities, gang membership, and delinquency." Amer. Soc.
          Rev. 30 (February): 56-67.
Spergel, I.
   1964   Racketville, Slumtown, Haulberg. Chicago: Univ. of Chicago Press.
Suttles, G.
   1968   Social Order of the Slum. Chicago: Univ. of Chicago Press.
Taylor, I., P. Walton, and J. Young
   1973   The New Criminology. New York: Harper & Row.
Toby, J.
   1959   "Book review." Amer. Soc. Rev. 22: 282-283.
          282-283.
Weber, Max
   1958   The Protestant Ethic and the Spirit of Capitalism. New York: Scribner's.
Wolfgang, M. E., R. M. Figlio, and T. Sellin
   1972   Delinquency in a Birth Cohort. Chicago: Univ. of Chicago Press.
Yablonsky, L.
   1962   The Violent Gang. New York: Free Press.
Zehr, H.
   1981   "The modernization of crime in Germany and France, 1830-1913," in L. I.
          Shelley (ed.) Readings in Comparative Criminology. Carbondale: Southern
          Illinois Univ. Press.

[6]

DELINQUENCY AND THE AGE STRUCTURE OF SOCIETY

DAVID F. GREENBERG

Much attention has been paid in research on the causes of delinquency to the role of such variables as class, sex, and race. By comparison, the relationship between age and criminality or delinquency, though noted in passing in many studies, has received little systematic attention. This paper will present a theoretical analysis of the age distribution of criminal involvement. In particular, I will attempt to show that the increasingly disproportionate involvement of juveniles in major crime categories, though not readily explained by current sociological theories of delinquency, can be understood as a consequence of the historically changing position of juveniles in industrial societies. This changing position, I will argue, has its origin, at least in Europe and the United States, in the long term tendencies of a capitalist economic system. Although the conceptual framework for this analysis is Marxist, the approach taken appropriates Marxian theory for criminology in a way that departs from earlier Marxist writings on crime. The nature of this departure will be spelled out explicitly in the concluding section.

Age and Criminal Involvement

As can be seen from Table 1, crime-specific arrest rates in the United States show substantial variation with age. For 1970, per capita arrest rates for vandalism and property crimes not involving confrontation with a person (burglary, grand larceny, auto theft) peak at age 15—16, fall to half their peak values in two to four years, and continue to decline rapidly. Arrest rates for narcotics violations and offenses involving confrontation with a person (homicide, forcible rape, aggravated assault, robbery) peak at age 19—21 and also decline with age, but less rapidly.

Studies of recidivism show that rearrest rates for those officially labeled as offenders also decline with age [1].

New York University, N.Y., U.S.A.

190

TABLE I

1970 Arrests Per 100,000 Population by Age*

AGE: OFFENSE	13–14	15	16	17	18	19	20	21	22	23	24	25–29	30–34	% under 18	% under 21
Murder and non-negligent manslaughter	3.5	13.2	20.1	25.2	35.8	35.5	35.2	*40.2*	35.3	36.6	37.8	30.7	24.4	10.2	24.5
Forcible rape	12.5	32.5	43.2	54.3	61.8	*64.7*	60.6	60.4	54.3	52.6	50.6	36.1	22.9	20.6	41.6
Robbery	164	274	340	373	393	*394*	358	346	293	250	250	154	82.5	32.2	55.3
Aggravated assault	109	189	243	272	309	317	320	347	328	316	*355*	284	240	17.6	30.5
Burglary	979	979	*1463*	1302	1176	968	788	697	585	527	505	320	191	50.9	69.8
Larceny over $50	2178	*2741*	2740	2408	2183	1788	1460	1309	1100	953	936	631	463	50.4	66.4
Auto theft	397	898	*965*	759	556	436	344	295	236	197	193	119	69.1	52.9	71.6
Vandalism	570	*613*	514	375	238	191	141	134	111	76.4	97.1	69	50.6	71.6	80.8
Narcotic drug laws	215	665	1169	1585	1971	*2073*	1187	1763	1447	1199	1039	587	312	22.0	52.2

*Arrests are based on F.B.I. statistics for 1970, population is number of males recorded in the 1970 census. The peak age in each offense category is set in italic type.

The risks in using agency-generated data to draw conclusions about group differences in rates of criminal involvement have been underscored repeatedly [2]. However, field and self-reporting studies of delinquency confirm that delinquents do abandon crime in late adolescence [3,4]. West, for example, found the average career length of his "serious thieves" to be about two years in his field study [5]. Evidence that declining arrest rates cannot be attributed to improved ability to escape apprehension is provided by Wilson [6], who found that self-reported participation in crime declined after age 15, with no relationship between age and probability of apprehension.

There is also evidence from self-reporting studies that recruitment to delinquency declines with age [7].

Already in nineteenth century United States, it had been noted that criminal involvement tended to decline with age [8], but fragmentary evidence suggests that the peak was higher than at present, and the decline gradual [9]. Tabulations of prosecutions, convictions and imprisonments for nineteenth century Europe show higher peak ages in agrarian nations like France, Italy and Austria than in industrialized nations like England [10]. The shift in arrest toward younger age brackets in recent decades in a number of other countries [11] is also suggestive of a relationship between the age distribution of crime and economic development.

In terms of delinquency theory, systematic variation in delinquent involvement with age requires explanation no less than other systematic differences. Indeed, age variation may help to test delinquency theories constructed to explain other sources of variation, such as class or sex. Since these other sources of variation can be explained in many ways, the adequacy with which rival theories explain age variation may help us to distinguish among them.

At a practical level, the rising volume of juvenile crime is creating public clamor for less lenient treatment of juvenile offenders. Intelligent response to this development requires an understanding of the social forces that have led to the increase.

Delinquency Theory and the Age Distribution of Crime

Since neither infants nor the elderly possess the prowess and agility required for some forms of crime, *some* association between age and criminal involvement can be expected on biological grounds alone. It is equally evident that the strong variation with age shown in Table 1 cannot be explained in these terms alone. Biological explanations based on other correlates of age than physical ability are equally weak. The Gluecks'

192

proposal that delinquency may be caused by delayed maturation [12] is inconsistent with the absence of any difference in physical maturity between delinquent and non-delinquent boys of the same age [13]. Moreover, any explanation of age variation in criminality based on psychological reactions to physiological changes accompanying adolescence would be difficult to reconcile with the great variation in delinquent involvement among juveniles as well as the lateness of peak involvement in violence offenses. If age is relevant to criminality, the link should lie primarily in its social significance.

Yet contemporary sociological theories of delinquency shed little light on the relationship between crime and age. If, for example, lower class male gang delinquence is simply a manifestation of a lower class subculture as Miller [14] has maintained, it would be mysterious why 21-year-olds act in conformity with the norms of their subculture so much *less* often than their siblings just a few years younger — unless the norms themselves were age-specific. While age-specific expectations may contribute to desistance from some forms of delinquent play, such as vandalism and throwing snowballs at cars, as Clark and Haurek [15] suggest, there is no social class in which felony, theft and violence receive general *approval* for persons of any age. Moreover, adult residents of high crime areas often live in fear of being attacked by teenagers, suggesting that if delinquency is subcultural, community does not form the basis of the subculture.

The difficulty of accounting for "maturational reform" within the framework of the motivational theories of Cloward and Ohlin [16] and Cohen [17] has already been noted by Matza [18]. In both theories, male delinquents cope with the problems arising from lower class status by entering into and internalizing the norms of a subculture which repudiates conventional rules of conduct and *requires* participation in crime. As with other subcultural theories, it is not at all clear why most subculture carriers abandon activities that are so highly prized within the subculture with such haste.

This desistance is doubly perplexing in anomie or opportunity theories [19] because the problem assumed to cause delinquency, namely the anticipation of failure in achieving socially inculcated success goals through legitimate means, does not disappear at the end of adolescence. At the onset of adulthood, few lower and working class youths are close to conventionally defined "success," and realization that opportunities for upward mobility are drastically limited can only be more acute. Students can perhaps entertain fantasies about their future prospects, but graduates or dropouts must come to terms with their chances. It is true that they can do this by reducing their aspirations and thus lessening anomie, but this seems to happen only slowly. According to Bachman [20], high school drop-outs' aspirations decline by about half a standard deviation over a four-year period, not fast enough to account for the rapid decline in theft involvement with age.

Cloward and Ohlin do note that many delinquents desist, but explain this in *ad hoc* terms unrelated to the main body of their theory. Writing of neighborhoods where violence is common, they assert,

As adolescents near adulthood, excellence in the manipulation of violence no longer brings status. Quite the contrary, it generally evokes extremely negative sanctions. What was defined as permissible or tolerable behavior during adolescence tends to be sharply proscribed in adulthood. New expectations are imposed, expectations of "growing up." of taking on adult responsibilities in the economic, familial, and community spheres. The effectiveness with which these definitions are imposed is attested by the tendency among fighting gangs to decide that conflict is, in the final analysis, simply "kid stuff." . . . In other words, powerful community expectations emerge which have the consequence of closing off access to previously useful means of overcoming status deprivation [21].

In view of Cloward and Ohlin's characterization of neighborhoods where gang violence is prevalent as so disorganized that no informal social controls limiting violence can be exercised [22], one can only wonder whose age-specific expectations are being described. Cloward and Ohlin do not say. This explanation, for which Cloward and Ohlin produce no supporting evidence, is inconsistent with their own larger theory of delinquent subcultures. In addition, it seems inconsistent with the *slowness* of the decline in the violence offense categories. Since recent panel studies [23] find no support for opportunity theory, the failure of the theory to explain the age distribution of crime is not surprising.

In a departure from the emphasis placed on social class membership in most motivational theories of delinquency, Bloch and Niederhoffer [24] interpret such forms of delinquency as adolescent drinking, sexual experimentation, and "wild automobile rides" as responses to the age status problems of adolescence. Denied the prerogatives of adulthood, but encouraged to aspire to adulthood and told to "act like adults," teenagers find in these activities a symbolic substitute which presumably is abandoned as soon as the genuine article is available. As an explanation for joy-riding and some status offenses, this explanation has manifest plausibility. For other categories it is more problemmatic, since it assumes that delinquents interpret activities behaviorally associated largely with adolescence as evidence of adult stature. When Bloch and Niederhoffer turn to more serious teenage crime, their explanations are vague and difficult to interpret, but in any event seem to depend less on the structural position of the juvenile.

In *Delinquency and Drift*, Matza [25] provides an alternative approach to the explanation of desistance. His assumption that many delinquents fully embrace neither delinquent nor conventional norms and values, but instead allow themselves to be easily influenced without deep commitment, makes

194

desistance possible when the delinquent discovers that his companions are no more committed to delinquency than he is. This discovery is facilitated by a reduction in masculinity anxiety that accompanies the attainment of adulthood. There are valuable insights in this account, but unresolved questions as well. Insofar as the discovery of a shared misunderstanding depends on chance events, as Matza suggests [26], *systematic* differences in desistance remain unexplained (I will cite evidence for such systematic differences below). Why does desistance from violence offenses occur later and more slowly than for theft offenses? Why are some juveniles so much more extensively involved in delinquency than others? Matza's remarkable presentation of the subjective elements in delinquency must be supplemented by an analysis of more "objective," structural elements in causation if such questions are to be answered.

That is the approach I will take. Working within the tradition established by Bloch and Niederhoffer, I will present an analysis of the structural position of juveniles in American society and elaborate the implications of that position for juvenile involvement in crime. Because the focus will be on age differences, no attempt will be made to address unresolved issues in delinquency theory that have no obvious relationship to age differences (e.g. does association with delinquents follow or precede delinquent acts); however, when the theory does predict variations in delinquency *within* an age-cohort, these will be noted and compared with the available empirical data.

The theory to be presented will have two major components. The first, a theory of motivation, locates sources of motivation toward criminal involvement in the structural position of juveniles in American society. The second, derived from a control theory perspective, suggests that the willingness to act on the basis of criminal motivation is distributed unequally among age groups because the costs of apprehension are different for persons of different ages. Although some of the theoretical ideas (e.g. control theory) on which I will be drawing have already appeared in the delinquency literature, each by itself is inadequate as a full theory of delinquence. When put together with some new ideas, however, a very plausible account of age and other systematic sources of variation in delinquent involvement emerges.

Anomie and the Juvenile Labor Market

Robert Merton's discussion of anomie [27] has provided a framework for a large volume of research on the etiology of crime. Although Merton observed that a disjunction between socially inculcated goals and legitimate means available for attaining them would produce a strain toward deviance *whatever the goal* [28], specific application of the perspective to de-linquency has been restricted to an assessment of the contribution to delinquency causation of the one cultural goal Merton considered in depth, namely occupational success. Cloward and Ohlin [29], for example, attribute lower class male delinquency to the anticipation of failure in achieving occupational success goals as adults. Their involvement in theft is interpreted as a strategy for gaining admission to professional theft and organized crime circles, that is, a way of obtaining the tutelage and organizational affiliations necessary for the successful pursuit of *career* crime, rather than for immediate financial return. Crime is thus seen as a means toward the attainment of *future* goals rather than *present* goals.

The assumption that delinquency is instrumentally related to the attainment of adult goals is plausible only for limited categories of delinquency, e.g. students who cheat on exams in the face of keen competition for admission to college or graduate school [30], and youths who save what they earn as pimps [31] or drug merchants [32] to capitalize investment in conventional business enterprises.

For other forms of delinquency this assumption is less tenable. Delinquents would have to be stupid indeed to suppose that shoplifting, joy-riding, burglary, robbery or drug use could bring the prestige or pecuniary rewards associated with high status lawful occupations. Nor is there evidence that most delinquents seek careers in professional theft or organized crime. In the face of Cohen's characterization of delinquents as short-run hedonists [33] and the difficulty parents and teachers encounter in attempting to engage delinquent youths in activities which could improve chances of occupational success (like school homework), the future orientation assumed in opportunity theory is especially farfetched.

The potential explanatory power of anomie theory, is, however, not exhausted by Cloward and Ohlin's formulation, because delinquency can be a response to a discrepancy between aspirations and expectations for the attainment of goals other than occupational ones. Most people have a multiplicity of goals, and only some of them are occupational. As the salience of different life goals can vary with stage of the life-cycle, our understanding of delinquency may be advanced more by an examination of those goals given a high priority by adolescents than by considering the importance attached to different goals in American culture generally.

The literature on youth reports a consensus that the transition from childhood to adolescence is marked by a heightened sensitivity to the expectations of peers, and concomitantly, a reduced concern with the fulfillment of parental expectations [34]. High value comes to be attached to popularity with peers, and exclusion from the most popular cliques becomes the occasion for acute psychological distress.

196

Adolescent peer groups and orientation to the expectations of peers are found in many societies [35]. In American society, the natural tendency of those who share common experiences and problems to prefer one another's company is accentuated by the importance parents and school attach to popularity and to the development of the social skills they believe will be necessary for later occupational success [36]. In addition, the exclusion of young people from adult work and leisure activity forces adolescents into virtually exclusive association with one another, cutting them off from alternative sources of validation for the self (as well as reducing the degree of adult supervision). A long run trend toward increased age segregation created by changing patterns of work and education has increased the vulnerability of teenagers to the expectations and evaluations of their peers [37].

This dependence on peers for approval is not itself criminogenic. In many tribal societies, age-homogeneous bands of youths are functionally integrated into the economic and social life of the tribe and are not considered deviant [38]. In America, too, many teenage clubs and cliques are not delinquent. Participation in teenage social life, however, requires resources. In addition to personal assets and skills (having an attractive appearance and "good personality," being a skilled conversationalist, being able to memorize song lyrics and learn dance steps, and in some circles, being able to fight), money is needed to purchase clothing, cosmetics, cigarettes, alcoholic beverages, narcotics, phonograph records, transistor radios, gasoline for cars and motorcycles, tickets to films and concerts, meals in restaurants [39], and for gambling. The progressive detachment of teenage social life from that of the family and the emergence of advertising directed toward a teenage market (this being a creation of postwar affluence for major sections of the population and the "baby boom") have increased the importance of these goods to teenagers and hence have inflated the costs of their social activities.

When parents are unable or unwilling to subsidize their children's social life at the level required by local convention, when children want to prevent their parents from learning of their expenditures, or when they are reluctant to incur the obligations created by taking money from their parents, alternative sources of funds must be sought. Full or part-time employment once constituted such an alternative.

The long-run, persistent decline in teenage employment and labor force participation has progressively eliminated this alternative. During the period from 1870 to 1920, many states passed laws restricting child labor and establishing compulsory education. Despite a quadrupling of the "gainfully employed" population from 1870 to 1930, the number of gainfully employed workers in the 10–15 year-old age bracket *declined*. The Great

Depression resulted in a further contraction of the teenage labor force and increased the school-leaving age [40]. Only in 1940 did the U.S. government stop counting all persons over the age of 10 as part of the labor force [41]. In recent years, teenage labor market deterioration has been experienced mainly by black teenagers. From 1950 to 1973, black teenage labor force participation declined from 67.8% to 34.7%, while white teenage labor force participation remained stable at about 63%. The current recession has increased teenage unemployment in the 16–19 year old age bracket to about 20%, with the rate for black teenagers being twice as high [42].

This process has left teenagers less and less capable of financing an increasingly costly social life whose importance is enhanced as the age segregation of society grows. Adolescent theft then occurs as a response to the disjunction between the desire to participate in social activities with peers and the absence of legitimate sources of funds needed to finance this participation.

Qualitative evidence supporting this explanation of adolescent theft is found in those delinquency studies that describe the social life of delinquent groups. Sherif and Sherif noted in their study of adolescent groups that theft was often instrumentally related to the group's leisure time social activities,

> In several groups. . ., stealing was not the incidental activity that it was in others. It was regarded as an acceptable and necessary means of getting needed possessions, or, more usually, cash. Members of the aforementioned groups frequently engaged in theft when they were broke, usually selling articles other than clothing, and *often using the money for group entertainment and treats* [43].

Carl Werthman reports that among San Francisco delinquents:

> Shoplifting . . . was viewed as a more instrumental activity, as was the practice of stealing coin changers from temporarily evacuated buses parked in a nearby public depot. In the case of shoplifting, most of the boys wanted and wore the various items of clothing they stole; and when buses were robbed, either the money was divided among the boys. or it was used to buy supplies for a party being given by the club [44].

Studies of urban delinquent gangs or individuals in England [45], Israel [46], Sweden [47], Taiwan [48] Holland [49] and Argentina [50] present a uniform picture: unemployed or employed but poorly paid male youths steal to support their leisure-time, group-centered social activities.

198

Joseph Weis' study of middle class delinquency using self-reports [51] is also consistent with the interpretation of adolescent theft presented here. Using key cluster analysis, Weis extracted three distinct factors from the correlation matrix for involvement in different forms of delinquency for the males in the sample. These oblique factors could be characterized as social, property, and aggression. The analysis for girls produced two factors: there was no aggression factor, while the other two factors were very similar to the social and property factors among the boys. For both boys and girls, the correlation between the oblique factor domains for social offenses (drinking, marijuana use, curfew violations, gambling use of false I.D. cards, drag racing, and similar offenses) and for property offenses (theft, burglary, shoplifting, etc.) was positive and moderately strong, as would be predicted if thefts are undertaken to finance peer-related social activities.

On the reasoning presented here, strain should be experienced most acutely by teenagers who are unable to achieve popularity on the basis of personal attributes and who lack alternative sources of self-esteem (e.g. school success or warm relationships with parents). Indeed, teenagers in this position may attempt to win friends by spending money on them [52]. Evidence that unpopular boys are more likely to become delinquent [53], and that delinquents tend to have unsatisfactory relations with peers [54] and parents [55] is consistent with my argument.

Where parents subsidize their children adequately, the incentive to steal is obviously reduced. Because the cost of social life can increase with class position, a strong correlation between social class membership and involve-ment in theft is not necessarily predicted. Insofar as self-reporting studies suggest that the correlation between participation in nonviolent forms of property acquisition and parental socio-economic status is not very high [56], this may be a strong point for my theory. By contrast the theories of Cohen, Miller, and Cloward and Ohlin all clash with the self-reporting studies.

In view of recent suggestions that increases in female crime and delinquency are linked with changing gender roles (of which the women's liberation movement is taken either as a cause or a manifestation), it is of interest to note that the explanation of adolescent theft presented here is applicable to boys and girls, and in particular, allows for female delinquency in support of *traditional* gender roles related to peer involvement.

Weis' work is consistent with this interpretation, as are differences in the forms of theft boys and girls undertake. Boys, who traditionally have paid girls' expenses on dates and therefore have a greater need for cash, are more likely to rob or to burglarize homes and stores, taking items for resale, while girls more often steal items (such as clothing and cosmetics) for personal use.

199

Increases in female crime which have occurred largely in those forms of theft in which female involvement has traditionally been high [57] are thus more plausibly attributed to the same deteriorating economic position in the face of escalating costs of social life that males confront, than to changes in gender role.

As teenagers get older, their vulnerability to the expectations of peers is reduced by institutional involvements that provide alternative sources of self-esteem; moreover, opportunities for acquiring money legitimately expand. Both processes reduce the motivation to engage in acquisitive forms of delinquent behavior. Consequently, involvement in theft should fall off rapidly with age, and it does.

Delinquency and the School

My explanation of juvenile theft in terms of structural obstacles to legitimate sources of funds at a time when peer-oriented leisure activities require access to financial resources implicitly characterizes this form of delinquency as instrumentally rational; the theory assumes that money and goods are stolen because they are useful. Acts of vandalism, thefts in which stolen objects are abandoned or destroyed, and interpersonal violence not necessary to accomplish a theft cannot be explained in this way. These are the activities that led Albert Cohen to maintain that much delinquency is "malicious" and "non-utilitarian" [58] and to argue that the content of the delinquent subculture arose in the lower class male's reaction to failure in schools run according to middle class standards.

Although Cohen can be criticized for not indicating the criteria used for assessing rationality – indeed, for failure to find out from delinquents themselves what they perceived the goals of their destructive acts to be – and though details of Cohen's theory (to be noted below) appear to be inaccurate, his observation that delinquency may be a response to school problems need not be abandoned. Indeed, the literature proposing a connection between one or another aspect of school and delinquency is voluminous [59]. I will concentrate on two features of the school experience, its denial of student autonomy and its subjection of some students to the embarrassment of public degradation ceremonies.

In all spheres of life outside the school, and particularly within the family, children more or less steadily acquire larger measures of personal autonomy as they mature. Over time, the "democratization" of the family has reduced the age at which given levels of autonomy are acquired. The gradual

200

extension of freedom that normally takes place in the family (not without struggle!) is not accompanied by parallel deregulation at school. Authoritarian styles of teaching, and rules concerning such matters as smoking, hair styles, manner of dress, going to the bathroom, and attendance, come into conflict with expectations students derive from the relaxation of controls in the family [60]. The delegitimation of hierarchical authority structures accomplished by the radical movements of the 1960s has sharpened student awareness of this contradiction.

The symbolic significance attached to autonomy exacerbates the inherently onerous burden of school restrictions. Parents and other adults invest age-specific rights and expectations with moral significance by disapproving "childish" behavior and by using privileges to reward behavior they label "mature." Because of this association, the deprivation of autonomy is experienced as "being treated like a baby," that is, as a member of a disvalued age-status.

All students are exposed to these restrictions, and to some degree, all probably resent them. For students who are at least moderately successful at their schoolwork, who excel at sports, participate in extra-curricular school activities, or who are members of popular cliques, this resentment is likely to be more than compensated by rewards associated with school attendance. These students tend to conform to school regulations most of the time, rarely collide with school officials, and are unlikely to feel overtly hostile to school or teachers. Students who are unpopular, and whose academic record, whether from inability or disinterest, is poor, receive no comparable compensation. For them, school can only be a frustrating experience: it brings no current gratification and no promise of future pay-off. Why then should they put up with these restrictions? These students often get into trouble, and feel intense hostility to the school.

Social class differences must of course be taken into account. Pre-adolescent and early adolescent middle and upper class children are supervised more closely than their working class counterparts, and thus come to expect and accept adult authority, while working class youths, who enter an unsupervised street life among peers at an early age have more autonomy to protect, and guard their prerogatives jealously [61]. To the extent that they see in the school's denial of their autonomy preparation for a future in occupations that also deny autonomy, and see in their parents' lives the psychic costs of that denial, they may be more prone to rebel than middle-class students, who can generally anticipate entering jobs that allow more discretion and autonomy.

Middle class youths also have more to gain by accepting adult authority than their working class counterparts. Comparatively affluent parents can control their children better because they have more resources they can withhold, and are in a better position to secure advantages for their children. Likewise, children who believe that their future chances depend on school success may conform regardless of whether they reject close regulation intellectually. Where returns on school success are reduced by class or racial discrimination, the school loses this source of social control. It similarly loses control over upper class children, whose inherited class position frees them from the necessity of doing well in school to guarantee their future economic status.

Only a few decades ago, few working class youths — or school failures with middle class family backgrounds — would have been exposed to a contradiction between their expectations of autonomy and the school's attempts to control them because a high proportion of students, especially working class students, left school at an early age. However, compulsory school attendance, low wages and high unemployment rates for teenagers, and increased educational requirements for entry-level jobs have greatly reduced dropout rates. Thus in 1920, 16.8% of the 17 year-old population were high school graduates; and in 1956, 62.3% [62]. In consequence, a greater proportion of students, especially those who benefit least from school, is exposed to this contradiction.

Common psychological responses to the irritation of the school's denial of autonomy range from affective disengagement to the school ("tuning out" the teacher) to smouldering resentment, and at the behavioral level from truancy to self-assertion through the flouting of rules. Such activities as getting drunk, using drugs, joy-riding, truanting, and adopting eccentric styles of dress, apart from any intrinsic gratification these activities may provide, can be seen as forms of what Gouldner has called "conflictual validation of the self" [63]. By helping students establish independence from authority (school, parental, etc.), these activities contribute to self-regard. Their attraction lies in their being forbidden.

As a status system, the school makes further contributions to the causation of delinquency. Almost by definition, status systems embody invidious distinctions. Where standards of evaluation are shared, and position is believed to reflect personal merit, occupants of lower statuses are likely to encounter problems in maintaining self-esteem [64]. The problem is somewhat alleviated by a strong tendency to restrict intimate association to persons of similar status. If one's associates are at roughly the same level as oneself, they provide the standards for self-evaluation [65]. In addition, "democratic" norms of modesty discourage the flaunting of success and boasting of personal merit, thereby insulating the less successful from an implied attribution of their failures to their own deficiencies.

202

These norms are not, however, universal in applicability. In our society, certification as a full-fledged social member is provided those whose commitment to the value of work and family is documented by spouse, home, car and job (for women, children have traditionally substituted for job). Institutional affiliations are thus taken as a mark of virtue, or positive stigma. Those who meet these moral tests are accorded standards of respect in face-to-face interaction not similarly accorded members of unworthy or suspect categories – e.g. prison and psychiatric hospital inmates, skid row bums, the mentally retarded, and unaccompanied women on the streets of New York. In particular, members are permitted to sustain self-presentations as dignified, worthy persons, regardless of what may be thought or said of them in private [66]. Students, however, especially failing students and those with lower class or minority origins, are accorded no comparable degree of respect. As they lack the appropriate institutional affiliations, their moral commitment to dominant institutions of society is suspect. In this sense, they are social strangers; we don't quite know what we can expect from them. They are, moreover, relatively powerless. In consequence, they are exposed to evaluations from which adults are ordinarily shielded.

This is especially true at school, where school personnel continuously communicate their evaluations of students through grades, honor rolls, track positions, privileges, and praise for academic achievement and proper deportment. On occasion, the negative evaluation of students conveyed by the school's ranking systems is supplemented by explicit criticism and denunciation on the part of teachers who act as if the academic performance of failing students could be elevated by telling them they are stupid, or lazy, or both. Only the most extreme failures in the adult world are subjected to degradation ceremonies of this kind.

The feelings of students subjected to this form of status derogation are well captured by a high school student describing a conversation with his school principal,

> I told him that the teacher was always trying to "put me down" in front of the class. I told him that the teacher knew I didn't like math so why did he keep calling on me – just to "put me down," to make me look bad. I'm not as dumb as he thinks so I "turned it around" on him and got the class to laugh at him. See how he likes being the fool. The principal said I was a wise guy, thought I was a "smart alec." He said that what I needed was a good old-fashioned talk behind the wood shed. I told him "Who're you going get to do it; better not try or somebody is going to get hurt, bad!" Man he turned white and started to shake, "You're suspended for threatening a school official." That's good, I said, this school, this school ain't worth a shit anyway [67].

Cohen [68] has argued that working class youths faced with this situation protect their self-esteem by rejecting conventional norms and values. Seeking out one another for mutual support, they create a delinquent subculture of opposition to middle-class norms in which they can achieve status. This subculture is seen as supporting the non-utilitarian acts of destructiveness that alleviate frustration.

There is little difficulty in finding evidence of adolescent destructiveness, however the choice of target may be more rational than Cohen allows. The large and growing volume of school vandalism and assaults on teachers indicate that delinquents often do see the school in antagonistic terms. Other targets, too may be chosen for clear reasons. In his study of gang violence, Miller found that,

> Little of the deliberately inflicted property damage represented a diffuse outpouring of accumulated hostility against arbitrary objects; in most cases the gang members injured the possession of properties of particular persons who had angered them, as a concrete expression of that anger (defacing automobile of mother responsible for having gang member committed to correctional institution; breaking windows of settlement house after eviction therefrom). There was thus little evidence of 'senseless' destruction; most property damage was directed and repressive [69].

Other targets may be chosen because of their symbolic value. e.g. membership in a despised racial group or class stratum, or in the adult world, which represents repressive authority. It is not unlikely that an unanticipated consequence of recent black nationalist movements has been an increase in crimes by minority group members that victimize whites.

Empirical research suggests the need for revision of other components of Cohen's theory as well. Delinquents do not necessarily reject conventional values or career goals except when in the presence of their peers [70]. A modern society contains numerous status systems that are not in competition with one another; acceptance of one need not require repudiation of others. In particular, students who do not reject the value system endorsed by parents and school officials but who do not succeed in its terms can nevertheless accept the value system of a subculture of delinquency (in the sense of Matza [71]) as a "second best" alternative on pragmatic grounds.

Self-reporting studies of delinquency indicate the association between class and most forms of delinquency to be weaker than Cohen supposed. School failure, though class-linked, is not the monopoly of any class, and the self-esteem problems of middle class youths who fail are not necessarily any less than those of working class schoolmates. Since parental expectations for academic achievement may be higher in middle class families, and since school failure may auger downward mobility, these problems could conceivably be worse. If delinquency restores self esteem lost through school failure, it may serve this function for students of all class backgrounds.

The impact of school degradation ceremonies is not limited to their effect on students' self-esteem. When a student is humiliated by a teacher the

204

student's attempt to present a favorable self to schoolmates is undercut. Even students whose prior psychological disengagement from the value system of the school leaves their self-esteem untouched by a teacher's disparagement may react with anger at being embarrassed before peers. The high school student quoted earlier complained of being ridiculed *in front of his class.* It is the situation of being in the company of others whose approval is needed for self-esteem that makes it difficult for teenagers to ignore humiliation that older individuals, with alternative sources of self-esteem, could readily ignore.

Visible displays of independence from, or rejections of authority can be understood as attempts to re-establish moral character in the face of affronts. This can be accomplished by direct attacks on teachers or school, or through daring illegal performances elsewhere. These responses may or may not reflect anger at treatment perceived to be unjust, may or may not defend the student against threats to self-esteem, may or may not reflect a repudiation of conventional conduct norms. What is crucial is that these activities *demonstrate* retaliation for injury and the rejection of official values to an audience whose own resentment of constituted authority causes it to be appreciative of rebels whom it would not necessarily dare to imitate. Secret delinquency and acts that entailed no risk would not serve this function.

Field research on the interaction between teachers and delinquent students [72] and responses of delinquent gangs and individuals to challenges to honor [73] support this dramaturgical interpretation of delinquency. Most gang violence seems not to erupt spontaneously out of anger, but is chosen and manipulated for its ability to impress others. Nonutilitarian forms of theft, property destruction and violence may well be understood as quite utilitarian if their purpose is the establishment or preservation of the claim to be a certain sort of person, rather than the acquisition of property.

Goffman [74] has called attention to the common features of activities in which participants establish moral character through risk-taking. Such activities as dueling, bull fighting, sky diving, mountain climbing, big game hunting, and gambling for high stakes are undertaken for the opportunity they provide to carve out a valued social identity by exhibiting courage, daring, pluck and composure.

These qualities are those the industrial system (factory and school) tend to disvalue or ignore: the concept of seeking out risks and "showing off" is antithetical to the traditional ethos of capitalism, where the emphasis has been placed on minimizing risk, using time productively, and suppressing the self to demonstrate moral character. Consequently, participants in action systems based on displays of risk-taking have traditionally been drawn

205

primarily from classes not subject to the discipline and self-denial of industrial production, e.g. the European nobility, bohemian populations, and the unemployed poor.

More recently, as production has come to require less sacrifice and self-denial from large sectors of the work force, and to require the steady expansion of stimulated consumption for its growth, the more affluent sectors of the labor force are increasingly encouraged to seek an escape from the routinicity of daily life through mild forms of risk-taking (e.g. gambling and skiing) as well as through the leisure use of drugs and sex.

The similarity between the subculture of delinquency and that of the leisurely affluent [75] makes sense in view of the position of the delinquent *vis à vis* the school. Like the factory, the school frequently requires monotonous and meaningless work. Regimentation is the rule. Expressions of originality and spontaneity are not only discouraged, but may be punished [76]. Students who reap no present rewards from school work or anticipate only the most limited occupational rewards in return for subordinating themselves to the discipline of the school are free to cultivate the self-expressive traits which the school fails to reward. As Downes [77] has pointed out, they may come to regard adults who work as defeated and lifeless because of their subordination to a routine that necessitates self-suppression, and hence try to avoid work because of the cost in self-alienation.

Traditionally this has been especially true of students with lower class backgrounds; Finestone [78] has described their adaptation and Rainwater [79] has interpreted the expressive features of lower class black male urban culture in these terms. However, when the political and occupational sectors of society lose their legitimacy, students of other classes may find the prospect of entering conventional careers in those sectors so repugnant that they lose the motivation to achieve in school, and also cultivate life styles based on self-expression or politically motivated risk-taking. The bright hippies and radicals from white middle-class backgrounds in the late 1960s are a case in point.

The similarity between delinquent and non-criminal recreational risk-taking warns us that the pursuit of status through risk-taking need not *necessarily* arise from problems in self-esteem. Once a status system rewarding delinquent activity exists, students may act with reference to it in order to *increase* prestige in the group, not only to prevent prestige from falling. Thus teachers may be provoked [80], gang rivals taunted, and daring thefts and assaults perpetrated, even in the absence of humiliation.

When students drop out or graduate from high school, they enter a world that, while sometimes inhospitable, does not restrict their autonomy and assault their dignity in the same way the school does. The need to engage in

206

crime to establish a sense of an autonomous self, and to preserve moral character through risk-taking is thus reduced. In addition, the sympathetic audience of other students of the same age is taken away. Thus school-leaving eliminates major sources of motivation toward delinquency.

In this respect, it is especially ironic that delinquency prevention programs have involved campaigns to extend the duration of schooling. American panel studies indicate that the self-esteem of dropouts rises after leaving school [81] and that dropping out produces an immediate decline in delinquency [82]. In England, when the school-leaving age was raised by one year, the peak age for delinquency also rose simultaneously by one year [83].

Despite this evidence that the school contributes to delinquency, it is hardly necessary. In Cordoba, Argentina, patterns of delinquency are fairly similar to those in the United States even though the school-leaving age for working-class children is 10, and delinquents report generally favorable attitudes toward school [84]. Unsatisfactory school experiences simply add to the economic motivations created by the exclusion of juveniles from the labor market.

Masculine Status Anxiety and Delinquency

Many observers have remarked on the disproportionate involvement of males in delinquent activity and the exaggerated masculine posturing that characterizes much male delinquency. Though sex differences in delinquency are not as pronounced in self-report studies as in arrest reports, and seem to be gradually narrowing, they nevertheless remain considerable, especially in the violence offense categories. Theoretical explanations for these differences not based on innate sex differences have alternatively emphasized differences in the socialization of boys and girls, which lead to differences in gender role [85], and "masculine protest" against maternal domination and identification [86], especially in the female-based households of the lower class [87]. In such households, the argument goes, boys will tend to identify with the mother, and hence will experience uncertainty and anxiety in later years in connection with their identification as a male. To allay this anxiety, they reject the "good" values of the mother and engage in "masculine" forms of delinquency.

Application of the theory to delinquency in the United States has not been entirely successful. Male delinquency does appear to be associated with what has been interpreted as anxiety over masculinity, but is independent of whether the household in which the child is raised lacked an adult male [88].

This finding points to the need for a revision in the argument.

Hannerz [89] has pointed out that children raised in homes without fathers may still have alternative male role models. Indeed, children raised in a community where adult male unemployment rates are high may spend more of their time in the company of adult males who could serve as role models than their middle class peers. I would argue, in addition, that Miller's adherence to the psycho-analytic framework blinds him to important sources of anxiety connected with masculinity that are unrelated to the family configuration in early childhood. Males who are not in doubt about their identity as males may nevertheless feel anxiety in connection with anticipated or actual inability to fulfill traditional sex role expectations concerning work and support of family. This masculine *status* anxiety can be generated by a father who is present but ineffectual, and by living in a neighborhood where, for social-structural reasons, many men are un-employed – regardless of whether one's own father is present in the household.

Men who experience such anxiety because they are prevented from fulfilling conventional male role expectations may attempt to alleviate their anxiety by exaggerating those traditionally male traits that *can* be expressed. Attempts to dominate women (including rape) and patterns of interpersonal violence can be seen in these terms. In other words, crime can be a response to masculine status anxiety no less than to anxiety over male identity; it can provide a sense of potency that is expected and desired but not achieved in other spheres of life.

In this interpretation, a compulsive concern with toughness and masculinity arises not from a hermetically sealed lower-class subculture "with an integrity of its own" nor from the psychodynamics of a female-headed household [90] but as a response to a contradiction between structural constraints on male status attainment imposed by the larger economic and political order, and the cultural expectations for men that permeate American society. The role of the subculture Miller describes is to make available the behavioral adaptations that previous generations have developed in response to this contradiction, and thus to shape those responses. We should therefore expect persons suffering from masculine status anxiety who were members of groups in which the structural sources of masculine status anxiety have been common and long-standing to develop more coherent and stereotyped adaptations than individuals who were not members of such groups, e.g. in lower class blacks as compared with recently unemployed white collar employees [91]. We should also expect those adaptations to attenuate in groups that ceased to encounter such contra-dictions, either because structural constraints to the fulfillment of traditional role expectations had been eliminated, or because expectations for men in the larger society had changed.

208

If I am correct in assuming that delinquents in the last years of elementary school and early years of high school are not excessively preoccupied with their occupational prospects, but become more concerned with their futures toward the end of high school – and there is some qualitative evidence to support this assumption [92] – then masculine anxiety during these early years must stem from other sources. One plausible source lies in the contradiction between the school's expectations of docility and submission to authority, and more widely communicated social expectations of masculinity. While the school represses both boys and girls, the message that girls get is consistent; the message boys receive is contradictory. This difference would help to explain sex differences in delinquency in early adolescence.

Most of the behavior that can be explained plausibly in this way – smoking, sexual conquests, joy-riding, vandalism, fighting between boys – is fairly trivial, and either becomes legal in mid to late adolescence, or abates rapidly. Anxiety over inability to fulfill traditional male occupational roles would show up late in adolescence. If I am correct in holding that such anxiety is an important source of criminal violations, the ratio of male to female participation should increase with age during adolescence, and there is evidence from self-reports that it does, at least among middle class youths [93].

One would expect masculine status anxiety to appear with greatest intensity and to decline most slowly in those segments of the population in which adult male unemployment is exceptionally high. This conforms to the general pattern of arrests for violence offenses such as homicide, forcible rape and assaults – offenses often unconnected with the pursuit of material gain, and hence most plausibly interpreted as a response to masculine status anxiety. Rates of arrest for these offenses peak in the immediate post-high school age brackets (several years later than for the property offenses) and the decline is slower than for property offenses. Moreover, blacks are over-represented in violence offense arrests to a much greater degree than in arrests for property offenses. Thus in 1973, the ratio of black to white arrests for burglary, larceny and auto theft was 0.45; for non-negligent homicide, forcible rape and aggravated assault, 0.85; for robbery, 1.79 [94]. This relative over-representation of blacks is confirmed in victimization studies [95] and in self-reporting studies of delinquency [96] and thus cannot be explained as a manifestation of racial differences in risk of apprehension.

Costs of Delinquency

So far some possible sources of variation with age in motivation to participate in common forms of criminal activity have been identified, but this is only half the story, for one may wish to engage in some form of behavior but nevertheless decide not to do so because the potential costs of participation are deemed unacceptably high. Costs can be a consequence of delinquency, and must be taken into account. Control theorists have begun to do so [97].

Costs can originate with internal or external sources of control. Superego restraints and favorable self-concepts and ideals exemplify internal sources of control [98]; they threaten the potential delinquent with guilt and shame. External costs can include parental disapproval and loss of privileges, school-imposed sanctions (ranging from teacher's disapproval to suspension or expulsion), loss of job and reduced prospects for future employment, acquisition of a police or juvenile court record, and deprivation of freedom through a reformatory sentence. Although external costs are actually imposed only on those who are caught, fear of incurring costs can inhibit potential delinquents and lead actual delinquents to desist.

To what extent can internal or external costs contribute to the age distribution of criminality? With the exception of those forms of minor delinquency considered far more discrediting to adults than to juveniles [99], it is unlikely that *internal* controls play a major role in generating age *differences* in criminal involvement, for it seems unlikely that moral inhibitions substantially increase from mid to late adolescence. Indeed, we generally expect people to take a more pragmatic view of morality as they get older.

External costs, however, are likely to vary with age. In early adolescence the potential costs of all but the most serious forms of delinquency are relatively slight. Parents and teachers are generally willing to write off a certain amount of misbehavior as "childish mischief," while enormous caseloads have forced juvenile courts in large cities to adopt a policy that comes very close to what Schur [100] has called "radical nonintervention" for all but the most serious cases. Moreover, the confidentiality of juvenile court records reduces the extent to which prospects are jeopardized by an arrest.

Given the slight risk of apprehension for any single delinquent act, the prevalence of motivations to violate the law, and the low costs of lesser violations, we should expect minor infractions to be common among juveniles, and the self-reporting studies generally suggest that they are. Where the risk of incurring costs does procure abstention, we should suppose fear of parental disapproval would be the most salient. Teenagers who have good relationships with parents would presumably be the most concerned with incurring their disapproval, and they do have lower rates of involvement in delinquency [101].

As teenagers get older, the potential costs of apprehension increase: victims may be more prone to file a complaint, and police to make an arrest.

210

Juvenile court judges are more likely to take a serious view of an older offender, especially one with a prior record. Older offenders risk prosecution in criminal court, where penalties tend to be harsher, and where an official record will have more serious consequences for later job opportunities.

Delinquents are acutely sensitive to these considerations. According to several youthful offenders testifying before the New York State Select Committee at a hearing on assault and robbery against the elderly,

> If you're 15 and under you won't go to jail ... That's why when we do a "Rush and Crib" – which means you rush the victim and push him or her into their apartment, you let the youngest member do any beatings. See, we know if they arrest him, he'll be back on the street in no time [102].

In interviews, former delinquents often attribute their own desistance to their unwillingness to risk the stiffer penalties they would receive if arrested and tried as adults [103]. Thus the leniency of the juvenile court contributes to high levels of juvenile crime.

Just as the costs of crime are escalating, new opportunities in the form of jobs, marriage, or enlistment in the armed forces create stakes in conformity and, as Matza points out [104], may also relieve problems of masculine status anxiety. Toward the end of high school, when student concern about the future increases, the anticipation of new opportunities is manifested in desistance from delinquency and avoidance of those who do not similarly desist. Consistent with this interpretation is the fact that in both England and the United States, the peak year for delinquent involvement is the year *before* school-leaving.

Labeling theorists have tended to emphasize the role that apprehension and official processing of delinquents may play in increasing their subsequent delinquent involvement, either through the effect of labeling on self-concept and attitudes [105] or because prospects for legitimate employment are jeopardized through stigmatization [106]. The evidence available does not suggest that this happens to any great extent [107]. This is not necessarily surprising. As Schur [108] has pointed out, children may develop psychological defenses that serve to neutralize the discrediting imputations of others. When the negative label is applied by adults who are perceived as antagonists (police, judges, jailers) it should not be difficult to avoid being deeply influenced by their evaluations. Moreover, the confidentiality of juvenile court records helps to shield delinquents from later stigma.

Those whose opportunities for lucrative employment are limited by obstacles associated with racial and/or class membership will have far less reason to desist from illegal activity than those whose careers are not similarly blocked. The kinds of jobs available to young members of the lower strata of the working class tend to be tedious and financially unrewarding (when they are available at all). Marriage may appear less appealing to young men whose limited prospects promise inability to fulfill traditional male expectations as breadwinner. Even an army career may be precluded by an arrest record, low intelligence test scores, physical disability, or illiteracy. Thus the legitimate opportunity structure, even if relatively useless for understanding entrance into delinquency, may still be helpful in understanding patterns of desistance.

The same may be said of the illegal opportunity structure. Those few delinquents who are recruited into organized crime or professional theft face larger rewards and less risk of serious penalty than those not so recruited, and their personal relationships with partners may be more satisfying. They should be less likely to desist from crime, but their offense patterns can be expected to change.

This reasoning suggests that the association between criminal involvement on the one hand and race and class on the other should be stronger for adults than for juveniles. If this is so, arrest rates in a given offense category should decline more rapidly for whites and youths with middle class backgrounds than for blacks and youths with working class and lower class backgrounds. In the male birth cohort studied by Wolfgang, Figlio and Sellin, whites were more likely to desist after an offense [109]. F.B.I. crime career data also suggest higher rearrest rates for blacks than for whites [110] and a number of studies of recidivism of released prisoners have found somewhat higher recidivism among black ex-prisoners than among white ex-prisoners. Though based on small samples, Chambliss' field study of delinquency [111] does indicate a much higher desistance rate for middle class delinquents.

If, as is often suggested, crimes of violence involve less reflection and deliberation than crimes of acquisition, violence offenses should respond less elastically to increased external costs than property offenses. For this reason, we should expect violence crime rates to decline less rapidly with age than property crime rates, and this prediction is verified (see Table I).

Delinquency and the Social Construction of the Juvenile

Among the structural sources of adolescent crime identified here, the exclusion of juveniles from the world of adult work plays a crucial role. It is this exclusion that simultaneously exaggerates teenagers' dependence on peers for approval and eliminates the possibility of their obtaining funds to support their intensive, leisure-time social activities. The disrespectful treatment students receive in school depends on their low social status, which in turn reflects their lack of employment. In late adolescence and

212

early adulthood, their fear that this lack of employment will persist into adulthood evokes anxiety over achievement of traditional male gender role expectations, especially among males in the lower levels of the working class, thus contributing to a high level of violence.

Institutionalized leniency to juvenile offenders, which reduces the potential costs of delinquency, stems from the belief that teenagers are not as responsible for their actions as adults [112]. The conception of juveniles as impulsive and irresponsible gained currency around the turn of the century (see for example, Hall [113]) when organized labor and Progressive reformers campaigned for child labor laws to save jobs for adults, a goal given high priority after the Depression of 1893. This conception was, in a sense, self-fulfilling. Freed from ties to conventional institutions, teenagers *have* become more impulsive and irresponsible.

The exclusion of teenagers from serious work is not characteristic of all societies. Peasant and tribal societies could not afford to keep their young idle as long as we do. In such societies, juvenile crime rates were low. Under feudalism, too, children participated in farming and handicraft production as part of the family unit beginning at a very early age.

In depriving masses of serfs and tenant farmers of access to the means of production (land), European capitalism in its early stages of development generated a great deal of crime, but in a manner that cut across age boundaries. Little of the literature on crime in Elizabethan and Tudor England singles out juveniles as a special category.

The industrial revolution in the first half of the nineteenth century similarly brought with it a great deal of misery, but its effect on crime was not restricted to juveniles. Children of the working class in that period held jobs at an early age and in some sectors of the economy were given preference. Only middle and upper class children were exempt from the need to work, and they were supervised much more closely than they are nowadays. As far as can be judged, juvenile crime in that period was a much smaller fraction of the total than at present, and was more confined to the lower classes than it is now [114].

In modern capitalist societies, children of all classes share, for a limited period, a common relationship to the means of production (namely exclusion) which is distinct from that of most adults, and they respond to their common structural position in fairly similar ways. Although there are class differences in the extent and nature of delinquency, especially violent delinquency, these are less pronounced than for adults, for whom occupational differentiation is much sharper.

The deteriorating position of juveniles in the labor market in recent years has been ascribed to a variety of causes, among them the inclusion of juveniles under minimum wage laws, changes in the structure of the economy (less farm employment), teenage preference for part-time work (to permit longer periods of education) which makes teenage labor less attractive to employers, and the explosion in the teenage labor supply created by the baby boom at a time when women were entering the labor market in substantial numbers [115]. Whatever contribution these circumstances may have made to shifting teenage employment patterns in the short-run, the exclusion of juveniles from the labor market has been going on for more than a century, and may more plausibly be explained in terms of the failure of the oligopoly-capitalist economy to generate sufficient demand for labor, than to these recent developments [116].

In both the United States and England, the prolongation of education has historically been associated with the contraction of the labor market [117], casting doubt on the view that more education is something that the general population has wanted for its own sake. Had this been true, the school leaving age would have jumped upward in periods of prosperity, when a larger proportion of the population could afford more education, not during depressions. Moreover, the functionalist argument that increased education is necessary as technology becomes more complex would apply at best to a small minority of students, and rests on the dubious assumption that full-time schooling is pedagogically superior to alternative modes of organizing the education of adolescents.

The present social organization of education, which I have argued contributes to delinquency, has also been plausibly attributed to the functional requirement of a capitalist economy for a docile, disciplined and stratified labor force [118], as well as to the need to keep juveniles out of the labor market.

Thus the high and increasing level of juvenile crime we are seeing in present-day United States and in other Western countries orginates in the structural position of juveniles in an advanced capitalist economy.

Delinquency is not, however, a problem of capitalism alone. Although there are many differences between crime patterns in the United States and the Soviet Union, the limited information available indicates that delinquency in the Soviet Union is often associated with leisure-time consumption activities on the part of youths who are academic failures, and who are either not working or studying, or are working at or preparing for unrewarding jobs [119]. This suggests that some of the processes described here may be at work in the Soviet Union. Since Soviet society is based on hierarchical domination and requires a docile, disciplined and stratified labor force, this parallel is not surprising.

One might, in fact, generalize from this analysis, to conclude that any

214

society that excluded juveniles from the world of adult work for long periods and imposed mandatory attendance at schools organized like ours would have a substantial amount of delinquency.

Criminology and Marxist Theory

For the first time in many decades, criminologists are again drawing on Marxian social theory. The small corpus of literature in this vein has thus far been devoted primarily to the analysis of criminal law and criminal justice administration [120], the criticism of liberal reform proposals [121], and the critique of non-Marxist contributions to the theory of crime causation [122].

Until recently, the only positive contribution this literature made to the theory of crime causation was the assertion that under capitalism crime is not pathological but rational [123]. The limitations of such an approach are manifest. When the mechanisms by which capitalism causes crime are left unspecified, only True Believers are likely to be persuaded of the connection, especially in the face of the persistence of crime in non-capitalist societies. In addition, other important questions about causation (why is there such variability in criminal behavior on the part of those who live in capitalist societies? Why does the amount and nature of crime undergo historical change?) are left unanswered.

However, several developments are leading radical criminologists to a new interest in questions of etiology. The prominence crime has assumed as a political issue has made it difficult for radicals trying to organize working class constituencies to dismiss the continuing rise in street crime by pointing out that crime is merely a "social construction" (feminist agitation over rape has had a similar effect), or by changing the subject to government and corporate crime. Within the discipline, the current reassessment of labeling theory is redirecting theoretical interest from secondary deviation resulting from labeling by law enforcement agencies to social structural sources of primary deviance [124]. Moreover, the recent Marxist critiques of phenomenology, existential sociology and symbolic interactionism as excessively voluntaristic, ahistorical and astructural [125] (paralleling the collapse of a New Left that emphasized voluntarism and subjectivity) has made radical criminologists more receptive to causal explanations of criminal behavior than has been the case in the recent past.

This paper has attempted to develop a Marxian perspective on the causation of crimes commonly committed by juveniles — for other recent Marxian work on causation see [126]. I have assumed throughout that there is no necessary contradiction between such traditional criminological concerns as the causal role of such institutions as family and school or psychological concepts like self-esteem and anxiety on the one hand, and Marxist theory on the other (although I have criticized elements in non-Marxist theories of delinquency, many of the points of criticism concern elements that are not crucial from the point of view of Marxism). Rather, Marxism compliments these traditional concerns by placing them in a larger framework.

Although not so fully developed that it can simply be "applied" to problems at hand, Marxism directs our attention to the manner in which changing modes and relations of production lead to historically changing criminogenic contradictions [127] within or between particular institutions. The analysis of these contradictions can only be carried out concretely, for particular historical epochs and particular forms of criminality. The same approach can be brought to the sociology of criminal law (which from this perspective need not be seen *solely* as an instrument of class rule), and can be of value in studying crime in non-capitalist as well as in capitalist societies. To leave off analysis with the statement that crime is rational and creative under capitalism is to fail to draw on the richness of the Marxist legacy.

From the point of view of theory, Marxism can serve to integrate criminology with questions central to macrosociological theory. The viewpoint I am recommending constitutes an implicit reproach to both consensus and conflict models in criminology. The conflict model, embraced by many radical criminologists in the 1960s in the face of massive social conflicts in American society (major statements of the conflict perspective can be found in [128]) fails to specify the lines along which conflicts appear, and where cooperation can be located. In that any society has elements of both consensus and dissensus, cooperation and conflict, varying historically in degree and form, both points of view distort social reality by omission, and by portraying a uniformity where diversity exists. Historical materialism provides the conceptual tools for investigating the degree of conflict present in a society and the forms it takes.

At the level of practice, the Marxist perspective exposes the limitations of liberal meliorism. For decades, criminologists have proposed such reforms as the elimination of poverty and racial discrimination in order to reduce crime, as if these social problems were mere oversights, little snags in a generally beneficial social order. Marxist theorists tend to see these problems largely as produced by and insoluble within the framework of a class society. My analysis of delinquency suggests that most proposed "solutions" to the delinquency problem would have little impact. A thorough integration of

216

teenagers into the labor force would require a major restructuring of work and education, and this is hardly to be expected in the foreseeable future.

Although I have argued for the general compatibility between Marxist and non-Marxist approaches to crime causation, there are points of tension which must be mentioned. Unlike positivists, Marxists have been concerned with the dynamic interplay between objective conditions and subjective consciousness. Responses to objective conditions – including criminal responses – are contingent on the level of group awareness of the origins of oppressive objective conditions in class dynamics and of the possibilities for engaging in collective action to change these conditions. My analysis of delinquency is implicitly predicated on the low level of such consciousness now present among most American teenagers. That could change, though the prospects of change in the immediate future do not appear especially bright.

Marxists have also approached the question of class differently from non-Marxists. In this essay, I have used the term "class" in the very imprecise manner of non-Marxist criminologists, to refer to position on a ranked scale. In applications to delinquency this usage is ordinarily extended to juveniles by assigning them to the class of their parents. This approach has been relatively unsuccessful in explaining delinquency; class, thus defined, is a poor predictor of delinquency.

Marxian theorists take class to be defined by relationship to the means of production [129], but have conceptualized such relationships too narrowly. Feminist theorists have pointed out the unique relationship to production of the housewife in a capitalist economy (for a summary of the major statements on this question, see Fee [130]) and here I have argued that juveniles in an advanced capitalist economy have a common, if temporary, relationship to the means of production, characterized by exclusion during a period of mandatory training for entry into the labor force. In Marxian terms, this means that juveniles can no more be assigned the class of their parents than housewives can be assigned the class of their husbands. The high rate of juvenile crime is largely a response to the conditions imposed on this class under conditions of weak class consciousness.

In this instance, at least, the Marxian perspective yielded insights into the nature of delinquency that non-Marxian approaches to class have failed to provide. It is not necessarily true, however, that all forms of crime originate *directly* in the problems confronting a particular class, even if class is defined in the flexible manner I propose. The dynamic functioning of a class society leads to social differentiation along many lines other than class, and the resulting differences in experiences, opportunities and costs may have great relevance for criminal involvement. The contribution of Marxism is to view such differentiation as the product of relations of production and reproduction, rather than as an *a priori* given.

Acknowledgements

I am grateful to Ava Baron, Eliot Freidson, Daniel Glaser, Irwin Goffman, Drew Humphreys, Caroline Persell, Edwin Schur and James Q. Wilson for helpful discussions and suggestions.

NOTES

1 Wolfgang, M.E., R.M. Figlio and T. Sellin (1972). *Delinquency in a Birth Cohort*. Chicago: University of Chicago Press; Glueck, S. and E. Glueck (1937). *Later Criminal Careers*. New York: The Commonwealth Fund; Glaser, D. (1964). *The Effectiveness of a Prison and Parole System*. Indianapolis: Bobbs-Merrill, 469–474.

2 Beattie, R.H. (1955). "Problems of Criminal Statistics in the United States," *Journal of Criminal Law, Criminology and Police Science* 55: 359–369; Kitsuse, J.I. and A.V. Cicourel (1963). "A Note on the Uses of Official Statistics." *Social Problems* 11: 131–139; Wolfgang, M.E. (1963). "Uniform Crime Reports: A Critical Appraisal," *University of Pennsylvania Law Review* 111: 708–738; Robinson, S.M. (1966). "A Critical View of Uniform Crime Reports," *Michigan Law Review* 64: 1031–1054; Wheeler, S. (1967). "Criminal Statistics: A Reformulation of the Problem," *Journal of Criminal Law, Criminology and Police Science* 58: 317–324.

3 Baittle, B. (1961). "Psychiatric Aspects of the Development of a Street Corner Group: An Exploratory Study," *American Journal of Orthopsychiatry* 31: 703–712; Miller, W.B. (1966). "Violent Crime in City Gangs," *Annals of the American Academy of Political and Social Science* 364: 96–112; Gold, M. (1970). *Delinquent Behavior in an American City*. Belmont, Cal.: Brooks Cole; Hindelang, M.J. (1971). "Age, Sex, and the Versatility of Delinquent Involvements," *Social Problems* 18: 522–535;

4 Offer, D. (1969). *The Psychological World of the Teenager: A Study of Normal Adolescent Boys*. New York: Basic Books.

5 West W.G. (1976). "Serious Thieves: Lower Class Adolescent Males in a Short-Term Deviant Occupation." Unpublished paper.

6 Wilson, N.K. (1972). *Risk Ratios in Juvenile Delinquency*. Ann Arbor: University Microfilms.

7 Private communication from Patricia Miller.

8 Michigan State Prison (1878). *Annual Report*.

9 Monkkonen. E. (1975). *The Dangerous Class: Crime and Poverty in Columbus Ohio 1860–1884*. Cambridge: Harvard University Press.

10 Neison, F.G.P. (1857). *Contributions to Vital Statistics*. Third Edition. Quoted in J.J. Tobias, *Nineteenth Century Crime: Prevention and Punishment*. Newton Abbott: David and Charles; Quetelet, A.J. (1831). *Recherches sur le Penchant au Crime aux Différents Ages*. Brussels: Académie Royale; Lombroso C. (1968). *Crime: Its Causes and Remedies*. Montclair, N.J.: Patterson Smith 175–177.

11 Normandeau A. (1968). *Trends and Patterns of Robbery*. Unpublished Ph. D. Dissertation University of Pennsylvania; McClintock, F.H., N.H. Avison and G.N.G. Rose (1968). *Crime in England and Wales* London: Heinemann Educational Books 179; Lopez-Rey, M. (1970). *Crime: An Analytical Approach*. New York: Praeger; Schichor, D. and A. Kirschenbaum (1975). "Juvenile Delinquency and New Towns: The Case of Israel." Paper presented to the American Society of Criminology.

12 Glueck, S. and E. Glueck (1968). *Delinquents and Non-delinquents in Perspective*. Cambridge: Harvard University Press 169–171.

13 Ferracuti F.. S. Dinitz and A. Esperanza (1975). *Delinquents and Nondelinquents in the Puerto Rican Slum Culture*. Columbus: Ohio State University Press.

14 Miller W B. (1958), "Lower Class Subculture as a Generating Milieu of Gang Delinquency " *Journal of Social Issues* 14: 5–19.

218

15 Clark J.P. and E.W. Haurek (1966). "Age and Sex Roles of Adolescents and their Involvement in Misconduct: A Reappraisal." *Sociology and Social Research* 50: 495–503

16 Cloward, R A. and L.E Ohlin (1960). *Delinquency and Opportunity: A Theory of Delinquent Gangs.* New York: Free Press.

17 Cohen, A.K. (1955). *Delinquent Boys.* New York: Free Press.

18 Matza, D. (1964). *Delinquency and Drift.* New York: Wiley 24–27.

19 Merton, R.K. (1957). *Social Theory and Social Structure.* Revised Edition. New York: Free Press; Cloward R. and L. Ohlin (1960), op cit.

20 Bachman, J.G., S. Green and I. Wirtanen (1972). *Dropping Out – Problem or Symptom.* Ann Arbor: Institute for Social Research.

21 Cloward, R. and L. Ohlin (1960). op. cit.

22 Ibid., 174–175.

23 Elliot, D.S. and H.L. Voss (1974). *Delinquency and Dropout.* Lexington, Mass.: Lexington Books; Quicker, J. (1974). "The Effect of Goal Discrepancy on Delinquency" *Social Problems* 22: 76–86; Lalli, M. and W. Roberts (1974). "The Strain Theory of Delinquency " Unpublished paper University of Pennsylvania.

24 Bloch, H.A. and A. Niederhoffer (1958). *The Gang.* New York: Philosophical Library 29–30.

25 Matza, D. (1964). Op. cit.

26 Ibid. 54–58.

27 Merton, R. (1957). Op. cit., 131 -194

28 Ibid., 166

29 Cloward, R. and L. Ohlin (1960), op. cit.

30 Perlin, L.I., M.R. Yarrow and H.A. Scarr (1967). "Unintended Effects of Parental Aspirations: The Case of Children's Cheating " *American Journal of Sociology* 73: 73–83, Bergman, D. (1974). "The Absence of Guilt in Cheating." Unpublished paper presented to the American Anthropological Association; Barnes, B. (1975). "School's Honor Code Gets an F," *New York Post* (September 24): 18.

31 Milner, R and C. Milner (1972). *Black Players: The Secret World of Black Pimps.* Boston: Little Brown, Ianni, F. (1974). *The Black Mafia.* New York: Simon and Schuster.

32 Woodley, R. (1972). *Dealer: Portrait of a Cocaine Merchant.* New York: Warner Paperback Library.

33 Cohen, A. (1955). Op.cit. 25.

34 Blos, P. (1941). *The Adolescent Personality: A Study of Individual Behavior.* New York: Appleton: Bowerman C.E. and J.W. Kinch (1959). "Changes in Family and Peer Orientation of Children between the Fourth and Tenth Grades," *Social Forces* 37: 206, Tuma, E. and N. Livson (1960). "Family Socioeconomic Status and Attitudes toward Authority," *Child Development* 31: 387; Conger, J.J. (1971). "A World They Never Knew: The Family and Social Change," *Daedalus* 100: 1105–1138; (1973). *Adolescence and Youth.* New York: Harper & Row 286–292.

35 Eisenstadt, S.N. (1956). *From Generation to Generation: Age Groups and Social Structure.* New York: Free Press; Bloch and Niederhoffer (1958), op. cit.

36 Mussen, P H., J.J. Conger and J. Kagan (1969). *Child Development and Personality.* New York: Harper & Row.

37 Panel on Youth of the President's Science Advisory Committee (1974). *Youth: Transition to Adulthood.* Chicago: University of Chicago.

38 Mead, M. (1939). *From the South Seas: Part III. Sex and Temperament in Three Primitive Societies.* New York: Morrow; Eisenstadt, S.N. (1956), op. cit., 56–92; Minturn, L. and W.W. Lambert (1964). *Mothers in Six Cultures: Antecedents of Child Rearing.* New York: Wiley.

39 Insofar as meals are not served regularly in some lower class families, biological and social needs here converge. Mertonian theory implicitly but erroneously assumes that the welfare state functions well enough to meet basic biological needs.

40 Panel on Youth (1974), op. cit., 36–38.

41 Tomson, B. and E.R. Fiedler (1975). "Gangs: A Response to the Urban World (Part II)," in Desmond S. Cartwright, Barbara Tomson and Herschey Schwartz (eds.), *Gang Delinquency.* Monterey, Cal.: Brooks/Cole.

42 Raskin, A.H. (1975). "The Teenage Worker is Hardest Hit," *New York Times* (May 4): F3.

43 Sherif, M. and C.W. Sherif (1964). *Reference Groups: Exploration into Conformity and Deviation of Adolescents*. New York: Harper & Row, 174.

44 Werthman, C. (1967). "The Function of Social Definitions in the Development of Delinquent Careers," in *Task Force Report: Juvenile Delinquency*. Washington, D.C.: Government Printing Office, 157.

45 Fyvel, T.R. (1962). *Troublemakers*. New York: Schocken Books; Parker, H.J. (1974), op. cit.

46 Toby, J. (1967), op. cit., 136–137.

47 Ibid., 137–138.

48 Lin, T. (1959), op. cit., 259.

49 Bauer, E.J. (1964). "The Trend of Juvenile Offenses in the Netherlands and the United States," *Journal of Criminal Law, Criminology and Police Science* 55: 359–369.

50 DeFleur, L. (1970), op. cit.

51 Weis, J. (1976). "Liberation and Crime: The Invention of the New Female Criminal." *Crime and Social Justice* 6: 17–27.

52 Parker, H.H. (1974), op. cit.; Toby (1967), op. cit., 137.

53 Rolf, M. and S.B. Sells (1968). "Juvenile Delinquency in Relation to peer Acceptance-Rejection and Socioeconomic Status." *Psychology in the Schools* 5: 3–18; West, D. (1973). "Are Delinquents Different?" *New Society* 26 (November 22): 456.

54 Rothstein, E. (1962). "Attributes Related to High Social Status: A Comparison of the Perceptions of Delinquents and Non-Delinquent Boys," *Social Problems* 10: 75–83; Short, J.F., Jr. and F.L. Strodtbeck (1965). *Group Process and Gang Delinquency*. Chicago: University of Chicago Press, 243–244; Hirschi, T. (1969). *The Causes of Delinquency*. Berkeley: University of California Press, 145–161.

55 Nye, F.I. (1958). *Family Relationships and Delinquent Behavior*. New York: Wiley, ch. 8; Hirschi, T. (1969), op. cit., 83–109.

56 Short, J.F., Jr. and F.I. Nye (1958). "Extent of Unrecorded Delinquency: Tentative Conclusions." *Journal of Criminal Law, Criminology and Police Science* 49: 296–302; Reiss, A.J., Jr. and A.L. Rhodes (1961). "The Distribution of Juvenile Delinquency in the Social Class Structure," *American Sociological Review* 26: 730–732; Dentler, R. and L.J. Monroe (1961). "Early Adolescent Theft," *American Sociological Review* 26: 733–743; Clark, J.P. and E.P. Wenninger (1962). "Socio-Economic Class and Area as Correlates of Illegal Behavior Among Juveniles," *American Sociological Review* 27: 826–834; Akers, R.L. (1964). "Socio-Economic Status and Delinquent Behavior: A Retest," *Journal of Research in Crime and Delinquency* 1: 38–46; Hirschi, T. (1969), op. cit., pp. 66–82.

57 Simon, R.J. (1975). *Women and Crime*. Lexington, Mass.: Lexington Books.

58 Cohen, A. (1955), op. cit., p. 25.

59 Schafer, W.E. and K. Polk (1967). "Delinquency and the Schools," in *Task Force Report: Juvenile Delinquency and Youth Crime*. Washington, D.C.: Government Printing Office; Polk, K. and W.E. Schafer (1972). *Schools and Delinquency*. Englewood Cliffs, N.J. Prentice-Hall.

60 These expectations are derived from young peoples' knowledge of family arrangements in our society generally, not only from their own family circumstances. When controls in their own family are not relaxed, this can provide an additional source of conflict.

61 Psathas, G. (1957). "Ethnicity, Social Class, and Adolescent Independence from Parental Control," *American Sociological Review* 22: 415–423. Kobrin, S. (1962). "The Impact of Cultural Factors in Selected Problems of Adolescent Development in the Middle and Lower Class," *American Journal of Orthopsychiatry* 33: 387–390; Werthman, C. (1967), op. cit.: Rainwater, L. (1970). *Behind Ghetto Walls*. Chicago: Aldine, 211–234; Ladner, J. (1971). *Tomorrow's Tomorrow: The Black Woman*. Garden City: Doubleday, 61–63; Elder, G. (1974). *Children of the Great Depression: Social Change in Life Experience*. Chicago: University of Chicago Press.

62 Toby, J. (1967), op. cit., 141.

63 Gouldner, A. (1970). *The Coming Crisis in Western Sociology*. New York: Basic Books, 221–222.

220

64 Cohen, A. (1955), op. cit., 112–113; Sennett, R. and J. Cobb (1972), *The Hidden Injuries of Class.* New York: Alfred A. Knopf.

65 Hyman, H.H. (1968). "The Psychology of Status," in H.H. Hyman and E. Singer (eds.), *Readings in Reference Group Theory and Research.* New York: Free Press, 147–168.

66 Goffman, E. (1955). "On Face-Work: An Analysis of Ritual Elements in Social Interaction," *Psychiatry* 18: 213–231.

67 Ellis, H.G. and S.M. Newman (1972). "The Greaser is a 'Bad Ass'; The Gowster is a 'Muthah'; An Analysis of Two Urban Youth Roles," in Thomas Kochman (ed.), *Rappin' and Stylin' Out: Communication in Black America.* Urbana: University of Illinois Press, 375–376.

68 Cohen, A. (1955), op. cit., 121–137.

69 Miller, W.B. (1966). "Violent Crime in City Gangs," *Annals of the American Academy of Political and Social Science* 364: 96–112.

70 Matza, D. (1964), op. cit., 33–68; Short, J.F., Jr. and F.L. Strodtbeck (1965), op.cit., 47–75.

71 Matza, D. (1964), op. cit., 33.

72 Werthman, C. (1967). op. cit.

73 Short, J.F., Jr. and F.L. Strodtbeck (1965), op. cit., 185–216, Horowitz, R. and G. Schwartz (1974). "Honor, Normative Ambiguity and Gang Violence," *American Sociological Review* 39: 238–251.

74 Goffman, E. (1974). "Where the Action Is," in *Interaction Ritual.* Garden City: Anchor Books, 149–270.

75 Matza, D. and G.M. Sykes (1961), "Juvenile Delinquency and Subterranean Values," *American Sociological Review* 26: 712–719.

76 Dennison, G. (1969). *The Lives of Children: The Story of the First Street School.* New York: Random House; Friedenberg, E.Z. (1964). *The Vanishing Adolescent.* Boston: Beacon Press; (1965). *Coming of Age in America: Growth and Acquiescence.* New York: Random House; Goodman, P. (1964). *Compulsory Miseducation.* New York: Horizon Press; Greene, M.F. and O. Ryan (1965). *The School Children: Growing Up in the Slums.* New York: Pantheon; Hargreaves, D.H. (1972). *Interpersonal Relations and Education.* London: Routledge and Kegan Paul; Hentoff, N. (1966). *Our Children Are Dying.* New York: Viking Press; Herndon, J. (1968). *The Way It Spozed to Be.* New York: Simon and Schuster; Jackson, P.W. (1968). *Life in Classrooms.* New York: Holt Rinehart and Winston; Kohl, H. (1967). *36 Children.* New York: New American Library; Nordstrom, C., E.Z. Friedenberg and H.A. Gold (1967). *Society's Children: A Study of Ressentiment in the Secondary School.* New York: Random House; Roberts, J.I. (1970). *Scene of the Battle: Group Behavior in Urban Classrooms.* Garden City: Doubleday; Webb, J. (1962). "The Sociology of a School," *British Journal of Sociology* 13: 264–272.

77 Downes, D.M. (1966). *The Delinquent Solution: A Study in Subcultural Theory.* New York: Free Press.

78 Finestone, H. (1957). "Cats, Kicks and Color," *Social Problems* 5: 3–13.

79 Rainwater, L. (1970), op. cit.

80 Werthman, C. (1967), op. cit.

81 Bachman, J.G., S. Green and I. Wirtanen (1972). *Dropping Out – Problem or Symptom.* Ann Arbor: Institute for Social Research.

82 Elliot, D.S. and H.L. Voss (1974). *Delinquency and Dropout.* Lexington, Mass.: Lexington Books, 115–122: Mukherjee, S.K. (1971). *A Typological Study of School Status and Delinquency.* Ann Arbor: University Microfilms.

83 McClean, J. D. and J.C. Wood (1969), op. cit.

84 DeFleur (1970), op. cit.

85 Grosser, G. (1952). *Juvenile Delinquency and Contemporary American Sex Roles.* Unpublished Ph.D. Dissertation, Harvard University.

86 Parsons, T. (1947). "Certain Primary Sources and Patterns of Aggression in the Social Structure of the Western World," *Psychiatry* 10: 167–181; Cohen, A. (1955), op. cit., 162–169.

87 Miller, W.B. (1958), op. cit.

88 Tennyson, R.A. (1967). "Family Structure and Delinquent Behavior," in M.W. Klein (ed.), *Juvenile Gangs in Context.* Englewood Cliffs, N.J.: Prentice-Hall; Monahan, T.P. (1957). "Family Status and the Delinquent Child: A Reappraisal and Some New Findings," *Social Forces* 35:

251–258; Rosen, L. (1969). "Matriarchy and Lower Class Negro Male Delinquency," *Social Problems* 17: 175–189.

89 Hannerz, U. (1969). *Soulside: Inquiries into Ghetto Culture.* New York: Columbia University Press.

90 Miller, W.B. (1958) op. cit.

91 A similar perspective on subcultures of violence and their relationship to masculinity has been developed by Curtis, L. (1975). *Violence, Race and Culture.* Lexington, Mass.: Lexington Books.

92 Werthman, C. (1967), op. cit.

93 Weis, J. (1967), op. cit.

94 Federal Bureau of Investigation (1974). *Crime in the United States. Uniform Crime Reports – 1973.* Washington, D.C.: Government Printing Office, 133.

95 Task Force Report (1967). *The Assessment of Crime.* Washington, D.C.: Government Printing Office.

96 Puntil, J.E. (n.d.). "Youth Survey Marginals." Chicago: Institute for Juvenile Research.

97 Briar, S. and I. Piliavin (1965). "Delinquency, Situational Inducements, and Commitment to Conformity," *Social Problems* 13: 35–45; Piliavin, I.M., A.C. Vadum and J.A. Hardyck (1969). "Delinquency, Personal Costs and Parental Treatment: A Test of a Reward-Cost Model of Juvenile Criminality," *Journal of Criminal Law, Criminology and Police Science* 60: 165–172; Hirschi, T. (1969), op. cit.; Ehrlich, I. (1973). "Participation in Illegitimate Activities: A Theoretical and Empirical Investigation," *Journal of Political Economy* 81: 521–565.

98 Reckless, W.C., S. Dinitz and E. Murray (1956). "Self Concept as an Insulator against Delinquency." *American Sociological Review* 21: 744–746.

99 Clark, J.P. and E.W. Haurek (1966), op. cit.

100 Schur, E.M. (1973). *Radical Nonintervention: Rethinking the Delinquency Problem.* Englewood Cliffs, N.J.: Prentice-Hall.

101 Hirschi, T. (1969), op. cit., 81–109.

102 Williams, L. (1976). "Three Youths Call Mugging the Elderly Profitable and Safe," *New York Times* (December 8): B2.

103 I have discussed the question of desistance with male juveniles on probation in Manhattan for theft offenses, and with a number of my students who have been involved in various forms of theft. The latter group includes both apprehended and unapprehended former thieves. No claim is made for the representativeness of this small sample.

104 Matza, D. (1964), op. cit., 55.

105 Tannenbaum, F. (1938). *Crime in the Community.* New York: Columbia University Press, 19–20.

106 Schwartz, R.D. and J.H. Skolnick (1962). "Two Studies of Legal Stigma," *Social Problems* 10: 133–142.

107 Hirschi, T. (1975). "Labelling Theory and Juvenile Delinquency: An Assessment of the Evidence," in Walter R. Gove (ed.), *Labeling of Deviance: Evaluating a Perspective.* New York: Halsted Press; Tittle, C.R. (1975). "Labelling and Crime: An Empirical Evaluation," in Walter R. Gove (ed.), *The Labelling of Deviance: Evaluating a Perspective.* New York: Halsted Press; Mahoney, A.R. (1974). "The Effect of Labeling upon Youths in the Juvenile Justice System: A Review of the Evidence," *Law and Society Review*, 8: 583–614.

108 Schur, E.M. (1973), op. cit., 125.

109 Wolfgang, M.E., R.M. Figlio and T. Sellin (1972), op. cit., 201.

110 Federal Bureau of Investigation (1972). *Crime in the United States. Uniform Crime Reports – 1971.* Washington D.C.: Government Printing Office, 138.

111 Chambliss, W.J. (1973). "The Saints and the Roughnecks," *Society* 11: 24–31.

112 This leniency has increased over the past decade, partly in response to the arguments of labeling theorists such as Schur, E.M. (1973), op. cit., that punishment of delinquents would be counter-rehabilitative, and because of the state's growing fiscal inability to cope with the social problems engendered by a deteriorating capitalist economy and polity. described by O'Connor. J. (1973). *The Fiscal Crisis of the State.* New York: St. Martin's Press. Scull, A. (1977). *Decarceration: Community Treatment and the Deviant – A Radical View.* Englewood Cliffs, N.J.: Prentice Hall, explicitly discusses the community corrections movement in these terms.

222

113 Hall, G.S. (1904). *Adolescence: Its Psychology and Its Relations to Physiology, Anthropology, Sociology, Sex, Crime, Religion, and Education.* New York: Appleton.

114 In nineteenth century England, juveniles were over-represented in crime statistics by comparison with the continent not because the social position of juveniles was very different, but because the age distribution of the English population was skewed toward the younger age brackets by the rapid growth in the English population during the nineteenth century. In the latter half of the century, juveniles were under-represented by comparison with their numbers in the English population, despite the high percentages of offenders who were juveniles; see, e.g. Lombroso, C. (1968), op. cit., 176; Tobias, J.J. (1972). *Urban Crime in Victorian England.* New York: Schocken Books, 78, 167.

115 Kalacheck, E. (1973). "The Changing Economic Status of the Young," *Journal of Youth and Adolescence* 2: 125–132.

116 Carson, R.B. (1972). "Youthful Labor Surplus in Disaccumulationist Capitalism," *Socialist Revolution* 9: 15–44; Bowers, N. (1975). "Youth and the Crisis of Monopoly Capitalism," in *Radical Perspectives on the Economic Crisis of Monopoly Capitalism.* New York: Union of Radical Political Economy.

117 Musgrove, F. (1965). *Youth and the Social Order.* Bloomington: Indiana University Press.

118 Cohen, D.K. and M. Lazerson (1972). "Education and the Corporate Order," *Socialist Revolution* 8: 47–72; Gorz, A. (1972). "Technologie, Techniker und Klassenkampf," in A. Gorz, *Schule and Fabrik.* Quoted in Gero Lenhardt, "On the Relationship between the Education System and Capitalist Work Organization." *Kapitalistate* 3: 128–146; Bowles S. and H. Gintis (1975). *Schooling in Capitalist America: Educational Reform and the Contradictions of Economic Life.* New York: Basic Books.

118 Connor, W. (1970). *Deviance in Soviet Society.* New York: Columbia University Press; Polk, K. (1972). "Social Class and the Bureaucratic Response to Youthful Deviance." Paper presented to the American Sociological Association.

120 Quinney, R. (1974). *Criminal Justice in America: A Critical Understanding.* Boston: Little, Brown; Quinney (1974). *Critique of Legal Order: Crime Control in Capitalist Society.* Boston: Little, Brown.

121 Platt, T. (1974). "Prospects for a Radical Criminology in the United States," *Crime and Social Justice: A Journal of Radical Criminology* 1: 2–10.

122 Taylor, I., P. Walton and J. Young (1973). *The New Criminology.* London: Routledge, Kegan Paul; Manders, D. (1975). "Labelling Theory and Social Reality: A Marxist Critique," *The Insurgent Sociologist* 6: 53–66.

123 Gordon, D. (1971). "Class and the Economics of Crime," *Review of Radical Political Economics* 3: 51–75; Taylor, I., P. Walton and J. Young (1973), op. cit.

124 Mankoff, M. (1971). "Societal Reaction and Career Deviance: A Critical Analysis." *Sociological Quarterly* 12: 204–218; Taylor, I., P. Walton and J. Young (1973), op. cit.; Manders, D. (1975), op. cit.

125 Lichtman, R. (1970). "Symbolic Interactionism and Social Reality: Some Marxist Queries." *Berkeley Journal of Sociology* 15: 75–94; McNall, S.G. and J.C.M. Johnson (1975). "The New Conservatives: Ethnomethodologists, Phenomenologists, and Symbolic Interactionists," *The Insurgent Sociologist* 5: 49–55; Grabiner, G. (1975). "The Situational Sociologies: A Theoretical Note." *The Insurgent Sociologist* 5: 80–81.

126 Seppilli, T. and G.G. Abbozzo, "The State of Research into Social Control and Deviance in Italy in the Post-War Period (1945–1973)," in Herman Bianchi, Mario Simoni and Ian Taylor (eds.), *Deviance and Control in Europe.* New York: Wiley, Pearce, F. (1975). *Crimes of the Powerful: Marxism, Crime and Deviance.* London: Pluto Press; Schwendinger, H. and J.R. Schwendinger (1976). "Delinquency and the Collective Varieties of Youth," *Crime and Social Justice* 5: 7–25.

127 I use this word, with some reservations, to indicate that steps taken to produce or reproduce social domination may be responded to in ways that interfere with that production or reproduction. Students may not be "cooled out" by low grades; they may rebel. Reservations are necessary because a Marxian contradiction has, at least potentially, the capability of overturning its source, not merely of being somewhat dysfunctional. The conventional sorts of crime

discussed in this paper do not have that capability; if anything, they tend to stabilize existing social arrangements, though in a manner that is disadvantageous for much of the population Only if the nature of the crimes were to change drastically would criminality be a manifestation of contradiction in the strict sense of the word. In that case we would be talking about a revolutionary movement.

128 Chambliss, W.J. (1976). "Functional and Conflict Theories of Crime: The Heritage of Emile Durkheim and Karl Marx," in William J. Chambliss and Milton Mankoff (eds), *Whose Law, What Order?* New York: Wiley; Denisoff, R.S. and C. McCaghy (1973). *Deviance, Conflict and Criminology.* Rand McNally.

129 Stolzman, J. and H. Gamberg (1973–1974). "Marxist Class Analysis versus Stratification Analysis as General Approaches to Social Inequality," *Berkely Journal of Sociology* 18: 105–126.

130 Fee. T. (1976). "Domestic Labor: An Analysis of Housework and Its Relation to the Production Process," *Review of Radical Political Economics* 8: 1–8.

Part III
General Strain Theory

[7]

FOUNDATION FOR A GENERAL STRAIN THEORY OF CRIME AND DELINQUENCY*

ROBERT AGNEW
Emory University

This paper presents a general strain theory of crime and delinquency that is capable of overcoming the criticisms of previous strain theories. In the first section, strain theory is distinguished from social control and differential association/social learning theory. In the second section, the three major types of strain are described: (1) strain as the actual or anticipated failure to achieve positively valued goals, (2) strain as the actual or anticipated removal of positively valued stimuli, and (3) strain as the actual or anticipated presentation of negatively valued stimuli. In the third section, guidelines for the measurement of strain are presented. And in the fourth section, the major adaptations to strain are described, and those factors influencing the choice of delinquent versus nondelinquent adaptations are discussed.

After dominating deviance research in the 1960s, strain theory came under heavy attack in the 1970s (Bernard, 1984; Cole, 1975), with several prominent researchers suggesting that the theory be abandoned (Hirschi, 1969; Kornhauser, 1978). Strain theory has survived those attacks, but its influence is much diminished (see Agnew, 1985a; Bernard, 1984; Farnworth and Leiber, 1989). In particular, variables derived from strain theory now play a very limited role in explanations of crime/delinquency. Several recent causal models of delinquency, in fact, either entirely exclude strain variables or assign them a small role (e.g., Elliott et al., 1985; Johnson, 1979; Massey and Krohn, 1986; Thornberry, 1987; Tonry et al., 1991). Causal models of crime/delinquency are dominated, instead, by variables derived from differential association/social learning theory and social control theory.

This paper argues that strain theory has a central role to play in explanations of crime/delinquency, but that the theory has to be substantially revised to play this role. Most empirical studies of strain theory continue to rely on the strain models developed by Merton (1938), A. Cohen (1955), and Cloward and Ohlin (1960). In recent years, however, a wealth of research in several fields has questioned certain of the assumptions underlying those theories and pointed to new directions for the development of strain theory. Most notable in this area is the research on stress in medical sociology and psychology, on equity/justice in social psychology, and on aggression in psychology—particularly recent versions of frustration-aggression and social

* I would like to thank Helene Raskin White and Karen Hegtvedt for their comments.

learning theory. Also important is recent research in such areas as the legiti-mation of stratification, the sociology of emotions, and the urban underclass. Certain researchers have drawn on segments of the above research to suggest new directions for strain theory (Agnew, 1985a; Bernard, 1987; Elliott et al., 1979; Greenberg, 1977), but the revisions suggested have not taken full advantage of this research and, at best, provide only incomplete models of strain and delinquency. (Note that most of the theoretical and empirical work on strain theory has focused on delinquency.) This paper draws on the above literatures, as well as the recent revisions in strain theory, to present the outlines of a general strain theory of crime/delinquency.

The theory is written at the social-psychological level: It focuses on the individual and his or her immediate social environment—although the macroimplications of the theory are explored at various points. The theory is also written with the empirical researcher in mind, and guidelines for testing the theory in adolescent populations are provided. The focus is on adoles-cents because most currently available data sets capable of testing the theory involve surveys of adolescents. This general theory, it will be argued, is capa-ble of overcoming the theoretical and empirical criticisms of previous strain theories and of complementing the crime/delinquency theories that currently dominate the field.

The paper is in four sections. In the first section, there is a brief discussion of the fundamental traits that distinguish strain theory from the other two dominant theories of delinquency: social control and differential association/ social learning theory (in the interest of brevity, the term *delinquency* is used rather than *crime and delinquency*). In the second section, the three major sources of strain are described. In the third section, guidelines for the mea-surement of strain are provided. And in the final section, the major adapta-tions to strain are listed and the factors influencing the choice of delinquent versus nondelinquent adaptations are discussed.

STRAIN THEORY AS DISTINGUISHED FROM CONTROL AND DIFFERENTIAL ASSOCIATION/SOCIAL LEARNING THEORY

Strain, social control, and differential association theory are all sociological theories: They explain delinquency in terms of the individual's social rela-tionships. Strain theory is distinguished from social control and social learn-ing theory in its specification of (1) the type of social relationship that leads to delinquency and (2) the motivation for delinquency. First, strain theory focuses explicitly on *negative relationships with others*: relationships in which the individual is not treated as he or she wants to be treated. Strain theory has typically focused on relationships in which others prevent the individual

A GENERAL STRAIN THEORY 49

from achieving positively valued goals. Agnew (1985a), however, broadened the focus of strain theory to include relationships in which others present the individual with noxious or negative stimuli. Social control theory, by contrast, focuses on the *absence of significant relationships with conventional others and institutions.* In particular, delinquency is most likely when (1) the adolescent is not attached to parents, school, or other institutions; (2) parents and others fail to monitor and effectively sanction deviance; (3) the adolescent's actual or anticipated investment in conventional society is minimal; and (4) the adolescent has not internalized conventional beliefs. Social learning theory is distinguished from strain and control theory by its focus on *positive relationships with deviant others.* In particular, delinquency results from association with others who (1) differentially reinforce the adolescent's delinquency, (2) model delinquent behavior, and/or (3) transmit delinquent values.

Second, strain theory argues that adolescents are *pressured into delinquency by the negative affective states—most notably anger and related emotions— that often result from negative relationships* (see Kemper, 1978, and Morgan and Heise, 1988, for typologies of negative affective states). This negative affect creates pressure for corrective action and *may* lead adolescents to (1) make use of illegitimate channels of goal achievement, (2) attack or escape from the source of their adversity, and/or (3) manage their negative affect through the use of illicit drugs. Control theory, by contrast, denies that outside forces pressure the adolescent into delinquency. Rather, the absence of significant relationships with other individuals and groups *frees the adolescent to engage in delinquency.* The freed adolescent either drifts into delinquency or, in some versions of control theory, turns to delinquency in response to inner forces or situational inducements (see Hirschi, 1969:31–34). In differential association/social learning theory, the adolescent commits delinquent acts because group forces lead the adolescent to *view delinquency as a desirable or at least justifiable form of behavior* under certain circumstances.

Strain theory, then, is distinguished by its focus on negative relationships with others and its insistence that such relationships lead to delinquency through the negative affect—especially anger—they sometimes engender. Both dimensions are necessary to differentiate strain theory from control and differential association/social learning theory. In particular, social control and social learning theory sometimes examine negative relationships— although such relationships are not an explicit focus of these theories. Control theory, however, would argue that negative relationships lead to delinquency not because they cause negative affect, but because they lead to a reduction in social control. A control theorist, for example, would argue that physical abuse by parents leads to delinquency because it reduces attachment to parents and the effectiveness of parents as socializing agents. Likewise, differential association/social learning theorists sometimes examine negative relationships—even though theorists in this tradition emphasize that imitation, reinforcement, and the internalization of values are less likely in negative relationships. Social learning theorists, however, would argue that negative relationships—such as those involving physically abusive parents—lead to delinquency by providing models for imitation and implicitly teaching the child that violence and other forms of deviance are acceptable behavior.

Phrased in the above manner, it is easy to see that strain theory complements the other major theories of delinquency in a fundamental way. While these other theories focus on the absence of relationships or on positive relationships, strain theory is the only theory to focus explicitly on negative relationships. And while these other theories view delinquency as the result of drift or of desire, strain theory views it as the result of pressure.

THE MAJOR TYPES OF STRAIN

Negative relationships with others are, quite simply, relationships in which others are not treating the individual as he or she would like to be treated. The classic strain theories of Merton (1938), A. Cohen (1955), and Cloward and Ohlin (1960) focus on only one type of negative relationship: relationships in which others prevent the individual from achieving positively valued goals. In particular, they focus on the goal blockage experienced by lower-class individuals trying to achieve monetary success or middle-class status. More recent versions of strain theory have argued that adolescents are not only concerned about the future goals of monetary success/middle-class status, but are also concerned about the achievement of more immediate goals—such as good grades, popularity with the opposite sex, and doing well in athletics (Agnew, 1984; Elliott and Voss, 1974; Elliott et al., 1985; Empey, 1982; Greenberg, 1977; Quicker, 1974). The focus, however, is still on the achievement of positively valued goals. Most recently, Agnew (1985a) has argued that strain may result not only from the failure to achieve positively valued goals, but also from the inability to escape legally from painful situations. If one draws on the above theories—as well as the stress, equity/justice, and aggression literatures—one can begin to develop a more complete classification of the types of strain.

Three major types of strain are described—each referring to a different type of negative relationship with others. Other individuals may (1) prevent one from achieving positively valued goals, (2) remove or threaten to remove positively valued stimuli that one possesses, or (3) present or threaten to present one with noxious or negatively valued stimuli. These categories of strain are presented as ideal types. There is no expectation, for example, that a factor analysis of strainful events will reproduce these categories. These categories,

A GENERAL STRAIN THEORY 51

rather, are presented so as to ensure that the full range of strainful events are considered in empirical research.

STRAIN AS THE FAILURE TO ACHIEVE POSITIVELY VALUED GOALS

At least three types of strain fall under this category. The first type encompasses most of the major strain theories in criminology, including the classic strain theories of Merton, A. Cohen, and Cloward and Ohlin, as well as those modern strain theories focusing on the achievement of immediate goals. The other two types of strain in this category are derived from the justice/equity literature and have not been examined in criminology.

STRAIN AS THE DISJUNCTION BETWEEN ASPIRATIONS AND EXPECTATIONS/ACTUAL ACHIEVEMENTS

The classic strain theories of Merton, A. Cohen, and Cloward and Ohlin argue that the cultural system encourages everyone to pursue the ideal goals of monetary success and/or middle-class status. Lower-class individuals, however, are often prevented from achieving such goals through legitimate channels. In line with such theories, adolescent strain is typically measured in terms of the disjunction between *aspirations* (or ideal goals) and *expectations* (or expected levels of goal achievement). These theories, however, have been criticized for several reasons (see Agnew, 1986, 1991b; Clinard, 1964; Hirschi, 1969; Kornhauser, 1978; Liska, 1987; also see Bernard, 1984; Farnworth and Leiber, 1989). Among other things, it has been charged that these theories (1) are unable to explain the extensive nature of middle-class delinquency, (2) neglect goals other than monetary success/middle-class status, (3) neglect barriers to goal achievement other than social class, and (4) do not fully specify why only *some* strained individuals turn to delinquency. The most damaging criticism, however, stems from the limited empirical support provided by studies focusing on the disjunction between aspirations and expectations (see Kornhauser, 1978, as well the arguments of Bernard, 1984; Elliott et al., 1985; and Jensen, 1986).

As a consequence of these criticisms, several researchers have revised the above theories. The most popular revision argues that there is a youth subculture that emphasizes a variety of immediate goals. The achievement of these goals is further said to depend on a variety of factors besides social class: factors such as intelligence, physical attractiveness, personality, and athletic ability. As a result, many middle-class individuals find that they lack the traits or skills necessary to achieve their goals through legitimate channels. This version of strain theory, however, continues to argue that strain stems from the inability to achieve certain ideal goals emphasized by the (sub)cultural system. As a consequence, strain continues to be measured in terms of the disjunction between *aspirations* and *actual achievements* (since we are dealing with immediate rather than future goals, actual achievements rather than expected achievements may be examined).

It should be noted that empirical support for this revised version of strain theory is also weak (see Agnew, 1991b, for a summary). At a later point, several possible reasons for the weak empirical support of strain theories focusing on the disjunction between aspirations and expectations/achievements will be discussed. For now, the focus is on classifying the major types of strain.

Strain as the Disjunction between Expectations and Actual Achievements

As indicated above, strain theories in criminology focus on the inability to achieve *ideal* goals derived from the cultural system. This approach stands in contrast to certain of the research on justice in social psychology. Here the focus is on the disjunction between *expectations* and *actual achievements* (rewards), and it is commonly argued that such expectations are existentially based. In particular, it has been argued that such expectations derive from the individual's past experience and/or from comparisons with referential (or generalized) others who are similar to the individual (see Berger et al., 1972, 1983; Blau, 1964; Homans, 1961; Jasso and Rossi, 1977; Mickelson, 1990; Ross et al., 1971; Thibaut and Kelley, 1959). Much of the research in this area has focused on income expectations, although the above theories apply to expectations regarding all manner of positive stimuli. The justice literature argues that the failure to achieve such expectations may lead to such emotions as anger, resentment, rage, dissatisfaction, disappointment, and unhappiness—that is, all the emotions customarily associated with strain in criminology. Further, it is argued that individuals will be strongly motivated to reduce the gap between expectations and achievements—with deviance being commonly mentioned as one possible option. This literature has not devoted much empirical research to deviance, although limited data suggest that the expectations-achievement gap is related to anger/hostility (Ross et al, 1971).

This alternative conception of strain has been largely neglected in criminology. This is unfortunate because it has the potential to overcome certain of the problems of current strain theories. First, one would expect the disjunction between expectations and actual achievements to be more emotionally distressing than that between aspirations and achievements. Aspirations, by definition, are *ideal* goals. They have something of the utopian in them, and for that reason, the failure to achieve aspirations may not be taken seriously. The failure to achieve expected goals, however, is likely to be taken seriously since such goals are rooted in reality—the individual has previously experienced such goals or has seen similar others experience such goals. Second,

A GENERAL STRAIN THEORY   53

this alternative conception of strain assigns a central role to the social comparison process. As A. Cohen (1965) argued in a follow-up to his strain theory, the neglect of social comparison is a major shortcoming of strain theory. The above theories describe one way in which social comparison is important: Social comparison plays a central role in the formation of individual goals (expectations in this case; also see Suls, 1977). Third, the assumption that goals are culturally based has sometimes proved problematic for strain theory (see Kornhauser, 1978). Among other things, it makes it difficult to integrate strain theory with social control and cultural deviance theory (see Hirschi, 1979). These latter theories assume that the individual is weakly tied to the cultural system or tied to alternative/oppositional subcultures. The argument that goals are existentially based, however, paves the way for integrations involving strain theory.[1]

STRAIN AS THE DISJUNCTION BETWEEN JUST/FAIR OUTCOMES AND ACTUAL OUTCOMES

The above models of strain assume that individual goals focus on the achievement of specific outcomes. Individual goals, for example, focus on the achievement of a certain amount of money or a certain grade-point average. A third conception of strain, also derived from the justice/equity literature, makes a rather different argument. It claims that individuals do not necessarily enter interactions with specific outcomes in mind. Rather, they enter interactions expecting that certain distributive justice rules will be followed, rules specifying how resources should be allocated. The rule that has received the most attention in the literature is that of equity. An equitable relationship is one in which the outcome/input ratios of the actors involved in an exchange/allocation relationship are equivalent (see Adams, 1963, 1965; Cook and Hegtvedt, 1983; Walster et al., 1978). Outcomes encompass a broad range of positive and negative consequences, while inputs encompass the individual's positive and negative contributions to the exchange. Individuals in a relationship will compare the ratio of their outcomes and inputs to the ratio(s) of specific others in the relationship. If the ratios are equal to one another, they feel that the outcomes are fair or just. This is true, according to equity theorists, even if the outcomes are low. If outcome/input ratios are

---

1. One need not assume that expectations are existentially based; they may derive from the cultural system as well. Likewise, one need not assume that aspirations derive from the cultural system. The focus in this paper is on *types* of strain rather than *sources* of strain, although a consideration of sources is crucial when the macroimplications of the theory are developed. Additional information on the sources of positively valued goals—including aspirations and expectations—can be found in Alves and Rossi, 1978; Cook and Messick, 1983; Hochschild, 1981; Jasso and Rossi, 1977; Martin and Murray, 1983; Messick and Sentis, 1983; Mickelson, 1990; and Shepelak and Alwin, 1986.

54   AGNEW

not equal, actors will feel that the outcomes are unjust and they will experience distress as a result. Such distress is especially likely when individuals feel they have been underrewarded rather than overrewarded (Hegtvedt, 1990).

The equity literature has described the possible reactions to this distress, some of which involve deviance (see Adams, 1963, 1965; Austin, 1977; Walster et al., 1973, 1978; see Stephenson and White, 1968, for an attempt to recast A. Cohen's strain theory in terms of equity theory). In particular, inequity may lead to delinquency for several reasons—all having to do with the restoration of equity. Individuals in inequitable relationships may engage in delinquency in order to (1) increase their outcomes (e.g., by theft); (2) lower their inputs (e.g., truancy from school); (3) lower the outcomes of others (e.g., vandalism, theft, assault); and/or (4) increase the inputs of others (e.g., by being incorrigible or disorderly). In highly inequitable situations, individuals may leave the field (e.g., run away from home) or force others to leave the field.[2] There has not been any empirical research on the relationship between equity and delinquency, although much data suggest that inequity leads to anger and frustration. A few studies also suggest that insulting and vengeful behaviors may result from inequity (see Cook and Hegtvedt, 1991; Donnerstein and Hatfield, 1982; Hegtvedt, 1990; Mikula, 1986; Sprecher, 1986; Walster et al., 1973, 1978).

It is not difficult to measure equity. Walster et al. (1978:234–242) provide the most complete guide to measurement.[3] Sprecher (1986) illustrates how

---

2. Theorists have recently argued that efforts to restore equity need not involve the specific others in the inequitable relationship. If one cannot restore equity with such specific others, there may be an effort to restore "equity with the world" (Austin, 1977; Stephenson and White, 1968; Walster et al., 1978). That is, individuals who feel they have been inequitably treated may try to restore equity in the context of a totally different relationship. The adolescent who is inequitably treated by parents, for example, may respond by inequitably treating peers. The concept of "equity with the world" has not been the subject of much empirical research, but it is intriguing because it provides a novel explanation for displaced aggression. It has also been argued that individuals may be distressed not only by their own inequitable treatment, but also by the inequitable treatment of others (see Crosby and Gonzalez-Intal, 1984; Walster et al., 1978.) We may have, then, a sort of vicarious strain, a type little investigated in the literature.

3. The equity literature has been criticized on a number of points, the most prominent being that there are a variety of distribution rules besides equity—such as equality and need (Deutsch, 1975; Folger, 1984; Mikula, 1980; Schwinger, 1980; Utne and Kidd, 1980). Much recent research has focused on the factors that determine the preference for one rule over another (Alves and Rossi, 1978; Cook and Hegtvedt, 1983; Deutsch, 1975; Hegtvedt, 1987, 1991a; Hochschild, 1981; Lerner, 1977; Leventhal, 1976; Leventhal et al., 1980; Schwinger, 1980; Walster et al., 1978). Also, the equity literature argues that individuals compare themselves with similar others with whom they are involved in exchange/allocation relations. However, it has been argued that individuals sometimes compare themselves with dissimilar others, make referential (generalized) rather than local (specific) comparisons, make internal rather than external comparisons, make group-to-group comparisons,

A GENERAL STRAIN THEORY 55

equity may be measured in social surveys; respondents are asked who contributes more to a particular relationship and/or who "gets the best deal" out of a relationship. A still simpler strategy might be to ask respondents how fair or just their interactions with others, such as parents or teachers, are. One would then predict that those involved in unfair relations will be more likely to engage in current and future delinquency.

The literature on equity builds on the strain theory literature in criminology in several ways. First, all of the strain literature assumes that individuals are pursuing some specific outcome, such as a certain amount of money or prestige. The equity literature points out that individuals do not necessarily enter into interactions with specific outcomes in mind, but rather with the expectation that a particular distributive justice rule will be followed. Their goal is that the interaction conform to the justice principle. This perspective, then, points to a new source of strain not considered in the criminology literature. Second, the strain literature in criminology focuses largely on the individual's outcomes. Individuals are assumed to be pursuing a specific goal, and strain is judged in terms of the disjuntion between the goal and the actual outcome. The equity literature suggests that this may be an oversimplified conception and that the individual's *inputs* may also have to be considered. In particular, an equity theorist would argue that inputs will condition the individual's evaluation of outcomes. That is, individuals who view their inputs as limited will be more likely to accept limited outcomes as fair. Third, the equity literature also highlights the importance of the social comparison process. In particular, the equity literature stresses that one's evaluation of outcomes is at least partly a function of the outcomes (and inputs) of those with whom one is involved in exchange/allocation relations. A given outcome, then, may be evaluated as fair or unfair depending on the outcomes (and inputs) of others in the exchange/allocation relation.

---

or avoid social comparison altogether (see Berger et al., 1972; Hegtvedt, 1991b; Martin and Murray, 1983; see Hegtvedt, 1991b, and Suls and Wills, 1991, for a discussion of the factors affecting the choice of comparison objects). Finally, even if one knows what distribution rule individuals prefer and the types of social comparisons they make, it is still difficult to predict whether they will evaluate their interactions as equitable. Except in unambiguous situations of the type created in experiments, it is hard to predict what inputs and outcomes individuals will define as relevant, how they will weight those inputs and outcomes, and how they will evaluate themselves and others on those inputs and outcomes (Austin, 1977; Hegtvedt, 1991a; Messick and Sentis, 1979, 1983; Walster et al., 1973, 1978). Fortunately, however, the above three problems do not prohibit strain theory from taking advantage of certain of the insights from equity theory. While it is difficult to predict whether individuals will define their relationships as equitable, it is relatively easy to measure equity after the fact.

56   AGNEW

SUMMARY: STRAIN AS THE FAILURE TO ACHIEVE POSITIVELY
VALUED GOALS

Three types of strain in this category have been listed: strain as the disjunction between (1) aspirations and expectations/actual achievements,
(2) expectations and actual achievements, and (3) just/fair outcomes and
actual outcomes. Strain theory in criminology has focused on the first type of
strain, arguing that it is most responsible for the delinquency in our society.
Major research traditions in the justice/equity field, however, argue that
anger and frustration derive primarily from the second two types of strain.
To complicate matters further, one can list still additional types of strain in
this category. Certain of the literature, for example, has talked of the disjunction between "satisfying outcomes" and reality, between "deserved" outcomes and reality, and between "tolerance levels" or minimally acceptable
outcomes and reality. No study has examined all of these types of goals, but
taken as a whole the data do suggest that there are often differences among
aspirations (ideal outcomes), expectations (expected outcomes), "satisfying"
outcomes, "deserved" outcomes, fair or just outcomes, and tolerance levels
(Della Fave, 1974; Della Fave and Klobus, 1976; Martin, 1986; Martin and
Murray, 1983; Messick and Sentis, 1983; Shepelak and Alwin, 1986). This
paper has focused on the three types of strain listed above largely because
they dominate the current literature.[4]

Given these multiple sources of strain, one might ask which is the most
relevant to the explanation of delinquency. This is a difficult question to
answer given current research. The most fruitful strategy at the present time
may be to assume that all of the above sources are relevant—that there are
several sources of frustration. Alwin (1987), Austin (1977), Crosby and Gonzalez-Intal (1984), Hegtvedt (1991b), Messick and Sentis (1983), and Tornblum (1977) all argue or imply that people often employ a variety of
standards to evaluate their situation. Strain theorists, then, might be best
advised to employ measures that tap all of the above types of strain. One
might, for example, focus on a broad range of positively valued goals and, for
each goal, ask adolescents whether they are achieving their ideal outcomes
(aspirations), expected outcomes, and just/fair outcomes. One would expect
strain to be greatest when several standards were not being met, with perhaps
greatest weight being given to expectations and just/fair outcomes.[5]

---

4. To add a still further complication, it has been suggested that anger may result
from the violation of *procedural* as well as distributive justice rules (Folger, 1984, 1986;
Lind and Tyler, 1988). Procedural justice does not focus on the fairness of outcomes, but
rather on the fairness of the procedures by which individuals decide how to distribute
resources. A central issue in procedural justice is whether all individuals have a "voice" in
deciding how resources will be distributed. One might, then, ask adolescents about the
fairness of the procedures used by parents, teachers, and others to make rules.

5. This strategy assumes that all standards are relevant in a given situation, which

A GENERAL STRAIN THEORY 57

STRAIN AS THE REMOVAL OF POSITIVELY VALUED STIMULI FROM THE INDIVIDUAL

The psychological literature on aggression and the stress literature suggest that strain may involve more than the pursuit of positively valued goals. Certain of the aggression literature, in fact, has come to de-emphasize the pursuit of positively valued goals, pointing out that the blockage of goal-seeking behavior is a relatively weak predictor of aggression, particularly when the goal has never been experienced before (Bandura, 1973; Zillman, 1979). The stress literature has largely neglected the pursuit of positively valued goals as a source of stress. Rather, if one looks at the stressful life events examined in this literature, one finds a focus on (1) events involving the loss of positively valued stimuli and (2) events involving the presentation of noxious or negative stimuli (see Pearlin, 1983, for other typologies of stressful life events/conditions).[6] So, for example, one recent study of adolescent stress employs a life-events list that focuses on such items as the loss of a boyfriend/girlfriend, the death or serious illness of a friend, moving to a new school district, the divorce/separation of one's parents, suspension from school, and the presence of a variety of adverse conditions at work (see Williams and Uchiyama, 1989, for an overview of life-events scales for adolescents; see Compas, 1987, and Compas and Phares, 1991, for overviews of research on adolescent stress).[7]

Drawing on the stress literature, then, one may state that a second type of strain or negative relationship involves the actual or anticipated removal (loss) of positively valued stimuli from the individual. As indicated above, numerous examples of such loss can be found in the inventories of stressful life events. The actual or anticipated loss of positively valued stimuli may lead to delinquency as the individual tries to prevent the loss of the positive stimuli, retrieve the lost stimuli or obtain substitute stimuli, seek revenge

---

may not always be the case. In certain situations, for example, one may make local comparisons but not referential comparisons (see Brickman and Bulman, 1977; Crosby and Gonzales-Intal, 1984). In other situations, social comparison processes may not come into play at all; outcomes may be evaluated in terms of culturally derived standards (see Folger, 1986).

6. The stress literature has also focused on positive events, based on the assumption that such events might lead to stress by overloading the individual. Accumulating evidence, however, suggests that it is only undesirable events that lead to negative outcomes such as depression (e.g., Gersten et al., 1974; Kaplan et al., 1983; Pearlin et al., 1981; Thoits, 1983).

7. Certain individuals have criticized the stress literature for neglecting the failure of individuals to achieve positively valued goals. In particular, it has been charged that the stress literature has neglected "nonevents," or events that are desired or anticipated but do not occur (Dohrenwend and Dohrenwend, 1974; Thoits, 1983). One major distinction between the strain literature in criminology and the stress literature in medical sociology, in fact, is that the former has focused on "nonevents" while the latter has focused on "events."

against those responsible for the loss, or manage the negative affect caused by the loss by taking illicit drugs. While there are no data bearing directly on this type of strain, experimental data indicate that aggression often occurs when positive reinforcement previously administered to an individual is withheld or reduced (Bandura, 1973; Van Houten, 1983). And as discussed below, inventories of stressful life events, which include the loss of positive stimuli, are related to delinquency.

STRAIN AS THE PRESENTATION OF NEGATIVE STIMULI

The literature on stress and the recent psychological literature on aggression also focus on the actual or anticipated presentation of negative or noxious stimuli.[8] Except for the work of Agnew (1985a), however, this category of strain has been neglected in criminology. And even Agnew does not focus on the presentation of noxious stimuli per se, but on the inability of adolescents to escape legally from noxious stimuli. Much data, however, suggest that the presentation of noxious stimuli may lead to aggression and other negative outcomes in certain conditions, even when legal escape from such stimuli is possible (Bandura, 1973; Zillman, 1979). Noxious stimuli may lead to delinquency as the adolescent tries to (1) escape from or avoid the negative stimuli; (2) terminate or alleviate the negative stimuli; (3) seek revenge against the source of the negative stimuli or related targets, although the evidence on displaced aggression is somewhat mixed (see Berkowitz, 1982; Bernard, 1990; Van Houten, 1983; Zillman, 1979); and/or (4) manage the resultant negative affect by taking illicit drugs.

A wide range of noxious stimuli have been examined in the literature, and experimental, survey, and participant observation studies have linked such stimuli to both general and specific measures of delinquency—with the experimental studies focusing on aggression. Delinquency/aggression, in particular, has been linked to such noxious stimuli as child abuse and neglect (Rivera and Widom, 1990), criminal victimization (Lauritsen et al., 1991), physical punishment (Straus, 1991), negative relations with parents (Healy and Bonner, 1969), negative relations with peers (Short and Strodtbeck, 1965), adverse or negative school experiences (Hawkins and Lishner, 1987), a wide range of stressful life events (Gersten et al., 1974; Kaplan et al., 1983; Linsky

---

8. Some researchers have argued that it is often difficult to distinguish the presentation of negative stimuli from the removal of positive stimuli (Michael, 1973; Van Houten, 1983; Zillman, 1979). Suppose, for example, that an adolescent argues with parents. Does this represent the presentation of negative stimuli, (the arguing) or the removal of positive stimuli (harmonious relations with one's parents)? The point is a valid one, yet the distinction between the two types of strain still seems useful since it helps ensure that all major types of strain are considered by researchers.

A GENERAL STRAIN THEORY 59

and Straus, 1986; Mawson, 1987; Novy and Donohue, 1985; Vaux and Ruggiero, 1983), verbal threats and insults, physical pain, unpleasant odors, disgusting scenes, noise, heat, air pollution, personal space violations, and high density (see Anderson and Anderson, 1984; Bandura, 1973, 1983; Berkowitz, 1982, 1986; Mueller, 1983). In one of the few studies in criminology to focus specifically on the presentation of negative stimuli, Agnew (1985a) found that delinquency was related to three scales measuring negative relations at home and school. The effect of the scales on delinquency was partially mediated through a measure of anger, and the effect held when measures of social control and deviant beliefs were controlled. And in a recent study employing longitudinal data, Agnew (1989) found evidence suggesting that the relationship between negative stimuli and delinquency was due to the *causal* effect of the negative stimuli on delinquency (rather than the effect of delinquency on the negative stimuli). Much evidence, then, suggests that the presentation of negative or noxious stimuli constitutes a third major source of strain.

Certain of the negative stimuli listed above, such as physical pain, heat, noise, and pollution, may be experienced as noxious largely for biological reasons (i.e., they may be unconditioned negative stimuli). Others may be conditioned negative stimuli, experienced as noxious largely because of their association with unconditioned negative stimuli (see Berkowitz, 1982). Whatever the case, it is assumed that such stimuli are experienced as noxious regardless of the goals that the individual is pursuing.

THE LINKS BETWEEN STRAIN AND DELINQUENCY

Three sources of strain have been presented: strain as the actual or anticipated failure to achieve positively valued goals, strain as the actual or anticipated removal of positively valued stimuli, and strain as the actual or anticipated presentation of negative stimuli. While these types are theoretically distinct from one another, they may sometimes overlap in practice. So, for example, the insults of a teacher may be experienced as adverse because they (1) interfere with the adolescent's aspirations for academic success, (2) result in the violation of a distributive justice rule such as equity, and (3) are conditioned negative stimuli and so are experienced as noxious in and of themselves. Other examples of overlap can be given, and it may sometimes be difficult to disentangle the different types of strain in practice. Once again, however, these categories are ideal types and are presented only to ensure that all events with the potential for creating strain are considered in empirical research.

Each type of strain increases the likelihood that individuals will experience one or more of a range of negative emotions. Those emotions include disappointment, depression, and fear. Anger, however, is the most critical emotional reaction for the purposes of the general strain theory. Anger results when individuals blame their adversity on others, and anger is a key emotion

60   AGNEW

because it increases the individual's level of felt injury, creates a desire for retaliation/revenge, energizes the individual for action, and lowers inhibitions, in part because individuals believe that others will feel their aggression is justified (see Averill, 1982; Berkowitz, 1982; Kemper, 1978; Kluegel and Smith, 1986: Ch. 10; Zillman, 1979). Anger, then, affects the individual in several ways that are conducive to delinquency. Anger is distinct from many of the other types of negative affect in this respect, and this is the reason that anger occupies a special place in the general strain theory.[9] It is important to note, however, that delinquency may still occur in response to other types of negative affect—such as despair, although delinquency is less likely in such cases.[10] The experience of negative affect, especially anger, typically creates a desire to take corrective steps, with delinquency being one possible response. Delinquency may be a method for alleviating strain, that is, for achieving positively valued goals, for protecting or retrieving positive stimuli, or for terminating or escaping from negative stimuli. Delinquency may be used to seek revenge; data suggest that vengeful behavior often occurs even when there is no possibility of eliminating the adversity that stimulated it (Berkowitz, 1982). And delinquency may occur as adolescents try to manage their negative affect through illicit drug use (see Newcomb and Harlow, 1986). The general strain theory, then, has the potential to explain a broad range of delinquency, including theft, aggression, and drug use.

Each type of strain may create a *predisposition* for delinquency or function as a *situational event* that instigates a particular delinquent act. In the words of Hirschi and Gottredson (1986), then, the strain theory presented in this paper is a theory of both "criminality" and "crime" (or to use the words of Clarke and Cornish [1985], it is a theory of both "criminal involvement" and "criminal events"). Strain creates a predisposition for delinquency in those cases in which it is chronic or repetitive. Examples include a continuing gap

---

9. The focus on blame/anger represents a major distinction between the general strain theory and the stress literature. The stress literature simply focuses on adversity, regardless of whether it is blamed on another. This is perhaps appropriate because the major outcome variables of the stress literature are inner-directed states, like depression and poor health. When the focus shifts to outer-directed behavior, like much delinquency, a concern with blame/anger becomes important.

10. Delinquency may still occur in the absence of blame and anger (see Berkowitz, 1986; Zillman, 1979). Individuals who accept responsibility for their adversity are still subject to negative affect, such as depression, despair, and disappointment (see Kemper, 1978; Kluegel and Smith, 1986). As a result, such individuals will still feel pressure to take corrective action, although the absence of anger places them under less pressure and makes vengeful behavior much less likely. Such individuals, however, may engage in inner-directed delinquency, such as drug use, and if suitably disposed, they may turn to other forms of delinquency as well. Since these individuals lack the strong motivation for revenge and the lowered inhibitions that anger provides, it is assumed that they must have some minimal disposition for deviance before they respond to their adversity with outer-directed delinquency (see the discussion of the disposition to delinquency).

A GENERAL STRAIN THEORY 61

between expectations and achievements and a continuing pattern of ridicule and insults from teachers. Adolescents subject to such strain are predisposed to delinquency because (1) nondelinquent strategies for coping with strain are likely to be taxed; (2) the threshold for adversity may be lowered by chronic strains (see Averill, 1982:289); (3) repeated or chronic strain may lead to a hostile attitude—a general dislike and suspicion of others and an associated tendency to respond in an aggressive manner (see Edmunds and Kendrick, 1980:21); and (4) chronic strains increase the likelihood that individuals will be high in negative affect/arousal at any given time (see Bandura, 1983; Bernard, 1990). A particular instance of strain may also function as the situational event that ignites a delinquent act, especially among adolescents predisposed to delinquency. Qualitative and survey data, in particular, suggest that particular instances of delinquency are often instigated by one of the three types of strain listed above (see Agnew, 1990; also see Averill, 1982, for data on the instigations to anger).

MEASURING STRAIN

As indicated above, strain theory in criminology is dominated by a focus on strain as goal blockage. Further, only one type of goal blockage is typically examined in the literature—the failure to achieve *aspirations*, especially aspirations for monetary success or middle-class status. The general strain theory is much broader than current strain theories, and measuring strain under this theory would require at least three sets of measures: those focusing on the failure to achieve positively valued goals, those focusing on the loss of positive stimuli, and those focusing on the presentation of negative stimuli. It is not possible to list the precise measures that should be employed in these areas, although the citations above contain many examples of the types of measures that might be used. Further, certain general guidelines for the measurement of strain can be offered. The guidelines below will also highlight the limitations of current strain measures and shed further light on why those measures are typically unrelated to delinquency.

DEVELOPING A COMPREHENSIVE LIST OF NEGATIVE RELATIONS

Strain refers to negative or adverse relations with others. Such relations are ultimately defined from the perspective of the individual. That is, in the final analysis adverse relations are whatever individuals say they are (see Berkowitz, 1982). This does not mean, however, that one must employ an idiosyncratic definition of adverse relations—defining adverse relations anew for each person one examines. Such a strategy would create serious problems for (1) the empirical study of delinquency, (2) the prediction and control of delinquency, and (3) efforts to develop the macroimplications of the general

62   AGNEW

strain theory. Rather, one can employ a strategy similar to that followed by stress researchers.

First, one can draw on theory and research to specify those objective situations that might reasonably be expected to cause adversity among adolescents. This parallels stress research, which relies on inventories of stressful life events, and several standard inventories are in wide use. The items in such inventories are based, to varying degrees, on the perceptions and judgments of researchers, on previous theory and research, and on reports from samples of respondents (see Dohrenwend, 1974). In developing inventories of strainful events, criminologists must keep in mind the fact that there may be important group differences in the types of strain or negative relations most frequently encountered. A list of negative relations developed for one group, then, may overlook certain negative relations important for another group (see Dohrenwend, 1974). It may eventually be possible, however, to develop a comprehensive list of negative relations applicable to most samples of adolescents.

Second, criminologists must recognize that individuals and groups may experience the strainful events in such inventories differently (see Thoits, 1983). Limited data from the stress literature, for example, suggest that the impact of family stressors is greatest among young adolescents, peer stressors among middle adolescents, and academic stressors among old adolescents (Compas and Phares, 1991). Stress researchers have responded to such findings not by abandoning their inventories, but by investigating those factors that determine why one group or individual will experience a given event as stressful and another will not. And researchers have identified several sets of variables that influence the perception and experience of negative events (e.g., Compas and Phares, 1991; Pearlin, 1982; Pearlin and Schooler, 1978). Many of the variables are discussed in the next section, and they represent a major set of conditioning variables that criminologists should consider when examining the impact of strainful events on delinquency.

EXAMINING THE CUMULATIVE IMPACT OF NEGATIVE RELATIONS

In most previous strain research in criminology, the impact of one type of negative relation on delinquency is examined with other negative relations ignored or held constant. So, for example, researchers will examine the impact of one type of goal blockage on delinquency, ignoring other types of goal blockage and other potential types of strain. This stands in sharp contrast to a central assumption in the stress literature, which is that stressful life events have a cumulative impact on the individual. Linsky and Straus (1986:17), for example, speak of the "accumulation theory," which asserts that "it is not so much the unique quality of any single event but the *cumulation* of several stressful events within a relatively short time span" that is

A GENERAL STRAIN THEORY 63

consequential. As a result, it is standard practice in the stressful life-events literature to measure stress with a composite scale: a scale that typically sums the number of stressful life events experienced by the individual.

The precise nature of the cumulative effect, however, is unclear. As Thoits (1983:69) points out, stressful events may have an additive or interactive effect on outcome variables. The additive model assumes that each stressor has a fixed effect on delinquency, an effect independent of the level of the other stressors. Somewhat more plausible, perhaps, is the interactive model, which assumes that "a person who has experienced one event may react with even more distress to a second that follows soon after the first . . . two or more events . . . results in more distress than would be expected from the simple sum of their singular effects."

Whether the effect is additive or interactive, there is limited support for the idea that the level of stress/strain must pass a certain threshold before negative outcomes result (Linsky and Straus, 1986; Thoits, 1983). Below that level, stress/strain is unrelated to negative outcomes. Above that level, stress/strain has a positive effect on negative outcomes, perhaps an additive effect or perhaps an interactive effect.

Given these arguments, one should employ a composite index of strain in all analyses or examine the interactions between strain variables. Examining interactions can become very complex if there are more than a few indicators of strain, although it does allow one to examine the differential importance of various types of strain. If stressors have an interactive effect on delinquency, the interaction terms should be significant or the composite index should have a nonlinear effect on delinquency (see the discussion of interactions and nonlinear effects in Aiken and West, 1991). If the effect is additive, the interaction terms should be insignificant or the composite index should have a linear effect on delinquency (after the threshold level is reached). These issues have received only limited attention in the stress literature (see the review by Thoits, 1983), and they should certainly be explored when constructing measures of strain for the purpose of explaining delinquency. At a minimum, however, as comprehensive a list of negative events/conditions as possible should be examined.

There is also the issue of whether positive events/experiences should be examined. If prior stressors can aggravate the negative effect of subsequent stressors, perhaps positive events can mitigate the impact of stressors. Limited evidence from the stress literature suggests that lists of negative events predict better than lists examining the balance of negative and positive events (usually negative events minus positive events) (see Thoits, 1983:58–59; Williams and Uchiyama, 1989:101; see Gersten et al., 1974, for a possible exception). This topic, however, is certainly in need of more research. In addition to looking at the *difference* between desirable and undesirable events, researchers may also want to look at the *ratio* of undesirable to desirable events.

It should be noted that tests of strain theory in criminology typically examine the disjunction between aspirations and expectations for one or two goals and ignore all of the many other types of strain. The tests also typically assume that strain has a linear effect on delinquency, and they never examine positive as well as negative events. These facts may constitute additional reasons for the weak empirical support given to strain theory in criminology.

EXAMINING THE MAGNITUDE, RECENCY, DURATION, AND CLUSTERING OF ADVERSE EVENTS

Limited research from the stress and equity literatures suggest that adverse events are more influential to the extent that they are (1) greater in magnitude or size, (2) recent, (3) of long duration, and (4) clustered in time.

MAGNITUDE

The magnitude of an event has different meanings depending on the type of strain being examined. With respect to goal blockage, magnitude refers to the size of the gap between one's goals and reality. With respect to the loss of positive stimuli, magnitude refers to the amount that was lost. And with respect to the presentation of noxious stimuli, magnitude refers to the amount of pain or discomfort *inflicted*.[11] In certain cases, magnitude may be measured in terms of a standard metric, such as dollars or volts delivered. In most cases, however, there is no standard metric available for measuring magnitude and one must rely on the perceptions of individuals (see Jasso, 1980, on quality versus quantity goods). To illustrate, researchers in the stress literature have asked judges to rate events according to the amount of readjustment they require or the threat they pose to the individual (see Thoits, 1983, for other weighting schemes). Such judgments are then averaged to form a magnitude score for each event. There is evidence, however, of subgroup differences in weights assigned (Thoits, 1983:53–55).

Magnitude ratings are then sometimes used to weight the events in composite scales. A common finding, however, is that lists of life events weighted by magnitude do *not* predict any better than unweighed lists (e.g., Gersten et al., 1974). This is due to the fact that the correlation between lists of

---

11. As Empey (1956) and others have pointed out, magnitude may also be measured in *relative* terms. For example, suppose an individual earning $10,000 a year and an individual earning $100,000 both lose $100 in a burglary. In absolute terms, the magnitude of their loss is the same. Relative to their current income, however, the magnitude of their loss is quite different. In most cases, it would be difficult to develop precise measures of relative magnitude. Nevertheless, researchers should at the very least be sensitive to this issue when analyzing and interpreting data.

A GENERAL STRAIN THEORY 65

weighted and unweighted events is typically so high (above .90) that the lists can be considered virtually identical (Thoits, 1983). Williams and Uchiyama (1989:99–100) explain this high correlation by arguing that severe life events, which are heavily weighted, have a low base rate in the population and so do not have a significant impact on scale scores. Studies that consider major and minor events separately tend to find that major events are in fact more consequential than minor events (Thoits, 1983:66).

It should be noted that the previous research on strain theory has paid only limited attention to the dimension of magnitude, even in those cases in which standard metrics for measuring magnitude were available. Samples, in fact, are often simply divided into strained and nonstrained groups, with little consideration of variations in the magnitude of strain.

RECENCY

Certain data suggest that recent events are more consequential than older events and that events older than three months have little effect (Avison and Turner, 1988). Those data focus on the impact of stress on depression, and so are not necessarily generalizable to the strain-delinquency relationship. Nevertheless, the data suggest that the recency of strain may be an important dimension to consider, and findings in this area might be of special use in designing longitudinal studies, in which the issue of the appropriate lag between cause and effect is central (although the subject of little research and theory).

DURATION

Much theory and data from the equity and stress literatures suggest that events of long duration (chronic stressors) have a greater impact on a variety of negative psychological outcomes (Folger, 1986; Mark and Folger, 1984; Pearlin, 1982; Pearlin and Lieberman, 1979; Utne and Kidd, 1980). Some evidence, in fact, suggests that discrete events may be unimportant except to the extent that they affect chronic events (Cummings and El-Sheikh, 1991; Gersten et al., 1977; Pearlin, 1983). Certain researchers in the equity/justice literature have suggested that the expected duration of the event into the future should also be considered (Folger, 1986; Mark and Folger, 1984; Utne and Kidd, 1980; see especially the "likelihood of amelioration" concept).

CLUSTERING

Data from the stress literature also suggest that events closely clustered in time have a greater effect on negative outcomes (Thoits, 1983). Such events, according to Thoits (1983), are more likely to overwhelm coping resources than events spread more evenly over time. Certain data, in particular, trace

66   AGNEW

negative outcomes such as suicide and depression to a series of negative
events clustered in the previous few weeks (Thoits, 1983).

ADAPTATIONS TO (COPING STRATEGIES FOR) STRAIN

The discussion thus far has focused on the types of strain that might promote delinquency. Virtually all strain theories, however, acknowledge that
only *some* strained individuals turn to delinquency. Some effort has been
made to identify those factors that determine whether one adapts to strain
through delinquency. The most attention has been focused on the adolescent's commitment to legitimate means and association with other strained/
delinquent individuals (see Agnew, 1991b).

The following discussion builds on this effort and is in two parts. First, the
major adaptations to strain are described. This discussion points to a number
of cognitive, emotional, and behavioral coping strategies that have not been
considered in the criminology literature. Second, those factors that influence
whether one adapts to strain using delinquent or nondelinquent means are
described. This discussion also expands on the criminology literature to
include several additional factors that affect the choice of adaptation.

ADAPTATIONS TO STRAIN

What follows is a typology of the major cognitive, emotional, and behavioral adaptations to strain, including delinquency.

COGNITIVE COPING STRATEGIES

Several literatures suggest that individuals sometimes cognitively reinterpret objective stressors in ways that minimize their subjective adversity.
Three general strategies of cognitive coping are described below; each strategy has several forms. These strategies for coping with adversity may be
summarized in the following phrases: "It's not important," "It's not that
bad," and "I deserve it." This typology represents a synthesis of the coping
strategies described in the stress, equity, stratification, and victimization literatures (Adams, 1963, 1965; Agnew, 1985b; Agnew and Jones, 1988; Averill,
1982; Della Fave, 1980; Donnerstein and Hatfield, 1982; Pearlin and
Schooler, 1978; Walster et al., 1973, 1978). The stress literature, in particular, was especially useful. Stress has been found to have a consistent,
although weak-to-moderate, main effect on outcome variables. Researchers
have tried to explain this weak-to-moderate effect by arguing that the impact
of stressors is conditioned by a number of variables, and much of the attention has been focused on coping strategies (see Compas and Phares, 1991;
Thoits, 1984).

A GENERAL STRAIN THEORY 67

Ignore/Minimize the Importance of Adversity. The subjective impact of objective strain depends on the extent to which the strain is related to the central goals, values, and/or identities of the individual. As Pearlin and Schooler (1978:7) state, individuals may avoid subjective strain "to the extent that they are able to keep the most strainful experiences within the least valued areas of their life." Individuals, therefore, may minimize the strain they experience by reducing the absolute and/or relative importance assigned to goals/values and identities (see Agnew, 1983; Thoits, 1991a).

In particular, individuals may claim that a particular goal/value or identity is unimportant in an absolute sense. They may, for example, state that money or work is unimportant to them. This strategy is similar to Merton's adaptations of ritualism and retreatism, and it was emphasized by Hyman (1953). Individuals may also claim that a particular goal/value or identity is unimportant in a relative sense—relative to other goals/values or identities. They may, for example, state that money is less important than status or that work is less important than family and leisure activities.

The strategy of minimizing strain by reducing the absolute and/or relative emphasis placed on goals/values and identities has not been extensively examined in the strain literature. Certain evidence, however, suggests that it is commonly employed and may play a central role in accounting for the limited empirical support for strain theory. In particular, research on goals suggests that people pursue a wide variety of different goals and that they tend to place the greatest absolute and relative emphasis on those goals they are best able to achieve (Agnew, 1983; McClelland, 1990; Rosenberg, 1979:265–269; Wylie, 1979).

Maximize Positive Outcomes/Minimize Negative Outcomes. In the above adaptation, individuals acknowledge the existence of adversity but relegate such adversity to an unimportant area of their life. In a second adaptation, individuals attempt to deny the existence of adversity by maximizing their positive outcomes and/or minimizing their negative outcomes. This may be done in two ways: lowering the standards used to evaluate outcomes or distorting one's estimate of current and/or expected outcomes.

Lowering one's standards basically involves lowering one's goals or raising one's threshold for negative stimuli (see Suls, 1977). Such action, of course, makes one's current situation seem less adverse than it otherwise would be. Individuals may, for example, lower the amount of money they desire (which is distinct from lowering the importance attached to money). This strategy is also related to Merton's adaptations of ritualism and retreatism, and many of the critics of strain theory in criminology have focused on it. Hyman (1953) and others have argued that poor individuals in the United States are not strained because they have lowered their success goals—bringing their aspirations in line with reality. The data in this area are complex, but they suggest that this adaptation is employed by some—but not all—lower-class individuals (see Agnew, 1983, 1986; Agnew and Jones, 1988; see Cloward and Ohlin, 1960, and Empey, 1956, for data on "relative" aspirations).

In addition to lowering their standards, individuals may also cognitively distort their estimate of outcomes. As Agnew and Jones (1988) demonstrate, many individuals exaggerate their actual and expected levels of goal achievement. Individuals with poor grades, for example, often report that they are doing well in school. And individuals with little objective chance of attending college often report that they *expect* to attend college. (See Wylie, 1979, for additional data in this area.) In addition to exaggerating positive outcomes, individuals may also minimize negative outcomes—claiming that their losses are small and their noxious experiences are mild.

The self-concept literature discusses the many strategies individuals employ to accomplish such distortions (see Agnew and Jones, 1988; Rosenberg, 1979). Two common strategies, identified across several literatures, are worth noting. In "downward comparisons," individuals claim that their situation is less worse or at least no worse than that of similar others (e.g., Brickman and Bulman, 1977; Gruder, 1977; Pearlin and Schooler, 1978; Suls, 1977). This strategy is compatible with the equity literature, which suggests that one's evaluation of outcomes is conditioned by the outcomes of comparison others. Temporal comparisons may also be made, with individuals claiming that their situation is an improvement over the past. Recent research on the social comparison process suggests that individuals often deliberately make downward comparisons, especially when self-esteem is threatened (Gruder, 1977; Hegtvedt, 1991b; Suls, 1977). In a second strategy, "compensatory benefits," individuals cast "about for some positive attribute or circumstance within a troublesome situation . . . the person is aided in ignoring that which is noxious by anchoring his attention to what he considers the more worthwhile and rewarding aspects of experience" (Pearlin and Schooler, 1978:6–7). Crime victims, for example, often argue that their victimization benefited them in certain ways, such as causing them to grow as a person (Agnew, 1985b).

Accept Responsibility for Adversity. Third, individuals may *minimize* the subjective adversity of objective strain by convincing themselves that they *deserve* the adversity they have experienced. There are several possible reasons why *deserved* strain is less adverse than undeserved strain. Undeserved strain may violate the equity principle, challenge one's "belief in a just world" (see Lerner, 1977), and—if attributed to the malicious behavior of another—lead one to fear that it will be repeated in the future. Such reasons may help explain why individuals who make internal attributions for adversity are less distressed than others (Kluegel and Smith, 1986; Mirowsky and Ross, 1990).

A GENERAL STRAIN THEORY 69

Drawing on equity theory, one may argue that there are two basic strategies for convincing oneself that strain is deserved. First, individuals may cognitively minimize their positive inputs or maximize their negative inputs to a relationship. Inputs are conceived as contributions to the relationship and/or status characteristics believed to be relevant to the relationship (see Cook and Yamagishi, 1983). Second, individuals may maximize the positive inputs or minimize the negative inputs of others. Della Fave (1980) uses both of these strategies to explain the legitimation of inequality in the United States. Those at the bottom of the stratification system are said to minimize their own traits and exaggerate the positive traits and contributions of those above them. They therefore come to accept their limited outcomes as just (also see Kluegel and Smith, 1986; Shepelak, 1987).

BEHAVIORAL COPING STRATEGIES

There are two major types of behavioral coping: those that seek to minimize or eliminate the source of strain and those that seek to satisfy the need for revenge.

Maximizing Positive Outcomes/Minimizing Negative Outcomes. Behavioral coping may assume several forms, paralleling each of the major types of strain. Individuals, then, may seek to achieve positively valued goals, protect or retrieve positively valued stimuli, or terminate or escape from negative stimuli. Their actions in these areas may involve conventional or delinquent behavior. Individuals seeking to escape from an adverse school environment, for example, may try to transfer to another school or they may illegally skip school. This rather broad adaptation encompasses Merton's adaptations of innovation and rebellion, as well as those coping strategies described in the equity literature as "maximizing one's outcomes," "minimizing one's inputs," and "maximizing the other's inputs."

Vengeful Behavior. Data indicate that when adversity is blamed on others it creates a desire for revenge that is distinct from the desire to end the adversity. A second method of behavioral coping, then, involves the taking of revenge. Vengeful behavior may also assume conventional or delinquent forms, although the potential for delinquency is obviously high. Such behavior may involve efforts to minimize the positive outcomes, increase the negative outcomes, and/or increase the inputs of others (as when adolescents cause teachers and parents to work harder through their incorrigible behavior).

EMOTIONAL COPING STRATEGIES

Finally, individuals may cope by acting directly on the negative emotions that result from adversity. Rosenberg (1990), Thoits (1984, 1989, 1990,

1991b), and others list several strategies of emotional coping. They include the use of drugs such as stimulants and depressants, physical exercise and deep-breathing techniques, meditation, biofeedback and progressive relaxation, and the behavioral manipulation of expressive gestures through playacting or "expression work." In all of these examples, the focus is on alleviating negative emotions rather than cognitively reinterpreting or behaviorally altering the situation that produced those emotions. Many of the strategies are beyond the reach of most adolescents (Compas et al., 1988), and data indicate that adolescents often employ illicit drugs to cope with life's strains (Labouvie, 1986a, 1986b; Newcomb and Harlow, 1986). Emotional coping is especially likely when behavioral and cognitive coping are unavailable or unsuccessful.

It should be noted that individuals may employ more than one of the above coping strategies (see Folkman, 1991). Also, still other coping strategies, such as distraction, could have been listed. It is assumed, however, that the above strategies constitute the primary responses to strain.

PREDICTING THE USE OF DELINQUENT VERSUS NONDELINQUENT ADAPTATIONS

The above typology suggests that there are many ways to cope with strain—only some of which involve delinquency. And data from the stress literature suggest that individuals vary in the extent to which they use the different strategies (Compas et al., 1988; Menaghan, 1983; Pearlin and Schooler, 1978). These facts go a long way toward explaining the weak support for strain theory. With certain limited exceptions, the strategies are not taken into account in tests of strain theory.

The existence of the above coping strategies poses a serious problem for strain theory. If strain theory is to have any value, it must be able to explain the selection of delinquent versus nondelinquent adaptations. This issue has, of course, been raised before. Critics contend that Merton and other strain theorists fail to explain adequately why only *some* strained individuals turn to delinquency. This issue, however, is all the more pressing when one considers the full range of nondelinquent adaptations to strain listed above. It is therefore important to specify those factors that influence the choice of delinquent versus nondelinquent coping strategies.

The following discussion of influencing factors draws on the aggression, equity, and stress literatures (see especially Adams, 1965; Menaghan, 1982; Pearlin and Shooler, 1978; Walster et al., 1978). The aggression literature in psychology is especially useful. Adversity is said to produce a general state of arousal, which can facilitate a variety of behaviors. Whether this arousal results in aggression is said to be determined by a number of factors, many of which are noted below (see Bandura, 1973, 1983; Berkowitz, 1978, 1982).

A GENERAL STRAIN THEORY 71

Those factors affect the choice of coping strategies by affecting (1) the constraints to nondelinquent and delinquent coping and (2) the disposition to engage in nondelinquent versus delinquent coping.

CONSTRAINTS TO NONDELINQUENT AND DELINQUENT COPING

While there are many adaptations to objective strain, those adaptations are not equally available to everyone. Individuals are constrained in their choice of adaptation(s) by a variety of internal and external factors. The following is a partial list of such factors.

Initial Goals/Values/Identities of the Individual. If the objective strain affects goals/values/identities that are high in absolute and relative importance, and if the individual has few alternative goals/values/identities in which to seek refuge, it will be more difficult to relegate strain to an unimportant area of one's life (see Agnew, 1986; Thoits, 1991a). This is especially the case if the goals/values/identities receive strong social and cultural support (see below). As a result, strain will be more likely to lead to delinquency in such cases.

Individual Coping Resources. A wide range of traits can be listed in this area, including temperament, intelligence, creativity, problem-solving skills, interpersonal skills, self-efficacy, and self-esteem. These traits affect the selection of coping strategies by influencing the individual's sensitivity to objective strains and ability to engage in cognitive, emotional, and behavioral coping (Agnew, 1991a; Averill, 1982; Bernard, 1990; Compas, 1987; Edmunds and Kendrick, 1980; Slaby and Guerra, 1988; Tavris, 1984). Data, for example, suggest that individuals with high self-esteem are more resistant to stress (Averill, 1982; Compas, 1987; Kaplan, 1980; Pearlin and Schooler, 1978; Rosenberg, 1990; Thoits, 1983). Such individuals, therefore, should be less likely to respond to a given objective strain with delinquency. Individuals high in self-efficacy are more likely to feel that their strain can be alleviated by behavioral coping of a nondelinquent nature, and so they too should be less likely to respond to strain with delinquency (see Bandura, 1989, and Wang and Richarde, 1988, on self-efficacy; see Thoits, 1991b, on perceived control).

Conventional Social Support. Vaux (1988) provides an extended discussion of the different types of social support, their measurement, and their effect on outcome variables. Thoits (1984) argues that social support is important because it facilitates the major types of coping. The major types of social support, in fact, correspond to the major types of coping listed above. Thus, there is informational support, instrumental support, and emotional support

72   AGNEW

(House, 1981). Adolescents with conventional social supports, then, should be better able to respond to objective strains in a nondelinquent manner.

Constraints to Delinquent Coping. The crime/delinquency literature has focused on certain variables that constrain delinquent coping. They include (1) the costs and benefits of engaging in delinquency in a particular situation (Clarke and Cornish, 1985), (2) the individual's level of social control (see Hirschi, 1969), and (3) the possession of those "illegitimate means" necessary for many delinquent acts (see Agnew, 1991a, for a full discussion).

Macro-Level Variables. The larger social environment may affect the probability of delinquent versus nondelinquent coping by affecting all of the above factors. First, the social environment may affect coping by influencing the importance attached to selected goals/values/identities. For example, certain ethnographic accounts suggest that there is a strong social and cultural emphasis on the goals of money/status among certain segments of the urban poor. Many poor individuals, in particular, are in a situation in which (1) they face strong economic/status demands, (2) people around them stress the importance of money/status on a regular basis, and (3) few alternative goals are given cultural support (Anderson, 1978; MacLeod, 1987; Sullivan, 1989). As such, these individuals should face more difficulty in cognitively minimizing the importance of money and status.

Second, the larger social environment may affect the individual's sensitivity to particular strains by influencing the individual's beliefs regarding what is and is not adverse. The subculture of violence thesis, for example, is predicated on the assumption that young black males in urban slums are taught that a wide range of provocations and insults are highly adverse. Third, the social environment may influence the individual's ability to minimize cognitively the severity of objective strain. Individuals in some environments are regularly provided with external information about their accomplishments and failings (see Faunce, 1989), and their attempts at cognitively distorting such information are quickly challenged. Such a situation may exist among many adolescents and among those who inhabit the "street-corner world" of the urban poor. Adolescents and those on the street corner live in a very "public world"; one's accomplishments and failings typically occur before a large audience or they quickly become known to such an audience. Further, accounts suggest that this audience regularly reminds individuals of their accomplishments and failings and challenges attempts at cognitive distortion.

Fourth, certain social environments may make it difficult to engage in behavioral coping of a nondelinquent nature. Agnew (1985a) has argued that adolescents often find it difficult to escape legally from negative stimuli, especially negative stimuli encountered in the school, family, and neighborhood. Also, adolescents often lack the resources to negotiate successfully with

A GENERAL STRAIN THEORY 73

adults, such as parents and teachers (although see Agnew, 1991a). Similar arguments might be made for the urban underclass. They often lack the resources to negotiate successfully with many others, and they often find it difficult to escape legally from adverse environments—by, for example, quitting their job (if they have a job) or moving to another neighborhood.

The larger social environment, then, may affect individual coping in a variety of ways. And certain groups, such as adolescents and the urban underclass, may face special constraints that make nondelinquent coping more difficult. This may explain the higher rate of deviance among these groups.

FACTORS AFFECTING THE DISPOSITION TO DELINQUENCY

The selection of delinquent versus nondelinquent coping strategies is not only dependent on the constraints to coping, but also on the adolescent's disposition to engage in delinquent versus nondelinquent coping. This disposition is a function of (1) certain temperamental variables (see Tonry et al., 1991), (2) the prior learning history of the adolescent, particularly the extent to which delinquency was reinforced in the past (Bandura, 1973; Berkowitz, 1982), (3) the adolescent's beliefs, particularly the rules defining the appropriate response to provocations (Bernard's, 1990, "regulative rules"), and (4) the adolescent's attributions regarding the causes of his or her adversity. Adolescents who attribute their adversity to others are much more likely to become angry, and as argued earlier, that anger creates a strong predisposition to delinquency. Data and theory from several areas, in fact, suggest that the experience of adversity is most likely to result in deviance when the adversity is blamed on another.[12] The attributions one makes are influenced by a variety of factors, as discussed in recent reviews by Averill (1982), Berwin (1988), R. Cohen (1982), Crittenden (1983, 1989), Kluegel and Smith (1986), and Utne and Kidd (1980). The possibility that there may be demographic and subgroup differences in the rules for assigning blame is of special interest (see Bernard, 1990; Crittenden, 1983, 1989).

A key variable affecting several of the above factors is association with delinquent peers. It has been argued that adolescents who associate with delinquent peers are more likely to be exposed to delinquent models and beliefs and to receive reinforcement for delinquency (see especially, Akers, 1985). It may also be the case that delinquent peers increase the likelihood that adolescents will attribute their adversity to others.

---

12. This is a major theme in the psychological research on aggression, in much of the recent research on equity, and in the emotions literature, and it is a central theme in Cloward and Ohlin's (1960) strain theory (e.g., Averill, 1982; Berkowitz, 1982; R. Cohen, 1982; Crosby and Gonzales-Intal, 1984; Garrett and Libby, 1973; Kemper, 1978; Leventhal, 1976; Mark and Folger, 1984; Martin and Murray, 1984; Weiner, 1982; Zillman, 1979).

74   AGNEW

The individual's disposition to delinquency, then, may condition the impact of adversity on delinquency. At the same time, it is important to note that continued experience with adversity may create a disposition for delinquency. This argument has been made by Bernard (1990), Cloward and Ohlin (1960), A. Cohen (1955), Elliott et al. (1979), and others. In particular, it has been argued that under certain conditions the experience of adversity may lead to beliefs favorable to delinquency, lead adolescents to join or form delinquent peer groups, and lead adolescents to blame others for their misfortune.

Virtually all empirical research on strain theory in criminology has neglected the constraints to coping and the adolescent's disposition to delinquency. Researchers, in particular, have failed to examine whether the effect of adversity on delinquency is conditioned by factors such as self-efficacy and association with delinquent peers. This is likely a major reason for the weak empirical support for strain theory.

CONCLUSION

Much of the recent theoretical work in criminology has focused on the integration of different delinquency theories. This paper has taken an alternative track and, following Hirschi's (1979) advice, has focused on the refinement of a single theory. The general strain theory builds upon traditional strain theory in criminology in several ways. First, the general strain theory points to several new sources of strain. In particular, it focuses on three categories of strain or negative relationships with others: (1) the actual or anticipated failure to achieve positively valued goals, (2) the actual or anticipated removal of positively valued stimuli, and (3) the actual or anticipated presentation of negative stimuli. Most current strain theories in criminology only focus on strain as the failure to achieve positively valued goals, and even then the focus is only on the disjunction between aspirations and expectations/ actual achievements. The disjunctions between expectations and achievements and just/fair outcomes and achievements are ignored. The general strain theory, then, significantly expands the focus of strain theory to include all types of negative relations between the individual and others.

Second, the general strain theory more precisely specifies the relationship between strain and delinquency, pointing out that strain is likely to have a cumulative effect on delinquency after a certain threshold level is reached. The theory also points to certain relevant dimensions of strain that should be considered in empirical research, including the magnitude, recency, duration, and clustering of strainful events.

Third, the general strain theory provides a more comprehensive account of the cognitive, behavioral, and emotional adaptations to strain. This account sheds additional light on the reasons why many strained individuals do *not*

A GENERAL STRAIN THEORY 75

turn to delinquency, and it may prove useful in devising strategies to prevent and control delinquency. Individuals, in particular, may be taught those non-delinquent coping strategies found to be most effective in preventing delinquency.

Fourth, the general strain theory more fully describes those factors affecting the choice of delinquent versus nondelinquent adaptations. The failure to consider such factors is a fundamental reason for the weak empirical support for strain theory.

Most of the above modifications in strain theory were suggested by research in several areas outside of traditional criminology, most notably the stress research in medical sociology and psychology, the equity/justice research in social psychology, and the aggression research in psychology. With certain exceptions, researchers in criminology have tended to cling to the early strain models of Merton (1938), A. Cohen (1955), and Cloward and Ohlin (1960) and to ignore the developments in related fields. And while these early strain models contain much of value and have had a major influence on the general strain theory in this paper, they do not fully exploit the potential of strain theory.

At the same time, it is important to note that the general strain theory is not presented here as a fully developed alternative to earlier theories. First, the macroimplications of the theory were only briefly discussed. It would not be difficult to extend the general strain theory to the macro level, however; researchers could focus on (1) the social determinants of adversity (for an example, see Bernard, 1990, on the urban underclass) and (2) the social determinants of those factors that condition the effect of adversity on delinquency. Second, the theory did not concern itself with the nonsocial determinants of strain, such as illness. It seems doubtful that adversity caused by nonsocial sources is a major source of delinquency because, among other things, it is unlikely to generate anger (see Averill, 1982). Nevertheless, nonsocial sources of adversity should be investigated. Third, the relationship between the general strain theory and other major theories of delinquency must be more fully explored. As hinted earlier, the relationship is rather complex. While the general strain theory is clearly distinct from control and differential association theory, strain may lead to low social control and association with delinquent others. Further, variables from the three theories may interact with one another in producing delinquency. Individuals with delinquent friends, for example, should be more likely to respond to strain with delinquency. The general strain theory then, is presented as a foundation on which to build.

It is not possible to test the general strain theory fully with currently available data sets, but it is possible to test core sections of the theory. Most data sets dealing with delinquency contain at least some measures of adversity and at least some measures of those factors said to condition the effect of adversity

76   AGNEW

on delinquency. Given this fact, researchers could focus on the following core hypotheses derived from the theory:

First, adverse relations with others will have a positive effect on both general and specific measures of delinquency, with measures of social control and differential association held constant. This is especially true of adverse relations that are severe and that provide limited opportunities for nondelinquent coping. Prime examples, as discussed earlier, are adverse relations involving family, school, and neighborhood. It is hoped research will point to several measures of strain that are especially relevant to delinquency. Such measures can then be made a routine part of delinquency research, just as the elements of the social bond and measures of differential association are now routinely included in empirical studies.

Second, adverse relations will have a cumulative impact on delinquency after a certain threshold level is reached. Further, this cumulative impact will likely be interactive in nature; each additional increment in strain will have a greater impact than the one before.

Third, the impact of strain or adverse relations on delinquency will be conditioned by several variables, as listed above.

Strain theory is the only major theory to focus explicitly on negative relations with others and to argue that delinquency results from the negative affect caused by such relations. As such, it complements social control and differential association/social learning theory in a fundamental way. It is hoped that the general strain theory will revive interest in negative relations and cause criminologists to "bring the bad back in."

REFERENCES

Adams, J. Stacy
   1963   Toward an understanding of inequity. Journal of Abnormal and Social
             Psychology 67:422–436.
   1965   Inequity in social exchange. In Leonard Berkowitz (ed.), Advances in
             Experimental Social Psychology. New York: Academic Press.

Agnew, Robert
   1983   Social class and success goals: An examination of relative and absolute
             aspirations. Sociological Quarterly 24:435–452.
   1984   Goal achievement and delinquency. Sociology and Social Research
             68:435–451.
   1985a   A revised strain theory of delinquency. Social Forces 64:151–167.
   1985b   Neutralizing the impact of crime. Criminal Justice and Behavior
             12:221–239.
   1986   Challenging strain theory: An examination of goals and goal-blockage.
             Paper presented at the annual meeting of the American Society of
             Criminology, Atlanta.
   1989   A longitudinal test of the revised strain theory. Journal of Quantitative
             Criminology 5:373–387.

A GENERAL STRAIN THEORY   77

1990   The origins of delinquent events: An examination of offender accounts. Journal of Research in Crime and Delinquency 27:267–294.

1991a   Adolescent resources and delinquency. Criminology 28:535–566.

1991b   Strain and subcultural crime theory. In Joseph Sheley (ed.), Criminology: A Contemporary Handbook. Belmont, Calif.: Wadsworth.

Agnew, Robert and Diane Jones

1988   Adapting to deprivation: An examination of inflated educational expectations. Sociological Quarterly 29:315–337.

Aiken, Leona S. and Stephen G. West

1991   Multiple Regression: Testing and Interpreting Interactions. Newbury Park, Calif.: Sage.

Akers, Ronald L.

1985   Deviant Behavior: A Social Learning Approach. Belmont, Calif.: Wadsworth.

Alves, Wayne M. and Peter H. Rossi

1978   Who should get what? Fairness judgments of the distribution of earnings. American Journal of Sociology 84:541–564.

Alwin, Duane F.

1987   Distributive justice and satisfaction with material well-being. American Sociological Review 52:83–95.

Anderson, Elijah

1978   A Place on the Corner. Chicago: University of Chicago Press.

Anderson, Craig A. and Dona C. Anderson

1984   Ambient temperature and violent crime: Tests of the linear and curvilinear hypotheses. Journal of Personality and Social Psychology 46:91–97.

Austin, William

1977   Equity theory and social comparison processes. In Jerry M. Suls and Richard L. Miller (eds.), Social Comparison Processes. New York: Hemisphere.

Averill, James R.

1982   Anger and Aggression. New York: Springer-Verlag.

Avison, William R. and R. Jay Turner

1988   Stressful life events and depressive symptoms: Disaggregating the effects of acute stressors and chronic strains. Journal of Health and Social Behavior 29:253–264.

Bandura, Albert

1973   Aggression: A Social Learning Analysis. Englewood Cliffs, N.J.: Prentice-Hall.

1983   Psychological mechanisms of aggression. In Russell G. Geen and Edward Donnerstein (eds.), Aggression: Theoretical and Empirical Reviews. New York: Academic Press.

1989   Human agency and social cognitive theory. American Psychologist 44:1175–1184.

Berger, Joseph, Morris Zelditch, Jr., Bo Anderson, and Bernard Cohen

1972   Structural aspects of distributive justice: A status-value formulation. In Joseph Berger, Morris Zelditch, Jr., and Bo Anderson (eds.), Sociological Theories in Progress. New York: Houghton Mifflin.

78   AGNEW

Berger, Joseph, M. Hamit Fisck, Robert Z. Norman, and David G. Wagner
    1983   The formation of reward expectations in status situations. In David M.
              Messick and Karen S. Cook (eds.), Equity Theory: Psychological and
              Sociological Perspectives. New York: Praeger.

Berkowitz, Leonard
    1978   Whatever happened to the frustration-aggression hypothesis? American
              Behavioral Scientist 21:691–708.
    1982   Aversive conditions as stimuli to aggression. In Leonard Berkowitz (ed.),
              Advances in Experimental Social Psychology. Vol. 15. New York:
              Academic Press.
    1986   A Survey of Social Psychology. New York: Holt, Rinehart & Winston.

Bernard, Thomas J.
    1984   Control criticisms of strain theories: An assessment of theoretical and
              empirical adequacy. Journal of Research in Crime and Delinquency
              21:353–372.
    1987   Testing structural strain theories. Journal of Research in Crime and
              Delinquency 24:262–280.
    1990   Angry aggression among the "truly disadvantaged." Criminology 28:73–96.

Blau, Peter
    1964   Exchange and Power in Social Life. New York: John Wiley & Sons.

Brewin, Chris R.
    1988   Explanation and adaptation in adversity. In Shirley Fisher and James
              Reason (eds.), Handbook of Life Stress, Cognition and Health. Chichester,
              England: John Wiley & Sons.

Brickman, Philip and Ronnie Janoff Bulman
    1977   Pleasure and pain in social comparison. In Jerry M. Suls and Richard L.
              Miller (eds.), Social Comparison Processes. New York: Hemisphere.

Clarke, Ronald V. and Derek B. Cornish
    1985   Modeling offenders' decisions: A framework for research and policy. In
              Michael Tonry and Norval Morris (eds.), Crime and Justice: An Annual
              Review of Research. Vol. 6. Chicago: University of Chicago Press.

Clinard, Marshall B.
    1964   Anomie and Deviant Behavior. New York: Free Press.

Cloward, Richard A. and Lloyd E. Ohlin
    1960   Delinquency and Opportunity. New York: Free Press.

Cohen, Albert K.
    1955   Delinquent Boys. New York: Free Press.
    1965   The sociology of the deviant act: Anomie theory and beyond. American
              Sociological Review 30:5–14.

Cohen, Ronald L.
    1982   Perceiving justice: An attributional perspective. In Jerald Greenberg and
              Ronald L. Cohen (eds.), Equity and Justice in Social Behavior. New York:
              Academic Press.

Cole, Stephen
    1975   The growth of scientific knowledge: Theories of deviance as a case study.
              In Lewis A. Coser (ed.), The Idea of Social Structure: Papers in Honor of
              Robert K. Merton. New York: Harcourt Brace Jovanovich.

A GENERAL STRAIN THEORY 79

Compas, Bruce E.
   1987   Coping with stress during childhood and adolescence. Psychological Bulletin
           101:393–403.

Compas, Bruce E., Vanessa L. Malcarne, and Karen M. Fondacaro
   1988   Coping with stressful events in older children and young adolescents.
           Journal of Consulting and Clinical Psychology 56:405–411.

Compas, Bruce E. and Vicky Phares
   1991   Stress during childhood and adolescence: Sources of risk and vulnerability.
           In E. Mark Cummings, Anita L. Greene, and Katherine H. Karraker (eds.),
           Life-Span Developmental Psychology: Perspectives on Stress and Coping.
           Hillsdale, N.J.: Lawrence Erlbaum.

Cook, Karen S., and Karen A. Hegtvedt
   1983   Distributive justice, equity, and equality. Annual Review of Sociology
           9:217–241.
   1991   Empirical evidence of the sense of justice. In Margaret Gruter, Roger D.
           Masters, Michael T. McGuire (eds.), The Sense of Justice: An Inquiry into
           the Biological Foundations of Law. New York: Greenwood Press.

Cook, Karen S. and David Messick
   1983   Psychological and sociological perspectives on distributive justice: Conver-
           gent, divergent, and parallel lines. In David M. Messick and Karen S. Cook
           (eds.), Equity Theory: Psychological and Sociological Perspectives. New
           York: Praeger.

Cook, Karen S. and Toshio Yamagishi
   1983   Social determinants of equity judgments: The problem of multidimensional
           input. In David M. Messick and Karen S. Cook (eds.), Equity Theory:
           Psychological and Sociological Perspectives. New York: Praeger.

Crittenden, Kathleen S.
   1983   Sociological aspects of attribution. Annual Review of Sociology 9:425–446.
   1989   Causal attribution in sociocultural context: Toward a self-presentational
           theory of attribution processes. Sociological Quarterly 30:1–14.

Crosby, Faye and A. Miren Gonzales-Intal
   1984   Relative deprivation and equity theories: Felt injustice and the undeserved
           benefits of others. In Robert Folger (ed.), The Sense on Injustice: Social
           Psychological Perspectives. New York: Plenum.

Cummings, E. Mark and Mona El-Sheikh
   1991   Children's coping with angry environments: A process-oriented approach.
           In E. Mark Cummings, Anita L. Greene, and Katherine H. Karraker (eds.),
           Life-Span Developmental Psychology: Perspectives on Stress and Coping.
           Hillsdale, N.J.: Lawrence Erlbaum.

Della Fave, L. Richard
   1974   Success values: Are they universal or class-differentiated? American Journal
           of Sociology 80:153–169.
   1980   The meek shall not inherit the earth: Self-evaluations and the legitimacy of
           stratification. American Sociological Review 45:955–971.

Della Fave, L. Richard and Patricia Klobus
   1976   Success values and the value stretch: A biracial comparison. Sociological
           Quarterly 17:491–502.

80   AGNEW

Deutsch, Morton
    1975   Equity, equality, and need: What determines which value will be used as the
            basis of distributive justice. Journal of Social Issues 31:137-149.

Dohrenwend, Bruce P.
    1974   Problems in defining and sampling the relevant population of stressful life
            events. In Barbara Snell Dohrenwend and Bruce P. Dohrenwend (eds.),
            Stressful Life Events: Their Nature and Effects. New York: John Wiley &
            Sons.

Dohrenwend, Barbara Snell and Bruce P. Dohrenwend
    1974   Overview and prospects for research on stressful life events. In Barbara
            Snell Dohrenwend and Bruce P. Dohrenwend (eds.), Stressful Life Events:
            Their Nature and Effects. New York: John Wiley & Sons.

Donnerstein, Edward and Elaine Hatfield
    1982   Aggression and equity. In Jerald Greenberg and Ronald L. Cohen (eds.),
            Equity and Justice in Social Behavior. New York: Academic Press.

Edmunds, G. and D.C. Kendrick
    1980   The Measurement of Human Aggressiveness. New York: John Wiley &
            Sons.

Elliott, Delbert and Harwin Voss
    1974   Delinquency and Dropout. Lexington, Mass.: Lexington Books.

Elliott, Delbert, Suzanne Ageton, and Rachel Canter
    1979   An integrated theoretical perspective on delinquent behavior. Journal of
            Research in Crime and Delinquency 16:3–27.

Elliott, Delbert, David Huizinga, and Suzanne Ageton
    1985   Explaining Delinquency and Drug Use. Beverly Hills, Calif.: Sage.

Empey, LaMar
    1956   Social class and occupational aspiration: A comparison of absolute and
            relative measurement. American Sociological Review 21:703–709.
    1982   American Delinquency: Its Meaning and Construction. Homewood, Ill.:
            Dorsey.

Farnworth, Margaret and Michael J. Leiber
    1989   Strain theory revisited: Economic goals, educational means, and delin-
            quency. American Sociological Review 54:263–274.

Faunce, William A.
    1989   Occupational status-assignment systems: The effect of status on self-esteem.
            American Journal of Sociology 95:378–400.

Folger, Robert
    1984   Emerging issues in the social psychology of justice. In Robert Folger (ed.),
            The Sense of Injustice: Social Psychological Perspectives. New York:
            Plenum.
    1986   Rethinking equity theory: A referent cognitions model. In Hans Werner
            Bierhoff, Ronald L. Cohen, and Jerald Greenberg (eds.), Justice in Social
            Relations. New York: Plenum.

A GENERAL STRAIN THEORY 81

Folkman, Susan
   1991   Coping across the life-span: Theoretical issues. In E. Mark Cummings, Anita L. Greene, and Katherine H. Karraker (eds.), Life-Span Developmental Psychology: Perspectives on Stress and Coping. Hillsdale, N.J.: Lawrence Erlbaum.

Garrett, James and William L. Libby, Jr.
   1973   Role of intentionality in mediating responses to inequity in the dyad. Journal of Personality and Social Psychology 28:21–27.

Gersten, Joanne C., Thomas S. Langer, Jeanne G. Eisenberg, and Lida Ozek
   1974   Child behavior and life events: Undesirable change or change per se. In Barbara Snell Dohrenwend and Bruce P. Dohrenwend (eds.), Stressful Life Events: Their Nature and Effects. New York: John Wiley & Sons.

Gersten, Joanne C., Thomas S. Langer, Jeanne G. Eisenberg, and Ora Smith-Fagon.
   1977   An evaluation of the etiological role of stressful life-change events in psychological disorders. Journal of Health and Social Behavior 18:228–244.

Greenberg, David F.
   1977   Delinquency and the age structure of society. Contemporary Crises 1:189–223.

Gruder, Charles L.
   1977   Choice of comparison persons in evaluating oneself. In Jerry M. Suls and Richard L. Miller (eds.), Social Comparison Processes. New York: Hemisphere.

Hawkins, J. David and Denise M. Lishner
   1987   Schooling and delinquency. In Elmer H. Johnson (ed.), Handbook on Crime and Delinquency Prevention. New York: Greenwood.

Healy, William and Augusta F. Bonner
   1969   New Light on Delinquency and Its Treatment. New Haven, Conn.: Yale University Press.

Hegtvedt, Karen A.
   1987   When rewards are scarce: Equal or equitable distributions. Social Forces 66:183–207.
   1990   The effects of relationship structure on emotional responses to inequity. Social Psychology Quarterly 53:214–228.
   1991a   Justice processes. In Martha Foschi and Edward J. Lawler (eds.), Group Processes: Sociological Analyses. Chicago: Nelson-Hall.
   1991b   Social comparison processes. In Edgar F. Borgotta and Marie E. Borgotta (eds.), Encyclopedia of Sociology. New York: Macmillan.

Hirschi, Travis
   1969   Causes of Delinquency. Berkeley: University of California Press.
   1979   Separate and unequal is better. Journal of Research in Crime and Delinquency 16:34–38.

Hirschi, Travis and Michael Gottfredson
   1986   The distinction between crime and criminality. In Timothy F. Hartnagel and Robert A. Silverman (eds.), Critique and Explanation. New Brunswick, N.J.: Transaction Books.

82   AGNEW

Hochschild, Jennifer L.
    1981   What's Fair: American Beliefs about Distributive Justice. Cambridge,
             Mass.: Harvard University Press.

Homans, George C.
    1961   Social Behavior: Its Elementary Forms. New York: Harcourt, Brace and
             World.

House, James S.
    1981   Work Stress and Social Support. Reading, Mass.: Addison-Wesley.

Hyman, Herbert
    1953   The value systems of the different classes: A social-psychological contribu-
             tion to the analysis of stratification. In Reinhard Bendix and Seymour
             Martin Lipset (eds.), Class, Status, and Power. New York: Free Press.

Jasso, Guillermina
    1980   A new theory of distributive justice. American Sociological Review 45:3-32.

Jasso, Guillermina and Peter H. Rossi
    1977   Distributive justice and earned income. American Sociological Review
             42:639-651.

Jensen, Gary
    1986   Dis-integrating integrated theory: A critical analysis of attempts to save
             strain theory. Paper presented at the annual meeting of the American
             Society of Criminology, Atlanta.

Johnson, Richard E.
    1979   Juvenile Delinquency and Its Origins. London: Cambridge University Press.

Kaplan, Howard B.
    1980   Deviant Behavior in Defense of Self. New York: Academic Press.

Kaplan, Howard B., Cynthia Robbins, and Steven S. Martin
    1983   Toward the testing of a general theory of deviant behavior in longitudinal
             perspective: Patterns of psychopathology. In James R. Greenley and
             Roberta G. Simmons (eds.), Research in Community and Mental Health.
             Greenwich, Conn.: Jai Press.

Kemper, Theodore D.
    1978   A Social Interactional Theory of Emotions. New York: John Wiley & Sons.

Kluegel, James R. and Eliot R. Smith
    1986   Beliefs about Inequality. New York: Aldine De Gruyter.

Kornhauser, Ruth Rosner
    1978   Social Sources of Delinquency. Chicago: University of Chicago Press.

Labouvie, Erich W.
    1986a   Alcohol and marijuana use in relation to adolescent stress. International
             Journal of the Addictions 21:333-345.
    1986b   The coping function of adolescent alcohol and drug use. In Rainer K.
             Silbereisen, Klaus Eyfeth and Georg Rudinger (eds.), Development as
             Action in Context. New York: Springer.

Lauritsen, Janet L., Robert J. Sampson, and John Laub
    1991   The link between offending and victimization among adolescents. Criminol-
             ogy 29:265-292.

A GENERAL STRAIN THEORY   83

Lerner, Melvin J.
   1977   The justice motive: Some hypotheses as to its origins and forms. Journal of
            Personality 45:1–52.

Leventhal, Gerald S.
   1976   The distribution of rewards and resources in groups and organizations. In
            Leonard Berkowitz and Elaine Walster (eds.), Advances in Experimental
            Social Psychology: Equity Theory: Toward a General Theory of Social
            Interaction. New York: Academic Press.

Leventhal, Gerald S., Jurgis Karuzajr, and William Rick Fry
   1980   Beyond fairness: A theory of allocation preferences. In Gerald Mikula (ed.),
            Justice and Social Interaction. New York: Springer-Verlag.

Lind, E. Allan and Tom R. Tyler
   1988   The Social Psychology of Procedural Justice. New York: Plenum.

Linsky, Arnold S. and Murray A. Straus
   1986   Social Stress in the United States. Dover, Mass.: Auburn House.

Liska, Allen E.
   1987   Perspectives on Deviance. Englewood Cliffs, N.J.: Prentice-Hall.

McClelland, Katherine
   1990   The social management of ambition. Sociological Quarterly 31:225–251.

MacLeod, Jay
   1987   Ain't No Makin' It. Boulder, Colo.: Westview Press.

Mark, Melvin M. and Robert Folger
   1984   Responses to relative deprivation: A conceptual framework. In Philip
            Shaver (ed.), Review of Personality and Social Psychology. Vol. 5. Beverly
            Hills, Calif.: Sage.

Martin, Joanne
   1986   When expectations and justice do not coincide: Blue collar visions of a just
            world. In Hans Weiner Bierhoff, Ronald L. Cohen, and Jerald Greenberg
            (eds.), Justice in Social Relations. New York: Plenum.

Martin, Joanne and Alan Murray
   1983   Distributive injustice and unfair exchange. In David M. Messick and Karen
            S. Cook (eds.), Equity Theory: Psychological and Social Perspectives. New
            York: Praeger.
   1984   Catalysts for collective violence: The importance of a psychological
            approach. In Robert Folger (ed.), The Sense of Injustice: Social Psychologi-
            cal Perspectives. New York: Plenum.

Massey, James L. and Marvin Krohn
   1986   A longitudinal examination of an integrated social process model of deviant
            behavior. Social Forces 65:106–134.

Mawson, Anthony R.
   1987   Criminality: A Model of Stress-Induced Crime. New York: Praeger.

Menaghan, Elizabeth
   1982   Measuring coping effectiveness: A panel analysis of marital problems and
            coping efforts. Journal of Health and Social Behavior 23:220–234.

84   AGNEW

1983   Individual coping efforts: Moderators of the relationship between life stress
            and mental health outcomes. In Howard B. Kaplan (ed.), Psychosocial
            Stress: Trends in Theory and Research. New York: Academic Press.

Merton, Robert
1938   Social structure and anomie. American Sociological Review 3:672–682.

Messick, David M. and Keith Sentis
1979   Fairness and preference. Journal of Experimental Social Psychology
            15:418–434.
1983   Fairness, preference, and fairness biases. In David M. Messick and Karen S.
            Cook (eds.), Equity Theory: Psychological and Sociological Perspectives.
            New York: Praeger.

Michael, Jack
1973   Positive and negative reinforcement, a distinction that is no longer necessary;
            or a better way to talk about bad things. In Eugene Ramp and George
            Semb (eds.), Behavior Analysis: Areas of Research and Application.
            Englewood Cliffs, N.J.: Prentice-Hall.

Mickelson, Roslyn Arlin
1990   The attitude-achievement paradox among black adolescents. Sociology of
            Education 63:44–61.

Mikula, Gerold
1980   Justice and Social Interaction. New York: Springer-Verlag.
1986   The experience of injustice: Toward a better understanding of its phenome-
            nology. In Hans Werner Bierhoff, Ronald L. Cohen, and Jerald Greenberg
            (eds.), Justice in Social Relations. New York: Plenum.

Mirowsky, John and Catherine E. Ross
1990   The consolation-prize theory of alienation. American Journal of Sociology
            95:1505–1535.

Morgan, Rick L. and David Heise
1988   Structure of emotions. Social Psychology Quarterly 51:19–31.

Mueller, Charles W.
1983   Environmental stressors and aggressive behavior. In Russell G. Geen and
            Edward I. Donnerstein (eds.), Aggression: Theoretical and Empirical
            Reviews. Vol. 2. New York: Academic Press.

Newcomb, Michael D. and L.L. Harlow
1986   Life events and substance use among adolescents: Mediating effects of
            perceived loss of control and meaninglessness in life. Journal of Personality
            and Social Psychology 51:564–577.

Novy, Diane M. and Stephen Donohue
1985   The relationship between adolescent life stress events and delinquent conduct
            including conduct indicating a need for supervision. Adolescence
            78:313–321.

Pearlin, Leonard I.
1982   The social contexts of stress. In Leo Goldberger and Shlomo Berznitz (eds.),
            Handbook of Stress. New York: Free Press.
1983   Role strains and personal stress. In Howard Kaplan (ed.), Psychosocial
            Stress: Trends in Theory and Research. New York: Academic Press.

A GENERAL STRAIN THEORY 85

Pearlin, Leonard I. and Carmi Schooler
1978 The structure of coping. Journal of Health and Social Behavior 19:2–21.

Pearlin, Leonard I. and Morton A. Lieberman
1979 Social sources of emotional distress. In Roberta G. Simmons (ed.), Research in Community and Mental Health. Vol. I. Greenwich, Conn.: Jai Press.

Pearlin, Leonard I., Elizabeth G. Menaghan, Morton A. Lieberman, and Joseph T. Mullan
1981 The stress process. Journal of Health and Social Behavior 22:337–356.

Quicker, John
1974 The effect of goal discrepancy on delinquency. Social Problems 22:76–86.

Rivera, Beverly and Cathy Spatz Widom
1990 Childhood victimization and violent offending. Violence and Victims 5:19–35.

Rosenberg, Morris
1979 Conceiving the Self. New York: Basic.
1990 Reflexivity and emotions. Social Psychology Quarterly 53:3–12.

Ross, Michael, John Thibaut, and Scott Evenback
1971 Some determinants of the intensity of social protest. Journal of Experimental Social Psychology 7:401–418.

Schwinger, Thomas
1980 Just allocations of goods: Decisions among three principles. In Gerald Mikula (ed.), Justice and Social Interaction. New York: Springer-Verlag.

Shepelak, Norma J.
1987 The role of self-explanations and self-evaluations in legitimating inequality. American Sociological Review 52:495–503.

Shepelak, Norma J. and Duane Alwin
1986 Beliefs about inequality and perceptions of distributive justice. American Sociological Review 51:30–46.

Short, James F. and Fred L. Strodtbeck
1965 Group Process and Gang Delinquency. Chicago: University of Chicago Press.

Slaby, Ronald G. and Nancy G. Guerra
1988 Cognitive mediators of aggression in adolescent offenders: 1. Developmental Psychology 24:580–588.

Sprecher, Susan
1986 The relationship between inequity and emotions in close relationships. Social Psychology Quarterly 49:309–321.

Stephenson, G.M. and J.H. White
1968 An experimental study of some effects of injustice on children's moral behavior. Journal of Experimental Social Psychology 4:460–469.

Straus, Murray
1991 Discipline and deviance: Physical punishment of children and violence and other crimes in adulthood. Social Problems 38:133–154.

Sullivan, Mercer L.
1989 Getting Paid. Ithaca, N.Y.: Cornell University Press.

86   AGNEW

Suls, Jerry M.
    1977   Social comparison theory and research: An overview from 1954. In Jerry
            M. Suls and Richard L. Miller (eds.), Social Comparison Processes. New
            York: Hemisphere.

Suls, Jerry M. and Thomas Ashby Wills
    1991   Social Comparison: Contemporary Theory and Research. Hillsdale, N.J.:
            Lawrence Erlbaum.

Tavris, Carol
    1984   On the wisdom of counting to ten. In Philip Shaver (ed.), Review of
            Personality and Social Psychology: 5. Beverly Hills, Calif.: Sage.

Thibaut, John W. and Harold H. Kelley
    1959   The Social Psychology of Groups. New York: John Wiley & Sons.

Thoits, Peggy
    1983   Dimensions of life events that influence psychological distress: An evalua-
            tion and synthesis of the literature. In Howard B. Kaplan (ed.),
            Psychosocial Stress: Trends in Theory and Research. New York: Academic
            Press.
    1984   Coping, social support, and psychological outcomes: The central role of
            emotion. In Philip Shaver (ed.), Review of Personality and Social
            Psychology: 5. Beverly Hills, Calif.: Sage.
    1989   The sociology of emotions. In W. Richard Scott and Judith Blake (eds.),
            Annual Review of Sociology. Vol. 15. Palo Alto, Calif.: Annual Reviews.
    1990   Emotional deviance research. In Theodore D. Kemper (ed.), Research
            Agendas in the Sociology of Emotions. Albany: State University of New
            York Press.
    1991a   On merging identity theory and stress research. Social Psychology Quarterly
            54:101–112.
    1991b   Patterns of coping with controllable and uncontrollable events. In E. Mark
            Cummings, Anita L. Greene, and Katherine H. Karraker (eds.), Life-Span
            Developmental Psychology: Perspectives on Stress and Coping. Hillsdale,
            N.J.: Lawrence Erlbaum.

Thornberry, Terence P.
    1987   Toward an Interactional Theory of Delinquency. Criminology 25:863–891.

Tonry, Michael, Lloyd E. Ohlin, and David P. Farrington
    1991   Human Development and Criminal Behavior. New York: Springer-Verlag.

Tornblum, Kjell Y.
    1977   Distributive justice: Typology and propositions. Human Relations 30:1–24.

Utne, Mary Kristine and Robert Kidd
    1980   Equity and attribution. In Gerald Mikula (ed.), Justice and Social
            Interaction. New York: Springer-Verlag.

Van Houten, Ron
    1983   Punishment: From the animal laboratory to the applied setting. In Saul
            Axelrod and Jack Apsche (eds.), The Effects of Punishment on Human
            Behavior. New York: Academic Press.

Vaux, Alan
    1988   Social support: Theory, Research, and Intervention. New York: Praeger.

A GENERAL STRAIN THEORY　　87

Vaux, Alan and Mary Ruggiero
　1983　Stressful life change and delinquent behavior. American Journal of
　　　　Community Psychology 11:169–183.

Walster, Elaine, Ellen Berscheid, and G. William Walster
　1973　New directions in equity research. Journal of Personality and Social
　　　　Psychology 25:151–176.

Walster, Elaine, G. William Walster, and Ellen Berscheid
　1978　Equity: Theory and Research. Boston: Allyn & Bacon.

Wang, Alvin Y. and R. Stephen Richarde
　1988　Global versus task-specific measures of self-efficacy. Psychological Record
　　　　38:533–541.

Weiner, Bernard
　1982　The emotional consequences of causal attributions. In Margaret S. Clark
　　　　and Susan T. Fiske (eds.), Affect and Cognition: The Seventeenth Annual
　　　　Carnegie Symposium on Cognition. Hillsdale, N.J.: Lawrence Erlbaum.

Williams, Carolyn L. and Craige Uchiyama
　1989　Assessment of life events during adolescence: The use of self-report
　　　　inventories. Adolescence 24:95–118.

Wylie, Ruth
　1979　The Self-Concept. Vol. 2. Lincoln: University of Nebraska Press.

Zillman, Dolf
　1979　Hostility and Aggression. Hillsdale, N.J.: Lawrence Erlbaum.

Robert Agnew is Associate Professor of Sociology at Emory University in Atlanta, Georgia. His research focuses on the causes of delinquency, particularly strain and social control theories. He is currently conducting an empirical test of the general strain theory with Helene Raskin White.

[8]

GENDER AND CRIME: A GENERAL STRAIN THEORY PERSPECTIVE

LISA BROIDY
ROBERT AGNEW

This study applies Agnew's general strain theory (GST) to two fundamental questions about gender and crime: (1) How can we explain the higher rate of crime among males? (2) How can we explain why females engage in crime? With respect to the first question, the authors suggest that gender differences in types of strain and the reaction to strain help one understand the gender gap in criminal behavior. With respect to the second question, it is argued that several types of strain may lead to female crime under the proper circumstances. In this area, GST has much in common with numerous accounts that explain female crime in terms of oppression.

Two questions dominate the theoretical literature on gender and crime: (1) How can we explain the higher rate of crime among males? and (2) How can we explain why females engage in crime? In particular, can the dominant theories of crime, developed primarily to explain male behavior, explain female crime? (For overviews of these two questions and data on gender differences in crime, see Box 1983; Canter 1982; Chesney-Lind and Shelden 1992; Daly and Chesney-Lind 1988; Klein 1973; Leonard 1982; Morris 1987; Naffine 1987; Steffensmeier and Allan 1995.) We argue that Agnew's (1992) general strain theory (GST) can offer insight into these two questions. With respect to the first question, we suggest that gender differences in types of strain and the reaction to strain help us understand the gender gap in crime. With respect to the second question, we argue that several types of female strain may lead to crime under the proper circumstances. In this area, GST has much in common with accounts that explain female crime in terms of oppression.

The classic strain theories of Merton (1938), Cohen (1955), and Cloward and Ohlin (1960) argue that crime stems from the inability to achieve the

---

This article is the result of a collaboration, with each author contributing equally to the final product. As such, the order of authorship was decided by the flip of a coin and does not reflect the authors' respective inputs.

276   JOURNAL OF RESEARCH IN CRIME AND DELINQUENCY

goals of monetary success, middle-class status, or both. These theories have been applied to the above two questions, although the results have not been satisfactory (for discussion see Agnew 1995; Agnew and Brezina 1997; Chesney-Lind and Shelden 1992; Leonard 1982; Messerschmidt 1993; Morris 1987; Naffine 1987). Several theorists, however, have argued that a broader version of strain theory may help shed light on the relation between gender and crime (Berger 1989; Cloward and Piven 1979:660-62; Leonard 1982:136, 190; Ogle, Maier-Katkin, and Bernard 1995). This argument, for example, is made by Naffine (1987) when she critiques those classic strain theorists who claim that women are under less strain or pressure.

> They ignore the evidence when they insist that women are insulated from the pressures of public life, that their role is less demanding than the male role and that they thus do not experience pressures causing them to deviate. . . . Research has since revealed that females are susceptible to frustrations of a more general nature and that these frustrations correlate positively with offending. . . . At the head of the feminist agenda for strain theory is the investigation of the concerns and goals and the frustrations of criminal and conforming women. (P. 23)

Agnew's (1992) general strain theory is much broader than classic strain theory: It recognizes that there are several sources of strain—not just the failure to achieve positively valued goals like monetary success. It also recognizes that there are a wide range of adaptations to strain—cognitive, behavioral, and emotional. Certain of these adaptations involve crime, whereas others do not. And it more fully describes the factors that influence the choice of criminal versus noncriminal adaptations. As such, GST is in a good position to exploit the observation that females suffer from a range of oppressive conditions and that this oppression is at the root of their crime. GST, in particular, allows us to significantly extend the work of classic strain theorists. It allows us to better explore the types of strain experienced by men and women, including but not limited to the economic strain identified by certain classic strain theorists. Furthermore, it allows us to more fully explore the factors that influence the reaction to this strain by men and women.

In the first section of this article, we examine how GST might explain the higher rate of male crime. In the second section, we examine how GST might explain the causes of female crime. We then discuss whether GST is equally applicable to males and females. These discussions draw heavily on the feminist literature on crime, the gender and stress literature in social psychology, and sociological research on gender. We then summarize the arguments that are presented by offering several hypotheses for further study.

WHY ARE MALES MORE CRIMINAL THAN FEMALES?

Much data indicate that males have higher crime rates than females, with the gender gap in crime being highest for serious violent and property crimes (except for family violence) and lowest for minor property crimes, drug use, and escapist behaviors like running away (e.g., Canter 1982; Chesney-Lind and Shelden 1992; Steffensmeier and Allan 1995). GST might explain the higher rate of male crime in four ways:

1. Males are subject to *more* strains or stressors than females.
2. Males are subject to *different* strains than females, with male strains being more conducive to crime.
3. Males have a different emotional response to strain, with the male response being more conducive to crime.
4. Males are more likely to respond to anger/strain with crime.

This section draws on the empirical literature to evaluate each of these explanations.

Are Males Subject to More Strain?

General Strain Theory identifies three major sources of strain: the failure to achieve positively valued goals, the loss of positively valued stimuli, and the presentation of negative stimuli. The first type of strain includes three subtypes: the failure to achieve aspirations or ideal goals, the failure to achieve expectations, and the failure to be treated in a just/fair manner. Classic strain theories focus exclusively on the failure to achieve aspirations. Such theories, in particular, focus on the inability of individuals and groups to achieve the culturally defined goals of monetary success, middle-class status, or both. GST, then, significantly broadens the scope of strain theory. It examines a broad range of goals—goals that derive from the cultural system as well as those that are existentially based. And, it considers types of strain other than goal blockage, such as the loss of positive stimuli like friends and romantic partners, and the presentation of negative stimuli like excessive demands and verbal/sexual/physical abuse. As such, GST allows us to better explore gender differences in the amounts and types of strain.

Are males more likely to experience the types of strain identified by GST than are females? The stress literature allows us to provide the best answer to this question because it contains systematic comparisons of the amounts of strain experienced by men and women. The most recent inventories of stressful events and conditions focus on numerous types of strain, particularly those dealing with the loss of positive stimuli and the presentation of negative stimuli: the two types of strain ignored by classic strain theory. The latest literature, based on the best samples and the broadest inventories of stressors, finds that females experience as much or more strain than do males (e.g., Barnett and Baruch 1987; Barnett, Biener, and Baruch 1987; Bush and Simmons 1987; Compas 1987; Compas, Davis, and Forsythe 1985; Gove and Herb 1974; Kessler and McLeod 1984; Kohn and Milrose 1993; LaCroix and Haynes 1987; Mirowsky and Ross 1995; Pearlin and Lieberman 1979; Petersen 1988; Thoits 1982; Turner, Wheaton, and Lloyd 1995; Wagner and Compas 1990). These findings apply to both adolescents and adults (some evidence suggests that male children experience more stressors than do female children). Further, certain data suggest that females subjectively rate these strainful events as more stressful or undesirable than do males (Compas 1987; Wagner and Compas 1990). Females, then, may be higher in both objective and subjective strain. These findings are especially convincing when one considers that the stress literature often overlooks stressors that may be of special relevance to females, like sexual abuse, abortion, gender-based discrimination, child care problems, and the burdens associated with nurturing others (see Aneshensel and Pearlin 1987; Makosky 1980).

The specific stressors experienced by females are described in more detail below. They fall into the three categories identified by GST. Certain of these stressors involve the failure to achieve positively valued goals, including economic and relational goals, as well as the failure to be treated in a just or equitable manner by others. Other stressors involve the loss of positively valued stimuli, including romantic partners, friends, and the opportunity to freely engage in a range of valued behaviors. Still other stressors involve the presentation of negative stimuli. Females are frequently subject to a wide range of abusive behaviors—verbal, sexual, and physical; they are the object of excessive demands by family members and others; and they often experience other aversive conditions at home, work, and in their neighborhoods.

Taken as a whole, these data suggest that GST cannot explain the higher rate of male crime by simply arguing that males experience more strain. Females experience as much if not more strain than males.

Are Males and Females Subject to Different Types of Strain?

Although differences in the *amount* of strain cannot explain gender differences in crime, perhaps differences in the *type* of strain can. Males experience somewhat different types of strain than females, and perhaps these types of strain are more likely to lead to crime. The stress literature suggests that different types of strain have substantially different impacts on emotional well-being and other outcome variables (e.g., Aneshensel, Rutter, and Lachenbruch 1991). GST is still in a primitive state, and we have little idea whether some types of strain are more likely to lead to crime than are other types. However, it is not unreasonable to suppose that this is the case.

It has been suggested that there are gender differences in the three types of strain identified in GST. First, males and females may have somewhat distinctive *goals and conceptions of fairness*. Several strain and feminist theorists have argued that males are more concerned with material success and extrinsic achievements, whereas females are more concerned with the establishment and maintenance of close relationships and with meaning/ purpose in life (see Cernkovich and Giordano 1979; Cohen 1955; Gilligan 1982; Gilligan, Lyons, and Hanmer 1989; Jordan 1995; Leonard 1982; J. Miller 1986; A. Morris 1987; R. Morris 1964). Tentative data provide for these arguments (Beutel and Marini 1995; Chesney-Lind and Shelden 1992; Gilligan 1982; Jones 1991; Mazur 1989; Rokeach 1973). Further, these arguments are compatible with the stress literature, which suggests that males more often report financial problems and are more upset when they experience financial and work problems. Females more often report network-related stressors (i.e., stressors involving family and friends) and are more upset when they experience network and interpersonal problems (Compas and Phares 1991; Conger et al. 1993; Kessler and McLeod 1984; Stark et al. 1989; Turner et al. 1995; Wethington, McLeod, and Kessler 1987). There also appear to be gender differences in evaluations of fairness (Gilligan 1982; Major and Deaux 1982). Males are said to be more concerned about the fairness of outcomes (distributive justice), whereas females seem to be more concerned about the fairness of the procedures by which outcomes are allocated (procedural justice). Males, then, focus more on the outcomes of interaction, whereas females focus more on how people involved in interactions are treated.

There are also gender differences in the experience of the second two types of strain: *the loss of positive stimuli and the presentation of negative stimuli*. In addition to experiencing more network-related stressors, females are more likely to report the following types of negative treatment: gender-based discrimination, low prestige in work and family roles, excessive demands from family members, and restrictions on their behavior—with females being more likely to be confined to the "private sphere" (e.g., Bush and Simmons 1987; Campbell 1984; Gove 1978; Gove and Herb 1974; Hagan, Simpson, and Gillis 1979; Messerschmidt 1986; Mirowsky and Ross 1989; Ogle et al. 1995; Thoits 1991). In addition to experiencing greater financial strain, males are said to experience more problems with peers. Males, in particular, are more likely to report that their relations with peers are characterized by conflict, competition, jealousy, and imbalance. Female relations with peers, however, are warmer and less competitive (see Campbell 1993; Giordano, Cernkovich, and Pugh 1986; Lempers and Clark-Lempers 1992). Finally, data suggest that males are more likely to be the victims of most types of crime—as well as the targets of others' aggression and anger (Eagly and Steffen 1986; Frodi, Macaulay, and Thome 1977; Frost and Averill 1982).

These differences in types of strain may help us explain gender differences in crime. The greater emphasis of males on material considerations and the greater financial stress of males may explain their higher rates of property crime. Females, however, may sometimes steal to finance their social activities or to provide assistance to their families (see Chesney-Lind and Shelden 1992:43; Morris 1987). Further, as argued shortly, females have come to experience increased levels of financial strain in recent years. This strain may help explain the increase in minor property crime by females (see Steffensmeier and Allan 1995). The interpersonal conflicts and criminal victimization more often experienced by males may explain their higher rates of violent crime. Many data suggest that interpersonal conflicts/victimizations are especially upsetting and that they play a central role in violent crime (see Ambert 1994; Avison and Turner 1988; Felson 1994; Luckenbill 1977). It is true that females experience relatively high levels of conflict with, and victimization by, family members, but it is in the area of family violence where gender differences in violence are smallest (Bowker 1978; Campbell 1993:103; Chesney-Lind and Shelden 1992:15; Mann 1984:21). The high levels of family violence experienced by females may also explain why gender differences in running away from home are so small (see Chesney-Lind and Shelden 1992).

The emphasis of females on ties to others and on procedural justice may help explain their lower rates of serious violent and property crime. Such a crime may be an effective way to obtain money or punish others, but it is a less effective vehicle for establishing ties to others or achieving procedural justice. The failure to achieve relational or justice goals, however, may be conducive to more self-destructive forms of illegitimate behavior, like drug use and eating disorders. Likewise, the other forms of strain more often experienced by females are *not* conducive to serious violent and property crime. With the exception of some types of gender discrimination, these strains involve excessive social control and a restriction of criminal opportunities. It is difficult to engage in serious violent and property crime when one spends little time in public, feels responsible for children and others, is burdened with the demands of others, and is under much pressure to avoid behaving in an aggressive manner. These types of strain, however, pose few barriers to self-destructive forms of behavior like drug use and criminal behavior compatible with female gender roles—like shoplifting. In fact, the above types of strain may foster such forms of deviance. Drug use, for example, allows females to "manage" their negative emotions without directly harming others. Minor property crime may allow females to finance social activities or better meet the demands of others.

Gender differences in types of strain, then, may help explain gender differences in types of crime.

Are There Gender Differences in the Emotional Response to Strain?

Not only may males and females experience different types of strain, but they may also differ in their emotional response to strain. Males, in particular, may be more likely to respond to a given strain in ways that are conducive to serious crime.

GST contends that what links strain to crime are the negative emotions individuals experience in response to strain. GST argues that strain increases one's level of negative affect, leading to emotions such as depression, anger, and frustration. These emotions, being unpleasant, create pressure for corrective action. Crime is one possible response. According to GST, the emotional reactions of anger and frustration are especially important because they increase the likelihood of a criminal response. As Agnew (1992:59-60) stated, anger energizes the individual for action, lowers inhibitions, and creates a desire for retaliation/revenge.

GST might explain the lower rate of female crime by arguing that females are more likely to respond to strain with depression rather than anger. As Mirowsky and Ross (1995) pointed out, it has been argued that women "respond to stressors with somewhat different emotions than men . . . men get angry and hostile—women get sad and depressed" (pp. 449, 451; also see Dornfeld and Kruttschnitt 1992; Frost and Averill 1982; Kopper and Epperson 1991; Ogle et al. 1995:175-76). The research on gender, stress, and emotion provides some support for this argument. Virtually all studies find that females are more depressed and anxious than are males. The higher depression of females is only partly explained by their greater exposure to stressors. With certain exceptions noted above, females are more likely to respond to a given stressor with depression than are males (e.g., Aneshensel 1992; Barnett et al. 1987; Bolger et al. 1989; Conger et al. 1993; Dohrenwend and Dohrenwend 1976; Gove 1978; Gove and Herb 1974; Kessler and McLeod 1984; Menaghan 1982; Newman 1986; Pearlin and Schooler 1978; Petersen 1988; Rosenfeld 1980; Ross and Huber 1985; Thoits 1982, 1987, 1991; Turner et al. 1995; Wheaton 1990).

Research on gender, stress, and anger, however, challenges the view that males are more angry than are females. In fact, data indicate that females are just as likely, or more likely, to respond to stress with anger than are males (Campbell 1993; Conger et al. 1993:78; Frost and Averill 1982; Gove 1978:189; Kopper and Epperson 1991).[1] In one of the best studies in this area, Mirowsky and Ross (1995) found that women reported feeling angry 28.7 percent more frequently than men. Anger was measured by asking respondents how often they felt angry, felt annoyed with things or people, and yelled at someone during the last seven days. Further, they found that depression and anger typically accompanied one another (also see White and Agnew 1992).

There is, however, some suggestion in the literature that the anger women experience is different from that experienced by men. In an extensive discussion of gender differences in anger, Campbell (1993) argued that the anger of women is typically accompanied by emotions such as fear, anxiety, guilt, and shame; the anger of men, on the other hand, is characterized by moral outrage. Other theorists have made similar arguments regarding the anger of women (see Kopper and Epperson 1991; Ogle et al. 1995:180). Data from the psychological literature support these arguments (Eagly and Steffen 1986; Frodi et al. 1977; Frost and Averill 1982). Such data, in particular, suggest that the anger of women is more likely to be accompanied by anxiety, hurt, and crying. These arguments are also compatible with Mirowsky and Ross (1995), who found that women are more likely to be *both* depressed and angry.

Several reasons are offered for this difference in the experience of anger. Women tend to blame themselves when adversely treated by others; they worry that their anger might lead them to harm others and jeopardize valued relationships—relationships central to their self-concept; and they view their anger as inappropriate and a failure of self-control (these arguments are said to be more true of White than African American women). Men, however, are quicker to blame others for their adversive treatment and to interpret such treatment as a challenge or deliberate insult. They are less concerned about hurting others or disrupting relationships, and they often view anger as an affirmation of their masculinity (see Adler 1975; Berger 1989; Box 1983; Campbell 1993; Chesney-Lind and Shelden 1992; Cloward and Piven 1979; Heidensohn 1985:193; Kopper and Epperson 1991; Messerschmidt 1986; Morris 1987:55, 64; Ogle et al. 1995; Rosenfeld 1980; Siddique and D'Arcy 1984 for fuller discussions). Research by Stapley and Haviland (1989) supports these explanations. They find that there are gender differences in the strains that most often provoke anger, as discussed above. Adolescent girls most often experience anger in affiliative interactions, whereas boys most often experience anger in situations in which performance is evaluated, such as in sports or at school. Further, there are gender differences in the experience of anger. The anger of boys is accompanied by contempt (suggesting externalization of anger), whereas the anger of girls is accompanied by surprise, shyness, shame, guilt, sadness, and self-hostility (suggesting internalization of anger).

These gender differences in the experience of anger may also help us explain gender differences in crime. The moral righteousness of the angry male may propel him into serious violent and property crime, whereas the depression and serious misgivings of the angry female may lead her into more self-destructive forms of deviance. White and Agnew (1992) found limited support for these arguments. They examined the effect of emotional state on crime and found that anger and depression interacted in their effect on delinquency, but not drug use. Anger was most likely to lead to delinquency when depression was low. Further research should more fully explore the experience of anger and other emotions in males and females and should examine the impact of the different constellations of emotions on different types of crime and other forms of deviance—such as eating disorders.

Are Males More Likely to
Respond to Strain/Anger with Crime?

As suggested above, one may argue that the types of strain and anger experienced by males are more conducive to many forms of crime. In addition, there is a fourth and final way that GST can explain higher rates of male crime. One might argue that males are more likely to respond to strain/anger with crime than are females. So, even if males and females experience the same emotional reactions to the same types of strain, males are still more likely to respond with crime—especially serious crime.

GST argues that the relationship between strain/anger and crime is conditioned by a number of factors, including coping resources, coping skills, social support, constraints to delinquent coping, and one's disposition toward delinquency—with this disposition being a function of certain temperamental variables, criminal beliefs, reinforcement for crime, and exposure to criminal models. Strained males may be more likely to engage in crime because of gender-related differences in these variables (also see Cloward and Piven 1979 for an excellent discussion in this area).

The stress literature has begun to explore gender differences in coping and social support. Although results do not indicate that females are significantly advantaged over males in these areas, they do offer some insight into why males may be more likely to respond to strain with serious crime than females.

**284	JOURNAL OF RESEARCH IN CRIME AND DELINQUENCY**

Certain data suggest that females are less likely to possess certain effective coping resources; especially a sense of mastery and positive self-esteem (Bush and Simmons 1987; Kobasa 1987; Miller and Kirsch 1987; Mirowsky and Ross 1989; Pearlin and Schooler 1978; Siddique and D'Arcy 1984; Thoits 1987; Wethington et al. 1987). Low mastery and self-esteem reduce women's ability to effectively cope with strain. However, these traits may also reduce the likelihood that women would respond to strain with serious crime, because they may not feel secure or confident enough to challenge behavioral proscriptions against such behaviors for women. Hence women low in mastery and self-esteem may be more likely to cope with strains using noncriminal and/or self-destructive, illegitimate coping strategies such as alcohol/drug abuse or disordered eating patterns (bingeing or starving oneself). Along with these differences in coping resources, there appear to be gender differences in coping skills. Data on gender differences in coping skills are mixed, with some studies showing that females are more likely to employ certain ineffective coping strategies, such as selective ignoring or defining away the problem (Brown et al., 1986; Compas, Malcarne, and Fondacaro 1988; Menaghan 1982; Pearlin and Schooler 1978). Such strategies seem to exacerbate rather than reduce stress. However, they are also less likely to trigger aggressive forms of criminal behavior. Rather, such strategies seem more conducive to escape-avoidance tactics such as drug use and eating disorders.

Research on gender differences in social support suggests that females are higher in emotional social support (Rosenthal and Gesten 1986; Stark et al. 1989). Data indicate that such support is often effective in reducing stress. The impact of this support on stress, however, is sometimes small. Further, involvement in intimate networks has costs as well as benefits—with the costs seeming to outweigh the benefits for females low in coping resources (Belle 1987). Involvement in interpersonal networks increases the likelihood of certain network-related strains, such as having a close friend or relative become seriously ill. Nevertheless, females who are more strongly invested in their intimate networks may try to avoid serious criminal behaviors that would threaten these ties. They may opt, instead, for various self-focused, nonconfrontational illegitimate coping strategies—like drug use.

The literature on gender, opportunities for crime, social control, and social learning also helps explain gender differences in the reaction to strain/anger (e.g., Berger 1989; Bottcher 1995; Box 1983; Burton et al. 1995; Campbell 1984, 1993; Cernkovich and Giordano 1987; Chesney-Lind and Shelden 1992; Figueria-McDonough 1981; Gilfus 1992; Giordano 1978; Giordano et al. 1986; Gora 1982; Hagan et al. 1979; Heidensohn 1985; Jensen and Eve

1976; Leonard 1982; Mann 1984; E. Miller 1986; Morash 1986; Morris 1987; Naffine 1987; Simons, Miller, and Aigner 1980; Smith 1979; Smith and Paternoster 1987; Sommers and Baskin 1993; Steffensmeier and Allan 1995; Torstensson 1990). Studies suggest that males have more opportunities for at least certain types of crime, that they are lower in at least certain types of social control, that they are more likely to possess certain temperamental traits conducive to crime, and that they are more likely to associate with deviant others. This is not to claim, however, that opportunity, social control, and social learning variables have a bigger impact on males than females. In most empirical research, such variables have a similar effect on males and females. Males, however, score higher on many of the variables that are conducive to a criminal response to strain.

The literature on gender differences in socialization reinforces the assertion that males may be more disposed to respond to strain/anger with crime. Males and females likely view certain behavioral responses as unavailable because they are inconsistent with gender stereotypes or their own gender identities. Several researchers suggest that the expression of anger is inconsistent with stereotypical beliefs about women and that women's anger is regarded as less appropriate than men's. Associated with this, women perceive greater costs for acting on their anger (e.g., Campbell 1993; Egerton 1988; Frost and Averill 1982; Kopper and Epperson 1991; Shields 1987). Evidence also suggests that these stereotypical beliefs about the appropriateness of anger and various responses to it are conditioned by gender role identification. Kogut, Langley, and O'Neal (1992) reported evidence that, for women, aggressive responses to provocation are more common among those high in gender role masculinity than low-masculinity subjects. This is despite similar levels of reported anger among both high- and low-masculinity subjects. Steenbarger and Greenberg (1990) also looked at the impact of women's gender identities on their coping responses. Their findings indicate that

> masculinity, facilitating coping through an externalization of threat, tends to protect against intrapersonal distress (depression), at the possible cost of interpersonal distress (hostility). Femininity, promoting an internalization of threat, mitigates against interpersonal stress at the possible cost of individual turmoil. (P. 66)

Males, then, may be more likely to respond to anger by aggressing against others, whereas females may be more likely to engage in self-directed illegitimate behaviors such as alcohol and drug abuse, and disordered eating practices.

286   **JOURNAL OF RESEARCH IN CRIME AND DELINQUENCY**

Gender differences in peer associations also suggest that males are more inclined to respond to strain/anger with crime. Thorne and Lupia (1986) pointed out that boys tend to congregate in large groups organized hierarchically and characterized by physical and competitive interaction. Girls, on the other hand, tend to interact in smaller groups or friendship pairs organized around cooperation. Conflict among boys tends to be overt and physical (i.e., fighting), whereas among girls conflict is typically indirect (i.e., talking behind people's backs). Further, groups of boys tend to be more likely to take risks and challenge authority.

> Girls are more likely to affirm the reasonableness of rules, and, when it occurs, rule breaking by girls is smaller scale. . . . Boys experience a shared, arousing context for transgression, with sustained gender group support for rule breaking. Girls' groups may engage in rule-breaking, but the gender group's support for repeated transgressions is far less certain. (Thorne and Lupia 1986:181)

If behavioral preferences are a function of the networks in which a person is embedded (see Smith-Lovin and McPherson 1993), then it is not surprising that women are less inclined to engage in deviant behaviors because their networks do not offer models or support for such behavior. However, this is not to say that female networks are entirely incompatible with all forms of illegitimate coping strategies. Noncompetitive, small friendship networks would facilitate nonaggressive, cognitive, and emotional coping strategies over the aggressive, behavioral ones that large, competitive male networks likely facilitate. So, whereas male networks would seemingly favor illegitimate behavioral coping strategies when legitimate strategies fail, female networks would favor cognitive or emotional ones. Males, then, would be more likely to have access to behaviorally deviant strategies such as violent/ aggressive delinquency. Females, on the other hand, would be more likely to have access to nondelinquent cognitive or emotional illegitimate strategies. Their networks stress rules, morals, and compassion, making overt delinquency less available. Deviance is more likely to take nondelinquent and/or nonconfrontational forms in such networks. Thus eating disorders, depression, and alcohol or drug use would be more probable responses to ineffective or blocked legitimate coping strategies among females.

The above arguments are reflected in certain theories of female aggression, which claim that females—facing greater barriers to aggression—must experience higher levels of provocation and anger before turning to aggression (e.g., Campbell 1993; Ogle et al. 1995; also see Klein 1973; Thoits 1991). These theories, then, argue that there is a curvilinear relationship between female anger and aggression, with anger only leading to aggression at very high levels (Campbell 1993; Ogle et al. 1995). The relationship between strain/anger and crime, then, should differ for males and females. Strain/anger should bear a stronger relationship to serious crime among males, because males have more opportunities for crime and are more disposed to deal with their problems through crime. Further, the relationship between anger and serious crime should be about linear for males, but curvilinear for females (see Campbell 1993:114).

Several studies have examined the relationship between gender, strain, and crime; with most such studies simply examining the linear effect of strain on crime. Experimental studies tend to suggest that males are more likely to respond to a given provocation with aggression, especially more serious forms of aggression (see the meta-analysis in Eagly and Steffen 1986; also see Frodi et al. 1977 and Frost and Averill 1982 for contradictory data). With certain exceptions, survey studies tend to find that the relationship between strain and crime is at least as strong for females as it is for males (Agnew and Brezina 1997; Cernkovich and Giordano 1987; Dornfeld and Kruttschnitt 1992; Grossman et al. 1992; Hoffman and Su forthcoming; MacEwen and Barling 1988; Rankin 1980; Simons et al. 1980; Vaux and Ruggiero 1983). Studies in this area, however, tend to suffer from certain problems. They only examine certain of the types of strain in GST, measures of negative emotions and coping strategies are limited or absent, and they tend to focus on less serious forms of aggression and/or crime.

Summary

GST can*not* explain the higher rate of male crime by arguing that males experience more strain than do females. GST, however, might explain gender differences in crime in three ways.

1. Males and females tend to experience different *types* of strain, with male strains being more conducive to serious violent and property crimes. Females' strains are conducive to family violence, to escape attempts like running away, and to more self-directed forms of crime, like drug use.
2. Males and females differ in their emotional response to strain. Although both males and females may experience anger in response to strain, the anger of females is more likely to be accompanied by depression, guilt, anxiety, and related states. Such accompanying states reduce the likelihood of aggressive or confrontational crimes and increase the likelihood of self-destructive and escapist offenses.
3. Males may be more likely to respond to a given level of strain or anger with serious property and violent crime because of differences in coping, social support, opportunities, social control, and the disposition to engage in crime.

Although many data provide indirect support for these arguments, there is a need for tests of GST that employ more comprehensive measures of strain and negative emotions, better measures of those factors that condition the reaction to anger/strain, and more comprehensive measures of crime and other deviant behaviors.

HOW CAN WE EXPLAIN FEMALE CRIME?

Not only can GST potentially account for the higher rate of male crime, it seems well suited for explaining female crime. In particular, it is very compatible with one of the central arguments in the feminist literature on crime: Female crime is rooted in the oppression of women (e.g., Carlen 1985, 1988; Daly and Chesney-Lind 1988; Gilfus 1992; Messerschmidt 1986; Naffine 1987). GST categorizes the types of oppression or strain that individuals experience and, like the feminist literature, argues that oppressed individuals may turn to crime in an effort to reduce their strain or manage the negative emotions associated with their strain.

The Strain Experienced by Females

In applying GST to the explanation of crime by females, it is first necessary to describe the major types of strain that are experienced by females. GST, as noted above, focuses on three types of strain, with the first type having three subcategories. The stress literature and the feminist literature on crime allow us to describe the particular types of strain experienced by females in these areas; with feminist studies of female offenders pointing to several types of strain that may bear a strong relation to crime.

The failure to achieve positively valued goals. Most tests of strain theory measure strain in terms of the disjunction between *aspirations* and expectations. According to GST, the failure to achieve aspirations or ideal goals is *not* a major source of strain. Aspirations have an element of the utopian in them, and we do not suffer serious distress when we fail to achieve them. Rather, serious distress is more likely when we experience a disjunction between our *expectations* or expected goals and actual achievements. Expectations are more firmly rooted in reality, and the failure to achieve them is likely to be quite upsetting. Serious distress is also likely when there is a disjunction between *just/fair outcomes* and actual outcomes. Many data indicate that individuals expect to be treated in a just or fair manner and they become upset when this is not the case.

GST, then, suggests that the failure to achieve positively valued goals be measured in at least two ways: (1) the disjunction between expectations and actual achievements, focusing on those goals that have high absolute and relative importance for the individual; and (2) the perception that one is being treated in a just or fair manner by others, including family, friends, co-workers, and employers (see Agnew 1992 for a fuller discussion of measurement strategies). There is reason to believe that many females would score high on these two measures of strain.

Although a particular woman may pursue a variety of goals, two goals have received much attention in the literature. First, numerous researchers contend that females are especially concerned with the achievement and maintenance of close interpersonal ties with others. Because of their socialization and structural position, females are said to have a strong desire for close relations with others and have certain expectations regarding the nature of those relations (Chesney-Lind and Shelden 1992; Conger et al. 1993; Gilfus 1992; Gilligan 1982; Klein 1973; Leonard 1982; J. Miller 1986; Morris 1964; Thoits 1991). Second, females are said to be becoming increasingly concerned with financial success/security. The increased concern with money may be in part culturally based, reflecting our increasingly consumerist culture and changing standards regarding female achievement (Berger 1989:387-88; Chapman 1980:63; Chesney-Lind and Shelden 1992:43). Adler (1975:94, 105), for example, argued that women are now more likely to be encouraged to strive for the same educational, occupational, and other goals as are males. And it may be in part structurally based, reflecting increased opportunities for achievement and the fact that increasing numbers of females live alone, head families, and/or have responsibility for supplying a substantial share of family income (Adler 1975; Figueira-McDonough and Selo 1980).

At the same time, many data indicate that the achievement of these goals is problematic for many females. The high rates of divorce and abuse in many intimate relationships mean that it is often difficult to satisfy the desire for interpersonal closeness. And qualitative studies suggest that abusive and failed relationships are a major source of strain in the lives of many female offenders. This strain, in turn, has been linked to their criminal behavior. Chesney-Lind (1986, 1989; Chesney-Lind and Shelden 1992), in fact, has constructed a theory of female delinquency that focuses on the abuse of adolescent females by family members. Chesney-Lind states that adolescent females are more subject to certain types of family abuse than are males, particularly sexual abuse. Adolescent females are unable to end this abuse through legal channels, so they often escape from it by running away. Their delinquent status forces them to turn to life on the street, where they confront a new set of strains. They have trouble obtaining legitimate employment and ultimately adapt to their economic problems through crime. In the process, they come to be exploited by a new set of actors (also see Daly 1992; Gilfus 1992; Mann 1984; E. Miller 1986). Joe and Chesney-Lind (1995) offer a similar explanation for gang involvement by females. Family and other problems are said to create a need for support and protection, and females adapt by joining a gang—which functions as a surrogate family (also see Campbell 1984, 1990). Case studies of adult female offenders report similar scenarios (e.g., Carlen 1988; E. Miller 1986; Sommers and Baskin 1993), although interpersonal problems are not the only problems implicated in crime.

Many females also have great difficulty achieving financial security/ success, even though limited data from the stress literature suggest that financial problems are more often experienced by men and have a greater psychological impact on men. Nevertheless, financial strain is quite common among women and is especially problematic for certain categories of women. Gender role socialization and discrimination direct most women into "pink-collar" jobs with low pay. It is true that the economic situation has improved for some women, but conditions have not changed as radically as many believe. There has been little change in the types of jobs most women hold or in the compensation they receive relative to men. Further, the situation has deteriorated for many women because of the "feminization of poverty." Increases in divorce and illegitimacy, coupled with changes in the job market, have dramatically increased the number of females who head households and live in poverty (Adler 1975; Box and Hale 1983, 1984; Carlen 1988; Leonard 1982:23; Mann 1984:96-98; Messerschmidt 1986; Morris 1987; Smart 1977; Steffensmeier and Allan 1995). Such financial stress is said to be a major source of female crime (Box 1983; Box and Hale 1983, 1984; Campbell 1984; Carlen 1988; Chapman 1980; Chesney-Lind and Shelden 1992; Gilfus 1992; Lewis 1981; Mann 1984:96; Messerschmidt 1986; E. Miller 1986; Naffine 1987; Simpson 1991).

Qualitative data confirm this argument, suggesting that financial problems are a major source of strain in the lives of female offenders and that they play a central role in their crime. Such offenders, in particular, have great trouble finding jobs that they like and that provide a satisfactory income. As a result, they often turn to illegal sources of income. Much female crime involves minor property offenses and, according to qualitative accounts, is committed for the income and the independence it provides (Campbell 1984, 1990;

Carlen 1985, 1988; Chapman 1980; Daly 1989, 1992; Gilfus 1992; Mann 1984:34; E. Miller 1986; Sommers and Baskin 1993).

Once again, more research is needed in this area. We must measure the financial goals of men and women, the absolute and relative importance attached to such goals, one's financial situation, and the level of dissatisfaction with one's financial situation. We would expect dissatisfaction to be highest among those who have high monetary expectations, attach high relative and absolute importance to such expectations, and are in a poor financial situation. Such dissatisfaction, in turn, should be related to crime.[2]

In addition to the pursuit of specific financial and interpersonal goals,[2] females (and males) have a more general desire to be treated in a just or fair manner. Many data, however, suggest that females are often treated in an inequitable manner by others. In the family, females (1) often perform low-skill, monotonous tasks that are not in keeping with their skills and qualifications; (2) routinely attend to the needs of their spouses and children but receive little attention to their own needs; and (3) do a disproportionate share of all housework, even if they are working full-time outside the home. At work, females are often employed in "pink-collar" jobs that are not commensurate with their skills and educational backgrounds. Further, they receive lower pay than do men in similar positions. And in interpersonal relations with males, females often give more than they receive. All of this is likely to create a sense of injustice, particularly given the increased emphasis on justice norms that stress *equal* treatment for males and females.

Unfortunately, these arguments have never received an adequate test. Cernkovich and Giordano (1979) did look at the relationship between gender discrimination and crime, but their study asked about perceptions of gender discrimination in general rather than whether the respondents had personally experienced such discrimination. As discussed in Agnew (1992), it is relatively easy to measure whether respondents believe they are being treated in an unjust or unfair manner. We would expect perceptions of injustice to be related to crime, particularly if the injustice involves relationships/roles that are central to the respondent.

The loss of positively valued stimuli. A second major category of strain involves the loss of positively valued stimuli, such as the loss of family members and friends through death and relocation and the loss of intimate others through divorce and separation.

This type of strain seems to be of special relevance to females. Data indicate that females are more likely to report and be affected by network events than are males (e.g., Kessler and McLeod 1984; Wethington et al. 1987)—with such events including the loss of family members and friends.

292   JOURNAL OF RESEARCH IN CRIME AND DELINQUENCY

Further, females often find it difficult to engage in many behaviors they may value. Females face certain barriers when it comes to participation in certain social settings and entering certain areas of the city—particularly when unaccompanied and at certain hours of the day (see Bottcher 1995; Hagan et al. 1979 regarding the restriction of women to the private sphere). Females also face certain barriers when it comes to behavior at work and behavior among family members, friends, and others. These barriers affect virtually every aspect of one's life; including appearance, conversation, physical and emotional expression, and sexual behavior. Females, in short, often are prevented or discouraged from engaging in a wide range of behaviors they may value. Theorists suggest that females first begin to experience this type of strain in a powerful way during adolescence (Bush and Simmons 1987; Gove and Herb 1974). After being allowed to participate in a range of "masculine behaviors," females suddenly face pressure to adopt the feminine role. Many previous forms of behavior, then, are abandoned or de-emphasized.

This type of strain has been ignored in quantitative studies in criminology and, with the exception of the network events listed above, it has been largely overlooked in the stress literature. This type of strain, however, does emerge in qualitative studies of women offenders. As Carlen (1988) stated, "[A] recurrent theme in the relatively few autobiographies and biographies of women criminals is the women's disdain and active dislike for the constricting social roles that have been systematically ascribed to women through the ages" (p. 18).

This strain may be measured by asking females about the extent to which others make it (or have made it) difficult for them to engage in various activities. We would expect females high in such strain to be more likely to engage in crime, particularly if they are prevented from engaging in highly valued behaviors. The relationship between this type of strain and crime, however, is complex. Females restricted to the private sphere may experience strain, but this strain may be offset by the limited opportunities for serious crime and the increased social control these females experience. Individuals *currently* high in this type of strain, then, may report higher levels of self-destructive behaviors and "gender-appropriate" crimes, such as shoplifting. They may not be higher in serious violent and property crimes, however. This type of strain might also be profitably explored with longitudinal data. Qualitative accounts of female offenders suggest that their crime is often accompanied by a more "open" or freer lifestyle. Nonetheless, their crime and lifestyle may be a function of the frustration they experienced with barriers imposed in the *past*.

The presentation of negatively valued stimuli. The third major type of strain involves the presentation of negatively valued stimuli. In this area, data suggest that females are often subject to varying types of abuse by family members and others, including emotional, physical, and sexual abuse. In addition to such blatant forms of victimization, females are subject to many other types of negative treatment.

Numerous commentators have focused on the negative stimuli associated with the role of housewife (see Aneshensel and Pearlin 1987; Mirowsky and Ross 1989 for overviews). Many females find this role monotonous, demeaning, highly demanding, and restrictive. It is little surprise that family life is more stressful for females than males (Barnett et al. 1987; Barnett and Baruch 1987; Campbell 1993:110-11; Gove 1978; Menaghan 1982). A large percentage of women, of course, have entered the labor force in recent years. Here too, however, women confront a variety of strains. They face discrimination in the job market, and their jobs often involve tedious and repetitive tasks, low authority and autonomy, limited upward mobility, and the underutilization of their skills and talents. And as is the case at home, they are often subject to sexual and other forms of harassment. Data indicate that pink-collar jobs, characterized by high demands and low control, are among the most stressful of all jobs (Barnett et al. 1987; Chapman 1980; Heidensohn 1985; LaCroix and Haynes 1987). Women, as indicated above, are more often affected by the adversive events that happen to others in their network. Such network events and the demands associated with them can also function as a major source of stress (Belle 1987; Turner et al. 1995). Finally, there is the background strain associated with the knowledge that the status of female is devalued in our society. As Leonard (1982) stated, females "are subject to the suffering caused by being viewed as inferior to one half of the population" (p. 136). (See Messerschmidt 1986; Ogle et al. 1995; Campbell 1984, 1993 for fuller discussions of the negative stimuli experienced by females.)

These strains do not affect all women equally, and we would expect that those women who are highest in such strains will be highest in crime. Limited data support this assertion. Several researchers have commented on the close connection between female victimization and female crime (e.g., Chesney-Lind and Shelden 1992; Daly 1992; Gilfus 1992). Also, data suggest that low-income, minority women are most likely to suffer from the above types of strain (Allen 1979; Campbell 1984, 1990; Carlen 1988; Chapman 1980; Chesney-Lind and Shelden 1992; Gilfus 1992; Hagan 1985; Joe and Chesney-Lind 1995; Lewis 1981; Morris 1987; Simpson 1991; Simpson and Ellis 1995). And it is these women who are most likely to be serious offenders.

294   JOURNAL OF RESEARCH IN CRIME AND DELINQUENCY

Factors Conditioning the Reaction to Strain

As numerous commentators have pointed out, not all strained individuals turn to crime. This is especially true of females. Females experience as much or more strain than do males but are less likely to engage in crime—especially serious crime. How, then, can we explain the fact that only a small portion of all strained females turn to crime? Part of the explanation may have to do with differences in the types of strain experienced. Although there are gender differences in the types of strain, it is still the case that many females experience those types of strain most conducive to serious crime—such as financial strain and victimization. Also, even though there are gender differences in the emotional response to strain, many females may respond to strain with the contemptuous anger that often characterizes males. As suggested, this may be more likely of females who are high in "masculinity." Finally, females differ from one another in those factors that condition the reaction to strain/anger; including coping, social support, opportunities for crime, and the disposition to engage in crime. Differences in the above areas, then, may help explain why some females are more likely than are other females to react to strain with crime—including serious crime.

The literature on female offenders provides some support for these arguments. Compared to females in general, female offenders have more opportunities for crime, are lower in social control, and/or are higher on those variables that predispose one to crime—such as criminal beliefs and association with deviant others than noncriminal females (Carlen 1985; Chesney-Lind and Shelden 1992; Daly 1992; Gilfus 1992; Giordano 1978; Jensen and Eve 1976; E. Miller 1986; Morash 1986; Simons et al. 1980; Sommers and Baskin 1993). Differences in these areas, as well as differences in the level and types of strain, have been used to explain the higher offending rates of minority and low-income females (Adler 1975:142-52; Lewis 1981; Mann 1984; Morris 1987:64; Simpson 1991). These differences may also explain why middle-class, White women are more likely than are low-income minority women to adopt self-destructive and typically noncriminal forms of illegitimate behavior.

Given the above arguments and data, we would expect the above factors to condition the impact of strain on crime. Data from the family violence literature suggest that this is the case. In particular, victimized females appear most likely to turn to crime when there are no or few legal options for dealing with their abuse (Chesney-Lind and Shelden 1992). Also, a recent study by Hoffman and Su (forthcoming) found that the impact of strain on crime was conditioned by certain of the above factors.

IS GENERAL STRAIN THEORY
APPLICABLE TO BOTH MALES AND FEMALES?

As indicated, a central question in the feminist literature is whether the same theories can explain both male and female crime. At a general level, it would appear that GST is applicable to the explanation of male and female crime. Both males and females experience the types of strain identified by GST, they often react to this strain with anger and related emotions, and research suggests that such strain leads some males and females to engage in crime. At a more specific level, data suggest that males and females (1) may be subject to somewhat different types of "objective" strain, (2) may differ in their subjective interpretation of particular types of strain (i.e., the extent to which these "objective" strains are interpreted as negative or stressful), (3) may differ in their emotional reaction to strain, and (4) may differ in their propensity to react to strain/anger with crime.

As indicated above, females appear more likely to experience network strains, gender-based discrimination, excessive demands from others, and low prestige in their work and family roles. Males appear more likely to experience financial strain, interpersonal conflicts with peers, and most types of criminal victimization. It is likely that additional research, employing better samples and broader inventories of strain, will reveal still other differences. Tentative data also suggest that females rate most types of strain as more stressful or negative than do males. Further, females are emotionally more vulnerable to network and interpersonal stressors, whereas males are emotionally more vulnerable to work and financial stressors. Again, additional research will likely reveal further gender differences in the emotional impact of specific stressors.

Males and females seem to react to strain with different constellations of emotions. Although both males and females may experience anger in response to certain types of strain, the anger of males is more often accompanied by moral outrage, whereas that of females is more often accompanied by self-deprecating emotions. Finally, experimental data suggest that males may be more likely than females to respond to provocations with serious aggression—although the survey data in this area are less supportive.

The above findings suggest that the underlying process identified by GST—that strain triggers negative emotions leading to coping behaviors, which can take legitimate or illegitimate (i.e., criminal/deviant) forms—is likely applicable to males and females. In other words, the theory can explain both male and female crime. However, different models of strain may be necessary for males and females to highlight gender differences in this

296   JOURNAL OF RESEARCH IN CRIME AND DELINQUENCY

underlying process. Hence empirical research on GST should examine males and females separately. Because of the gender differences described above, we may find that a particular type of strain leads to crime among one gender but has little or no effect on crime in the other gender (see, e.g., Aneshensel et al. 1991; Hoffman and Su forthcoming). Whether gender differences do, in fact, shape individuals' experiences with strain and their subsequent responses (both deviant and nondeviant) must be assessed through future empirical analyses. Such analyses will be able to assess whether separate models of male and female deviance are necessary.

At the same time, it is important to note that the above gender differences, to the extent that they exist, involve differences in *degree* rather than *kind*. It is not the case, for example, that females are exclusively concerned with interpersonal relations and males are exclusively concerned with the achievement sphere. As Morris (1987:62) argued, we are simply talking about different degrees of emphasis. Further, as Thoits (1991) and others point out, we may ultimately be able to develop more sophisticated models of stress/strain that allow us to treat males and females together. Such models would take account of those factors that explain gender differences in the reaction to strain. We are already aware of many of these factors, such as differences in criminal opportunities, level of social control, and the predisposition to crime. And research continues to point to other factors. Thoits (1991), for example, argued that the individual's salient role identities strongly condition the reaction to strain.

In sum, if asked whether GST can explain both male and female crime, the answer is yes, but we must pay attention to the way in which gender conditions the processes described by GST.

CONCLUSION

Agnew (1992) did not present a fully developed theory of crime when he first introduced GST. Rather, as suggested in the title of his article, he presented a foundation on which such a theory could be constructed. Agnew described several potential sources of strain, several modes of coping with such strain, and several factors that influence whether criminal versus noncriminal coping strategies are employed. Further research is necessary to develop the specifics of this general theory. That is, further research must specify (1) how much and what types of strain are experienced by different groups; (2) how different groups cope with the strain they experience, including the extent to which they cope in criminal versus noncriminal ways; and (3) why groups cope with strain in the manner in which they do (see

Agnew 1997 for an effort to address these issues regarding age groups). This article attempted to address these issues regarding gender groups. In doing so, GST was applied to the two central questions about gender and crime: Why do males engage in more crime than females, and how can we explain female crime? The research highlighted in this article suggests that GST can potentially answer both questions. On the basis of the preceding discussions, we can advance several tentative hypotheses.

First, regarding differences in rates of male and female crime, we hypothesize that males and females experience different *types* of strain, which leads to distinct behavioral outcomes. The research discussed above suggests that males are more often subject to types of strain that are conducive to serious crime. Among other things, research indicates that males are more often subject to financial strain, which is conducive to property crime, and to severe interpersonal conflict, which is conducive to violence. With certain exceptions, the types of strain most common among women involve high levels of social control and a restriction of criminal opportunities (e.g., the burdens of nurturing others like family members, the restriction to the private sphere). These types of strain may be conducive to self-destructive forms of behavior, such as drug use. However, it should be noted that females are often subject to family violence—which may explain why gender differences in the commission of family violence are relatively small. Also, financial strain is becoming a more serious problem for women, which may explain why gender differences in minor property crime are relatively small.

Second, we hypothesize that differences in rates of crime among males and females are, in part, a function of their distinct emotional responses to strain. Although both males and females are likely to respond to strain with anger, the anger of females is more likely to be accompanied by emotions such as depression, guilt, anxiety, and shame. Such emotions reduce the likelihood of other-directed crime. Rather, they often lead to self-destructive forms of deviance, such as drug use and eating disorders. This may help explain why gender differences in many types of drug use are small and why eating disorders are significantly more common among females than males. A third hypothesis is that females are less likely to respond to strain/anger with crime than are males. This is due to gender differences in social support and coping styles as well as differences in opportunities for crime, social control, and the disposition for crime.

In offering these hypotheses, it should be emphasized that GST does *not* argue that gender differences in crime are a function of differences in the *amount* of strain males and females experience. Certain researchers, drawing on classic strain theories, did make this argument (see Agnew 1995 for an overview). GST, however, recognizes a much broader range of strainful

298   JOURNAL OF RESEARCH IN CRIME AND DELINQUENCY

events and conditions than does classic strain theory. And, the data strongly suggest that compared with males, females are as likely or more likely to experience these types of strain.

With respect to the causes of female crime, GST also suggests several tentative hypotheses. First, women's oppression in various social arenas may play an important role in the generation of strain, and ultimately criminal behavior. In the preceding discussion, we argued that the following types of strain may be especially conducive to crime among females: the failure to achieve financial and interpersonal expectations; the failure to be treated in a just and fair manner by others, including family members, intimate others, and employers; the loss of positive ties to others; a broad range of restrictions on behavior—including restrictions on appearance, conversation, physical and emotional expression, sexual behavior, travel, and social life; the experience of emotional, physical, and sexual abuse; and the role-related strains often associated with "pink-collar" jobs and the housewife role. Women, of course, differ in the extent to which they experience these strains, with most being more common among low-income, minority women.

Second, women are more likely to respond to strain with crime (or other deviant adaptations) when nondeviant coping mechanisms are ineffective or unavailable, when they have criminal/deviant opportunities, when they are low in social control, and when they are predisposed to crime/deviance (i.e., have deviant beliefs and associates, are reinforced for deviance).

The above hypotheses advance the literature in several ways. They pull together and synthesize the theory and research from several areas, providing a more precise statement of those variables that may be important in explaining gender differences in crime and the causes of female crime. Further, they point to a range of new variables for empirical researchers to consider. Empirical researchers, particularly quantitative researchers, have largely neglected the several types of strain outlined in this article in their attempts to explain female crime. Finally, this article and the larger literature on GST provide some guidance as to how empirical researchers should go about testing these hypotheses (also see Agnew and White 1992; Hoffman and Su forthcoming; Paternoster and Mazerolle 1994).

Unfortunately, no currently available data set that we are aware of allows anything close to a full test of the above hypotheses. In particular, most data sets contain only a small portion of the types of strainful events and conditions described above. It is even more difficult to find a crime/delinquency data set with good measures of emotions such as anger and depression. Several data sets, however, allow for partial tests of certain of the hypotheses listed above. It is our hope that this article will stimulate researchers to collect better data on the above issues and to once again give serious consideration to strain theory when focusing on issues of gender and crime.[3]

NOTES

1. The issue of causal order may be relevant here. Men may initially experience more anger than women, but their higher level of crime/aggressiveness may subsequently reduce their anger. Women, being less likely to act on their anger, may experience further negative treatment and grow even more angry (see Brezina 1996; Campbell 1993; Ogle, Maier-Katkin, and Bernard 1995). Limited data from the psychological literature, however, suggest that females are just as likely as males to respond to provocations with anger (see Averill 1983; Frost and Averill 1982).

2. Females obviously pursue other goals beyond the interpersonal and financial ones just described, and research should focus on such goals. It has been suggested, however, that the lives of females are often more restricted than those of males. Females, in particular, have fewer arenas for achievement than men have. If true, this might also contribute to female strain. Individuals who pursue a smaller number of goals are probably more likely to experience strain because they "place all their eggs in one basket"—leaving themselves fewer alternatives should they fail to achieve their goals in a particular area. Related research in the stress literature suggests that multiple role performance tends to reduce rather than increase stress (Barnett and Baruch 1987; Barnett, Biener, and Baruch 1987). It is theorized that this is because multiple roles provide alternative avenues for the development of self-esteem and alternative sources of gratification.

3. GST is a social-psychological theory and so does not address the macro-level sources of strain and coping. Some effort was made to discuss these sources in the article, such as differences in socialization and in the structural position of men and women. Future research should also devote more attention to the ways in which gender structures one's exposure to strain and reaction to strain. GST is compatible with several macro-level theories of crime, including most of the macro theories regarding gender and crime (see Messerschmidt 1993 for a summary), the anomie theories of Bernard (1990) and Messner and Rosenfeld (1994), Messerschmidt's theory of masculinities and crime, left realism (Young and Matthews 1992), and the recent work of Hagan (1994). All of these theories provide excellent starting points for this type of analysis.

REFERENCES

Adler, Freda. 1975. *Sisters in Crime*. New York: McGraw-Hill.

Agnew, Robert. 1992. "Foundation for a General Strain Theory of Crime and Delinquency." *Criminology* 30:47-87.

———. 1995. "Gender and Crime: A General Strain Theory Perspective." Paper presented at the 1995 annual meeting of the American Society of Criminology, November 15-18, Boston.

———. 1997. "Stability and Change in Crime over the Life Course: A Strain Theory Explanation." Pp. 101-32 in *Developmental Theories of Crime and Delinquency*, vol. 7, *Advances in Criminological Theory*, edited by Terence P. Thornberry. New Brunswick, NJ: Transaction Books.

Agnew, Robert and Timothy Brezina. 1997. "Relational Problems with Peers, Gender, and Delinquency." Unpublished manuscript.

300   JOURNAL OF RESEARCH IN CRIME AND DELINQUENCY

Agnew, Robert and Helene Raskin White. 1992. "An Empirical Test of General Strain Theory." *Criminology* 30:475-99.

Allen, Walter R. 1979. "Family Roles, Occupational Statuses, and Achievement Orientations among Black Women in the United States." *Signs: Journal of Women in Culture and Society* 4:670-86.

Ambert, Anne-Marie. 1994. "A Qualitative Study of Peer Abuse and Its Effects: Theoretical and Empirical Implications." *Journal of Marriage and the Family* 56:119-30.

Aneshensel, Carol S. 1992. "Social Stress: Theory and Research." *Annual Review of Sociology* 18:15-38.

Aneshensel, Carol S. and Leonard I. Pearlin. 1987. "Structural Contexts of Sex Differences in Stress." Pp. 75-95 in *Gender and Stress*, edited by Rosalind C. Barnett, Lois Biener, and Grace K. Baruch. New York: Free Press.

Aneshensel, Carol S., Carolyn M. Rutter, and Peter A. Lachenbruch. 1991. "Social Structure, Stress, and Mental Health: Competing Conceptual and Analytic Models." *American Sociological Review* 56:166-78.

Averill, James R. 1983. "Studies on Anger and Aggression." *American Psychologist* 38:1145-60.

Avison, William R. and R. Jay Turner. 1988. "Stressful Life Events and Depressive Symptoms: Disaggregating the Effects of Acute Stressors and Chronic Strains." *Journal of Health and Social Behavior* 29:253-64.

Barnett, Rosalind C. and Grace K. Baruch. 1987. "Social Roles, Gender, and Psychological Distress." Pp. 122-43 in *Gender and Stress*, edited by Rosalind C. Barnett, Lois Biener, and Grace K. Baruch. New York: Free Press.

Barnett, Rosalind C., Lois Biener, and Grace K. Baruch, eds. 1987. *Gender and Stress*. New York: Free Press.

Belle, Deborah. 1987. "Gender Differences in the Social Moderators of Stress." Pp. 257-77 in *Gender and Stress*, edited by Rosalind C. Barnett, Lois Biener, and Grace K. Baruch. New York: Free Press.

Berger, Ronald J. 1989. "Female Delinquency in the Emancipation Era: A Review of the Literature." *Sex Roles* 21:375-99.

Bernard, Thomas J. 1990. "Angry Aggression among the 'Truly Disadvantaged.' " *Criminology* 28:73-96.

Beutel, Ann M. and Margaret Mooney Marini. 1995. "Gender and Values." *American Sociological Review* 60:436-48.

Bolger, Niall, Anita DeLongis, Ronald C. Kessler, and Elizabeth A. Schilling. 1989. "Effects of Daily Stress on Negative Mood." *Journal of Personality and Social Psychology* 57:808-17.

Bottcher, Jean. 1995. "Gender as Social Control: A Qualitative Study of Incarcerated Youths and Their Siblings in Greater Sacramento." *Justice Quarterly* 12:33-57.

Bowker, Lee H. 1978. *Women, Crime, and the Criminal Justice System*. Lexington, MA: Lexington Books.

Box, Steven. 1983. *Power, Crime, and Mystification*. London: Tavistock.

Box, Steven and Chris Hale. 1983. "Liberation and Female Criminality in England and Wales." *British Journal of Criminology* 23:35-49.

————. 1984. "Liberation/Emancipation, Economic Marginalization, or Less Chivalry: The Relevance of Three Theoretical Arguments to Female Crime Patterns in England and Wales, 1951-1980." *Criminology* 22:473-97.

Brown, Jude M., Jennifer O'Keefe, Steven H. Sanders, and Beverly Baker. 1986. "Developmental Changes in Children's Cognition to Stressful and Painful Situations." *Journal of Pediatric Psychology* 11:343-57.

Brezina, Timothy, 1996. "Adapting to Strain: An Examination of Delinquent Coping Responses." *Criminology* 34:39-60 .

Burton, Velmer S., Jr., Francis T. Cullen, T. David Evans, and R. Gregory Dunaway. 1995. "Gender, Self-control, and Crime." Unpublished manuscript.

Bush, Diane Mitsch and Roberta Simmons. 1987. "Gender and Coping with Entry into Early Adolescence." Pp. 185-218 in *Gender and Stress*, edited by Rosalind C. Barnett, Lois Biener, and Grace K. Baruch. New York: Free Press.

Campbell, Anne. 1984. *The Girls in the Gang*. New York: Basil Blackwell.

———. 1990. "Female Participation in Gangs." Pp. 163-82 in *Gangs in America*, edited by C. Ronald Huff. Newbury Park, CA: Sage.

———. 1993. *Men, Women, and Aggression*. New York: Basic Books.

Canter, Rachel. 1982. "Sex Differences in Self-Reported Delinquency." *Criminology* 20:373-93.

Carlen, Pat, ed. 1985. *Criminal Women: Autobiographical Accounts*. Cambridge: Polity.

———. 1988. *Women, Crime and Poverty*. Milton Keynes, England: Open University Press.

Cernkovich, Stephen A. and Peggy C. Giordano. 1979. "Delinquency, Opportunity, and Gender." *Journal of Criminal Law and Criminology* 70:145-51.

———. 1987. "Family Relationships and Delinquency." *Criminology* 25:295-321.

Chapman, Jane Roberts. 1980. *Economic Realities and the Female Offender*. Lexington, MA: Lexington Books.

Chesney-Lind, Meda. 1986. "Women and Crime: The Female Offender." *Signs: Journal of Women in Culture and Society* 12:78-96.

———. 1989. "Girls' Crime and Woman's Place: Toward a Feminist Model of Female Delinquency." *Crime & Delinquency* 35:5-29.

Chesney-Lind, Meda and Randall G. Shelden. 1992. *Girls, Delinquency, and Juvenile Justice*. Pacific Grove, CA: Brooks/Cole.

Cloward, Richard A. and Lloyd E. Ohlin. 1960. *Delinquency and Opportunity*. New York: Free Press.

Cloward, Richard A. and Frances Fox Piven. 1979. "Hidden Protest: The Channeling of Female Innovation and Resistance." *Signs: Journal of Women in Culture and Society* 4:651-69.

Cohen, Albert K. 1955. *Delinquent Boys*. New York: Free Press.

Compas, Bruce E. 1987. "Stress and Life Events during Childhood and Adolescence." *Clinical Psychology Review* 7:275-302.

Compas, Bruce E., Glen E. Davis, and Carolyn J. Forsythe. 1985. "Characteristics of Life Events during Adolescence." *American Journal of Community Psychology* 13:677-91.

Compas, Bruce E., Vanessa L. Malcarne, and Karen M. Fondacaro. 1988. "Coping with Stressful Events in Older Children and Young Adolescents." *Journal of Consulting and Clinical Psychology* 56:405-11.

Compas, Bruce E. and Vicky Phares. 1991. "Stress during Childhood and Adolescence: Sources of Risk and Vulnerability." Pp. 111-30 in *Life Span Developmental Psychology*, edited by Mark E. Cummings, Anita L. Greene, and Katherine H. Karraker. Hillsdale, NJ: Lawrence Erlbaum.

Conger, Rand D., Frederick O. Lorenz, Glen H. Elder, Jr., Ronald L. Simons, and Xiaojia Ge. 1993. "Husband and Wife Differences in Response to Undesirable Life Events." *Journal of Health and Social Behavior* 34:71-88.

Daly, Kathleen. 1989. "Gender and Varieties of White-Collar Crime." *Criminology* 27:769-94.

———. 1992. "Women's Pathways to Felony Court: Feminist Theories of Lawbreaking and Problems of Representation." *Review of Law and Women's Studies* 2:11-52.

Daly, Kathleen and Meda Chesney-Lind. 1988. "Feminism and Criminology." *Justice Quarterly* 5:497-538.

302   JOURNAL OF RESEARCH IN CRIME AND DELINQUENCY

Dohrenwend, Bruce P. and Barbara Snell Dohrenwend. 1976. "Sex Differences in Psychiatric Disorders." *American Journal of Sociology* 81:1447-54.

Dornfeld, Maude and Candace Kruttschnitt. 1992. "Do the Stereotypes Fit? Mapping Offender-Specific Outcomes and Risk Factors." *Criminology* 30:397-419.

Eagly, Alice H. and Valerie J. Steffen. 1986. "Gender and Aggressive Behavior: A Meta-Analytical Review of the Social Psychological Literature." *Psychological Bulletin* 100:309-28.

Egerton, M. 1988. "Passionate Women and Passionate Men: Sex Differences in Accounting for Angry Weeping Episodes." *British Journal of Social Psychology* 27:51-66.

Felson, Marcus. 1994. *Crime and Everyday Life*. Thousand Oaks, CA: Pine Forge.

Figueria-McDonough, Josefina. 1981. "Normal Deviance: Gender Similarities in Adolescent Subcultures." Pp. 17-45 in *Comparing Male and Female Offenders*, edited by Marquerite Q. Warren. Beverly Hills, CA: Sage.

Figueira-McDonough, Josefina and Elaine Selo. 1980. "A Reformulation of the 'Equal Opportunity' Explanation of Female Delinquency." *Crime & Delinquency* 26:333-43.

Frodi, Ann, Jacqueline Macaulay, and Pauline Ropert Thome. 1977. "Are Women Always Less Aggressive Than Men? A Review of the Experimental Literature." *Psychological Bulletin* 84:634-60.

Frost, W. Douglas and James R. Averill. 1982. "Differences between Men and Women in the Everyday Experience of Anger." Pp. 281-315 in *Anger and Aggression*, edited by James R. Averill. New York: Springer-Verlag.

Gilfus, Mary E. 1992. "From Victims to Survivors to Offenders: Women's Routes of Entry and Immersion into Street Crime." *Women and Criminal Justice* 4:63-89.

Gilligan, Carol. 1982. *In a Different Voice*. Cambridge. MA: Harvard University Press.

Gilligan, Carol, Nona P. Lyons, and Trudy J. Hanmer. 1989. *Making Connections*. Troy, NY: Emma Willard School.

Giordano, Peggy C. 1978. "Girls, Guys and Gangs: The Changing Social Context of Female Delinquency." *Journal of Criminal Law and Criminology* 69:126-32.

Giordano, Peggy C., Stephen A. Cernkovich, and M. D. Pugh. 1986. "Friendships and Delinquency." *American Journal of Sociology* 91:1170-1292.

Gora, JoAnn Gennaro. 1982. *The New Female Criminal: Empirical Reality or Social Myth*. New York: Praeger.

Gove, Walter R. 1978. "Sex Differences in Mental Illness among Adult Men and Women: An Evaluation of Four Questions Raised Regarding the Evidence on the Higher Rates of Women." *Social Science and Medicine* 12B:187-98.

Gove, Walter R. and Terry R. Herb. 1974. "Stress and Mental Illness among the Young: A Comparison of the Sexes." *Social Forces* 53:256-65.

Grossman, F. K., J. Beinashowitz, M. Sakurai, L. Finnin, and M. Flaherty. 1992. "Risk and Resilience in Young Adolescents." *Journal of Youth and Adolescence* 21:529-50.

Hagan, John. 1985. "Toward a Structural Theory of Crime, Race, and Gender: The Canadian Case." *Crime & Delinquency* 31:129-46.

———. 1994. *Crime and Disrepute*. Thousand Oaks, CA: Pine Forge.

Hagan, John, John H. Simpson, and A. R. Gillis. 1979. "The Sexual Stratification of Social Control: A Gender-Based Perspective on Crime and Delinquency." *British Journal of Sociology* 30:25-38.

Heidensohn, Frances. 1985. *Women and Crime*. Loundmills, England: Macmillan.

Hoffman, John P. and S. Susan Su. Forthcoming. "The Conditional Effects of Stress on Delinquency and Drug Use: A Strain Theory Assessment of Sex Differences." *Journal of Research in Crime and Delinquency*.

Jensen, Gary J. and Raymond Eve. 1976. Sex Differences in Delinquency. *Criminology* 13:427-48.

Joe, Karen A. and Meda Chesney-Lind. 1995. " 'Just Every Mother's Angel.' An Analysis of Gender and Ethnic Variations in Youth Gang Membership." *Gender & Society* 9:408-31.

Jones, C. 1991. "Age Related Differences in College Students' Values." *College Student Journal* 24:292-95.

Jordan, Judith V. 1995. "A Relational Approach to Psychotherapy." *Woman and Therapy* 16:51-61.

Kessler, Ronald C. and Jane D. McLeod. 1984. "Sex Differences in Vulnerability to Undesirable Life Events." *American Sociological Review* 49:620-31.

Klein, Dorie. 1973. "The Etiology of Female Crime: A Review of the Literature." *Issues in Criminology* 8:3-30.

Kobasa, Suzzane C. Ouellette. 1987. "Stress Responses and Personality." Pp. 308-29 in *Gender and Stress*, edited by Rosalind C. Barnett, Lois Biener, and Grace K. Baruch. New York: Free Press.

Kogut, Diane, Travis Langley, and Edgar O'Neal. 1992. "Gender Role Masculinity and Angry Aggression in Women." *Sex Roles* 26:355-68.

Kohn, Paul M. and Jill A. Milrose. 1993. "The Inventory of High-School Students' Recent Life Experiences: A Decontaminated Measure of Adolescent Hassles." *Journal of Youth and Adolescence* 22:43-55.

Kopper, Beverly A. and Douglas L. Epperson. 1991. "Women and Anger." *Psychology of Women Quarterly* 15:7-14.

LaCroix, Andrea Z. and Suzanne G. Haynes. 1987. "Gender Differences in the Health Effects of Workplace Roles." Pp. 96-121 in *Gender and Stress*, edited by Rosalind C. Barnett, Lois Biener, and Grace K. Baruch. New York: Free Press.

Lempers, Jacques D. and Dania S. Clark-Lempers. 1992. "Young, Middle, and Late Adolescents' Comparisons of the Functional Importance of Five Significant Relationships." *Journal of Youth and Adolescence* 21:53-96.

Leonard, Eileen B. 1982. *Women, Crime and Society: A Critique of Theoretical Criminology.* New York: Longman.

Lewis, Diane K. 1981. "Black Women Offenders and Criminal Justice: Some Theoretical Considerations." Pp. 89-105 in *Comparing Male and Female Offenders*, edited by Marguerite Q. Warren. Beverly Hills, CA: Sage.

Luckenbill, David F. 1977. "Criminal Homicide as a Situated Transaction." *Social Problems* 25:176-86.

MacEwen, Karyl E. and Julian Barling. 1988. "Multiple Stressors, Violence in the Family of Origin, and Marital Aggression: A Longitudinal Investigation." *Journal of Family Violence* 3:73-87.

Major, Brenda and Kay Deaux. 1982. "Individual Differences in Justice Behavior." Pp. 43-76 in *Equity and Justice in Social Behavior*, edited by Jerald Greenberg and Ronald L. Cohen. New York: Academic Press.

Makosky, Vivian Parker. 1980. "Stress and the Mental Health of Women: A Discussion of Research and Issues." In *The Mental Health of Women*, edited by Marcia Guttentag, Susan Salasin, and Deborah Belle. New York: Academic Press.

Mann, Coramae Richey. 1984. *Female Crime and Delinquency.* University of Alabama Press.

Mazur, Elizabeth. 1989. "Predicting Gender Differences in Same-Sex Friendships from Affiliation Motive and Value." *Psychology of Women Quarterly* 13:277-291.

Menaghan, Elizabeth. 1982. "Measuring Coping Effectiveness: A Panel Analysis of Marital Problems and Coping Effects." *Journal of Health and Social Behavior* 23:220-34.

Merton, Robert. 1938. "Social Structure and Anomie." *American Sociological Review* 3:672-82.

304 JOURNAL OF RESEARCH IN CRIME AND DELINQUENCY

Messerschmidt, James W. 1986. *Capitalism, Patriarchy, and Crime.* Totowa, NJ: Rowman & Littlefield.

———. 1993. *Masculinities and Crime.* Lanham, MD: Rowman & Littlefield.

Messner, Steven F. and Richard Rosenfeld. 1994. *Crime and the American Dream.* Belmont, CA: Wadsworth.

Miller, Eleanor M. 1986. *Street Woman.* Philadelphia: Temple University Press.

Miller, Jean Baker. 1986. *Toward a New Psychology of Women.* Boston: Beacon.

Miller, Suzanne M. and Nicholas Kirsch. 1987. "Sex Differences in Cognitive Coping with Stress." Pp. 278-307 in *Gender and Stress,* edited by Rosalind C. Barnett, Lois Biener, and Grace K. Baruch. New York: Free Press.

Mirowsky, John and Catherine E. Ross. 1989. *Social Causes of Psychological Distress.* New York: Aldine de Gruyter.

———. 1995. "Sex Differences in Distress: Real or Artifact?" *American Sociological Review* 60:449-68.

Morash, Merry. 1986. "Gender, Peer Group Experiences, and Seriousness of Delinquency." *Journal of Research in Crime and Delinquency* 23:43-67.

Morris, Allison. 1987. *Women, Crime and Criminal Justice.* Oxford, England: Basil Blackwell.

Morris, Ruth R. 1964. "Female Delinquency and Relational Problems." *Social Forces* 43:82-89.

Naffine, Ngaire. 1987. *Female Crime: The Construction of Women in Criminology.* Sydney: Allen & Unwin.

Newman, Joy P. 1986. "Gender, Life Strains, and Depression." *Journal of Health and Social Behavior* 27:161-78.

Ogle, Robin S., Daniel Maier-Katkin, and Thomas J. Bernard. 1995. "A Theory of Homicidal Behavior among Women." *Criminology* 33:173-93.

Paternoster, Raymond and Paul Mazerolle. 1994. "General Strain Theory and Delinquency: A Replication and Extension." *Journal of Research in Crime and Delinquency* 31:235-63.

Pearlin, Leonard I. and Morton A. Lieberman. 1979. "Social Sources of Emotional Distress." In *Research in Community and Mental Health,* vol. 1, edited by Roberta G. Simmons. Greenwich, CT: JAI.

Pearlin, Leonard I. and Carmi Schooler. 1978. "The Structure of Coping." *Journal of Health and Social Behavior* 19:2-21.

Petersen, Anne C. 1988. "Adolescent Development." *Annual Review of Psychology* 39:583-607.

Rankin, Joseph H. 1980. "School Factors and Delinquency: Interactions by Age and Sex." *Sociology and Social Research* 64:420-34.

Rokeach, Milton. 1973. *The Nature of Human Values.* New York: Free Press.

Rosenfeld, Sarah. 1980. "Sex Differences in Depression: Do Women Always Have Higher Rates?" *Journal of Health and Social Behavior* 21:33-42.

Rosenthal, Karen R. and Ellis L. Gesten. 1986. "Gender and Sex Role Differences in the Perception of Social Support." *Sex Roles* 14:481-99.

Ross, Catherine E. and Joan Huber. 1985. "Hardship and Depression." *Journal of Health and Social Behavior* 26:312-27.

Shields, S. 1987. "The Dilemma of Emotion." Pp. 223-54 in *Sex and Gender,* edited by P. Shaver and C. Hendrick. Newbury Park, CA: Sage.

Siddique, C. M. and Carl D'Arcy. 1984. "Adolescence, Stress, and Psychological Well-Being." *Journal of Youth and Adolescence* 13:459-73.

Simons, Ronald L., Martin G. Miller, and Stephen M. Aigner. 1980. "Contemporary Theories of Deviance and Female Delinquency: An Empirical Test." *Journal of Research in Crime and Delinquency* 17:42-53.

Simpson, Sally S. 1991. Caste, Class, and Violent Crime: Explaining Differences in Female Offending. *Criminology* 29:115-35.

Simpson, Sally S. and Lori Ellis. 1995. "Doing Gender: Sorting Out the Caste and Class Conundrum." *Criminology* 33:47-81.

Smart, Carol. 1977. *Women, Crime and Criminology: A Feminist Critique*. London: Routledge & Kegan Paul.

Smith, Douglas A. 1979. "Sex and Deviance: An Assessment of Major Sociological Variables." *Sociological Quarterly* 20:183-95.

Smith, Douglas A. and Raymond Paternoster. 1987. "The Gender Gap in Theories of Deviance: Issues and Evidence." *Journal of Research in Crime and Delinquency* 24:140-72.

Smith-Lovin, Lynn and J. Miller McPherson. 1993. "You Are Who You Know: A Network Approach to Gender." Pp. 223-54 in *Theory on Gender/Feminism on Theory*, edited by Paula England. New York: Aldine de Gruyter.

Sommers, Ira and Deborah R. Baskin. 1993. "The Situational Context of Violent Female Offending." *Journal of Research in Crime and Delinquency* 30:136-62.

Stark, Lori J., Anthony Spirito, Connie A. Williams, and David C. Guevremont. 1989. "Common Problems and Coping Strategies: Findings with Normal Adolescents." *Journal of Abnormal Child Psychology* 17:203-21.

Stapley, Janice C. and Jeanette M. Haviland. 1989. "Beyond Depression: Gender Differences in Normal Adolescents' Emotional Experiences." *Sex Roles* 20:295-308.

Steenbarger, Brett N. and Roger P. Greenberg. 1990. "Sex Roles, Stress, and Distress: A Study of Person by Situation Contingency." *Sex Roles* 22:59-68.

Steffensmeier, Darrell and Emile Allan. 1995. "Criminal Behavior: Gender and Age." Pp. 83-113 in *Criminology: A Contemporary Handbook*, edited by Joseph F. Sheley. Belmont, CA: Wadsworth.

Thoits, Peggy A. 1982. "Life Stress, Social Support, and Psychological Vulnerability: Epidemiological Considerations." *Journal of Community Psychology* 10:341-62.

———. 1987. "Gender and Marital Status Differences in Control and Distress: Common Stress versus Unique Stress Explanations." *Journal of Health and Social Behavior* 28:7-22.

———. 1991. "On Merging Identity Theory and Stress Research." *Social Psychology Quarterly* 54:101-12.

Thorne, Barrie and Zella Lupia. 1986. "Sexuality and Gender in Children's Daily Worlds." *Social Problems* 33:177-90.

Torstensson, Marie. 1990. "Female Delinquents in a Birth Cohort: Tests of Some Aspects of Control Theory." *Journal of Quantitative Criminology* 6:101-15.

Turner, R. Jay, Blair Wheaton, and Donald A. Lloyd. 1995. "The Epidemiology of Social Stress." *American Sociological Review* 60:104-25.

Vaux, Alan and Mary Ruggiero. 1983. "Stressful Life Change and Delinquent Behavior." *American Journal of Community Psychology* 11:169-83.

Wagner, Barry M. and Bruce E. Compas. 1990. "Gender, Instrumentality, and Expressivity: Moderators of the Relation between Stress and Psychological Symptoms during Adolescence." *American Journal of Community Psychology* 18:383-406.

Wethington, Elaine, Jane D. McLeod, and Ronald C. Kessler. 1987. "The Importance of Life Events for Explaining Sex Differences in Psychological Distress." Pp. 144-58 in *Gender and Stress*, edited by Rosalind C. Barnett, Lois Biener, and Grace K. Baruch. New York: Free Press.

Wheaton, Blair. 1990. "Life Transitions, Role Histories, and Mental Health." *American Sociological Review* 55:209-23.

306   JOURNAL OF RESEARCH IN CRIME AND DELINQUENCY

White, Helene Raskin and Robert Agnew. 1992. "The Role of Negative Affect in Adolescent Delinquency and Drug Use." Paper presented at the annual meeting of the American Society of Criminology, November 4-7, New Orleans, LA.

Young, Jock and Roger Matthews. 1992. *Rethinking Criminology: The Realist Debate*. London: Sage.

[9]

BUILDING ON THE FOUNDATION OF GENERAL STRAIN THEORY: SPECIFYING THE TYPES OF STRAIN MOST LIKELY TO LEAD TO CRIME AND DELINQUENCY

ROBERT AGNEW

General strain theory (GST) is usually tested by examining the effect of strain on crime. Researchers, however, have little guidance when it comes to selecting among the many hundreds of types of strain and have trouble explaining why only some of them are related to crime. This article builds on GST by describing the characteristics of strainful events and conditions that influence their relationship to crime. Strains are said to be most likely to result in crime when they (1) are seen as unjust, (2) are seen as high in magnitude, (3) are associated with low social control, and (4) create some pressure or incentive to engage in criminal coping. Drawing on these characteristics, it is predicted that some types of strain will not be related to crime, including types that have dominated the research on strain theory, and that others will be related to crime, including types that have been neglected by empirical researchers.

General strain theory (GST) argues that strains or stressors increase the likelihood of negative emotions like anger and frustration. These emotions create pressure for corrective action, and crime is one possible response (Agnew 1992). Crime may be a method for reducing strain (e.g., stealing the money you desire), seeking revenge, or alleviating negative emotions (e.g., through illicit drug use). GST builds on previous strain theories in several ways: most notably, by pointing to several new categories of strain, including the loss of positive stimuli (e.g., loss of a romantic partner, death of a friend), the presentation of negative stimuli (e.g., physical assaults and verbal insults), and new categories of goal blockage (e.g., the failure to achieve justice goals). Recent research demonstrates that many of the specific strains falling under these categories are related to crime and delinquency (see Agnew 2001a for a summary; Aseltine, Gore, and Gordon 2000; Mazerolle et al. 2000; Piquero and Sealock 2000). The specification of these new categories of strain is GST's greatest strength.

320 JOURNAL OF RESEARCH IN CRIME AND DELINQUENCY

This strength, however, is also GST's biggest weakness. GST is so broad that researchers have little guidance as to the specific types of strain to examine in their research. Hundreds of types of strain fall under the major categories of strain listed by GST, as reflected in recent inventories of stressful life events, chronic stressors, and daily life events or hassles (see Cohen, Kessler, and Gordon 1995; Herbert and Cohen 1996 for overviews). And even these inventories do not measure many of the strains described by GST. Furthermore, the broadness of GST makes it difficult to falsify. As Jensen (1995) stated, "if strain can be defined in so many different ways, then strain theory is virtually unfalsifiable. There is always a new measure that might salvage the theory" (p. 152).

It is therefore crucial that GST more precisely specify the types of strain most likely to lead to crime and delinquency. This article represents an attempt to do that. First, strain is defined. Although Agnew (1992) presented a general definition of strain, the term has nevertheless been used in different ways by researchers and it is important to clarify its meaning. Second, previous tests of GST are reviewed to determine what they say about the types of strain most likely to lead to crime. Third, the characteristics of those types of strain most likely to lead to crime are described. Briefly, such strains (1) are seen as unjust, (2) are seen as high in magnitude, (3) are associated with low social control, and (4) create some pressure or incentive to engage in crime. Fourth, these characteristics are then used to predict the likelihood that several types of strain will result in crime. Fifth, suggestions for empirical research are provided.

WHAT IS STRAIN?

Before discussing the types of strain most likely to lead to crime, it is first necessary to clarify what is meant by the term *strain*. Agnew (1992) stated that strain refers to "relationships in which others are not treating the individual as he or she would like to be treated" (p. 48). Even so, researchers use the term in different ways. Some refer to an objective event or condition (e.g., the infliction of physical abuse, the receipt of poor grades at school), some to the individual's evaluation of an event or condition (e.g., whether juveniles like the way their parents or teachers treat them), and some to the emotional reaction to an event or condition (e.g., whether respondents are angry at how others treat them). To help clarify the meaning of strain, the following definitions are proposed.

Objective strains refer to events or conditions that are disliked by most members of a given group. So, if we state that an individual is experiencing objective strain, we mean that he or she is experiencing an event or condition that is usually disliked by members of his or her group. Many events and conditions are disliked by most people, regardless of group membership (e.g., physical assault, lack of adequate food and shelter). The evaluation of other events and conditions varies with group characteristics, such as gender and age (e.g., Broidy and Agnew 1997; Elder, George, and Shanahan 1996). It is, of course, important for researchers to consider the possibility of such group differences when constructing measures of objective strain.

Empirically, it is possible to determine the objective strains for group members in several ways. Observational research is one method. Anderson (1999), for example, described many of the objective strains in a poor, inner-city, African American community. Surveying a representative sample of group members or people familiar with the group is another method, and both have been employed in the stress research (Turner and Wheaton 1995). In particular, respondents can be asked whether they (or group members) would dislike a range of events and conditions. It is important to present respondents with preestablished lists of events/conditions and to ask them to list events/conditions not on the list. This helps to ensure that a complete list of objective strains is developed.[1]

Subjective strains refer to events or conditions that are disliked by the people who are experiencing (or have experienced) them. So, if we state that individuals are experiencing subjective strain, we mean that they are experiencing an event or condition that *they* dislike. One of the key findings to emerge from the stress research is that individuals often differ in their subjective evaluation of the same objective strains. For example, people differ in how they subjectively evaluate such objective strains as divorce and the death of a family member. The subjective evaluation of an objective strain is a function of a range of factors, including individual traits (e.g., irritability), personal and social resources (e.g., self-esteem, self-efficacy, social support), goals/values/identities, and a range of life circumstances (for overviews, see Dohrenwend 1998; Kaplan 1996; Lazarus 1999). Wheaton (1990), for example, found that the quality of ones' prior marriage strongly influenced how people evaluated their divorce, with people in bad marriages evaluating their divorce in positive terms. It is also important to note that an individual's evaluation of an objective strain frequently changes over time as the individual copes with the strain. So, although there is a relationship between objective and subjective strain, it is far from perfect.

Most of the research on strain theory employs measures of objective strain (although see Agnew and White 1992). Researchers ask individuals whether they have experienced a certain event or condition (e.g., Did you fail any classes? Do your parents yell at you?); no effort is made to measure the individual's subjective evaluation of this event/condition. This may cause researchers to underestimate the support for strain theory because objective strains sometimes create little subjective strain. This does not mean, however, that researchers should simply employ subjective measures of strain. It is important to examine objective strains as well because this allows us to better distinguish external events from the subjective evaluation of such events. We can then examine individual and group differences in both the exposure to external events/conditions likely to cause strain and the subjective evaluation of those events/conditions. Furthermore, we can explore the factors that influence individual and group differences in the subjective evaluation of the same external events and conditions. This is critical if we are to fully explain individual and group differences in crime. As an illustration, Bernard (1990) argued that poor, inner-city residents have higher rates of violence not only because they experience more objective strains but also because they are more sensitive to such strains (also see Thoits 1995 on individual and group differences in the "vulnerability" to stressors).

The emotional response to an event or condition is closely linked to subjective strain. Subjective strain deals with the individual's evaluation of an event or condition. There are many definitions of emotion, but most state that a central component of an emotion is an evaluation of or an affective response to some object or behavior or idea. Most theorists, however, go on to state that emotions involve more than an evaluation or affective response. For example, they also involve changes in physiological or bodily sensations (see Berkowitz 1993; Smith-Lovin 1995; Thoits 1989). Building on this argument, I would contend that subjective strain is distinct from the full emotional reaction to strain.

Two individuals may evaluate an event/condition in the same way; that is, they may both dislike it an equal amount. So, they have the same level of subjective strain. One may become angry in response to the strain, however, whereas the other may become depressed. And they may differ in the degree to which they experience certain emotions, so one may become quite angry, whereas the other may experience only mild anger. So the same subjective strain may result in rather different emotional reactions. Again, a range of individual and environmental factors influences the emotional reaction to subjective strain. The potential utility of distinguishing between subjective strain and the emotional reaction to strain is highlighted by Broidy and Agnew (1997). They argued that males and females often differ in their emotional reaction to subjective strains. Although both males and females may experience anger, the anger of females is more likely to be accompanied by feelings of guilt, depression, and anxiety. These additional emotions are said to reduce the likelihood of other-directed crime, thereby helping us explain gender differences in such crime.

RESEARCH ON THE TYPES OF STRAIN MOST LIKELY TO LEAD TO CRIME AND DELINQUENCY

Agnew (1992) described those types of events and conditions most likely to be classified as objective strains and to result in subjective strain. Such events/conditions involve goal blockage, the loss of positive stimuli, and/or the presentation of negative stimuli. They are also high in magnitude (degree), recent, and of long duration. But as indicated earlier, hundreds of events/conditions meet these criteria, and so there are potentially hundreds of objective and subjective strains. Agnew did *not* discuss whether certain of these strains are more likely to result in crime than others. Rather, he treated these strains as more or less equivalent in terms of their impact on crime. He argued that whether they result in crime is largely a function of the characteristics of the individuals experiencing the strain. In particular, strain is most likely to lead to crime when individuals lack the skills and resources to cope with their strain in a legitimate manner, are low in conventional social support, are low in social control, blame their strain on others, and are disposed to crime. This article builds on Agnew by arguing that the effect of strain on crime is not only a function of individual characteristics but also of the type of strain experienced by the individual. Certain types of strain—either objective or subjective strain—are more likely to result in crime than other types.

Previous research on GST provides some information about the types of strain most likely to lead to crime, although much of this research suffers from two problems that severely limit its utility. First, most tests of GST only examine a small portion of the strains described by Agnew (1992). These tests tend to make use of existing data sets, which were not collected for the purpose of testing GST. As a consequence, many key strain measures are missing—particularly measures of the types of goal blockage described by Agnew and measures of certain types of negative treatment, like peer abuse and experiences with racial discrimination and prejudice. So we have little idea whether these types of strain are related to delinquency. Second, most tests of GST examine the effect of a single, cumulative strain measure on delinquency. In some cases, a measure of stressful life events is employed. Hoffmann and associates, for example, tested GST using a 16- to 18-item measure that focuses on events like "death, illness, or accidents among family or friends; changes in school or residence; parental divorce or separation; and family financial problems" (Hoffmann and Cerbone 1999; Hoffmann and Miller 1998; Hoffmann and Su 1997; also see Aseltine et al. 2000). In other cases, the cumulative strain measure is a composite of several scales and/or items measuring a range of different types of strain, such as neighborhood problems, negative relations with adults, the failure to achieve educational and occupational goals, breaking up with a romantic partner or friend, and getting lower grades than you deserve (e.g., Mazerolle 1998; Mazerolle et al. 2000; Mazerolle and Piquero 1997). The use of such cumulative measures means that we lack information on the effect of the individual strain measures.

Researchers employ cumulative measures of strain because Agnew (1992) argued that it is not the effect of one specific strain or stressor that is important; rather, it is the cumulative effect of all the strains experienced by the individual. He recommended combining individual strain measures into a single scale so as to better estimate this cumulative effect (pp. 62-63). It is assumed that all or most of the individual strain measures in the cumulative scale make some contribution to crime. As will be argued below, there is good reason to question this assumption. Most cumulative measures encompass a wide range of strains, and it is likely that some contribute to crime and some do not. Given this fact, it is not surprising that most cumulative measures have only a moderate impact on crime. A consideration of different types of strain, however, might reveal that some have a strong impact on crime, whereas others have little or no impact.

Some tests of GST do examine the impact of different types of strain on crime among adolescents. Agnew and White (1992) examined the effect of eight strain measures on delinquency, including both general and specific measures. They found that negative life events, life hassles, negative relations with adults, and parental fighting are significantly associated with delinquency. Neighborhood problems, unpopularity with the opposite sex, occupational strain, and clothing strain are not associated with delinquency. Paternoster and Mazerolle (1994) examined the effect of five strain measures on delinquency. They found that neighborhood problems, negative life events, school/peer hassles, and negative relations with adults are significantly associated with subsequent delinquency, whereas a measure of educational and occupational expectations is not (see Mazerolle 1998 for information on gender differences in the effect of these strain measures). Aseltine et al. (2000) found that family and peer conflict (through anger) are related to selected types of delinquency. Agnew and Brezina (1997) found that poor relations with peers is related to delinquency, whereas unpopularity with peers is not. Piquero and Sealock (2000) found that physical and emotional abuse in the household (toward the juvenile and others) is related to delinquency (also see Brezina 1999). Tests of classic strain theory typically find that the failure to achieve educational and occupational goals is *not* related to delinquency (see Agnew 1995a). The failure to achieve economic goals, however, may be related to delinquency (Burton and Dunaway 1994).

Many other studies have not set out to test GST but have examined types of strain that fall under the theory. Several studies found that adolescent crime is significantly related to criminal victimization; parental abuse and neglect; parental rejection; disciplinary techniques that are excessive, very strict, erratic, and/or punitive (e.g., nagging, yelling, threats, insults, and/or hitting); family conflict; parental divorce/separation; and negative experiences at school (low grades, poor relations with teachers, and the perception that school is boring and a waste of time). Summaries of these studies are provided in Agnew (1992, 1995b, 1997, 2001a, 2001b). Studies of adults suggest that crime is related to marital problems, work in the secondary labor market, unemployment in certain cases, and possibly the failure to achieve economic goals (Agnew et al. 1996; Baron and Hartnagel 1997; Cernkovich, Giordano, and Rudolph 2000; Colvin 2000; Crutchfield and Pitchford 1997; Sampson and Laub 1993; Uggen 2000). There has not been enough good research on other types of strain to draw any firm conclusions about their relationship to crime.

The above studies, then, suggested that certain types of strain are related to crime whereas others are not. At this point, it seems safe to conclude that crime is related to verbal and physical assaults, including assaults by parents, spouses/partners, teachers, and probably peers. Crime is also related to parental rejection, poor school performance, and work problems, including work in the secondary labor market. Crime is not related to the expected failure to achieve educational/occupational success or to unpopularity with peers. Beyond that, the relationship between various strains and crime is unclear.

These data pose a major problem for GST: Why is it that only some types of strain are related to crime? At present, GST offers little guidance in this area. GST, for example, does not allow us to explain why verbal and physical assaults are related to crime, but the failure to achieve educational/occupational goals and unpopularity with peers is not. All of these strains fall under the categories listed by Agnew (1992), and they are frequently high in magnitude (degree), recent, and of long duration.

Recent versions of GST do argue that certain types of strain are especially relevant to crime (Agnew and Brezina 1997; Broidy and Agnew 1997). Agnew (1997, 2001a, 2001b), for example, argued that although many types of goal blockage may lead to delinquency, the failure to achieve monetary, autonomy, and "masculinity" goals are of special importance. And he argued that although a range of negative or noxious stimuli may cause delinquency, physical and verbal assaults are of special importance. These suggestions, however, are not derived from theory. Rather, they represent ad hoc attempts to explain empirical findings or to incorporate other theoretical and empirical work into GST. Much theoretical and empirical work, for example, suggests that threats to one's status, particularly one's masculine status, contribute to crime in certain groups (Anderson 1999; Messerschmidt 1993). Likewise, some theoretical and empirical work suggests that the blockage of autonomy goals contributes to delinquency (Agnew 1984; Moffitt 1993; Tittle 1995).

And although empirical research is starting to point to those types of strain that are and are not related to delinquency, it is not wise to depend on such research to fully resolve this issue. There are hundreds of specific types of strain; it will take empirical researchers a long while to determine their relative importance (although observational research and open-ended, intensive interviews can be of some help here). Furthermore, we would still lack an explanation of why some types of strain have a greater effect on crime than other types. The lack of such an explanation might cause us to overlook certain important types of strain. It is therefore important for GST to better explain why some types of strain are more likely to lead to crime than other types.

THE CHARACTERISTICS OF THOSE TYPES OF STRAIN MOST LIKELY TO LEAD TO CRIME

Individuals may cope with strain in a number of ways, only some of which involve crime (see Agnew 1992). Individuals may cope using a variety of cognitive strategies, most of which attempt to redefine strainful events and conditions in ways that minimize their adversity. Individuals may employ behavioral coping strategies that are intended to terminate, reduce, or escape from the strainful events and conditions. Certain of these strategies involve conventional behaviors (e.g., negotiating with the people who harass you), whereas others involve crime (e.g., assaulting the people who harass you). And they may employ emotional coping strategies that are intended to alleviate the negative emotions that result from strain. Certain of these strategies involve conventional actions (e.g., listening to music), whereas others involve crime (e.g., illicit drug use). It is argued here that some types of strain are more likely to result in crime than other types because they influence the ability to cope in a noncriminal versus criminal manner, the perceived costs of noncriminal versus criminal coping, and the disposition for noncriminal versus criminal coping. (As indicated above, these factors are also affected by a range of individual characteristics.)

The characteristics of those types of strain most likely to result in crime are discussed in this section, with the discussion referring to both objective and subjective strains. In brief, it is argued that strains are most likely to result in crime when they (1) are seen as unjust, (2) are seen as high in magnitude, (3) are associated with low social control, and (4) create some pressure or incentive to engage in criminal coping. These characteristics are derived primarily from the stress, justice, and emotions literatures (see references below); the social interactionist theory of coercive behavior (Tedeschi and Felson 1994); defiance theory (Sherman 1993); reintegrative-shaming theory (Briathwaite 1989); frustration-aggression theory (Berkowitz 1993); techniques of neutralization or moral disengagement theory (Bandura 1990; Sykes and Matza 1957); differential coercion theory (Colvin 2000); social control theory; social-learning theory; and the routine activities perspective (Cullen and Agnew 1999). There is a discussion of why these characteristics are important and how researchers can determine whether specific types of strain possess these characteristics. In the next section, these characteristics are used to predict the likelihood that several specific types of strain will result in crime.

The Strain Is Seen as Unjust

Agnew (1992) presented unjust treatment as a distinct category of strain, classified under "the failure to achieve positively-valued goals." In particular, Agnew spoke of the disjunction between just/fair outcomes and actual outcomes. It is here argued that unjust treatment is *not* a special type of strain distinct from the other types. The issue of injustice applies to all types of strain; that is, it is possible to classify any type of strain according to the extent to which it is seen as unjust. Those types of strain seen as unjust should be more likely to lead to crime, primarily because they are more likely to provoke emotions conducive to crime like anger.

Much data from the emotions and justice literatures indicate that there is a strong link between unjust treatment and anger (see Agnew 1992, 68-69; Averill 1982, 1993; Berkowitz 1993; Hegtvedt and Cook forthcoming; Hegtvedt and Markovsky 1995; Mikula 1986; Mikula, Petri, and Tanzer 1990; Tedeschi and Felson 1994; Tedeschi and Nesler 1993; Tyler 1994; Tyler et al. 1997). And limited data suggest that anger increases the likelihood of crime, particularly violent crime (Agnew 1985; Aseltine et al. 2000; Berkowitz 1993; Brezina 1998; Mazerolle et al. 2000; Mazerolle and Piquero 1998; Piquero and Sealock 2000; Tedeschi and Felson 1994; Tyler et al. 1997). Anger fosters crime because it disrupts cognitive processes in ways that impede noncriminal coping; for example, it leads individuals to disregard information that may help resolve the situation, and it reduces the ability to clearly express grievances. Anger also reduces the actual and perceived costs of crime; for example, angry individuals are less likely to feel guilt for their criminal behavior because they believe that the injustice they suffered justifies crime. Finally, anger energizes the individual for action, creates a sense of power or control, and creates a desire for revenge or retribution—all of which lead individuals to view crime in a more favorable light (see Agnew

328 JOURNAL OF RESEARCH IN CRIME AND DELINQUENCY

1992; Averill 1982, 1993; Cloward and Ohlin 1960; Gottfredson and Hirschi 1990; Tedeschi and Felson 1994; Tedeschi and Nesler 1993; see Tyler et al. 1997 on retributive justice).

Measuring injustice. There are several ways to measure the perceived injustice of particular strains. The perceived injustice of objective strains can be estimated by (1) researchers, with such researchers drawing on the justice and attributions literature (see below) and their knowledge of the group being examined; (2) a panel of judges familiar with the group being examined, with such judges being asked to estimate the likelihood that various strains will be seen as unjust by group members; and/or (3) a representative sample of group members, with such members being asked to rate the injustice of various strains (see Mikula 1993; Mikula et al. 1990). The ratings of judges and group members can be averaged. It is best to provide judges and group members with moderately specific descriptions of the strains being rated because the specific features of the strain can have a large impact on ratings of injustice (see below). For example, instead of asking individuals to rate the injustice of "a close friend dying," it is better to ask them to rate the injustice of "a close friend being shot to death by a rival gang." Data suggest that raters tend to underestimate the extent to which victims perceive the strains they experience as unjust (see Mikula 1986), so these measurement strategies will likely provide conservative estimates of perceived injustice.

The perceived injustice of subjective strains can be estimated by asking victims to rate the injustice of the strains they have experienced. Such ratings will reflect both the characteristics of the strains and the characteristics of the victims. Most notably, victims with attributional biases of the type described by Dodge and Schwartz (1997) will be more likely to rate given strains as unjust. Studies focusing on subjective strains should therefore control for relevant individual characteristics when examining the effect of the perceived injustice of strain on crime (see Herbert and Cohen 1996; Turner and Wheaton 1995).[2]

Factors influencing perceptions of injustice. It is important for GST to describe why some strains are more likely to be perceived as unjust than others. This allows researchers to better explain individual and group differences in perceptions of injustice, better predict whether given strains will be seen as unjust, and better develop policies that address perceptions of injustice. Several literatures devote much attention to the factors influencing perceptions of injustice, with the justice and attributions literature being most relevant (for overviews, see Crittenden 1983, 1989; Hegtvedt and Cook forthcoming; Hegtvedt and Markovsky 1995; Mikula 1986, 1993; Tedeschi and Felson 1994; Tedeschi and Nesler 1993; Tyler 1990; Tyler et al. 1997).

These literatures suggest that a strainful event or condition is most likely to be seen as unjust when individuals believe that it involves *the voluntary and intentional violation of a relevant justice norm*. This belief is influenced by a range of individual characteristics, most of which are described in the justice and attributions literature *and* by the nature of the strainful event or condition. Most strainful events and conditions involve a perpetrator who does something to a victim in a particular setting or collection of settings. The likelihood that a strainful event will be seen as unjust partly depends on the characteristics of the perpetrator and victim, what the perpetrator does to the victim, what the victim does to the perpetrator, the relationship between the perpetrator and victim, and the setting(s) in which the strain occurs. Perceptions of injustice are also influenced by the interpretation of the event/condition provided by others, especially trusted others, and by (sub)cultural beliefs associated with the event/condition. The contribution of these factors is described below, with the central point being that some strainful events and conditions are more likely than others to be perceived as unjust—holding individual characteristics constant.

Voluntary/intentional. Strainful events and conditions are most likely to be attributed to the voluntary, intentional behavior of others when the following occurs:

1. There is good evidence that the victim's strain was in large measure caused by the behavior of others (as opposed to being caused by the victim's own behavior, bad luck or chance, natural/impersonal forces, or forces of uncertain origin). Such evidence includes the following: A perpetrator directly inflicts the strain on the victim (e.g., punches or insults the victim), a perpetrator is identified by trusted others, and/or (sub)cultural beliefs attribute the victim's strain to the behavior of others.
2. There is good evidence that the perpetrator voluntarily intended to inflict the strain (i.e., freely chose to treat the victim in a way that they knew would probably be disliked). Conversely, there is little evidence that the behavior of the perpetrator was the result of constraint, reasonable accident, or reasonable ignorance. Such evidence includes the following:

   Behavior of the perpetrator. The perpetrator states his or her intention to inflict strain, as sometimes happens in cases involving physical and verbal assault. The perpetrator devotes much effort to or incurs high costs in inflicting the strain. The perpetrator violates normative expectations in inflicting strain. The perpetrator does not excuse, apologize for, or express remorse over the harm he or she has caused. Conversely, the perpetrator expresses pleasure or pride over his behavior (see Averill 1993; Tedeschi and Felson 1994; Tedeschi and Nesler 1993).

Severity of harm. Attributions of intent are more likely the greater the actual or intended harm to the victim (see Tedeschi and Felson 1994; Tedeschi and Nesler 1993).

Characteristics of the perpetrator and the relationship between the perpetrator and victim. The perpetrator has the personal and social resources to voluntarily and intentionally inflict the strain (e.g., has sufficient power, is aware of the harmful consequences of his or her behavior). The perpetrator has a known history of intentionally harming the victim or others. The perpetrator is disliked by the victim or has a negative reputation, making attributions of malicious intent more likely. This dislike/negative reputation may be related to the characteristics of the perpetrator (e.g., race, gang membership; see Tedeschi and Felson 1994; Tedeschi and Nesler 1993).

Audience reaction. Others, especially trusted others, tell the victim that the harm inflicted by the perpetrator was intentional.

(Sub)cultural beliefs or causal schema. (Sub)cultural beliefs or causal schema define the strainful event or condition as one that is usually the result of intent.

Criterion 1 is necessary for attributions of intent, and the factors under criterion 2—although not necessary—substantially increase the likelihood of attributions of intent.[3]

The violation of relevant justice rules. Voluntary and intentional efforts to inflict strain are not necessarily seen as unjust. For example, parents, teachers, employers, and the police voluntarily and intentionally inflict strain on a routine basis, but the victims of such strain often do not view the actions of these others as unjust. The intentional infliction of strain is most likely to be seen as unjust when it is believed to violate a relevant justice norm. We must consider norms related to distributive, procedural, interactional, and retributive justice (for overviews, see Hegtvedt and Markovsky 1995: Mikula 1993; Mikula et al. 1990; Tedeschi and Felson 1994; Tyler et al. 1997).[4] Drawing on the justice literature, as well as the related literature on the techniques of neutralization/rules of moral disengagement (Bandura 1990; Sykes and Matza 1957), it can be argued that the voluntary and intentional infliction of strain is likely to be seen as unjust to the extent that

A. Victims believe their strain is *undeserved*. In the United States, victims are more likely to believe that their strain is deserved if it is the result of negatively valued behavior on their part (e.g., a child is punished for misbehaving) or if it is the result of the possession of certain negatively evaluated characteristics—usually achieved characteristics—deemed relevant in the particular situation (e.g., a job applicant gets turned down because he or she does not possess relevant work experience). Furthermore, the strain must not be excessive given the negatively evaluated behavior or characteristics of the victim. Violations of these conditions foster the impression that strain is undeserved.

B. Victims believe their strain is *not in the service of a higher cause or authority*—such as God, country, or gang. The infliction of strain is often justified by appeals to higher purposes or authorities; for example, nations may ask individuals to serve in combat to protect their country or gangs may ask members to risk injury for the protection of "turf."

C. Victims believe their strain *will result in much net harm to them.* The infliction of strain is often justified by claiming that the strain was minor or negligible—in absolute and/or relative terms. Victims, for example, may be told that they suffered little actual harm or that they suffered much less harm than similar others. Perpetrators may also justify the strain they inflict by claiming that victims will achieve a net benefit from it. Parents, for example, may claim that they need to limit the autonomy of their children to protect them from greater harm. Such claims are most likely to be made and accepted in settings in which personal welfare and development are major goals.

D. Victims believe that the *process used to decide whether to inflict their strain was unjust.* Victims are more likely to make attributions of procedural injustice when (1) they have no voice in the decision to inflict their strain, (2) they do not accord legitimacy to those who inflict their strain, (3) they do not trust those who inflict their strain—believing they are biased or dishonest, (4) they believe that those inflicting their strain do not make use of accurate or complete information, (5) they believe that different procedures are followed for similar others, (6) they are not treated in a polite or respectful manner, (7) the decision-making process is incompatible with fundamental moral and ethical values, (8) no rationale is given for the decision that was made, and/or (9) there are no mechanisms available to correct bad decisions.

E. The strain involves treatment perceived as disrespectful, inconsiderate, or aggressive.

F. The strain violates strongly held social norms, especially those embodied in certain criminal laws (see Tyler et al. 1997).

Perceptions of injustice are likely if criteria A, B, *and* C are satisfied (having to do with distributive justice); criterion D is satisfied (procedural justice); criterion E is satisfied (interactional justice); *and/or* criterion F is satisfied (retributive justice). The characteristics of the strainful event/condition often allow us to roughly judge the likelihood that victims will hold the beliefs listed in criteria A through E. For example, a criminal victimization is more likely to generate the beliefs outlined above than is the failure of a poorly educated person to obtain a highly paid job. In addition, the justice literature suggests that we pay special attention to the following factors when trying to estimate the likelihood that individuals hold the above beliefs (e.g., believe their strain is undeserved or involves disrespectful treatment):

1. Do (sub)cultural beliefs define the strain as just or as unjust for one or more of the reasons listed in A through F? Laws defining the strainful treatment as illegal are especially relevant, particularly when the treatment involves the violation of criminal laws with severe penalties.
2. Do others, especially trusted others, support or hinder the adoption of the above beliefs (e.g., tell the victim that their negative treatment is undeserved or disrespectful)? The actions of family and friends, audience members who witness the negative treatment, and the perpetrator of the negative treatment are especially important. For example, victims are less likely to adopt the above beliefs if the perpetrator is a trusted other who offers a convincing justification for their behavior (see Crittenden 1989).
3. Is the victims's negative treatment very different from their past treatment in similar circumstances and/or from the treatment of similar others? Comparisons to past treatment and to the treatment of similar others are especially important in situations in which there are no strong standards defining what is just or fair. Comparison others may include specific others, groups, or more generalized others or "referential structures" (see Hegtvedt and Markovsky 1995). Unfortunately, it is often difficult to predict the comparison others that are selected and the nature of the comparison process—although some progress is being made in this area (see Hegtvedt and Cook forthcoming).

The Strain Is Seen as High in Magnitude

A second factor influencing the likelihood that strainful events and conditions will lead to crime is the perceived magnitude of the strain. Strain that is high in magnitude influences the ability to cope in a noncriminal manner, the perceived costs of noncriminal versus criminal coping, and the disposition to engage in criminal coping. It is more difficult to cognitively minimize the impact of severe strain, emotional coping techniques of a noncriminal nature may be less effective, and behavioral coping of a noncriminal nature may be more difficult (e.g., it is more difficult to legally cope with a large rather than small financial problem). Furthermore, not only is it more difficult to legally cope with severe strain, but such strain often reduces the ability to cope. For example, the victims of severe strain are more likely to suffer from depression, which impedes their ability to cope. Finally, severe strain generates more anger and so also influences the perceived costs of crime and the disposition to engage in crime.

Measuring magnitude. The magnitude of *objective* strains can be estimated by (1) researchers, with such researchers taking account of the factors listed below; (2) a panel of judges familiar with the group, with these judges being asked to estimate the extent to which various strains are likely to be disliked (or seen as undesirable, harmful/threatening, etc.); and/or (3) a representative sample of group members, with such members being asked to rate the extent to which they dislike various strains. Again, it is best to provide individuals with specific information about the strains being rated.

The magnitude of *subjective* strains can be estimated by asking victims to rate the extent to which they dislike the strains they have experienced. These ratings will reflect both the characteristics of the strains and the characteristics of the victims. In particular, the same strainful event/condition might be seen as high in magnitude by one victim but low by another—depending on such things as the victim's goals/activities/identities, coping ability and resources, and level of social support (see Cohen et al. 1995; Kessler et al. 1995; Lazarus 1999; Taylor and Aspinwall 1996; Thoits 1995; Wheaton 1996). Studies focusing on subjective strains should therefore control for relevant individual characteristics when examining the effect of the perceived magnitude of strain on crime (see Herbert and Cohen 1996 and Turner and Wheaton 1995 for a fuller discussion).

Factors influencing perceptions of magnitude. Drawing on Agnew (1992) and the stress literature, there is reason to believe that several features of the strainful event/condition influence perceptions of magnitude. These include the degree or amount of strain inflicted; the duration and frequency of the strain, including the expected duration into the future; the recency of the strain; and the centrality of the strain, which refers to the extent to which the strain threatens the core goals, needs, values, activities, and/or identities of the victim. At present, it is unclear how these factors combine to influence overall judgments of magnitude.

Degree of strain. The degree or amount of strain inflicted influences judgments of magnitude. As Agnew (1992) pointed out, it is sometimes possible to measure the degree of strain inflicted in terms of a standard metric, like the severity of the physical injuries inflicted or the amount of money lost. This is not possible for many types of strain, however. Furthermore, the metrics used to measure the degree of strain vary from one type of strain to another, making it difficult to make comparisons across types of strain. These problems can be dealt with using techniques from the stress research. Individuals can rate the degree or amount of strain inflicted for different types of strain using a common scale. Such ratings likely reflect the objective characteristics of the strain (e.g., amount of money lost, injury inflicted), (sub)cultural beliefs regarding the degree of strain (e.g., beliefs regarding what is a small versus large financial loss, a minor versus serious insult), audience reactions to the strain (where applicable), and individual characteristics (especially when dealing with subjective strains).

Duration/frequency of strain. The duration and frequency of strain are also likely to influence the perceived magnitude of strain. As Agnew (1992) pointed out, data suggest that strains of long duration (chronic stressors) and/or high frequency have a greater negative impact on the individual (also see Lepore 1995; Turner and Wheaton 1995). Furthermore, data from the stress literature suggest that unresolved strains have a much greater impact on the individual than resolved strains (Herbert and Cohen 1996; Turner and Avison 1992). It is therefore important to determine whether the strain has been resolved. If the strain has not been resolved, it is also important to estimate its expected duration. That is, will the strain be resolved shortly or continue for some time, perhaps increasing in frequency and/or degree? The importance of estimating the expected duration of strain is illustrated in the work of Anderson (1999). As Anderson emphasized, seemingly trivial strains like a negative remark or a stare often generate much distress among inner-city residents, partly because they signal future conflicts of a more serious nature.

Recency. As Agnew (1992) noted, the impact of strains or stressors dissipates over time. Therefore, recent strains should have a larger impact on judgments of magnitude than older strains. At the same time, it is important to note that severe childhood strains may sometimes contribute to later criminal behavior (Elder et al. 1996; Kessler et al. 1995, 1997; Widom 1998).

Centrality of strain. Two individuals might be similar to one another in the degree, duration/frequency, and recency of their strain; yet they may differ dramatically in the perceived magnitude of their strain. One reason for this has to do with the centrality of the strain: Does the strain threaten the core goals, needs, values, activities, and/or identities of the individual? For example, two individuals may perceive the same monetary loss differently because they differ in the value they place on money.

Centrality is conceived of in different ways depending on the researcher and/or research tradition. Classic strain theorists, frustration-aggression theorists, and certain stress researchers focus on the importance of the goals, needs, or terminal values that are blocked or threatened (Berkowitz 1993; Cloward and Ohlin 1960; Cohen 1955; Dohrenwend 2000; Kaplan 1996; Lazarus 1999; Merton 1938; Wethington, Brown, and Kessler 1995). Certain stress researchers focus on the extent to which the strain leads to change (or negative change) in the usual or core activities of daily life (e.g., Dohrenwend 1998; Wheaton 1996). Still others—including strain, stress, social interactionist, and identity theorists—focus on the extent to which strains threaten the core identities of individuals or threaten efforts to establish positive identities (e.g., Berkowitz 1993; Burke 1996; Cohen 1997; Kaplan 1996;

Tedeschi and Felson 1994; Thoits 1991; Tyler 1994; Tyler et al. 1997; Wheaton 1996). These perspectives overlap to a large degree (see Burke 1996; Dohrenwend 1998; Kaplan 1996). For example, one's core identities are in large measure defined in terms of one's goals, values, and activities. In any event, GST can accommodate all these perspectives: Strain is central to the extent that it threatens core goals, needs, values, activities, and/or identities.

Judgments regarding the centrality of strain are partly influenced by the characteristics of the strain. For example, certain strainful events/conditions are such that they threaten a broad range of goals, values, needs, identities, and activities, so they are likely to be high in centrality for the overwhelming majority of people who experience them. Examples include "extreme stressors" (Dohrenwend 1998, 2000) and "traumatic events" (Wheaton, Roszell, and Hall 1997). As Dohrenwend (2000) stated, extreme stressors are such that "all usual activities are disrupted and all of the individual's goals are in jeopardy" (p. 8). Judgments regarding centrality are also influenced by the (sub)cultural beliefs associated with the strainful event/condition and how the event/condition is interpreted by others (e.g., whether audience members define an insult as trivial or a serious challenge to one's manhood).

The Strain Is Caused by or Associated with Low Social Control

A third factor affecting the likelihood that strain will lead to crime is the level of social control associated with the strain. Certain strains are caused by or associated with low social control, such as the strain caused by erratic parental discipline (low direct control), parental rejection (low attachment), work in the secondary labor market (low commitment), or homelessness (low direct control, attachment, and commitment). Such strains are more likely to result in crime because the low social control associated with them reduces the costs of crime. Also, low social control may reduce the ability to cope in a noncriminal manner. Individuals low in direct control, conventional attachments, and conventional commitments generally lack the social supports and resources that facilitate noncriminal coping.

Conversely, certain strains stem from or are associated with high social control. For example, much adolescent strain stems from the efforts of parents to supervise their children (direct control), much parental strain stems from the demands associated with childcare (attachment), and much occupational strain stems from the long working hours and difficult tasks associated with many professional/business jobs (commitment). Such strains are less likely to result in crime because the high social control associated with them increases the costs of crime. High social control may also increase the ability to cope in a noncriminal manner. High control is frequently associated with the provision of social support and the possession of personal and financial resources that facilitate noncriminal coping.

An excellent illustration of the association between strain and social control is provided in Hirschi's (1969) and Kornhauser's (1978) discussion of classic strain theory. Classic strain theorists focus on one type of strain: the inability to achieve conventional success goals—like educational and occupational success—through legitimate channels. Hirschi and Kornhauser argued that the pursuit of such goals implies some level of social control. As Kornhauser stated,

> if the child is sufficiently socialized to have a strong desire for conventional goals, he should be well enough socialized also to have the internalized values governing the conventional means of achieving them. . . . He should also be strongly enough attached to conventional persons and institutions to resist the temptation to use nonnormative means. (P. 47)

The pursuit of conventional success goals therefore implies at least moderately high levels of attachment, commitment, and belief (in conventional norms). And this may explain why the inability to achieve educational and occupational goals is unrelated to crime in most studies (Agnew 1995a).

Measuring social control. Researchers should estimate the extent to which the type of strain being examined is associated with (1) supervision or direct control by conventional others, (2) attachment to conventional others, (3) commitment to conventional institutions, and (4) the acceptance of conventional beliefs, especially beliefs condemning crime. This is easily done in certain cases; for example, the strain being examined stems from or is associated with employment in prestigious, well-paid jobs that indicate a strong commitment to conventional society. In other cases, researchers can employ observational or survey research to determine the association between strain and social control. For example, survey data can be used to determine whether individuals who desire educational and occupational success are high in such types of social control as attachment to conventional others and beliefs condemning crime.

The Strain Creates Some Pressure or
Incentive to Engage in Criminal Coping

A final factor affecting the likelihood that strain will lead to crime is the extent to which the strain creates some pressure or incentive to engage in criminal coping. Drawing on social-learning and routine activities theories, it can be argued that the type of strain experienced influences the availability and appeal of noncriminal and criminal coping options—thereby affecting the pressure/incentive to engage in crime. Certain types of strain are associated with exposure to others who model crime, reinforce crime, and/or present beliefs favorable to crime (e.g., child abuse, being bullied by peers). More directly, certain types of strain are associated with exposure to others who model criminal coping to that type of strain and present beliefs favorable to criminal coping *to that type of strain*. Furthermore, criminal coping may be the only or the most effective way to address the perceived injustice and reduce the perceived magnitude of that type of strain (see Brezina 2000). Anderson's (1999) discussion of life in a poor, inner-city community provides an example.

Anderson (1999) argued that young males in this community are under much pressure to respond to one type of strain—disrespectful treatment— with violence. The perpetrators of disrespectful treatment and others in the community frequently model and present beliefs favorable to criminal coping. And violence is often the only effective way to respond to disrespectful treatment. Efforts to ignore disrespectful treatment or reason with the perpetrators of such treatment often result in further abuse—by both the perpetrator and others in the community. Victims cannot rely on the police or others to intervene on their behalf (also see Black 1983). And the efforts of victims to cognitively reinterpret their strain or engage in emotional coping are also ineffective. The perpetrators of the strain typically escalate their level of abuse, others regularly remind the victim of the disrespectful treatment they have experienced, and subcultural beliefs define such treatment as unjust and high in magnitude. Cognitive reinterpretation is therefore difficult. Violent coping, however, reduces feelings of injustice, reduces the likelihood of further disrespectful treatment, and allows the victim to protect or enhance their identity/status.

Measuring the pressure or incentive for criminal coping. Researchers should consider the following factors when determining whether a particular instance of strain creates some pressure or incentive for criminal coping.

1. Does the strain stem from or is it associated with exposure to others who model, reinforce, and/or present beliefs favorable to crime?
2. What behavioral options of a noncriminal and criminal nature are available to members of the group experiencing the strain in question? Are these options frequently modeled by others? Do they have (sub)cultural support? How effective will these options be in reducing the perceived injustice and magnitude of the strain?
3. What cognitive options of a noncriminal criminal nature are available to members of the group experiencing the strain? Efforts to cognitively cope with

strain usually involve attempts to minimize the injustice, degree, duration/frequency, recency, and/or centrality of the strain. It is more difficult to cognitively minimize the injustice and/or magnitude of some types of strain than others. In particular, minimization is more difficult when (1) the victim receives clear and frequent information on the injustice and magnitude of their strain, with this information coming from such sources as trusted others, witnesses to the strainful event or condition, and members of the community; (2) (sub)cultural beliefs define the strain as unjust and high in magnitude; (3) there is strong (sub)cultural and structural support for the goals, needs, values, activities, and/or identities being challenged; and (4) the strain is unresolved, perhaps increasing in frequency and/or degree.

Information in the above areas can be obtained from observational studies, intensive interviews, and surveys.

CLASSIFYING TYPES OF STRAIN ACCORDING TO THEIR LIKELIHOOD OF LEADING TO CRIME

In sum, strainful events and conditions are most likely to lead to crime when they (1) are seen as unjust, (2) are seen as high in magnitude, (3) are associated with low social control, and (4) create some pressure or incentive for criminal coping. At present, I would argue that all four of these characteristics are roughly equal in importance and that the absence of any one characteristic substantially reduces the likelihood that strain will result in crime—unless the strain is seen as extraordinarily unjust and high in magnitude (see below). These characteristics are next used to predict the relative likelihood that different types of strain will result in crime. Drawing on the existing research where possible, I roughly estimate the likelihood that these strains are seen as unjust, are seen as high in magnitude, are associated with low social control, and create some pressure or incentive for criminal coping. It would of course be desirable to verify my judgments using the research strategies described above.

It is not possible in this short article to make predictions for all types of strain. Instead, I consider several broad types of strain. These types of strain were selected for several reasons: They encompass many of the major types of strain that people face—including family, peer, school, and work-related strains; they include most of the strains examined in tests of classic and GST, as well as certain strains neglected by empirical researchers; and most of these strains can be examined with currently available data sets. The focus on broad types of strain, however, does reduce the accuracy of the predictions. As indicated, it is more difficult to classify broadly defined types of strain on the above characteristics. For example, it is difficult to predict whether unemployment will be related to crime. As many researchers argue, the relationship between unemployment and crime depends on the circumstances associated with the unemployment. Limited evidence suggests that unemployment is most likely to lead to crime when it is persistent (i.e., high in magnitude) and blamed on others (i.e., seen as unjust) (see Baron and Hartnagel 1997; Box 1987; Colvin 2000; Hagan and McCarthy 1997; Uggen 2000). As a result, the strains below are simply sorted into two groups: those predicted to be unrelated or weakly related to crime and those predicted to be more strongly related to crime.

Types of Strain Unrelated or Weakly Related to Crime

The first condition (strain seen as unjust) allows us to predict that a wide range of strains will be unrelated to crime. At the most general level, these include those types of strain that are clearly the result of reasonable accident or chance, reasonable ignorance, reasonable constraint, the victim's own behavior, or natural causes like extreme weather and disease (as opposed to those types of strain resulting from the voluntary and intentional violation of justice norms). Many of the strains commonly included in the stressful life events scales used to test GST likely fall into this category, like accident, serious illness or injury, serious illness or injury of brother or sister, brother or sister leaving home for college or a job, and family member dying.

The second condition (strain seen as high in magnitude) allows us to predict that strains that are low in magnitude will be unrelated to crime. Certain types of strain are more likely to be seen as low in magnitude than other types. For example, those strains that threaten peripheral goals are more likely to be seen as low in magnitude than those that threaten core goals. There are data ranking the importance of various goals in the United States as a whole and among certain groups (e.g., Rokeach 1973). Such data can be used as a guide in predicting the likelihood that specific strains will be seen as low or high in magnitude (more below). At the same time, it is important to note that many seemingly serious strains—like the death of a family member—may be perceived as low or high in magnitude depending on the circumstances (see Wethington et al. 1995; Wheaton 1990). So, it is important for researchers to estimate the magnitude of the strains they are examining, something that is rarely done in the criminology research.

Considerations of injustice and magnitude—as well the third and fourth conditions (the strain is associated with low social control and creates some pressure or incentive for criminal coping)—allow us to predict that several other types of strain will not be related to crime. These include types of strain that have dominated the research on strain theory.

The failure to achieve those goals that result from conventional socialization and that are difficult to achieve through illegitimate channels. These goals include educational success, occupational success, and middle-class status. Although the inability to achieve these goals may result in strain of high magnitude, such strain is unlikely to be seen as unjust. Among other things, the failure to achieve such goals is typically blamed on the victim. As Merton (1968) stated, the cultural system in the United States conveys the message that "success or failure are wholly results of personal qualities; that he who fails has only himself to blame" (p. 222; also see Merton 1968:191, 201-03). And much research on the legitimation of stratification suggests that people tend to accept responsibility for their place in the stratification system (see Agnew 1992; Hegtvedt and Markovsky 1995; see below for the argument that minority-group members in the United States may sometimes blame others for their failure to achieve conventional success goals). Furthermore, as argued above, the pursuit of conventional success goals implies some level of social control. Finally, the inability to achieve these goals is not likely to create strong pressure for criminal coping. In particular, these goals are not easily achieved through criminal means, like theft and violence. In fact, criminal behavior may undermine the achievement of these goals. Therefore, criminal coping is not likely to be reinforced. These arguments may help explain why empirical research typically finds that crime is unrelated to the disjunction between educational and/or occupational aspirations and expectations (see Agnew 1995a for an overview; Jensen 1995).[5]

Supervision/discipline by parents, teachers, criminal justice officials, and other conventional authority figures that is (1) not overly strict, (2) consistent, (3) contingent on negative behavior, (4) not excessive given the infraction, and (5) not verbally or physically abusive. Such supervision/discipline may generate much strain (e.g., juveniles being grounded, offenders being arrested and sent to prison). But this strain is not likely to be seen as unjust because it is deserved, is administered in a fair way by legitimate authority figures, and is not aggressive or disrespectful. Furthermore, such supervision/discipline creates a high level of direct control and reduces the likelihood of association with delinquent others. Much data demonstrate that parental and school supervision/discipline of the above type is associated with lower levels of delinquency (Agnew 2001b; Sampson and Laub 1993). And some data suggest that this may be true for supervision/discipline by criminal justice officials as well (Lanza-Kaduce and Radosevich 1987; Sherman 1993, 2000; Tyler 1990).

The burdens associated with the care of conventional others to whom one likely has a strong attachment, like children and sick/disabled spouses. Although such care may create great strain, it is not likely to be viewed as unjust. There is a strong cultural expectation that one is supposed to care for children and sick/disabled spouses, an expectation likely to be supported by others in the person's network. In fact, one is usually labeled a bad parent or spouse if such care is not provided. This type of strain implies at least a moderate level of social control: the "victim" may be closely supervised by others inside and outside the family, the victim likely has a strong emotional bond to conventional others, and cultural beliefs strongly support the provision of adequate care. This type of strain also does not create much pressure or incentive for most forms of criminal coping. Caregivers have little opportunity to engage in crime, except for family violence, neglect, certain types of illicit drug use, and possibly shoplifting. Crime is not an effective solution to this type of strain. And the burdens associated with care giving limit association with criminal others.

The impact of this type of strain on crime has not been well examined. Data from the stress literature, however, indicate that females are more likely than males to experience this type of strain (see Broidy and Agnew 1997). This may partly explain gender differences in crime. It may also help explain why such differences are smallest for the crimes of family violence, larceny, and certain types of illicit drug use, such as the misuse of prescription drugs.

The excessive demands associated with conventional pursuits that provide rewards like high pay, prestige, and/or intrinsic satisfaction (or that have a strong likelihood of providing access to such rewards in the future). The prime examples of such pursuits are work in prestigious and/or well-paid jobs (or work in the primary labor market) and attending college. Excessive demands include long working (or studying) hours and work on difficult tasks. Such strain may be seen as high in magnitude, but it is not likely to be seen as unjust. The voluntary or quasi-voluntary nature of these conventional pursuits contributes to self-blame, and the victims of such strain may feel that the excessive demands made on them are justified or offset by the rewards they receive. Such strain is frequently caused by or associated with high social control, including commitment to conventional activities (e.g., one's job or educational pursuits) and supervision (i.e., much time is spent on structured tasks that are closely monitored). And such strain does not create pressure or incentives for criminal coping. The excessive demands limit the opportunity for association with criminal others. Furthermore, crime is typically not an effective solution to such demands (with the exception of cheating and certain types of white-collar crime). This type of strain has not been well examined, although we do know that time spent studying is negatively related to crime (Agnew 2001b; Hirschi 1969).

Unpopularity with or isolation from peers, especially criminal peers. Such strain may be high in magnitude and may also be seen as unjust. In particular, individuals may blame their unpopularity/isolation on peers who unfairly reject them or on parents who unfairly limit their social life. Such strain, however, may contribute to an increase in social control by increasing time spent with parents or other conventional figures. Also, such strain does not create much pressure or incentive for crime. Little time is spent with peers who may reinforce crime, model crime, and foster beliefs conducive to crime. And related to this, there are fewer opportunities for crime. Data support this prediction: Crime is less common among juveniles who report that they are unpopular with peers, have few close friends, have few delinquent friends, never or seldom date, or seldom engage in unsupervised social activities with peers (Agnew 2001b; Agnew and Brezina 1997; Agnew and Petersen 1989; Osgood et al. 1996).

Isolation from those situations or environments conducive to crime. Such strain is closely related to strain from unpopularity or isolation from peers because these situations/environments are typically settings where unsupervised peers gather. Likewise, this type of strain often stems from peer rejection and the efforts of parents to supervise their children (e.g., setting curfews, prohibiting attendance at parties). This type of strain is unlikely to lead to crime for the reasons indicated in the previous paragraph. Data support this prediction (Agnew 2001b; Agnew and Petersen 1989; Osgood et al. 1996). And the fact that females are more likely to experience this type of strain than males may help explain gender differences in crime (Broidy and Agnew 1997; Jensen and Brownfield 1986; Osgood et al. 1996).

Extreme instances of the above types of strain. Certain of the above types of strain may lead to crime in extreme cases. Extraordinary demands at work or school and extraordinary demands for the care of conventional others may be viewed as unjust because they are far outside the range of past experience or the experience of similar others, they may severely tax efforts at conventional coping, and they may eventually undermine conventional attachments and commitments. As such, these extraordinary demands may lead to crime. This argument finds indirect support in the work of Wells and Rankin (1988), who found a curvilinear relationship between parental supervision and delinquency. Increases in parental supervision up to a point reduce delinquency, but very strict supervision increases delinquency.

Types of Strain More Strongly Related to Crime

As indicated, strainful events and conditions are unlikely to lead to crime *unless* they are (1) seen as unjust, (2) seen as high in magnitude, (3) associated with low social control, *and* (4) create some pressure or incentive for criminal coping. Such strains are likely to include (but are not limited to) the following.

The failure to achieve core goals that are not the result of conventional socialization and that are easily achieved through crime. Such goals include money—particularly the desire for much money in a short period of time (as opposed to the gradual accumulation of savings), thrills/excitement, high levels of autonomy, and masculine status (see Agnew 1997, 2001a, 2001b; Agnew et al. 1996; Anderson 1999; Cernkovich et al. 2000; Colvin 2000; Katz 1988; Matza and Sykes 1961; Messerschmidt 1993; Moffitt 1993; Tittle 1995). These are core goals for at least certain segments of the population. It is difficult to predict whether the failure to achieve these goals will be seen as unjust, although it has been suggested that this is the case where barriers to success are visible and such barriers involve discrimination based on acquired characteristics—like "the mere fact of birth into a particular race, religion, social class, or family" (Cloward and Ohlin 1960:119; also see Anderson 1999; Blau and Blau 1982; Messerschmidt 1993). The pursuit of these goals does *not* imply conventional socialization or high social control. Rather, the pursuit of these goals frequently stems from the possession of certain individual traits, like sensation seeking (White, Labouvie, and Bates 1985), exposure to "subterranean' traditions" or subcultural groups (see Matza and Sykes 1961), and structural conditions—like poverty in the midst of plenty (see Kornhauser 1978). In this area, Cernkovich et al. (2000) demonstrated that the desire for material success does not function as a form of social control. Furthermore, these goals—unlike educational and occupational success—are easily achieved through crime. Crime is frequently used to get money (Agnew et al. 1996; Cernkovich et al. 2000; Colvin 2000), obtain thrills/excitement (Katz 1988), demonstrate or obtain autonomy (Agnew 1984; Moffitt 1993; Tittle 1995), and "accomplish" masculinity (Anderson 1999; Messerschmidt 1993).

Parental rejection. Parents who reject their children do not express love or affection for them, show little interest in them, provide little support to them, and often display hostility toward them. Parental rejection is likely to create much strain because it may seriously threaten many of the child's goals, values, needs, activities, and/or identities. Parental rejection is likely to be seen as unjust given cultural expectations and the experiences of other children. Parental rejection is associated with very low rather than high social control. And rejection creates some pressure or incentive to engage in crime, largely because rejected children are more likely to be exposed to deviant/aggressive behaviors by their parents and associate with delinquent peers. Data indicate that parental rejection is strongly related to delinquency (Agnew 2001b; Sampson and Laub 1993).

Supervision/discipline that is very strict, erratic, excessive given the infraction, and/or harsh (use of humiliation/insults, threats, screaming, and/or physical punishments). Such supervision/discipline is likely to be seen as high in magnitude, particularly if the individual is exposed to it on a regular basis by parents, school officials, criminal justice officials, or others. It is likely to be seen as unjust because it violates one or more justice norms. It is associated with low social control; sanctions administered in the above manner do not function as effective direct controls, and they frequently undermine attachments and commitments to conventional others and institutions. Such supervision/discipline also creates some pressure or incentive for crime because the sanctioning agents frequently model aggressive behavior, implicitly or explicitly foster beliefs conducive to aggression, and sometimes reinforce aggression (see Patterson, Reid, and Dishion 1992). This type of discipline is also likely to promote association with delinquent peers. Data indicate that parents, school officials, and possibly criminal justice officials who employ this type of discipline/supervision increase the likelihood of crime (Agnew 2001b; Colvin 2000; Lanza-Kaduce and Radosevich 1987; Patterson et al. 1992; Sampson and Laub 1993; Sherman 1993, 2000; Tyler 1990).

Child neglect and abuse. Child neglect and abuse represent extreme forms of parental rejection and harsh parental discipline, and abuse/neglect should be related to crime for all the reasons listed above for these forms of strain. Data support this prediction (Smith and Thornberry 1995; Widom 1998).

Negative secondary school experiences. Negative school experiences include low grades, negative relations with teachers (e.g., teachers treat unfairly, belittle/humiliate), and the experience of school as boring and a waste of time. These experiences are likely to be seen as high in magnitude given the central role that school plays in the lives of juveniles. They *may* be seen as unjust. The compulsory nature of school and the dependent status of juveniles contribute to external blame. Also, juveniles may feel that school personnel ask much of them (several hours of their time and attention each day) but give little in return—which contributes to feelings of distributive injustice. Feelings of injustice are especially likely when students believe they are discriminated against because of ascribed characteristics. Negative school experiences are associated with low rather than high social control. And negative experiences may foster association with delinquent peers. Data indicate that negative school experiences are related to delinquency (Agnew 2001b; Sampson and Laub 1993).

Work in the secondary labor market. Such work commonly involves unpleasant tasks (e.g., simple, repetitive work; physically demanding work; work that requires a subservient stance), little autonomy, coercive control (e.g., threats of being fired), low pay, few benefits, little prestige, and very limited opportunities for advancement. Furthermore, such work is often intermittent in nature. Such work is likely to create much strain, especially given the central role of work for adults. Such work may be seen as unjust. Although individuals often accept responsibility for their position in the stratification system, the high demands and meager benefits of such work are likely to be seen as unjust by many. Such work is associated with low rather than high social control (Crutchfield and Pitchford 1997). And such work may create some pressure or incentive for criminal coping. Crime is often an effective remedy to the problems associated with work in the secondary labor market. And such work often increases the likelihood of exposure to others who are disposed to crime (Colvin 2000; Crutchfield and Pitchford 1997). Data suggest that work in the secondary labor market is associated with crime (Colvin 2000; Crutchfield and Pitchford 1997).

Homelessness, especially youth homelessness. This type of strain is likely to be seen as very high in magnitude because it represents a major challenge to a broad range of goals, needs, values, activities, and identities. Furthermore, homelessness dramatically increases the likelihood that many other types of strain will be experienced, particularly conflicts with and victimization by others (Baron and Hartnagel 1997; Davis 1999; Hagan and McCarthy 1997). Homelessness may be seen as unfair, particularly among youth—whose homelessness is often the result of parental abuse and neglect (Davis 1999; Hagan and McCarthy 1997). And homelessness is strongly associated with low social control and the social learning of crime, as demonstrated in several recent studies (Baron and Hartnagel 1997; Davis 1999; Hagan and McCarthy 1997). Data indicate that homelessness and its attendant problems are associated with crime (Baron and Hartnagel 1997; Hagan and McCarthy 1997).

Abusive peer relations, especially among youth. Peer abuse has been neglected as a type of strain, although data suggest that it is widespread and that it often has a devastating effect on victims (e.g., Ambert 1994: Lockwood 1997). Such abuse may involve insults/ridicule, gossip, threats, attempts to coerce, and physical assaults. Peer abuse is likely to be seen as high in magnitude, especially among youth, where peers are of central importance. Peer abuse is likely to be seen as unjust because it frequently violates one or more justice norms (e.g., is excessive given the infraction, is disrespectful or aggressive, is not administered by legitimate sanctioning agents). Peer abuse is not associated with high social control. Peer abuse among juveniles, in particular, often occurs away from sanctioning agents like parents and teachers. And such abuse is often associated with some pressure or incentive to engage in crime. Peer abuse is especially common in delinquent peer groups and gangs, where the victim is regularly exposed to others who model crime, present beliefs favorable to crime, and reinforce crime (see Agnew 2001b; Colvin 2000). Furthermore, peers often model criminal coping in response to abuse, present beliefs that encourage criminal coping in response to abuse, and differentially reinforce criminal coping in response to abuse.

Criminal victimization. Victimization is typically seen as unjust and high in magnitude. Victimization is not associated with high social control; in fact, victimization is most likely to occur in settings in which social control is low—such as settings where young, unsupervised males gather (Jensen and Brownfield 1986; Lauritsen, Sampson, and Laub 1991; Meier and Miethe 1993). Furthermore, victimization may reduce concern with internal and external sanctions because criminal victimization often provides a justification for crime in the eyes of the victim and others. Finally, criminal victimization is often associated with the social learning of crime. Victimization is more common in delinquent peer groups and gangs, and victimization by definition involves exposure to a criminal model (Lauritsen et al. 1991). Limited data suggest that criminal victimization is strongly related to criminal offending (see Dawkins 1997; Esbensen and Huizinga 1991; Jensen and Brownfield 1986; Lauritsen et al. 1991; Lauritsen, Laub, and Sampson, 1992; Sampson and Lauritsen 1993).

Experiences with prejudice and discrimination based on ascribed characteristics, like race/ethnicity. Data indicate that racial prejudice and discrimination are quite common in the United States (Ambert 1994; Forman, Williams, and Jackson 1997). This type of strain is likely to be seen as unjust and high in magnitude, particularly given the strong cultural emphasis in the United States on egalitarianism. Prejudice/discrimination may reduce social control, particularly attachment and commitment to those individuals and institutions associated with the prejudice and discrimination. Prejudice/discrimination may also create some pressure or incentive to engage in crime because the victim is exposed to others who violate strongly held social norms. Data indicate that experiences with prejudice and discrimination contribute to psychological distress (Finch, Kolody, and Vega 2000; Schulz et al. 2000), and certain qualitative studies have linked prejudice and discrimination to crime (e.g., Anderson 1999). Quantitative studies, however, have not devoted much attention to experiences with prejudice and discrimination.

Summary

The above list represents the most comprehensive attempt to identify those types of strain that are and are not related to crime. It incorporates and extends the work of classic and contemporary strain theorists. Building on the classic strain theorists, it argues that the inability to achieve certain success goals—particularly educational and occupational goals—is not related to crime, whereas the inability to achieve other success goals—like the rapid acquisition of much money—is related to crime. The list also includes many of the strains that contemporary researchers have identified—like the denial of autonomy needs (Moffitt 1993; Tittle 1995); threats to masculine status (Anderson 1999; Messerschmidt 1993); disrespectful, unfair, or abusive police practices (Sherman 1993, 2000); and the types of coercion discussed in Colvin's (2000) theory of differential coercion.[6] The list also contains types of strain that have not been extensively discussed in the strain literature—noting which are related to crime and which are not. The general principles listed in the previous section allow us to group all of these strains under one theoretical umbrella.

HOW DO WE TEST THE ABOVE ARGUMENTS?

Strain is most likely to lead to crime when it is seen as unjust, is seen as high in magnitude, is associated with low social control, and creates some pressure or incentive to engage in criminal coping. If these arguments are correct, types of strain that meet these conditions should be more strongly related to crime than types that do not (although the precise relationship between strain and crime is a function of the characteristics of *both* the strain and the people experiencing the strain). So at the most basic level, researchers should test the above arguments by classifying strains on the above characteristics and then examining the relative impact of these strains on crime. The classification of strains just presented can be used as a staring point for such research. Ideally, researchers should compare the criminal behavior of people who have experienced the above strains. As an alternative, researchers can present people with vignettes describing these types of strain and then ask how likely they or others would be to respond to them with crime (see Mazerolle and Piquero 1997 for a model).

The Cumulative Effect of Strain

This strategy for testing strain theory differs from the approach now taken by most researchers, who examine the impact of cumulative measures of strain on crime—with these cumulative measures often containing types of strain that differ widely on the above characteristics. Although researchers should not ignore the argument that strains may have a cumulative effect on crime, it is most important at this point to determine which types of strain are most strongly related to crime. Once this is determined, researchers can then explore the cumulative impact of strain on crime. Cumulative scales can be created by combining those types of strain that have a significant impact on crime—perhaps weighting them by their regression coefficients. A similar strategy has been successfully employed in the stress literature (Herbert and Cohen 1996; Turner and Wheaton 1995; Wheaton et al. 1997; also see Agnew and White 1992). Or researchers can determine whether strains interact with one another in their impact on crime through the creation of interaction terms (see Wheaton et al. 1997; note the argument that moderate levels of prior stress sometimes *reduce* the negative effects of current stressors).

Distinguishing Strain from Social Control and Social Learning

Researchers testing GST all confront a major problem: Many of the "strain" measures they use—like low grades or harsh parental discipline—can also be taken as social control or social-learning measures. Researchers usually deal with this problem by assigning some measures to the strain camp, some to the social control camp, and some to the social-learning camp. They then try to justify these assignments, although their arguments are often less than convincing. Agnew (1995c) explained why this is so, noting that most variables have implications for strain, social control, *and* social-learning theories. Harsh discipline, for example, is often classified as a type of strain, but some claim that it leads to crime by reducing attachment to parents or implicitly teaching the child that violence is acceptable under certain conditions (see Brezina 1998). It is therefore difficult to classify an independent variable as a purely strain, social control, or social-learning variable. This article makes the same argument: Most types of strain have implications for social control and the social learning of crime. Furthermore, it is argued that those types of strain most likely to lead to crime are those that are associated with low social control and the social learning of crime.

This argument raises a major problem: If those types of strain most strongly related to crime are associated with low control and the social learning of crime, how do we know whether these strains affect crime for reasons related to strain, social control, or social-learning theories? Agnew's (1995c) solution to this problem was to examine the intervening processes described by these theories. Although these theories have many of the same independent variables in common, they differ in terms of their specification of intervening processes. Strain theory argues that these variables increase crime through their effect on negative emotions, control theory argues that they lower the perceived costs of crime, and social-learning theory argues that they influence the perceived desirability of crime. A few studies have attempted to examine such intervening processes, and they typically find that the processes associated with all three theories are operative (see Agnew 1985; Brezina 1998).[7] Unfortunately, most existing data sets do not allow for the proper examination of these intervening processes (see Schieman 2000 and Stone 1995 for discussions of certain of the problems involved in measuring the key negative emotion of anger).

There is a second strategy that may be employed to determine if a strain measure affects crime for reasons related to strain, social control, or social-learning theory. Certain strain measures may affect crime because they reduce social control and/or foster the social learning of crime. As indicated, harsh discipline is said to reduce attachment to parents and foster beliefs conducive to violence. In such cases, we can examine the effect of the strain measure on crime while controlling for the relevant social control and social-learning variables. For example, we can examine the effect of harsh discipline on crime while controlling for parental attachment and beliefs conducive to violence. Or we can examine the effect of teacher conflicts while controlling for attachment to teachers, attachment to school, and grades. If the strain measure still affects crime after such controls, support for strain theory is increased. This strategy cannot be followed in all cases, however. Certain strain measures—like low grades—directly index the respondent's level of social control or social learning. Therefore, it is not possible to control for the relevant control or social-learning variables. Also, there is some risk in arguing that the *direct* effect of the strain measure on crime is best explained by strain theory. Researchers may have failed to control for or properly measure all relevant social control and social-learning variables. And it is possible that the strain measure affects crime for reasons other than those offered by strain, social control, and social-learning theories (e.g., genetic factors may influence both exposure to strain and levels of crime).

350   JOURNAL OF RESEARCH IN CRIME AND DELINQUENCY

Finally, a third strategy sometimes allows us to determine whether strain variables affect crime for reasons distinct from those offered by social control theory. According to the logic of control theory, neutral relationships with other individuals and groups should have the same effect on crime as negative relationships. For example, a juvenile who does not care about her parents should be just as delinquent as a juvenile who dislikes or hates her parents. Both juveniles are equally free to engage in delinquency; that is, both have nothing to lose through delinquency. According to the logic of strain theory, however, the juvenile who hates her parents should be higher in delinquency than the juvenile who does not care about her parents. This is because the juvenile who hates her parents is under more strain. Her hatred likely stems from unpleasant relations with her parents, and it is stressful to live with people you hate. This prediction is easily tested with certain data sets, but researchers rarely compare juveniles who dislike/hate their parents with juveniles who neither like nor dislike their parents (see Nye 1958 for an exception). Similar analyses can be conducted in other areas. For example, researchers can compare the criminal behavior of individuals who hate their grades or jobs with those who do not care about their grades or jobs. If strain theory is correct, individuals who hate their grades or jobs should be higher in crime.

None of these strategies allows us to perfectly determine whether strain variables affect crime for reasons related to strain, social control, or social-learning theories, but taken together they can shed much light on this problem.

Measuring Strain

Many current measures of strain are quite simplistic; single-item measures of specific strains are often employed, with these measures providing little information about the magnitude, injustice, or other dimensions of the strain. A similar situation characterizes the stress literature, although stress researchers are starting to collect more detailed information on stressors to better estimate things like their magnitude. For example, some stress researchers have abandoned simple checklist measures and are employing intensive interviews with semistructured probes (see Herbert and Cohen 1996; Wethington et al. 1995; Wheaton 1996). Such techniques were developed because respondents often report trivial stressors when checklist measures are used—even when such checklists attempt to focus on serious stressors (Dohrenwend 2000; Herbert and Cohen 1996; Wethington et al. 1995). Also, many stress researchers now recognize that the circumstances associated with the stressor have an important effect on its impact. It is difficult to employ intensive interviews in the large-scale surveys often conducted by criminologists, but criminologists can do a much better job of measuring strain in such surveys. As an illustration, one need only compare the measures of economic strain typically employed by criminologists with those commonly used in the family research. Economic strain is not simply measured in terms of low income or a two- or three-item index of socioeconomic status. Rather, family researchers examine such things as (1) family per capita income; (2) unstable work history, which includes changing to a worse job, demotions, and being fired or laid off; (3) debt-to-asset ratio; and (4) increases or decreases in family income in the past year. Furthermore, researchers recognize that these types of economic strain do not affect all families in the same way. So, more direct measures of economic strain are sometimes employed as well. For example, parents are asked about the extent to which the family has enough money for clothing, food, medical care, and bills. They are also asked about the changes they have had to make to cope with economic hardship, like moving, taking an additional job, canceling medical insurance, and obtaining government assistance (e.g., Conger et al. 1992; Fox and Chancey 1998; Voydanoff 1990; also see Agnew et al. 1996; Cernkovich et al. 2000).

CONCLUSION

GST is usually tested by examining the effect of selected types of strain on crime. Researchers, however, have little guidance when it comes to selecting among the many hundreds of types of strain that might be examined. And they have trouble explaining why only some of the strains they do examine are related to crime. This article builds on GST by describing the characteristics of strainful events and conditions that influence their relationship to crime. As indicated, strains are most likely to lead to crime when they (1) are seen as unjust, (2) are seen as high in magnitude, (3) are associated with low social control, and (4) create some pressure or incentive to engage in criminal coping. Based on these characteristics, it is argued that certain types of strain will be unrelated or only weakly related to crime. Such strains include the failure to achieve educational and occupational success, the types of strain that have dominated the research on strain theory. Such strains also include many of the types of strain found in stressful life events scales, which are commonly used to test GST. And it is argued that other types of strain will be more strongly related to crime, including types that have received much attention in the criminology literature (e.g., parental rejection; erratic, harsh parental discipline; child abuse and neglect; negative school experiences) and types that have received little attention (e.g., the inability to achieve selected goals, peer abuse, experiences with prejudice and discrimination).

The arguments presented in this article should have a fundamental impact on future efforts to test GST because they identify those types of strain that should and should not be related to crime. And in doing so, these arguments make it easier to falsify GST. Furthermore, these arguments help explain the contradictory results of past research on strain theory; for example, they help explain why the failure to achieve educational and occupational success is usually not related to crime, whereas verbal and physical assaults usually have a relatively strong relationship to crime.

These arguments also have important policy implications. Agnew (1992) argued that two major policy recommendations flow from GST: reduce the exposure of individuals to strain and reduce the likelihood that individuals will cope with strain through crime (by targeting those individual characteristics conducive to criminal coping). This article suggests a third recommendation: alter the characteristics of strains in ways that reduce the likelihood they will result in crime. Despite our best efforts, many individuals will be exposed to strain. For example, parents, teachers, and criminal justice officials will continue to sanction individuals in ways that are disliked. We can, however, alter the ways in which these sanctions are administered so as to reduce the likelihood that they will (1) be seen as unjust, (2) be seen as high in magnitude, (3) reduce social control, and (4) create some pressure or incentive to engage in crime. In fact, this is one of the central thrusts behind the restorative justice and related movements (see Bazemore 1998; Briathwaite 1989; Sherman 1993, 2000; Tyler 1990). These movements point to ways in which criminal justice officials can increase the perceived justice of sanctions, reduce the perceived magnitude of sanctions, sanction in ways that increase rather than reduce social control, and sanction in ways that create little pressure or incentive for crime. Recommendations in these areas include treating offenders with respect; making them aware of the harm they have caused; giving them some voice in determining sanctions; tempering the use of severe, punitive sanctions; and reintegrating offenders with conventional society through a variety of strategies—like reintegration ceremonies and the creation of positive roles for offenders. Certain parent-training and school-based programs are also structured in ways that reduce the likelihood that strains like disciplinary efforts will be administered in ways that increase the likelihood of criminal coping (see Agnew 1995d, 2001b).

This article, then, extends Agnew's (1992) GST in a way that substantially improves its ability to explain and control crime. Although Agnew (1992) argues that the reaction to strain is largely a function of individual characteristics, this article argues that the reaction to strain is a function of both individual characteristics and the characteristics of the strain that is being experienced. Strain is most likely to lead to crime when individuals possess characteristics conducive to criminal coping (as described in Agnew 1992) and they experience types of strain conducive to criminal coping (as described above). This extension of strain theory parallels recent developments in the stress literature. Like Agnew (1992), stress researchers argued that the impact of stressors on outcome variables was largely a function of individual characteristics like coping skills and social support. Stress researchers, however, have increasingly come to realize that stressors do not have comparable impacts on outcome variables. Certain stressors are significantly related to outcome variables—most often measures of mental and physical health—whereas others are not (e.g., Aseltine et al. 2000; Aseltine, Gore, and Colten 1998; Brown 1998; Wethington et al. 1995; Wheaton et al. 1997; Dohrenwend 1998). So we must consider both the nature of the stressor and the characteristics of the individual experiencing the stressor.

Like Agnew's (1992) original statement of GST, however, the arguments in this article are in need of further research and elaboration. The predictions regarding the impact of specific types of strain on crime are tentative. Researchers should use the methods described in this article to better determine the extent to which these and other types of strain are seen as unjust, are seen as high in magnitude, are associated with low social control, and create some pressure or incentive for crime. Such research should improve the accuracy of the predictions that are made. Furthermore, researchers should pay attention to the impact of group membership in such research. For example, it is likely that there are group differences in the extent to which certain strains are seen as unjust or high in magnitude.[8] In addition, researchers should examine whether particular strains have a greater impact on some types of crime than other types. For example, some research suggests that certain strains are more strongly related to aggression/violence than to other types of crime (e.g., Agnew 1990; Aseltine et al. 1998, 2000; Mazerolle et al. 2000; Mazerolle and Piquero 1997). (Likewise, the stress research reveals that some stressors are more strongly related to some types of negative outcomes than to others.) The arguments presented in this article, then, are still in need of much development, but that does not diminish their central thrust—some strains are more likely than others to result in crime.

NOTES

1. Most of the research in criminology simply assumes that certain events or conditions are disliked by most of the people being studied. This is probably a reasonable assumption in most cases (e.g., criminal victimization), although it is a more questionable assumption in other cases (e.g., changing schools). A potentially more serious problem with the criminology research is that researchers rarely employ a complete or comprehensive list of objective strains. Researchers usually only examine a few types of objective strain—often overlooking many of the most important types. For example, interviews with adolescents suggest that peer conflict and abuse

are among the most important types of objective strain in this group, but such conflict/abuse is rarely considered by researchers (although see Agnew 1997; Agnew and Brezina 1997; Ambert 1994; Aseltine, Gore, and Gordon 2000; Seiffge-Krenke 1995). Likewise, experiences with racial prejudice and discrimination are seldom considered by researchers, despite evidence that such experiences are a major type of objective strain among African Americans and others (Ambert 1994; Anderson 1999). Recent research suggests that the failure to examine the full range of stressors can lead researchers to substantially underestimate the effect of stress or strain (Turner, Wheaton, and Lloyd 1995).

2. This is much less of a problem when judges or group members are rating the injustice of objective strains because these ratings are averaged across judges or group members.

3. Attributions of recklessness and negligence may also lead to perceptions of unjust treatment, although they result in less blame than attributions of intent. See Tedeschi and Felson (1994) and Tyler et al. (1997) for discussions in this area.

4. The distributive justice literature focuses on norms governing the distribution of outcomes, with outcomes broadly defined. Such outcomes include the types of strain considered in general strain theory (GST): the blockage of goal-seeking behavior, the removal of positively valued stimuli, and the presentation of negatively valued stimuli. Several rules govern the distribution of outcomes (e.g., equity, need, equality). And a range of factors influences the choice of the most relevant rule(s) and the determination of whether the rule(s) has been violated—with self-interest being a major factor (Hegtvedt and Cook forthcoming; Hegtvedt and Markovsky 1995; Tyler et al. 1997). The procedural justice literature focuses on the process by which people decide how to distribute outcomes. Several factors have been found to influence judgments about the fairness or justice of this process, although the relative importance of these factors varies by type of situation and other variables (Hegtvedt and Markovsky 1995; Lind and Tyler 1988; Sherman 2000; Tyler 1994; Tyler et al. 1997). The interactional justice literature focuses on the norms governing interaction between people, with data indicating that people have a strong desire to be treated in a polite, respectful, considerate, nonaggressive manner (Mikula 1986, 1993; Mikula, Petri, and Tanzer 1990; Tedeschi and Felson 1994). The retributive justice literature focuses on the factors that influence the reaction to people who break social rules, with research indicating that people feel a need to sanction those who intentionally violate rules and with the sanction being proportional to the harm intended or inflicted (Tedeschi and Felson 1994; Tyler et al. 1997). Violations of distributive, procedural, interactional, and retributive justice norms may each influence overall evaluations of justice, although the relative importance of each type of justice varies according to several factors (Tyler et al. 1997).

5. Agnew (1992) argued that the inability to achieve educational and occupational goals would be related to crime if researchers focused on the disjunction between expectations or expected goals and actual achievements. He claimed that expectations are taken more seriously than aspirations. An empirical study by Jensen (1995), however, failed to find support for this argument—although further tests would be useful.

6. Colvin's (2000) theory of differential coercion essentially described a general type of strain—coercion—said to be especially conducive to crime (the theory also presented excellent discussions of the many ways that coercion may contribute to crime and the cultural and structural sources of coercion). Coercion involves "the use or threat of force and intimidation aimed at creating compliance through fear," including the "actual or threatened removal of social supports," and "pressure arising from structural arrangements and circumstances that seem beyond individual control," creating "a sense of desperation that seems to compel an individual toward immediate action." This broad definition includes most or all of the types of strain said to lead to crime but may also include many of the strains not predicted to affect crime—such as the inability to achieve conventional success goals, demands for the care of conventional others, and isolation from peer groups and situations conducive to crime.

7. One should also take account of the possibility that anger may indirectly affect crime by reducing the perceived costs of crime and increasing the perceived desirability of crime, as indicated earlier in this article.

8. Explaining the origins of such differences is, of course, central to any effort to develop the macro-side of GST (see the excellent discussions in Anderson 1999; Bernard 1990; Colvin 2000; and Messerschmidt 1993).

REFERENCES

Agnew, Robert. 1984. "Autonomy and Delinquency." *Sociological Perspectives* 27:219-36.

————. 1985. "A Revised Strain Theory of Delinquency." *Social Forces* 64:151-67.

————. 1990. "The Origins of Delinquent Events: An Examination of Offender Accounts." *Journal of Research in Crime and Delinquency* 27:267-94.

————. 1992. "Foundation for a General Strain Theory of Crime and Delinquency." *Criminology* 30:47-87.

————. 1995a. "Strain and Subcultural Theories of Criminality." In *Criminology: A Contemporary Handbook*, edited by Joseph F. Sheley. Belmont, CA: Wadsworth.

————. 1995b. "The Contribution of Social-Psychological Strain Theory to the Explanation of Crime and Delinquency." In *The Legacy of Anomie Theory, Advances in Criminological Theory*, Vol. 6, edited by Freda Adler and William S. Laufer. New Brunswick, NJ: Transaction.

————. 1995c. "Testing the Leading Crime Theories: An Alternative Strategy Focusing on Motivational Processes." *Journal of Research in Crime and Delinquency* 32:363-98.

————. 1995d. "Controlling Delinquency: Recommendations from General Strain Theory." In *Crime and Public Policy*, edited by Hugh D. Barlow. Boulder, CO: Westview.

————. 1997. "Stability and Change in Crime over the Life Course: A Strain Theory Explanation." In *Developmental Theories of Crime and Delinquency, Advances in Criminological Theory*, Vol. 7, edited by Terence P. Thornberry. New Brunswick, NJ: Transaction.

————. 2001a. "An Overview of General Strain Theory." In *Explaining Criminals and Crime*, edited by Raymond Paternoster and Ronet Bachman. Los Angeles: Roxbury.

————. 2001b. *Juvenile Delinquency: Causes and Control*. Los Angeles: Roxbury.

Agnew, Robert and Timothy Brezina. 1997. "Relational Problems with Peers, Gender and Delinquency." *Youth and Society* 29:84-111.

Agnew, Robert, Francis T. Cullen, Velmer S. Burton, Jr., T. David Evans, and R. Gregory Dunaway. 1996. "A New Test of Classic Strain Theory." *Justice Quarterly* 13:681-704.

Agnew, Robert and David M. Petersen. 1989. "Leisure and Delinquency." *Social Problems* 36:332-50.

Agnew, Robert and Helene Raskin White. 1992. "An Empirical Test of General Strain Theory." *Criminology* 30:475-99.

Ambert, Ann-Marie. 1994. "A Qualitative Study of Peer Abuse and Its Effects: Theoretical and Empirical Implications." *Journal of Marriage and the Family* 56:119-30.

Anderson, Elijah. 1999. *Code of the Street*. New York: Norton.

Aseltine, Robert H., Jr., Susan Gore, and Mary Ellen Colten. 1998. "The Co-occurrence of Depression and Substance Abuse in Late Adolescence." *Development and Psychopathology* 10:549-70.

Aseltine, Robert H., Jr., Susan Gore, and Jennifer Gordon. 2000. "Life Stress, Anger and Anxiety, and Delinquency: An Empirical Test of General Strain Theory." *Journal of Health and Social Behavior* 41:256-75.

356 JOURNAL OF RESEARCH IN CRIME AND DELINQUENCY

Averill, James R. 1982. *Anger and Aggression: An Essay on Emotion.* New York: Springer-Verlag.

————. 1993. "Illusions of Anger." In *Aggression and Violence*, edited by Richard B. Felson and James T. Tedeschi. New York: Springer-Verlag.

Bandura, Albert. 1990. "Selective Activation and Disengagement of Moral Control." *Journal of Social Issues* 46:27-46.

Baron, Stephen W. and Timothy F. Hartnagel. 1997. "Attributions, Affect, and Crime: Street Youths' Reactions to Unemployment." *Criminology* 35:409-34.

Bazemore, Gordon. 1998. "Restorative Justice and Earned Redemption." *American Behavioral Scientist* 41:768-813.

Berkowitz, Leonard. 1993. *Aggression: Its Causes, Consequences, and Control.* New York: McGraw-Hill.

Bernard, Thomas J. 1990. "Angry Aggression among the 'Truly Disadvantaged.' " *Criminology* 28:73-96.

Black, Donald. 1983. "Crime as Social Control." *American Sociological Review* 48:34-45.

Blau, Judith R. and Peter M. Blau. 1982. "The Cost of Inequality: Metropolitan Structure and Violent Crime." *American Sociological Review* 47:114-29.

Box, Steven. 1987. *Recession, Crime and Punishment.* Basingstoke, UK: Macmillan.

Briathwaite, John. 1989. *Crime, Shame, and Reintegration.* Cambridge, UK: Cambridge University Press.

Brezina, Timothy. 1998. "Adolescent Maltreatment and Delinquency: The Question of Intervening Processes." *Journal of Research in Crime and Delinquency* 35:71-99.

————. 1999. "Teenage Violence toward Parents as an Adaptation to Family Strain." *Youth and Society* 30:416-44.

————. 2000. "Delinquent Problem-Solving: An Interpretative Framework for Criminological Theory and Research." *Journal of Research in Crime and Delinquency* 37:3-30.

Broidy, Lisa and Robert Agnew. 1997. "Gender and Crime: A General Strain Theory Perspective." *Journal of Research in Crime and Delinquency* 34:275-306.

Brown, George W. 1998. "Loss and Depressive Disorders." In *Adversity, Stress, and Psychopathology*, edited by Bruce P. Dohrenwend. New York: Oxford University Press.

Burke, Peter J. 1996. "Social Identities and Psychosocial Stress." In *Psychosocial Stress*, edited by Howard B. Kaplan. San Diego, CA: Academic Press.

Burton, Velmer S., Jr. and R. Gregory Dunaway. 1994. "Strain, Relative Deprivation, and Middle-Class Delinquency." In *Varieties of Criminology*, edited by Greg Barak. Westport, CT: Praeger.

Cernkovich, Stephen A., Peggy C. Giordano, and Jennifer L. Rudolph. 2000. "Race, Crime, and the American Dream." *Journal of Research in Crime and Delinquency* 37:131-70.

Cloward, Richard A. and Lloyd E. Ohlin. 1960. *Delinquency and Opportunity.* New York: Free Press.

Cohen, Albert K. 1955. *Delinquent Boys.* New York: Free Press.

————. 1997. "An Elaboration of Anomie Theory." In *The Future of Anomie Theory*, edited by Nikos Passas and Robert Agnew. Boston: Northeastern University Press.

Cohen, Sheldon, Ronald C. Kessler, and Lynn Underwood Gordon. 1995. *Measuring Stress.* New York: Oxford University Press.

Colvin, Mark. 2000. *Crime and Coercion: An Integrated Theory of Chronic Criminality.* New York: St. Martin's.

Conger, Rand D., Katherine J. Conger, Glen H. Elder, Jr., Frederick O. Lorenz, Ronald L. Simons, and Lee B. Whitbeck. 1992. "A Family Process Model of Economic Hardship and Adjustment of Early Adolescent Boys." *Child Development* 63:526-41.

Crittenden, Kathleen S. 1983. "Sociological Aspects of Attribution." *Annual Review of Sociology* 9:425-46.

———. 1989. "Causal Attribution in Sociocultural Context." *Sociological Quarterly* 30:1-14.

Crutchfield, Robert D. and Susan R. Pitchford. 1997. "Work and Crime: The Effects of Labor Stratification." *Social Forces* 76:93-118.

Cullen, Francis T. and Robert Agnew. 1999. *Criminological Theory: Past to Present*. Los Angeles: Roxbury.

Davis, Nanette J. 1999. *Youth Crisis*. Westport, CT: Praeger.

Dawkins, Nicola. 1997. "Striking Back: An Empirical Test of the Impact of Victimization on Violent Crime." Presented at the annual meeting of the American Society of Criminology, San Diego, CA.

Dodge, Kenneth A. and D. Schwartz. 1997. "Social Information Processing Mechanisms in Aggressive Behavior." In *Handbook of Antisocial Behavior*, edited by David M. Stoff, James Breiling, and Jack D. Maser. New York: John Wiley.

Dohrenwend, Bruce P. 1998. *Adversity, Stress, and Psychopathology*. New York: Oxford University Press.

———. 2000. "The Role of Adversity and Stress in Psychopathology: Some Evidence and Its Implications for Theory and Research." *Journal of Health and Social Behavior* 41:1-19.

Elder, Glen H., Jr., Linda K. George, and Michael J. Shanahan. 1996. "Psychosocial Stress over the Life Course." In *Psychosocial Stress*, edited by Howard B. Kaplan. San Diego, CA: Academic Press.

Esbensen, Finn-Aage and David Huizinga. 1991. "Juvenile Victimization and Delinquency." *Youth and Society* 23:202-28.

Finch, Brian Karl, Bohdan Kolody, and William A. Vega. 2000. "Perceived Discrimination and Depression among Mexican-Origin Adults in California." *Journal of Health and Social Behavior* 41:295-313.

Forman, Tyrone A., David R. Williams, and James S. Jackson. 1997. "Race, Place, and Discrimination." *Perspectives on Social Problems* 9:231-61.

Fox, Greer Linton and Dudley Chancey. 1998. "Sources of Economic Distress." *Journal of Family Issues* 19:725-49.

Gottfredson, Michael R. and Travis Hirschi. 1990. *A General Theory of Crime*. Stanford, CA: Stanford University Press.

Hagan, John and Bill McCarthy. 1997. *Mean Streets*. Cambridge, UK: Cambridge University Press.

Hegtvedt, Karen A. and Karen S. Cook. Forthcoming. "Distributive Justice: Recent Theoretical Developments and Applications." In *The Justice Reader*, edited by Joseph Sanders and V. Lee Hamilton. New York: Plenum..

Hegtvedt, Karen A. and Barry Markovsky. 1995. "Justice and Injustice." In *Sociological Perspectives on Social Psychology*, edited by Karen S. Cook, Gary Alan Fine, and James S. House. Needham Heights, NY: Allyn and Bacon.

Herbert, Tracy B. and Sheldon Cohen. 1996. "Measurement Issues in Research on Psychosocial Stress." In *Psychosocial Stress*, edited by Howard B. Kaplan. San Diego, CA: Academic Press.

Hirschi, Travis. 1969. *Causes of Delinquency*. Berkeley: University of California Press.

Hoffmann, John P. and Felice Gray Cerbone. 1999. "Stressful Life Events and Delinquency Escalation in Early Adolescence." *Criminology* 37:343-74.

Hoffmann, John P. and Alan S. Miller. 1998. "A Latent Variable Analysis of Strain Theory." *Journal of Quantitative Criminology* 14:83-110.

358 JOURNAL OF RESEARCH IN CRIME AND DELINQUENCY

Hoffmann, John P. and S. Susan Su. 1997. "The Conditional Effects of Stress on Delinquency and Drug Use: A Strain Theory Assessment of Sex Differences." *Journal of Research in Crime and Delinquency* 34:46-78.

Jensen, Gary F. 1995. "Salvaging Structure through Strain: A Theoretical and Empirical Critique." In *The Legacy of Anomie Theory, Advances in Criminological Theory*, Vol. 6, edited by Freda Adler and William S. Laufer. New Brunswick, NJ: Transaction.

Jensen, Gary F. and David Brownfield. 1986. "Gender, Lifestyles, and Victimization: Beyond Routine Activity." *Violence and Victims* 1:85-99.

Kaplan, Howard B. 1996. "Psychosocial Stress from the Perspective of Self Theory." In *Psychosocial Stress*, edited by Howard B. Kaplan. San Diego, CA: Academic Press.

Katz, Jack. 1988. *Seductions of Crime*. New York: Basic Books.

Kessler, Ronald C., Jacquelyn Gillis-Light, William J. Magee, Kenneth S. Kendler, and Lindon J. Eaves. 1997. "Childhood Adversity and Adult Psychopathology." In *Stress and Adversity over the Life Course*, edited by Ian H. Gottlib and Blair Wheaton. Cambridge, UK: Cambridge University Press.

Kessler, Ronald C., James S. House, Renee R. Anspach, and David R. Williams. 1995. "Social Psychology and Health." In *Sociological Perspectives on Social Psychology*, edited by Karen S. Cook, Gary Alan Fine, and James S. House. Needham Heights, NY: Allyn and Bacon.

Kornhauser, Ruth Rosner. 1978. *Social Sources of Delinquency*. Chicago: University of Chicago Press.

Lanza-Kaduce, Lonn and Marcia J. Radosevich. 1987. "Negative Reactions to Processing and Substance Use among Young Incarcerated Males." *Deviant Behavior* 8:137-48.

Lauritsen, Janet L., John Laub, and Robert J. Sampson. 1992. "Conventional and Delinquent Activities: Implications for the Prevention of Violent Victimization among Adolescents." *Violence and Victims* 7:91-108.

Lauritsen, Janet L., Robert J. Sampson, and John H. Laub. 1991. "The Link between Offending and Victimization among Adolescents." *Criminology* 29:265-92.

Lazarus, Richard S. 1999. *Stress and Emotion: A New Synthesis*. New York: Springer.

Lepore, Stephen J. 1995. "Measurement of Chronic Stressors." In *Measuring Stress*, edited by Sheldon Cohen, Ronald C. Kessler, and Lynn Underwood Gordon. New York: Oxford University Press.

Lind, E. Allan and Tom R. Tyler. 1988. *The Social Psychology of Procedural Justice*. New York: Plenum.

Lockwood, Daniel. 1997. *Violence among Middle School and High School Students: Analysis and Implications for Prevention*. Washington, DC: National Institute of Justice.

Matza, David and Gresham Sykes. 1961. "Juvenile Delinquency and Subterranean Beliefs." *American Sociological Review* 26:713-19.

Mazerolle, Paul. 1998. "Gender, General Strain, and Delinquency: An Empirical Examination." *Justice Quarterly* 15:65-91.

Mazerolle, Paul, Velmer S. Burton, Jr., Francis T. Cullen, T. David Evans, and Gary L. Payne. 2000. "Strain, Anger, and Delinquency Adaptations: Specifying General Strain Theory." *Journal of Criminal Justice* 28:89-101.

Mazerolle, Paul and Alex Piquero. 1997. "Violent Responses to Strain: An Examination of Conditioning Influences." *Violence and Victims* 12:323-43.

———. 1998. "Linking Exposure to Strain with Anger: An Investigation of Deviant Adaptations." *Journal of Criminal Justice* 26:195-211.

Meier, Robert F. and Terence D. Miethe. 1993. "Understanding Theories of Criminal Victimization." *Crime and Justice: A Review of Research* 17:465-95.

Merton, Robert K. 1938. "Social Structure and Anomie." *American Sociological Review* 3:672-82.

————. 1968. *Social Theory and Social Structure*. New York: Free Press.

Messerschmidt, James W. 1993. *Masculinities and Crime*. Lanham, MD: Rowman and Littlefield.

Mikula, Gerold. 1986. "The Experience of Injustice: Toward a Better Understanding of Its Phenomenology." In *Justice in Social Relations*, edited by Hans Werner Bierhoff, Ronald L. Cohen, and Jerald Greenberg. New York: Plenum.

————. 1993. "On the Experience of Injustice." *European Journal of Social Psychology* 4:223-44.

Mikula, Gerold, Birgit Petri, and Norbert Tanzer. 1990. "What People Regard as Unjust: Types and Structures of Everyday Experiences of Injustice." *European Journal of Social Psychology* 2:133-49.

Moffitt, Terrie E. 1993. " 'Life-Course Persistent' and 'Adolescent-Limited' Antisocial Behavior: A Developmental Taxonomy." *Psychological Review* 100:674-701.

Nye, Ivan. 1958. *Family Relationships and Delinquent Behavior*. New York: John Wiley.

Osgood, D. Wayne, Janet K. Wilson, Patrick M. O'Malley, Jerald G. Bachman, and Lloyd D. Johnston. 1996. "Routine Activities and Individual Deviant Behavior." *American Sociological Review* 61:635-55.

Paternoster, Raymond and Paul Mazerolle. 1994. "General Strain Theory and Delinquency: A Replication and Extension." *Journal of Research in Crime and Delinquency* 31:235-63.

Patterson, Gerald R., John B. Reid, and Thomas J. Dishion. 1992. *Antisocial Boys*. Eugene, OR: Castalia.

Piquero, Nicole Leeper and Miriam D. Sealock. 2000. "Generalizing General Strain Theory: An Examination of an Offending Population." *Justice Quarterly* 17:449-84.

Rokeach, Milton. 1973. *The Nature of Human Values*. New York: Free Press.

Sampson, Robert J. and John H. Laub. 1993. *Crime in the Making*. Cambridge, MA: Harvard University Press.

Sampson, Robert J. and Janet L. Lauritsen. 1993. "Violent Victimization and Offending: Individual-, Situational-, and Community-Level Risk Factors." In *Understanding and Preventing Violence*, Vol. 3, *Social Influences*, edited by the National Research Council. Washington, DC: National Research Council.

Schieman, Scott. 2000. "Education and the Activation, Course, and Management of Anger." *Journal of Health and Social Behavior* 41:20-39.

Schulz, Amy, David Williams, Barbara Israel, Adam Becker, Edith Parker, Sherman A. James, and James Jackson. 2000. "Unfair Treatment, Neighborhood Effects, and Mental Health in the Detroit Metropolitan Area." *Journal of Health and Social Behavior* 41:314-32.

Seiffge-Krenke, Inge. 1995. *Stress, Coping, and Relationships in Adolescence*. Mahwah, NJ: Lawrence Erlbaum.

Sherman, Lawrence W. 1993. "Defiance, Deterrence, and Irrelevance: A Theory of Criminal Sanctions." *Journal of Research in Crime and Delinquency* 30:445-73.

————. 2000. "The Defiant Imagination: Consilience and the Science of Sanctions." Presented at the University of Pennsylvania, Philadelphia.

Smith, Carolyn and Terence P. Thornberry. 1995. "The Relationship between Childhood Maltreatment and Adolescent Involvement in Delinquency." *Criminology* 33:451-81.

Smith-Lovin, Lynn. 1995. "The Sociology of Affect and Emotion." In "Sociological Perspectives on Social Psychology, edited by Karen S. Cook, Gary Alan Fine, and James S. House. Needham Heights, NY: Allyn and Bacon.

360 JOURNAL OF RESEARCH IN CRIME AND DELINQUENCY

Stone, Arthur A. 1995. "Measurement of Affective Response." In *Measuring Stress*, edited by Sheldon Cohen, Ronald C. Kessler, and Lynn Underwood Gordon. New York: Oxford University Press.

Sykes, Gresham M. and David Matza. 1957. "Techniques of Neutralization: A Theory of Delinquency." *American Sociological Review* 22:664-70.

Taylor, Shelley E. and Lisa G. Aspinwall. 1996. "Mediating and Moderating Processes in Psychosocial Stress: Appraisal, Coping, Resistance, and Vulnerability." In *Psychosocial Stress*, edited by Howard B. Kaplan. San Diego, CA: Academic Press.

Tedeschi, James T. and Richard B. Felson. 1994. *Violence, Aggression, and Coercive Actions*. Washington, DC: American Psychological Association.

Tedeschi, James T. and Mitchell S. Nesler. 1993. "Grievances: Development and Reaction." In *Aggression and Violence*, edited by Richard B. Felson and James T. Tedeschi. Washington, DC: American Psychological Association.

Thoits, Peggy A. 1989. "The Sociology of Emotions." *Annual Review of Sociology* 15:317-42.

———. 1991. "On Merging Identity Theory and Stress Research." *Social Psychology Quarterly* 54:101-12.

———. 1995. "Stress, Coping, and Social Support Processes: Where Are We? What Next?" *Journal of Health and Social Behavior* (Extra Issue):53-79.

Tittle, Charles R. 1995. *Control Balance: Toward a General Theory of Deviance*. Boulder, CO: Westview.

Turner, Jay R. and William R. Avison. 1992. "Innovations in the Measurement of Life Stress: Crisis Theory and the Significance of Event Resolution." *Journal of Health and Social Behavior* 33:36-50.

Turner, R. Jay and Blair Wheaton. 1995. "Checklist Measurement of Stressful Life Events." In *Measuring Stress*, edited by Sheldon Cohen, Ronald C. Kessler, and Lynn Underwood Gordon. New York: Oxford University Press.

Turner, R. Jay, Blair Wheaton, and Donald A. Lloyd. 1995. "The Epidemiology of Social Stress." *American Sociological Review* 60:104-25.

Tyler, Tom. 1990. *Why People Obey the Law*. New Haven, CT: Yale University Press.

———. 1994. "Psychological Models of the Justice Process: Antecedents of Distributive and Procedural Justice." *Journal of Personality and Social Psychology* 67:850-63.

Tyler, Tom R., Robert J. Boeckmann, Heather J. Smith, and Yuen J. Huo. 1997. *Social Justice in a Diverse Society*. Boulder, CO: Westview.

Uggen, Christopher. 2000. "Work as a Turning Point in the Life Course of Criminals: A Duration Model of Age, Employment, and Recidivism." *American Sociological Review* 67:529-46.

Voydanoff, Patricia. 1990. "Economic Distress and Family Relations: A Review of the Eighties." *Journal of Marriage and the Family* 52:1099-115.

Wells, Edward L. and Joseph H. Rankin. 1988. "Direct Parental Controls and Delinquency." *Criminology* 26:263-84.

Wethington, Elaine, George W. Brown, and Ronald C. Kessler. 1995. "Interview Measurement of Stressful Life Events." In *Measuring Stress*, edited by Sheldon Cohen, Ronald C. Kessler, and Lynn Underwood Gordon. New York: Oxford University Press.

Wheaton, Blair. 1990. "Life Transitions, Role Histories, and Mental Health." *American Sociological Review* 55:209-24.

———. 1996. "The Domains and Boundaries of Stress Concepts." In *Psychosocial Stress*, edited by Howard B. Kaplan. San Diego, CA: Academic Press.

Wheaton, Blair, Patricia Roszell, and Kimberlee Hall. 1997. "The Impact of Twenty Childhood and Adult Traumatic Stressors on the Risk of Psychiatric Disorder." In *Stress and Adversity over the Life Course: Trajectories and Turning Points*, edited by Ian H. Gottlib. New York: Cambridge University Press.

White, Helene Raskin, Erich W. Labouvie, and Marsha E. Bates. 1985. "The Relationship between Sensation Seeking and Delinquency: A Longitudinal Analysis." *Journal of Research in Crime and Delinquency* 22:197-211.

Widom, Cathy Spatz. 1998. "Childhood Victimization: Early Adversity and Subsequent Psychopathology." In *Adversity, Stress, and Psychopathology*, edited by Bruce P. Dohrenwend. New York: Oxford University Press.

Part IV
The Development
of Subcultural Theory

[10]

Delinquent Subcultures: Sociological Interpretations of Gang Delinquency

By David J. Bordua

ABSTRACT: Group delinquency has been of theoretical interest to American sociology for more than half a century. During that time, four major interpretations of the origins of gang delinquency and delinquent subcultures have emerged. The classical view developed by Thrasher focuses on the development of spontaneous groups under conditions of weak social control and social disorganization. Two other views, somewhat akin, emphasize the adjustment problems of lower class boys and stress respectively the status deprivation of such boys when they fail to place well according to the middle class measuring rod and the alienation produced when opportunities to achieve universally demanded success goals are denied lower class boys. Another view is that of the lower class street gang and its way of life as the adolescent version of a more general adult life style, namely, lower class culture. There is a noticeable tendency in the recent theories to emphasize irrational explanations of gang delinquency, to view the boys who participate as driven rather than attracted, and polemical pressures have tended to produce extreme theoretical interpretations.

David J. Bordua, Ph.D., Ann Arbor, Michigan, is Assistant Professor in the Department of Sociology at the University of Michigan. He received his doctorate from Harvard in 1957 and has published on theories of delinquency, authoritarianism, college aspirations of high school youth, and the use of formal selection instruments to detect delinquents at an early age.

THE problem of group delinquency has been a subject of theoretical interest for American sociologists and other social observers for well over a half century. In the course of that period, the group nature of delinquency has come to be a central starting point for many theories of delinquency, and delinquency causation has been seen by some sociologists as pre-eminently a process whereby the individual becomes associated with a group which devotes some or all of its time to planning, committing, or celebrating delinquencies and which has elaborated a set of lifeways —a subculture—which encourages and justifies behavior defined as delinquent by the larger society.

In addition to the processes whereby an individual takes on the beliefs and norms of a pre-existing group and thereby becomes delinquent—a process mysterious enough in itself in many cases—there is the more basic, and in many respects more complex, problem of how such groups begin in the first place. What are the social conditions that facilitate or cause the rise of delinquency-carrying groups? What are the varying needs and motives satisfied in individuals by such groups? What processes of planned social control might be useable in preventing the rise of such groups or in redirecting the behavior and moral systems of groups already in existence? All these questions and many others have been asked for at least two generations. Within the limits of this brief paper, it is impossible to present and analyze in detail the many answers to these questions which have been put forward by social scientists. What I can do is single out a few of the major viewpoints and concentrate on them.

In its more well-developed and extreme forms, gang or subcultural delinquency has been heavily concentrated in the low status areas of our large cities.

The theoretical interpretations I will discuss all confine themselves to gang delinquency of this sort.

THE CLASSICAL VIEW

Still the best book on gangs, gang delinquency, and—though he did not use the term—delinquent subcultures is *The Gang* by Frederick M. Thrasher, and his formulations are the ones that I have labeled "the classical view." Not that he originated the basic interpretative framework, far from it, but his application of the theoretical materials available at the time plus his sensitivity to the effects of social environment and his willingness to consider processes at all behavioral levels from the basic needs of the child to the significance of the saloon, from the nature of city government to the crucial importance of the junk dealer, from the consequences of poverty to the nature of leadership in the gang still distinguish his book.[1]

Briefly, Thrasher's analysis may be characterized as operating on the following levels. The ecological processes which determine the structure of the city create the interstitial area characterized by a variety of indices of conflict, disorganization, weak family and neighborhood controls, and so on. In these interstitial areas, in response to universal childhood needs, spontaneous play groups develop. Because of the relatively uncontrolled nature of these groups—or of many of them at least—and because of the presence of many attractive and exciting opportunities for fun and adventure, these groups engage in a variety of activities, legal and illegal, which are determined, defined, and directed by the play group itself rather than by conventional adult supervision.

The crowded, exciting slum streets teem with such groups. Inevitably, in

[1] Frederick M. Thrasher, *The Gang* (Chicago: University of Chicago Press, 1927).

a situation of high population density, limited resources, and weak social control, they come into conflict with each other for space, playground facilities, reputation. Since many of their activities, even at an early age, are illegal, although often not feloniously so—they swipe fruit from peddlers, turn over garbage cans, stay away from home all night and steal milk and cakes for breakfast, play truant from school—they also come into conflict with adult authority. Parents, teachers, merchants, police, and others become the natural enemies of this kind of group and attempt to control it or to convert it to more conventional activities. With some groups they succeed, with some they do not.

If the group continues, it becomes part of a network of similar groups, increasingly freed from adult restraint, increasingly involved in intergroup conflict and fighting, increasingly engaged in illegal activities to support itself and to continue to receive the satisfactions of the "free" life of the streets. Conflict, especially with other groups, transforms the play group into the gang. Its illegal activities become more serious, its values hardened, its structure more determined by the necessity to maintain eternal vigilance in a hostile environment.

By middle adolescence, the group is a gang, often with a name, usually identified with a particular ethnic or racial group, and usually with an elaborate technology of theft and other means of self-support. Gradually, the gang may move in the direction of adult crime, armed robbery, perhaps, or other serious crimes.

Prior to that time, however, it is likely to have engaged in much stealing from stores, railroad cars, empty houses, parents, drunks, almost anywhere money or goods are available. The ready access to outlets for stolen goods is of major importance here. The junk dealer, especially the junk wagon peddler, the convenient no-questions-asked attitudes of large numbers of local adults who buy "hot" merchandise, and the early knowledge that customers are available all help to make theft easy and profitable as well as morally acceptable.[2]

Nonutilitarian?

It is appropriate at this point to deal with a matter that has become important in the discussion of more recent theories of group delinquency. This is Albert K. Cohen's famous characterization of the delinquent subculture as nonutilitarian, by which he seems to mean that activities, especially theft, are not oriented to calculated economic ends.[3]

Thrasher makes a great point of the play and adventure quality of many illegal acts, especially in the pregang stages of a group's development, but he also describes many cases where theft has a quite rational and instrumental nature, even at a fairly early age.

The theft activities and the disposition of the loot make instrumental sense in the context of Thrasher's description of the nature of the group or gang. Much theft is essentially for the purpose of maintaining the group in a state of freedom from adult authority. If a group of boys lives days or even weeks away from home, then the theft of food

---

[2] One of the charms of Thrasher's old-time sociology is the fashion in which fact intrudes itself upon the theorizing. For example, he tells us that there were an estimated 1,700 to 1,800 junk wagon men in Chicago, most of whom were suspected of being less than rigid in inquiring about the source of "junk." *Ibid.*, p. 148. He also does some other things that seem to have gone out of style, such as presenting information on the age and ethnic composition of as many of the 1,313 gangs as possible. *Ibid.*, pp. 73, 74, 191–193.

[3] Albert K. Cohen, *Delinquent Boys: The Culture of the Gang* (Glencoe: The Free Press, 1955), pp. 25, 26.

or of things which are sold to buy food is hardly nonutilitarian. If such a group steals from freight cars, peddles the merchandise to the neighbors for movie money, and so on, this can hardly be considered nonutilitarian. The behavior makes sense as instrumental behavior, however, only after one has a picture of the general life led by the group. Boys who feed themselves by duplicating keys to bakery delivery boxes, creep out of their club rooms right after delivery, steal the pastry, pick up a quart of milk from a doorstep, and then have breakfast may not have a highly developed sense of nutritional values, but this is not nonutilitarian.

Such youngsters may, of course, spend the two dollars gained from selling stolen goods entirely on doughnuts and gorge themselves and throw much of the food away. I think this largely indicates that they are children, not that they are nonutilitarian.[4]

[4] The examples cited above are all in Thrasher along with many others of a similar nature. In general, views of the nature of gang activity have shifted quite fundamentally toward a more irrationalist position. Thus, the gang's behavior seems to make no sense. Underlying this shift is a tendency to deal almost entirely with the gang's subculture, its values, beliefs, and the like, to deal with the relationships between this subculture and presumed motivational states which exist in the potential gang members before the gang or protogang is formed, and to deal very little with the developmental processes involved in the formation of gangs. Things which make no sense without consideration of the motivational consequences of gang membership are not necessarily so mysterious given Thrasher's highly sensitive analysis of the ways in which the nature of the gang as a group led to the development—in relation to the local environment—of the gang culture. Current theory focuses so heavily on motive and culture to the exclusion of group process that some essential points are underemphasized. It would not be too much of a distortion to say that Thrasher saw the delinquent subculture as the way of life that would be developed by a group becoming a gang and that some recent theorists look at the gang as the kind of group

Let us look a little more systematically at the Thrasher formulations, however, since such an examination can be instructive in dealing with the more recent theories. The analysis proceeds at several levels, as I have mentioned.

Levels of analysis

At the level of the local adult community, we may say that the social structure is permissive, attractive, facilitative, morally supportive of the gang development process.

It is permissive because control over children is weak; attractive because many enjoyable activities are available, some of which are illegal, like stealing fruit, but all of which can be enjoyed only if the child manages to evade whatever conventional controls do exist.

In another sense, the local environment is attractive because of the presence of adult crime of a variety of kinds ranging from organized vice to older adolescents and adults making a living by theft. The attraction lies, of course, in the fact that these adults may have a lot of money and live the carefree life and have high status in the neighborhood.

The local environment is facilitative in a number of ways. There are things readily available to steal, people to buy them, and places to hide without adult supervision.

The environment is morally supportive because of the presence of adult crime, as previously mentioned, but also for several additional reasons. One is the readiness of conventional adults to buy stolen goods. Even parents were discovered at this occasionally. The prevalence of political pull, which not only objectively protected adult crime but tended to undercut the norms against crime, must be mentioned then as now. The often bitter poverty which

that would develop if boys set about creating a delinquent subculture.

turned many situations into matters of desperate competition also contributed.

Additionally, many gang activities, especially in the protogang stage, are not seriously delinquent and receive adult approval. These activities include such things as playing baseball for "side money" and much minor gambling such as penny pitching. Within limits, fighting lies well within the local community's zone of tolerance, especially when it is directed against members of another ethnic group.

At the level of the adolescent and preadolescent groups themselves, the environment is essentially coercive of gang formation. The presence of large numbers of groups competing for limited resources leads to conflict, and the full-fledged adolescent gang is pre-eminently a conflict group with a high valuation of fighting skill, courage, and similar qualities. Thus, the transition from spontaneous group to gang is largely a matter of participating in the struggle for life of the adolescent world under the peculiar conditions of the slum.

At the level of the individual, Thrasher assumes a set of basic needs common to all children. He leans heavily on the famous four wishes of W. I. Thomas, security, response, recognition, and new experience, especially the last two. Gang boys and boys in gang areas are, in this sense, no different from other boys. They come to choose different ways of satisfying these needs. What determines which boys form gangs is the differential success of the agencies of socialization and social control in channeling these needs into conventional paths. Thus, due to family inadequacy or breakdown or school difficulties, coupled with the ever present temptations of the exciting, adventurous street as compared to the drab, dull, and unsatisfying family and school, some boys are more available for street life than others.

Finally, it should be pointed out that the gang engages in many activities of a quite ordinary sort. Athletics are very common and highly regarded at all age levels. Much time is spent simply talking and being with the gang. The gang's repertory is diverse—baseball, football, dice, poker, holding dances, shooting the breeze, shoplifting, rolling drunks, stealing cars.

This is more than enough to give the tenor of Thrasher's formulations. I have purposely attempted to convey the distinctive flavor of essentially healthy boys satisfying universal needs in a weakly controlled and highly seductive environment. Compared to the deprived and driven boys of more recent formulations with their status problems, blocked opportunities (or psychopathologies if one takes a more psychiatric view), Thrasher describes an age of innocence indeed.

This is, perhaps, the most important single difference between Thrasher and some—not all—of the recent views. Delinquency and crime were attractive, being a "good boy" was dull. They were attractive because they were fun and were profitable and because one could be a hero in a fight. Fun, profit, glory, and freedom is a combination hard to beat, particularly for the inadequate conventional institutions that formed the competition.

WORKING CLASS BOY AND MIDDLE CLASS MEASURING ROD

If Thrasher saw the gang as being formed over time through the attractiveness of the free street life and the unattractiveness and moral weakness of the agencies of social control, Albert K. Cohen sees many working class boys as being driven to develop the delinquent subculture as a way of recouping the self-esteem destroyed by middle-class-dominated institutions.

Rather than focusing on the gang and

its development over time, Cohen's theory focuses on the way of life of the gang—the delinquent subculture. A collective way of life, a subculture, develops when a number of people with a common problem of adjustment are in effective interaction, according to Cohen. The bulk of his basic viewpoint is the attempted demonstration that the common problem of adjustment of the lower class gang boys who are the carriers of the delinquent subculture derives from their socialization in lower class families and their consequent lack of preparation to function successfully in middle class institutions such as the school.

The institutions within which the working class boy must function reward and punish him for acceptable or unacceptable performance according to the child-assessing version of middle class values. The middle class value pattern places great emphasis on ambition as a cardinal virtue, individual responsibility (as opposed to extreme emphasis on shared kin obligations, for example), the cultivation and possession of skills, the ability to postpone gratification, rationality, the rational cultivation of manners, the control of physical aggression and violence, the wholesome and constructive use of leisure, and respect for property (especially respect for the abstract rules defining rights of access to material things).[5]

The application of these values adapted to the judgment of children constitutes the "middle class measuring rod" by which all children are judged in institutions run by middle class personnel—the school, the settlement house, and the like. The fact that working class children must compete according to these standards is a consequence of what Cohen, in a most felicitous phrase, refers to as the "democratic status universe" characteristic of American society. Everyone is expected to strive,

[5] Albert K. Cohen, *op. cit.*, pp. 88–93.

and everyone is measured against the same standard. Not everyone is equally prepared, however, and the working class boy is, with greater statistical frequency than the middle class boy, ill prepared through previous socialization.

Cultural setting

Social class for Cohen is not simply economic position but, much more importantly, a set of more or less vertically layered cultural settings which differ in the likelihood that boys will be taught the aspirations, ambitions, and psychological skills necessary to adjust to the demands of the larger institutions.

Cohen goes on to describe this predominantly lower working class cultural setting as more likely to show restricted aspirations, a live-for-today orientation toward consumption, a moral view which emphasizes reciprocity within the kin and other primary groups and correlatively less concern with abstract rules which apply across or outside of such particularistic circumstances. In addition, the working class child is less likely to be surrounded with educational toys, less likely to be trained in a family regimen of order, neatness, and punctuality. Of particular importance is the fact that physical aggression is more prevalent and more valued in the working class milieu.

When a working class boy thus equipped for life's struggle begins to function in the school, the settlement, and other middle-class-controlled institutions and encounters the middle class measuring rod, he inevitably receives a great deal of disapproval, rejection, and punishment. In short, in the eyes of the middle class evaluator, he does not measure up. This is what Cohen refers to as the problem of status deprivation which constitutes the fundamental problem of adjustment to which the delinquent subculture is a solution.

Self-derogation

But this deprivation derives not only from the negative evaluations of others but also from self-derogation. The working class boy shares in this evaluation of himself to some degree for a variety of reasons.[6] The first of these is the previously mentioned democratic status universe wherein the dominant culture requires everyone to compete against all comers. Second, the parents of working class boys, no matter how adjusted they seem to be to their low status position, are likely to project their frustrated aspirations onto their children. They may do little effective socialization to aid the child, but they are, nevertheless, likely at least to want their children to be better off than they are. Third, there is the effect of the mass media which spread the middle class life style. And, of course, there is the effect of the fact of upward mobility as visible evidence that at least some people can make the grade.

In short, the working class boy is subjected to many social influences which emphasize the fact that the way to respect, status, and success lies in conforming to the demands of middle class society. Even more importantly, he very likely has partly accepted the middle class measuring rod as a legitimate, even superior, set of values. The profound ambivalence that this may

[6] In presenting the theoretical work of someone else, it is often the case that the views of the original author are simplified to his disadvantage. I have tried to guard against this. At this point in Cohen's formulation, however, I may be oversimplifying to his benefit. In view of the considerable struggle over the matter of just what the working class boy is sensitive to, I should point out that Cohen is less than absolutely clear. He is not as unclear, however, as some of his critics have maintained. For the best statement in Cohen's work, see *Delinquent Boys*, pp. 121–128.

lead to in the individual is simply a reflection of the fact that the larger culture penetrates the lower working class world in many ways.

Thus, to the external status problem posed by devaluations by middle class functionaries is added the internal status problem of low self-esteem.

This, then, is the common problem of adjustment. Given the availability of many boys similarly situated, a collective solution evolves, the delinquent subculture. This subculture is characterized by Cohen as nonutilitarian, malicious, and negativistic, characterized by versatility, short-run hedonism, and an emphasis on group autonomy, that is, freedom from adult restraint.

These are, of course, the direct antitheses of the components of the middle class measuring rod. The delinquent subculture functions simultaneously to combat the enemy without and the enemy within, both the hated agents of the middle class and the gnawing internal sense of inadequacy and low self-esteem. It does so by erecting a counterculture, an alternative set of status criteria.

Guilt

This subculture must do more than deal with the middle-class-dominated institutions on the one hand and the feelings of low self-esteem on the other. It must also deal with the feelings of guilt over aggression, theft, and the like that will inevitably arise. It must deal with the fact that the collective solution to the common problem of adjustment is an illicit one in the eyes of the larger society and, certainly, also in the eyes of the law-abiding elements of the local area.

It must deal, also, with the increasing opposition which the solution arouses in the police and other agencies of the conventional order. Over time, the subculture comes to contain a variety of definitions of these agents of conventionality which see them as the aggressors, thus legitimating the group's deviant activities.

Because of this requirement that the delinquent subculture constitute a solution to internal, psychological problems of self-esteem and guilt, Cohen sees the group behavior pattern as being overdetermined in the psychological sense and as linking up with the mechanism of reaction formation.

Thus, the reason for the seeming irrationality of the delinquent subculture lies in the deeply rooted fears and anxieties of the status deprived boy. I have already discussed the shift from Thrasher's view of delinquency as attractive in a situation of weak social control to the views of it as more reactive held by some modern theorists. Cohen, of course, is prominent among these latter, the irrationalists. It is extremely difficult to bring these viewpoints together at all well except to point out that Cohen's position accords well with much research on school failure and its consequences in damaged self-esteem. It does seem unlikely, as I will point out later in another connection, that the failure of family, school, and neighborhood to control the behavior of Thrasher's boys would result in their simple withdrawal from such conventional contexts without hostility and loss of self-regard.

Cohen emphasizes that not all members of an ongoing delinquent group are motivated by this same problem of adjustment. Like any other protest movement, the motives which draw new members at different phases of its development will vary. It is sufficient that a core of members share the problem.

The analysis of the delinquent subculture of urban working class boys set forth in *Delinquent Boys* has been elaborated and supplemented in a later article by Cohen and James F. Short.[7]

Other delinquent subcultures

Responding to the criticism that there seemed a variety of kinds of delinquent subcultures, even among lower class urban youth, Cohen and Short distinguish the parent-male subculture, the conflict-oriented subculture, the drug addict subculture, and a subculture focused around semiprofessional theft.[8]

The parent subculture is the now familiar subculture described in *Delinquent Boys*. Cohen and Short describe it as the most common form.[9]

We refer to it as the parent sub-culture because it is probably the most common variety in this country—indeed, it might be called the "garden variety" of delinquent sub-culture—and because the characteristics listed above seem to constitute a common core shared by other important variants.

In discussing the conditions under which these different subcultures arise, Cohen and Short rely on a pivotal paper published in 1951 by Solomon Kobrin.[10] Dealing with the differential location of the conflict-oriented versus the semiprofessional theft subculture, Kobrin pointed out that delinquency areas vary

[7] Albert K. Cohen and James F. Short, Jr., "Research in Delinquent Sub-Cultures," *Journal of Social Issues*, Vol. 14 (1958), No. 3, pp. 20–36.

[8] For criticism in this vein as well as for the most searching general analysis of material from *Delinquent Boys*, see Harold L. Wilensky and Charles N. Lebeaux, *Industrial Society and Social Welfare* (New York: Russell Sage Foundation, 1958), Chap. 9.

[9] Cohen and Short, *op. cit.*, p. 24. The characteristics are those of maliciousness and so on that I have listed previously.

[10] Solomon Kobrin, "The Conflict of Values in Delinquency Areas," *American Sociological Review*, Vol. 16 (October 1951), No. 5, pp. 653–661.

in the degree to which conventional and criminal value systems are mutually integrated. In the integrated area, adult criminal activity is stable and organized, and adult criminals are integral parts of the local social structure —active in politics, fraternal orders, providers of employment. Here delinquency can form a kind of apprenticeship for adult criminal careers with such careers being relatively indistinct from conventional careers. More importantly, the interests of organized criminal groups in order and a lack of police attention would lead to attempts to prevent the wilder and more untrammeled forms of juvenile violence. This would mean, of course, that crime in these areas was largely of the stable, profitable sort ordinarily associated with the rackets.

LOWER CLASS BOY AND LOWER CLASS CULTURE

The interpretation of the delinquent subculture associated with Albert Cohen that I have just described contrasts sharply in its main features with what has come to be called the lower class culture view associated with Walter B. Miller.[11] Miller disagrees with the Cohen position concerning the reactive nature of lower class gang culture.[12]

In the case of "gang" delinquency, the cultural system which exerts the most

[11] See the following papers, all by Walter B. Miller: "Lower Class Culture as a Generating Milieu of Gang Delinquency," *Journal of Social Issues*, Vol. 14 (1958), No. 3, pp. 5–19; "Preventive Work with Street Corner Groups: Boston Delinquency Project," *The Annals of the American Academy of Political and Social Science*, Vol. 322 (March 1959), pp. 97–106; "Implications of Urban Lower Class Culture for Social Work," *The Social Service Review*, Vol. 33 (September 1959), No. 3, pp. 219–236.

[12] Walter B. Miller, "Lower Class Culture as a Generating Milieu of Gang Delinquency," *op. cit.*, pp. 5, 6.

direct influences on behavior is that of the lower class community itself—a long-established, distinctively patterned tradition with an integrity of its own—rather than a so-called "delinquent sub-culture" which has arisen through conflict with middle class culture and is oriented to the deliberate violation of middle class norms.

What, then, is the lower class culture Miller speaks of and where is it located? Essentially, Miller describes a culture which he sees as emerging from the shaking-down processes of immigration, internal migration, and vertical mobility. Several population and cultural streams feed this process, but, primarily, lower class culture represents the emerging common adaptation of unsuccessful immigrants and Negroes.

It is the thesis of this paper that from these extremely diverse and heterogeneous origins (with, however, certain common features), there is emerging a relatively homogeneous and stabilized native-American lower class culture; however, in many communities the process of fusion is as yet in its earlier phases, and evidences of the original ethnic or locality culture are still strong.[18]

In his analysis, Miller is primarily concerned with what he calls the hard

[18] Walter B. Miller, "Implications of Urban Lower Class Culture for Social Work," *op. cit.*, p. 225. Miller seems to be saying that the processes of sorting and segregating which characterized American industrial cities in the period referred to by Thrasher are beginning to show a product at the lower end of the status order. In this, as in several other ways, Miller is much more the inheritor of the classical view, as I have called it, than are Cohen or Cloward and Ohlin. Miller shows much the same concern for relatively wholistic description of the local community setting and much the same sensitivity to group process over time. Whether his tendency to see lower class culture in terms of a relatively closed system derives from differences in fact due to historical change or primarily to differences in theoretical perspective is hard to say.

core group in the lower class—the same very bottom group referred to by Cohen as the lower-lower class. The properties of this emerging lower class culture as described by Miller may be divided into a series of social structural elements and a complex pattern of what Miller calls focal concerns.

Focal concerns

The first of the structural elements is what Miller calls the female-based household, that is, a family form wherein the key relationships are those among mature females (especially those of different generations but, perhaps, also sisters or cousins) and between these females and their children. The children may be by different men, and the biological fathers may play a very inconsistent and unpredictable role in the family. Most essentially, the family is not organized around the expectation of stable economic support provided by an adult male.

The relationship between adult females and males is characterized as one of serial mating, with the female finding it necessary repeatedly to go through a cycle of roles of mate-seeker, mother, and employee.

Closely related to and supportive of this form of household is the elaboration of a system of one-sex peer groups which, according to Miller, become emotional havens and major sources of psychic investment and support for both sexes and for both adolescents and adults. The family, then, is not the central focus of primary, intimate ties that it is in middle class circles.

In what is surely a masterpiece of cogent description, Miller presents the focal concerns of lower class culture as trouble, toughness, smartness, excitement, fate, and autonomy. His description of the complexly interwoven patterns assumed by these focal concerns

cannot be repeated here, but a brief discussion seems appropriate.[14]

Trouble is what life gets you into—especially trouble with the agents of the larger society. The central aspect of this focal concern is the distinction between law-abiding and law-violating behavior, and where an individual stands along the implied dimension either by behavior, reputation, or commitment is crucial in the evaluation of him by others. Toughness refers to physical prowess, skill, masculinity, fearlessness, bravery, daring. It includes an almost compulsive opposition to things seen as soft and feminine, including much middle class behavior, and is related, on the one hand, to sex-role identification problems which flow from the young boy's growing up in the female-based household and, on the other hand, to the occupational demands of the lower class world. Toughness, along with the emphasis on excitement and autonomy, is one of the ways one gets into trouble.

Smartness refers to the ability to "con," outwit, dupe, that is, to manipulate things and people to one's own advantage with a minimum of conventional work. Excitement, both as an activity and as an ambivalently held goal, is best manifested in the patterned cycle of the week end night-on-the-town complete with much drink and sexual escapades, thereby creating the risk of fighting and trouble. Between week ends, life is dull and passive. Fate refers to the perception by many lower class individuals that their lives are determined by events and forces over which they have little or no control. It manifests itself in widespread gambling

[14] This description of the focal concern is taken from Walter B. Miller, "Lower Class Culture as a Generating Milieu of Gang Delinquency," *op. cit.*, especially Chart 1, p. 7. In this case especially, the original should be read.

and fantasies of "when things break for me." Gambling serves multiple functions in the areas of fate, toughness, smartness, and excitement.

The last focal concern described by Miller is that of autonomy—concern over the amount, source, and severity of control by others. Miller describes the carrier of lower class culture as being highly ambivalent about such control by others. Overtly, he may protest bitterly about restraint and arbitrary interference while, covertly, he tends to equate coercion with care and unconsciously to seek situations where strong controls will satisfy nurturance needs.

Growing up

What is it like to grow up in lower class culture? A boy spends the major part of the first twelve years in the company of and under the domination of women. He learns during that time that women are the people who count, that men are despicable, dangerous, and desirable. He also learns that a "real man" is hated for his irresponsibility and considered very attractive on Saturday night. He learns, too, that, if he really loves his mother, he will not grow up to be "just like all men" but that, despite her best efforts, his mother's pride and joy will very likely turn out to be as much a "rogue male" as the rest. In short, he has sex-role problems.

The adolescent street group is the social mechanism which enables the maturing boy to cope with a basic problem of feminine identification coupled with the necessity of somehow growing up to be an appropriately hated and admired male in a culture which maximizes the necessity to fit into all male society as an adult. The seeking of adult status during adolescence, then, has a particular intensity, so that manifestations of the adult culture's focal concerns tend to be overdone. In addition, the street group displays an exaggerated concern with status and belongingness which is common in all adolescent groups but becomes unusually severe for the lower class boy.

The street group, then, is an essential transition mechanism and training ground for the lower class boy. Some of the behavior involved is delinquent, but the degree to which the group engages in specifically delinquent acts, that is, constructs its internal status criteria around the law-violating end of the trouble continuum, may vary greatly depending on local circumstances. These include such things as the presence and salience of police, professional criminals, clergy, functioning recreational and settlement programs, and the like.

Like Thrasher, Miller emphasizes the wide range of activities of a nondelinquent nature that the gang members engage in, although, unlike Thrasher's boys, they do not do so because of poor social control, but because of the desire to be "real men."

Participation in the lower class street group may produce delinquency in several ways:[15]

1. Following cultural practices which comprise essential elements of the total pattern of lower class culture automatically violates certain legal norms.
2. In instances where alternative avenues to similar objectives are available, the non-law-abiding avenue frequently provides a greater and more immediate return for a relatively smaller investment of energy.
3. The "demanded" response to certain situations recurrently engendered within lower class culture involves the commission of illegal acts.

Impact of middle class values

Miller's approach, like the approaches of Thrasher and Cohen, has its strengths

[15] Walter B. Miller, "Lower Class Culture as a Generating Milieu of Gang Delinquency," *op. cit.*, p. 18.

and weaknesses. Miller has not been very successful in refuting Cohen's insistence on the clash between middle class and lower class standards as it affects the sources of self-esteem. To be sure, Cohen's own presentation of just what the lower class boy has or has not internalized is considerably confused. As I have remarked elsewhere, Cohen seems to be saying that a little internalization is a dangerous thing.[16] Miller seems to be saying that the involvements in lower class culture are so deep and exclusive that contacts with agents of middle class dominated institutions, especially the schools, have no impact.

Actually, resolution of this problem does not seem so terribly difficult. In handling Cohen's formulations, I would suggest that previous internalization of middle class values is not particularly necessary, because the lower class boys will be told about them at the very time they are being status-deprived by their teachers and others. They will likely hate it and them (teachers and values), and the process is started. On the other hand, it seems unlikely that Miller's lower class boys can spend ten years in school without some serious outcomes. They should either come to accept middle class values or become even more antagonistic or both, and this should drive them further into the arms of lower class culture.

This would be especially the case because of the prevailing definition of school work as girlish, an attitude not at all limited to Miller's lower class culture. With the sex-role identification problems Miller quite reasonably poses for his boys, the demands of the middle class school teacher that he be neat and

[16] David J. Bordua, *Sociological Theories and Their Implications for Juvenile Delinquency* (Children's Bureau, Juvenile Delinquency: Facts and Facets, No. 2; Washington, D. C.: U. S. Government Printing Office, 1960), pp. 9–11.

clean and well-behaved must be especially galling.[17] In short, it seems to me inconceivable that the objective conflict between the boys and the school, as the most crucial example, could end in a simple turning away.

Miller also seems to be weak when he insists upon seeing what he calls the hard core of lower class culture as a distinctive form and, at the same time, must posit varieties of lower class culture to account for variations in behavior and values. This is not necessarily a factually untrue position, but it would seem to underemphasize the fluidity and variability of American urban life. It is necessary for him to point out that objectively low status urban groups vary in the degree to which they display the core features of lower class culture, with Negroes and Irish groups among those he has studied displaying it more and Italians less.

Validity of female base

Miller seems so concerned that the features of lower class culture, especially the female-based household, not be seen as the disorganization of the more conventional system or as signs of social pathology that he seems to overdo it rather drastically. He is very concerned to show that lower class culture is of ancient lineage and is or was functional in American society. Yet, at the same time, he says that lower class culture is only now emerging at the bottom of the urban heap. He also forgets that none of the low status groups in the society, with the possible exception of low status Negroes, has any history of

[17] For evidence that lower class Negro girls seem to do much better than boys in adjusting to at least one middle class institution, see Martin Deutsch, *Minority Group and Class Status as Related to Social and Personality Factors in School Achievement* (Monograph No. 2, The Society for Applied Anthropology; Ithaca, New York: The Society, 1960).

SOCIOLOGICAL INTERPRETATIONS OF GANG DELINQUENCY 131

his female-based household, at least not in the extreme form that he describes.[18]

A closely related problem is posed by Miller's citation of cross-cultural evidence, for example, "The female-based household is a stabilized form in many societies—frequently associated with polygamy—and is found in 21 per cent of world societies."[19] I do not doubt the figure, but I question the implication that the female-based household as the household form, legitimated and normatively supported in societies practicing polygamy, can be very directly equated with a superficially similar system existing on the margins of a larger society and clearly seen as deviant by that larger society. Surely, in primitive societies, the household can count on the stable economic and judicial base provided by an adult male. The very fact that such a household in the United States is under continuous and heavy pressure from the law, the Aid to Dependent Children worker, and nearly all other agents of the conventional order must make for a very different situation than in societies where it is the accepted form. In such societies, would mothers generally regard men as "unreliable and untrustworthy" and would the statement "all men are no good" be common?[20] Surely, such an attitude implies some awareness that things should be otherwise.

All this is not to argue that tendencies of the sort Miller describes are not present nor to underestimate the value of his insistence that we look at this way of life in its own terms—a valuable contribution indeed—but only to ask for somewhat greater awareness

of the larger social dynamics that produce his lower class culture.

Danger of tautology

Finally, a last criticism of Miller's formulations aims at the use of the focal concerns material. There seems more than a little danger of tautology here if the focal concerns are derived from observing behavior and then used to explain the same behavior. One would be on much safer ground to deal in much greater detail with the structural roots and reality situations to which lower class culture may be a response. Thus, for example, Miller makes no real use of the vast literature on the consequences of prolonged instability of employment, which seems to me the root of the matter.

These criticisms should not blind us to very real contributions in Miller's position. Most importantly, he tells us what the lower class street boys are for, rather than just what they are against. In addition, he deals provocatively and originally with the nature of the adult culture which serves as the context for adolescent behavior. Finally, he alerts us to a possible historical development that has received relatively little attention—the emergence of something like a stable American lower class. This possiblity seems to have been largely neglected in studies of our increasingly middle class society.

SUCCESS GOALS AND OPPORTUNITY STRUCTURES

The last of the major approaches to the problem of lower class group delinquency to be considered here is associated with Richard A. Cloward and Lloyd E. Ohlin.[21] Stated in its briefest

[18] E. Franklin Frazer, *The Negro Family in the United States* (Chicago: University of Chicago Press, 1939).

[19] Walter B. Miller, "Implications of Urban Lower Class Culture for Social Work," *op. cit.*, p. 225 fn.

[20] *Ibid.*, p. 226.

[21] The full statement of the approach is in Richard A. Cloward and Lloyd E. Ohlin, *Delinquency and Opportunity* (Glencoe: The Free Press, 1960); see also Richard A. Cloward "Illegitimate Means, Anomie and

form, the theory is as follows: American culture makes morally mandatory the seeking of success goals but differentially distributes the morally acceptable means to these success goals, the legitimate opportunities that loom so large in the approach.[22]

This gap between culturally universalized goals and structurally limited means creates strain among lower class youths who aspire to economic advancement. Such strain and alienation leads to the formation of delinquent subcultures, that is, normative and belief systems that specifically support and legitimate delinquency, among those boys who blame the system rather than themselves for their impending or actual failure. The particular form of delinquent subculture—conflict, criminal, or retreatist (drug-using)—which results depends on the nature of the local neighborhood and, especially, on the availability of illegitimate opportunities, such as stable crime careers as models and training grounds.

The criminal subculture develops in stable neighborhoods with much regularized crime present; the conflict form develops in really disorganized neighborhoods where not even illegitimate opportunities are available; the retreatist, or drug-use, subculture develops among persons who are double failures due either to internalized prohibitions against violence or theft or to the objective unavailability of these solutions.

Intervening between the stress due to blocked aspirations and the creation of the full-fledged subculture of whatever type is a process of collectively supported "withdrawal of attributions of legitimacy from established social norms."

This process, coupled with the collective development of the relevant delinquent norms, serves to allay whatever guilt might have been felt over the illegal acts involved in following the delinquent norms.

Since the argument in *Delinquency and Opportunity* is, in many ways, even more complicated than those associated with Cohen, Short, and Miller, I will discuss only a few highlights.[23]

Potential delinquents

On the question of who aspires to what, which is so involved in the disagreements between Cohen and Miller, Cloward and Ohlin take the position that it is not the boys who aspire to middle class status—and, therefore, have presumably partially internalized the middle class measuring rod—who form the raw material for delinquent subculture, but those who wish only to improve their economic status without any change in class membership. Thus, it is appropriate in their argument to say that the genitors of the delinquent subcultures are not dealing so much with an internal problem of self-esteem as with an external problem of injustice. Cohen says, in effect, that the delinquent subculture prevents self-blame for failure from breaking through, the reaction formation function of the delinquent subculture. Cloward and Ohlin say that the delinquent norm systems are generated by boys who have already

Deviant Behavior," *American Sociological Review,* Vol. 24 (April 1959), No. 2, pp. 164–176.

[22] For the original version of this formulation, see Robert K. Merton, *Social Theory and Social Structure* (rev. and enl.; Glencoe: The Free Press, 1951), Chaps. 4, 5.

[23] Large segments of *Delinquency and Opportunity* are devoted to refutations of other positions, especially those of Cohen and Miller. I felt that, at least for the present paper, criticizing in detail other people's refutations of third parties might be carrying the matter too far. It should be pointed out, however, that the tendency to take extreme positions as a consequence of involvement in a polemic which is apparent in Miller's work seems even more apparent in the Cloward and Ohlin book.

determined that their failures, actual or impending, are the fault of the larger social order.[24]

This insistence that it is the "system blamers" who form the grist for the subcultural mill leads Cloward and Ohlin into something of an impasse, it seems to me. They must, of course, then deal with the determinants of the two types of blame and choose to say that two factors are primarily relevant. First, the larger culture engenders expectations, not just aspirations, of success which are not met, and, second, there exist highly visible barriers to the fulfillment of these expectations, such as racial prejudice, which are defined as unjust.

These do not seem unreasonable, and, in fact, in the case of Negro youth, perhaps, largely fit the case. Cloward and Ohlin, however, are forced for what seems overwhelmingly polemical reasons into a position that the feeling of injustice must be objectively correct. Therefore, they say (1) that it is among those actually fitted for success where the sense of injustice will flourish and (2) that delinquent subcultures are formed by boys who do not essentially differ in their capacity to cope with the larger institutions from other boys. This point deserves some attention since it is so diametrically opposed to the Cohen position which states that some working class boys, especially lower working class boys, are unable to meet the demands of middle-class-dominated institutions.

It is our impression that a sense of being unjustly deprived of access to opportunities to which one is entitled is common among those who become participants in

delinquent subcultures. Delinquents tend to be persons who have been led to expect opportunities because of their potential ability to meet the formal, institutionally-established criteria of evaluation. Their sense of injustice arises from the failure of the system to fulfill these expectations. Their criticism is not directed inward since they regard themselves in comparison with their fellows as capable of meeting the formal requirements of the system. It has frequently been noted that delinquents take special delight in discovering hypocrisy in the operation of the established social order. They like to point out that it's "who you know, not what you know" that enables one to advance or gain coveted social rewards. They become convinced that bribery, blackmail, fear-inspiring pressure, special influence, and similar factors are more important than the publicly avowed criteria of merit.[25]

Delinquents and nondelinquent peers

On the same page in a footnote, the authors go on to say that the research evidence indicates "the basic endowments of delinquents, such as intelligence, physical strength, and agility, are the equal of or greater than those of their non-delinquent peers."

The material in these quotations is so riddled with ambiguities it is difficult to know where to begin criticism, but we can at least point out the following. First, Cloward and Ohlin seem to be confusing the justificatory function of delinquent subcultures with their causation. All of these beliefs on the part of gang delinquents have been repeatedly reported in the literature, but, by the very argument of *Delinquency and Opportunity*, it is impossible to tell whether they constitute compensatory ideology or descriptions of objective reality.

Second, Cloward and Ohlin seem to be victims of their very general tend-

[24] Richard A. Cloward and Lloyd E. Ohlin, *Delinquency and Opportunity, op. cit.* For the problem of types of aspiration and their consequences, see, especially, pp. 86–97. For the matter of self-blame and their system blame for failure, see pp. 110–126.

[25] *Ibid.*, p. 117.

ency to ignore the life histories of their delinquents.[26] Thus, there is no way of knowing really what these subcultural beliefs may reflect in the experience of the boys. Third, and closely related to the ignoring of life history material, is the problem of assessing the degree to which these gang boys are in fact prepared to meet the formal criteria for success. To say that they are intelligent, strong, and agile is to parody the criteria for advancement. Perhaps Cohen would point out that intelligent, agile, strong boys who begin the first grade using foul language, fighting among themselves, and using the school property as arts and crafts materials do not meet the criteria for advancement.

It is quite true that members of highly sophisticated delinquent gangs often find themselves blocked from whatever occupational opportunities there are, but this seems, often, the end product of a long history of their progressively cutting off opportunity and destroying their own capacities which may begin in the lower class family, as described by either Cohen or Miller, and continue through school failure and similar events. By the age of eighteen, many gang boys are, for all practical purposes, unemployable or need the support, instruction, and sponsorship of trained street-gang workers. Participation in gang delinquency in itself diminishes the fitness of many boys for effective

functioning in the conventional world.[27]

If, indeed, Cloward and Ohlin mean to include the more attitudinal and characterological criteria for advancement, then it seems highly unlikely that any large number of boys trained and prepared to meet these demands of the occupational world could interpret failure exclusively in terms which blame the system. They would have been too well socialized, and, if they did form a delinquent subculture, it would have to perform the psychological function of mitigating the sense of internal blame. This, of course, would make them look much like Cohen's boys.

In short, Cloward and Ohlin run the risk of confusing justification and causation and of equating the end with the beginning.

All of this is not to deny that there are real obstacles to opportunity for lower class boys. There are. These blocks on both the performance and learning sides, are a major structural feature in accounting for much of the adaptation of lower class populations. But they do not operate solely or even primarily on the level of the adolescent. They create a social world in which he comes of age, and, by the time he reaches adolescence, he may find himself cut off from the larger society. Much of the Cloward and Ohlin approach seems better as a theory of the origins of Miller's lower class culture. Each generation does not meet and solve anew the problems of class structure barriers to opportunity but begins with

[26] This is the most fundamental weakness in the book. The delinquents in Thrasher, Cohen, and Miller were, in varying degrees, once recognizably children. Cloward and Ohlin's delinquents seem suddenly to appear on the scene sometime in adolescence, to look at the world, and to discover, "Man, there's no opportunity in my structure." It is instructive in this connection to note that the index to *Delinquency and Opportunity* contains only two references to the family. One says that the family no longer conducts occupational training; the other criticizes Miller's ideas on the female-based household.

[27] Here, again, Thrasher seems superior to some of the modern theorists. He stressed the fact that long-term involvement in the "free, undisciplined" street life with money at hand from petty theft and with the days devoted to play was not exactly ideal preparation for the humdrum life of the job. Again, Thrasher's sensitivity to the attitudinal and subcultural consequences of the gang formation and maintenance process truly needs reintroduction.

the solution of its forebears.[28] This is why reform efforts can be so slow to succeed.

Some insights

The positive contributions of the Cloward-Ohlin approach seem to me to lie less on the side of the motivational sources of subcultural delinquency, where I feel their attempts to clarify the ambiguities in Cohen have merely led to new ambiguities, but more on the side of the factors in local social structure that determine the type of subcultural delinquency.

The major innovation here is the concept of illegitimate opportunities which serves to augment Kobrin's almost exclusive emphasis on the differentially controlling impact of different slum environments. I do think that Cloward and Ohlin may make too much of the necessity for systematic, organized criminal careers in order for the illegitimate opportunity structure to have an effect, but the general argument has great merit.

In addition to the concept of illegitimate opportunities and closely related to it is the description, or speculation, concerning historical changes in the social organization of slums. Changes in urban life in the United States may have truly produced the disorganized slum devoid of the social links between young and old, between children and

[28] Parenthetically, the Cloward and Ohlin position has great difficulty in accounting for the fact that lower class delinquent subculture carriers do not avail themselves of opportunities that do exist. The mixed success of vocational school training, for example, indicates that some fairly clear avenues of opportunity are foregone by many delinquent boys. For Negro boys, where avenues to the skilled trades may indeed be blocked, their argument seems reasonable. For white boys, I have serious question. In fact, the only really convincing case they make on the aspiration-blockage, system-blame side is for Negroes.

older adolescents which characterized the slums described by Thrasher. Certainly, the new conditions of life seem to have created new problems of growing up, though our knowledge of their precise impact leaves much to be desired.

CONCLUSION

This paper should not, I hope, give the impression that current theoretical interpretations of lower class, urban, male subcultural delinquency are without value. Such is far from the case. Many of my comments have been negative since each of the theorists quite ably presents his own defense, which should be read in any case. In fact, I think that this problem has led to some of the most exciting and provocative intellectual interchange in all of sociology in recent years. I do believe, however, that this interchange has often been marred by unnecessary polemic and, even more, by a lack of relevant data.

As I have indicated, there have been some profound changes in the way social theorists view the processes of gang formation and persistence. These, I believe, derive only partially, perhaps even unimportantly, from changes in the facts to be explained. Indeed, we must wait for a study of gangs which will approach Thrasher's in thoroughness before we can know if there are new facts to be explained. Nor do I believe that the changes in viewpoint have come about entirely because old theories were shown to be inadequate to old facts. Both Cohen and Cloward and Ohlin feel that older theorists did not deal with the problem of the origins of delinquent subcultures, but only with the transmission of the subculture once developed.[29]

[29] Albert K. Cohen, *Delinquent Boys, op. cit.,* p. 18; Richard A. Cloward and Lloyd E. Ohlin, *Delinquency and Opportunity, op. cit.,* p. 42.

A careful reading of Thrasher indicates that such is not the case.

All in all, though, it does not seem like much fun any more to be a gang delinquent. Thrasher's boys enjoyed themselves being chased by the police, shooting dice, skipping school, rolling drunks. It was fun. Miller's boys do have a little fun, with their excitement focal concern, but it seems so desperate somehow. Cohen's boys and Cloward and Ohlin's boys are driven by grim economic and psychic necessity into rebellion. It seems peculiar that modern analysts have stopped assuming that "evil" can be fun and see gang delinquency as arising only when boys are driven away from "good." [30]

[30] For a more thorough commentary on changes in the view of human nature which, I think, partly underlie the decline of fun in theories of the gang, see Dennis Wrong, "The Oversocialized View of Man," *American Sociological Review*, Vol. 26 (April 1961), No. 3, pp. 183–193.

[11]

SUB-CULTURAL THEORY:
VIRTUES AND VICES

Jock Young

The roots of modern subcultural theory arose in the extraordinary creative ferment which occurred in American sociology of deviance in the late middle of the twentieth century. (Ferrell et al, 2008). Here the influences of Durkheim and Merton became melded with the work of Edwin Sutherland, whilst learning from the phenomenological perspectives which accrued around labelling theory. And this first wave of American subcultural theorization became reinterpreted within a Marxist rubric in the extraordinary fertile developments in subcultural theory centring around work at the Centre for Contemporary Cultural Studies in Britain in the seventies.

Subcultural approaches to crime and deviance have a long history; to talk of criminal subcultures and to graphically describe their activities and values was commonplace amongst Victorian writers such as Booth and Mayhew who depicted the 'dangerous classes', the underlife of nineteenth century London. Central to this type of analysis is that crime is normal behaviour, it is not a product of lack of socialization and culture but of different cultures and values. In the twentieth century, for example, Walter Miller (1958) talks about the focal values of lower working class culture, 'toughness', 'excitement', 'fate', 'trouble', etc. and relates these to crime. What is distinctive about early subcultural theorization, however, is its purely descriptive nature. It describes values, it argues how these are *transmitted* in a normal process of socialization, but it does not explain their *origins*. It is the combination of explaining both the origins and transmission of deviant subcultures which is the hallmark of what I will term 'mature subcultural theory'. Such an approach commenced with the pioneering work of Albert Cohen, Richard Cloward and Lloyd Ohlin in the late fifties and early sixties.

Mature subcultural theory attempts to deal with the fundamental problems of social analysis: how to relate the subjective meanings of actions to an objective assessment of their situation, how to relate the individual actions to the values of his or her group, how to relate the macro-structure of society to the microcosm of human action, how to understand the voluntarism of human action in determinate circumstances, how to tackle problems of rationality and irrationality, of social organization and disorganization and how to relate the past to the present predicament. In many ways it reflects the framework set up by C. Wright Mills in *The Sociological Imagination* (1959; see Young 2010). In attempting this project individual subcultural theorists frequently are unable to adequately straddle these dichotomies. For example, they grant actors creative freedom, but end up describing them as acting out a prescribed cultural essence or they are fascinated by human subjectivity but project on their subjects their own preoccupations. I will start by looking at the promises of subcultural theory, but I will also point to the pitfalls.

The Concept of Subculture

David Downes, in his study of working class delinquency in Stepney and Poplar, invokes the definition of culture formulated by C.S. Ford, namely: 'learned problem solutions'. That is subcultural responses are jointly elaborated solutions to collectively experienced problems. Deviant behaviour is viewed as being a meaningful attempt to solve the problems faced by a group or an isolated individual – it is not a meaningless pathology. It is necessary, therefore, to explore and understand the subjective experience of the actor. Thus Downes writes: 'Whatever factors and circumstances combine to produce a problem derive from wither the individual's frame of reference – the way he looks at the world – or the 'situation' he confronts – the world he lives in and where he is located in the world', (1966, p.6). To achieve this aim it is necessary to delineate how new situations – and with them new problems – are assessed from the point of view of the culture that the individuals *already* embrace. In short: subcultures emerge from the moral springboard of already existing cultures and are the solutions to problems perceived within the framework of these initial cultures. (See Young, 1999).

Culture is seen as the ways people have evolved to tackle the problems which face them in every day life. It includes language, ways of dress, moral standards, political institutions, art forms, work norms, modes of sexuality – in sum all human behaviour. That is, people find themselves in particular structural positions in the world; their age, class, gender, race, for instance, and in order to solve the problems thus posed, certain cultural solutions are evolved to attempt to tackle them. That is, people in each particular structural position evolve their own subculture. And, of course, the major structural axes are those of age, class, ethnicity and gender. They shape people's levels in the context of the particular space they occupy (e.g. the inner city, or rural), their occupational setting and the particular time and country we are talking about. Thus the structural predicaments which give rise to problems for particular groups are varied and stratified throughout society. Subcultures, of course, overlap, they are not distinct normative ghettos: the subculture of young black working class men will overlap a great deal with their female counterparts. But there will also be distinct differences stemming from the predicaments of gender. And, of course, people in the same structural position can evolve different subcultures and these will change over time. Mods, rockers, teds, punks, may all be varieties of attempts by working class youth to deal with similar problems. For subcultures are human creations and can vary as widely as the imagination of the participants involved.

All human beings create their own subcultural forms and although we tend to use the term for the young and the deviant, it is important to note how this is just a matter of focus. Policemen and Army Officers, for example, form their own subcultures which are in their way as developed and exotic as those that exist in the underworld. It is important to stress then that not only deviants but agents of social control exist in subcultures. Thus the encounter in the street late at night between kids and cops, is an encounter between two subcultures. Indeed the dyadic nature of deviance – the necessity of explaining both actors and reactors – necessitates so to speak, a collision of subcultures. (See Young, 2010).

In order to see clearly how this perspective differs from more conventional approaches to human deviance, I will look at five contrasts. And closely associated with these contrasts are the dichotomies which the theory of subcultures attempts to transcend.

(1) The Meaning of Discontent: The Subjective and the Objective, The Rational and the Irrational

In subcultural theory deviant subcultures are viewed not as pathological groupings of maladjusted individuals who lack culture, but rather as meaningful attempts to solve problems faced by the individuals concerned. Whether it is juvenile vandalism or the latest teenage style, cultural responses are meaningful rather than meaningless. In contrast a whole series of terms have evolved which, rather than explaining deviant behaviour, in fact attempt to *explain it away*. Terms like mob, psychopath, undersocialized, hyper-active, primitive, animal, mindless (as in 'mindless' violence), immature, mad – all serve one purpose. They take the observer's values as obvious and 'normal' and they castigate other people's values as not meaningful alternatives but a lack of value, meaning and rationality. In contrast subcultural theory would argue that human behaviour is fundamentally meaningful and differences in behaviour represent the *different* problems and solutions to these problems which particular subcultures have evolved.

A riot, for instance, is not a situation where a mob of people have taken leave of their senses, but a response understandable in terms of the subculture concerned. This is not to say that it is necessarily the most effective method of achieving the aims of the individuals, but rather it makes sense given their limitations and their understanding of the situation. It is, in fact, a common method of voicing protest by relatively powerless groups. As the socialist historian Eric Hobsbawn commented. (1964, p. 379):

> No other European country has so strong a tradition of rioting as Britain; and one which persisted well past the middle of the nineteenth century. The riot, as a normal part of collective bargaining, was well-established in the eighteenth century.

Or take a different type of behaviour: the outstanding study of classroom 'misbehaviour' by Paul Willis (*Learning to Labour,* 1977) dismisses pathological interpretations such as 'hyperactivity' and analyzes how the lower stream of the class – 'the Lads' – realize that they are destined for low skilled jobs where academic achievement is irrelevant. Their structural problem is that they are being asked to compete against middle class standards for which their own background ill prepares them, in order to achieve academic qualifications irrelevant to their future jobs. They culturally 'solve' the problem by playing up in the classroom, rejecting the teacher's discipline, by despising 'swots' – 'earoles' – whilst at the same time evolving a subculture which gives high status to manliness and physical toughness. That is, they begin to evolve a culture which rejects standards which threaten their self-esteem and more relevantly fits their future work as labourers. They turn their misfortune into a virtue. Similarly Ken Pryce, in his study of young blacks in Bristol (*Endless Pressure,* 1979), notes how a proportion reject 'shit work' – they evolve a leisure culture which helps them survive unemployment, racism and the few and menial jobs available to them.

Thus explanations of classroom behaviour which reduce the activities of kids to the defects and failings of individuals are rejected. These can be, and of course often are, phrased in quasi-scientific language (e.g. 'hyperactivity', 'underachievement', 'low IQ') and they can be at times associated with progressive, caring views (e.g. lead poisoning in the inner cities). None of this makes them, from a subcultural point of view, any the less suspect. In all these instances subcultural theorists, instead of viewing deviant behaviour as pathological, irrational or lacking in meaning, are interpreting it as a socially evolved activity with a definite meaningful rationality. To start with the theorist is seeing the problem through the eyes of the people in the subculture. That is, he or she is granting the group being analyzed a subjectivity instead of invoking spurious 'objective' notions of pathology or sickness unrelated to their interpretations of their situation. But this does not imply a rejection of an objective assessment of the situation; rather to disagree with much of what passes as objective accounts – they are in fact most often attempts to belittle subcultures of discontent. By denying the meaning and reason they are unable to to encompass the vital component of human subjectivity necessary in the explanation of human behaviour in contrast to explanations of animal behaviour or inanimate movement.

But to take the opposite viewpoint and elevate the particular actors subjective interpretations of a situation without objectivity also poses enormous problems. Are we to say, for instance, that a Pentecostalist, a Rastafarian or a Primitive Methodist have, in fact, grasped the nature of the world they live in a correct fashion? This is the road to relativism; however 'democratic' it might seem to put the actor's interpretation on a par with that of the theorist, it has obvious pitfalls. At the very least, for instance, the three groups above would conflict about the same social predicament. They would argue vehemently about what is happening around them. It is important therefore not to take subcultures at face value – one must start from these values but put them in a more objective context. One must never lose the values – for unlike animal behaviour or inanimate movement – it is impossible to explain human action without retaining their values. But these values have to be interpreted or – 'read' – from a wider objectivity.

Therefore, to understand present day Rastafarianism or 19th century Methodism one must understand the concepts that the devotees of both religions use – but we would be wrong to limit our study of them to these terms alone. And riots, for instance, represent a collective response to particular predicaments facing groups of individuals; they must be understood in terms of the alternative ranges of responses available to them, but they are not understood merely by interviewing rioters as to the assessments of the motives expressed by them at the time. You cannot understand the revolution of a riot without subjectivity, but equally you cannot make a shibboleth about the views of the participants.

Subcultural theory then attempts to bridge the problem of subjectivity and objectivity – it grants its actors meaning within a world of choice and probability which can be objectively assessed.

(2) The Shape of Discontent: The Present and the Past

Discontent can take on a myriad of shapes, and these forms may change during the biographies of individuals or the social trajectories of groups. It can involve the self-debasement of hard drug use, the elaborate style of a deviant youth culture, the studied pose of the hustler, the other-worldliness of the religious cult, the obsessive nationalism of the fascist, the dedication of the revolutionary, the spontaneous rebellion of the oppressed.

From a subcultural perspective these responses are neither an obvious result of the present predicament of a group nor are they a simple reflex of its past cultural tradition. Subcultures constantly change under the impact of circumstances and they constantly reinterpret circumstances. Tradition brings a series of interpretations to the present but the present itself changes and, in turn, changes tradition.

The rioting in Brixton, South London in 1981, for example, was not an 'obvious' response to the predicament of the Caribbean population as many writers on the left suggested , nor is it simply part of a tradition of anti-colonial struggle carried over from the West Indies as another commentator maintained (P. Gilroy, 1983). It is a response to the present predicament from the perspective of a particular cultural tradition (which is why many other immigrant groups were in low profile at the riots). And it is also the creation of a form of rioting in a specific situation with particular motives which are in no way an identikit replay of events in Kingston, Jamaica three decades ago.

Similarly, crime is not – as I have argued – a simple and obvious response to the problem of being poor irrespective of culture, nor is it part of a working class tradition as some writers, such as Walter Miller, would presume. To take the *reductio ad absurdum* of the two instances, suddenly becoming poor and facing the immediate predicament of poverty may often result in a hangover of honesty and even being desperately poor for six generations in certain foolhardy cultures may result in a remarkable constancy of respect for the law.

'Identical' conditions become different conditions when viewed through the social spectacles of a particular subculture. What is poverty for a resident of Harlem is wealth for a citizen of New Delhi. And the 'pains of imprisonment' depend on what group is experiencing the prison. Thus Ward and Kassebaum, in their study of women's prisons (1965), show how women and men experience greatly differing problems when imprisoned. And the often remarkably contrasting inmate subcultures which occur in male and female prisons are a response to the problem of the regimentation of life in a total institution as experienced from a male and female perspective.

What we must understand is the cultural trajectory of a group, how their material circumstances change (or remain constant) and how their understandings of their situation fluctuate (or have an air of consistency).

(3) The Causes of Discontent: Creativity and Determinism

Much discontent is a product of *relative* not *absolute* deprivation. This notion of causality is at the heart of subcultural theory. Sheer poverty, for example, does not necessarily lead to a subculture of discontent – it may, just as easily, lead to quiescence and fatalism. Discontent occurs when comparisons are made which suggest that injustices are occurring which are artificial when contrasting one group to another which is comparable. If the distribution of wealth is seen as natural and just – however disparate it is – it will be accepted. An objective history of exploitation, or even a history of increased exploitation, does not explain disturbances. Exploitative cultures have existed for generations without friction – it is the perception of justice – *relative deprivation* – which counts. A key influence here is, of course, Mertonian anomie theory and the notion of the disjunction between culturally induced aspirations and the structurally limited opportunities of achieving them experienced by a particular subgroup. That is, people experience relative deprivation in terms of consensual goals and their actual rewards. (Merton, 1938).

The concept of relative deprivation manages to capture the creative and determined parts of the process of being human; it refuses to compromise in terms of either moment. That is, it is totally opposed to simple deterministic ideas of crime. These theories suggest that he or she is criminal because of circumstances, so that one could, with enough effort, come up with laws of human deviance like one can come up with natural laws of the physical universe. Of course, many positivist writers have pronounced such laws. Thus broken homes are said, because of the paternal deprivation that they involve, to lead to delinquency. And these statements are made as if they were natural laws like, say, Boyles Law. But from the perspective of subcultural theory such statements are implausible – and, indeed, impossible – because they miss out the human factor. For however objective one may be about the figures for broken homes and the statistics of the incidence of delinquency (and many criminologists quite rightly would dispute the 'objectivity' of both of these), a subjective factor interposes itself in between the two facts: namely how do particular individuals and groups experience, and interpret, their broken homes.

For one child a broken home may be a bit of luck: an unwitting escape from domestic violence and tyranny. For the other it may involve the loss of a parent who would have been a civilising influence on his or her life. Each child must (and will) creatively make something of this fact – it is not a determinant shove that pushes a human being in an ineluctable direction. But what of the high correlation that occurs between broken homes and delinquency? Is this not proof of such simple determinacy? No, for two reasons: firstly, it may be true that for a *specified* period a sizeable proportion of human beings placed in particular circumstances make similar choices. But this is not the same as a physical law. Tables do not choose which way to go when they are pushed: consciousness does not intervene in the process – human beings do. Secondly, and more subtly, the process of collecting criminal statistics involves human subjectivity: what is crime or delinquency is a subjective decision. Undoubtedly the vandalism of lower working class kids (who have a greater proportion of broken homes) is more likely to be considered delinquent than the vandalism of middle class youth. Thus, spraying 'Sex Pistols' on a wall may be delinquent whilst painting 'Peace Now' – both graffiti, involve equal cost to remove – may be seen as an unfortunate but understandable lapse due to political idealism. Now, all agencies of social control: the police, social workers and the courts, are inundated with offenders. There are too many delinquents and not enough people to cope with them or places to put them. Decisions have to be made in order to distinguish who is a 'real' delinquent from a kid who is merely experimenting or acting atypically. In order to make these decisions social control agencies use theories of delinquency – a particularly potent one being the theory which links paternal deprivation to delinquency. That is, when confronted with a youth who has committed an offence, they decide whether he or she is a 'serious' case by utilization of case history reports in which a broken home is a crucial factor in making the decision whether to proceed with the case or, indeed, incarcerate the youth. In short, if we apply subcultural theory to control agencies, we are able to see how social workers confronted with their work problems make decisions about the classification of juvenile misbehaviour based on a theory which has become part of their culture in this period which would self-fulfil the correlation between juvenile delinquency and broken homes.

All of this, involving human subjectivity, both in the commission – or not – of delinquent acts or the classification – or not – of acts as delinquents – the fundamental dyad of realism – is far removed from the formation of physical laws of inanimate objects.

(4) The Social Context of Discontent: The Individual and the Social

Subcultural theory attempts to place the behaviour of people in the context of the wider society. It does not explain human action in terms of the propensity of particular individuals (e.g. he is violent because he is a 'psychopath', she has a large number of sexual partners because she is a 'nymphomaniac', he is greedy because he is 'evil'). Rather it suggests that individuals can only be understood in terms of the subcultures of which they are a part. As an instance let us look at the explanation of the relatively high level of drug addiction amongst physicians:

> Take the example of the doctor who faces the problem of overwork combined with a painful gastro-intestinal disorder. As a member of the subculture of medicine he has a considerable knowledge of drugs, both in terms of their effects and also in terms of their required prescription. He also has high accessibility to a multitude of drugs. Secretly, therefore, he prescribes himself daily shots of morphine. He does not see himself as likely to become addicted, as his expertise in medicine equips him with the belief that he can control its use. He will take the opiate in order to pursue ends compatible with his profession (i.e. to continue working) rather than for pleasure as with the lower-class addict. If he becomes, eventually, dependent on morphine the addiction will be shaped, timed, administered and resolved in terms of his culture. All in all, therefore, the solution to his problem is understandable only in terms of the subculture of medicine to which he belongs. (Young, 1971, p. 92).

Note that the physician addict, in contrast, say, to the street junkie, acts as an isolated individual, yet his or her response is explicable in terms of belonging to a medical subculture. Similarly, the isolated suburban housewife addicted to valium or experiencing persistent domestic violence may not know that their situation is comparatively common, yet will interpret what is happening to her from the perspective of the subculture of middle class femininity to which she belongs.

Both the isolated individual and the individual in a group evolving collective norms must be understood in terms of their subculture. And behaviour 'objectively' identical becomes dissimilar, depending on the context. Thus, to explain the addiction of the street addict, one must turn to the particular lower working class culture to which he or she belongs. It is only this way the extremely contrasting life-styles of two groups who are both heavily addicted to opiates (the doctor usually much more so than the street addict, incidentally) can be explained. (see Young, 1988).

(5) The Global Context of Discontent: The Macro and the Micro: Consensus and Diversity

Thus subcultural theory focuses on the group rather than the individual; but it then places the group in the context of the total society. The delinquent gang is not to be understood in terms of the values of an isolated group somewhere in the ghetto: but the gang must be understood in the ghetto and the ghetto within the culture, politics and economy of an advanced capitalist society. And Punk is not just an interesting youth style evolved out of the blue in the early eighties, but related to and was caused by, the particular problems of unemployment and disillusionment in Britain at that time. All three dimensions, discussed above, are given relevance by this insistence on viewing the micro-level (subculture) within the context of the macro-level (the total society). Thus the subcultural meanings given by the actors – the subjective level – become more capable of being seen objectively from the viewpoint of the total society. The history of a subcultural group has to be viewed as the trajectory through a changing wider social order. And the subcultural group is creative within the compass of a surrounding and determining totality. (See Mills, 1959).

Subcultural theory maintains that people are satisfied or dissatisfied dependent on the comparisons they make. The relationship between the total society and the group is crucial here. People simply do not make comparisons and say 'that is just', 'that is unfair' on their own, as it were. Rather the standards and comparisons are structured by forces arising at the level of the wider social order, which not only provides universal criteria by which to make comparisons, but actually on which people are grouped together in terms of physical proximity. That is, the social order facilitates or obfuscates – either intentionally or, more usually, unintentionally – this process. And, if we turn once again to the topic of crime, that a fundamental irony is that what is seen as the most basic example of anti-social behaviour is itself a product of the dominant values and economic pressures of conforming to society. (See Merton, 1938).

Crime, then, can only be understood in the context of the wider society: it is a product of forces within the totality; at times it epitomizes values which stem from the most law-abiding virtues of that society. At others contra-cultural values are seen as a product of reaction to the wider values. In this way consensus and diversity of value are seen to intimately relate to each other.

Subcultural Theory: Its Virtues and Its Views

Without a doubt subcultural theory represents a significant advance in the study of crime. As a way of viewing juvenile crime and youth cultures, in particular, it has had enormous influence. In the act of granting the offenders meaning, it has dominated progressive criminology over the last fifty or more years.

Mature subcultural theorization occurred in two major waves: a liberal current in American sociology of the early 1960s and a Marxist version, particularly in Britain, in the late 1970s. Both remain considerable influences today. The American work was pioneered by writers such as Albert Cohen, Richard Cloward and Lloyd Ohlin. The British work was epitomized by the writings stemming from the Centre for Contemporary Cultural Studies at the University of Birmingham. Examples of the latter work are *Policing the Crisis* (S. Hall *et al.* 1978) and *Resistance Through Rituals* (S. Hall and T. Jefferson [eds] 1975). In the Table below I have chronicled – admittedly pretty selectively – the development of subcultural theory.

THE DEVELOPMENT OF SUBCULTURAL THEORY

FIRST WAVE

U.S. 1955 Albert Cohen *Delinquent Boys: The Culture of the Gang*

U.S. 1960 R. Cloward & L. Ohlin *Delinquency and Opportunity*

U.K. 1964 J.B. Mays *Crime and Social Structure*

U.K. 1966 David Downes *The Delinquent Solution*

PERIOD OF SYNTHESIS AND CRITICISM

U.S 1964 David Matza *Delinquency and Drift*

U.S. 1964 Albert Cohen 'The Sociology of the Deviant Act'

U.S. 1966 David Matza *Becoming Deviant*

U.S. 1966 D. Ward & Kassebaum *Women and Prison*

U.S. 1968 C. Valentine *Culture and Poverty*

U.K. 1971 Jock Young *The Drugtakers*

U.K. 1972 Stan Cohen *Folk Devils and Moral Panics*

SECOND WAVE

U.K. 1976 Phil Cohen 'Working Class Youth Cultures in East London'

U.K. 1975 John Clarke *et al. Resistance Through Ritual*

U.K. 1977 Paul Willis *Learning to Labour*

U.K. 1978 S. Hall *et al. Policing the Crisis*

U.K. 1978 P. Cohen & D. Robins *Knuckle Sandwich*

U.K. 1979 Paul Corrigan *Schooling the Smash Street Kids*

U.K. 1979 Dick Hebdidge *Subculture: The Theory of Style*

U.K. 1979 Ken Pryce *Endless Pressure*

U.K. 1980 Mike Brake *The Sociology of Youth Culture*

U.S. 1985 H. & J. Schwendinger *Adolescent Subcultures and Delinquency*

The new Marxist subcultural theorists of the second wave tended to see themselves as radically different from the 'bourgeois' structural functionalists who preceded them but there are many convergences. In particular note the remarkable similarities between Albert Cohen's 1955 book, *Delinquent Boys: the Culture of the Gang* and Paul Willis' *Learning to Labour,* written at the beginning of the Marxist second wave, twenty two years later. For whilst there were important differences, there were core similarities. As Stan Cohen astutely noted:

> When new subcultural theory appeared in Britain at the beginning of the seventies it was concerned to show how radically it differed from tradition. And it could hardly have looked more different.

> It was not just the switch from functionalist to Marxist language but the sense conveyed of why this switch 'had' to take place. The context was light years away from America in the mid-fifties: a sour, post welfare state Britain which had patently not delivered the goods; the cracking of all those interdependent myths of classlessness, embourgeoisement, consumerism and pluralism; the early warnings of economic recession and high (particularly juvenile) unemployment; the relative weakness of recognizably political resistance.

> History and political economy became open rather than hidden; the 'problem' of the working class adolescent was seen not in terms of adjustment, or providing more opportunities to buy a larger share of the cake, but of bitter conflict, resistance and strife. The delinquent changed from 'frustrated social climber' to cultural innovator and critic. What was really happening on the beaches of Brighton and Clacton – as well as earlier at the Teddy Boy dance halls and later on the football terraces and punk concerts – was a drama of profound symbolic resonance. Subculture was, no less, a political battleground between the classes.

> It is worth noting, though, that for all its obvious novelty and achievement....the new theory shares a great deal more with the old than it cared to admit. Both work with the same 'problematic'.... growing up in a class society; both identify the same vulnerable group: the urban male working-class late adolescent; both see delinquency as a collective solution to a structurally imposed problem. (S. Cohen, 1980, pp. iii–iv).

I have, hopefully, made clear this common core of both subcultural theories in terms of the attempts to encompass the five dichotomies of subjectivity and objectivity, present and past, creativity and determinism, individual and social, micro and macro levels of analysis. Such an analysis which attempts to give meaning, rationality and voluntarism to deviant actors within a determinate world stands apart from a host of more conservative understandings of crime, youth and delinquency. As Cohen puts it:

> These common assumptions must be emphasized precisely because they do *not* appear in the rhetoric of moral panics or in conventional criminology or in the official control culture. (*Ibid*, p.iv).

But, as with many a theory, its virtues led to its vices. For the attempts to encompass the dichotomies often lead to a fake emphasis on one pole at the expense of the other. And just as the two waves of theory had common, though concealed, similarities, they not surprisingly had the same failings. Thus Marxist subcultural theory tends to unwittingly replicate the mistakes of bourgeois subcultural theory. Let us examine the problems:

(1) The Problem of Over-Rationality

In attempting to grant the human actor a sense of making his or her history in a determinate world not of their own choosing there is a tendency to bestow over-rationality on them. That is, to see the subcultural project as necessarily involving much reasoning, or distancing from the determining circumstances which surround the individuals involved is making an optimistic assumption. All too often what happens is an unreflective bouncing off the conditions which confront them. This can range from being so beset by circumstances that the person allows his or her self to give way to them. He or she is, in David Matza's phrase, 'free to drift' (*Delinquency and Drift*, 1964). The alcoholic gives in to his alcoholism, the petty criminal robs the next door neighbour's gas meter, the kids hang around on the street trying to survive. All of this might involve reason, and often a subcultural context, but the rationality may be simply borrowed from the more predatory portion of conventional reason and what is more, it may simply not work. For to grant rationality is not to maintain that the activities which ensue are particularly tenable. They may keep things going for a while, they may purchase survival at the expense of others in the same fate or they may, in fact, make matters worse. Rationality may be encumbered: so that people act *as if* they were determined actors, rationality may be borrowed from the meanest conventions of society, and it may undermine the possibilities of genuine freedom for oneself and others. Take street crime as an instance: pimping does not create freedom for the sister, dealing in hard drugs does not aid the brother on the streets, burglary does not help the problems of one's neighbour on the block. And as for the hustlers themselves? As Malcolm X put it, when writing about his old fellow-hustlers in Harlem:

> Hearing the usual fates of so many others. Bullets, knives, prison, dope, diseases, insanity, alcoholism... so many of the survivors whom I knew as tough hyenas and wolves of the streets in the old days now were so pitiful. They had known all the angles but beneath that surface they were poor, ignorant, untrained black men; life had eased up on them and hyped them. I ran across close to twenty-five of these old-timers I had known pretty well, who in the space of nine years had been reduced to the ghetto's minor, scavenger hustles to scratch up room for rent and food money. Some now worked downtown, messengers, janitors, things like that. (*The Autobiography of Malcolm X*).

There are two tendencies in Marxist views of crime, both of them prefigured in Engel's *Conditions of the Working Class in England.*(1969/1844). For Engels the working man could be so brutalized as to become a determined creature: 'as much a thing without volition as water' (p. 159). For:

> There is no cause for surprise if the workers, treated as brutes, actually become such. (p. 144).

Where volition does occur, it is the rationality of the market place:

> In this country, social war is under full headway, everyone stands for himself against all comers, and whether or not he shall injure all the others who are his declared foes, depends upon a cynical calculation as to what is most advantageous for himself. (*Ibid*, p.161).

Against this, Engels recognizes that some forms of crime can in fact be a primitive form of protest – a proto-revolutionary act:

It was not clear to his mind why he, who did more for society than the rich idler, should be the one to suffer under these conditions. Want conquered his inherited respect for the sacredness of property, and he steals....That was the most primitive form of protest. (*Ibid.* p.240).

As he notes, even in this last instance:

Crime did not help matters. The criminal could protest against the existing order of society only singly, as one individual; the whole might of society was brought to bear upon each criminal and crushed him with its immense superiority. (*Ibid*, p. 240).

These two Marxist perspectives on crime have remained with us: on the one hand, crime as a product of demoralization, a reflection of capitalism, a determination of the market, where rationality, at its best, follows that of individualism which is sooner or later an untenable enterprise; or crime as a pre-figurative form of rebellion, the Robin Hood or 'Primitive Rebel', who has seen through the fakeness of society and inarticulately creates his own destiny. If, furthermore, in the first case rationality is either absent or limited, in the second it is the *criminal* who is the rational minority amongst a mass of people who are irrationally and automatically accepting oppression. On the one side the notion of the lumpenproletariat; on the other the romantic hero. And, of course, even outside of Marxism such a contradiction also exists. The appeal of the working class professional criminal as a hero is enormous: witness the media attention given to the Krays in Britain and the American romanticisation of the Mafia in *The Godfather*.

I shall return to this theme later; let us note that such a contradiction remains unresolved. For the moment Steven Marcus's comment on the discussion is extremely pertinent in its application to crime and to subcultural theories of deviancy in general:

An inescapable part of the meaning of crime is its essential failure. *It is insufficiently rational and excessively, or too purely, symbolic and symptomatic.* Most of all, in it the criminal remains socially untransformed: he is still an isolated individual pursuing activities in an underground and alternate marketplace; if he is successful, he is a small-time entrepreneur; at best he is a member or leader of a gang. In no instance is he capable of organizing a movement to withstand the institutional forces that are arrayed against him. He lives in a parallel and parasitic world whose horizon is bounded and obscured by the larger society upon which it depends. (1975, pp. 223–4).

(2) The Problem of Overcoherence

Constantly in subcultural theory there has been a tendency to draw a picture which was much more coherent than reality. For by granting full subjectivity to the actors involved in a deviant enterprise they tended to present this subjectivity as of necessity coherence and non-contradictory. It is as if one were completing one of those games in a children's comic where you join up all the dots to make a face. In the comic all the dots are there; they are all equally emphasised and there is only one face. But in terms of a subculture, the researcher in reality finds that some of the dots are missing, some are extremely feint and there is often more than one face. The temptation, however, is in the interests of granting the actors a culture: to find a face to depict a coherent, well thought out, non-contradictory subculture where nothing of the sort exists. (See Young, 2010).

To the question, then, 'what are delinquents?' the American theorists would talk about 'the delinquent subculture' with well-drawn codes of honour based on 'rep' and the mobilization of violence. Whilst the British theorists describe punks, teds, mods or what have you, with a clear definition of their style which ignores the lack of clarity of the actors themselves.

One of the few subcultural theorists to recognise this is Paul Corrigan, in his study of Sunderland kids. Thus he writes:

> For most kids where it's at is the street; not the romantic action-packed streets of the ghetto, but the wet pavements of Wigan, Shepherds Bush and Sunderland. The major activity in this venue, the main action of British subculture is, in fact, 'doing nothing'.
>
> What sort of thing do you do with your mates?
>
> DUNCAN: Just stand around talking about footy. About things.
>
> Do you do anything else?
>
> DUNCAN: Joke, lark about, carry on. Just what we feel like really.
>
> What's that?
>
> DUNCAN: Just doing things. Last Saturday someone started throwing
>
> bottles and we all got in.
>
> What happened?
>
> DUNCAN: Nothing really.
>
> All these activities come under the label of 'doing nothing' and they represent the largest and most complex youth subculture. In fighting boredom the kids do not choose the street as a wonderfully lively place, rather they look on it as the place where there is the most chance that something will happen. Doing nothing on the street must be compared with the alternatives: for example, knowing that nothing will happen with Mum and Dad in the front room; being almost certain that the youth club will be full of boredom. This makes the street the place where something might just happen, if not this Saturday, then surely next. (1976, pp. 103–4).

In the area of crime and delinquency the problem of overcoherence leads to a blindness towards the sporadic and drifting nature of much deviancy. In particular it encourages an overestimation of the level of commitment of the actors involved.

But it is not only in the dilemmas of half-heartedness that such mistaken assumptions are made. More seriously there is a tendency to ignore the fact that crime and delinquency can occur where there is genuine social breakdown. As I have argued previously:

> The new deviancy theorists accused those who operated with notions of social disorganisation of belittling, or denying the authenticity, of alternative forms of social organization developed in pursuit of other than dominant goals. However important this accusation may have been in pointing to the plurality of social organizations in a divided society, the fact remains that certain...areas *are* disorganized; and that this disorganization relates both to the external and internal forces acting on such areas (for example, on skid-row, or in 'hippie' communities)... And it is absurd to deny that phenomena like marital breakdown are irrelevant, at the micro-level of interaction, in the aetiology of deviant behaviour. To accord subcultural solution authenticity is not equivalent to endowing it with health. (1975, p. 73).

Ken Pryce, in his study of the West Indian area of Bristol, castigates those who confuse social disorganization with the notion of an alternative community:

> The lack of community in St Paul's is often not apparent to strangers visiting the area for the first time, especially students and intellectuals with their tendency to romanticize the deviant and the exotic. Diverse groups with vastly dissimilar backgrounds do mingle freely in close physical interaction in St Paul's. But this is deceptive, for mingling of this kind does not automatically create a sense of conformity, consensus, and vigilance about community standards. The only unity is an external one, in the form of common services utilized by all.

> Beneath the romantic's illusion of a tight-knit, friendly, organic, warm, harmonious community, the divisions are deep. There is much suspicion between groups. The very fact that in St Paul's people are 'not fussy' (which is what attracts middle-class students 'n' intellectuals), the very fact that there are no constraining community standards, no overriding considerations that people are forced to adhere to, is one reason why St Paul's is a shanty town. The social heterogeneity of the neighbourhood and the suspicion reigning between groups, especially different ethnic groups, gives rise to a sort of 'anything goes' atmosphere, in which one group tends to view members from other groups as easy prey and fair game for exploitation. There is no melting-pot morality combining disparate elements into one. (1979, pp. 29–30).

The 'community' which occurs, Pryce notes, echoing Simmel, is 'bound only by commerce' – social behaviour is united only by the silver threads of the market place.

Once again, a virtue of subcultural theory: its emphasis on creativity, authenticity and alternative forms of organization creates a blindness about the absolute opposite. To distinguish the two moments: that of the generation of alternative norms and that of the disintegration of social behaviour is extremely difficult. But distinguish them we *must*.

Drug use and sale may, for example, be part of an apathy which has spread through a community. It may proselytize in a fashion that creates around it further demoralization and generates organized crime and predatory criminality. It may, on the other hand, be part of a positive culture which is affirmative of the community, of enjoyment and of the need for change. It may be inconsequential, it may have profoundly negative or important positive effects on the community.

It is thus an extremely, easy task to project onto a subculture an organized system of values where there are none, or one which ignores crucial contradictions or ones which are, in fact, the very opposite of reality. I shall further explore the latter point in the next section.

(3) The Problem of the Existence of Contracultures

A classic distinction in subcultural theory is between subcultures and contracultures. A subculture, strictly speaking, is in the case of youth, for example, one which arises out of the concerns of young people (eg. mating, dating), but does not isolate the central values of society. A contraculture – or counterculture – has as its central concerns values and behaviour which are oppositional to the status quo.

In the first wave of subcultural theory in the United States, such oppositional cultures were seen as centring around delinquency and gang violence. Thus, a youth belonging to such a contraculture, saw stealing and violence as a central part of his lifestyle (compared to the 'honesty' and 'docility' of the wider American Society) and he acted out such values as a member of a gang. Crime which was seen as, by definition, an anathema to American Values became thus celebrated in the oppositional values of youth. But where were these contraculture? Criminologists looked everywhere but they could not find them.

It was into this controversy that David Matza's book, *Delinquency and Drift* entered as an important counterbalance to the excesses of subcultural theory. We have already seen, in our discussion of rationality, how Matza counterposed to the notion of the well worked out subcultural project the concept of drift. Often the delinquency merely drifted, sporadically into crime, neither have the ideas been well formulated, nor is any great distance achieve from conventional values and situations. He developed this further; the subculture of delinquency, he argues, is:

> facilitated and perhaps even dependent on support and reinforcement from conventional sources. (It) is buttressed by beliefs that flourish influential sectors of the normative order. These views... include the professional ideology of criminology, psychiatry and social work, an emergent ideology of leisure...the cult of cowboy masculinity in the mass media. (1964, p. 62).

The subcultural theorists are in agreement with more orthodox views on crime on one thing. That is that crime is carried out by criminals who positively embrace illegality. For the conservative theorist it is because the person is either willfully evil or lacks a sense of legality; for the subcultural theorist it is because a culture has emerged which elevates criminality to a virtue. Both of these are – in the vast majority of instances – wrong.

If delinquent youth cultures were genuinely contracultural then crime would be justified in terms of a conflict with propertied society, as a redistribution of wealth or even as a means of hitting out at the system. In fact, such a situation is rarely come across. There are, of course, youths and adults who have committed crimes for explicitly political reasons. Socialist and nationalist groups from the Bolsheviks at the beginning of the century to the Provisional IRA, more recently, have in a fairly disciplined fashion, robbed banks to raise money for such purposes as the purchase of arms. They have been explicit in their criminality: they have also invariably been scathing in their attitudes to petty crime and anti-social behaviour within their own communities. But the average offender – whether youthful or adult – is far from radically articulate about their infractions. The way in which the bind of law is neutralized is, in fact, as Matza argues, in strictly conventional terms. That is where violation of the law is brought about paradoxically because of concerns about legality.

There are two ways in which an initial commitment to legality leads to the breaking of laws. The first – and the most immediate – is where the individual feels wronged by others because of their illegal actions towards him or her. An act of domestic violence occurs towards a wife and she hits back; a person steals from his friend and he or she seeks redress in a fight; trust is broken – the police are seen to be ineffective in acting on behalf of the person concerned – so he or she acts in order to restore the balance of justice. Here a commitment to legality leads directly to illegality. There are, however, more indirect, yet extremely significant ways which such a commitment can lead to its opposite. The role of the police is crucial here. The police are the most obvious and intrusive representatives of law and order in the community. As I have argued throughout, one of the most decisive events in the breaking of a young person's bond to the status quo is the experience of illegal and unjust activities by the police. Police violence, arbitrary arrest, prejudiced and abusive behaviour create the conditions by which young people are able to detach themselves from the ranks of the orderly. Bad policing leads to crime. But it leads to crime, not because of some contraculture which has evolved out of the blue or, in the case of black youth, some culture carried over unchanged from the West Indies. Rather it is a culture of discontent which righteously foments over the violation of its rights and whose rhetoric centres around legality. It is not couched, like a *Socialist Worker* editorial, in terms of the sham of bourgeois legality: rather it is the palpable violation of civil rights which are prized and esteemed which fuels the rebellion of youth against authority. It is not a commitment to illegality but a violation of legality which precipitates the individual into crime. Nowhere is this seen more blatantly than in the instance of young blacks. Police racism so palpably violates notions of equality under the law which black youth manifestly and quite rightly demand. It is the degree to which they identify themselves as citizens, with rights which have been violated, rather than alien immigrants which fuels this anger.

I have traced the fashion in which people drift into crime and I have been severely critical of those theorists who see crime as a product of alternative values of contracultures. Rather we have seen that both the causes of crime and the circumstances which facilitate the commission of crime are closely related to conventional values. Furthermore, the eventual values which the criminal embraces are a caricature of convention.

I wish to argue that in the second, radical, wave of subcultural theory precisely the same error occurred. For if it were true that we live in a class divided society, then it was to be expected that certain segments of the population would experience this most acutely. Thus, just as with the first wave, the focus became on working class youth culture. Here, whether it was with Punks or Skinheads, or Rastas, the contraculture was to be found. In the second wave, such a contraculture would be constructed not around anti-social events such as gang violence, but around more radical 'insights' into the world. The new subcultural theorist then had as a task 'reading' the varied youth styles in a fashion which revealed the underlying radical symbolism of its adherents. On one level the virtue of subcultural theory of stressing human creativity and meaning produced some amazingly perceptive insights into the world of deviant youth. On the other, the vice of a blindness to determination and conventionality was frequently evidenced. The relationship of youth culture to the straight world is thus played down and downright examples of conservatism interpreted as radical. As Stan Cohen shrewdly notes, there is a:

constant impulse to decode the style in terms only of opposition and resistance. This means that instances are sometimes missed when the style is conservative or supportive: in other words, not reworked or reassembled but taken over intact from dominant commercial culture. Such instances are conceded, but then brushed aside because – as we all know – the style is a *bricolage* of inconsistencies and, anyway, things are not what they seem and so the apparently conservative meaning really hides just the opposite. (1980, p.xii).

The degree of commitment of youth to their deviant cultures is given precious little consideration. Much of youth culture involves 'bricollaging', borrowing from the available cultural stock in order to lever out an identity of difference. But this difference is not necessarily a qualitative one. The white youth wearing a Che Guevara sweatshirt is not necessarily yearning to fight in the sierras. The black youth with dreadlocks is probably not a fully fledged and committed Rastafarian. As Cashmore and Troyna put it:

The street-corner gang member may have lived at home quite satisfactorily in comfortable domestic circumstances; he may have attended black discotheques yet have had a white girlfriend; he may have hung around with others who disregarded the educational systems and still carried on at school or college; he may have criticised the oppressive white dominance of Babylon, but still have worked as an electrical engineer in a white-owned company from 9 till 5. He may, as one youth we knew, have held very vehement views on the exploitative structures of white control until that day, yet continue to work sedulously taking advantage of government training schemes to improve his professional qualifications.

Basically, our point is simple: young blacks always had and still have, their fingers in a number of cultural pies and to assign them to specific lifestyles...is tantamount to freezing a frame and studying it while the movie is still running – you miss the interesting bits. Our investigations indicate that black youth did not and does not adopt one cultural lifestyle but mix many. So it would be feasible to expect the ostensibly docile bakery worker to be a hostile critic of white society, a part-time pimp, a Pentecostalist church member and the organiser of an all-black, self-help group. He does not have to belong to one culture; he may belong to many. (1982, p. 27).

For there is much 'posing' in youth styles. They, as Simon Frith puts it, 'pass through groups, change identities and play their leisure roles for fun.' (1978, p. 53).

This process of overplaying the contracultural nature of a phenomenon, can be seen on various levels. We do not examine the contradictions in the most vivid examples of youth rebellion: that is in their conventional *as well* as their radical motifs.

And finally, it does not capture the drifting, testing – or perhaps a better word is 'tasting' – of youthful commitment. The most obvious danger of such a plethora of subcultural forms is that it presents the theorist – whether sociologist or journalist – with the maximum possible potential for projecting his or her own preconceptions. It also allows for the radical and fake optimism as to the revolutionary potential of the future. But, in the area of crime, the effect on young people themselves is more dramatic. Because, as conventional wisdom on both left and right stresses commitment, it over-emphasizes the criminal identification of youth. That is, it sees people who commit offences as criminals and acts towards them with commensurate severity. The reality is the opposite: commitment only occurs as a result of prolonged social reaction to the offender, itself a product of such beliefs.

(4) The Problem of Consensus and Diversity

The problem of the relationship between a pointed dominant culture and the subcultures of subordinate groups is central to sociology. Studies of working class culture have debated the area vigorously, seeking, like criminologists, and with equal uncertainty, for genuine oppositional cultures (see N. Abercrombie *et al*, 1980; F. Parkin, 1972; M. Mann, 1973). The debate about the culture of poverty is beset with identical problems (see C. Valentine, 1968).

As we have seen, the contraculture of the gang was seldom to be found. Even worse, contracultures occurred in all the wrong places. In youth culture it was the middle class hippie, not the working class delinquent who formed the more genuine contracultures. Whilst in studies of class consciousness rather than the working class embracing Marxist ideas, it was middle class intellectuals. And it is not amongst the most hardly pressed women at the bottom of the social structure that radical feminist ideas arose, but amongst relatively well off professional women. None of this, in fact, contradicts the relative deprivation theory, the message of which is that discontent is greatest where relative inequalities are most visible and blocked opportunities are most apparent. More importantly, it points to the relative rarity of well thought out contracultural values. As Abercrombe *et al* point out in their discussion of the search for alternative ideologies amongst the working class:

> [These writers] demand what would seem to be unreasonably straight conditions for the rejection of the dominant ideology. [They seem] to be unaware that the possession of a coherent, well-formed and clearly articulated philosophy is a rarity even in the dominant class, and is probably found only among certain intellectual groups. (1980, p.141).

Instead they argue that what occurs is the partial rejection and embracing of dominant ideas, the contradictory nature of class consciousness and the inarticulate and non-abstract nature of much opposition. Charles Valentine, in his parallel analysis of the culture of poverty, comes to very similar conclusions:

> One further consideration has received little attention in the relevant literature, probably because the stress on subcultural distinctiveness has inhibited its exploration. This is the possibility that commitment to values, norms, and other cultural themes may often involve ambiguity, ambivalence, and the simultaneous holding of alternative or contradictory beliefs. Some of these possibilities are suggested by Rodman's ingenious idea of 'value-stretch'. Lee Rainwater has recently followed this up by exploring thoughtfully how 'conventional society manages somehow to inculcate its norms even in those persons who are not able to achieve successfully in terms of them,' including groups who are thought to live within a poverty subculture. This consideration needs empirical development through ethnographic field work so that we may see more clearly how subcultural elements and total-system universals can coexist as simultaneously available alternatives. (1968, p. 120).

Later in his book he contrasts his model of the culture of poverty with both those versions that see the culture of the poor as an underclass lacking culture and thus of an unremittingly anti-social nature, or those which see it as a distinct, alternative culture which is a positive, social response to aggression:

> The lower-class poor possess some distinct subcultural patterns, even though they also subscribe to norms of the middle class or the total system in some of the same areas of life and are quite

nondistinctive in other areas; there is variation in each of these dimensions from one ethnic group to another.

> The distinctive patterns of the poverty subcultures, like those of the other subsocieties, include not only pathogenic traits but also healthy and positive aspects, elements of creative adaptation to conditions of deprivation. (Ibid, p. 142–3).

There is much that criminological subculture theory can learn from this and, indeed, it is a position which key critics of subcultural theory, particularly David Matza, have pointed us towards.

But a further problem remains, for if diversity is a less obvious phenomenon than would appear at first, so too is consensus. The notion of a dominant ideology embraced by the population and endorsed by both Parsonian Functionalist and Marxist theorists has been roundly criticized by Nicholas Abercrombie and Bryan Turner. Consensual values as a social cement which binds society together applauded by Functionalists and lamented as the prime source of false consciousness by Althusserian Marxists, simply exaggerates the coherentness and over-emphasizes the non-contradictory nature of dominant values in advanced capitalist societies. Further, to this I would add (1) it over-emphasizes the level of which élite values which percolate down to subordinate groups and under-emphasizes the fashion in which the values of subordinate groups rise up; (2) it puts too great an emphasis on the role of ideas as moulding people's consciousness and too little on their everyday experience of material reality.

(5) The Problem of Objectivity

> I sometimes have a sense of working-class kids suffering an awful triple fate. First, their actual current prospects are grim enough; then their predicament is used, shaped and turned to financial profit by the same interests which created it – and then – the final irony – they find themselves patronized in the latest vocabulary imported from the Left Bank. (S. Cohen, 1980, pp. xxviii).

Subcultural theory insists on being 'appreciative' of taking the subjective meanings that criminal values have seriously. Their account, it is argued, is a vital part of the explanation. First, give your actors the chance to speak for themselves and then place their beliefs in the objective centre which the theorist has worked out. The irony is that what often happens is that the subjectivity which the theorist recounts to the reader is, in fact, very largely a projection of his own 'objective' vision. That is, just as too much coherence is teased out of subcultures, so often this teasing is very selective and creative on the part of the theorist.

Sometimes, the actors themselves cannot understand the interpretation. It reminds one of Genet's rueful comment that he could not understand a word of the biography that Sartre wrote of him. Stan Cohen puts this point well:

> This leads on to the vexing issue of consciousness and intent.... Now it would be as absurd to demand here that every bearer of symbols walk around with structuralist theory in his head, as it would be to expect the oppressed to have a detailed knowledge of dialectical materialism. It seems to me, though, that *somewhere* along the line, symbolic language implies a knowing subject, a subject at least dimly

aware of what the symbols are supposed to mean. To be really tough-minded about this, our criterion for whether or not to go along with a particular symbolic interpretation should be Beckett's famous warning to his critics: 'no symbols where none intended'. (Ibid, pp. xiii–xiv).

This problem is one of methodology involving the 'dangers of the forest of symbols without a method'. (p. xvii). Thus, Cohen takes issue with Dick Hebdige's assertion that the use of swastikas by punks was really not a sign of Fascist inclinations – for, in fact, they tended to support anti-Fascist movements. That is, the symbol was 'read' the opposite of its usual meaning. This, he points out, goes:

> right against widespread findings about the racism and support for restrictive immigration policies among substantial sections of working class youth....We are given no clue about how these particular actors manage the complicated business of distancing and irony. In the end, there is no basis whatsoever for choosing between this particular sort of interpretation and any others: say, that for many or most of the kids walking around with swastikas on their jackets, the dominant context is simple conformity, blind ignorance or knee-jerk racism. (Ibid, pp. xvii–xviii).

There is, thus, a danger that such groups become sort of subcultural Rorschach blobs onto which the theorist projects his or her own private definitions of objectivity. At the very least, then, one must proceed with an adequate methodology. It is a pity that we have so soon forgotten the demand, so frequent in the sixties, that sociological research should be fed back to the subjects of investigation to see if they recognized themselves in the accounts of the social scientist. Very often – they cannot; and very often, as David Matza has indicated, they protest, in very conventional terms, over the manner in which their behaviour was being interpreted.

(6) The Problem of Causality

In the process of giving history to a particular subculture the present ongoing events often become overwhelmed by the causality of the past. The delinquent gang thus acts out an essence formed in the past: black youth are given plenty of causality *in the past* (for example, in their African roots), but that causality in the past is seen to override the present. This is cultural essentialism, which is very similar in form to Freudianism. It is not that it denies causality – far from it – but it puts it in the past where the mould has formed. Events after that become merely precipitating circumstances. For example, the importance of changes in policing is underestimated in the causality of alienation. In some of the theories the kids seem to replay the problems of their parents as if they were characters in an Ibsen play.

The focus on subculture as an essence that unfolds, often loses sight of the importance of the ongoing trajectory. The way in which administrative agencies can impact and change the path of a subculture; and the way in which subcultures can creatively change. It is as if the subculture was granted creativity by the theorist when concentrating on the first causes, but thereafter is denied it.

The focus on subculture not only denies the impact of administrative agencies, it also denies the structural reality of the agencies themselves. That is, there is no *symmetry* in the understanding of the world. The subcultural actors exist in a different order of existence than the agencies of control that surround them. thus, for example, a subcultural approach to the police would note how the police – like juvenile delinquents, for example, exist in a particular structural pattern in the world which carries with it certain problems. Their problem of dealing with what is perceived as rising street crime, for instance, together with a plethora of performance indicators. The police evolve a subculture which attempts to understand and solve these problems. The material problems change over time and so does the police subculture and the effect that such changes have on the police and public. Such an approach attempts to both see police practices in the context of shifting beliefs and practices. It parallels and interacts with the analysis of delinquent subcultures themselves. It is rarely attempted in radical subcultural literature which tends to approach the police from an extraordinarily unsophisticated angle. That is, causality is seen as being extremely distinct, very obvious and ineluctable. It is the needs of capital which generates an ineluctable swing towards the strong state. Policing is one vital part of such a movement. But once such an unexplicated, disconnected, ex cathedra causality has been briefly hinted at – then a full-blown voluntarism becomes the order of the day. Chief Commissioners supposedly act out the logic of capital with a precision which would be the envy of any economist.

It is causality which generates major problems for subcultural theories. Here all its virtues, all its attempts to transcend the dichotomies of subjectivity-objectivity, past-present, creativity-determination and the macro- and micro-levels seem to come adrift. I will deal with the more serious of these problems, all of which centre around the tendency towards cultural essentialism, that is, seeing a subculture as a fixed essence which unfolds rather than one which is a continuous human creation. Essentialism occurs in all the disciplines which deal with human behaviour. In subcultural theory it ironically parallels genetic essentialism which views people as playing out the destiny of their genes; instead of this we must view subculture as a creative and, above all, a non-static state.

Subculture as a Non-Static State

A.K. Cohen's perceptively critical article on subcultural theory, written in 1965, noted the assumption of discontinuity implicit in its frequent formulations. 'It treats the deviant act', he writes, 'as though it were an abrupt change of state, a leap from a state of strain or anomie to a state of deviance'. Thus it deals with initial states and eventual outcomes, but neglects the interactive process that occurs between these stages. Instead:

> Human action, deviant or otherwise, is something that typically develops and grows in a tentative, groping, advancing, backtracking, sounding-out process. People taste and feel their way along. They begin an act and do not complete it. They start doing one thing and end up by doing another. They extricate themselves from progressive involvement or become further involved to the point of commitment. (1965, p. 5).

This type of analysis is in the tradition of labelling theorists such as Becker and Lemert; and it is this notion of a gradual process that must be wedded to anomie theory with which to tackle a major flaw in subcultural theory. Merton, for example, moves from anomie to delinquency in a sharp discontinuous fashion, intervening variables determine the form of the deviancy it is true, but these are once and for all interventions which are not considered in processual terms.

Cohen's innovation was to formulate a framework for analyzing the nature of such a process described above by utilising the Mertonian notion of opportunity structure, but giving it a new flexibility suitable for an interaction theory. 'The history of the deviant act', he writes, 'is a history of an interaction process. The antecedents of the act are an unfolding sequence of acts contributed by a set of actors. A makes a move, possibly in a deviant direction; B responds; A responds to B's response etc .... The disjunction between goals and means and the choice of adaptions depends on the opportunity structure. The opportunity structure consists in or is the result of, the actions of other people. These, in turn, are in part reactions to ego's behaviour and may undergo change in response to that behaviour. The development of ego's action can, therefore, be conceptualised as a series of responses on the part of ego, to a series of changes in the opportunity structure resulting from ego's actions. More specifically, altered responses may open up, close off, or leave unaffected legitimate opportunities for ego, and they may do the same to illegitimate opportunities.' (1965; pp. 9–10).

Thus the interaction process between the ego and the environment can be seen in terms of changes in the opportunity structure which the environment presents to the individual. That is, the disjunction between the aspirations and possibilities (i.e. anomie) of the actor, will fluctuate as both the aspirations of ego and the possibilities presented by the environment change. For example, anomie can lead to deviant action which can, because of societal reaction, reduce the existing possibilities of realisation of ego's aspirations, causing an *increase* in the anomie of the actor and a spiral of increasing deviance.

Thus we have a model where the degree of anomie of the actors in a particular structural position is in flux. Such a situation is suggested by Lindesmith and Gagnon in their criticism of subcultural theory:

> The use of drugs is supposed to reduce or eliminate the inner strain resulting from anomie. Yet it is clear that the primary effect of addiction is to widen substantially the gap between aspirations and the means of achievement and to intensify rather than resolve inner anomie-generated conflict. (1964, p. 6).

This movement in the degree of anomie experienced by individuals may, of course, proceed in either direction, dependent partly on the configuration or opportunities available to the actor. I have chosen examples where anomie is intensified merely for illustrative purposes. Labelling theory studies the building up of deviant behaviour in the form of a process; I am postulating that inherent in this very process is the varying degree of anomie of the action which is, in turn, a function of the interaction system.

Thus what occurs in reality is a constant interaction between the actions of the deviant individual and the societal reactions of his or her environment. Solutions to particular initial problems create new problems, generated internally by the inherent contradiction existing in the emerging subculture, and externally by the nature and degree of societal reaction which the solution has evoked from society. New solutions create new contradictions and social responses, and the change in the latter represents a new environment – and therefore problems – for the group. Groups evolve hypotheses as to the nature of their situation and the likely solutions to their problems; they test these hypotheses out in praxis, and, in the conflict between them and the wider society, re-view their situation and formulate alternative hypotheses – however inarticulate – which are, once again, applied to their situation. In the seventies, at a very articulate level, the movement of the ghetto American black from the hedonistic culture of the 'cat' and the 'hustle', to the disciplined puritanism of the Muslims, to the revolutionary stance of the Black Panthers and beyond to a further regroupment after the onslaught of the FBI, is a paradigm instance of this process.

Subcultural Theory Today

Subcultural theory flourishes today everywhere from urban anthropology, to postmodern studies of youth culture to the realms of cultural criminology. It is the implicit base of much of the most influential ethnographies, for example Phillipe Bourgois' *In Search of Respect* (1995), Elijah Anderson's *Code of the Street* (1999) Jay McLeod's *Ain't No Makin'It* (1995). It is the almost forgotten roots of the 'post-subcultural theory of cultural studies and the sociology of youth' (Muggleton and Weinzierl, 2003; Muggleton, 2000; Thornton, 1995). And here it is true to say that this third wave of subcultural theorisation exhibits both the virtues of a stress on creativity and social construction whilst stumbling, once more, on some of the problems – or vices – which we have discussed.

There has been overall a lack of attention about theory; the tentative steps forward which evolved in the sixties and seventies, have simply not been well developed. Sadly just as positivism in American criminology disdained theory, more progressive currents are only just recently turning attention to building on past gains. The importance of subcultural theory which grants crime and deviance meaning and human creativity in the context of a positivism which does just the opposite should not be downplayed. A major aspect of the new cultural criminology emerging in the last few years (Ferrell and Saunders, 1995; Presdee, 2000; Ferrell et al., 2008) is that it fully recognises its lineage in subcultural theory as it attempts to respond to the condition of late modernity in which we now live.

Bibliography

Abercrombie N. and Turner B. (1980), *The Dominant Ideology Thesis*, London: Allen and Unwin.

Anderson, E. (1999), *Code of the Street*. New York: W W Norton.

Bourgois, P. (1995), *In Search of Respect*. Cambridge: Cambridge University Press.

Bourgois, P. (1998), 'Just Another Night in a Shooting Gallery', *Theory, Culture and Society* 15(2), pp. 37–66.

Brake, M. (1980), *The Sociology of Youth Culture and Youth Subcultures: Sex and drugs and Rock n Roll*. London: Routledge and Kegan Paul.

Brake, M. (1985), *Comparative youth culture: The sociology of youth cultures and youth subcultures in America, Britain, and Canada*. London: Routledge and Kegan Paul.

Brotherton, D and Barrios, L. (2004), *The Almighty Latin King and Queen Nation*. New York: Columbia University Press.

Cashmore E and Troyna B. (1982), *Black Youth in Crisis*, London: Allen and Unwin.

Cloward, R. and Ohlin, L. (1961), *Delinquency and Opportunity*. London: Routledge and Kegan Paul.

Cohen, A.K. (1955), *Delinquent Boys: The Culture of the Gang*. New York: The Free Press.

Cohen, A.K. (1965), 'The Sociology of the Deviant Act: Anomie Theory and Beyond', *American Sociological Review*, 30, pp. 5–14.

Cohen, P. (1972), 'Subcultural Conflict and Working Class Community', Centre for Contemporary Culture Studies, *Working Papers* 2, pp. 5–53 (reprinted in Cohen, P. 1997).

Cohen, S. (1972), *Folk Devils and Moral Panics*. London: McGibbon and Kee. Second Edition, 1987.

Cohen, S. (1981), 'Footprints in the Sand' in Fitzgerald, M., McLennan, G. and Pawson, J. (1981), *Crime and society*. London: Routledge and Kegan Paul.

Cohen, S. (1997), 'Intellectual Scepticism and Political Commitment' in P. Walton and J. Young (eds) *The New Criminology Revisited*. London: Macmillan.

Corrigan, P. (1976), *Schooling the Smash Street Kids*. London: Macmillan.

Downes, D. (1966), *The Delinquent Solution*. London: Routledge and Kegan Paul.

Downes, D. (1988), 'The Sociology of Crime and Social Control in Britain 1960–1987' in P Rock (ed.) *The History of British Criminology*. Oxford: Oxford University Press.

Downes, D. and Rock, P. (1988), *Understanding Deviance*. Oxford: Clarendon Press.

Engels, F. (1969) [1844], *Conditions of the Working Class in England in 1844*. London: Panther.

Erikson, K. (1966), *Wayward Puritans*. New York: John Wiley.

Ferrell, J. (1999), 'Cultural Criminology', *Annual Review of Sociology*, 25, pp. 395–418.

Ferrell, J. (2000), 'Making Sense of Crime: Review Essay on Jack Katz's Seductions of Crime, *Social Justice*, 19(3), pp. 111–123.

Ferrell, J. (2004), 'Boredom, Crime and Criminology', *Theoretical Criminology*, 8(3), pp. 287–302.

Ferrell, J. (2005), 'Cultural Criminology', *Blackwell Encyclopaedia of Sociology*. Oxford: Blackwell.

Ferrell, J. and Sanders, C. (1995), 'Culture, Crime and Criminology', in J. Ferrell and C. Sanders (eds) *Cultural Criminology*. Boston: Northeastern University Press.

Ferrell, J. Hayward, K., Young J. (2008), *Cultural Criminology: An Invitation*, London:Sage

Frith S. (1978), *The Sociology of Rock*, London: Constable.

Frith, S. (1983), *Sound Effects: Youth, Leisure and the Politics of Rock 'n' Roll*. London: Constable.

Gaines, D. (1998), *Teenage Wasteland: Suburbia's Dead End Kids*. Chicago: University of Chicago Press.

Galbraith, J.K. (1992), *The Culture of Contentment*. London: Sinclair-Stevenson.

Gans, H. (1995), *The War Against the Poor*. New York: Basic Books.

Goffman, E. (1968), *Asylums*. Harmondsworth: Penguin.

Goode, E. (1994), *Deviant Behaviour* (4th ed) Englewood Cliffs NJ: Prentice Hall.

Hall, S. (Steve) (1997), 'Visceral Culture and Criminal Practices', *Theoretical Criminology* 1(4) pp. 453–78.

Hall, S., Ancrum, C., and Winlow, S. (2007), *Criminal Identities and Consumer Culture*. Cullompton: Willan.

Hall S., Chritcher C. Jefferson T. Clarke J. and Roberts B. (1978), *Policing the Crisis,* London: Macmillan.

Hall, S. and Jefferson, T. (eds) (1975), *Resistance Through Ritual*. London: Hutchinson.

Hayward, K. and Young, J. (2004), 'Cultural Criminology: Some Notes on the Script', *Theoretical Criminology* 8, pp. 259–273.

Hebdige, D. (1979), *Subcultures: The Meaning of Style*. London: Methuen.

Hebdige, D. (1988), *Hiding in the Light*. London: Routledge.

Hebdige, D. (1990), 'Fax to the Future', *Marxism Today* (Jan), pp. 18–23.

Hobsbawm, E. (1964), Labouring Man: Studies in the History of Labour, London: Weidenfeld and Nicolson.

Lemert, E. (1967), *Human Deviance, Social Problems and Social Control*. New Jersey: Pretence Hall.

Lindesmith A. and Gagnon S. (1964), 'Anomie and Drug Addiction' in M.Clinard(ed) *Anomie and Deviant Behavior*, New York: The Free Press.

MacLeod, J. (1995), *Ain't No Makin' It*. Boulder, CO: Westview.

Maffesoli, M. (1996), *The Time of Tribes*. London: Sage.

Maffesoli, M. (2004), 'Everyday Tragedy and Creation', *Cultural Studies,* 18(2/3), pp. 201–210.

Malcolm X. (1987), *Autobiography*, London: Penguin.

Marcus, S. (1975), *Engels, Manchester and the Working Class,* New York: Random House.

Matza, D. (1964), *Delinquency and Drift*, New York: Wiley.

Matza, D. (1969), *Becoming Deviant*. Englewood Cliffs, NJ: Prentice Hall.

Matza, D. and Sykes, G. (1961), 'Juvenile Delinquency and Subterranean Values', *American Sociological Review*, 26, pp. 712–719.

Merton, R.K. (1938), 'Social Structure and Anomie', *American Sociological Review*, 3, pp. 672–82.

Merton, R. (1957), *Social Theory and Social Structure* Rev. Ed. Glencoe: Free Press.

Miller, W. (1958), 'Lower Class Culture as a Generating Milieu of Gang Delinquency', *Journal of Social Issues*, 14(3), pp. 17–23.

Mills, C.W. (1959), *The Sociological Imagination*. New York: Oxford University Press.

Muggleton, D. (2000), *Inside Subculture: The Postmodern Meaning of Style*, Oxford: Berg.

Muggleton D. and Weinzierl, R. (2003), *The Post-subcultures Reader*, Oxford: Berg.

Muncie, J. (1999), *Youth and Crime*. London: Sage.

Nightingale, C. (1993), *On the Edge*. New York: Basic Books.

Parkin F. (1972), *Class Inequality and Political Order*, London: McGibbon and Kee.

Pitts, J. (2001), *The New Politics of Youth Crime*. London: Palgrave.

Pitts, J. (2003), 'New Labour and the Racialisation of Youth Crime', in J. Hagedorn (ed.) *Gangs in the Global City: The Limitations of Criminology*. Champaign, Illinois: University of Illinois Press.

Polsky, N. (1967), *Hustlers, Beats, and Others*. Observations. Chicago: Aldine.

Pountain, D. and Robins, D. (2000), *Cool Rules: Anatomy of an Attitude*. London: Reaktion.

Presdee, M. (2000), *Cultural Criminology and the Carnival of Crime*. London: Routledge.

Pryce K. (1979), *Endless Pressure*, London: Penguin.

Robins, D. (1992), *Tarnished Vision*. Oxford: Oxford University Press.

Schwendinger, H. and Schwendinger, J. (1985), *Adolescent Subcultures and Delinquency*. New York: Praeger.

Sykes, G. (1958), *The Society of Captives*. Princeton NJ: Princeton University Press.

Sykes, G. and Matza, D. (1957), 'Techniques of Neutralization', *American Sociological Review*, 22, pp. 664–670.

Taylor, I., Walton, P. and Young, J. (1973), *The New Criminology*. London: Routledge and Kegan Paul.

Thornton, S. (1995), *Club Cultures: Music, Media, and Subcultural Capital*. Cambridge, UK: Polity Press.

Valentine, C. (1968), *Culture and Poverty*. Chicago: University of Chicago Press.

Ward, D. and Kassebaum G. (1965), *Women and Prison*, London: Weidenfeld and Nicolson.

Willis, P. (1977), *Learning to Labour*. Aldershot: Gower.

Willis, P. (1990), *Common Culture*. Milton Keynes: Open University Press.

Willis, P. (2000), *The Ethnographic Imagination*. Cambridge: Polity.

Yablonsky, L. (1962), *The Violent Gang*. New York: Macmillan.

Young, J. (1971a), 'The Role of Police as Amplifiers of Deviancy, Negotiators of Reality and Translators of Fantasy', in S. Cohen (ed.) *Images of Deviance*. Harmondsworth: Penguin.

Young, J. (1971b), *The Drugtakers*. London: Paladin.

Young, J. (1973), 'The Hippie Solution: An Essay in the Politics of Leisure', in I. Taylor and L. Taylor (eds) *The Politics of Deviancy*. London: Penguin.

Young, J. (1988), 'Deviance and Drugs', in *The New Introductory Sociology* (ed.) P. Worsley, London: Penguin.

Young, J. (1999), *The Exclusive Society*. London: Macmillan.

Young, J. (2003), 'Merton with Energy, Katz with Structure', *Theoretical Criminology,* 7(3) pp. 389–414.

Young, J. (2007a), *The Vertigo Of Late Modernity*, London: Sage.

Young, J. (2007b), *Voodoo Criminology and the Art of Skating on Thin Ice*.

Young, J. (2009), 'Robert Merton and Albert Cohen' in *Fifty Key Thinkers in Criminology* (eds) K. Hayward, S. Maruna and J. Mooney, London: Routledge.

Young, J. (2010), *The Criminological Imagination*, Cambridge: Polity.

Part V
Contemporary Subcultural Theories

[12]

ANGRY AGGRESSION AMONG THE "TRULY DISADVANTAGED"*

THOMAS J. BERNARD
Pennsylvania State University

Violent incidents arising out of trivial conflicts and insults have been explained by subcultural theories of violence, but empirical support for those theories has been lacking. Recent cognitively oriented research on anger and aggression is combined in this analysis with W. Wilson's (1987) arguments about the "truly disadvantaged" to revise those theories. An individual-level theory explains the violent incidents, and an aggregate-level theory explains the distribution of those incidents among social groups. A subculture of angry aggression arises under conditions of social isolation, when multiple feedback loops result in concentration effects.

Those who examine events that are officially defined as violent crimes, especially murders, find that a large portion arise out of seemingly trivial conflicts and insults (e.g., Lundsgaarde, 1977; Toch, 1969; Wilbanks, 1984; Wolfgang, 1958). This is the largest single category of homicide in the United States and the most variable category historically and cross-culturally (Daly and Wilson, 1988:283–286). This type of event occurs most frequently between unrelated, lower class males, especially blacks. These actions do not appear to be in the persons' interests, so theories explaining them focus on shared deviant values and can be described as subcultural theories of violence (Curtis, 1975; Gastil, 1971; Hackney, 1969; Lundsgaarde, 1977; Silberman, 1978; Wolfgang and Ferracuti, 1981).

Empirical evidence for such values has not been found, however, even among highly violent groups (Baker and Ball, 1969; Ball–Rokeach, 1973; Erlanger, 1974). This has led to three types of criticisms: that the theories are circular (e.g., Nettler, 1984), that the theories fail to consider the structural sources of the cultural values (e.g., Berkowitz, 1982), and that weak values free people to engage in violence but that no one values violence itself (e.g., Kornhauser, 1978).

Recent biological and psychological research supports the view that cognitions are central to explaining anger and aggression (for reviews, see Averill, 1979, 1982; Novaco, 1979). That research is used in this paper to revise and extend subcultural theories of violence.[1]

---

* An earlier version of this paper was presented at the 1988 annual meeting of the American Society of Criminology. I wish to thank Stephen Messner, Richard Rosenfeld, Francis Cullen, Neil Alan Weiner, and R. Richard Ritti for helpful comments on this paper.

1. Similar research was used by Mawson (1987) to explain transient criminality.

74   BERNARD

The new theory predicts high levels of angry aggression among the group described by W. Wilson (1987) as the "truly disadvantaged," even if that group does not possess any abnormal biological or psychological characteristics. Specifically, three social factors (urban environment, low social position, and racial and ethnic discrimination) increase the likelihood of frequent or intense physiological arousal. This directly increases the likelihood of angry aggression. It also indirectly increases it through its effect on cognitions related to anger and aggression. A fourth social factor (social isolation) concentrates the effects of the first three through multiple feedback loops. The result is a "peak" of angry aggression comparable to learned helplessness (Seligman, 1975). The theory therefore explains the high rates of angry aggression among the "truly disadvantaged" by hypothesizing variation only in social, but not in biological and psychological, characteristics. The theory also predicts that certain biological and psychological characteristics increase the likelihood of angry aggression among individuals. Existing research indicates that all of these factors are associated with increased levels of violence and crime.

This new theory avoids the three types of criticism of the subcultural theories, thus providing a more adequate explanation of a particular form of violent crime. Beyond that, the theory uses recent biological and psychological research to develop an individual-level theory of crime, and it proposes a fully social aggregate-level theory to explain the distribution of that crime among social groups. Thus, this theory models a possible relation between biological/psychological explanations and social explanations of crime, as well as a relation between individual- and aggregate-level explanations of crime.

The analysis begins with an individual-level theory of angry aggression. This section considers the physiological and cognitive bases of angry aggression in the context of normal biological and psychological characteristics. The second section develops an aggregate-level theory about the distribution of rates among social groups by focusing on the social circumstances in which the "truly disadvantaged" live. The individual-level theory predicts that people who live under such circumstances will exhibit high levels of angry aggression even if they do not possess any abnormal biological or psychological characteristics. The third section considers abnormal or unusual biological and psychological characteristics that the theory predicts would increase levels of angry aggression among individuals. Existing research finds that each of these characteristics is associated with increased rates of violence and crime.

AN INDIVIDUAL-LEVEL THEORY OF ANGRY AGGRESSION[2]

Recent biological and psychological research is used in this section to construct an individual-level theory suited to explaining a particular form of crime: violent incidents that arise over trivial insults and conflicts. In the next section, this theory is combined with certain abnormal social conditions to produce a social theory of the distribution of this type of crime.

PHYSIOLOGICAL AROUSAL

A variety of situations increase the level of physiological arousal within an organism (see Canon, 1929; Mason, 1975; Selye, 1976).[3] These generally are situations to which the organism must respond in order to survive and thrive both individually and as a species. The increased states of arousal are biologically based mechanisms that energize the organism to respond to these conditions.

Arousal is implemented involuntarily through the autonomic nervous system, but recent research has emphasized the role of cognitive appraisal in determining the level and type of arousal (Burchfield, 1979, Lazarus, 1966). The ultimate goal of the actions energized by arousal is to reduce the state of arousal itself, a process described as *coping* (Lazarus and Averill, 1972). Despite some debate about the reasons, researchers agree that successful efforts to reduce arousal are highly reinforcing (Ursin, 1978) and that unsuccessful efforts lead to a variety of physical and psychological pathologies (Weiss, 1972).

SITUATIONAL AROUSAL

Researchers agree that anger involves physiological arousal that is activated in response to some event or situation in the external environment. Researchers often use terms that suggest interpretations of that event or situation, for example, *annoyance* (Zillmann, 1979) and *provocation* (Averill, 1982). For the types of crimes that are the focus of this paper, those terms suggest that the victims annoyed or provoked the criminals, which often is not the case. In contrast, I use the term *situational arousal*, which suggests only that the aggressor becomes physiologically aroused in response to an external event or situation. Terms like *annoyance* and *provocation* actually

---

2. A lengthier presentation of this individual-level theory can be found in Bernard (in press).

3. For a brief review of the history of research on arousal (or "stress" or "activation"), see Ursin (1978). Current research has resulted in a proliferation of definitions and a broadening of the concept (Elliott and Eisdorfer, 1982).

76   BERNARD

incorporate   the   cognitive   components   of   anger: causality   and
blameworthiness.

COGNITIVE COMPONENTS OF ANGER

Physiological arousal generated in response to external situations differs
from the cognitive processing that interprets that arousal as anger.[4] Even
those who describe anger as a "biologically and psychologically innate affect"
(e.g., Tompkins, 1981) acknowledge the impact of past learning and social
norms and rules in constituting and regulating anger.

The cognition associated with anger is that the situational arousal is caused
by some morally blameworthy action or inaction by the target of the anger
(see Averill, 1982). Blameworthiness may be attributed to the target when
the angry person assumes that the arousal resulted from an intent to harm
(e.g., injure, irritate, embarrass, humiliate) or from recklessness or negligence
(see Daly and Wilson, 1988:254–258).

Attributing causality and blameworthiness may be nonrational or irrational, as is often the case in the violent crimes this paper is designed to
explain.. Nevertheless, if a person is angry with someone else, that person has
attributed causality and blameworthiness to the other person in connection
with some situational arousal. The cognitive attribution of causality and
blameworthiness is not a correlate of anger, but it is an element in its
definition.

INTENTIONAL HARM AND ANGRY AGGRESSION

Many psychologists link anger to aggression, and it is clear that there is an
enormous range of empirical connections between the two (see Averill, 1982).
Baron (1977:7) points out that, after years of controversy, "many social scientists have now moved toward acceptance of a definition (of aggression) . . .
involving the intention as well as the actual delivery of harm or injury to
others." For purposes of clarity, I therefore link anger to *intentional harm*
rather than to *aggression* as a response.

Aggression that is motivated by the intent to harm (i.e., to reduce the target's well-being) is defined herein as *angry aggression*. Angry aggression is a
subset of violent crime (Megargee, 1982) and a subset of aggression (Buss,
1961, 1971), but the majority of actions in those larger categories probably
are instrumental, that is, motivated by attempts to increase the aggressor's
well-being.

---

4.   Behaviorally oriented definitions of anger, such as by Berkowitz (1972), identify
the state of arousal itself as anger and eliminate the "inferential" cognitions. More
recently, however, Berkowitz (e.g., 1981) has added elements, such as intention, that have a
cognitive flavor.

ANGRY AGGRESSION   77

COGNITIVE RULES OF ANGER

A common cultural imperative is that people should not intentionally harm others, but a second common imperative is that they should retaliate against those who intentionally harm them (Averill, 1982). Because retaliation involves intentionally harming others, the two cultural imperatives contradict. The contradiction is resolved through various decision rules that indicate the specific circumstances under which retaliation may be exacted. Those decision rules vary historically and cross-culturally, and attempts have been made to describe their content in contemporary America (e.g., Blumenthal et al., 1972, 1975; Williams, 1981).

Averill (1982:342–345) argues that the "rules of anger" are both regulative and constitutive—they define not only the appropriate responses to anger but also the situations and circumstances in which it is appropriate to become angry in the first place. In terms of a theory of angry aggression, constitutive rules describe when a person believes it is appropriate to attribute to another person causality and blameworthiness for a state of high arousal. These rules determine the conditions under which the person becomes angry and how angry the person becomes. Regulative rules define the nature and amount of intentional harm that must be inflicted on the target for the angry person to feel "satisfied" (i.e., for angry arousal to be reduced). These are the individual's rules for retribution.

ANGRY AROUSAL

Zillman (1979:320–321) argues that "in a state of acute annoyance, the individual presumably rehearses his or her grievance and thereby perpetuates both the state of elevated excitation and the dependent, intense feelings of anger." He then reviews research that shows that promoting such rehearsal prolongs the arousal and disrupting it results in a rapid decay. In terms of the present theory, the "acute annoyance" is the situational arousal, and the "grievance" lies in the attribution of causality and blameworthiness for that arousal to a target. Zillmann interprets the cognitive reiteration of grievances as maintaining and extending the situational arousal, so that he implies that the cognitions do not cause the arousal.

But in the kinds of violent crimes this paper addresses, trivial situations and events lead to extremely high levels of physiological arousal. In such crimes, the level of arousal appears to be influenced by the cognitions themselves. I therefore define *angry arousal* as the physiological arousal a person experiences once causality and blameworthiness for the situational arousal have been attributed to the target. This definition leaves open the possibility (although it does not require) that the cognitions may generate, rather than merely maintain or extend, physiological arousal.

Hypothesizing that the cognitions generate arousal is consistent with related research (Burchfield, 1979; Lazarus, 1966; Schachter, 1964, 1971) and with arguments that cognitive restructuring can reduce anger (e.g., Goldstein and Glick, 1988; Lerner, 1985; Tavris, 1982). It may be troublesome, however, to behaviorists who explain physiological responses with behavioral rather than cognitive stimuli.[5]

TRANSFER OF CAUSALITY AND BLAMEWORTHINESS

Organisms do not have a physiological mechanism that identifies the source of the arousal or the response that will reduce it. Those are determined by a cognitive appraisal of the situation (Schacter, 1964, 1971). Thus, different responses may be energized by identical states of arousal, and physiological arousal generated by various sources may be combined in a cognitive appraisal and jointly attributed to a single source (for a review, see Dienstbier, 1979). Researchers can arouse an organism using one source, and they can structure the situation so that the organism attributes the arousal to an unrelated source (Zillmann, 1979:335–347). Psychoanalysts describe a similar phenomenon as *displacement* (e.g., Hartmann et al., 1964:68–69), which suggests there may be unconscious or preconscious purposes to the transfer (see also Averill, 1982:138–139).

Whether or not such transfers are purposeful, angry arousal can be reduced by harming targets who are not the source of the situational arousal so long as the angry person attributes causality and blameworthiness to that target. Two tendencies with respect to such transfers are relevant to the present theory (see Zillmann, 1979:337). First, in situations in which there is no blameworthy source of the arousal or the actual source is not apparent within the perceptions of the organism, causality and blameworthiness may be transferred to some other organism that is apparent within the perception of the angry organism. That is, transfer tends to occur from a less visible to a more visible target. Second, in situations in which there is reason to believe that the proper source of the arousal could effectively create additional high arousal if so motivated (i.e., retaliate), causality and blameworthiness may be transferred to some other organism that lacks this capacity. That is, transfer tends to occur from a less vulnerable to a more vulnerable target.

Figure 1 summarizes the individual-level theory of angry aggression. Three behavioral elements form the causal chain (situational arousal, angry arousal, and angry aggression), and two cognitive elements mediate the causal linkages between the behavioral elements (constitutive and regulative rules).

---

5. Zillmann's (1979) behavioral orientation underlies his position that cognitions cannot generate physiological arousal. Later, however, Zillmann (1984) argues that sexual arousal, which shares the same autonomic nervous system pathways as angry arousal, can have cognitive origins.

ANGRY AGGRESSION   79

FIGURE 1.
INDIVIDUAL-LEVEL THEORY OF ANGRY
AGGRESSION

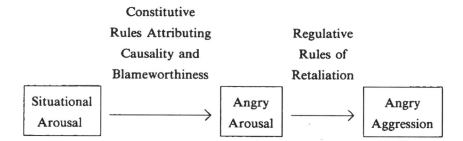

AN AGGREGATE-LEVEL THEORY OF THE
DISTRIBUTION OF ANGRY AGGRESSION

In the individual-level theory of angry aggression, any factor that increases physiological arousal, broadens the constitutive rules, or increases the aggressiveness of regulative rules also increases the likelihood of angry aggression. Such factors could be biological, psychological, or social.

This section focuses on social factors. It explains the concentration of angry aggression among a particular social group solely by hypothesizing variations in socially structured situations. The following section focuses on biological and psychological factors that would increase or decrease the likelihood that individuals within particular social situations would engage in angry aggression.

SOCIAL SOURCES OF SITUATIONAL AROUSAL

In the above theory, frequent or intense arousal directly increases the probability of angry aggression.[6] Research indicates that modern urban environments, low social position, and racial and ethnic discrimination all increase arousal.

Hamilton (1983:247) describes people who live in modern urban environments as experiencing a wide variety of stressors that increase arousal, including population density and crowding, noise, pollution, technological innovations imposed on nontechnological populations, elaborations of institutional organizations and their regulations, design of housing complexes on the basis of efficiency and space-utilizing criteria, restrictions in recreational

---

6. In general, Berkowitz (1961, 1969, 1972, 1981, 1982, 1986) focuses on the link between arousal and aggression.

space, the anonymity of central and local bureaucracies, the power structure
of industrial relationships, and the demands of repetitive work performance
in situations inducing excessive and unavoidable degrees of fatigue. The complexity of urban situations often results in blocking of goal-directed behavior
(e.g., being stuck in a traffic jam), and the density of people increases the
probability of interpersonal conflicts (Blau, 1977). Finally, urban environments tend to be more dangerous (e.g., Campbell, 1986). All these factors
increase arousal, which would increase the likelihood of angry aggression
even if modern urban people do not hold broad constitutive or aggressive
regulative rules of anger.

A second social factor that increases arousal is low social position. Summarizing research, Kohn (1976:178) argues that

> people in lower social classes live in more stressful conditions, they have
> little money or power to employ in coping with the consequences of
> stress, there are fewer institutional resources available to them for escap-
> ing stressful situations or mitigating the consequences of stress, and
> lower-class conditions of life limit individuals' internal resources for
> dealing with stressful or problematic situations.[7]

Higher arousal increases the likelihood of angry aggression even if people in
low social positions do not hold broad constitutive or aggressive regulative
rules of anger.

Racial and ethnic discrimination involves intentionally harming, threatening, or insulting people and intentionally blocking their goal-directed activities (Allport, 1954:51–65).[8] People respond to such experiences with
increased arousal, which increases the likelihood of angry aggression (see Allport, 1954:142–161) whether or not they hold broad constitutive or aggressive
regulative rules of anger.

Two additional elements feed back from later points in the causal chain.
First, a highly aggressive environment increases physiological arousal; nothing is so arousal-inducing as being in danger of physical injury or death. Such
an environment would occur when a chronically aroused group is socially
isolated, since everyone in the group would be more likely to exhibit angry
aggression.

Second, chronic high arousal reduces the ability to cope with arousal,
which results in more arousal (see Ursein, 1978, and Lazarus, 1985). Fisher
(1984:184–202) describes the situation as multiple stress feedback loops that

---

7. See also Brown (1979), Brown et al. (1973), Rutter and Quinton (1976), and
Vance (1988).

8. In terms of this theory, discrimination involves intentional harm and can be
explained as a form of angry aggression—the discriminating group is in a state of high
arousal for some reason and attributes causality and blameworthiness to those they dis-
criminate against. See Allport (1954:343–353).

culminate in total incompetence and crisis. Others describe the end point of this downward spiral as learned helplessness (Seligman, 1975), hopelessness (Lazarus, 1976), or incompetence (White, 1959). Thus, situations that combine several arousing-inducing factors may generate an interactive effect on arousal (and therefore on angry aggression) beyond the additive effects of the various factors.

For example, modern urban life is most stress-inducing for the lower class, and lower class life is most stress-inducing in modern urban environments. Thus, lower class people in modern urban areas would engage in angry aggression at a rate that exceeds the additive effects of the two factors, independent of whether they also hold broad constitutive and aggressive regulative rules of anger. If those people are socially isolated, an aggressive environment would be produced by concentrating a large number of aggression-prone people in a single location. That would feed back to create even more arousal and more aggression.

Prisoners also occupy a low social position and may experience deliberate discrimination in environments that contain many of the most stress-inducing features of a modern city. They would be expected to exhibit angry aggression at a rate that exceeds the additive effects of the three factors, independent of whether they also hold broad constitutive and aggressive regulative rules of anger. Prisoners also are socially isolated, and the resulting aggressive environment would feed back to create even more arousal and more aggression.

The above discussion suggests three social sources of high physiological arousal, plus two additional sources that feed back from later points in the causal chain. This argument is summarized in Figure 2.

SOCIAL SOURCES OF BROAD CONSTITUTIVE RULES

Constitutive rules are cognitions by which individuals determine whether to attribute causality and blameworthiness to a target in connection with a situation of high arousal. People with broad constitutive rules attribute causality and blameworthiness in a greater variety of situations and, therefore, are more likely to engage in angry aggression. Research indicates that subcultural views, high arousal, and the likelihood of an aggressive response influence the breadth of the constitutive rules.

Averill (1982:142), summarizing research, argues that people in an aroused state have a lowered threshold for perceived wrong or injury. That is, in addition to its direct effect of increasing the likelihood of aggression, high arousal indirectly increases aggression by expanding constitutive rules for anger. In terms of the present theory, people who are already aroused attribute causality and blameworthiness in situations in which other people do not.

In addition, the likelihood of an aggressive response influences constitutive

82   BERNARD

FIGURE 2.
SOCIAL SOURCES OF SITUATIONAL
AROUSAL

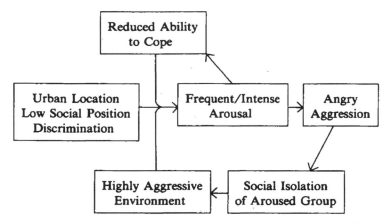

rules. Aggression is motivated by a wide range of factors, but when people aggress for any reason, they tend to interpret their aggression as motivated by anger, retrospectively attributing causality and blameworthiness to the target. Thus, Averill (1982:142), after reviewing research, concludes that "any factor that increases the likelihood of an aggressive response will also increase the likelihood of anger." This includes past instrumental or vicarious learning, the presence of relevant situational cues or target characteristics, and the ingestion of drugs or alcohol. Averill (1982:143) suggests that this creates a feedback loop in which people interpret themselves as angry (i.e., broaden their constitutive rules) in order to justify their aggressive response and then escalate the aggression because they now interpret themselves as angry. This is consistent with observations that criminals often blame the victim for the crime (e.g., Bandura, 1976; Sykes and Matza, 1957). In terms of the present theory, they aggress against the victims and then retrospectively attribute causality and blameworthiness to them (i.e., get angry) as a means of justifying the aggression.

Because these are cognitive rules, the most direct influence would be interpersonal transmission in primary groups. Some social groups may transmit constitutive rules that attribute causality and blameworthiness in many high arousal situations.[9] Hackney (1969), for example, describes "a Southern

---

9.   Wolfgang (1958:188–189) found an increased variety of situations in which homicide offenders become angry, and this finding was reported in Wolfgang and Ferracuti's subculture of violence theory (1981:153). However, that theory focuses on more aggressive regulative rules (i.e., violence as a preferred response to anger, as opposed to alternative responses) rather than on the broadening of the constitutive rules.

ANGRY AGGRESSION   83

world view that defines the social, political, and physical environment as hostile and casts the white Southerner in the role of the passive victim of malevolent forces." He then uses these subcultural views to explain high rates of southern violence (see also Lundsgaarde, 1977). Curtis (1975) and Silberman (1978) argue that similar subcultural views are found among blacks in the United States, and they similarly link those views to violent behaviors. In terms of the present argument, these subcultures increase the likelihood of attributing causality and blameworthiness and therefore increase the likelihood of angry aggression, independent of increases in the likelihood of arousal or in the aggressiveness of regulative rules.

The above referenced researchers describe the origins of these subcultures as situations in which groups of people were socially isolated and chronically aroused, but in which the true sources of the arousal were neither visible nor vulnerable. This suggests an interpretation of how subcultures originated. Individuals placed in such situations broaden their constitutive rules for anger and transfer causality and blameworthiness to visible and vulnerable targets in the immediate environment. In social isolation, these cognitions can be transmitted from person to person and generalize into a cultural phenomenon. This creates a feedback loop by increasing aggressiveness in the environment, which further increases physiological arousal and further enhances the tendency to expand constitutive rules of anger.

The above discussion suggests that there are three social sources of broad constitutive rules, all of which are implicated in feedback loops involving social isolation. This argument is summarized in Figure 3.

SOCIAL SOURCES OF AGGRESSIVE REGULATIVE RULES

Regulative rules are the individual's rules for retribution—they define the amount of harm considered appropriate to inflict on the target in retaliation for the situational arousal. To the extent that angry arousal is generated by cognitions, regulative rules are the cognitive framework for arousal reduction—that is, what the person must do to feel satisfied. Research indicates that subcultural views, aggressive environments, and past frequent or intense arousal influence the aggressiveness of regulative rules.

In highly aggressive environments, aggressive regulative rules of anger are acquired through vicarious learning and maintained through direct reinforcement and instrumental learning (Bandura, 1973, 1976). Aggressive regulative rules are also elicited from reasonable expectations that physical aggression is necessary for personal safety, due to the dangerousness of the situation. Finally, social isolation of groups of people with aggressive regulative rules would result in a highly aggressive environment, which then would feed back to make the regulative rules even more aggressive.

People who have been subject to frequent or intense arousal in the past

84   BERNARD

FIGURE 3.
SOCIAL SOURCES OF BROAD CONSTITUTIVE RULES

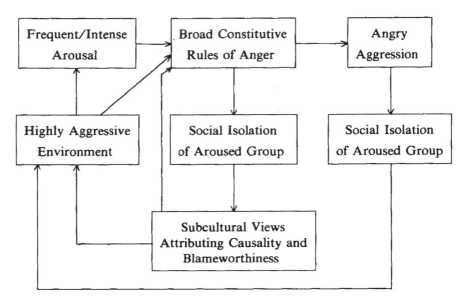

become more likely to respond with aggression than other people (Berkowitz, 1962:51–72, 1969, 1972). That is, the factors that increase the likelihood of high arousal also expand the regulative rules for anger. Those who are more frequently aroused tend to respond with aggression to a greater variety of situations than those who are less frequently aroused. This results in a feedback loop under conditions of social isolation, since the expanded regulative rules result in a highly aggressive environment, which would then increase arousal and further expand the regulative rules.

Because the regulative rules are cognitive, the most direct influence would be the learning of these rules through interpersonal transmission in primary groups. Some social groups transmit regulative rules that specify higher levels of intentional harm as appropriate retaliation for lower levels of arousal, and they support those rules with the awarding or withholding of status and prestige. Such subcultural rules are described as a "subculture of violence" by Wolfgang and Ferracuti (1981).

Wolfgang and Ferracuti (1981:162–163) speculate that there may be several causal paths resulting in these subcultures. The research cited above suggests one possible path. When socially isolated people are frequently and intensely aroused, they tend to develop more aggressive regulative rules for anger. This leads to a highly aggressive environment, as individuals both engage in angry aggression and transfer it to visible and vulnerable targets in the isolated group. The regulative rules would be transmitted interpersonally within the group and generalize into a cultural phenomenon.

The above discussion indicates that three factors lead to aggressive regulative rules, all of which are involved in feedback loops. The argument is summarized in Figure 4.

FIGURE 4.
SOCIAL SOURCES OF AGGRESSIVE
REGULATIVE RULES

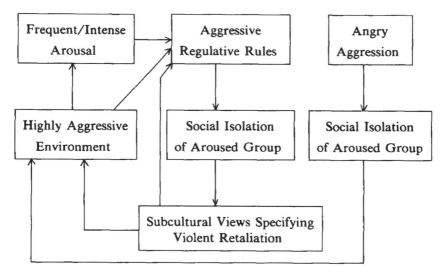

THE OVERALL CAUSAL CHAIN

Figure 5 combines Figures 2-4 and summarizes the entire causal chain. In this figure, an additional role for social isolation is hypothesized. When people in socially isolated groups are highly aroused and have broad constitutive and aggressive regulative rules, they are likely to transfer arousal and intentionally harm visible and vulnerable targets, who necessarily will be other members of the socially isolated group. That increases the overall aggressiveness of the environment, which then feeds back into the causal chain by further increasing physiological arousal, broadening the constitutive rules, and making the regulative rules more aggressive.

There are only four independent variables in this causal chain, but there are a large number of feedback loops. Three of the independent variables are sources of physiological arousal (urban environment, low social position, discrimination), and the fourth (social isolation) concentrates their effects. This suggests that there may be a critical mass of arousal, which if surpassed,

FIGURE 5.
OVERALL CAUSAL CHAIN OF ANGRY AGGRESSION

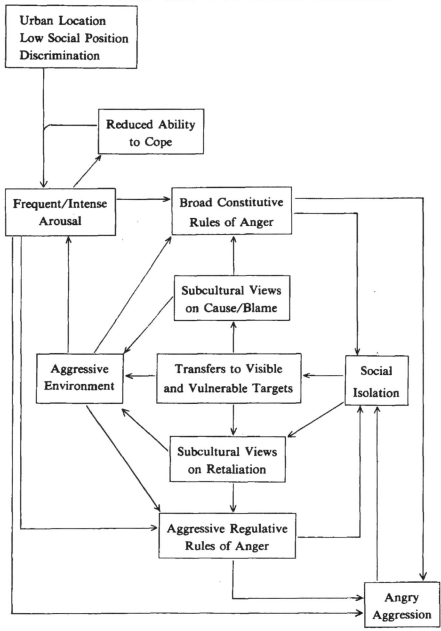

ANGRY AGGRESSION   87

could result in extremely high rates of angry aggression brought on by the concentration effects associated with the multiple feedback loops. Such a "peak" of angry aggression would be similar to the learned helplessness that also results from multiple feedback loops.

Social isolation and concentration effects are concepts used by W. Wilson (1987) to describe "the truly disadvantaged." Wilson argues that this group experiences the four independent variables associated with angry aggression, and that it exhibits the high levels of angry aggression predicted by the feedback loops within the theory. I describe this phenomenon as *the subculture of angry aggression*.

THE SUBCULTURE OF ANGRY AGGRESSION

W. Wilson (1987) describes the truly disadvantaged as consisting of a socially isolated group of urban people of low social position who experience discrimination. Consider how the theory of angry aggression would apply to this group, assuming the members have no abnormal or unusual biological or psychological characteristics.

First, angry aggression in this group would be an additive effect of each of the social factors: urban environment, low social position, and racial and ethnic discrimination. The social isolation of this group would concentrate the aggressive effects of the above factors, resulting in a highly aggressive environment. The aggressive environment would then generate a feedback loop that would further increase the likelihood of aggression through vicarious and instrumental learning and through reasonable expectations of dangerousness.

Second, in such an environment, each individual's constitutive and regulative rules for anger would tend to expand, so that people would become angry in a greater range of situations and respond with more violence when angry. This would result in an even more aggressive environment, one also feeding back on itself through vicarious and instrumental learning and reasonable expectations of dangerousness.

Third, the social isolation of the group would mean that the broad constitutive and aggressive regulative rules for anger would tend to become subcultural through interpersonal transmission, becoming independent of the structural conditions that gave rise to them. Those subcultural rules would then interact with individual experiences, each shaping and reinforcing the other. These subcultural rules, thus, would increase the overall aggressiveness of the environment, which would then feed back on itself through vicarious and instrumental learning and reasonable expectations of dangerousness.

Fourth, social isolation would result in a tendency to transfer arousal to visible and vulnerable people in the immediate environment, especially because the true sources of the arousal are largely invisible and invulnerable.

That is, people in this situation would tend to harm each other rather than others. This would increase the aggressiveness of the environment, feeding back on itself through instrumental and vicarious learning and through reasonable expectations of dangerousness.

The result of these four processes would be a high rate of angry aggression, even if there were no abnormal or unusual biological or psychological characteristics among "truly disadvantaged" people.

INDIVIDUAL DIFFERENCES

The causal chain in Figure 5 does not hypothesize any variations in biological and psychological factors, but it is possible to consider them in the context of the theory. As with social factors, there are three possible types of biological/psychological factors that could influence angry aggression: those influencing the likelihood of arousal, those influencing the constitutive rules, and those influencing the regulative rules.

The likelihood of physiological arousal is influenced by several biological and psychological factors, each of which is shown by research to be further associated with increased violence and aggression. "Type A" personality is associated with excessive physiological arousal (see Dembroski et al., 1985) and with high aggressiveness (Glass, 1977). People with low autonomic nervous system functioning are said to seek out high-arousal situations (Eysenck, 1964; Mednick, 1977) and also exhibit increased aggressiveness (Mednick et al., 1982). People with low intelligence may be more frequently and intensely aroused because of inadequate coping skills (Hamilton, 1983; Ursin et al., 1978), and this apparently is associated with increased criminality (J. Wilson and Herrnstein, 1985). Premenstrual syndrome is associated with increased arousal in women and is also correlated with increased incidence of crime (Shah and Roth, 1974).

The constitutive rules of anger (i.e., the attribution of causality and blameworthiness) may be influenced by two psychological factors, but evidence linking those to violence and aggression is weak. Paranoid ideation (see Bartol, 1980:153–155) is a cognitive framework associated with attributing causality and blame. This has been used in some theories of violence (e.g., Yablonsky, 1970). Some research has found that violent people are more paranoid than others (Toch, 1969), that violent criminals are more paranoid than nonviolent criminals (Mefferd et al., 1981), and that paranoid people are more violent than people with other mental illnesses (Berger and Gulevich, 1981). However, the connection between paranoia and violence is weak (Hodgins, 1988). An external locus of control (Rotter, 1966) would be associated with the attribution of causality, and research finds high levels of externality among black and poor people (Battle and Rotter, 1963; Lefcourt and Ludwig, 1965; Rotter et al., 1962). Baron (1977:184–187) suggests that such people engage mainly in angry aggression because they perceive little utility in instrumental aggression.

Finally, two sex-related factors may affect the regulative rules of anger. Bernardez–Bonesatti (1978) and Lerner (1985) argue that women hold "cultural" views that strongly inhibit becoming angry and also inhibit aggressive responses once the woman is angry. Averill (1982:297–311) reviewed research and concluded that women become angry in as many situations as men, but that once angry they rarely engage in aggressive responses. That is, women may have restricted regulative rules of anger.

In contrast, people who have physical strength and skill have a greater tendency to reduce angry arousal through intentional harm than people who are physically weak and unskilled, since such actions are reinforced only when they also prevent retaliation (Bandura, 1976). A similar situation exists when bystanders intervene in a criminal event (e.g., Huston et al., 1981; Shotland and Stebbins, 1980). Physical strength and skill are associated with men rather than women, with younger rather than older people, and with mesomorphs rather than ectomorphs and endomorphs, all of which are correlated with violence and aggression.

These biological and psychological variables are associated with aggression and violence at the individual level, but Mark (1978) suggests that these types of factors are randomly distributed among social groups and do not affect the social distribution of violent crime. Similarly, Mednick et al. (1982:22, 55, 68) argue that biological explanations of aggression and violence are appropriate only when social explanations are not available.

These types of factors, therefore, could be used to explain individual differences in angry aggression within similar social situations. They would not be useful in explaining the distribution of angry aggression among social groups, however, unless it could be demonstrated that they are distributed similarly among social groups and that the social explanation presented above is inadequate.

CONCLUSION

The theory of angry aggression avoids three types of criticisms (noted at the beginning of this paper) that have been directed at other subcultural theories of violence. First, the theory is testable rather than circular. All of the specific causal links are supported by existing empirical research. Individual-level research can determine whether the probability of engaging in angry aggression is associated with the breadth of constitutive rules and the aggressiveness of regulative rules of anger. Aggregate-level research can determine whether broader and more aggressive rules are found in social situations that generate frequent and intense arousal, including urban environments, low social position, and racial and ethnic discrimination.

90   BERNARD

Second, no assertion is made that criminals "value" violence. Rather, all people have constitutive and regulative rules of anger, but those rules are extended and distorted under certain social conditions. It is those extended and distorted rules that underlie angry aggression. In addition, the theory provides a more complex view of these cognitive rules. Earlier subcultural theories focus on the aggressiveness of the regulative rules, but it is often noted that violent criminals attribute causality and blameworthiness in a wider variety of situations than nonviolent people (e.g., Wolfgang, 1958:188–189). Earlier subcultural theories did not emphasize this aspect.

Third, the theory of angry aggression is primarily a structural theory, in which the major causal forces are found in structural sources of high arousal: modern urban environment, low social position, and racial and ethnic discrimination. A fourth structural factor, social isolation, concentrates the effects of these factors, which accounts for the high levels of angry aggression. Other elements flow from these structural sources, including the subcultural and cognitive elements. Thus, the policy implications of the theory focus on changing the structural elements rather than the subcultural or cognitive ones (cf. W. Wilson, 1987).

Finally, much criminological theory and research focuses on social structural conditions (see Vold and Bernard, 1986), but the specific mechanisms that mediate between those conditions and the resulting violence and crime are not usually identified. This theory identifies such a mechanism and thus complements that theory and research.

REFERENCES

Allport, Gordon W.
    1954   The Nature of Prejudice. Reading, Mass.: Addison–Wesley.

Averill, James R.
    1982   Anger and Aggression. New York: Springer–Verlag
    1979   Anger. In H.E. Howe, Jr., and R.A. Dienstbier (eds.), Nebraska Symposium on Motivation 1978. Vol. 26. Lincoln: University of Nebraska Press.

Baker, R.K. and Sandra J. Ball
    1969   The actual world of violence. In Violence and the Media. Vol. 9. Staff report to the National Commission on the Causes and Prevention of Violence. Washington, D.C.: Government Printing Office.

Ball-Rokeach, Sandra J.
    1973   Values and violence: A test of the subculture of violence thesis. American Sociological Review 38:736–749.

Bandura, Albert
    1973   Aggression: A Social Learning Analysis. Englewood Cliffs, N.J.: Prentice-Hall.
    1976   Social learning analysis of aggression. In Emilio Ribes-Inesta and Albert Bandura (eds.), Analysis of Delinquency and Aggression. Hillsdale, N.J.: Erlbaum.

ANGRY AGGRESSION 91

Baron, Robert A.
   1977   Human Aggression. New York: Plenum.

Bartol, Curt R.
   1980   Criminal Behavior. Englewood Cliffs, N.J.: Prentice-Hall.

Battle, Esther and Julian B. Rotter
   1963   Children's feelings of personal control as related to social class and ethnic
           groups. Journal of Personality 31:482–490.

Berger, Philip A. and George D. Gulevich
   1981   Violence and mental illness. In David A. Hamburg and Michelle B.
           Trudeau (eds.), Biobehavioral Aspects of Aggression. New York: Alan R.
           Liss.

Berkowitz, Leonard
   1962   Aggression. New York: McGraw-Hill.
   1969   The frustration-aggression hypothesis revisited. In Leonard Berkowitz (ed.),
           Roots of Aggression. New York: Atherton.
   1972   The contagion of violence: An S-R mediational analysis of some effects of
           observed aggression. In W.J. Arnold and M.M. Page (eds.), Nebraska
           Symposium on Motivation 1971. Vol. 19. Lincoln: University of Nebraska
           Press.
   1981   The concept of aggression. In Paul Brain and D. Benton (eds.), Multidis-
           ciplinary Approaches to Aggression Research. Amsterdam: Elsevier/North-
           Holland.
   1982   Violence and rule-following behavior. In Peter Marsh and Anne Campbell
           (eds.), Aggression and Violence. Oxford: Basil Blackwell.
   1986   Some varieties of human aggression. In Anne Campbell and John J. Gibbs
           (eds.), Violent Transactions. Oxford: Basil Blackwell.

Bernard, Thomas J.
   In press The intent to harm: Angry aggression as a form of violent crime. In Anna
           F. Kuhl (ed.), The Dynamics of the Victim-Offender Interaction. Cincinnati:
           Anderson.

Bernardez–Bonesatti, Teresa
   1978   Women and anger. Journal of the American Medical Women's Association
           33:215–219.

Blau, Peter M.
   1977   Inequality and Heterogeneity. New York: Free Press.

Blumenthal, Monica D., Robert L. Kahn, Frank M. Andrews, and Kendra B. Head
   1972   Justifying Violence. Ann Arbor, Mich.: Institute for Social Research.

Blumenthal, Monica D., Letha B. Chadiha, Gerald A. Cole, and Toby Epstein Jayaratne
   1975   More About Justifying Violence. Ann Arbor, Mich.: Institute for Social
           Research.

Brown, George W.
   1979   The social etiology of depression. In R.A. Depue (ed.), The Psychobiology
           of the Depressive Disorders. New York: Academic Press.

Brown, George W., T.O. Harris, and J. Peto
   1973   Life events and psychiatric disorders. Psychological Medicine 3:159–176.

Burchfield, Susan R.
   1979   The stress response. Psychosomatic Medicine 41:661–672.

92   BERNARD

Buss, Arnold H.
   1961   The Psychology of Aggression. New York: John Wiley & Sons.
   1971   Aggression pays. In Jerome L. Singer (ed.), The Control of Aggression and
            Violence. New York: Academic Press.

Campbell, Anne
   1986   The streets and violence. In Anne Campbell and John J. Gibbs (eds.),
            Violent Transactions. Oxford: Basil Blackwell.

Cannon, Walter B.
   1929   Bodily Changes in Pain, Hunger, Fear, and Rage. New York: Appleton-
            Century.

Curtis, Lynn A.
   1975   Violence, Race, and Culture. Lexington, Mass.: D.C. Heath.

Daly, Martin and Margo Wilson
   1988   Homicide. New York: Aldine de Gruyter.

Dembroski, Theodore M., James M. MacDougall, Robert S. Eliot, and James C. Buell
   1985   A social-psycho-physiological model of biobehavioral factors and coronary
            heart disease. In C.D. Spielberger and I.G. Sarason (eds.), Stress and
            Anxiety. Vol. 9. Washington, D.C.: Hemisphere.

Dienstbier, R.A.
   1979   Emotion-attribution theory. In H.E. Howe, Jr., and R.A. Dienstbier (eds.),
            Nebraska Symposium on Motivation. Vol. 26. Lincoln: University of
            Nebraska Press.

Elliott, Glen R. and Carl Eisdorfer (eds.)
   1982   Stress and Human Health. New York: Springer-Verlag.

Erlanger, Howard S.
   1974   The empirical status of the subculture of violence thesis. Social Problems
            22(4):280–292.

Eysenck, Hans
   1964   Crime and Personality. Boston: Houghton Mifflin.

Fisher, Shirley
   1984   Stress and the Perception of Control. Hillsdale, N.J.: Erlbaum.

Gastil, Raymond D.
   1971   Homicide and a regional culture of violence. American Sociological Review
            36:412-427.

Glass, David C.
   1977   Stress and Coronary Prone Behavior. Hillsdale, N.J.: Erlbaum.

Goldstein, Arnold P. and Barry Glick
   1988   Aggression Replacement Training. Champaign, Ill.: Research Press.

Hackney, Sheldon
   1969   Southern violence. In Hugh Davis Graham and Ted Robert Gurr (eds.),
            Violence in America. Beverly Hills, Calif.: Sage.

Hamilton, Vernon
   1983   The Cognitive Structures and Processes of Human Motivation. New York:
            John Wiley & Sons.

Hartmann, Heinz, Ernst Kris, and Rudolph Loewenstein
1964   Notes on the theory of aggression. In H. Hartmann, E. Kris, and R. Loewenstein (eds.), Papers on Psychoanalytic Psychology. Vol. 4. New York: International Universities Press.

Hodgins, S.
1988   Antisocial behavior and persons suffering from mental disorders. In Wouter Buikhuisen and Sarnoff A. Mednick (eds.), Explaining Criminal Behavior. Leiden: Brill.

Huston, Ted L., Mary Ruggiero, Ross Conner, and Gilbert Geis
1981   Bystander intervention into crime. Social Psychology Quarterly 44:14–23.

Kohn, Melvin L.
1976   The interaction of social class and other factors in the etiology of schizophrenia. American Journal of Psychiatry 133:177–180.

Kornhauser, Ruth Rosner
1978   Social Sources of Delinquency. Chicago: University of Chicago Press.

Lazarus, Richard S.
1966   Psychological Stress and the Coping Process. New York: McGraw-Hill.
1976   Patterns of Adjustment. New York: McGraw-Hill.
1985   Toward an understanding of efficiency and inefficiency in human affairs. In Michael Frese and John Sabini (eds.), Goal Directed Behavior: The Concept of Action in Psychology. Hillsdale, N.J.: Erlbaum.

Lazarus, Richard S. and James R. Averill
1972   Emotion and cognition. In C.D. Spielberger (ed.), Anxiety: Current Trends in Theory and Research. Vol. 2. New York: Academic Press.

Lefcourt, Herbert M. and Gordon W. Ludwig
1965   The american negro. Journal of Personality and Social Psychology 1:377–380.

Lerner, Harriet
1985   The Dance of Anger. New York: Harper & Row.

Lundsgaarde, Henry P.
1977   Murder in Space City. New York: Oxford University Press.

Mark, Vernon
1978   Sociobiological theories of abnormal aggression. In I.L. Kutash, S.B. Kutash, and L.B. Schlesinger (eds.), Violence. San Francisco: Jossey-Bass.

Mason, John W.
1975   A historical view of the stress field. Journal of Human Stress 1:6–12ff.

Mawson, Anthony R.
1987   Transient Criminality. New York: Praeger.

Mednick, Sarnoff A.
1977   A bio-social theory of the learning of law-abiding behavior. In Sarnoff A. Mednick and Karl O. Christiansen (eds.), Biosocial Bases of Criminal Behavior. Beverly Hills, Calif.: Sage.

Mednick, Sarnoff A., Vicki Pollock, Jan Volavka, and William F. Gabrielli, Jr.
1982   Biology and violence. In Marvin E. Wolfgang and Neil Alan Weiner (eds.), Criminal Violence. Beverly Hills, Calif.: Sage.

94   BERNARD

Mefferd, Roy B., John M. Lennon, and Nancy E. Dawson
    1981   Violence—the ultimate noncoping behavior. In J.R. Hays, T.K. Roberts,
              K.S. Solway, and L. Feldman (eds.), Violence and the Violent Individual.
              New York: Spectrum.

Megargee, Edwin I.
    1982   Psychological determinants and correlates of criminal violence. In Marvin
              E. Wolfgang and Neil Alan Weiner (eds.), Criminal Violence. Beverly Hills,
              Calif.: Sage.

Nettler, Gwynne
    1984   Killing One Another. Cincinnati: Anderson.

Novaco, Raymond W.
    1979   The cognitive regulation of anger and stress. In P. Kendall and S. Hollon
              (eds.), Cognitive-Behavioral Interventions. New York: Academic Press.

Rotter, Julian B.
    1966   Generalized expectancies for internal versus external control of reinforce-
              ment. Psychological Monographs 80:609.

Rotter, Julian B., M. Seeman, and S. Liverant
    1962   Internal versus external control of reinforcement. In N.F. Washburne (ed.),
              Decisions, Values and Groups. Vol. 2. Oxford: Pergamon.

Rutter, Michael L. and D. Quinton
    1976   Psychiatric disorders: Ecological factors and concepts of causation. In H.
              McGurk (ed.), Ecological Factors in Human Development. Amsterdam:
              North-Holland.

Schachter, Stanley
    1964   The interaction of cognitive and psychological determinants of emotional
              state. In Leonard Berkowitz (ed.), Advances in Experimental Social
              Psychology. New York: Academic Press.
    1971   Emotion, Obesity, and Crime. New York: Academic Press.

Seligman, Martin E.P.
    1975   Helplessness. San Francisco: Freeman, Cooper.

Selye, Hans
    1976   The Stress of Life. New York: McGraw-Hill.

Shah, Saleem A. and Loren H. Roth
    1974   Biological and psychophysiological factors in criminality. In Daniel Glaser
              (ed.), Handbook of Criminology. Chicago: Rand McNally.

Shotland, R. Lance and Charles A. Stebbing
    1980   Bystander response to rape. Journal of Applied Social Psychology
              10:510–527.

Silberman, Charles E.
    1978   Criminal Violence, Criminal Justice. New York: Random House.

Sykes, Gresham M. and David Matza
    1957   Techniques of neutralization. American Sociological Review 22:667–670.

Tavris, Carol
    1982   Anger: The Misunderstood Emotion. New York: Simon & Schuster.

Toch, Hans
    1969   Violent Men. Chicago: Aldine.

Tompkins, Silvan S.
1981   The quest for primary motives. Journal of Personality and Social Psychology 41:306–329.

Ursin, Holger
1978   Activation, coping and psychosomatics. In Holger Ursin, Eivind Baade, and Seymour Levine (eds.), Psychobiology of Stress. New York: Academic Press.

Ursin, Holger, Eivind Baade, and Seymour Levine (eds.)
1978   Psychobiology of Stress. New York: Academic Press.

Vance, Elizabeth Taylor
1988   A typology of risks and the disabilities of low status. In G.W. Albee, J.M. Joffe, and L.A. Dusenbury (eds.), Prevention, Powerlessness and Politics. Beverly Hills, Calif.: Sage.

Vold, George B. and Thomas J. Bernard
1986   Theoretical Criminology. New York: Oxford University Press.

Weiss, J.M.
1972   Influence of psychological variables on stress-induced pathology. In Ciba Foundation, Symposium: Physiology, Emotion and Psychosomatic Illness. Amsterdam: Elsevier.

White, Robert W.
1959   Motivation reconsidered: The concept of competence. Psychological Review 66:297–333.

Wilbanks, William
1984   Murder in Miami. Lanham, Md.: University Press of America.

Williams, Robin
1981   Legitimate and illegitimate uses of violence: A review of ideas and evidence. In Willard Gaylin, Ruth Macklin, and Tabitha M. Powledge (eds.), Violence and the Politics of Research. New York: Plenum.

Wilson, James Q. and Richard J. Herrnstein
1985   Crime and Human Nature. New York: Simon and Schuster.

Wilson, William Julius
1987   The Truly Disadvantaged. Chicago: University of Chicago Press.

Wolfgang, Marvin E.
1958   Patterns in Criminal Homicide. Philadelphia: University of Pennsylvania Press.

Wolfgang, Marvin E. and Franco Ferracuti
1981   The Subculture of Violence. Beverly Hills, Calif.: Sage.

Yablonsky, Lewis
1970   The Violent Gang. New York: Penguin.

Zillmann, Dolf
1979   Hostility and Aggression. Hillsdale, N.J.: Erlbaum.
1984   Connections Between Sex and Aggression. Hillsdale, N.J.: Erlbaum.

Thomas J. Bernard is Associate Professor of Administration of Justice at Pennsylvania

96   **BERNARD**

State University. His research interests are in criminological theory and juvenile justice.
He is currently writing a book on the history, philosophy, and law of juvenile justice.

[13]
THE CODE OF THE STREETS

by ELIJAH ANDERSON

*In this essay in urban anthropology
a social scientist takes us inside a world
most of us glimpse only in grisly headlines—
"Teen Killed in Drive-By Shooting"—
to show us how a desperate
search for respect governs
social relations among
many African-American
young men*

O F all the problems besetting the poor inner-city black community, none is more pressing than that of interpersonal violence and aggression. It wreaks havoc daily with the lives of community residents and increasingly spills over into downtown and residential middle-class areas. Muggings, burglaries, carjackings, and drug-related shootings, all of which may leave their victims or innocent bystanders dead, are now common enough to concern all urban and many suburban residents. The inclination to violence springs from the circumstances of life among the ghetto poor—the lack of jobs that pay a living wage, the stigma of race, the fallout from rampant drug use and drug trafficking, and the resulting alienation and lack of hope for the future.

Simply living in such an environment places young people at special risk of falling victim to aggressive behavior. Although there are often forces in the community which can counteract

AT THE HEART OF THE CODE IS THE ISSUE OF RESPECT—LOOSELY DEFINED

the negative influences, by far the most powerful being a strong, loving, "decent" (as inner-city residents put it) family committed to middle-class values, the despair is pervasive enough to have spawned an oppositional culture, that of "the streets," whose norms are often consciously opposed to those of mainstream society. These two orientations—decent and street—socially organize the community, and their coexistence has important consequences for residents, particularly children growing up in the inner city. Above all, this environment means that even youngsters whose home lives reflect mainstream values—and the majority of homes in the community do—must be able to handle themselves in a street-oriented environment.

This is because the street culture has evolved what may be called a code of the streets, which amounts to a set of informal rules governing interpersonal public behavior, including violence. The rules prescribe both a proper comportment and a proper way to respond if challenged. They regulate the use of violence and so allow those who are inclined to aggression to precipitate violent encounters in an approved way. The rules have been established and are enforced mainly by the street-oriented, but on the streets the distinction between street and decent is often irrelevant; everybody knows that if the rules are violated, there are penalties. Knowledge of the code is thus largely defensive; it is literally necessary for operating in public. Therefore, even though families with a decency orientation are usually opposed to the values of the code, they often reluctantly encourage their children's familiarity with it to enable them to negotiate the inner-city environment.

At the heart of the code is the issue of respect—loosely defined as being treated "right," or granted the deference one deserves. However, in the troublesome public environment of the inner city, as people increasingly feel buffeted by forces beyond their control, what one deserves in the way of respect becomes more and more problematic and uncertain. This in turn further opens the issue of respect to sometimes intense interpersonal negotiation. In the street culture, especially among young people, respect is viewed as almost an external entity that is hard-won but easily lost, and so must constantly be guarded. The rules of the code in fact provide a framework for negotiating respect. The person whose very appearance—including his clothing, demeanor, and way of moving—deters transgressions feels that he possesses, and may be considered by others to possess, a measure of respect. With the right amount of respect, for instance, he can avoid "being bothered" in public. If he is bothered, not only may he be in physical danger but he has been disgraced or "dissed" (disrespected). Many of the forms that dissing can take might seem petty to middle-class people (maintaining eye contact for too long, for example), but to those invested

in the street code, these actions become serious indications of the other person's intentions. Consequently, such people become very sensitive to advances and slights, which could well serve as warnings of imminent physical confrontation.

This hard reality can be traced to the profound sense of alienation from mainstream society and its institutions felt by many poor inner-city black people, particularly the young. The code of the streets is actually a cultural adaptation to a profound lack of faith in the police and the judicial system. The police are most often seen as representing the dominant white society and not caring to protect inner-city residents. When called, they may not respond, which is one reason many residents feel they must be prepared to take extraordinary measures to defend themselves and their loved ones against those who are inclined to aggression. Lack of police accountability has in fact been incorporated into the status system: the person who is believed capable of "taking care of himself" is accorded a certain deference, which translates into a sense of physical and psychological control. Thus the street code emerges where the influence of the police ends and personal responsibility for one's safety is felt to begin. Exacerbated by the proliferation of drugs and easy access to guns, this volatile situation results in the ability of the street-oriented minority (or those who effectively "go for bad") to dominate the public spaces.

DECENT AND STREET
FAMILIES

ALTHOUGH almost everyone in poor inner-city neighborhoods is struggling financially and therefore feels a certain distance from the rest of America, the decent and the street family in a real sense represent two poles of value orientation, two contrasting conceptual categories. The labels "decent" and "street," which the residents themselves use, amount to evaluative judgments that confer status on local residents. The labeling is often the result of a social contest among individuals and families of the neighborhood. Individuals of the two orientations often coexist in the same extended family. Decent residents judge themselves to be so while judging others to be of the street, and street individuals often present themselves as decent, drawing distinctions between themselves and other people. In addition, there is quite a bit of circumstantial behavior—that is, one person may at different times exhibit both decent and street orientations, depending on the circumstances. Although these designations result from so much social jockeying, there do exist concrete features that define each conceptual category.

Generally, so-called decent families tend to accept mainstream values more fully and attempt to instill them in their

AS BEING TREATED "RIGHT," OR GRANTED THE DEFERENCE ONE DESERVES.

children. Whether married couples with children or single-parent (usually female) households, they are generally "working poor" and so tend to be better off financially than their street-oriented neighbors. They value hard work and self-reliance and are willing to sacrifice for their children. Because they have a certain amount of faith in mainstream society, they harbor hopes for a better future for their children, if not for themselves. Many of them go to church and take a strong interest in their children's schooling. Rather than dwelling on the real hardships and inequities facing them, many such decent people, particularly the increasing number of grandmothers raising grandchildren, see their difficult situation as a test from God and derive great support from their faith and from the church community.

Extremely aware of the problematic and often dangerous environment in which they reside, decent parents tend to be strict in their child-rearing practices, encouraging children to respect authority and walk a straight moral line. They have an almost obsessive concern about trouble of any kind and remind their children to be on the lookout for people and situations that might lead to it. At the same time, they are themselves polite and considerate of others, and teach their children to be the same way. At home, at work, and in church, they strive hard to maintain a positive mental attitude and a spirit of cooperation.

So-called street parents, in contrast, often show a lack of consideration for other people and have a rather superficial sense of family and community. Though they may love their children, many of them are unable to cope with the physical and emotional demands of parenthood, and find it difficult to reconcile their needs with those of their children. These families, who are more fully invested in the code of the streets than the decent people are, may aggressively socialize their children into it in a normative way. They believe in the code and judge themselves and others according to its values.

In fact the overwhelming majority of families in the inner-city community try to approximate the decent-family model, but there are many others who clearly represent the worst fears of the decent family. Not only are their financial resources extremely limited, but what little they have may easily be misused. The lives of the street-oriented are often marked by disorganization. In the most desperate circumstances people frequently have a limited understanding of priorities and consequences, and so frustrations mount over bills, food, and, at times, drink, cigarettes, and drugs. Some tend toward self-destructive behavior; many street-oriented women are crack-addicted ("on the pipe"), alcoholic, or involved in complicated relationships with men who abuse them. In addition, the seeming intractability of their situation, caused in large part by the lack of well-paying jobs and the persistence of racial discrimination, has engendered

deep-seated bitterness and anger in many of the most desperate and poorest blacks, especially young people. The need both to exercise a measure of control and to lash out at somebody is often reflected in the adults' relations with their children. At the least, the frustrations of persistent poverty shorten the fuse in such people—contributing to a lack of patience with anyone, child or adult, who irritates them.

In these circumstances a woman—or a man, although men are less consistently present in children's lives—can be quite aggressive with children, yelling at and striking them for the least little infraction of the rules she has set down. Often little if any serious explanation follows the verbal and physical punishment. This response teaches children a particular lesson. They learn that to solve any kind of interpersonal problem one must quickly resort to hitting or other violent behavior. Actual peace and quiet, and also the appearance of calm, respectful children conveyed to her neighbors and friends, are often what the young mother most desires, but at times she will be very aggressive in trying to get them. Thus she may be quick to beat her children, especially if they defy her law, not because she hates them but because this is the way she knows to control them. In fact, many street-oriented women love their children dearly. Many mothers in the community subscribe to the notion that there is a "devil in the boy" that must be beaten out of him or that socially "fast girls need to be whupped." Thus much of what borders on child abuse in the view of social authorities is acceptable parental punishment in the view of these mothers.

Many street-oriented women are sporadic mothers whose children learn to fend for themselves when necessary, foraging for food and money any way they can get it. The children are sometimes employed by drug dealers or become addicted themselves. These children of the street, growing up with little supervision, are said to "come up hard." They often learn to fight at an early age, sometimes using short-tempered adults around them as role models. The street-oriented home may be fraught with anger, verbal disputes, physical aggression, and even mayhem. The children observe these goings-on, learning the lesson that might makes right. They quickly learn to hit those who cross them, and the dog-eat-dog mentality prevails. In order to survive, to protect oneself, it is necessary to marshal inner resources and be ready to deal with adversity in a hands-on way. In these circumstances physical prowess takes on great significance.

In some of the most desperate cases, a street-oriented mother may simply leave her young children alone and unattended while she goes out. The most irresponsible women can be found at local bars and crack houses, getting high and socializing with other adults. Sometimes a troubled woman will leave very young children alone for days at a time. Reports of crack addicts abandoning their children have become common in drug-infested inner-city communities. Neighbors or relatives discover the abandoned children, often hungry and distraught over the absence of their mother. After repeated absences, a friend or relative, particularly a grandmother, will often step in to care for the young children, sometimes petitioning the authorities to send her, as guardian of the children, the mother's welfare check, if the mother gets one. By this time, however, the children may well have learned the first lesson of the streets: survival itself, let alone respect, cannot be taken for granted; you have to fight for your place in the world.

CAMPAIGNING FOR RESPECT

THESE realities of inner-city life are largely absorbed on the streets. At an early age, often even before they start school, children from street-oriented homes gravitate to the streets, where they "hang"—socialize with their peers. Children from these generally permissive homes have a great deal of latitude and are allowed to "rip and run" up and down the street. They often come home from school, put their books down, and go right back out the door. On school nights eight- and nine-year-olds remain out until nine or ten o'clock (and teenagers typically come in whenever they want to). On the streets they play in groups that often become the source of their primary social bonds. Children from decent homes tend to be more carefully supervised and are thus likely to have curfews and to be taught how to stay out of trouble.

When decent and street kids come together, a kind of social shuffle occurs in which children have a chance to go either way. Tension builds as a child comes to realize that he must choose an orientation. The kind of home he comes from influences but does not determine the way he will ultimately turn out—although it is unlikely that a child from a thoroughly street-oriented family will easily absorb decent values on the streets. Youths who emerge from street-oriented families but develop a decency orientation almost always learn those values in another setting—in school, in a youth group, in church. Often it is the result of their involvement with a caring "old head" (adult role model).

In the street, through their play, children pour their individual life experiences into a common knowledge pool, affirming, confirming, and elaborating on what they have observed in the home and matching their skills against those of others. And they learn to fight. Even small children test one another, pushing and shoving, and are ready to hit other children over circumstances not to their liking. In turn, they are readily hit by other children, and the child who is toughest prevails. Thus the violent resolution of disputes, the hitting and cursing, gains social reinforcement. The child in effect is initiated into a system that is really a way of campaigning for respect.

In addition, younger children witness the disputes of old-er children, which are often resolved through cursing and abusive talk, if not aggression or outright violence. They see that one child succumbs to the greater physical and mental abilities of the other. They are also alert and attentive witnesses to the verbal and physical fights of adults, after which they compare notes and share their interpretations of the event. In almost every case the victor is the person who physically won the altercation, and this person often enjoys the esteem and respect of onlookers. These experiences reinforce the lessons the children have learned at home: might makes right, and toughness is a virtue, while humility is not. In effect they learn the social meaning of fighting. When it is left virtually unchallenged, this understanding becomes an ever more important part of the child's working conception of the world. Over time the code of the streets becomes refined.

Those street-oriented adults with whom children come in contact—including mothers, fathers, brothers, sisters, boyfriends, cousins, neighbors, and friends—help them along in forming this understanding by verbalizing the messages they are getting through experience: "Watch your back." "Protect yourself." "Don't punk out." "If somebody messes with you, you got to pay them back." "If someone disses you, you got to straighten them out." Many parents actually impose sanctions if a child is not sufficiently aggressive. For example, if a child loses a fight and comes home upset, the parent might respond, "Don't you come in here crying that somebody beat you up; you better get back out there and whup his ass. I didn't raise no punks! Get back out there and whup his ass. If you don't whup his ass, I'll whup your ass when you come home." Thus the child obtains reinforcement for being tough and showing nerve.

While fighting, some children cry as though they are doing something they are ambivalent about. The fight may be against their wishes, yet they may feel constrained to fight or face the consequences—not just from peers but also from caretakers or parents, who may administer another beating if they back down. Some adults recall receiving such lessons from their own parents and justify repeating them to their children as a way to toughen them up. Looking capable of taking care of oneself as a form of self-defense is a dominant theme among both street-oriented and decent adults who worry about the safety of their children. There is thus at times a convergence in their child-rearing practices, although the rationales behind them may differ.

SELF-IMAGE BASED ON "JUICE"

BY the time they are teenagers, most youths have either internalized the code of the streets or at least learned the need to comport themselves in accordance with its rules, which chiefly have to do with interpersonal communication. The code revolves around the presen-

AMONG THE HARD-CORE STREET-ORIENTED, THE CLEAR RISK OF MEETING

tation of self. Its basic requirement is the display of a certain predisposition to violence. Accordingly, one's bearing must send the unmistakable if sometimes subtle message to "the next person" in public that one is capable of violence and mayhem when the situation requires it, that one can take care of oneself. The nature of this communication is largely determined by the demands of the circumstances but can include facial expressions, gait, and verbal expressions—all of which are geared mainly to deterring aggression. Physical appearance, including clothes, jewelry, and grooming, also plays an important part in how a person is viewed; to be respected, it is important to have the right look.

Even so, there are no guarantees against challenges, because there are always people around looking for a fight to increase their share of respect—or "juice," as it is sometimes called on the street. Moreover, if a person is assaulted, it is important, not only in the eyes of his opponent but also in the eyes of his "running buddies," for him to avenge himself. Otherwise he risks being "tried" (challenged) or "moved on" by any number of others. To maintain his honor he must show he is not someone to be "messed with" or "dissed." In general, the person must "keep himself straight" by managing his position of respect among others; this involves in part his self-image, which is shaped by what he thinks others are thinking of him in relation to his peers.

Objects play an important and complicated role in establishing self-image. Jackets, sneakers, gold jewelry, reflect not just a person's taste, which tends to be tightly regulated among adolescents of all social classes, but also a willingness to possess things that may require defending. A boy wearing a fashionable, expensive jacket, for example, is vulnerable to attack by another who covets the jacket and either cannot afford to buy one or wants the added satisfaction of depriving someone else of his. However, if the boy forgoes the desirable jacket and wears one that isn't "hip," he runs the risk of being teased and possibly even assaulted as an unworthy person. To be allowed to hang with certain prestigious crowds, a boy must wear a different set of expensive clothes—sneakers and athletic suit—every day. Not to be able to do so might make him appear socially deficient. The youth comes to covet such items—especially when he sees easy prey wearing them.

In acquiring valued things, therefore, a person shores up his identity—but since it is an identity based on having things, it is highly precarious. This very precariousness gives a heightened sense of urgency to staying even with peers, with whom the person is actually competing. Young men and women who are able to command respect through their presentation of self—by allowing their possessions and their body language to speak for them—may not have to campaign for regard but may, rather, gain it by the force of their manner. Those who are unable to command respect in this way must actively campaign for it—and are thus particularly alive to slights.

One way of campaigning for status is by taking the possessions of others. In this context, seemingly ordinary objects can become trophies imbued with symbolic value that far exceeds their monetary worth. Possession of the trophy

A VIOLENT DEATH MAY BE PREFERABLE TO BEING "DISSED" BY ANOTHER.

can symbolize the ability to violate somebody—to "get in his face," to take something of value from him, to "dis" him, and thus to enhance one's own worth by stealing someone else's. The trophy does not have to be something material. It can be another person's sense of honor, snatched away with a derogatory remark. It can be the outcome of a fight. It can be the imposition of a certain standard, such as a girl's getting herself recognized as the most beautiful. Material things, however, fit easily into the pattern. Sneakers, a pistol, even somebody else's girlfriend, can become a trophy. When a person can take something from another and then flaunt it, he gains a certain regard by being the owner, or the controller, of that thing. But this display of ownership can then provoke other people to challenge him. This game of who controls what is thus constantly being played out on inner-city streets, and the trophy—extrinsic or intrinsic, tangible or intangible—identifies the current winner.

An important aspect of this often violent give-and-take is its zero-sum quality. That is, the extent to which one person can raise himself up depends on his ability to put another person down. This underscores the alienation that permeates the inner-city ghetto community. There is a generalized sense that very little respect is to be had, and therefore everyone competes to get what affirmation he can of the little that is available. The craving for respect that results gives people thin skins. Shows of deference by others can be highly soothing, contributing to a sense of security, comfort, self-confidence, and self-respect. Transgressions by others which go unanswered diminish these feelings and are believed to encourage further transgressions. Hence one must be ever vigilant against the transgressions of others or even *appearing* as if transgressions will be tolerated. Among young people, whose sense of self-esteem is particularly vulnerable, there is an especially heightened concern with being disrespected. Many inner-city young men in particular crave respect to such a degree that they will risk their lives to attain and maintain it.

The issue of respect is thus closely tied to whether a person has an inclination to be violent, even as a victim. In the wider society people may not feel required to retaliate physically after an attack, even though they are aware that they have been degraded or taken advantage of. They may feel a great need to defend themselves *during* an attack, or to behave in such a way as to deter aggression (middle-class people certainly can and do become victims of street-oriented youths), but they are much more likely than street-oriented people to feel that they can walk away from a possible altercation with their self-esteem intact. Some people may even have the strength of character to flee, without any thought that their self-respect or esteem will be diminished.

In impoverished inner-city black communities, however, particularly among young males and perhaps increasingly among females, such flight would be extremely difficult. To run away would likely leave one's self-esteem in tatters. Hence people often feel constrained not only to stand up and at least attempt to resist during an assault but also to "pay back"—to seek revenge—after a successful assault on their person. This may include going to get a weapon or even getting relatives involved. Their very identity and self-respect, their honor, is often intricately tied up with the way they perform on the streets during and after such encounters. This outlook reflects the circumscribed opportunities of the inner-city poor. Generally people outside the ghetto have other ways of gaining status and regard, and thus do not feel so dependent on such physical displays.

BY TRIAL OF MANHOOD

ON the street, among males these concerns about things and identity have come to be expressed in the concept of "manhood." Manhood in the inner city means taking the prerogatives of men with respect to strangers, other men, and women—being distinguished as a man. It implies physicality and a certain ruthlessness. Regard and respect are associated with this concept in large part because of its practical application: if others have little or no regard for a person's manhood, his very life and those of his loved ones could be in jeopardy. But there is a chicken-and-egg aspect to this situation: one's physical safety is more likely to be jeopardized in public *because* manhood is associated with respect. In other words, an existential link has been created between the idea of manhood and one's self-esteem, so that it has become hard to say which is primary. For many inner-city youths, manhood and respect are flip sides of the same coin; physical and psychological well-being are inseparable, and both require a sense of control, of being in charge.

The operating assumption is that a man, especially a real man, knows what other men know—the code of the streets. And if one is not a real man, one is somehow diminished as a person, and there are certain valued things one simply does not deserve. There is thus believed to be a certain justice to the code, since it is considered that everyone has the opportunity to know it. Implicit in this is that everybody is held responsible for being familiar with the code. If the victim of a mugging, for example, does not know the code and so responds "wrong," the perpetrator may feel justified even in killing him and may feel no remorse. He may think, "Too bad, but it's his fault. He should have known better."

So when a person ventures outside, he must adopt the code—a kind of shield, really—to prevent others from "messing with" him. In these circumstances it is easy for people to think they are being tried or tested by others even when this is not the case. For it is sensed that something extremely valuable is at stake in every interaction, and people are encouraged to rise to the occasion, particularly with strangers. For people who are unfamiliar with the code—generally people who live outside the inner city—the concern with respect in the most ordinary interactions can be frightening and incomprehensible. But for those who are invested in the code, the clear object of their demeanor is to discourage strangers from even thinking about testing their manhood. And the sense of power that attends the ability to deter others can be alluring even to those who know the code without being heavily invested in it—the decent inner-city youths. Thus a boy who has been leading a basically decent life can, in trying circumstances, suddenly resort to deadly force.

Central to the issue of manhood is the widespread belief that one of the most effective ways of gaining respect is to manifest "nerve." Nerve is shown when one takes another person's possessions (the more valuable the better), "messes with" someone's woman, throws the first punch, "gets in someone's face," or pulls a trigger. Its proper display helps on the spot to check others who would violate one's person and also helps to build a reputation that works to prevent future challenges. But since such a show of nerve is a forceful expression of disrespect toward the person on the receiving end, the victim may be greatly offended and seek to retaliate with equal or greater force. A display of nerve, therefore, can easily provoke a life-threatening response, and the background knowledge of that possibility has often been incorporated into the concept of nerve.

True nerve exposes a lack of fear of dying. Many feel that it is acceptable to risk dying over the principle of respect. In fact, among the hard-core street-oriented, the clear risk of violent death may be preferable to being "dissed" by another. The youths who have internalized this attitude and convincingly display it in their public bearing are among the most threatening people of all, for it is commonly assumed that they fear no man. As the people of the community say, "They are the baddest dudes on the street." They often lead an existential life that may acquire meaning only when they are faced with the possibility of imminent death. Not to be afraid to die is by implication to have few compunctions about taking another's life. Not to be afraid to die is the quid pro quo of being able to take somebody else's life—for the right reasons, if the situation demands it. When others believe this is one's position, it gives one a real sense of power on the streets. Such credibility is what many inner-city youths strive to achieve, whether they are decent or street-oriented, both because of its practical defensive value and because of the positive way it makes them feel about themselves. The difference between the decent and the street-oriented youth is often that the decent youth makes a conscious decision to appear tough and manly; in another setting—

with teachers, say, or at his part-time job—he can be polite and deferential. The street-oriented youth, on the other hand, has made the concept of manhood a part of his very identity; he has difficulty manipulating it—it often controls him.

GIRLS AND BOYS

INCREASINGLY, teenage girls are mimicking the boys and trying to have their own version of "manhood." Their goal is the same—to get respect, to be recognized as capable of setting or maintaining a certain standard. They try to achieve this end in the ways that have been established by the boys, including posturing, abusive language, and the use of violence to resolve disputes, but the issues for the girls are different. Although conflicts over turf and status exist among the girls, the majority of disputes seem rooted in assessments of beauty (which girl in a group is "the cutest"), competition over boyfriends, and attempts to regulate other people's knowledge of and opinions about a girl's behavior or that of someone close to her, especially her mother.

A major cause of conflicts among girls is "he say, she say." This practice begins in the early school years and continues through high school. It occurs when "people," particularly girls, talk about others, thus putting their "business in the streets." Usually one girl will say something negative about another in the group, most often behind the person's back. The remark will then get back to the person talked about. She may retaliate or her friends may feel required to "take up for" her. In essence this is a form of group gossiping in which individuals are negatively assessed and evaluated. As with much gossip, the things said may or may not be true, but the point is that such imputations can cast aspersions on a person's good name. The accused is required to defend herself against the slander, which can result in arguments and fights, often over little of real substance. Here again is the problem of low self-esteem, which encourages youngsters to be highly sensitive to slights and to be vulnerable to feeling easily "dissed." To avenge the dissing, a fight is usually necessary.

Because boys are believed to control violence, girls tend to defer to them in situations of conflict. Often if a girl is attacked or feels slighted, she will get a brother, uncle, or cousin to do her fighting for her. Increasingly, however, girls are doing their own fighting and are even asking their male relatives to teach them how to fight. Some girls form groups that attack other girls or take things from them. A hard-core segment of inner-city girls inclined toward violence seems to be developing. As one thirteen-year-old girl in a detention center for youths who have committed violent acts told me, "To get people to leave you alone, you gotta fight. Talking don't always get you out of stuff." One major difference between girls and boys: girls rarely use guns. Their fights are therefore not life-or-death struggles. Girls are not often willing to put their lives on the line for "manhood." The ultimate form of respect on the male-dominated inner-city street is thus reserved for men.

"GOING FOR BAD"

IN the most fearsome youths such a cavalier attitude toward death grows out of a very limited view of life. Many are uncertain about how long they are going to live and believe they could die violently at any time. They accept this fate; they live on the edge. Their manner conveys the message that nothing intimidates them; whatever turn the encounter takes, they maintain their attack—rather like a pit bull, whose spirit many such boys admire. The demonstration of such tenacity "shows heart" and earns their respect.

This fearlessness has implications for law enforcement. Many street-oriented boys are much more concerned about the threat of "justice" at the hands of a peer than at the hands of the police. Moreover, many feel not only that they have little to lose by going to prison but that they have something to gain. The toughening-up one experiences in prison can actually enhance one's reputation on the streets. Hence the system loses influence over the hard core who are without jobs, with little perceptible stake in the system. If mainstream society has done nothing *for* them, they counter by making sure it can do nothing *to* them.

At the same time, however, a competing view maintains that true nerve consists in backing down, walking away from a fight, and going on with one's business. One fights only in self-defense. This view emerges from the decent philosophy that life is precious, and it is an important part of the socialization process common in decent homes. It discourages violence as the primary means of resolving disputes and encourages youngsters to accept nonviolence and talk as confrontational strategies. But "if the deal goes down," self-defense is greatly encouraged. When there is enough positive support for this orientation, either in the home or among one's peers, then nonviolence has a chance to prevail. But it prevails at the cost of relinquishing a claim to being bad and tough, and therefore sets a young person up as at the very least alienated from street-oriented peers and quite possibly a target of derision or even violence.

Although the nonviolent orientation rarely overcomes the impulse to strike back in an encounter, it does introduce a certain confusion and so can prompt a measure of soul-searching, or even profound ambivalence. Did the person back down with his respect intact or did he back down only to be judged a "punk"—a person lacking manhood? Should he or she have acted? Should he or she have hit the other person in the mouth? These questions beset many young men and women during public confrontations. What is the "right" thing to do? In the quest for honor, respect, and local status—which few young people are uninterested in—common sense most often prevails, which leads many to opt for the tough approach, enacting their own particular versions of the display of nerve. The presentation of oneself as rough and tough is very often quite acceptable until one is tested. And then that presentation may help the person pass the test, because it will cause fewer questions to be asked about what he did and why. It is hard for a person to explain why he lost the fight or why he backed down. Hence many will strive to appear to "go for bad," while hoping they will never be tested. But when they are tested, the outcome of the situation may quickly be out of their hands, as they become wrapped up in the circumstances of the moment.

AN OPPOSITIONAL CULTURE

THE attitudes of the wider society are deeply implicated in the code of the streets. Most people in inner-city communities are not totally invested in the code, but the significant minority of hard-core street youths who are have to maintain the code in order to establish reputations, because they have—or feel they have—few other ways to assert themselves. For these young people the standards of the street code are the only game in town. The extent to which some children—particularly those who through upbringing have become most alienated and those lacking in strong and conventional social support—experience, feel, and internalize racist rejection and contempt from mainstream society may strongly encourage them to express contempt for the more conventional society in turn. In dealing with this contempt and rejection, some youngsters will consciously invest themselves and their considerable mental resources in what amounts to an oppositional culture to preserve themselves and their self-respect. Once they do, any respect they might be able to garner in the wider system pales in comparison with the respect available in the local system; thus they often lose interest in even attempting to negotiate the mainstream system.

At the same time, many less alienated young blacks have assumed a street-oriented demeanor as a way of expressing their blackness while really embracing a much more moderate way of life; they, too, want a nonviolent setting in which to live and raise a family. These decent people are trying hard to be part of the mainstream culture, but the racism, real and perceived, that they encounter helps to legitimate the oppositional culture. And so on occasion they adopt street behavior. In fact, depending on the demands of the situation, many people in the community slip back and forth between decent and street behavior.

A vicious cycle has thus been formed. The hopelessness and alienation many young inner-city black men and women feel, largely as a result of endemic joblessness and persistent racism, fuels the violence they engage in. This violence serves to confirm the negative feelings many whites and some middle-class blacks harbor toward the ghetto poor, further legitimating the oppositional culture and the code of the streets in the eyes of many poor young blacks. Unless this cycle is broken, attitudes on both sides will become increasingly entrenched, and the violence, which claims victims black and white, poor and affluent, will only escalate. 🦋

The following images by Edmund Guy and poem by Brooks Haxton have been omitted from this article due to restrictions of copyright and facsimile reproduction.

Page 80 – Power Play

Page 87 – Trophies

Page 88 – The Body of my Brother Osiris is in the Mustard Seed

Page 93 – Drive By

[14]

UP IT UP: GENDER AND THE ACCOMPLISHMENT OF STREET ROBBERY*

JODY MILLER
University of Missouri-St. Louis

Attempts to understand women's participation in violence have been plagued by a tendency either to overemphasize gender differences or to downplay the significance of gender. The goal of this research is to reconcile these approaches through an examination of the experiences of female and male street robbers in an urban setting. Based on in-depth interviews with active offenders, the study compares women's and men's accounts of why they commit robbery, as well as how gender organizes the commission of the crime. The research suggests that while women and men articulate similar motives for robbery, their enactment of the crime is strikingly different—a reflection, in part, of practical choices women make in the context of a gender-stratified street setting.

With the exception of forcible rape, robbery is perhaps the most gender differentiated serious crime in the United States. According to the Federal Bureau of Investigation's Uniform Crime Report for 1995, women accounted for 9.3% of robbery arrestees, while they were 9.5%, 17.7%, and 11.1% of arrestees for murder/manslaughter, aggravated assault, and burglary, respectively (Federal Bureau of Investigation, 1996). And while recently there has been considerable attention among feminist scholars to the question of why males are more violent than females, there have been few attempts to examine women's participation in these "male" crimes. Though their numbers are small, women who engage in violent street crime have something significant to teach us about women's place in the landscape of the urban street world.

Simpson (1989:618; see also Kelly, 1991; White and Kowalski, 1994) recently noted that feminist scholars' "reticence [to address issues concerning women's criminality] leaves the interpretive door open to less critical perspectives." Nowhere is this more the case than with the issue of

* Thanks to Richard Wright and Scott Decker for so generously allowing me to re-read their data with a feminist eye; to Richard Wright for his feedback throughout the writing process; and to the anonymous reviewers at *Criminology* for their helpful suggestions on an earlier draft. The research on which the article is based was funded jointly by the Harry Frank Guggenheim Foundation and the National Institute of Justice (NIJ grant 94-IJ-CX-0030). Opinions expressed are those of the author and do not necessarily reflect those of the funding agencies.

women's participation in violent street crime. Sensational accounts of the "new violent female offender" (e.g., Sikes, 1997; see Chesney-Lind, 1993), which draw heavily on racial imagery of young women of color, must be countered with accurate, nuanced accounts of women's use of violence in the contexts of racial and economic inequalities. This research compares the experiences of male and female robbers active in an urban underclass environment with the goal of expanding understanding of women's use of violence in nondomestic street settings.

MASCULINITIES AND CRIME: ROBBERY AS GENDER ACCOMPLISHMENT

In the late 1980s, feminist sociologists began theorizing about gender as situated accomplishment (West and Fenstermaker, 1995; West and Zimmerman, 1987). According to these authors, gender is "much more than a role or an individual characteristic: it is a mechanism whereby situated social action contributes to the reproduction of social structure" (West and Fenstermaker, 1995:21). Women and men "do gender" in response to normative beliefs about femininity and masculinity. These actions are "the interactional scaffolding of social structure" (West and Zimmerman, 1987:147) such that the performance of gender is both an indication and a reproduction of gendered social hierarchies.

This approach has been incorporated into feminist accounts of crime as a means of explaining differences in women's and men's offending (Messerschmidt, 1993, 1995; Newburn and Stanko, 1994; Simpson and Elis, 1995). Here, violence is described as "a 'resource' for accomplishing gender—for demonstrating masculinity within a given context or situation" (Simpson and Elis, 1995:50). Further, it is suggested that although some women may engage in violent behavior, because their actions transgress normative conceptions of femininity, they will "derive little support for expressions of masculine violence from even the most marginal of subcultures" (Braithwaite and Daly, 1994:190).

Several authors suggest that robbery epitomizes the use of crime to construct masculine identity (Katz, 1988; Messerschmidt, 1993). Messerschmidt argues as follows:

> The robbery setting provides the ideal opportunity to construct an "essential" toughness and "maleness"; it provides a means with which to construct that certain type of masculinity—hardman. Within the social context that ghetto and barrio boys find themselves, then, robbery is a rational practice for "doing gender" and for getting money (Messerschmidt, 1993:107).

UP IT UP   39

Moreover, given the disproportionate use of robbery by African-American versus white men (Federal Bureau of Investigation, 1996), the masculinity that robbery constructs may be one that fits particularly well in urban underclass settings, which are unique from areas in which poor whites live (see Sampson and Wilson, 1995). Katz, in fact, suggests that "for some urban, black ghetto-located young men, the stickup is particularly attractive as a distinctive way of being black" as well as male (1988:239).

Examining violence as masculine accomplishment can help account for women's lack of involvement in these crimes, just as this approach offers explanation for women's involvement in crime in ways scripted by femininity (e.g., prostitution). However, it leaves unexplained women's participation in violent street crime, except as an anomaly. Perhaps this is because femininity in this approach is conceived narrowly—specifically "within the parameters of the white middle class (i.e., domesticity, dependence, selflessness, and motherhood)" (Simpson and Elis, 1995:51). Given urban African-American women's historical patterns of economic self-sufficiency and independence, this passive feminine ideal is unlikely to have considerable influence and is "much more relevant (and restrictive) for white females" (Simpson and Elis, 1995:71).

Messerschmidt himself has recently recognized this oversight. Given that urban African-American females are involved in violent street crime at higher rates than other females, he suggests that "theory must not universalize female crime" (1995:171) and must consider significant women's involvement in presumably "male" crime. Simpson (1991:129; see also White and Kowalski, 1994) concludes: "The simplistic assertion that males are violent and females are not contains a grain of truth, but it misses the complexity and texture of women's lives."

WOMEN'S VIOLENCE AS RESISTANCE TO MALE OPPRESSION

Feminist scholars who address the use of street violence by women often suggest that women's violence differs from that of men's—women use violence in response to their vulnerability to or actual victimization in the family and/or at the hands of men (Campbell, 1993; Joe and Chesney-Lind, 1995; Maher, 1997; Maher and Curtis, 1992; Maher and Daly, 1996). In her ethnography of a Brooklyn drug market, Maher notes that women adopt violent presentations of self as a strategy of protection. She explains, "'Acting bad' and 'being bad' are not the same. Although many of the women presented themselves as 'bad' or 'crazy,' this projection was a street persona and a necessary survival strategy" (1997:95; see also

40   JODY MILLER

Maher and Daly, 1996). These women were infrequently involved in violent crime and most often resorted to violence in response to threats or
harms against them. She concludes that "unlike their male counterparts,
for women, reputation was about 'preventing victimization'" (Maher,
1997:95–96; see also Campbell, 1993). In this account, even when women's
aggression is offensive, it can still be understood as a defensive act,
because it emerges as resistance to victimization.

Maher's research uncovered a particular form of robbery—"viccing"—
in which women involved in the sex trade rob their clients. Although the
phenomenon of prostitutes robbing tricks is not new, Maher's work docu-
ments the proliferation of viccing as a form of resistance against their
greater vulnerability to victimization and against cheapened sex markets
within the drug economy. Comparing viccing with traditional forms of
robbery, Maher and Curtis conclude, "The fact that the act [of viccing]
itself is little different to any other instrumental robbery belies the reality
that the motivations undergirding it are more complex and, indeed, are
intimately linked with women's collective sense of the devaluation of their
bodies and their work" (1992:246). However, it is likely that not all of
women's street violence can be viewed as resistance to male oppression;
instead, some women may be motivated to commit violent crimes for
many of the same reasons some men are. In certain contexts, norms
favorable to women's use of violence may exist, and they are not simply
about avoiding victimization, but also result in status and recognition.

RACE, CLASS AND GENDER: WOMEN'S VIOLENCE AS SITUATED ACTION

It is necessary to consider that some of women's participation in violent
street crime may stem from "the frustration, alienation, and anger that are
associated with racial and class oppression" (Simpson, 1989:618). The
foregrounding of gender is important; however, there are structural and
cultural underpinnings related to racial and economic inequalities that
must simultaneously be addressed when one considers women's involvement in violent street crime (Simpson, 1991).

Research suggests that urban African-American females are more likely
to engage in serious and violent crime than their counterparts in other
racial groups and/or settings (Ageton, 1983; Hill and Crawford, 1990; Laub
and McDermott, 1985; Mann, 1993). Ageton's analysis of the National
Youth Survey found little difference across race or class in girls' incidence
of crimes against persons, but she reports that "lower class females report
. . . the greatest involvement in assaultive crime . . . [and] a consistently
higher proportion of black females are involved in crimes against persons
for all five years surveyed" (1983:565). This is not to suggest that African-

UP IT UP   41

American women's participation in these offenses parallel or converge with that of urban African-American males (see Chesney-Lind and Shelden, 1992:21–24; Laub and McDermott, 1985). Rather, my point is to highlight the contexts in which these women negotiate their daily lives. Violence is extensive in the lives and communities of African-American women living in the urban underclass. As a result, some women in these circumstances may be more likely than women who are situated differently to view violence as an appropriate or useful means of dealing with their environment. As Simpson (1991:129) notes,

> Living daily with the fact of violence leads to an incorporation of it into one's experiential self. Men, women, and children have to come to terms with, make sense of, and respond to violence as it penetrates their lives. As violence is added to the realm of appropriate and sanctioned responses to oppressive material conditions, it gains a sort of cultural legitimacy. But not for all.

Evidence of the significance of the link between underclass conditions and African-American women's disproportionate involvement in violence may be found in recent research that examines factors predicting women's criminal involvement. Hill and Crawford (1990) report that structural indicators appear to be most significant in predicting the criminal involvement of African-American women, while social-psychological indicators are more predictive for white women. They conclude that "the unique position of black women in the structure of power relations in society has profound effects not shared by their white counterparts" (Hill and Crawford, 1990:621). In fact, Baskin et al. (1993:413) suggest that "women in inner city neighborhoods are being pulled toward violent street crime by the same forces that have been found to affect their male counterparts. As with males, neighborhood, peer and addiction factors have been found to contribute to female initiation into violence."

This is not to suggest, however, that gender does not matter. Gender remains a salient aspect of women's experiences in the urban street milieu, and must remain—along with race and class—at the forefront of attempts to understand their involvement in violent crime. Some research that stresses race and economic oppression as factors in women's criminality overlooks the significance of gender oppression in these contexts. For instance, Baskin et al. (1993:415) argue that "women's roles and prominence have changed in transformed neighborhoods" such that there exist "new dynamics of crime where gender is a far less salient factor" (p. 417).

However, there is overwhelming evidence that gender inequality remains a salient feature of the urban street scene (Anderson, 1994; Maher, 1997; Maher and Curtis, 1992; Maher and Daly, 1996; Oliver, 1994; Steffensmeier, 1983; Steffensmeier and Terry, 1986; Wilson, 1996). As

42   JODY MILLER

Maher notes, for scholars who suggest that gender has lost its relevance, women's "activity is confused with [their] equality" (1997:18). Research that examines women's participation in violent street crime without paying sufficient attention to the gendered nature of this participation or the ways in which "gendered status structures this participation" (Maher, 1997:13) cannot adequately describe or explain these phenomena.

The strength of the current study is its comparative analysis of women's *and* men's accounts of the accomplishment of one type of violent crime— street robbery. In comparing both the question of *why* women and men report engaging in robbery, and *how* gender organizes the commission of robbery, this research provides insight into the ways in which gender shapes women's involvement in what is perhaps the typification of "masculine" street crime. As such, it speaks to broader debates about women's place in the contemporary urban street world.

METHODOLOGY

The study is based on semistructured in-depth interviews with 37 active street robbers. The sample includes 14 women and a comparative sample of 23 men, matched approximately by age and age at first robbery.[1] The respondents range in age from 16 to 46; the majority are in their late teens to mid-twenties.[2] All of the men are African-American; 12 of the women are African-American and 2 are white.[3] See the appendix for a fuller description of each respondent.

Respondents were recruited on the streets through the use of snowball sampling (Watters and Biernacki, 1989) in impoverished urban neighborhoods in St. Louis, Missouri. An ex-offender was hired to serve as a street ethnographer; he culled from his former criminal associates in order to generate the initial respondents for the study (see also Decker and Van Winkle, 1996; Wright and Decker, 1994). These respondents were then

---

1.   The original study (Wright and Decker, 1997) contained 86 interviews, 72 of which were with males. From these, the matched sample of males for the current study was drawn prior to data analysis to avoid sampling biases.

2.   This age distribution differs from that of the larger sample, which included a sizable number of older male robbers. Eighteen of the males in the current sample were under 25 (78%), while only 35 of the 72 males in the larger sample (49%) were under 25.

3.   One white male was interviewed for the original study but was excluded from this analysis because he didn't fit the matching criteria (age, age at first robbery) and had only committed one robbery, which was retaliatory in nature. He was 30 years old and had recently been ripped off by someone, whom he robbed in order to get his money back. Notably though, the physicality of his style in committing the robbery—"I had my left hand on his neck and the gun on his cheekbone"—paralleled the predominant style of the male robbers included.

UP IT UP   43

asked to refer other friends or associates who might be willing to be interviewed, and the process continued until an appropriate sample was built.

Criteria for inclusion in the sample included the following: the individual had committed a robbery in the recent past, defined him- or herself as currently active, and was regarded as active by other offenders.[4] Though it is not possible to determine the representativeness of this sample of active offenders (see Glassner and Carpenter, 1985), the approach nonetheless overcomes many of the shortcomings associated with interviewing ex-offenders or offenders who are incarcerated (see Agar, 1977). In fact, in the current study snowball sampling allowed for the purposive over-sampling of both female and juvenile robbers.

Perhaps the greatest limitation of the sample is the overrepresentation of African-American robbers and the near absence of white offenders. According to the St. Louis Metropolitan Police Department's (1994) *Annual Report*, whites were 18% of robbery arrestees in that year. As Wright and Decker (1997:11) explain,

> No doubt the racial composition of our sample is a reflection of the social chasm that exists between blacks and whites in the St. Louis underworld. Black and white offenders display a marked tendency to "stick to their own kind" and seldom are members of the same criminal networks. Successfully making contact with active black armed robbers proved to be of almost no help to us in locating white offenders.

This problem was exacerbated because the hired street ethnographer was African-American and was unable to provide any initial contacts with white robbers. In fact, both of the white females interviewed in the study were referred by their African-American boyfriends.

Each respondent was paid $50 for participation in the research and was promised strict confidentiality.[5] Respondents were paid an additional $10

---

4. All but five of the respondents reported that they had committed at least one robbery within the month prior to being interviewed. These five included three men (Woods, C-Loco, and Tony Wright) and two women (Quick and Kim Brown). All nonetheless considered themselves active robbers.

5. Because the project was partially supported by funds from the National Institute of Justice, respondents' confidentiality was protected by federal law. In addition, completed interviews were kept in a locked file cabinet. For a fuller discussion of human subjects' protections, see Wright and Decker (1997). In regard to confidentiality, one clarification is in order. One of the young women (Tish) was referred by her boyfriend, who had previously been interviewed for the project. They insisted that he be present during her interview, and he occasionally interjected to offer his own clarifications of her responses. Though his presence may have made her more hesitant or self-conscious in answering, his own comments were illuminating regarding the gendered nature of their robberies, as both of them downplayed the seriousness of her involvement.

for each successful referral (i.e., a cooperative participant who was currently an active robber). Interviews lasted one to two hours and included a range of questions about the respondents' involvement in robbery, with particular focus on "their thoughts and actions during the commission of their crimes" (Wright and Decker, 1997:8). Respondents were asked to describe their typical approach when committing robbery, as well as to describe in detail their most recent offense; the goal was to gain a thorough understanding of the contexts of these events (see Wright and Decker, 1997, for a full discussion of the research process).

Because this research is concerned with the situational accomplishment of robbery, it does not provide a means to explore fully the contexts of offending as they relate to respondents' life circumstances. Nonetheless, it is worthwhile to situate their discussions with a brief description of the milieu from which they were drawn. As noted above, respondents were recruited from impoverished urban neighborhoods in St. Louis. St. Louis typifies the midwestern city devastated by structural changes brought about by deindustrialization. With tremendous economic and racial segregation, population loss, and resulting social isolation, loss of community resources, and concentrated urban poverty among African-Americans, the neighborhoods the respondents were drawn from are characteristic of "underclass" conditions (Sampson and Wilson, 1995; Wilson, 1996). These conditions no doubt shape respondents' offending through the interactive effects of structural barriers and resulting cultural adaptations (see Sampson and Wilson, 1995). Thus, they should remain in the foreground in examining the accomplishment of robbery.

MOTIVATIONS TO COMMIT ROBBERY

In this study, active robbers' articulation of the reasons they commit robbery is more a case of gender similarities than differences. What they get out of robbery, why they choose robbery instead of some other crime, why particular targets are appealing—the themes of these discussions are overlapping in women's and men's accounts. For both, the primary motivation is to get money or material goods. As Libbie Jones notes, "You can get good things from a robbery." For some, the need for money comes with a strong sense of urgency, such as when the individual is robbing to support a drug addiction—a situation more prevalent among older respondents than younger ones. But for the majority of women and men in this sample, robberies are committed to get status-conferring goods such as gold jewelry, spending money, and/or for excitement.[6] For instance, T-

---

6. This pattern is somewhat different from that of the larger sample of 86 active robbers, more of whom described robbing with a greater sense of desperation for money (Wright and Decker, 1997). This difference results from the differences in age

UP IT UP   45

Bone says he decides to commit robberies when he's "tired of not having money." When the idea comes about, he is typically with friends from the neighborhood, and he explains, "we all bored, broke, mad." Likewise, CMW says she commits robberies "out of the blue, just something to do. Bored at the time and just want to find some action." She explains, "I be sitting on the porch and we'll get to talking and stuff. See people going around and they be flashing in they fancy cars, walking down the street with that jewelry on, thinking they all bad, and we just go get 'em." For both males and females, robberies are typically a means of achieving conspicuous consumption.

If anything, imperatives to gain money and material goods through robbery appear to be stronger for males than females, so that young men explain that they sometimes commit robberies because they feel some economic pressure, whereas young women typically do not. Masculine street identity is tied to the ability to have and spend money, and included in this is the appearance of economic self-sufficiency. Research has documented women's support networks in urban communities, including among criminally involved women (see Maher, 1997; Stack, 1974). This may help explain why the imperative for young men is stronger than for young women: Community norms may give women wider latitude for obtaining material goods and economic support from a variety of sources, including other females, family members, and boyfriends; whereas the pressure of society's view of men as breadwinners differentially affects men's emotional experience of relying on others economically. This may explain why several young men specifically describe that they do not like relying on their parents in order to meet their consumer needs. As Mike J. notes, "My mother, she gives me money sometimes but I can't get the stuff like I want, clothes and stuff . . . so I try to get it by robbery." Though both males and females articulate economic motives for robbery, young men,

---

structure of the current sample compared to the original sample. Because the majority of female respondents were teenagers or young adults (10 of the 14), the matched sample of males drawn for this study was younger than the larger sample of males (see note 2). Older robbers were more likely to be supporting drug habits and were more likely to have children or family that they made efforts to provide for.

Sommers and Baskin's (1993) study of female robbers offers much the same conclusion regarding motivation. In their study of 44 female robbers, 89% describe committing the crime for money, and 11% for noneconomic reasons such as excitement or vengeance. Of women who committed robbery for money, 81% did so to support drug habits, and only 19% did so to get commodities such as jewelry and clothes. These differences are likely the case because their sample is older than the current sample and because they were incarcerated at the time of the interview, and thus likely represent less successful robbers (perhaps because of their drug habits). In fact, when giving life-history accounts, two-thirds of Sommers and Baskin's sample reported that their initial reasons for committing robbery were less economic and more oriented toward thrill seeking and excitement.

46   JODY MILLER

more than young women, describe feeling compelled to commit robberies because they feel "broke."

Asked to explain why they commit robberies instead of other crimes with similar economic rewards, both women and men say that they choose robberies, as Cooper explains, because "it's the easiest." Libbie Jones reports that robbery provides her with the things she wants in one quick and easy step:

> I like robbery. I like robbery 'cause I don't have to buy nothing. You have a herringbone, I'm gonna take your herringbone and then I have me a herringbone. I don't have to worry about going to the store, getting me some money. If you got some little earrings on I'm gonna get 'em.

The ease with which respondents view the act of robbery is also reflected in their choice of victims—most frequently other street-involved individuals, who are perceived as unlikely to be able to go to the police, given their own criminal involvement. In addition, these targets are perceived as likely to have a lot of money, as well as jewelry and other desirable items. Less frequently, respondents report targeting individuals who are perceived as particularly easy marks, such as older citizens. However, most robberies, whether committed by females or males, occur in the larger contexts of street life, and their victims reflect this—most are also involved in street contexts, either as adolescents or young adults who hang out on the streets and go to clubs, or as individuals involved (as dealers and/or users) in the street-level drug economy. Because of this, it is not uncommon for robbers to know or at least know of their victims (for more on target selection, see Wright and Decker, 1997:Ch. 3).

In addition to the economic incentives that draw the respondents toward robbery, many also derive a psychological or emotional thrill from committing robberies. Little Bill says, "when my first robbery started, my second, the third one, it got more fun . . . if I keep on doing it I think that I will really get addicted to it." Likewise, Ne-Ne's comment illustrates the complex dynamics shaping many respondents' decisions to commit robberies, particularly the younger ones: "I don't know if it's the money, the power or just the feeling that I know that I can just go up and just take somebody's stuff. It's just a whole bunch of mixture type thing." Others describe a similar mixture of economic and emotional rewards. Buby notes, "you get like a rush, it be fun at the time."

When individuals on the street are perceived as "high-catting" or showing off, they are viewed by both male and female robbers as deserving targets. Ne-Ne describes the following dialogue between herself and a young woman she robbed: "[The girl] said 'if you take my money then I'm gonna get in trouble because this is my man's money.' He told you to keep it, not showboat. You talking 'nigger I got $800 in my pocket,' pulling it out. Yeah, you wanted us to know." Likewise, describing a woman he robbed at a gas station, Treason Taylor says, "really I didn't like the way she came out. She was like pulling out all her money like she think she hot shit." A few respondents even specifically target people they don't like, or people who have insulted or hurt them in the past.

For both women and men, then, motivations to commit robbery are primarily economic—to get money, jewelry, and other status-conferring goods, but they also include elements of thrill seeking, attempting to overcome boredom, and revenge. Most striking is the continuity across women's and men's accounts of their motives for committing robbery, which vary only by the greater pressure reported by some young men to have their own money to obtain material goods. As discussed in the next sections, there are clear differences in the accomplishment of robbery by gender; however, these differences are apparently not driven by differences in motivation.

MEN'S ENACTMENTS OF STREET ROBBERY

Men accomplish street robberies in a strikingly uniform manner. Respondents' descriptions of their robberies are variations around one theme—using physical violence and/or a gun placed on or at close proximity to the victim in a confrontational manner. This is reflected in Looney's description of being taught how to commit his first robbery, at the age of 13, by his stepbrother:

> We was up at [a fast food restaurant] one day and a dude was up there tripping. My stepbrother had gave me a .22 automatic. He told me to walk over behind him and put the gun to his head and tell him to give me all his stuff. That's what I did. I walked up to him and said man, this is a jack, man, take off all your jewelry and take you money out of your pockets, throw it on the ground and walk off. So that's what he did. I picked up the money and the jewelry and walked away.

By far the most common form of robbery described by male respondents entails targeting other men involved in street life—drug dealers, drug users, gang members, or other men who look "flashy" because of their clothes, cars, and/or jewelry. Twenty-two respondents (96%) report committing robberies in these contexts, which involve accosting people on the streets or accosting them in their cars. Only Little Bill, who is an addict, does not describe engaging in these types of robberies. Instead, he only targets non-street-involved citizens, whom he feels safer confronting.[7]

---

7. This may be a low estimate. Sometimes it is difficult to discern whether victims are street involved; robbers simply view them as an individual likely to have money

48   JODY MILLER

Seven men (30%) describe robbing women as well as men.

All of the men in this sample report using guns when they rob, though not everyone uses a gun every time.[8] The key is to make sure that the victim knows, as Syco says, "that we ain't playing." This is accomplished either through the positioning of the gun or by physically assaulting the victim. If the victim appears to resist, the physical assault is more severe, a shot is fired in the air or to the side of the victim, or the victim is shot—typically in the foot or the leg. Again, what is striking across men's interviews is the continuity of their approach toward street robberies. Upon spotting a target, they swiftly run up on the victim and physically confront him or her, telling the victim "up it up," "come up off it," or some similar phrase. These robberies frequently are committed with partners, but sometimes are committed alone.

For many male robbers, cooperation is achieved simply by the presence and positioning of the gun. Bob Jones confronts his victims by placing the gun at the back of their head, where "they feel it," and says, "give it up, motherfucker, don't move or I'll blow your brains out." Explaining the positioning of the gun, he says, "when you feel that steel against your head . . . that pistol carries a lot of weight." Describing one of his robberies, Looney says, "I creeped up behind him, this time I had a 12 gauge, I pointed it to the back of his head, told him to drop it." Big Prod notes that he will "have the gun to his head, can't do nothing but respect that." Likewise, Treason Taylor explains that he will "grab [the victim] by the neck and stick the gun to they head. Sometimes I don't even touch them I just point the gun right in front of they face. That really scares people." Prauch says, "I don't even have to say nothing half the time. When they see that pistol, they know what time it is."

A number of respondents report using some measure of physical confrontation, even when using a weapon, in order to ensure the victim's cooperation and/or the robber's getaway. Cooper says, "you always got to either hit 'em, slap 'em or do something to let them know you for real." T-Bone says, "I just hit them with the gun and they give it up quick." Likewise, Mike J. says, "you might shake them a little bit. If there is more than one of you, you can really do that kind of stuff like shake them up a little bit to show them you're not messing around." Sometimes physical confrontation is simply part of the thrill. Damon Jones says that while he typically doesn't physically assault his victims, a friend he often robs with "always do something stupid like he'll smash somebody with the pistol,

---

because of their physical appearance, dress, and jewelry. In the larger sample, Wright and Decker estimated that 30 of the 86 robbers (35%) targeted citizens.

8.   In the larger sample, approximately 90% of respondents used guns to commit robberies.

you know what I'm saying. He'll hit them in the head or something just, I guess, just to do it."

When the victim hesitates or is seen as uncooperative, the respondents describe using a variety of physical measures to ensure the completion of the robbery. The mildest version is described by Carlos Reed: "If I have a revolver, I'll cock it back, that will be the warning right there. If I run up to you like this and then you hesitate I'm gonna cock it back." Others use physical violence to intimidate the victim. Redwood says, "if they think I'm bullshitting I'll smack them up in they motherfucking head." Likewise, Tony Wright notes, "you would be surprised how cooperative a person will be once he been smashed across the face with a .357 Magnum." Other respondents describe shooting the gun, either past the victim or in the leg or foot, in order to ensure cooperation. Prauch says, "one gun shot, they ass in line. If I hit them a couple of times and that don't work, one gun shot by they ear and they in line." And Cooper notes, "If I see he just trying to get tough then sometimes I just straight out have to shoot somebody, just shoot 'em."

Though most robberies involve the use of a weapon, several men also report engaging in strong-arm robberies, sometimes when an opportunity presents itself and there is no time to retrieve a weapon. These robberies involve a great deal of physical violence. Taz says, "if it's a strong-arm, like I'll just get up on them and I'll just hit 'em and [my partner] will grab them or like he will hit them and I'll grab 'em and we keep on hitting them until they fall or something . . . we just go in his pockets, leave him there, we gone." Likewise, Swoop describes a strong-arm robbery he was involved in:

> Me and my two partners saw this dude and he had on a lot of jewelry. I wanted them chains and my partner wanted the rings. We didn't have a weapon. We strong-armed him. . . He was coming from off the lot [at a fast food restaurant], he actually was going to his car so I ran up on him . . . and I hit him in the face. He tried to run. My partner ran and kicked him in the mouth. He just let us, I took the chains off of him, my partner took his rings, my partner took his money, we split the money and that was all it took.

Seven men describe robbing women as well as men. However, male respondents—both those who have robbed women and those who have not—clearly state that robbing women is different from robbing men. Robbing women is seen as less dangerous, and women are believed to be less likely to resist. The following dialogue with Looney is illustrative:

Interviewer: Do you rob men or women more?

Looney: I rob men.

Interviewer: Why?

50   JODY MILLER

Looney: They got money.

Interviewer: Do men behave differently than women?

Looney: Nope. Men gonna try to act like the tough guy, when they
    see the gun, then they give it up quick. But a lady, I just tell them
    to give it up and they give me they whole purse or whatever they
    got.

While physical violence is often used in men's robberies of other men,
respondents do not describe assaulting women routinely, typically only if
they are seen as resisting. It appears not to be deemed a necessary part of
the transaction with female victims. Taz, whose robberies of men typically
involve a great deal of physical violence (see above), says, "I did a girl
before but I didn't hurt her or nothing, we just robbed her. She was too
scared." Having women present is also seen as making male targets more
vulnerable. Swoop explains: "If he like by himself or if he with a girl then
that's the best time, but if he with two dudes, you know they rolling
strapped so you wait." Unlike when a street-involved target is with other
males and needs to maintain an air of toughness, Swoop says "you know
they ain't gonna try to show off for the little gals, they gonna give it all
up."

It is notable that women are widely perceived, as C-Loco says, as "easy
to get," and yet as a rule they are not targeted for street robberies. Partly
this is because women are perceived as less likely to have a lot of money
on them. Moreover, women are not viewed as real players in the action of
the streets; they are peripheral, and thus not typically part of the masculine game of street robbery. Antwon Wright sums this up in the following
dialogue about the use of physical violence:

Interviewer: Do you hit everybody?

Antwon Wright: It depends. It depends on who is there and how
    many. If it's a dude and a gal we might hit the dude and leave the
    girl.

Interviewer: Why?

Antwon Wright: 'Cause a girl is no threat for real to us. A girl is no
    threat. We just worry about dudes. Girls is no threat. But if it's
    about six dudes, man we gonna hit everybody. We gonna get every-
    body on the ground, bam, bam. Then if they want to get back up
    we just keep on hitting.

Male robbers, then, clearly view the act of robbery as a masculine
accomplishment in which men compete with other men for money and
status. While some rob women, those robberies are deviations from the
norm of "badass" against "badass" that dominates much of men's discussions of street robbery (see Katz, 1988). The routine use of guns, physical

contact, and violence in male-on-male robberies is a reflection of the masculine ideologies shaping men's robberies. Women's enactment of robbery is much more varied than that of men's and provides a telling contrast about the nature of gender on the streets.

WOMEN'S ENACTMENTS OF STREET ROBBERY

The women in the sample describe three predominant ways in which they commit robberies: targeting female victims in physically confrontational robberies, targeting male victims by appearing sexually available, and participating with males during street robberies of men. Ten women (71%) describe targeting female victims, usually on the streets but occasionally at dance clubs or in cars. Seven (50%) describe setting up men through promises of sexual favors, including two women who do so in the context of prostitution. Seven (50%) describe working with male friends, relatives, or boyfriends in street robberies; three (21%) report this as their exclusive form of robbery.

ROBBING FEMALES

The most common form of robbery reported by women in the study is robbing other females in a physically confrontational manner. Ten of the 14 female respondents report committing these types of offenses. Of those who do not, three only commit robberies by assisting men, whose targets are other males (see below), and one only robs men in the context of prostitution. Typically, women's robberies of other females occur on the streets, though a few young women also report robbing females in the bathrooms or parking lots of clubs, and one robs women in cars. These robberies are sometimes committed alone, but usually in conjunction with one or several additional women, but not in conjunction with men. In fact, Ne-Ne says even when she's out with male friends and sees a female target, they don't get involved: "They'll say 'well you go on and do her.'"

Most robberies of females either involve no weapon or they involve a knife. Four women report having used a gun to rob women, only one of whom does so on a regular basis.[9] Women are the victims of choice because they are perceived as less likely to be armed themselves and less likely to resist or fight back. CMW explains, "See women, they won't

---

9.   This is Yolanda Smith, who robs older women by offering to give them rides in her car. Describing a typical robbery, she says: "I asked her did she need a ride. I said 'if you give me one dollar for gas I'll take you to work.' So she jumped in the car. I took her about three or four blocks and then I said 'do you have any more money?' She had this necklace on so I put a gun up to her head and said 'give it up.'" Her approach was unlike any other woman's in the sample, both in terms of how she approached the victim and in her routine use of a firearm.

really do nothing. They say, 'oh, oh, ok, here take this.' A dude, he might try to put up a fight." Yolanda Smith reports that she only robs women because "they more easier for me to handle." Likewise, Libbie Jones says, "I wouldn't do no men by myself," but she says women victims "ain't gonna do nothing because they be so scared." The use of weapons in these assaults is often not deemed necessary. Quick explains that she sometimes uses a knife, "but sometimes I don't need anything. Most of the time it be girls, you know, just snatching they chains or jewelry. You don't need nothing for that." Quick has also used a gun to rob another female. She and a friend were driving around when they spotted a young woman walking down the street with an expensive purse they liked. "We jumped out of the car. My friend put a gun up to her head and we just took all of her stuff." However, this approach was atypical.

On occasion, female victims belie the stereotype of them and fight back. Both Janet Outlaw and Ne-Ne describe stabbing young women who resisted them. Janet Outlaw describes one such encounter:

> This was at a little basketball game. Coming from the basketball game. It was over and we were checking her out and everything and she was walking to her car. I was, shit fuck that, let's get her motherfucking purse. Said let's get that purse. So I walked up to her and I pulled out the knife. I said "up that purse." And she looked at me. I said "shit, do you think I'm playing? Up that purse." She was like "shit, you ain't getting my purse. Do what you got to do." I was like "shit, you must be thinking I'm playing." So I took the knife, stabbed her a couple of times on the shoulder, stabbed her on the arm and snatched the purse. Cut her arm and snatched the purse. She just ran, "help, help." We were gone.

Ne-Ne describes a similar incident that occurred after an altercation between two groups of young women. When one young woman continued to badmouth her, she followed the girl to her car, pulled out a knife, "headed to her side and showed the bitch [the knife]." The girl responded, "I ain't giving you shit," and Ne-Ne said, "please don't make me stick you." Then, "She went to turn around and I just stuck it in her side. . . She was holding her side, just bleeding. And so when she fell on the ground one of my partners just started taking her stuff off of her. We left her right there."

As with pulling guns on women, stabbing female victims is a rare occurrence. Nonetheless, women's robbery of other women routinely involves physical confrontation such as hitting, shoving, or beating up the victim. Describing a recent robbery, Nicole Simpson says, "I have bricks in my purse and I went up to her and hit her in the head and took her money." Kim Brown says that she will "just whop you and take a purse but not

UP IT UP 53

really put a gun to anybody's face." Libbie Jones says she has her victims throw their possessions on the ground, "then you push 'em, kick 'em or whatever, you pick it up and you just burn out." Likewise, CMW describes a recent robbery:

> I was like with three other girls and we was like all walking around . . . walking around the block trying to find something to do on a Saturday night with really nothing to do and so we started coming up the street, we didn't have no weapons on us at the time. All we did was just start jumping on her and beating her up and took her purse.

According to Janet Outlaw, "We push 'em and tell them to up their shit, pushing 'em in the head. Couple of times we had to knock the girls down and took the stuff off of them." She explains the reason this type of physical force is necessary: "It's just a woman-to-woman thing and we just like, just don't, just letting them know like it is, we let them know we ain't playing." As discussed below, this approach is vastly different from women's approaches when they rob men, or when they commit robberies with males. It appears to be, as Janet Outlaw says, "a woman-to-woman thing."

As noted above, sometimes female-on-female robberies occur in or around night clubs, in addition to on the streets. Libbie Jones explains, "you just chill in the club, just dance or whatever, just peep out people that got what you want. And then they come out of the club and you just get them." Likewise, Janet Outlaw says, "we get a couple of drinks, be on the blow, party, come sit down. Then be like, damn, check that bitch out with all this shit on." Libbie Jones came to her interview wearing a ring she had gotten in a robbery at a club the night before, telling the interviewer, "I like this on my hand, it looks lovely." She describes the incident as follows:

> This girl was in the bathroom. I seen the rings on her hands. Everybody was in there talking and putting their makeup on, doing their hair. So I went and got my godsister. She came back with her drink. She spilled it on her and she was like, "oh, my fault, my fault." She was wiping it off her. I pulled out my knife and said "give it up." The girl was taking the rings off her hand so when we got the rings we bounced up out of the club.

Though most of the women who rob females are teenagers or young adults and rob other young women, two women in the sample—Lisa Wood and Kim Brown—also describe targeting middle-aged or older citizens. It is notable that both are older (in their late 30s) and that both describe robbing in order to support drug habits, which make them more

54   JODY MILLER

desperate.[10] As with the younger women who choose to rob other young women because they believe them unlikely to resist, both of these women choose older targets because they won't fight back. Lisa Wood says sometimes they accomplish these robberies of non-street-involved citizens by getting victims to drop their guard when they are coming out of stores. She describes approaching the person, "say 'hi, how you doing,' or 'do you need any help?' A lot of times they will say yeah. They might have groceries to take to they car and get it like that." She says once they drop their guard she will "snatch they purse and take off running."

To summarize, notable elements of women's robberies of other women are that they most frequently occur within street-oriented settings, do not include male accomplices, and typically involve physical force such as hitting, shoving and kicking, rather than the use of a weapon. When weapons are used, they are most likely to be knives. In these contexts, women choose to rob other females rather than males because they believe females are less likely to fight back; they typically do not use weapons such as guns because they perceive female targets as unlikely to be armed.

SETTING UP MALES BY APPEARING SEXUALLY AVAILABLE

Women's robberies of men nearly always involve guns.[11] They also do not involve physical contact. Janet Outlaw, who describes a great deal of physical contact in her robberies of other women (see above), describes her robberies of men in much different terms: "If we waste time touching men there is a possibility that they can get the gun off of us, while we wasting time touching them they could do anything. So we just keep the gun straight on them. No touching, no moving, just straight gun at you." The circumstances surrounding the enactment of female-on-male robberies differ as well. The key, in each case, is that women pretend to be sexually interested in their male victims, whose guard drops, providing a safe opportunity for the crime to occur. Two women—Jayzo and Nicole Simpson—rob men in the context of prostitution. The other five typically choose a victim at a club or on the streets, flirt and appear sexually interested, then suggest they go to a hotel, where the robbery takes place. These robberies may involve male or female accomplices, but they are just as likely to be conducted alone.

Nicole Simpson prostitutes to support her drug habit, but sometimes she

---

10.   These two are also the only women who report having had male accomplices when robbing women in this way.

11.   The only exception to this pattern was Nicole Simpson, who used a knife to rob tricks in the context of prostitution. These findings parallel those of Sommers and Baskin (1993:147), who found that women were not likely to rob men without weapons, but were likely to rob other women without them.

UP IT UP   55

"just don't be feeling like doing it," and will rob her trick rather than complete the sexual transaction. Sometimes she does this alone, and other times has a female accomplice. She chooses tricks she feels will make safe victims. She explains, "like I meet a lot of white guys and they be so paranoid they just want to get away." When Nicole Simpson is working alone, she waits until the man is in a vulnerable position before pulling out her knife. As she explains, "if you are sucking a man's dick and you pull a knife on them, they not gonna too much argue with you." When she works with a female partner, Nicole Simpson has the woman wait at a designated place, then takes the trick "to the spot where I know she at." She begins to perform oral sex, then her partner jumps in the car and pulls a knife. She explains, "once she get in the car I'll watch her back, they know we together. I don't even let them think that she is by herself. If they know it's two of us maybe they won't try it. Because if they think she by herself they might say fuck this, it ain't nothing but one person." Jayzo's techniques parallel those of Nicole Simpson, though she uses a gun instead of a knife and sometimes takes prospective tricks to hotels in addition to car dating.

Young women who target men outside the context of prostitution play upon the men's beliefs about women in order to accomplish these robberies—including the assumptions that women won't be armed, won't attempt to rob them, and can be taken advantage of sexually. Quick explains, "they don't suspect that a girl gonna try to get 'em. You know what I'm saying? So it's kind of easier 'cause they like, she looks innocent, she ain't gonna do this, but that's how I get 'em. They put they guard down to a woman." She says when she sets up men, she parties with them first, but makes sure she doesn't consume as much as them. "Most of the time, when girls get high they think they can take advantage of us so they always, let's go to a hotel or my crib or something." Janet Outlaw says, "they easy to get, we know what they after—sex." Likewise, CMW and a girlfriend often flirt with their victims: "We get in the car then ride with them. They thinking we little freaks . . . whores or something." These men's assumptions that they can take advantage of women lead them to place themselves at risk for robbery. CMW continues: "So they try to take us to the motel or whatever, we going for it. Then it's like they getting out of the car and then all my friend has to do is just put the gun up to his head, give me your keys. He really can't do nothing, his gun is probably in the car. All you do is drive on with the car."

Several young women report targeting men at clubs, particularly dope dealers or other men who appear to have a lot of money. Describing one such victim, Janet Outlaw says she was drawn to him because of his "jewelry, the way he was dressed, little snakeskin boots and all. . . I was like, yeah, there is some money." She recounts the incident as follows:

> I walked up to him, got to conversating with him. He was like, "what's up with you after the club?" I said "I'm down with you, whatever you want to do." I said "we can go to a hotel or something." He was like "for real?" I was like, "yeah, for real." He was like, "shit, cool then." So after the club we went to the hotel. I had the gun in my purse. I followed him, I was in my own car, he was in his car. So I put the gun in my purse and went up to the hotel, he was all ready. He was posted, he was a lot drunk. He was like, "you smoke weed?" I was like, "yeah shit, what's up." So we got to smoking a little bud, he got to taking off his little shit, laying it on a little table. He was like, "shit, what's up, ain't you gonna get undressed?" I was like "shit, yeah, hold up" and I went in my purse and I pulled out the gun. He was like "damn, what's up with you gal?" I was like, "shit, I want your jewelry and all the money you got." He was like, "shit, bitch you crazy. I ain't giving you my shit." I said, "do you think I'm playing nigger? You don't think I'll shoot your motherfucking ass?" He was like, "shit, you crazy, fuck that, you ain't gonna shoot me." So then I had fired the thing but I didn't fire it at him, shot the gun. He was like "fuck no." I snatched his shit. He didn't have on no clothes. I snatched the shit and ran out the door. Hopped in my car.

Though she did this particular robbery alone, Janet Outlaw says she often has male accomplices, who follow her to the hotel or meet her there. While she's in the room, "my boys be standing out in the hallway," then she lets them in when she's ready to rob the man. Having male backup is useful because men often resist being robbed by females, believing that women don't have the heart to go through with what's necessary if the victim resists. Janet Outlaw describes one such incident. Having flirted with a man and agreed to meet him, she got in his car then pulled her gun on him:

> I said "give me your stuff." He wasn't gonna give it to me. This was at nighttime. My boys was on the other side of the car but he didn't know it. He said "I ain't gonna give you shit." I was like, "you gonna give me your stuff." He was like "I'll take that gun off of your ass." I was like, "shit, you ain't gonna take this gun." My boy just pulled up and said, "give her your shit." I got the shit.

In the majority of these robberies, the victim knows that the woman has set him up—she actively participates in the robbery. Ne-Ne also describes setting up men and then pretending to be a victim herself. Her friends even get physical with her to make it appear that she's not involved. She explains:

> I'll scam you out and get to know you a little bit first, go out and eat

UP IT UP   57

and let you tell me where we going, what time and everything. I'll go in the restroom and go beep them [accomplices] just to let them know what time we leaving from wherever we at so they can come out and do their little robbery type thing, push me or whatever. I ain't gonna leave with them 'cause then he'll know so I still chill with him for a little while.

Only Ne-Ne reports having ever engaged in a robbery the opposite of this—that is, one in which her male partners flirted with a girl and she came up and robbed her. She explains:

I got some [male friends] that will instigate it. If I see some girl and I'm in the car with a whole bunch of dudes, they be like "look at that bitch she have on a leather coat." "Yeah, I want that." They'll say "well why don't you go get it?" Then you got somebody in the back seat [saying] "she's scared, she's scared." Then you got somebody just like "she ain't scared, up on the piece" or whatever and then you got some of them that will say well, "we gonna do this together." It could be like two dudes they might get out like "what's up baby," try to holler at her, get a mack on and they don't see the car. We watching and as soon as they pulling out they little pen to write they number, then I'll get out of the car and just up on them and tell them, the dudes be looking like, damn, what's going on? But they ain't gonna help 'cause they my partners or whatever.

STREET ROBBERIES WITH MALE ROBBERS

As the previous two sections illustrate, women's accomplishment of robbery varies according to the gender of their victims. As a rule, women and men do not rob females together, but do sometimes work together to set up and rob males. In addition, half of the women interviewed describe committing street robberies—almost always against males—with male accomplices. In these robberies, women's involvement either involves equal participation in the crime or assisting males but defining their role as secondary. Three women in the sample—Buby, Tish, and Lisa Jones— describe working with males on the streets as their only form of robbery, and each sees her participation as secondary. The rest engage in a combination of robbery types, including those described in the previous two sections, and do not distinguish their roles from the roles of male participants in these street robberies.

Lisa Jones and Tish each assist their boyfriends in the commission of robberies; Buby goes along with her brother and cousins. Lisa Jones says "most of the time we'll just be driving around and he'll say 'let's go to this neighborhood and rob somebody.'" Usually she stays in the car while he approaches the victim, but she is armed and will get out and assist when necessary. Describing one such incident, she says, "One time there was two guys and one guy was in the car and the other guy was out of the car and I seen that one guy getting out of the car I guess to help his friend. That's when I got out and I held the gun and I told him to stay where he was." Likewise Buby frequently goes on robberies with her brother and cousins but usually chooses to stay in the car "because I be thinking that I'm gonna get caught so I rather stay in the back." She has never done a robbery on her own and explains, "I know what to do but I don't know if I could do it on my own. I don't know if I could because I'm used to doing them with my brother and my cousins." Though her role is not an active one, she gets a cut of the profits from these robberies.

Tish and Lisa Jones are the only white respondents in the study. Each robs with an African-American boyfriend, and—though they commit armed robberies—both reject the view of themselves as criminals. Lisa Jones, for instance, downplays her role in robberies, as the following dialogue illustrates:

> Interviewer: How many armed robberies have you done in your life?
> Lisa Jones: I go with my boyfriend and I've held the gun, I've never actually shot it.
> Interviewer: But you participate in his robberies?
> Lisa Jones: Yeah.
> Interviewer: How many would you say in your whole life?
> Lisa Jones: About fifteen.
> Interviewer: What about in the last month?
> Lisa Jones: Maybe five or six.
> Interviewer: What other crimes have you done in your life, or participated with others?
> Lisa Jones: No, I'm not a criminal.

It is striking that this young woman routinely engages in robberies in which she wields a weapon, yet she defines herself as "not a criminal." Later in the interview, she explains that she would stop participating in armed robberies "if I was to stop seeing him." She and Tish are the only respondents who minimize the implications of their involvement in armed robbery, and it is probably not coincidental that they are young white women—their race and gender allow them to view themselves in this way.

Both also describe their boyfriends as the decision makers in the robberies—deciding when, where, and whom to rob. This is evident in Tish's interview, as her boyfriend, who is present in the room, frequently interjects to answer the interviewer's questions. The following dialogue is revealing:

> Interviewer: How do you approach the person?
> Tish: Just go up to them.

UP IT UP 59

Interviewer: You walk up to them, you drive up to them?

Boyfriend: Most of the time it's me and my partner that do it. Our gals, they got the guns and stuff but we doing most of the evaluating. We might hit somebody in the head with a gun, go up to them and say whatever. Come up off your shit or something to get the money. The girls, they doing the dirty work really, that's the part they like doing, they'll hold the gun and if something goes wrong they'll shoot. We approach them. I ain't gonna send my gal up to no dude to tell him she want to rob him, you know. She might walk up to him with me and she might hit him a couple of times but basically I'm going up to them.

These respondents reveal the far end of the continuum of women's involvement in robbery, clearly taking subordinate roles in the crime and defining themselves as less culpable as a result. Tish's boyfriend also reveals his perception of women as secondary actors in the accomplishment of robbery. For the most part, other women who participate in street robberies with male accomplices describe themselves as equal participants. Older women who rob citizens to support their drug habits at times do so with male accomplices. For instance, Lisa Woods sometimes commits her robberies with a male and female accomplice and targets people "like when they get they checks. Catch them coming out of the store, maybe trip 'em, go in they pocket and take they money and take off running." Among the younger women, robberies with male accomplices involve guns and typically come about when a group of people are driving around and spot a potential victim. Janet Outlaw describes a car jacking that occurred as she and some friends were driving around:

Stop at a red light, we was looking around, didn't see no police, we was right behind them [the victims]. . . So one of my boys got out and I got out. Then the other boy got up in the driver's seat that was with them. My boy went on one side and I went on the other side and said "nigger get out of the car before we shoot you." Then the dudes got out. It was like, shit, what's up, we down with you all. No you ain't down with us, take they jewelry and shit off. It was like, damn, why you all tripping? Then my boy cocked the little gun and said take it off now or I'm gonna start spraying you all ass. So they took off the little jewelry, I hopped in, put it in drive and pulled on off.

Likewise, Ne-Ne prefers committing street robberies with males rather than females. She explains:

I can't be bothered with too many girls. That's why I try to be with dudes or whatever. They gonna be down. If you get out of the car and if you rob a dude or jack somebody and you with some dudes then you know if they see he tryin' to resist, they gonna give me some help. Whereas a girl, you might get somebody that's scared and might drive off. That's the way it is.

It is not surprising, then, that Ne-Ne is the only woman interviewed to report having ever committed this type of street robbery of a male victim on her own. Her actions parallel those of male-on-male robbers described above. Ne-Ne explicitly indicates that this robbery was possible because the victim did not know she was a woman. Describing herself physically, she says, "I'm big, you know." In addition, her dress and manner masked her gender. "I had a baseball cap in my car and I seen him. . . I just turned around the corner, came back down the street, he was out by himself and I got out of the car, had the cap pulled down over my face and I just went to the back and upped him. Put the gun up to his head." Being large, wearing a ballcap, and enacting the robbery in a masculine style (e.g., putting a gun to his head) allowed her to disguise the fact that she was a woman and thus decrease the victim's likelihood of resisting. She says, "He don't know right now to this day if it was a girl or a dude."

DISCUSSION

Feminist scholars have been hesitant to grapple with the issue of women's violence, both because a focus on women's violence draws attention away from the fact that violence is a predominantly male phenomenon and because studying women's violence can play into sensationalized accounts of female offenders. Nonetheless, as this and other studies have shown, "gender alone does not account for variation in criminal violence" (Simpson, 1991:118). A small number of women are involved in violent street crime in ways that go beyond "preventing victimization," and appear to find support among their male and female peers for these activities. To draw this conclusion is not to suggest that women's use of violence is increasing, that women are "equals" on the streets, or that gender does not matter. It does suggest that researchers should continue developing feminist perspectives to address the issue.

What is most notable about the current research is the incongruity between motivations and accomplishment of robbery. While a comparison of women's and men's motivations to commit robbery reveals gender similarities, when women and men actually commit robbery their enactments of the crime are strikingly different. These differences highlight the clear gender hierarchy that exists on the streets. While some women are able to carve out a niche for themselves in this setting, and even establish partnerships with males, they are participating in a male-dominated environment, and their actions reflect an understanding of this.

To accomplish robberies successfully, women must take into account the gendered nature of their environment. One way they do so is by targeting other females. Both male and female robbers hold the view that females are easy to rob, because they are less likely than males to be armed and because they are perceived as weak and easily intimidated. Janet Outlaw describes women's robbery of other women as "just a woman to woman thing." This is supported by Ne-Ne's description that her male friends do not participate with her in robberies of females, and it is supported by men's accounts of robbing women. While women routinely rob other women, men are less likely to do so, perhaps because these robberies do not result in the demonstration of masculinity.

At the same time that women articulate the belief that other women are easy targets, they also draw upon these perceptions of women in order to rob men. Two of the women describe committing robberies much in keeping with Maher's (1997) descriptions of "viccing." In addition, a number of women used men's perceptions of women as weak, sexually available, and easily manipulated to turn the tables and manipulate men into circumstances in which they became vulnerable to robbery—by flirting and appearing sexually interested in them. Unlike women's robberies of other women, these robberies tend not to involve physical contact but do involve the use of guns. Because they recognize men's perceptions of women, they also recognize that men are more likely to resist being robbed by a female, and thus they commit these robberies in ways that minimize their risk of losing control and maximize their ability to show that they're "for real."

West and Zimmerman (1987:139) note that there are circumstances in which "parties reach an accommodation that allow[s] a woman to engage in presumptively masculine behavior." In this study, it is notable that while both women and men recognize the urban street world as a male-dominated one, a few of the women interviewed appear to have gained access to male privilege by adopting male attitudes about females, constructing their own identities as more masculine, and following through by behaving in masculine ways (see also Hunt, 1984). Ne-Ne and Janet Outlaw both come to mind in this regard—as women who completed robberies in equal partnerships with men and identified with men's attitudes about other women. Other women, such as Lisa Jones and Tish, accepted not only women's position as secondary, but their own as well. While Ne-Ne and Janet Outlaw appeared to draw status and identity from their criminality in ways that went beyond their gender identity, Lisa Jones and Tish used their gender identity to construct themselves as noncriminal.

In sum, the women in this sample do not appear to "do robbery" differently than men in order to meet different needs or accomplish different goals. Instead, the differences that emerge reflect practical choices made in the context of a gender-stratified environment—one in which, on the whole, men are perceived as strong and women are perceived as weak.

JODY MILLER

Motivationally, then, it appears that women's participation in street violence can result from the same structural and cultural underpinnings that shape some of men's participation in these crimes, and that they receive rewards beyond protection for doing so. Yet gender remains a salient factor shaping their actions, as well as the actions of men.

Though urban African-American women have higher rates of violence than other women, their participation in violent crime is nonetheless significantly lower than that of their male counterparts in the same communities (Simpson, 1991). An important line of inquiry for future research is to assess what protective factors keep the majority of women living in underclass settings from adopting violence as a culturally legitimate response. While research shows that racial and economic oppression contribute to African-American women's greater participation in violent crime, they do not ensure its occurrence. Daly and Stephens (1995:208) note: "Racism in criminological theories occurs when racial or cultural differences are overemphasized or mischaracterized *and* when such differences are denied." Future research should strive to strike this balance and attend to the complex issues surrounding women's participation in violence within the urban street world.

REFERENCES

Agar, Michael H.
  1977   Ethnography in the streets and in the joint: A comparison. In Robert S. Weppner (ed.), Street Ethnography: Selected Studies of Crime and Drug Use in Natural Settings. Beverly Hills, Calif.: Sage.

Ageton, Suzanne S.
  1983   The dynamics of female delinquency, 1976-1980. Criminology 21(4):555—584.

Anderson, Elijah
  1994   The code of the streets. Atlantic Monthly 273:81—94.

Baskin, Deborah, Ira Sommers, and Jeffrey Fagan
  1993   The political economy of violent female street crime. Fordham Urban Law Journal 20:401—417.

Braithwaite, John and Kathleen Daly
  1994   Masculinities, violence and communitarian control. In Tim Newburn and Elizabeth A. Stanko (eds.), Just Boys Doing Business? New York: Routledge.

Campbell, Anne
  1993   Men, Women and Aggression. New York: Basic Books.

Chesney-Lind, Meda
  1993   Girls, gangs and violence: Anatomy of a backlash. Humanity & Society 17(3):321—344.

UP IT UP   63

Chesney-Lind, Meda and Randall G. Shelden
   1992   Girls, Delinquency and Juvenile Justice. Pacific Groves, Calif.: Brooks/
          Cole.

Daly, Kathleen and Deborah J. Stephens
   1995   The "dark figure" of criminology: Towards a black and multi-ethnic feminist
          agenda for theory and research. In Nicole Hahn Rafter and Frances
          Heidensohn (eds.), International Feminist Perspectives in Criminology:
          Engendering a Discipline. Philadelphia: Open University Press.

Decker, Scott and Barrik Van Winkle
   1996   Life in the Gang. New York: Cambridge University Press.

Federal Bureau of Investigation
   1996   Crime in the United States, 1995. Washington, D.C.: U. S. Government
          Printing Office.

Glassner, Barry and Cheryl Carpenter
   1985   The feasibility of an ethnographic study of adult property offenders.
          Unpublished report prepared for the National Institute of Justice, Washing-
          ton, D.C.

Hill, Gary D. and Elizabeth M. Crawford
   1990   Women, race, and crime. Criminology 28(4):601—623.

Hunt, Jennifer
   1984   The development of rapport through the negotiation of gender in field work
          among police. Human Organization 43(4):283—296.

Joe, Karen A. and Meda Chesney-Lind
   1995   Just every mother's angel: An analysis of gender and ethnic variations in
          youth gang membership. Gender & Society 9(4):408—430.

Katz, Jack
   1988   Seductions of Crime. New York: Basic Books.

Kelly, Liz
   1991   Unspeakable Acts. Trouble and Strife 21:13—20.

Laub, John H. and M. Joan McDermott
   1985   An analysis of serious crime by young black women. Criminology
          23(1):81—98.

Maher, Lisa
   1997   Sexed Work: Gender, Race and Resistance in a Brooklyn Drug Market.
          Oxford: Clarendon Press.

Maher, Lisa and Richard Curtis
   1992   Women on the edge of crime: Crack cocaine and the changing contexts of
          street-level sex work in New York City. Crime, Law and Social Change
          18:221—258.

Maher, Lisa and Kathleen Daly
   1996   Women in the street-level drug economy: Continuity or change? Criminol-
          ogy 34(4):465—492.

Mann, Coramae Richey
   1993   Sister against sister: Female intrasexual homicide. In C.C. Culliver (ed.),
          Female Criminality: The State of the Art. New York: Garland Publishing.

64   JODY MILLER

Messerschmidt, James W.
    1993   Masculinities and Crime. Lanham, Md.: Rowman & Littlefield.
    1995   From patriarchy to gender: Feminist theory, criminology and the challenge
            of diversity. In Nicole Hahn Rafter and Frances Heidensohn (eds.), Inter-
            national Feminist Perspectives in Criminology: Engendering a Discipline.
            Philadelphia: Open University Press.

Newburn, Tim and Elizabeth A. Stanko (eds.)
    1994   Just Boys Doing Business? New York: Routledge.

Oliver, William
    1994   The Violent Social World of Black Men. New York: Lexington Books.

Sampson, Robert J. and William Julius Wilson
    1995   Toward a theory of race, crime, and urban inequality. In John Hagan and
            Ruth D. Peterson (eds.), Crime and Inequality. Stanford, Calif.: Stanford
            University Press.

Sikes, Gini
    1997   8 Ball Chicks: A Year in the Violent World of Girl Gangsters. New York:
            Anchor Books.

Simpson, Sally
    1989   Feminist theory, crime and justice. Criminology 27(4):605—631.
    1991   Caste, class and violent crime: Explaining difference in female offending.
            Criminology 29(1):115—135.

Simpson, Sally and Lori Elis
    1995   Doing gender: Sorting out the caste and crime conundrum. Criminology
            33(1):47—81.

Sommers, Ira and Deborah R. Baskin
    1993   The situational context of violent female offending. Journal of Research on
            Crime and Delinquency 30(2):136—162.

St. Louis Metropolitan Police Department
    1994   Annual Report—1993/1994.

Stack, Carol B
    1974   All Our Kin: Strategies for Survival in a Black Community. New York:
            Harper & Row.

Steffensmeier, Darrell J.
    1983   Organization properties and sex-segregation in the underworld: Building a
            sociological theory of sex differences in crime. Social Forces 61:1010—1032.

Steffensmeier, Darrell J. and Robert Terry
    1986   Institutional sexism in the underworld: A view from the inside. Sociological
            Inquiry 56:304-323.

Watters, John and Patrick Biernacki
    1989   Targeted sampling: Options for the study of hidden populations. Social
            Problems 36:416—430.

West, Candace and Sarah Fenstermaker
    1995   Doing difference. Gender & Society 9(1):8—37.

West, Candace and Don H. Zimmerman
    1987   Doing gender. Gender & Society 1(2):125—151.

UP IT UP 65

White, Jacquelyn W. and Robin M. Kowalski
  1994   Deconstructing the myth of the nonaggressive woman: A feminist analysis. Psychology of Women Quarterly 18:487-508.

Wilson, William Julius
  1996   When Work Disappears: The World of the New Urban Poor. New York: Alfred A. Knopf.

Wright, Richard T. and Scott Decker
  1994   Burglars on the Job: Streetlife and Residential Break-Ins. Boston: Northeastern University Press.
  1997   Armed Robbers in Action: Stickups and Street Culture. Boston: Northeastern University Press.

Jody Miller is Assistant Professor of Criminology and Criminal Justice at the University of Missouri-St. Louis. She is currently completing a book based on her research about gender dynamics in youth gangs.

66   JODY MILLER

Appendix.   List of Interviewees ($N = 37$)

Name*	Sex	Race	Age (years)	Age at 1st Robbery (years)
CMW	Female	African-American	16	14
Buby	Female	African-American	17	17
Libbie Jones	Female	African-American	18	12
Tish	Female	White	18	17
Lisa Jones	Female	White	18	17
Quick	Female	African-American	19	15
Ms. Berry	Female	African-American	19	17
Janet Outlaw	Female	African-American	20	15
Ne-Ne	Female	African-American	20	16
Yolanda Smith	Female	African-American	22	19
Nicole Simpson	Female	African-American	26	17
Lisa Wood	Female	African-American	37	18
Kim Brown	Female	African-American	37	28
Jayzo	Female	African-American	43	27
Syco	Male	African-American	17	12
Cooper	Male	African-American	17	13
Taz	Male	African-American	17	14
Swoop	Male	African-American	17	16
K-Money	Male	African-American	17	16
Looney	Male	African-American	18	13
Beano	Male	African-American	18	16
Mike J.	Male	African-American	18	17
Woods	Male	African-American	18	17
Redwood	Male	African-American	19	14
Antwon Wright	Male	African-American	19	14
T-Bone	Male	African-American	19	16
Big Prod	Male	African-American	19	18
C-Loco	Male	African-American	20	14
Little Bill	Male	African-American	20	18
Damon Jones	Male	African-American	21	19
Treason Taylor	Male	African-American	22	18
Carlos Reed	Male	African-American	24	15
Prauch	Male	African-American	36	22
C.K.	Male	African-American	36	28
Bob Jones	Male	African-American	39	17
Tony Wright	Male	African-American	43	25
Wyman Danger	Male	African-American	46	21

* Pseudonyms supplied by respondents.

Part VI
The Development
of Anomie Theory

-

[15]

MERTON'S "SOCIAL STRUCTURE AND ANOMIE": THE ROAD NOT TAKEN

STEVEN F. MESSNER
State University of New York at Albany

The thesis of this paper is that Robert Merton's essay "Social Structure and Anomie" contains two analytically distinct theoretical arguments, a theory of social organization and a theory of deviant motivation. The theory of social organization discusses the articulation of components of social systems, whereas the theory of deviant motivation addresses the sources of pressures on individuals to violate social norms. These two theories employ similar terms and are joined to deal with a principal substantive concern for Merton, namely, the distribution of deviant behavior within a social structure. I argue, however, that the two theories are not logically interdependent. Evidence inconsistent with one is thus not necessarily inconsistent with the other. Moreover, I suggest that the theory of social organization warrants greater attention than it has received to date because it is the more original and lucid of the two theoretical arguments, and because it has the potential for generating a promising research agenda.

An earlier version of this paper was presented at the Thirty-eighth Annual Meeting of the American Society of Criminology, Atlanta, Georgia, October 29 – November 1, 1986. I would like to thank Allen Liska, Maurice Richter, Steven Seidman, and David Wagner for helpful comments on drafts of this manuscript. I have also benefited from the remarks offered by Albert Cohen as a discussant of the ASC session which included this paper.

S. F. MESSNER

Robert Merton's theory of social structure and anomie has been the source of persistent commentary throughout the fifty year period since its publication in 1938. The continued influence of this theoretical perspective in the study of crime and deviance may seem rather surprising at first glance given the hostile treatment it has received at the hands of some of its critics. Over twenty years ago, Scott and Turner expressed total exasperation over the attention and admiration devoted to this theory. They wrote: "that this essay should be regarded as a first rate example of sociological theorizing remains to us a mystery" (1965, p. 234). Only slightly more charitable in tone is the influential assessment of anomie theory by Ruth Kornhauser, an assessment that is frequently cited in textbook summaries of the anomie or strain perspective. Kornhauser confidently concludes that strain theory has been "disconfirmed" by the relevant data (1978, p. 180, see also p. 253). She further asserts that the empirical facts on the relationship between strain and delinquency, taken in conjunction with the alleged theoretical flaws inherent in this perspective, "compel [emphasis added] the conclusion that criminologists should turn their attention to the development of alternative theories of delinquency" (1978, p. 180).

A very different position, however, has been argued by Thomas Bernard (1984). After a careful review of previous theoretical and empirical criticisms of strain theory, including those raised in Kornhauser's critique, Bernard concludes that these theories have been "prematurely closed off." He accordingly advises that strain theories "deserve a resurgence of interest in criminology" (1984, p. 369), and by extension, in the sociological study of deviance more generally.

The purpose of this paper is to try to promote a resurgence of interest in strain theories by redirecting attention to a relatively neglected aspect of Merton's original theoretical statement. I will argue that Merton presents two analytically distinct theories in his essay to address two distinct substantive problems. One of these theories might be referred to as a theory of social organization and the other as a theory of deviant motivation. These two theories seem on the surface to be intimately intertwined, but they are not in fact logically interdependent. The bulk of the extensive commentary and research dealing with Merton's theory, I will further propose, has been concerned with the latter theory and is in large measure irrelevant to the former. This is highly unfortunate because the theory of social organization is considerably more lucid and original than is the theory of deviant motivation. Furthermore, the theory of social organization contains intriguing research implications. In view of these considerations, I will suggest that there is indeed ample justification for renewed efforts to refine and test the "organizational variant" of Merton's theory of social structure and anomie.

Merton's Two Theories in "Social Structure and Anomie"

Merton's general objective in the "Social Structure and Anomie"
(hereafter SS&A) essay can be stated quite simply. He intends to
develop a sociological explanation for deviant behavior as an
alternative to psychological, and particularly Freudian, explanations.
He proclaims at the onset that "our perspective is sociological"
(1968c, p. 186). This entails the formulation of special kinds of
questions and the utilization of special kinds of data for purposes
of evaluating the answers to these questions.

Merton poses the sociological questions to be addressed in an
explicit contrast with those likely to be of concern in other
disciplines. He writes:

> For whatever the role of biological impulses, there
> still remains the further question of why it is that
> the frequency of deviant behavior varies within
> different social structures and how it happens that
> the deviations have different shapes and patterns in
> different social structures (1968c, p. 185).

This passage identifies two distinct substantive concerns for
sociological inquiry into deviant behavior.[1] One is the distribution
of deviant behavior within a social collectivity, and the other is
the "shape and pattern" of deviant behavior across different social
collectivities. Merton does not elaborate on the meaning of "shapes
and patterns," but it is clear from subsequent discussions that a
major concern for him lies with overall levels of deviant behavior.[2]
Both of these questions focus attention on population aggregates
rather than individuals. The first is concerned with the aggregate
number of occupants of the positions constituting the social
structure. The second question deals with the total number of
members of the collectivity. The nature of these questions implies
that the answers must be cast in terms of rates of behavior for these
aggregates, and the assessment of the answers must involve the
comparison of such rates (1968c, p. 186).

---

[1]It is interesting to note that Merton refers in the quoted passage
to "the further question" (singular) rather than to "further
questions" (plural). The lack of a clear demarcation between these
two questions probably contributes to the mistaken impression that
the theoretical arguments developed in response to them are
necessarily interdependent.

[2]Consider, for example, Merton's argument that it is only under
certain combinations of social and cultural conditions that "deviant
behavior ensues on a large scale" (emphasis added) (1968c, p. 200).
See, also, Hilbert and Wright (1979, p. 151).

There is an additional implication of Merton's formulation of his questions in sociological terms. The answers will be best formulated in terms of sociological concepts. Merton accordingly introduces a series of sociological concepts and develops a highly abstract analytical model describing the inter-relationships between these concepts.

At the heart of Merton's analytical model is the conceptualization of a social system as being comprised of two fundamental components: a cultural structure and a social structure. These concepts are not fully defined in the initial SS&A article, but their meanings are clarified in Merton's subsequent essay, "Continuities in the Theory of Social Structure and Anomie" (1968a). Merton explains:

> cultural structure may be defined as that organized set of normative values governing behavior which is common to members of a designated society or group. And by social structure is meant that organized set of social relationships in which members of the society or group are variously implicated" (1968, p. 216).

Every social system can thus be described in terms of these properties; that is, the cultural values and the patterned social relationships.

The cultural component of any social system can itself be further subdivided into two distinctive elements. "The first consists of culturally defined goals, purposes, and interests, held out as legitimate objects for all or for diversely located members of society" (1968c, p. 186), while the "second element of cultural structure defines, regulates and controls the acceptable modes of reaching out for these goals" (1968c, p. 187). This latter element can be referred to as the "normative means."[3] The importance placed on the cultural component of social systems derives from Merton's firm belief that human action can only be fully understood within the context of the concrete, socio-cultural environment.

---

[3]Merton is not always consistent in his use of terms to describe this second element of cultural structure. He uses "institutionalized norms" and "institutionalized means" interchangeably (1968c: 187). The concept evidently is intended to refer to the socially approved procedures for realizing goals. Hence, the term "normative means" seems to best capture the meaning of the concept.

MERTON'S SOCIAL STRUCTURE AND ANOMIE   37

It is with these basic concepts - social structure, cultural structure, goals, and means - that Merton formulates his theory of the organization of social systems. His basic premise, which might be regarded as an underlying "principle of social organization," is that a collectivity is well organized when social structural relationships enable members of that collectivity to realize the culturally approved goals via the normatively prescribed means.[4] When social structure and cultural structure exhibit such a harmonious inter-relationship, satisfactions accrue to individuals as a normal consequence of conformity to cultural mandates (see especially Merton 1968c, p. 188). It thus seems reasonable to postulate that levels of deviant behavior will tend to be low in social systems that are characterized by strong social organization in this particular sense.

Not all societies are, of course, strongly organized. Merton cites American society as a case in point. The American social system exhibits pronounced disjuncture, and it does so in two different spheres. At the level of the social system, there is disjuncture between social structural arrangements and cultural prescriptions. The cultural structure extols common success goals, while the social structure restricts access to the normative means (1968c, p. 200). This essentially constitutes a violation of the "principle of social organization." Satisfactions are not likely to accure to individuals as a natural consequence of conformity to the cultural mandates. Because of this, the cultural structure is prone to a "breakdown" (1968a, p. 216), wherein the norms begin to lose "their savor and their force" (1964, p. 226). This situation, which can be described as a state of anomie, is conducive to high rates of deviant behavior.

American society also exhibits disjuncture within the cultural structure itself. There is an imbalance between the two components of culture. In Merton's words, American culture approximates an extreme type "in which great emphasis upon certain success-goals occurs without equivalent emphasis upon institutional means" (1968c, p. 190). American society, in other words, exhibits both disjuncture at the system level (that is, a discrepancy between social structure and cultural structure) and imbalance within the cultural component of the social system (that is, an exaggerated emphasis on goals in comparison with the emphasis on means).

There is some ambiguity in Merton's discussion with respect to how these two kinds of disjuncture interrelate to generate high levels of anomie and high rates of deviant behavior. At one point in the text, Merton seems to imply that high levels of deviant behavior can

---

[4]A fairly detailed exposition of Merton's views on social organization and disorganization is presented in his essay "Social Problems and Sociological Theory" (1971, pp. 818-838). See also Rosenfeld's (1985, p. 3) discussion of the anomie argument as "classic disorganization theory."

be explained simply in terms of a cultural imbalance. He speculates that behavior becomes unpredictable as a result of an "imperfect coordination" of the "goals-and-means phases of the social structure" (1968c, p. 213).[5] Elsewhere, however, Merton cautions that "other aspects of social structure, besides the extreme emphasis on pecuniary success (that is, the overemphasis on goals vis-a-vis means), must be considered if we are to understand the social sources of deviant behavior" (1968c, p. 200). Considering the argument as a whole, it seems clear that Merton intends to highlight the role of a system-component disjuncture as a principal source of high overall rates of deviant behavior. Indeed, an imbalanced state of the cultural structure, such as that observed in the United States, might be best viewed as a consequence of system-component disjuncture. When social structural arrangements make it difficult to behave in accordance with cultural values, the cultural structure is "strained" and is susceptible to "breakdown." The balance in the emphasis on cultural goals and norms thereby becomes highly precarious.

Merton's theory of social organization thus provides an answer to one of the two questions guiding his inquiry. It explains why some societies tend to exhibit higher levels of deviant behavior than do others, and it poses this explanation in terms of the fundamental properties of social systems. Merton has an additional objective, however. He hopes to account for the distribution of deviant behavior within a social system. To deal with this question, he introduces a theory of deviant motivation and combines this theory with insights from his theory of social organization.

The most distinctive feature of Merton's theory of deviant motivation is the emphasis on socially generated pressures. In his introduction to the SS&A chapter in Social Theory and Social Structure (1968b), Merton explains that his kind of analysis, in contrast with Freudian interpretations, "conceives of the social structure as active, as producing fresh motivations which cannot be predicted on the basis of knowledge about man's native drives" (1968b, pp. 175-6). This approach attempts "to determine how the social and cultural structure generates pressure for socially deviant

---

[5]Kornhauser (1978, pp. 145-6) elaborates on some of the implications of this theoretical ambiguity. She wonders: if anomie is produced simply by an imbalance in the emphasis on goals and means, what is the role of social structure? Would not a society with an exaggerated emphasis on goals and only a minor emphasis on means exhibit high rates of deviance irrespective of social structural arrangements? Kornhauser's argument, it seems to me, fails to recognize the extent to which the integrity of the cultural structure depends upon the compatibility of the cultural and structural components of society. This oversight is perhaps responsible for Kornhauser's rather surprising assertion that strain theory "neglects social structure" (1978, p. 167).

behavior upon people variously located in that structure" (1968b, pp. 175-6). In other words, the primary motivation for deviant behavior does not emanate from within but is imposed from the outside. Consequently, as Bernard puts it, crime and deviance are largely the product of social forces driving individuals to do things that they normally would not do (1984, p. 353).

The type of social situation that tends to generate such forces or pressures is one in which individuals confront restricted opportunities despite cultural injunctions to aspire to lofty goals. Persons confronting such situations are likely to experience severe relative deprivation (for similar interpretations, see Box 1981, pp. 99-100, and Davis 1980, p. 135). In so far as they continue to abide by the normative means, they will be deprived relative to the goals that are deemed culturally appropriate for them. It is precisely this experience of relative deprivation, along with the concomitant sense of frustration (see Merton 1968a, p. 232), that often pressures individuals into deviant adaptations.

Merton's theory of deviant motivation thus involves a rather simple social psychological model. Individuals who are relatively deprived become frustrated and angered (see also Empey 1982, p. 233), which drives them to "do things that they normally would not do" (Bernard 1984, p. 353). This simple social psychological model can be joined fairly easily with Merton's theory of social organization to provide a plausible account for the distribution of deviant behavior within a social system. When a social system is characterized by both universal goals and restricted opportunities (a particular form of system-component disjuncture), the degree of relative deprivation can be expected to vary inversely with the distribution of legitimate opportunities. Those positions characterized by few opportunities are likely to be characterized by high levels of relative deprivation. Furthermore, because relative deprivation tends to generate deviant motivations, social positions with restricted opportunities and severe relative deprivation should exhibit high rates of deviant behavior. Merton in this way explains why the distribution of deviant behavior within the kind of "disjunctured" social system under examination is systematic and not random – it reflects the structured opportunities to employ the normatively approved means.

Although Merton's speculations about the social sources of deviant motivations and the social distribution of deviance are in many respects highly plausible, the empirical adequacy of these

speculations has been explicitly challenged.[6] The most important
empirical critiques have addressed two primary concerns. First, do
rates of deviant behavior in American society vary across the social
structure in the manner suggested by Merton's theory? Secondly, do
social conditions affect the likelihood of deviant behavior in a
manner consistent with Merton's social psychological model of deviant
motivation?[7]

The first issue involves the claim that there is in fact an inverse
relationship between social class and rates of deviance. Critics
charge that Merton's theory underestimates the volume of deviance
among the well-to-do and overestimates the volume among the lower
classes (for example, Empey 1982, p. 256; Liska 1981, p. 54;
Taylor et al. 1973, pp. 106-7). This criticism has been based
largely on the observation that the relationship between class and
various forms of deviant behavior are very modest or trivial when
self-report measures are used rather than measures based on
official statistics (see especially Tittle et al. 1978). The actual
relationship between class and rates of deviant behavior remains
an open question (cf. Braithwaite 1981; Elliot and Huizinga 1983),
but it is clear that the lack of any genuine, inverse relationship
between class and rates of deviant behavior would contradict Merton's
arguments about the social distribution of deviance precisely because
these arguments are introduced to explain such an assumed relationship.

The second issue that has received considerable attention in the
empirical literature is the extent to which individual perceptions
of blocked opportunities do in fact motivate deviant acts. The

---

[6]It is perhaps ironic that despite the extensive citations to Merton's
work, the number of efforts to evaluate formally aspects of his
theory is actually very small. Stephen Cole (1975, p. 207) reports
that only 9 articles attempting to test Merton's theory or derivative
theories appeared in the four leading sociology journals between 1950
and 1972. Note also Kornhauser's remark that "strain models are
relatively easy to test, and yet there have been surprisingly few
definitive tests of strain theory" (1978, p. 167).

[7]Research has also examined Merton's claim that the goals in American
society apply universalistically. For example, Hyman (1966) reports
that the proportions of persons adhering to goals vary by social
class. Merton (1968a) responds that absolute numbers may be more
important than proportions in the explanation of the social
distribution of deviance. In any event, this debate centers around
the accuracy of Merton's description of the content of the culture
structure in American society rather than the adequacy of the
general theoretical model.

conventional analytical strategy has been to examine the relationship between "discrepancy scores," based on reports of aspirations and expectations, and involvement in deviant behavior (Kornhauser 1978, p. 168). Underlying this procedure is the premise that, according to the logic of strain theory, individuals in disadvantaged positions will aspire to goals that cannot be realized. Awareness of this state of affairs should generate the frustration and anger that allegedly motivate deviant behavior. Critics have charged that the evidence, especially with respect to delinquency, fails to support the "strain" hypothesis (Kornhauser 1978, pp. 174–180; Liska 1971). Once again, there is controversy surrounding the assessment of the evidence (for an evaluation favorable to strain theory, see Bernard 1984). Nevertheless, the hypothesis of a goal–discrepancy–deviance relationship follows logically from Merton's theory of deviant motivation, and thus the lack of any such relationship would challenge this theory.

To summarize, Merton formulates a theory of social organization to explain the variation in rates of deviant behavior across social systems. The theory stipulates that disjuncture between the structural and cultural components of social systems creates a strain towards anomie and produces high rates of deviance. He also introduces a theory of deviant motivation that cites the frustration of socially generated expectations as a force driving individuals to commit deviant acts. He then combines the two arguments to explain an assumed inverse relationship between social class and rates of deviant behavior in American society. Critical assessments of Merton's work have been concerned primarily with the plausibility of his arguments about the sources of deviant motivations and the class distribution of deviance. In the section that follows, I will argue that the validity of Merton's general theory of social organization is by no means contingent on the validity of either his theory of deviant motivation or his explanation of the relationship between class and deviance.

The Logical Independence of the Organizational and Motivational Theories

As previously noted, Merton's theory of deviant motivation is formulated in an explicit contrast with Freudian theories. He criticizes the view of Freud and Freudian "revisionists" that the "structure of society primarily restrains the free expression of man's fixed native impulses and that, accordingly, man periodically breaks into open rebellion against these restraints to achieve freedom" (1968b, p. 175). The notion of innate, anti-social impulses is for Merton thoroughly unacceptable. Hence, he seeks to explain the social origins of deviant motivation, and he does so with reference to structural sources of relative deprivation and accompanying feelings of anger and frustration.

Merton's theory of deviant motivation is also opposed to other theoretical orientations that share Freudian premises about human nature. The most influential contemporary theory of this type is unquestionably control theory. As Hirschi (1969, pp. 16-34) explains, control theorists adopt the position that people are naturally predisposed to misbehave and hence that the motivation for deviance is unproblematic. Deviance must be explained in terms of the ineffectiveness of controls. According to this perspective, certain individuals are not driven to do things that they ordinarily would not do; rather, they feel free to do things we all would do if only "we dared" (Hirschi 1969, p. 34).

A fundamental conflict clearly exists between Merton's theory of deviant motivation and control theories of deviant motivation. There is no such conflict, however, between control approaches and Merton's theory of social organization. On the contrary, it is possible to link the two, and efforts to do so have appeared in the literature.

Control theorists who have attempted to incorporate elements of strain theory hypothesize that strain may be related to the nature and strength of social controls (Kornhauser 1978, p. 140; see also Cohen 1985, pp. 236-7, and Elliott et al. 1985, pp. 17-21). This argument contends that structurally induced strain impedes the development of controls and also undermines the effectiveness of existing controls. Individuals are then "free" to engage in deviance. Note that according to this account, the deviant impulses themselves are not socially generated. Consequently, Merton's theory of deviant motivation is rejected. The argument does permit, however, an important contribution of system-component disjuncture in the production of deviant behavior. Such disjuncture may affect observed levels of deviant behavior by influencing the restraining capacity of social controls. In essence, Merton's theory of social organization is employed in these arguments for purposes of explaining why social controls develop or fail to develop, while the operation of these controls continues to be the proximate determinant of the probability of deviant behavior.

It is interesting to observe that, despite Merton's persistent and often polemical attacks on Freudian motivational perspectives, he seems to anticipate the possibility of joining his theory of social organization with these alternative motivational approaches. Near the conclusion of the SS&A essay, Merton proposes that system disjuncture produces an "attenuation of institutional controls" and "a situation in which calculations of personal advantage and fear of punishment are the only regulating agencies" (1968, p. 211). In other words, poor social organization weakens social controls and thereby frees individuals to pursue their own personal (natural?) desires. Similarly, in his concluding chapter in Clinard's extensive review of anomie theory, Merton emphasizes that the anomie resulting from system disjuncture deprives norms of their "legitimacy." Consequently, "there is no longer a widely shared sense within the social system...of what goes and what does not go, of what is justly allowed by way of behavior and of what is justly prohibited, of what might be legitimately expected in the course of social interaction" (1964, p. 226). System disjuncture, in other words, promotes ambiguity about the social rules. Without any firm understanding of

such rules (that is, without controls), members of society are free
to engage in a wide range of behavior, including deviant behavior.

In short, there is no necessary, logical interconnection between
Merton's theory of social organization and his theory of deviant
motivation. The organizational argument is in principle compatible
with alternative theories of deviant motivations, including theories,
such as control theories, that are fundamentally at odds with Merton's
primary position on the origins of deviant impulses. It follows
that evidence either in support of or opposed to Merton's theory of
deviant motivation, such as the evidence on goal frustration and
deviance, is essentially irrelevant in the assessment of the
validity of Merton's theory of social organization.

The same point can be made with respect to evidence on the
distribution of deviant behavior within the social structure.
The prediction of an inverse social class-deviance relationship
derives largely from Merton's motivational argument--it is expected
that members of the lower classes will experience greater relative
deprivation and frustration and as a consequence will be driven to
deviant behavior. Adoption of an alternative theory of motivation,
however, could very well imply a different social class-deviance
relationship. The disjuncture between the cultural and social
structural component could undermine the legitimacy of social norms
in a general way (Merton, 1964, p. 226) and thereby provide the
"freedom to deviate" for all members of society irrespective of their
locations in the social structure (cf. Box 1981, p. 99). Merton's
organizational argument does not require that there be an inverse
relationship between social class and rates of deviant behavior; it
requires only that overall levels of deviant behavior vary
systematically with the degree of disjuncture between the component
elements of social systems.[8]

In sum, Merton's theory of deviant motivation and his theory of social
organization are logically independent. There is accordingly no valid
reason for rejecting the latter because of doubts about the
theoretical or empirical adequacy of the former. In the section that
follows, I will argue that, of the two theories, only the theory of
social organization incorporates the sociological concept of "anomie"
in an original and consistent manner.

The Concept of "Anomie" in Merton's Theories

Despite the centrality of the concept of "anomie" in Merton's SS&A
essay, he never really provides an explicit definition of this
concept in the course of his discussion (cf. Gibbs 1985, p. 42;

---

[8]Charles Tittle also concludes that anomie theory does not require
an inverse relationship between social class and crime rates,
although his arguments differ somewhat from mine. See Tittle
(1983, pp. 336-339).

Scott and Turner 1965, p. 234). He notes briefly that an unstable
society develops "what Durkheim called 'anomie' (or normlessness)"
(1968c, p. 189), but he does not elaborate on the precise meaning
or meanings of normlessness anywhere in the SS&A article.
Elsewhere, Merton does provide further clues about the nature of
"anomie." He suggests that the distinguishing feature of a state
of normlessness is the widespread de-legitimation of social norms:

> "withdrawal of allegiance from one or another part of
> prevailing social standards is what we mean, in the
> end, by anomie" (Merton 1964, p. 218);

> "When a high degree of anomie has set in, the rules
> once governing conduct have lost their savor and their
> force. Above all else, they are deprived of legitimacy"
> (1964, p. 226);

> "In a word, the degree of anomie in a social system is
> indicated by the extent to which there is a lack of
> consensus on norms judged to be legitimate"
> (1964, p. 227).

Merton seems to be saying that anomie refers to collective judgments
about the legitimacy of the prevailing norms. When norms are widely
regarded as legitimate, anomie is low. Conversely, when norms are
incapable of sustaining the allegiance of the population, anomie is
high.

This conceptualization of anomie can be introduced into Merton's
general theory of social organization quite readily to construct
Merton's explanation for levels of deviance. To recapitulate
briefly, disjuncture between the cultural and social structural
elements of a social system tends to de-legitimize social norms.
Cultural prescriptions are at odds with structural realities,
thereby promoting the withdrawal of allegiance from social norms
and high rates of deviant behavior. Note, however, that Merton's
other theory, the theory of deviant motivations, can be expressed
easily without reference to the concept of anomie. Experiences
of relative deprivation could conceivably generate anger and
frustration leading to deviant behavior irrespective of the degree
of legitimacy of social norms.

The conspicuous absence of any central role of "anomie" in the
theory of deviant motivations is understandable in view of the fact
that "anomie" and "motivations" are typically conceptualized at
different levels of analysis. Motivations are usually regarded as
properties of individuals, whereas anomie is defined as a property
of collectivities. Indeed, Merton repeatedly calls attention to the
collective character of the concept of anomie:

"As initially developed by Durkheim, the concept of
anomie referred to a condition of relative normlessness
in a society or group. Durkheim made it clear that
this concept referred to a property of the social
and cultural structure, not to a property of individuals
confronting that structure" (1968a, p. 215).

"The first thing to note about the sociological concept
of anomie is that it is - sociological. Anomie refers
to a property of a social system, not to the state of
mind of this or that individual within the system"
(1964, p. 226).

"Anomie, then, is a condition of the social surround,
not a condition of particular people" (1964, p. 227).

Anomie is a property of a social system that should be useful for
explaining other features of social systems such as rates of
deviant behavior (see Cohen 1985, p. 230; Short 1979, pp. 28–29).[9]
Given such a conceptualization of anomie, there can be no direct
link between "anomie" and deviant motivations for the simple reason
that motivations of any sort are not properties of social systems.
Only human actors, not systems, can be properly regarded as being
"motivated."[10]

In short, Merton's conceptualization of anomie as a property of
social systems enables him to incorporate the concept into his
general theoretical model of social organization, a model expressed
entirely in terms of system properties. The model explains aggregate
rates of deviant behavior with reference to the basic structural
and cultural properties of these systems. Merton's arguments
concerning the origins of deviant motivations, in contrast, do not
invoke the concept of anomie in any rigorous manner. Indeed, given
Merton's conceptualization of anomie as a system property, it is

---

[9]Merton does not always heed his admonitions to treat anomie as a
system property. He suggests, for example, that class structures are
differentially subject to anomie (1968a, p. 217), as if anomie were
a property of class positions. Social positions, however, are not
social systems in Merton's sense of the term, and hence such usage
of the anomie concept seems inappropriate.
[10]It is of course possible to formulate concepts that are intended
to serve as individual-level counterparts to "anomie." Merton
(1964) acknowledges this possibility with reference to Srole's
distinction between "anomie" and "anomia." Anomia is defined in
terms of individual experiences in a situation of anomie. An anomia
theory of deviant motivation is possible in principle, but the utility
of developing an individual-level analogue to anomie is by no means
self-evident.

difficult to imagine how anomie could be used to explain variation
in deviant motivations within a social system. Any specified
system presumably has a unique value on the anomie variable which
reflects the condition of the larger environment confronting all
members of that system. Anomie, therefore, constitutes a constant,
not a variable, for members of a given system, and it is not
relevant to the explanation of variation in motivations or behaviors
among the members of that system.

Finally, Merton's arguments pertaining to deviant motivations are
not especially original but rather entail references to certain
factors (that is, conditions of relative deprivation and feelings
of frustration) whose potential for producing deviance has long
been suspected.[11] Merton's theory of social organization is thus
not only logically independent of his theory of deviant motivations,
as argued in the previous section. The organization theory
constitutes Merton's most coherent and original contribution to the
development of an anomie perspective on deviant behavior.

A Research Agenda for the Future

My final argument on behalf of Merton's theory of social organization
concerns its potential for opening up a promising research agenda.
Merton's theory is much too sketchy and "discursive" to permit the
logical deduction of unambiguous test implications (Gibbs 1985).
Nevertheless, the basic analytical model at the core of SS&A, and the
central theoretical proposition contained therein, can contribute
to the research enterprise in three important ways. First, the
analytical model provides guidance in the selection of units of
analysis that are justifiable on theoretical grounds. More
specifically, the model offers a cogent justification for <u>macro</u>
level research on deviant behavior. Secondly, the analytical model
directs attention to the kinds of variables, if not the specific
variables, that are likely to be required for a satisfactory
explanation of variation in levels of deviance. Finally, the central
theoretical proposition of SS&A implies that the effects of
independent variables on levels of deviance will assume a distinctive,
but typically unexamined, form.

James Short (1985) has recently argued that a major source of
controversy in the sociology of deviance is confusion over "levels
of explanation." Protagonists of research at one level of
explanation are often inclined to criticize others working at a
different level for not attending to the set of variables and
processes which the former consider to be particularly significant.

---

[11]See for example Radzinowicz's (1971) discussion of the work on
relative deprivation by the "moral statisticians" of the early 19th
century and Cohen's (1966) review of the numerous efforts to link
frustration with anti-social behavior.

MERTON'S SOCIAL STRUCTURE AND ANOMIE 47

The problem here is that by not recognizing differences in theoretical purposes, participants in scholarly debates are likely to "talk past each other," which tends to lead in turn "to faulty communication and to misunderstanding" (Short 1985, p. 56).

An important implication of Short's argument is that researchers should make explicit precisely what it is that they intend to explain, and they should select units of analysis which are compatible with these intentions. Merton's theory of social organization provides useful guidelines in this regard. The units of analysis for research informed by Merton's theory must be population aggregates rather than individual persons. This follows because, as noted at several points in the discussion above, the theory is stated in terms of properties which are intrinsically "collective" rather than "individual" (Lazardsfeld and Menzel 1972). Moreover, the aggregates under investigation must be "social collectivities," rather than mere statistical aggregates, in the sense that these entities must be organized in some meaningful way. Merton's theory thus offers a clear rationale for conducting a particular kind of macro level research on deviant behavior, that is, research on organized, social collectivities. Scholars might legitimately disagree over the relative utility of constructing different kinds of explanations of deviance, but the application of the Mertonian framework in macro level research on deviance should forestall unproductive debates over the advantages and disadvantages of aggregate versus individual-level data.

Merton's theory also identifies the kinds of variables which are likely to be required for a comprehensive analysis of deviance. As Rosenfeld (1986) observes, Merton's theory exhibits a "sociological completeness" that is lacking in most other perspectives on deviant behavior. Research inspired by this theory will by necessity attend to both structural and cultural properties of social collectivities because it is the poor articulation between these properties that is the hypothesized causal factor in the genesis of a strain toward deviant behavior. Hence, it seems reasonable to expect that models derived from Merton's theory will offer more powerful explanations of deviance than will those that focus exclusively on either one or the other of these major components of social organization.

Finally, the distinctive prediction to be derived from Merton's theory is that structural and cultural variables affect rates of deviant in an "interactive" manner. The theory stipulates that certain structural conditions, in combination with certain cultural conditions, generate anomie and high rates of deviant behavior.

One simple way to express the logic of this argument is in terms of a multiple regression equation with product terms:[12]

$$Y = a + b_1 X_1 + b_2 X_2 + b_3 (X_1 * X_2)$$

where Y = the rate of deviant behavior;

X_1 = a structural property;

X_2 = a cultural property.

To apply this model in empirical research, specific structural and cultural conditions must be identified which are expected to produce interactive effects on the level of a given form of deviant behavior. The parameter "b_3" then becomes the focus of attention in the assessment of the structural strain argument.

The kind of research just described has not been pursued to any significant degree to date. However, there is some evidence in the literature on homicide that is at least suggestive of the utility of this approach. For example, in a previous study on regional differences in the economic correlates of the homicide rate, I report evidence which is consistent with Merton's general theory (Messner 1983). The principal hypothesis in this study is that poverty should have a weaker effect on homicide rates in Southern than in non-Southern cities. This hypothesis is based on the premise that the South is characterized by less "universalistic" value orientations than is the non-south, and on the theoretical claim that the criminogenic consequences of economic deprivation should be greatest when value orientations are strongly universalistic. (The premise about differences in values between the South and other parts of the U.S. derives from John Shelton Reed's work (1972; 1982) on regional cultures).

With respect to the regression model presented above, the research strategy in this empirical study involves treating regional location as a proxy for certain value orientations (a cultural property). A regional difference in the effects of poverty (a structural variable) then represents the hypothesized interaction between these two variables. The results for a sample of 347 American cities in 1969-71 support the hypothesis. The effect of poverty on homicide rates is significantly weaker in Southern than in non-Southern cities.

---

[12]This equation treats "anomie" as an unmeasured construct. If valid indicators of this variable were to be developed, then a path model could be estimated in which anomie serves as an intervening variable which statistically interprets the effects of structural and cultural properties on rates of deviance. Unfortunately, the prospects for developing non-tautological indicators of anomie in the near future are not particularly promising.

Another piece of evidence which suggests the utility of the Mertonian framework can be found in Krahn et al.'s (1986) cross-national study of income inequality and homicide rates. These researchers discover an interaction between a measure of income inequality, an indicator of democracy, and national homicide rates. Specifically, "income inequality is found to have a more pronounced effect on homicide in more democratic societies" (Krahn et al. 1986, p. 285).

Krahn et al. interpret this finding by speculating that "income inequality might be more likely to generate violent behavior in more democratic societies because of the coexistence of high material inequality in an egalitarian value system" (p. 288). What they are suggesting, in other words, is that it is the presence of certain structural conditions (income inequality) in combination with certain cultural conditions (egalitarian values) that seems to be particularly conducive to high rates of this severe form of deviant behavior (homicide). This is, of course, precisely the kind of effect that would be expected on the basis of Merton's general theory.

In short, Merton's theory calls for a distinctive kind of research on the determinants of levels of deviant behavior. This research will involve the macro-level analysis of the interactions between social structural variables and cultural variables. The sparse evidence in the literature on deviant behavior, such as homicide, which is directly relevant to the claims of Merton's theory indicates that such a research agenda has considerable promise.

Summary and Conclusions

I have argued that there are both organizational and motivational theories contained in Merton's classic SS&A essay and that these two theories are logically independent. The validity of one does not, therefore, depend on the validity of the other. Moreover, the focus of critical attention devoted to the anomie perspective has been restricted mainly to the motivational theory and is basically irrelevant to the organizational theory. This is unfortunate because only the organizational theory applies the concept of anomie in a coherent and original manner, and because the organizational theory has interesting but largely unexplored research implications. The premature abandonment of the anomie perspective noted above can be attributed in large measure to the longstanding preoccupation with the more problematic elements of Merton's essay, that is, his theory of deviant motivations and the application of this theory in the explanation of the social distribution of deviant behavior in

American society.[13] In view of these considerations, a resurgence
of interest in the anomie perspective, and particularly in Merton's
theory of social organization, seems amply justified.

Two important qualifications of my basic argument should be noted
before closing. First, although Merton's theory of social
organization is not logically dependent on his theory of deviant
motivations, the organizational theory must be compatible with
some motivational theory of deviance. Deviant behavior is in the
final analysis behavior that is enacted by motivated individuals.
I have indicated very briefly how Merton's organizational theory
might be joined with alternative motivational theories, such as
control theories, but clearly a more rigorous articulation of the
linkages between Merton's system-level processes and individual
motivations and behaviors is required for the development of a
truly comprehensive explanation of the phenomenon of deviance.

Second, even with respect to the organizational theory itself,
Merton leaves unanswered a host of pressing questions, only a few
of which can be noted here. What specific kinds of inter-
relationships between structural and cultural components of social
systems constitute a state of disjuncture? What are the principal
causes of system disjuncture? How do different forms of disjuncture
bear upon the integrity of the cultural structure? Are there types
of system-component disjuncture, for example, that promote a
cultural imbalance characterized by an overemphasis on means
vis-a-vis goals? How is the "normal" balance between goals and
means specified? Finally, why is anomie manifested in certain forms
of deviant behavior rather than others (cf. Cullen 1984)?

The challenges that must be confronted in any effort to translate
Merton's discursive and sketchy arguments into a rigorous and
testable theory are obviously formidable (Gibbs 1985).
Nevertheless, the potential returns are great. Rehabilitation of the
anomie perspective offers an opportunity to reverse the reductionist
trends in research that have accompanied the "growth of
individualist behaviorism" (Coleman 1986, p. 1313) in sociology in
general. The theory of SS&A underscores the importance of looking
beyond the individual characteristics of the members of social
collectivities to the structural interrelationships among them and
to the shared beliefs that govern these interrelationships. In
short, Merton's theory of social organization promises to lead to a
distinctively sociological explanation of levels of crime and
deviance, an explanation that systematically incorporates both
cultural and structural dynamics (cf. Rosenfeld 1986). This promise

----

[13]Hilbert and Wright argue persuasively that the preoccupation with
Merton's discussion of a social class-deviance relationship on the
part of sociologists reflects a widespread value commitment to
equality of opportunity as a solution to the problem of high rates
of deviance. See Hilbert and Wright (1979).

sets Merton's theory apart from most other approaches that inform contemporary research on crime and deviance, and because of this promise, SS&A warrants continued attention in the years ahead.

REFERENCES

Bernard, Thomas J.
　1984　"Control criticisms of strain theories:　An assessment of theoretical and empirical adequacy."　Journal of Research in Crime and Delinquency 21:353-372.
Box, Steven
　1981　Deviance, Reality, and Society.　London:　Holt, Rinehart, and Winston.
Braithwaite, John
　1981　"The myth of social class and criminality reconsidered." American Sociological Review 46:36-57.
Cohen, Albert K.
　1966　Deviance and Control.　Englewood, Cliffs, New Jersey: Prentice-Hall.
　1985　"The assumption that crime is a product of environ- ments:　Sociological approaches."　Pp. 223-243 in Robert F. Meier (ed.), Theoretical Methods in Criminology.　Beverly Hills, California:　Sage.
Cole, Stephen
　1975　"The growth of scientific knowledge:　Theories of deviance as a case study."　Pp. 175-220 in Lewis A. Coser (ed.), The Idea of Social Structure:　Papers in Honor of Robert K. Merton.　New York:　Harcourt Brace Jovanovich.
Coleman, James S.
　1986　"Social theory, social research, and a theory of action."　American Journal of Sociology 91:1309-1335.
Cullen, Francis T.
　1984　Rethinking Crime and Deviance Theory:　The Emergence of a Structuring Tradition.　Totowa, New Jersey: Rowman and Allanheld.
Davis, Nanette J.
　1980　Sociological Constructions of Deviance:　Perspectives and Issues in the Field, 2nd edition.　Dubuque, Iowa: Brown.
Elliott, Delbert S. and David Huizinga
　1983　"Social class and delinquent behavior in a national youth panel, 1976-1980."　Criminology 21:149-177.
Elliott, Delbert S., David Huizinga, and Suzanne S. Ageton
　1985　Explaining Delinquency and Drug Use.　Beverly Hills, California:　Sage.
Empey, Lamar T.
　1982　American Delinquency:　Its Meaning and Construction. Homewood, Illinois:　Dorsey.
Gibbs, Jack P.
　1985　"The methodology of theory construction in criminology." Pp. 23-50 in Robert F. Meier (ed.), Theoretical Methods in Criminology.　Beverly Hills, California:　Sage.

Hilbert, R. E. and Charles W. Wright
    1979   "Representations of Merton's theory of anomie." The
            American Sociologist 14:150-156.
Hirschi, Travis
    1969   Causes of Delinquency. Berkeley, California:
            University of California.
Kornhauser, Ruth R.
    1978   Social Sources of Delinquency: An Appraisal of
            Analytic Models. Chicago: University of Chicago.
Krahn, Harvey, Timothy Hartnagel, and John Gartrell
    1986   "Income inequality and homicide rates: Cross-
            national data and criminological theories."
            Criminology 24:269-295.
Lazarsfeld, Paul F. and Herbert Menzel
    1972   "On the relationship between individual and collective
            properties." Pp. 225-237 in Paul F. Lazarsfeld, Ann
            Pasanella, and Morris Rosenberg (eds.), Continuities
            in the Language of Social Research. New York: Free
            Press.
Liska, Allen E.
    1971   "Aspirations, expectations and delinquency: Stress
            and additive models." Sociological Quarterly 12:
            99-107.
    1981   Perspectives on Deviance. Englewood Cliffs, New
            Jersey: Prentice-Hall.
Merton, Robert K.
    1964   "Anomie, anomia, and social interaction: Contexts of
            deviant behavior." Pp. 213-242 in Marshall B. Clinard
            (ed.), Anomie and Deviant Behavior: A Discussion and
            Critique. New York: Free Press.
    1968a   "Continuities in the theory of social structure and
            anomie." Pp. 215-248 in Robert K. Merton, Social
            Theory and Social Structure. New York: Free Press.
    1968b   "Part II. Studies in social and cultural structure.
            Introduction." Pp. 175-184 in Robert K. Merton,
            Social Theory and Social Structure. New York: Free
            Press.
    1968c   "Social structure and anomie." Pp. 185-214 in Robert
            K. Merton, Social Theory and Social Structure. New
            York: Free Press.
    1971   "Epilogue: Social problems and sociological theory."
            Pp. 793-845 in Robert K. Merton and Robert Nisbet
            (eds.), Contemporary Social Problems, 3rd edition.
            New York: Harcourt Brace Jovanovich.
Messner, Steven F.
    1983   "Regional differences in the economic correlates of
            the urban homicide rate: Some evidence on the
            importance of the cultural context." Criminology 21:
            477-488.
Radzinowicz, Leon
    1971   "Economic pressures." Pp. 429-442 in Leon Radzinowicz
            and Marvin E. Wolfgang (eds.), Crime and Justice, Vol.
            1. New York: Basic.

Reed, John S.
  1972   The Enduring South. Lexington, Massachusetts: D. C.
            Heath.
  1982   One South. Baton Rouge: Louisiana State University
            Press.
Rosenfeld, Richard
  1985   "Contradiction, consumption, and crime: A synthesis
            of Marxist and Mertonian perspectives." Presented at
            the Annual Meeting of the American Society of
            Criminology, November 16, San Diego, California.
  1986   "Rereading Merton: The strain perspective and con-
            temporary sociological theories of crime." Presented
            at the Annual Meeting of the American Society of
            Criminology, October 29-November 1, Atlanta, Georgia.
Scott, Marvin B. and Ray Turner
  1965   "Weber and the anomie theory of deviance."
            Sociological Quarterly 6:233-240.
Short, James S.
  1979   "On the etiology of delinquent behavior." Journal of
            Research in Crime and Delinquency 16:28-33.
  1985   "The level of explanation problem in criminology."
            Pp. 51-72 in Robert F. Meier (ed.), Theoretical
            Methods in Criminology. Beverly Hills, California:
            Sage.
Taylor, Ian, Paul Walton, and Jock Young
  1973   The New Criminology: For a Social Theory of Deviance.
            New York: Harper Colophon Books.
Tittle, Charles R.
  1983   "Social class and criminal behavior: A critique of
            the theoretical formulation." Social Forces 62:334-358.
Tittle, Charles R. and Wayne J. Villemez
  1978   "The myth of social class and criminality: An
            empirical assessment of the empirical evidence."
            American Sociological Review 43:643-656.

*Request reprints from Dr. Steven F. Messner, Department
of Sociology, State University of New York at Albany,
Albany, NY 12222.*

[16]

Global Anomie, Dysnomie, and Economic Crime: Hidden Consequences of Neoliberalism and Globalization in Russia and Around the World

Nikos Passas

Introduction

TRANSNATIONAL CRIME HAS RECENTLY ACQUIRED A PROMINENT PLACE IN PUBLIC debates. It is commonly presented as the most significant crime problem at the turn of the millennium (Myers, 1995–1996; Shelley, 1995). Many have even suggested that it represents a serious domestic and international security threat (Paine and Cillufo, 1994; Williams, 1994). The argument is also made that a wave of transnational crime undermines neoliberal policies and the functioning of an increasing number of market economies around the globe (Handelman, 1995; Shelley, 1994). As a consequence, the proposed remedies are often quite drastic and involve undercover operations, privacy-piercing approaches, and the participation of intelligence services in the fight against global crime (Andreas, 1997; Naylor, 1999; Passas and Blum, 1998; Passas and Groskin, 1995).

Yet, little attention and virtually no systematic research has been devoted to understanding the causes, structure, extent, and effects of serious cross-border misconduct (Passas, 1998). The risks it poses may be grossly exaggerated (Naylor, 1995; Lee, 1999). The draconian measures being contemplated and implemented in different countries, therefore, are essentially an exercise in shooting in the dark. Chances are good that the target will be missed and substantial "collateral damage" may be caused by ill-conceived policies in this "war" on crime. This risk is

NIKOS PASSAS is Associate Professor in the Department of Criminal Justice at Temple University (529 Gladfelter Hall, Philadelphia, PA 19122; e-mail: npassas@nimbus.temple.edu). The author specializes in the study of white-collar crime, corruption, organized crime, and international crime. He is the author of *Informal Value Transfer Systems and Criminal Organizations: A Study into So-called Underground Banking Networks* (1999) and the editor of *The Future of Anomie Theory* (1997), *Transnational Crime* (1999), and *Organized Crime* (1995). Dr. Passas has authored numerous papers and research reports. He serves as Northeastern University Press series editor on transnational crime. He has acted as a consultant to various bodies, including the United Nations Centre for International Crime Prevention, the Commission of the European Union, the German Parliament, and a number of governments. The author wishes to thank warmly Bob Weiss for his constructive feedback and patience.

particularly high in countries in transition toward a market democracy. It would be much wiser, thus, to carefully study the problem before taking ineffective and possibly damaging actions.

This article seeks to make a contribution by concentrating on the causes of transnational economic crime. The main argument is that, contrary to conventional wisdom, neoliberalism and globalization contribute to processes leading to global anomie, dysnomie, and, ultimately, economic misconduct. They do so by activating the criminogenic potential of economic, political, legal, and cultural asymmetries, as well as by creating new such asymmetries (Passas, 1999). These asymmetries cause crime by furnishing opportunities for misconduct, by generating motives for actors to take advantage of such opportunities, and by weakening social controls. More specifically, means-ends disjunctions are systematically created, as neoliberal policies foster new needs and desires that are all too often left unfulfilled. Promises of more freedom, prosperity, and happiness for a larger number of people have turned out to be chimerical. Economic and power inequalities have widened within and across countries in the last two decades. The number of poor has reached unprecedented levels, while welfare programs and safety nets are reduced or abolished. Enormous populations have become more vulnerable to exploitation, criminal victimization, and recruitment in illicit enterprises or rebel and fundamentalist groups. Normative standards and control mechanisms are weak or completely absent exactly when they are needed the most.

This article begins with some basic conceptual clarifications and outlines the theoretical framework so far applied to the analysis of U.S. organizational and individual deviance. Then, the main features of globalization and neoliberalism are presented, followed by a contrast of promises made by proponents of neoliberal policies and their actual consequences. Attention then shifts to specific criminogenic effects of these outcomes and the case of Russia, which illustrates the different stages in the processes leading up to serious misconduct and anomie. The chief policy implication of this analysis is that the recently unleashed forces of neoliberalism need to be reined in and held in check, while government policies ought to better shield the least privileged from the adverse effects of globalization.

Some Conceptual Clarifications

Although there is no universally accepted definition of transnational crime, many commentators seem to think of it as a globalized form of the stereotypical "organized crime." This, however, leaves out corporate and governmental crimes, whose effects can be far more harmful than those of "professional" criminals and ethnic groups involved in the business of illegal goods and services. We therefore need a definition that is inclusive enough without becoming too relativistic and subjective. For our purposes, transnational crime refers to cross-border misconduct that entails avoidable and unnecessary harm to society, is serious enough to warrant state intervention, and is similar to other kinds of acts criminalized in the countries concerned or by international law. Crime will be viewed as transnational when the offenders or victims are located in or operate through more than one country (Passas, 1999).

Globalization is another term that is often used without clear definition. In the simplest sense, it refers to a growing interconnectedness and multilateral linkages across national borders. According to Keohane and Nye (2000: 104),

> globalism is a state of the world involving networks of interdependence at multicontinental distances. The linkages occur through flows and influences of capital and goods, information and ideas, and people and forces, as well as environmentally and biologically relevant substances (such as acid rain or pathogens).

Globalism has several dimensions, such as economic, cultural, environmental, or military, not all of which take place at the same time. So, whenever globalism increases and becomes thicker or more intense, we can speak of globalization. When globalism decreases, we can speak of de-globalization.

Finally, the term "criminogenic asymmetries" refers to structural discrepancies and inequalities in the realms of the economy, law, politics, and culture. Such asymmetries are produced in the course of interactions between unequal actors (individual or organizational) or systems with distinctive features. All asymmetries contain some criminogenic potential. Durkheim argued that crime cannot be eliminated, because we are and always will be different from each other. Even in a society of saints, minor deviations would be considered serious offenses. In modern societies, crimes are those behavioral differences (asymmetries) that have been outlawed by legislative bodies. There is always the opportunity for powerful actors to victimize less privileged ones (economic, political, and power asymmetries). This potential is not always materialized. Criminal opportunities are not necessarily taken advantage of. Mostly this is because actors do not always seek or wish to make use of illegal opportunities. They may not regard such action as appropriate (due to socialization, internalization of norms) or fear adverse consequences. The criminogenic potential is most likely to be activated when opportunities, motives, and weak controls are all present.

For example, a combination of legal/regulatory asymmetries with economic and political asymmetries has given rise to a huge illicit market for toxic waste disposal. Many Third World countries either did not regulate toxic waste or did so much less rigorously than did industrialized states. This provided an opportunity for maximum-profit-seeking companies to get rid of their hazardous waste in areas where rules were lax or nonexistent (Center for Investigative Reporting and Moyers, 1990; Critharis, 1990). Power and economic asymmetries between rich and poor countries have led waste recipients to allow this to go on because of their dependence on foreign investment, the need for cash to service external debt, or the desire to create jobs (Korten, 1995). Economic and knowledge asymmetries also shaped the motivation of local participants in this questionable trade. The decision to go along reflects an incomplete understanding of the extent or nature of the hazard, their desperate need for additional income, an effort to be competitive and attractive to foreign companies (race to the bottom), or corruption.

Anomie and Deviance

Both Durkheim (1983) and Merton (1968) have stressed how high rates of deviance should be expected when social expectations are out of balance with realistic opportunities to reach the desired goals. According to Durkheim, this means-ends discrepancy is caused by society's inability to regulate people's naturally limitless desires. This problem was particularly acute in the commercial and business sector, in which anomie was chronic during the industrial revolution, opening up new horizons and undermining society's ability to contain aspirations. A similar situation can be observed in contemporary societies, where electronic, information, and biological technologies constantly redefine what is possible and break new ground.

According to Merton, unrealistic hopes and expectations are not simply natural, but socially constructed and promoted. Structural problems are at the heart of the means-ends disjunction. The U.S. culture and the ideology of the American Dream encourage lofty expectations, while society fails to provide equal access to legal opportunities. Meanwhile, there is a cultural overemphasis on success goals at the expense of normative behavior (as further elaborated by Messner and Rosenfeld, 1994). Both of these factors make for deviance and anomie.

Without ignoring the differences between the two sociologists, it has been possible to use an elaborated version of their anomie theories to explain corporate crime in the context of capitalist economies (Passas, 1990). Regardless of whether people strive for "more" due to natural drives or because of cultural encouragement, the point is that market economies cannot perform without lofty aspirations, consumerism, emphasis on material/monetary goals, and competition. All this leads to the pursuit of constantly moving targets and systematic sources of frustration. A synthesis of anomie theory with reference group analysis made clear how means-ends discrepancies are socially generated and experienced by people in all social strata. It also showed how this theoretical framework is applicable to the analysis of crime without strain or problems (i.e., anomie theory is not a strain theory) and to "organized crime" even after discrimination or blockage of legitimate opportunities no longer affects minority groups (Passas, 1997).

In brief, the dynamic social process leading to structurally induced strain, anomie, and deviance without strain is as follows. Means-ends discrepancies are caused by a strong cultural emphasis on monetary or material success goals for all members of society, while a good number of them do not have a realistic chance to attain them. Socially distant comparative referents are constantly introduced and sustained through the school, family, politics, workplace, media, advertising, and even religion (Passas, 1994). Regardless of their social background and the social capital available to them, people are urged to desire more than they have. Success stories of going from rags to riches make the American Dream even more believable. As this cultural theme is internalized, competitive forces and consumerism foster normative referents on what is "normal" and appropriate. The widely internalized egalitarian discourse clashes in practice with widespread inequality (power and economic asymmetries). Consequently, those members who fail to meet such comparative and normative standards are likely to experience relative deprivation and frustration. This strain, combined with the culturally induced overemphasis on goals and the concomitant underemphasis on the proper methods, makes for deviance of various types (see Merton's typology). A good part of the deviance is an individual search for a solution to these structural problems. If the deviant solution is successful (i.e., perpetrators are not caught or adequately punished), this adaptation may become normative for others in a similar social context. To the extent that this solution is available to them (demand for illicit goods or services, access to illegitimate opportunity structures), they may adopt this role model — and may be expected by their significant others to follow this path — even though the original source of strain has by now been eclipsed. Unless effective control measures are taken, this process continues in a vicious circle toward higher rates of deviance and widespread anomie (for a schematic representation of this process, see Figure 1 at the end of the article).

In the literature, anomie is often conceptually confused with its causes or effects. To keep its explanatory potential, this mistake should be avoided. Anomie is a withdrawal of allegiance from conventional norms and a weakening of these norms' guiding power on behavior. This is caused by structural contradictions and affects deviance in two ways. One is associated with strain, the other is not. The former is caused by relative deprivation, frustrations, and the almost obsessive focus on goals. This makes deviance thinkable, as conventional norms are regarded as nonbinding, at least temporarily. Rationalizations enable departures from otherwise accepted/internalized social rules, as actors convince themselves that in their particular circumstances an exception is acceptable (Aubert, 1968; Sykes and Matza, 1957). Through interactive processes, techniques of neutralization and rationalizations contribute to a context in which newly socialized actors may adopt normative referents and deviant behavior as a matter of course. If "this is the way business is done around here," people may engage in price fixing or misleading advertising without experiencing any prior frustration or problem.

Globalization and Neoliberalism

These structural problems have been most prominent in the USA. However, a very similar process is now being reproduced throughout the world through globalism and neoliberalism. Promises are made that are not fulfilled. People's expectations are exalted at a time when economic and power asymmetries increase and become less justifiable and intolerable in the eyes of the people affected. The logic of the market permeates popular thinking and introduces rationalizations, making the adoption of a criminal or unethical solution more acceptable. The horizontal lines in Figure 1, rather than representing controlling influences, at the global level point to the criminogenic impact of globalization and neoliberal policies.

Nowadays, globalism and neoliberalism seem to be indistinguishable empirically or even conceptually (Cox, 1993; Stewart and Berry, 1999). Nevertheless, I think it is useful to try to separate them analytically. As noted earlier, globalism refers to the degree of interconnectedness and the increase or decrease of linkages. By contrast, neoliberalism refers to an economic and political school of thought on the relations between the state on the one hand, and citizens and the world of trade and commerce on the other. Because it espouses minimal or no state interference in the market and promotes the lifting of barriers to trade and business transactions across regional and national borders, it certainly becomes a motor of globalization.

Globalization in the last two decades shows clear signs of deeper and thicker interconnections that affect many more people than ever before. The effects are now much faster, as shown by the financial crisis in Thailand in 1997. The world has shrunk and become "one place," with global communications and media, transnational corporations, supranational institutions, and integrated markets and financial systems that trade around the clock (McGrew, 1992; Sklair, 1995). The cultural landscape has changed under the influence of mass media. Through their ads, TV programs, movies, and music, they contribute to cultural globalism, target young children, and foster consumerism (e.g., "Image Is Everything," "Just Do It," or "Coke Is It"). Information technology is making for "distant encounters and instant connections" (Yergin and Stanislaw, 1998). Fresh normative and comparative ideals are thus promoted, legitimated, and presented as attainable. Scholars attribute the momentum of this process to the forces of capitalism (Wallerstein, 1983), technology (Rosenau, 1990), the presence of a hegemon (Gilpin, 1987), or a combination of them all (Giddens, 1990).

Neoliberalism, in particular, has made a major contribution to the dynamic and contradictory processes of globalization since the elections of Ronald Reagan, Margaret Thatcher, and Helmut Kohl. During the 1950s and 1960s, the dominant concerns revolved around distributive justice, neocolonialism, and dependency theory. These were displaced in the 1980s and into the 1990s by discourses of "free markets," individualism, and self-help (Woods, 1999). Policies of deregulation, privatization of state assets, and removal of tariffs implemented the doctrine that the state should get out of the way of free enterprise. Unemployment, inequality, and poverty were no longer explained by structural contradictions or constraints. The problems became individualized and blamed on corrupt administrations or on the poor themselves. The proposed medicine was more liberalization of the economy, free competition, privatization of inefficiently managed government agencies, abolition of capital controls, and permitting foreign capital to enter all markets.

The ideological underpinning of globalization, thus, has been the primacy of economic growth, which is thought to be benefiting the whole planet. Consistent with that prime directive, country after country has been persuaded (or forced) to promote "free trade" and consumerism, to reduce government regulation of business, and to adopt the same economic model regardless of local specificities and differences between industrialized and developing countries (Bello, 1999; Mander, 1996).

More specifically, shifts in the North, the East, and the South have been quite remarkable. In the North, the welfare state that used to care for citizens "from cradle to grave" has been replaced by a "pay as you go" social service system. Even public utilities have been privatized and have begun to charge "economic prices," as former subsidization systems were abolished. Further, "industrial intervention-ism and labour protection have given way to laissez-faire; and...tax systems whose major purpose was to correct inequalities have been transformed into systems mainly intended to promote incentives and economic efficiency" (Stewart and Berry, 1999: 151).

In developing countries, similar shifts took place as a result of hegemonic influences from the North. Western-educated Third World "technocrats" returned to their home countries eager to introduce neoliberal policies (Burbach et al., 1997: 86; *Newsweek*, June 15, 1992). As the bandwagon of liberalization took off, few countries wished to be left out. As a World Bank official warned, "lagging countries risk being left farther behind.... For economies that remain inward-looking, the risk of being marginalized is greater than ever" (cited in Klak, 1998: 21).

Yet, the shifts have not always been voluntary. A host of measures and conditions consistent with the neoliberal agenda were imposed on countries through international institutions, such as the International Monetary Fund (IMF), the World Bank, the OECD, the European Union, the G7, etc. Countries drowning in external debt sought additional loans to pay off their older ones — chiefly to banks from the industrialized world. Billions of dollars were made available to them, but only if they introduced Structural Adjustment Programs (SAPs). Despite important differences among the various economies, SAPs shared the same basic elements: long-term "structural" reforms to deregulate the economy, liberaliza-tion of trade, removal of restrictions on foreign investment, promotion of an export orientation of the economy, wage reductions and controls, privatization of state enterprises, and short-term stabilization measures such as cutbacks in government spending, high interest rates, and currency devaluation (Bello, 1996; 1999).

Changes along these lines also took place in the East, where the switch from state-managed economies toward "free market" and parliamentary democracy has been quite drastic and swift (Glinkina, 1994; Woods, 1999). The problem is that the introduction of global neoliberalism has brought about enormous economic and political asymmetries, as its promises and theoretical expectations remain unfulfilled.

The Promises of Global Neoliberalism

The supporters of global neoliberalism make a series of claims. For instance, the world is shrinking following greater connectivity (IBM claims to offer "solutions for a smaller planet"). The distinction between core and periphery states is presumed to be getting fuzzier and irrelevant, as there are only winners from now on. Investment, trade, and development opportunities are more widely distributed around the world. There is a marked convergence into one world economy, in which everyone can find a market niche. Media and cultural influences are more widespread and multilateral, as foods, music, and art are imported to the North and integrated into local cultures. Finally, people are more integrated thanks to telecommunication technologies and immigration (Klak, 1998).

To economists, all these trends are positive, even if short-term hardship is deemed necessary for some parts of the population. Global welfare is expected to be enhanced, as the forces of free competition within and between countries will encourage more efficient resource allocation and bring about higher productivity (Oman, 1999). A more open, trade-creating world should, therefore, benefit everyone, if unevenly. Trickle-down effects of wealth creation would ensure that virtually everyone will participate in this welcome trend (Korten, 1996).

The objective of SAPs was to render developing economies more efficient, drive up growth rates, and provide foreign exchange that could be used to repay debt. Higher growth rates are empirically associated with comparatively more equal income distribution (Alesina and Rodrik, 1994). Hence, neoliberal policies would bring about not only more economic growth, productivity, a better division of labor (multistate production and wider participation), lower unemployment, more wealth and prosperity, but also more democracy, less poverty, and fewer inequalities. Unfortunately, in most countries, these virtuous circles did not occur.

The Consequences of Global Neoliberalism

Throughout the world, the expectations raised by neoliberal theorists have not materialized despite the extensive application of their policy recommendations. Instead, most economies "fell into a hole" of low investment, decreased social spending and consumption, low output, decline and stagnation. Both the World Bank and the IMF retreated from SAPs and acknowledged their failure (Bello, 1999; Katona, 1999; *Multinational Monitor*, June 2000; Watkins, 1997).

In the North, GDP growth was lower in the 1980 to 1990 period than in the 1950s and 1960s. We also witness a higher volatility in growth (e.g., booms and busts). Lost in all the talk about huge technological advances ushering in the computer and Internet era is the fact that productivity growth now is half that of levels in the 1950s and 1960s. Unemployment in OECD (Organization for Economic Cooperation and Development) countries has risen from eight million in 1970 to 35 million in 1994. In the midst of U.S. prosperity and economic expansion, inequalities increased. The number of people living under the officially defined poverty level grew from 11.4% of the population in 1978 to 13.5% in 1990. Almost one in four new babies in the U.S. are born into poverty, while the top one percent of Americans saw their real income shoot up by 50% (Levy, 1998; Wilterdink, 1995). Also noteworthy is that U.S. and Western European international trade relative to GDP was greater a century ago than in recent years (Hirst and Thompson, 1996).

Neoliberal dreams proved to be even more chimerical in the South. Role models, like South Korea, Malaysia, and Indonesia plunged into crises in the 1990s. Mexico and Brazil, which faced their own scary periods, experienced growth of three percent in the last two decades, whereas that rate was six percent during the *dirigiste* period of 1950 to 1980. Wage gaps widened. Even in Costa Rica and Chile, models of success in Latin America, the results have been an unmitigated disaster for the lower social classes. The number of Costa Ricans below the poverty line rose from 18.6% in 1987 to 24.4% in 1991, while 42% of all Chileans are also living in poverty (Burbach et al., 1997: 86). Half of the investment flows to developing countries went to just three countries (China, Mexico, and Argentina). In addition, some investments had negative local effects. For instance, as diverse agriculture was converted into monocultures or to export-oriented flower plantations, self-sufficiency was undermined (Clinard, 1990; Klak, 1998).

Moreover, the core-periphery distinction is as relevant as ever. Its real meaning relates to power, authority, and the accumulation of wealth, where the gaps (asymmetries) are increasing. Although production (of certain items) is more dispersed, the concentration of power, control, and benefits has become more pronounced. In 1991, 81% of the world stock of direct foreign investment was in the core triad of the USA, the European Union, and Japan — up from 69% in 1967. The appearance of integrated markets also obscures the fact that 80% of all world trade is within the core triad, in which resides less than 20% of the planet's population (Hirst and Thompson, 1996; Klak, 1998).

In Latin America, debt jumped from $230 billion in 1980 to $600 billion in 1997. Capital had been fleeing those countries up to the early 1990s, when net inflows were the result of casino capital — seeking short-term gains and likely to abandon those countries at the first hint of trouble. Consequently, new debts were created with a new round of borrowing (Robinson, 1998–1999). An important reason why developing countries cannot pay off their debt is that trade protectionism in the North has kept them from penetrating those markets. Trade liberalization has been inconsistent in that rich countries demand more open markets abroad, while continuing to subsidize their own economic sectors, such as agriculture (Andreas, 1999; UNDP, 2000; Watkins, 1997). Compounding these problems, aid to poor countries has been cut back. Whatever assistance is offered comes with strings attached, including the reduction of state intervention, which could have softened the effects for the most vulnerable (Watkins, 1997; Woods, 1999). These policies further undercut food security, cause poverty, and increase economic and power asymmetries. For instance, the cost of living in the Caribbean and the U.S. is quite comparable. In 1997, however, per capita income in Trinidad and Tobago, the richest Caribbean state, was less than half that of Mississippi, the poorest U.S. state. The gap between skilled and unskilled workers widened even more: Haitian workers made clothing with Disney logos for less than 60 cents per hour, while Disney's CEO made $9,700 per hour (Klak, 1998).

The claim of multilateral and even cultural influences also masks tremendous asymmetries. Even though we listen to reggae in the North, 95% of TV programs in St. Lucia come from the U.S. The most widely read newspaper in the Caribbean is the *Miami Herald*. Consequently,

> U.S. affluence and opportunity, often romanticized, is especially well-known, deeply ingrained, and alluring to the Caribbean...[where] people are prone to set their living standard goals in accordance with what the U.S. media ascribe to the United States. And the imbalance in media flows is increasing with the Caribbean's economic crisis and neoliberalism, as local media have been slashed (Klak, 1998: 11).

As dreams of consumption are disseminated, 86% of total private consumption expenditures is accounted for by 20% of the world's people in industrialized countries (UNDP, 1998). For the people who live outside the consumption geographical area, big banks offer credit to only 10% of the people in developing countries, whereas ads for credit cards and consumer items are omnipresent (Barnet and Cavanagh, 1994). Well over one billion people are deprived of basic consumption needs. For hundreds of millions, basic sanitation, clean water, adequate housing, and health services are unattainable luxuries. Two billion people live on less than two dollars a day and 1.3 billion on less than one dollar a day (ICFTU, 2000). Struggling to survive, some decide to sell their body parts to make ends meet, which is the ultimate symbol of commodification (Scheper-Hughes, 2000).

A negative effect of the Internet is that it alters the relationship between our place of residence and our cultural preferences, experiences, and identities. A spreading global virtual reality disconnects locality from culture, weakens the bonds to particular communities, and estranges people from each other (Minda, 2000). Ladakh, a Himalayan province that prospered for a millennium despite harsh weather conditions, illustrates how (especially cultural) globalization devastated local communities (Norberg-Hodge, 1996). In 1962, isolated Ladakh was linked to the rest of India by an army-built road. The modernization that began in 1975 took about a decade to change the pride Ladakhis felt until then into a collective inferiority complex. Tourism and the media conveyed a picture of wealth, technology, power, and work that was alien and irresistible to them. Village life by comparison began to appear "primitive, silly, and inefficient" (*Ibid.*: 35). Ladakhis felt ashamed of their culture and strove for consumer items that symbolize modern life, such as sunglasses and Walkmans. As Western educational standards penetrated Ladakh, the intergenerational learning experience that helped them provide for themselves in their rough terrain gave way to schools that used texts imitating Indian and British models that were completely irrelevant to their lives (e.g., figuring out the angle of the Tower of Pisa and learning how to keep a London-like bedroom tidy). There used to be no such thing as a "paying job"; there was no money economy. Gradually, however, unemployment — previously nonexistent — became a serious problem, because naturally available resources were abandoned, cheap imports made local farming redundant, and people flocked to the cities to compete for scarce jobs. Radios and TVs chased away the traditions of singing together and group story telling. The points of reference ceased to be real people living nearby, but geographically and socially remote ideals. Consumerism bred new "needs," which could hardly be materialized. Family and other bonds disintegrated and divisions emerged between old and young, Buddhists and Muslims. The result was unprecedented violence, community breakdown, and anomie.

Criminogenic Effects: Systemic Strains and Global Anomie

What makes the ideology of the American Dream unique is a focus on money and material goods, a strong emphasis on "winning" (often, by all means), and success for everyone in a society where many opportunities for material advancement are available and plenty of "rags to riches" stories lend legitimacy and credibility to the egalitarian discourse. Legal opportunities, however, for achieving the lofty goals are inaccessible to most Americans. In such a consumption-driven culture, which highly values competition and individualism, the means-ends disjunction has entailed a significant criminogenic risk, much greater than in the rest of the world. Crime has been the flip side of economic growth, innovation, and better living standards for certain segments of the population. What sheltered other countries from this negative potential were things absent or minimized in the USA, such as rigid social stratification, low rates of social mobility, less materialism and time spent before TV boxes, safety nets for the underprivileged, more emphasis on other priorities (e.g., solidarity), etc.

This made it possible to explain the higher crime rates in the U.S. compared to other developed or developing countries. These protective factors, however, are now being gradually lost. Disjunctions between socially induced goals and legal means are few in societies that do not encourage high social mobility. In such societies, people may not feel that they are lacking anything, even when they are "objectively" deprived. Economic or other asymmetries are unknown or not experienced and perceived as intolerable. Global neoliberalism breaks down societal barriers and encourages new needs, desires, and fashions. It promotes the adoption of nonmembership reference groups for comparisons that can be unfavorable and upsetting. New normative reference groups define what is "cool" to do. People's ideals in the South and the East may not be about getting from "a log cabin to the White House." However, they are being systematically driven to abandon old ways and values in order to consume. They do not necessarily think that they can be "like Mike," but they do fancy those pricey athletic shoes. So, fresh normative and comparative models create new "needs," together with the expectation that the fulfillment of such needs is vital and achievable.

Yet, as needs and normative models are "harmonized," people become conscious of economic and power asymmetries, and directly experience their impact. Globalization and neoliberalism heightened this awareness, further widened the asymmetries, and fostered the interpretation of them as unnecessary and changeable. In the end, most people realize that the attainment of their lofty goals and lifestyles is beyond reach, if they are to use legitimate means. The success in spreading neoliberalism has brought about a series of failures: more poverty, bigger economic asymmetries, ecosystem deterioration, slower and unsustainable growth patterns. At the time that societies most needed the shield of the state to cushion these effects, welfare programs, safety nets, and other assistance to the poor (individuals, companies, and states alike) forcibly declined or disappeared. Thus, global neoliberalism systematically causes relative deprivation as well as absolute immiseration of masses of people. In effect, it has generated new sources of criminogenesis and removed existing antidotes to it.

All this provides multiple motivations for criminality, as many would turn left and right for solutions and illicit opportunity structures become more international and accessible. At the same time, many weak states lose their autonomy, come to depend more on international organizations and transnational capital, and are unable to cope with emerging crime threats from criminal enterprises and powerful corporations. So, globalism and neoliberalism replace the "egalitarian discourse" of the American Dream in the scheme represented in Figure 1 in a process occurring in the industrialized world, developing countries, and those in transition from Communism to market democracies. Nowhere are these results more clearly visible than in the former USSR.

The Case of Russia

No one argues that there was no appetite for consumer goods in the years of the USSR or that such goods were widely available. Crime, corruption, illegal markets, and even underground factories could be found behind the official facade of the command system before *glasnost* and *perestroika*, although black marketers were not numerous and lived modestly. The government turned a blind eye to these activities, because they served as a safety valve in an inefficient system (Gleason, 1990; Handelman, 1995; Naylor, 1999b). Discontent, enormous structural problems, and an inability to deal with them characterized the pre-transition years. This is particularly true for the 1960s, when Khrushchev pledged that the USSR would overtake the U.S. in the production of industrial goods by the 1980s. Yet, as inefficiencies precluded such progress, demands for more consumer items "from an increasingly educated, by now self-assured, population, started to put pressure on government…as a loyal expression of the citizens' request for the gradual delivery of promised well-being" (Castells, 2000: 25).

In the 1990s, however, the rates of fraud, prostitution, drug trafficking and abuse, alcoholism, smuggling, white-collar crime, violence, and corruption skyrocketed (Castells, 2000; Handelman, 1995; Holmes, 1997; Lee, 1994; Shelley, 1994). To be sure, Russia is unique in the degree of chaos and disintegration that accompanied the transition to a market economy and the implementation of neoliberal reforms. Few countries have experienced the speed and intensity of privatization, deregulation, and the lack of political leadership and administrative skills we witness in Russia. Indeed, it is the closest we can come to a social state of anomie, without a total collapse and anarchy. This does not mean that Russia is atypical. Very similar, albeit less intense, processes have occurred throughout the world (Lee, 1999; Mander and Goldsmith, 1996; van Duyne et al., 2000). Nevertheless, precisely because it is such an extreme case, it illustrates the theoretical points made here and the process toward anomie and economic crime.

Enter Neoliberalism

In the 1985 to 1989 period, reforms took place while the Communist Party was still in control. The Law on Cooperatives (1986) and the Law on Individual Labor Activity (1987) paved the way for further reforms, such as legalization of small businesses in 1989. Between 1990 and 1991, the USSR Supreme Soviet, with Yeltsin as chairman, introduced laws that made state and private enterprises equal, allowed state companies relative independence from government managers, abolished most restrictions on property bought by citizens, promoted privatization, and allowed foreign companies to operate in Russia. Such reforms did not take place at the same pace throughout the USSR. This set Russia apart from the Union and Yeltsin from Gorbachev. Legal asymmetries made the task of law enforcers impossible, as they did not know which laws to prioritize and apply (Afanasyef, 1994). Up to the 1991 coup and the collapse of the USSR, reforms were cautious and gradual, and had not challenged the core of the command economy system. Following the failed coup and under Yeltsin, however, this changed dramatically. Demagogy and erroneous judgments on the feasibility of a swift transition to a market democracy compounded the problem. The Russian government was warned of the dire consequences of a speedy transition to a market economy without previous establishment of the necessary institutions and legal infrastructure. The chairman of an international advisory committee, which repeatedly issued warnings in 1992, was told that "forces in the Kremlin" favored a less "regulatory approach that would provide greater freedom of manoeuvre. Gaidar, supported by the IMF, believed firmly in the intrinsic capacity of market forces to remove obstacles by themselves, and people could use their vouchers to acquire shares" (Castells, 2000: 188). Prices were liberalized, imports and exports became free, domestic trade restrictions were abolished, government intervention was minimized, and public property was massively privatized. By June 1994, officials were self-congratulatory over the fact that 70% of state assets had passed into private hands (Kuznetsova, 1994).

New Normative and Comparative Referents

The reforms initiated by Andropov and Gorbachev (*perestroika* and *glasnost*) allowed some freedom of speech and openness that let globalization and media influences into the USSR. The post-1991 changes, however, offered new hope out of the severe problems people were facing. Russian leaders fostered heightened aspirations by declaring that the country would soon be modernized and join the "civilized world." Authorities in the former Soviet republics made the same promise, arguing that "'since we got rid of the Russians,' all obstacles to prosperity have been removed and Western standards are within reach" (Burbach et al., 1997: 118). There were forceful and impressive presentations of consumerist lifestyles as "desirable," "modern," and feasible. Distant comparative and normative referents were thus promoted by the media and advertising. Indeed, the yearning for Western lifestyles and consumption items made the initial acceptance of neoliberalism by the population much easier (*Ibid.*). Neoliberalism strengthened that desire and made consumerist dreams appear realistic. Even young Russians now would like to be like Mike and wear the same type of shoes or eat the same breakfast. As Glinkina (1994: 385) put it, an important factor contributing to the criminalization of the economy has been "a drastic stratification of the population's standard of living with a simultaneous loss, in a considerable part (especially among the youth), of socially important goals — replacing them with consumption ideals...."

It must be noted that the normative shift was far more radical in the former USSR and Eastern Europe than it was in Third World countries. The transition from socialism to capitalism by overzealous authorities espousing the new dogma of neoliberalism has had its own direct anomic effects, as will be seen below.

The Consequence: Means-Ends Discrepancies

The worldwide consequences of neoliberal policies were replicated in Russia. However, the effects have been far more disastrous than elsewhere: lower productivity, high unemployment, much steeper inequalities, increased levels of absolute poverty, disappearance of familiar safety nets, and administrations paralyzed by ineptness and corruption. The ensuing means-ends discrepancies are far more than a theoretical construct. They are painfully experienced by large numbers of people who realize that they simply cannot attain their goals. Within one year, inflation wiped out most people's life savings, while the buying power of most wages dropped to the level of the 1950s. In the winter of 1993, funds were often insufficient to heat residential buildings (Burbach et al., 1997; Handelman, 1993).

As a new bourgeoisie emerged from the ashes of the Communist regime, one-third of the population became impoverished. The gap between the rich and the poor opened up suddenly and grew out of proportion. Official data indicate that in 1994 the difference between them was elevenfold. Researchers argue that the difference between the top 10% and the bottom 10% is 28-fold (Kuznetsova, 1994). Even the chair of the Privatization Commission admitted that the process created "pauper-proprietors" who "cannot survive without state protection" (cited in Burbach et al., 1997: 120).

Relative and Absolute Deprivation

The rising expectations of the 1960s led to disenchantment with Communism and paved the way for radical social change. The abandonment of the Soviet conservative model and very rapid implementation of neoliberal policies fueled hopes that a much better future was within reach. Russians rejected rigid stratification and strove for a socially mobile ideal. As has been noted,

> [the middle classes] believed that capitalism could offer even more. Thus, the modernization that had been promised by the neoliberals was perceived by the majority of the population as the modernization of consumption.... The Western model of consumption has finally triumphed, at least in the main cities. But for the majority of the people, the price is that even the former Soviet way of life has become an unattainable dream (Burbach et al., 1997: 124).

The aspiring yuppies have ended up as "dumpies," while a growing polarization makes them see a few of their compatriots enjoy luxuries attained by looting the remnants of the former USSR.

Thus, the post-Soviet Russian dream turned out to be a nasty nightmare (Handelman, 1995). As happened in many other countries, austerity, belt tightening, and lower (in some cases, no) salaries were imposed as consumerism took hold. The impact of these experiences on personal feelings is much more widespread, intense, and unpleasant due to the higher expectations. Even people who are not objectively deprived now feel relatively deprived. Comparisons between their present and past situations are unfavorable: "Formerly privileged sections of the Russian population, such as teachers, doctors, miners, and workers in the oil and gas industry, went on strike, for they could no longer survive on 50 to 70 dollars per month salaries" (Burbach et al., 1997: 125–126).

East-West political and administrative asymmetries, economic asymmetries, and relative deprivation in the aftermath of the collapse of the USSR and disillusionment with Western policies and capitalism have been clearly crimino-genic (Handelman, 1994; Shelley, 1994). Motives for various types of crime became abundant, illegal opportunity structures multiplied, and control systems have been seriously damaged and undermined. The Mertonian category of "conformity" has almost become a rarity, as crime rates increased sharply. Even worse is the problem of economic crime. Recorded economic crimes rose almost 23% during the first seven months of 2000, compared with the same period in 1999 (Radio Free Europe/Radio Liberty, August 17, 2000). Strains and discontent have translated into a range of predatory misconduct, corruption, political violence, a variety of illegal markets, and expressive misconduct.

Search for Solutions and Anomie

In this context, many can be expected to "innovate," to employ illegal methods for survival or the satisfaction of their basic and newly acquired needs. Methods range from petty property crimes and prostitution to criminal enter-prises and white-collar crime, depending on the social position of the offender. An electronics engineer, for example, could not live on his three dollars per month and moonlighted as a taxi driver. When his taxi broke down, he turned to selling poppy straw (OGD, 1996). Unpaid and depressed professionals with access to more valuable commodities, such as nuclear material, pose an even more serious threat (Lee, 1999). Consumerist teasing increased demand for goods made unavailable (e.g., cars or electronics) by the economic collapse, fueling smug-gling operations, black market networks, and associated illegal enterprises. Shortages of other desired goods are artificially created by quickly adapting entrepreneurs.

Similar conditions outside Russia explain the illegal car trade between Eastern and Western Europe (van Duyne et al., 2000) and the illegal trade in various commodities between China and Hong Kong before unification (Vagg, 1992). In Russia, many took advantage of such supply-demand asymmetries, including the *vory v zakonye* (commonly described as "thieves in law"), who had been the dominant type of professional offenders in the USSR. Structural changes and globalization, however, brought about more competition from ethnic groups (Armenians, Azeris, Chechens, Georgians, etc.) in drugs and arms trafficking, as well as from loose and ad hoc associations of criminals in certain locations or industries. Unsettling reports assert a symbiotic relationship between criminal groups and active or retired intelligence officials. Deteriorating economic condi-tions have facilitated recruitment for employees in growing illegal markets.

Criminal enterprises, for instance, have "...invested heavily in the opium business, financing much of the new cultivation by hiring peasants and even entire villages to plant and protect the poppy crops" (Lee, 1994: 401).

Another source of criminal opportunities sprang from the disintegration of institutions and the disarray in law enforcement. Legitimate businesses are exposed to blackmail and other criminal victimization, but the authorities are unable to assist them. Consequently, many domestic and foreign companies deal with criminal groups and seek their protection, rather than rely on the government (Lee, 1994). Not surprisingly, the majority of Russian experts consider the strengthening of criminal groups to be a "very significant" social consequence of the market reforms introduced in 1992 (Afanasyef, 1994).

Other illicit opportunities were furnished by the privatization process, such as selling state assets at extremely low prices or driving down the prices of privatized companies so as to cheaply purchase vouchers owned by individuals desperate to make ends meet. Privatization in countries with an existing bourgeoisie and experienced managers and entrepreneurs facilitated certain corporate crimes and abuses of power by respected professionals. In Russia, the mix of offenders was different: former company directors, the *nomenklatura*, professional criminals, and new entrepreneurs with a black market background (Glinkina, 1994; Kuznetsova, 1994; Shelley, 1994). The attempt of former Communist officials to dominate this field did not prove lasting. Many were not competent to run private businesses and had to sell them or lose control. The main beneficiaries seem to be former black marketers and outsiders to the old order (Naylor, 1999b). The abuse of privatization has had an anomic effect as the impunity of offenders became widely known, to the point that Russians began to refer to privatization (*privatizatsiya*) as *prikhvatizatsiya*, which means "grabbing" (Handelman, 1995: 104).

Crime and corruption in the midst of privatization fervor are not unique to Russia. (On other previously Communist states, see Popescu-Birlan, 1994; on Latin America, see Saba and Manzetti, 1996–1997.) As a former World Bank official put it, "everything we did from 1983 onward was based upon our new sense of mission to have the south privatized or die; towards this end we ignominiously created economic bedlam in Latin America and Africa" (cited in Katona, 1999). Another similarity with other parts of the world is the degree of authoritarianism that accompanied neoliberal policies. While stimulating rapid accumulation of private capital, the role of the state is reduced to implementing financial austerity. When people started to oppose such measures, "Yeltsin resorted, with Western support, to establishing a semi-authoritarian regime. Making Russian 'reformers' invincible to political and legal challenges inside the country contributed to further criminalization of the Russian State, which acquired an oligarchic character" (Beare, 2000: 6). As similar processes occurred around the world, from Pinochet's Chile to Suharto's Indonesia, one wonders if such reforms would have been possible in a democracy.

Legal organizations also "innovate" by cutting corners and breaking the law due to the environment created by unsystematic legal reforms. Unable to navigate a sea of legal gaps and inconsistencies, "...most managers of private as well as state-owned enterprises cannot run their businesses without committing crimes" (Afanasyef, 1994: 437). Many companies cannot handle the competitive challenges generated by globalism and require state protection. The subsidization of privatized companies, however, introduces further regulatory and price asymmetries that foster the smuggling of goods across newly created borders within the former USSR (see below on nonferrous materials). Enterprises that do not enjoy state intervention are at a disadvantage and may be forced into bankruptcy or crime as a last resort. This is analogous to the situation in all countries that abolish trade barriers, let transnational corporations in, and eliminate preferential treatment for domestic industries.

High-level corruption and banking crimes have become quite common, as the networks of mobsters, financiers, businessmen, and high-level officials extend beyond Eurasia (Beare, 2000). The ongoing investigations into billions of dollars (possibly IMF-provided funds) laundered through the Bank of New York have expanded to include British, Swiss, and Italian entities and actors.

Moreover, pyramid schemes and other frauds have devastated gullible investors, as is the case with other post-Communist countries. Independent Oil, Lenin Trade and Financial Corporation, Aldzher (a security corporation), and other companies defrauded more than a million depositors and investors. Just as the Lincoln Savings and Loan frauds were committed in midst of obsessive deregulation in the U.S. against "the weak, the meek, and the old," Russian pensioners have been the main fraud victims (Glinkina, 1994).

Economic asymmetries among countries produce another set of criminal opportunities, as many become strongly motivated to flee the problem and search for a better future in the West, where the "goodies" are available. However, neoliberalism has promoted the free movement of everything but labor. Quotas and restrictions in promised lands generate demand for illegal services such as the smuggling of humans (Chin, 1999). This leads to opportunities for criminal exploitation, corruption, child/cheap labor, slavery, and forced prostitution.

Women, who are increasingly breadwinners but make up two-thirds of the newly unemployed in Russia, are even more vulnerable in this respect. Economic desperation drives many of them to prostitution or high risk taking. Lack of opportunity makes Russians and East Europeans softer targets for human traffickers. They are more likely to be lured to the West with promises of well-paying, respectable jobs only to end up blackmailed, beaten up, and forced into prostitution (Bruinsma, 1999; Shelley, 1994). The same problems faced by Thai, Mexican, and other women in the U.S. have led to a public hearing before the House Subcommittee on International Operations and Human Rights (September 14, 1999).

Relative deprivation and experience of injustice have a revolutionary potential too. International communications convey the message that injustice and inequality are avoidable. Events in one corner of the earth affect feelings and encourage people elsewhere to rebel against aggression. This may inspire change and foster rebellion. Just as the ideals of the French Revolution led to rebellions in the Balkans against the Ottoman rule (Hovannisian, 1994), the independence of the Baltic states and the U.N. response to Iraq's invasion of Kuwait inspired the East Timorese to fight against the Indonesian autocratic rule (Dunn, 1994). The uprising of Zapatistas in Mexico was deliberately started on January 1, 1994, the day NAFTA went into effect, "as a highly symbolic way to protest neoliberalism and globalisation in Mexico and Latin America" (Robinson, 1998-1999: 123–124).

Repressed nationalism, globalism, and bad times have jointly contributed to several armed conflicts and rebellions in the former USSR (the Caucasus, Moldova, Crimea, Tajikistan, and Chechnya). Rebellion and illegal markets become interconnected, as armed conflicts necessitate training, weapons, intelligence, and financing. The cases of Chechnya, Tajikistan, Afghanistan, and Colombia show how political revolts are associated with corruption, money laundering, the traffic in arms, drugs, and even nuclear material and other crimes that go unpunished (Kuznetsova, 1994: 445; Lee, 1999; Naylor, 1999b; OGD, 1996). Chechnya, which survives thanks to donations from criminal organizations based in other parts of Russia, has become such a paradise for these activities that some depict the war there as "a crusade against a 'mafia republic,'" while others think of it as "a conflict between opposing criminal elites for the control of oil and the financial resources held by the government in Grozny" (Politi, 1998: 44).

Finally, "retreatism" is the only option left to those lacking access to illegal opportunities or who are unwilling to assume the associated risks of violence and arrest. Hence, expressive crimes could be expected. More important, the rates of alcohol and drug abuse (further facilitated by the decriminalization of drug use in Russia in 1991) increased geometrically, especially in the cities, and fueled the demand for things provided in illegal markets (Lee, 1994; OGD, 1996).

Anomie

The transition from a command to a market economy practically legalized large parts of the black market and made legal business dependent on criminals' protection. The dismantling of borders and increased contact among previously isolated ethnic groups contributed to the formation of new, wider networks of illegality (Politi, 1998) The result was that one could hardly tell criminals from businessmen, particularly when some outlaw groups act on instructions from government officials or the police (Handelman, 1993). Given official efforts to ensure that the transition to a market economy would occur before substantial opposition could build and that the changes would be irreversible, too many shady actors were allowed to take advantage of this official shield (Glinkina, 1994; Naylor, 1999b). In this light, common views on government-criminal interfaces and symbiosis are plausible, although difficult to prove. Surveys in 1994 showed that the concern of Russians over organized crime was second only to their fears of triple-digit inflation (Afanasyef, 1994). At the perceptual level, therefore, this interface is real and has real consequences: demoralization and anomie.

The corrupted process of privatization has generated widespread rationalizations, such as, "it is OK to steal from the state" or "everyone is doing the same thing." Taking an example pointing to international security risks, Lee (1999: 21) has noted that, "perhaps the most serious problem is the growth of a privatization mentality within the nuclear complex. Economic reform has meant a license to steal. This has resulted in broad systemic corruption and a variety of insider threats and conspiracies."

An additional sign of anomie is what has been described as a "culture of urgency" among young killers:

> For them there is no hope in society, and everything, particularly politics and politicians, is rotten. Life itself has no meaning, and their life has no future.... So, only the moment counts, immediate consumption, good clothing, good life, on the run, together with the satisfaction of inducing fear, of feeling powerful with their guns (Castells, 2000: 210).

Only effective social controls can halt the process toward further deviance and a higher degree of anomie (deviance without strain). Unfortunately, in Russia and elsewhere, a decreased level of autonomy for certain states, the increased power of international organizations and transnational corporations, and dysnomie add to the fuel.

Dependence, Deregulation, and the Race to the Bottom

> "Just between you and me, shouldn't the World Bank be encouraging more migration of the dirty industries to the LDCs (lesser developed countries)?" "I think the economic logic behind dumping a load of toxic waste in the lowest wage country is impeccable and we should face up to that.... I've always thought that underpopulated countries in Africa are vastly under-polluted; their air quality is vastly inefficiently low compared to Los Angeles or Mexico City" (1991 memo attributed to World Bank official Lawrence Summers, who later became U.S. Secretary of Treasury; it is widely believed that he did not write it, even though he has accepted responsibility for it. At any rate, this illustrates the neoliberal mindset).

The loss of autonomy and reduced sovereignty of the state relative to capital referred to earlier (Korten, 1996; Watkins, 1997) is particularly acute in the former

Communist countries. Speculative capital will quickly flee each country at the first sign trouble or wavering over neoliberal reforms. External debt grew in all former Communist countries, but especially in Russia, which bears the marks of Africa-like dependent capitalism and "colonial subjugation. The country exports fewer and fewer industrial products and more and more raw materials. Meanwhile, it imports low-quality mass consumption goods, obsolete and hence cheap technology, luxury items and radioactive waste" (Burbach et al., 1997: 120–121). An instance of the direct and blatant interference of foreign governments and transnational corporations in domestic matters was when Chase Manhattan urged the Mexican government to crush the Zapatista rebellion to calm down U.S. investors (Silverstein and Cockburn, 1995; see also Clinard, 1990).

Ironically, the higher degree of dependency in the South and East has lowered the accountability of politicians and corporations. They can now blame globalization for the loss of jobs and lower wages, and prescribe more "efficiency," deregulation, short-term austerity, and declining levels of public spending so as to keep capital in place or attract more. Thus, economic and political leaders appear to be protectors of the public interest and a stabilizing force, while they dismantle existing safety nets (economic neoliberalism has also undermined political liberalism; Klak, 1998).

The Russian government's aversion to regulation (Glinkina, 1994) is observable in other countries, where deregulation turned into competitive deregulation and a race to the bottom. Even in the U.S., the savings and loan disaster and the asymmetric regulation of hazardous wastes demonstrate how criminogenic this process has been. This made it possible to dump legally in Pennsylvania what was prohibited in New Jersey, in what has been termed "crimes without law violations" (Passas, 1999). Such crimes are most likely in the global context given the overwhelming influence of TNCs over national laws and macroeconomic policies. This has prompted some to speak of "rationalized corporate colonialism" (Mander, 1996). Such asymmetries of power make for legal norms that allow overseas that which is, for good reason, criminalized in the base country (e.g., toxic waste dumping, testing drugs on humans, bribery, tax evasion, as well as the patenting of life forms by biotechnology companies and other outrageous practices) (see King and Stabinsky, 1998–1999; Shiva, 1997). The legal asymmetries and uneven power of transnational corporations that create or perpetuate these and other asymmetries give rise to crimes without law violations. Thus, entire countries become vulnerable to victimization by TNCs, a significant problem that is often neglected in conventional discussions of transnational crime. The volatile combination of low wages, bad working conditions, tax breaks only for the rich/corporations, lower environmental standards, deregulation, and less corporate and political accountability with the government relegated to the protection of the international free trade system has predictably made for crises (e.g., Korea, Malaysia, Indonesia, Mexico, and Brazil). It also makes for dysnomie.

Dysnomie and Further (Global) Anomie

Dysnomie literally means "difficulty to govern" and obtains when the following three conditions are present: a lack of a global norm-making mechanism,
inconsistent enforcement of existing international rules, and the existence of a
regulatory patchwork of diverse and conflicting legal traditions and practices.
Russia is in this respect a microcosm that reflects what is happening in the entire
world.

Since reforms took place at an uneven pace in each Soviet Republic, an
asymmetry grew wider following the collapse of the USSR. In addition, this
collapse suddenly created thousands of miles of new borders that had to be policed,
just as state resources were diminished. This made for porous borders that offered
no resistance to smugglers. This is how Estonia became the largest exporter of
nonferrous materials, even though it does not produce any (Glinkina, 1994).
Extensive legal changes accelerated the transition to a market economy, but they
were marked by inconsistencies and lacked the necessary legal and institutional
infrastructure (Handelman, 1995). For example, the law against private entrepre-
neurship and commercial mediations was repealed only on December 5, 1991. The
law against black market transactions, which defined them as "the buying up and
reselling of goods or other items for profit-making," was first amended in February
1990 to increase penalties for certain offenses, was then officially reinterpreted to
refer only to trade in commodities sold at state-fixed prices (October 1990), and
was finally repealed in February 1991 (Afanasyef, 1994: 429). Lack of resources
made the problem worse, as underpaid, ill-equipped, and outgunned police could
not be expected to do an effective job.

Weak controls allow criminals to get away and to regard themselves as
successful. Deviant "solutions" came to be seen as keys to "success." Successful
deviance then becomes a normative referent, contributing to a wider normative
breakdown and overemphasis on goals at the expense of normative means. In the
context of massive cultural shifts — from the criminalizing of private profit and
the hiring of labor outside the household to making them central values for a new
social order — the sense of right and wrong became fuzzy. As the deputy minister
of Internal Affairs admitted at a 1992 press conference, "even our specialists find
it difficult to determine the legal from the illegal — to determine, for instance, what
is profiteering and what is honest trade" (cited in Handelman, 1993). Corruption
grew so much that up to 30% of illegal gains are reportedly paid to government
officials (Glinkina, 1994; Lee, 1999). In the end, distinctions between white-collar
crime, organized crime, corruption, and legitimate business are almost impossible
to make. Lawbreaking behavior and success are fused. As a businessman told
Handelman (1995: 139), "the truth is, everything you see around you, all our
success, is not thanks to our wonderful economic laws. It's thanks to the fact that
we do not obey them."

Dysnomic conditions also bring about anomie at the global level. As argued elsewhere (Passas, 1999), international law is more essential now than ever for the maintenance of world order and security. Yet, big powers are reluctant to contribute to the required pooling of sovereignty and have been blocking the development of an international criminal code and specific legislation to restrain their corporations. Dependent on rich countries for its operations, the U.N. has not been overly aggressive in pursuing these aims or in establishing a permanent international criminal tribunal. Globalism has thus run ahead of the creation of a desperately needed normative and enforcement infrastructure.

Existing international laws are applied selectively and never against one of the permanent members of the U.N. Security Counsel. This ad hoc approach and the extraterritorial application of national laws undermine the legitimacy of current laws and procedures. We are left with a legal patchwork of inconsistent and conflicting rules. An example of the effect of such asymmetries is the secrecy and anonymity available in certain jurisdictions that hinder investigative work by covering the tracks and proceeds of global offenders, de facto shielding them against prosecution and punishment. By exploiting the cracks between diverse state rules, companies continually commit crimes without law violation. Globalism also leads to a relativization of norms and facilitates law violations with a clear conscience (rationalizations and techniques of neutralization).

Finally, the border-policing problem in the former USSR is not unique, even if the underlying causes were specific to it and other European countries (Yugoslavia, Czechoslovakia). More generally, borders become porous, as technology and mobility enabled people, money, goods, and ideas to travel quickly and cheaply. Criminals can take advantage of this shrinking world, but law enforcement agencies are constrained by parochial laws and procedures. Though the reasons for the porousness may differ, the process and results are the same.

Conclusion

Tremendous structural strains have overwhelmed even the usually patient and submissive Russians. The economic situation deteriorated further, hopes were dashed, opportunities for criminal gain and for looting the USSR's assets multiplied, and the anomic societal context offered no assistance to anyone seeking to restore some law and order. In Russia and around the world, the neoliberal operation was successful, but the patients are being systematically frustrated, are starving, and subject to exploitation by corporations, criminal enterprises, and corrupt politicians. In short, globalization and neoliberalism spread analytically similar criminogenic processes that were once unique to the U.S. culture of the American Dream in a context of structural inequalities. Just as the world supposedly became freer, wealthier, more democratic, more enjoyable, and more equal, people find themselves poorer, more exploited, and facing increased hardships. Just as the need for strong normative guidance grows, norms break down or lose their legitimacy. Just as effective controls become necessary to slow down or stop the vicious cycle leading to higher rates of crime, a dysnomic regulatory patchwork remains in place largely because of nationalist insistence on sovereignty and states' unwillingness to allow the introduction of common principles and law enforcement mechanisms.

Two main points need to be reiterated here. First, it appears that global neoliberalism and serious crime go hand in hand. However, it would be erroneous to argue that stereotypical organized criminals are giving capitalism a bad name and undermining neoliberal policies. The implication is that, were we to rid ourselves of some very bad apples, everything would be fine. Rather, it appears that serious organizational misconduct is a consequence of such policies. Second, when we discuss transnational crime, we should bear in mind that it is not just the stereotyped ethnics who cause most problems. It may be that the biggest threat emanates from legitimate corporations and other organizations.

Detailed discussion of policy implications is beyond the scope of this article. The horizontal arrows in Figure 1 hint at the points of possible policy intervention. Myriad concrete ideas can be found in the literature, ranging from legal changes to informal controls, grass-roots movements, integration of economic growth with environmental and social protection, relocalization of production and consumption, etc. The most important ray of hope, however, is implicit in the foregoing analysis. Neoliberal policies and globalization are largely the fruit of (some) governments. They affect and are affected by governance. Therefore, governments have the ability to reverse some of these processes and to mitigate their adverse consequences. Otherwise, the current processes of globalization and neoliberalism will prove to be unsustainable and at a huge cost.

Figure 1:
Social Processes Leading to Anomie and Deviance

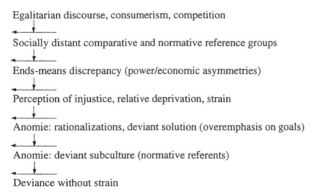

Egalitarian discourse, consumerism, competition

Socially distant comparative and normative reference groups

Ends-means discrepancy (power/economic asymmetries)

Perception of injustice, relative deprivation, strain

Anomie: rationalizations, deviant solution (overemphasis on goals)

Anomie: deviant subculture (normative referents)

Deviance without strain

The horizontal lines point to policy implications. This is where interventions can be attempted in order to block this process and prevent misbehavior. In the context of neoliberal globalism, they represent criminogenic influences.

REFERENCES

Afanasyef, V.
1994   "Organized Crime and Society." *Demokratizatsiya* 2,3: 426–441.
Alesina, A. and D. Rodrik
1994   "Distributive Politics and Economic Growth." *Quarterly Journal of Econom-ics* 109,2: 465–490.
Andreas, P.
1999   "Smuggling Wars: Law Enforcement and Law Evasion in a Changing World." T. Farer (ed.), *Transnational Crime in the Americas*. London: Routledge: 85–98.
1997   "The Rise of the American Crimefare State." *World Policy Journal* 14,3: 37–45.
Aubert, V.
1968   "White-Collar Crime and Social Structure." G. Geis (ed.), *White-Collar Criminal: The Offender in Business and the Professions*. New York: Atherton Press: 173–184.
Barnet, R.J. and J. Cavanagh
1994   *Global Dreams: Imperial Corporations and the New World Order*. New York: Simon and Schuster.
Beare, M.
2000   "Russian (East European) Organized Crime Around the Globe." Paper presented at the "Transnational Crime Conference," organized by the Australian Institute of Criminology, Australian Customs Service, and Australian Federal Police, Canberra.
Bello, W.
1999   "Is the 'Structural Adjustment' Approach Really and Truly Dead?" *BusinessWorld, Internet Edition* (November 8), downloaded from Internet site http://www.bworld.com.ph/current/today.html.
1996   "Structural Adjustment Programs: 'Success' for Whom?" J. Mander and E. Goldsmith (eds.), *The Case Against the Global Economy*. San Francisco: Sierra Club Books: 285–293.
Bruinsma, G.J.N. and G. Meershoek
1999   "Organized Crime and Trafficking in Women from Eastern Europe in the Netherlands." *Transnational Organized Crime* 4: 105–118.
Burbach, R., O. Núñez, and B. Kagarlitsky
1997   *Globalization and Its Discontents*. London: Pluto Press.
Castells, M.
2000   *End of Millennium* (2nd ed.). Oxford: Blackwell.
Center for Investigative Reporting and B. Moyers
1990   *Global Dumping Ground: The International Traffic in Hazardous Waste*. Washington, D.C.: Seven Locks Press.
Chin, K.L.
1999   *Smuggled Chinese: Clandestine Immigration to the United States*. Philadel-phia: Temple University Press.
Clinard, M.B.
1990   *Corporate Corruption: The Abuse of Power*. New York: Praeger.
Cox, R.W.
1993   "Structural Issues of Global Governance: Implications for Europe." S. Gill (ed.), *Gramsci, Historical Materialism, and International Relations*. Cambridge: Cambridge University Press.
Critharis, M.
1990   "Third World Nations Are Down in the Dumps: The Exportation of Hazardous Waste." *Brooklyn Journal of International Law* 6,2: 311–339.

Dunn, J.
    1994   "East Timor: A Case of Cultural Genocide?" G.J. Andreopoulos (ed.),
                    Genocide: Conceptual and Historical Dimensions. Philadelphia: University of
                    Pennsylvania Press: 171–190.
Durkheim, E.
    1983   *Le Suicide*. Paris: Presses Universitaires de France. (Originally published
                    1930.)
Gambetta, D.
    1993   *The Sicilian Mafia*. Cambridge: Harvard University Press.
Giddens, A.
    1990   *The Consequences of Modernity*. Cambridge: Polity.
Gilpin, R.
    1987   *The Political Economy of International Relations*. Princeton: Princeton
                    University Press.
Gleason, G.
    1990   "Nationalism or Organized Crime? The Case of the 'Cotton Scandal' in the
                    USSR." *Corruption and Reform* 5: 87–108.
Glinkina, S.P.
    1994   "*Privatizatsiya* and *Kriminalizatsiya*: How Organized Crime Is Hijacking
                    Privatization." *Demokratizatsiya* 2,3: 385–391.
Handelman, S.
    1995   *Comrade Criminal*. New Haven: Yale University Press.
    1994   "The Russian 'Mafiya.'" *Foreign Affairs* 73,2: 83-96.
    1993   "Why Capitalism and the Mafia May Mean Business." *The New York Times*
                    (January 24).
Hirst, P. and G. Thompson
    1996   *Globalisation in Question: The International Economy and the Possibilities of
                    Governance*. Cambridge: Polity.
Holmes, L.
    1997   "Corruption and the Crisis in the Post-Communist State." *Crime, Law, and
                    Social Change* 27: 275–297.
Hovannisian, R.G.
    1994   "Etiology and Sequelae of the Armenian Genocide." G.J. Andreopoulos (ed.),
                    Genocide: Conceptual and Historical Dimensions. Philadelphia: University of
                    Pennsylvania Press: 111–140.
ICFTU (International Confederation of Free Trade Unions)
    2000   *Globalising Social Justice: Trade Unionism in the 21st Century*. Durban:
                    ICFTU.
Katona, D.
    1999   "Challenging the Global Structure Through Self-Determination: An African
                    Perspective." *American University International Law Review* 14: 1439–1472.
Keohane, R.O. and J.S. Nye
    2000   "Globalization: What's New? What's Not? (And So What?)." *Foreign Policy*
                    118: 104–119.
King, J. and D. Stabinsky
    1998-99   "Biotechnology Under Globalisation: The Corporate Expropriation of Plant,
                    Animal, and Microbial Species." *Race and Class* 40,2–3: 73-89.
Klak, T.
    1998   "Thirteen Theses on Globalization and Neoliberalism." T. Klak (ed.),
                    Globalization and Neoliberalism. Lanham, MD: Rowman and Littlefield: 3–
                    23.
Klak, T. and G. Myers
    1998   "How States Sell Their Countries and Their People." T. Klak (ed.), *Globaliza-
                    tion and Neoliberalism*. Lanham, MD: Rowman and Littlefield: 87–109.

Korten, D.C.
    1996   "The Failures of Bretton Woods." J. Mander and E. Goldsmith (eds.), *The
                    Case Against the Global Economy.* San Francisco: Sierra Club Books: 20–30.
    1995   *When Corporations Rule the World.* West Hartford, CT: Kumarian Press.
Krasner, S.D.
    1985   *Structural Conflict: The Third World Against Global Liberalism.* Berkeley:
                    California University Press.
Kuznetsova, R.W.L.F.
    1994   "Crime in Russia: Causes and Prevention." *Demokratizatsiya* 2,3: 442–452.
Lee, R.W.
    1999   "Transnational Organized Crime: An Overview." T. Farer (ed.), *Transnational
                    Crime in the Americas.* London: Routledge: 1–38.
    1994   "The Organized Crime Morass in the Former Soviet Union." *Demokratizatsiya*
                    2,3: 392–411.
Levy, F.
    1998   *The New Dollars and Dreams: American Incomes and Economic Change.*
                    New York: Russell Sage Foundation.
Mander, J.
    1996   "Facing the Rising Tide." J. Mander and E. Goldsmith (eds.), *The Case
                    Against the Global Economy.* San Francisco: Sierra Club Books: 3–19.
Mander, J. and E. Goldsmith (eds.)
    1996   *The Case Against the Global Economy.* San Francisco: Sierra Club Books.
McGrew, T.
    1992   "A Global Society?" S. Hall, D. Held, and T. McGrew (eds.), *Modernity and
                    Its Futures.* Cambridge: Open University Press: 62–102.
Merton, R.K.
    1968   *Social Theory and Social Structure.* New York: The Free Press.
Messner, S.F. and R. Rosenfeld
    1994   *Crime and the American Dream.* Belmont, CA: Wadsworth.
Minda, G.
    2000   "Book Review: The Globalization of Culture." *Colorado Law Review* 71:
                    589–643.
Myers, W.H.
    1995–1996   "The Emerging Threat of Transnational Organized Crime from the East."
                    Crime, Law, and Social Change 24,3: 181–222.
Naylor, R.T.
    1999a   "Wash-out: A Critique of Follow-the-Money Methods in Crime Control
                    Policy." *Crime, Law, and Social Change* 32,1: 1–57.
    1999b   *Patriots and Profiteers: On Economic Warfare, Embargo Busting, and State-
                    Sponsored Crime.* Toronto: McClelland and Stewart.
    1995   "From Cold War to Crime War: The Search for a New 'National Security'
                    Threat." *Transnational Organized Crime* 1,4: 37–56.
Norberg-Hodge, H.
    1996   "The Pressure to Modernize and Globalize." J. Mander and E. Goldsmith
                    (eds.), *The Case Against the Global Economy.* San Francisco: Sierra Club
                    Books: 33–46.
OGD, Observatoire Géopolitique des Drogues
    1996   *The Geopolitics of Drugs.* Boston: Northeastern University Press.
Oman, C.
    1999   "Globalization, Regionalization, and Inequality." Ngaire Woods and A.
                    Hurrell (eds.), *Inequality, Globalization, and World Politics.* Oxford: Oxford
                    University Press: 36–65.
Paine, L.P. and F.J. Cilluffo (eds.)
    1994   *Global Organized Crime: The New Empire of Evil.* Washington, D.C.: CSIS.

Passas, N.
    1999   "Globalization, Criminogenic Asymmetries, and Economic Crime." *European Journal of Law Reform* 1,4: 399–423.
    1998   "Transnational Crime: The Interface Between Legal and Illegal Actors." Presented at the National Research Council Workshop on "Transnational Organized Crime." Washington, D.C.
    1997   "Anomie, Reference Groups, and Relative Deprivation." N. Passas and R. Agnew (eds.), *The Future of the Anomie Tradition*. Boston: Northeastern University Press: 62–94.
    1994   "The Market for Gods and Services: Religion, Commerce, and Deviance." *Religion and Social Order* 4: 217–241.
    1990   "Anomie and Corporate Deviance." *Contemporary Crises* 14,3: 157–178.
Passas, N. and J. Blum
    1998   "Intelligence Services and Undercover Operations: The Case of Euromac." S. Field and C. Pelser (eds.), *Invading the Private? Accountability and the New Policing in Europe*. Aldershot: Dartmouth.
Passas, N. and R.B. Groskin
    1995   "International Undercover Operations." G. Marx and C. Fijnaut (eds.), *Undercover: Police Surveillance in Comparative Perspective*. Amsterdam: Kluwer: 291–312.
Politi, A.
    1998   "Russian Organised Crime and European Security." E.U. Directorate-General for External Relations (ed.), *Illicit Trade and Organised Crime: New Threats to Economic Security?* Luxembourg: European Communities: 31–57.
Popescu-Birlan, L.
    1994   "Privatization and Corruption in Romania." *Crime, Law, and Social Change* 21,4: 375–379.
Robinson, W.I.
    1998–1999   "Latin America and Global Capitalism." *Race and Class* 40,2–3: 111–131.
Rosenau, J.
    1990   *Turbulence in World Politics*. Brighton: Harvester Wheatsheaf.
Saba, R.P. and L. Manzetti
    1996–1997   "Privatization in Argentina: The Implications for Corruption." *Crime, Law, and Social Change* 25,4: 353–369.
Scheper-Hughes, N.
    2000   "The Global Traffic in Human Organs." *Current Anthropology* 41,2: available on the Internet at http://www.journals.uchicago.edu/CA/journal/issues/v41n2/002001/002001.html.
Shelley, L.
    1995   "Transnational Crime: An Imminent Threat to the Nation-State?" *Journal of International Affairs* 48,2: 463–489.
    1994   "Post-Soviet Organized Crime." *Demokratizatsiya* 2,3: 341–358.
Shiva, V.
    1997   *Biopiracy: The Plunder of Nature and Knowledge*. Boston: South End Press.
Silverstein, K. and A. Cockburn
    1995   "Major U.S. Bank Urges Zapatista Wipe-Out: 'A Litmus Test for Mexico's Stability.'" *Counterpunch* 2,3.
Sklair, L.
    1995   *Sociology of the Global System* (2nd ed.). New York and London: Prentice Hall and Harvester Wheatsheaf.
Stewart, F. and A. Berry
    1999   "Globalization, Liberalization, and Inequality: Expectations and Experience." Ngaire Woods and A. Hurrell (eds.), *Inequality, Globalization, and World Politics*. Oxford: Oxford University Press: 150–186.

44   PASSAS

Sykes, G.M. and D. Matza
    1957   "Techniques of Neutralization: A Theory of Delinquency." *American Sociological Review* 22,6: 664–670.
UNDP (United Nations Development Programme)
    2000   *Poverty Report*. New York: Oxford University Press.
    1998   *Human Development Report: Consumption for Human Development*. New York: United Nations.
Vagg, J.
    1992   "The Borders of Crime." *British Journal of Criminology* 32,3: 310–328.
van Duyne, P.C., V. Ruggiero, M. Scheinost, and W. Valkenburg (eds.).
    2000   *Cross-Border Crime in a Changing Europe*. Tilburg and Prague: Tilburg University and Prague Institute of Criminology and Social Prevention.
Wallerstein, I.
    1983   *Historical Capitalism*. London: Verso.
Watkins, K.
    1997   *Globalisation and Liberalisation: Implications for Poverty, Distribution, and Inequality*. Occasional Paper 32: U.N. Development Program.
Williams, P.
    1994   "Transnational Criminal Organisations and International Security." *Survival* 36,1: 96–113.
Wilterdink, N.
    1995   "Increasing Income Inequality and Wealth Concentration in the Prosperous Societies of the West." *Studies in Comparative International Development* 30,3: 3–23.
Woods, N.
    1999   "Order, Globalization, and Inequality in World Politics." Ngaire Woods and A. Hurrell (eds.), *Inequality, Globalization, and World Politics*. Oxford: Oxford University Press: 8–35.
Yergin, D. and J. Stanislaw
    1998   *The Commanding Heights: The Battle Between Government and the Marketplace That Is Remaking the Modern World*. New York: Simon and Schuster.

Part VII
Institutional-Anomie Theory

Political Restraint of the Market and Levels of Criminal Homicide: A Cross-National Application of Institutional-Anomie Theory *

STEVEN F. MESSNER, *University at Albany, SUNY*
RICHARD ROSENFELD, *University of Missouri — St. Louis*

Abstract

This article examines the effects on national homicide rates of political efforts to insulate personal well-being from market forces. Drawing upon recent work by Esping-Andersen and the institutional-anomie theory of crime, we hypothesize that levels of homicide will vary inversely with the "decommodification of labor." We develop a measure of decommodification based on levels and patterns of welfare expenditures and include this measure in a multivariate, cross-national analysis of homicide rates. The results support our hypothesis and lend credibility to the institutional-anomie perspective. The degree of decommodification is negatively related to homicide rates, net of controls for other characteristics of nations.

Interest in explaining differences among nations in rates of crime and violence is as old as the sociology of crime itself. The quantitative measurement of these differences by the nineteenth-century moral statisticians Quetelet and Guerry marks the beginning of scientific criminological inquiry (Beirne 1993). Marx also refers to national crime data in the course of developing his critique of the inherent flaws of capitalism. "There must be something rotten in the very core of a social system," Marx (1859) writes, "which increases its wealth without diminishing its misery, and increases in crimes even more rapidly than in numbers" (*New York Daily Tribune*).

In recent decades, there has been a resurgence of interest in cross-national criminological inquiry as reflected in a growing body of literature on the structural determinants of homicide rates.[1] Although there are some

Presented at the 46th annual meeting of the American Society of Criminology, 9-12 November, 1994, Miami, FL. We are grateful to the anonymous referees for helpful comments on an earlier draft of this manuscript. Direct correspondence to Steven F. Messner, Department of Sociology, SUNY-Albany, Albany, NY 12222.

1394 / *Social Forces* 75:4, June 1997

discrepancies in this literature, the research is supportive of Marx's general suspicion that fundamental features of the economic system affect societal levels of crime. A finding that has emerged with remarkable consistency is that high rates of homicide tend to accompany high levels of inequality in the distribution of income (Krahn, Hartnagel & Gartrell 1986; Neuman & Berger 1988). The cross-national research also indicates that there are additional features of a society's political economy, beyond that of income dispersion, that are systematically related to homicide rates. For example, evidence suggests that levels of homicide are associated with measures of the degree of economic discrimination against social groups (Messner 1989) and measures of the generosity of social welfare policies (Fiala & LaFree 1988; Gartner 1990, 1991).

The present article explores further the relationship between basic features of the economic and political systems of societies and levels of criminal homicide. Our specific focus is on the role of the market as a mechanism for distributing the material resources for personal well-being. Markets play a vital role in all capitalist societies, but, in some of these, physical survival and social position are not as dependent on market considerations as in others. Esping-Andersen (1990) has recently used the concept of the "decommodification of labor" to refer to policies that promote reliance on, or insulation from, pure market forces, and he has developed techniques for measuring this concept for a small sample of advanced capitalist nations. In this research, we build upon Esping-Andersen's work and propose a proxy measure of the decommodification of labor that can be used in multivariate analyses for a reasonably large sample of nations. We link the decommodification of labor specifically with crime by drawing upon a recently proposed macrosocial perspective in criminology: institutional-anomie theory. Our basic hypothesis is that homicide rates and decommodification vary inversely: the higher the level of political protection from the vicissitudes of the market, the lower the national homicide rate.

Decommodification and Crime in Market Society

Esping-Andersen's work on decommodification is part of a long standing intellectual and political tradition that emphasizes the importance of the welfare state in stabilizing market societies (e.g., Bellah et al. 1992; Marshall 1950; Polanyi 1944; Tawney 1920). Decommodification refers in the most general sense to the empowerment of the citizenry against the forces of the market. Decommodified social policies permit actions and choices by citizens — to get married, have children, seek higher education, engage in political activity — that are, in principle, unconstrained by market considerations. Decommodification frees people from the market.

There is some irony in this conception of the interrelation between the market and the state. In the classical writings of Enlightenment thinkers such as Adam Smith and David Hume, markets are depicted as social arrangements that liberate individuals from the restraints imposed by traditional institutions: the "free market" is an arena for the unfettered pursuit of self-interest (see Hirschman 1992). That the market itself impedes the exercise of free choice is a key intellectual claim of Marxist and social-democratic critics of modern capitalism. That citizens possess social rights and entitlements that transcend market considerations is the principal institutional claim made on the modern capitalist economy by the welfare state (Marshall 1950).

The basic issue of accommodating the market to the functioning of other social institutions is also relevant to the concerns of modernization theorists. In Parsons's (1966) influential formulation, modernization entails the increasing differentiation and interdependence of institutional subsystems. The decommodification policies of the welfare state can be viewed from this perspective as an equilibrating mechanism in highly differentiated societies.[2] In general, the concept of decommodification has been highly useful in attempts to understand the institutional functioning of modern market societies.

In Esping-Andersen's usage, decommodification refers to the granting of services and resources to citizens as a matter of right, thereby reducing their reliance on the market for sustenance and support (1990). It entails "emancipation" of citizens from the market in the most fundamental sense: "citizens can freely, and without potential loss of job, income, or general welfare, opt out of work when they themselves consider it necessary" (23). Decommodification involves considerably more than a society's level of expenditure on social welfare policies and programs. It reflects the quality as well as the quantity of social rights and entitlements. Three essential dimensions of entitlements are encompassed by decommodification: ease of access to them, their income-replacement value, and the range of social statuses and conditions they cover (Esping-Andersen 1990).

It is useful to think of a continuum of decommodified social policies along which societies may be arrayed. Near one end would be societies with highly decommodified policies, defined by nearly universal and nonconditional entitlements, with benefit levels close to average market incomes[3], covering most or all of the relevant causes and conditions for assistance (e.g., sickness, old age, unemployment, parenthood). Societies located near the other end would display correspondingly weaker decommodification, reflected in strict eligibility criteria for assistance, benefit levels well below prevailing market incomes, and a narrow range of statuses and conditions meriting assistance. At the extremes, fully decommodified policies would pay everyone a "social wage" guaranteeing a socially acceptable level of earnings regardless of market participation, and fully "commodified" policies would require strict and complete dependence on the market for the resources necessary for survival. Although no existing society can be found at either of the ideal-typical extremes of the continuum, market societies are enormously variable with respect to the level and types of social assistance available to their populations and the associated degree of decommodification.

Esping-Andersen does not relate the notion of decommodification directly to the phenomenon of crime. However, Messner and Rosenfeld's institutional-anomie perspective provides a plausible theoretical basis for predicting a relationship between the levels of serious crime in market society and the extent to which labor has been decommodified.

Institutional-anomie theory builds upon the classical anomie tradition, attributing high levels of crime to interrelated cultural and structural dynamics (Messner & Rosenfeld 1997; Rosenfeld & Messner 1994; cf. Chamlin & Cochran 1995). With respect to culture, a basic premise of the theory is that market mechanisms and arrangements are conducive to anomic pressures. Markets presuppose a materialistic goal-orientation among actors, and they promote a calculating, utilitarian orientation towards social relationships (Hirschman 1992:139). When these orientations develop to an extreme degree, anomie in the Mertonian sense is likely to ensue (Merton 1968). Goals — especially, but not exclusively, materialistic ones — receive strong cultural support, whereas the normative means regulating conduct begin to lose "their savor and their force" (Merton 1964:226). In such an anomic environment, actors are preoccupied with "outcomes" (Merton 1968:211), and the efficiency rather than the legitimacy of the means governs behavior. The resulting attenuation of normative controls is likely to lead to high levels of deviant behavior, including crime.[4]

Institutional-anomie theory also assigns a critical role to structural dynamics and, more specifically, to the balance among major social institutions (e.g., the economy, the family, the polity). In all societies of any complexity, the integration of social institutions is inherently problematic. This is because the claims of the social roles associated with the respective institutions are potentially contradictory and competing. For example, the demands and value-orientations associated with economic roles are at times incompatible with those of familial roles. The resolution of these conflicting claims in the course of ongoing social interaction yields a distinctive pattern of institutional relationships for the society at large — a distinctive "institutional balance of power" (Messner & Rosenfeld 1997:68-79).

According to institutional-anomie theory, the form of institutional structure that is particularly conducive to high levels of crime is one in which the economy dominates the institutional balance of power.[5] Economic dominance occurs when: (1) economic goals are assigned high priority in comparison with noneconomic goals; (2) the claims of economic roles are typically honored at the expense of those of noneconomic roles when conflicts occur; (3) social standing tends to be more highly dependent on the performance of economic roles than of noneconomic roles; and (4) the calculating, utilitarian logic of the marketplace penetrates other institutional realms.[6]

Economic dominance leads, in turn, to high rates of crime via two complementary processes. First, this type of institutional imbalance provides fertile soil for the growth of the anomic cultural pressures associated with market arrangements. This is because the noneconomic institutions that bear primary responsibility for cultivating respect for social norms, such as families and schools, are less capable of fulfilling their distinctive socialization functions. Second, economic dominance weakens the external social controls associated with institutional attachments. When the economy dominates the institutional balance of power, noneconomic roles become relatively unattractive. The result is relatively tenuous institutional engagement, weak social control, and high rates of crime.

This concept of economic dominance in the institutional balance of power, we propose, can be joined with Esping-Andersen's notion of decommodification to derive a hypothesis about societal levels of crime. As noted above, decommodification signals that the balance of institutional power in market society has shifted from the economy toward the polity; it implies that purely economic values and criteria are accommodated to collective, political considerations. The market is not permitted to operate according to its inherent logic alone but rather is subjected to political restraints. In other words, the decommodification of labor can serve as an indicator of one important dimension of the institutional balance of power — the balance between the economy and the polity. A greater degree of decommodification indicates a lower level of economic dominance in this particular institutional interrelationship. Given the general logic of institutional-anomie theory, then, the decommodification of labor should vary inversely with societal levels of crime, including the most serious of crimes — homicide.

We are aware of no previous efforts to join institutional-anomie theory with the concept of decommodification in the analysis of cross-national variation in homicide rates. Nevertheless, there is evidence consistent with our basic hypothesis. Fiala & LaFree (1988) find that measures of welfare expenditures are inversely related to child homicide rates in a cross-sectional analysis of 39 developed countries. Research by Gartner (1990) indicates that these beneficial effects of welfare policies apply to homicide victimization more generally. In a pooled, cross-sectional time-series analysis of 18 capitalist societies observed at five-year intervals between 1950-80, Gartner discovers significant negative effects of indicators of welfare spending on homicide rates for all age-sex-specific groups. Finally, Pampel and Gartner (1995) have examined the effects of a scale of "collectivism" on homicide rates in a cross-national analysis of the same 18 advanced capitalist societies studied by Gartner. The collectivism scale combines Esping-Andersen's decommodification index with indicators of corporatism, consensus government, Leftist political rule, and "governability" (the absence of violent political conflict). The collectivism scale has negative main effects on homicide rates, and it reduces the positive effect of the relative size of the youthful population on annual changes in homicide rates.

1398 / *Social Forces* 75:4, June 1997

These studies lend plausibility to our general hypothesis, but they are limited in important respects. As noted, the research by Fiala & LaFree (1988) is restricted to child homicide (see also Gartner 1991), while the results of the research by Gartner (1990) and Pampel & Gartner (1995) pertain only to the experiences of the 18 most advanced capitalist nations (albeit with observations for multiple time periods). The present study goes beyond these earlier efforts by developing a theoretically grounded measure of decommodification that can be employed in a multivariate analysis of overall homicide rates for a reasonably large sample of contemporary nations.

Before describing our measure of decommodification, it is important to confront a key conceptual issue. Esping-Anderson (1990) explicitly focuses his analyses on "advanced" nations and, more specifically, on the "advanced capitalist democracies" (1-2). He does so because these are the nations with the economic and political capacity to achieve a high degree of decommodification. The advanced capitalist democracies have sufficiently large economic surpluses to enable appreciable segments of the population to withdraw from the market, and they have political structures that are conducive to the emergence of class coalitions supportive of decommodification.

A legitimate question to raise, therefore, is whether the very concept of decommodification can be applied to a heterogeneous sample of nations at very different levels of development. We base our analysis on the assumption that decommodification is a meaningful property with which to describe industrial and industrializing nations in general because the provision of basic social security is a concern in virtually all such societies. This assumption is consistent with the underlying rationale for the comparative data sets on social transfers published by the International Labour Office (ILO), which serve as the source for our proxy measure of decommodification. The ILO observes that social security has become an important feature of the economy for member states in "nearly every country" (ILO 1992:3). To assess the applicability of decommodification to industrial nations generally, we have examined whether the effects of our decommodification measure on homicide rates differ significantly for the 18 nation subsample studied by Esping-Andersen and the remaining subsample of nations. As reported below, comparable effects are observed across these subsamples, which is consistent with our assumption that the concept of decommodification can be usefully applied to lesser-developed nations as well as to the advanced capitalist democracies.

Data and Methods

MEASURING DECOMMODIFICATION

Esping-Andersen's measure of decommodification encompasses three primary dimensions of the underlying concept: the ease of access to welfare

Institutional-Anomie Theory / 1399

benefits, their income-replacement value, and the expansiveness of coverage across different statuses and circumstances. A complex scoring system is used to operationalize each of these dimensions of decommodification for the three most important social welfare programs: pensions, sickness benefits, and unemployment compensation (1990). This scoring system reflects the "prohibitiveness" of conditions for eligibility, the disincentives for and duration of entitlements, and the degree to which benefits replace normal levels of earnings (1990). The indices for these three types of social welfare programs are then aggregated into a combined index reflecting the overall decommodification characteristic of a given nation's social welfare system.

Esping-Andersen is able to operationalize decommodification in this unique way by using highly detailed information on social policies from an original data source — the Svensk Socialpolitik i International Bleysning (the SSIB data files). The data were collected at the Swedish Institute for Social Research over an eight-year period, beginning in 1981, through contacts with numerous officials in government departments and statistical offices in different nations (1990). Although Esping-Andersen's approach to measuring decommodification is highly appealing from a theoretical standpoint, his measure has been constructed for only 18 capitalist nations. The explanatory scope using this measure will therefore apply to only the most highly developed market societies, and the small size of the resulting sample will seriously limit the possibilities for including decommodification in multivariate statistical analyses. Moreover, the procedures employed by Esping-Andersen to construct his index require data on social policies that are not available in published sources.

To overcome these limitations, we have developed a proxy measure of decommodification for an appreciably larger sample of nations (maximum $N = 45$). The proxy measure is based on data compiled by the International Labor Office (ILO) on the financial operations of national social security systems. These data include information on absolute and relative levels of expenditures for social security programs, on funding sources for these programs, and on the distribution of the expenditures across different program types (e.g., unemployment benefits, family allowances, work-related injuries). Our approach is based on the assumption that general expenditure patterns reflect the underlying logic of social welfare systems. Consequently, indicators of these general patterns are likely to be correlated with the more refined and theoretically informed measure of decommodification developed by Esping-Andersen.

We have examined the relationships between Esping-Andersen's decommodification index and a variety of indicators of social security expenditures in the 1980s for the 18 advanced capitalist nations included in the SSIB data files. The indicators encompass four important features of the social security systems: (1) the priority given to social welfare spending, as reflected in expenditures as a percent of total gross domestic product (ILO 1992, Table 3); (2) the generosity of social welfare spending, as reflected in

1400 / *Social Forces* **75:4, June 1997**

average annual expenditures per head of population in U.S. dollars (Table 5); (3) the financing of social security systems, as reflected in the percentage of total receipts according to origin (Table 8); and (4) the range of entitlements, as reflected in the percentage distribution of benefit expenditures across different program types (Table 10).[7]

Esping-Andersen's decommodification index is strongly associated with three of the indicators of expenditure patterns. Expenditure levels as a percent of GDP and average annual expenditures per capita exhibit large positive correlations with the decommodification index (.75 and .81, respectively). An indicator of the distribution of expenditures across program types — the percent of total benefit expenditures allocated to employment injuries — also yields a sizeable correlation with the decommodification index: $r = .-.67$. The negative sign of this coefficient is theoretically meaningful because it implies that a large share of welfare benefits is not available to all citizens as a basic entitlement but, rather, is contingent on participation in the labor market. Only employed workers can receive benefits for employment injuries. Welfare systems that impose this type of restriction on access are therefore less decommodifying than those covering a wider range of circumstances independent of market participation (e.g., programs such as family allowances and maternity benefits).

Analogous results are obtained in a principal components factor analysis of the decommodification index and the full range of expenditure indicators. The decommodification index, average annual benefits per household, expenditures as a percent of GDP, and the percent of benefit expenditures allocated to employment injuries all load highly on the same factor. These four measures thus exhibit a high level of shared variance, suggesting that they converge on a common, underlying dimension.[8]

Given these results, we have computed a proxy decommodification index by summing the z-scores for the three indicators of expenditure patterns that are highly intercorrelated with Esping-Andersen's index and that cluster along the same dimension.[9] The resulting composite index is highly correlated with Esping-Andersen's original decommodification measure: $r = .84$. Our proxy measure thus exhibits strong predictive validity for the 18 nations with data from the Swedish data source, the SSIB.

It is possible to compute the decommodification proxy measure for a fairly large sample of nations (a maximum of 55) using ILO (1992) data for the mid-1980s. The presence of missing data on other variables (explained below) limits the sample size for the analysis to 45 cases. The proxy measure of decommodification yields a respectable level of reliability for this sample: alpha coefficient = .702.

DEPENDENT VARIABLE

The dependent variable for the analysis is the homicide rate per 100,000 population as reported in the World Health Organization's (WHO) *World*

Institutional-Anomie Theory / 1401

Health Statistics Annual (various years). WHO defines homicide as death by injury purposely inflicted by others. One limitation of the WHO data on homicide is that underdeveloped nations, especially those in Africa and Asia, are not well represented in this data source (Krahn, Hartnagel & Gartrell 1986). Therefore caution should be exercised in generalizing our findings to the larger population of nations. In addition, the WHO data on homicide may be biased because they necessarily exclude deaths with undetermined cause, some of which may be homicides. Nevertheless, Kalish (1988) argues that the WHO data serve as the best source of information on homicide for international comparisons because they are "based on an actual count of deceased persons" and therefore are not susceptible to biases resulting from intercountry differences in the treatment of "attempted homicides."[10]

To minimize the effect of random yearly fluctuations in homicide levels, we follow the conventional practice of computing multi-year averages (Kick & LaFree 1985; Krahn, Hartnagel & Gartrell 1986). The averages refer to the 1980-90 period, or in cases with missing data, to the subset of years within that period for which data are available. We employ an extended time period for measuring homicide (a maximum of 11 years) because decommodification is conceptualized as a basic structural feature of societies that is not likely to vary in a meaningful way over the short run.

Examination of the univariate distribution for homicide rates reveals considerable skewness. The value for the highest nation (Colombia, 41.2) is approximately 6.5 times the mean value for the sample at large (6.27). We accordingly convert homicide rates to natural logarithms to reduce skewness and induce homogeneity in error variance.[11] Although the log transformation successfully reduces the overall degree of skewness in the homicide distribution, a possible outlier remains at the lower tail of the distribution. The logged value for Syria (-3.00; untransformed value = .05) is considerably smaller than the value for the nation (Egypt) with the next smallest value (-.38; untransformed value = .69). The possibility that this case is an atypical one that distorts the regression estimates is addressed in the statistical analysis.

CONTROL VARIABLES

Data have also been collected on additional characteristics of nations to serve as controls. Previous comparative research on homicide typically includes some combination of indicators of the general economic well-being of national populations and of demographic structure (see LaFree & Kick 1986, and Neuman & Berger 1988, for comprehensive reviews). Consistent with this research, we have collected information on the following socioeconomic and demographic characteristics of nations:[12] gross national product per capita in U.S. dollars; infant mortality rate (under age 1); life expectancy at birth; percent of the population over 64 years of age; average annual population growth 1980-85; percent of the population urban; males per 100 females.

1402 / Social Forces 75:4, June 1997

GNP per capita and the sex ratio are logged transformed to reduce the effect of cases with extreme values. With the exception of the measure of population growth, the time of measurement for these socioeconomic and demographic characteristics is 1985, the midpoint of the 1980-90 period, or the closest year with available data. The sources for the sex ratio and percent over 64 years of age are the Population Reference Bureau's (1987) *Population Data Sheet* and United Nations' (various years) *Demographic Yearbook*. The other measures are taken from the World Bank's (1987) *World Development Report*.

In the comparative homicide literature, age structure is typically measured by an indicator of the relative size of the young population. This approach is based on the assumption that the young population is at a relatively high risk of offending (see Krahn, Hartnagel & Gartrell 1986). We employ a measure of the relative size of the elderly population because this variable has been identified as a key determinant of welfare expenditures (Wilensky 1975; see also Pampel, Williamson & Stryker 1990), and because the elderly are likely to have low homicide offending rates (thereby creating the possibility of spuriousness in the bivariate relationship between homicide rates and social welfare measures). Not surprisingly, measures of the youthful population and the elderly population are strongly correlated. The correlation between percent less than 15 years of age and the percent over 64 for the sample of 45 nations is -.90. Thus, the results of our regression analyses are highly similar if the former measure of age structure is substituted for the latter.

Several of the control variables are strongly intercorrelated. To simplify the regressor space and lessen the problem of multicollinearity (Land, McCall & Cohen 1990), a principal components analysis has been performed on these socioeconomic and demographic variables. The results reveal that all the measures except the sex ratio cluster along a single dimension (the eigenvalue for the principal component is 4.2, and the variance explained is 71%). The positive pole of this dimension reflects socioeconomic development, as indicated by high life expectancy, high GNP/capita, low infant mortality, relatively large elderly populations, slow population growth, and high levels of urban development. These measures have been combined into a "development index" using the loadings from the principal components analysis as weights.

Two additional variables are also relevant to the analysis on both empirical and theoretical grounds. As noted earlier, previous cross-national research indicates that economic inequality is one of the more important structural correlates of homicide rates. It seems likely that decommodification and economic inequality are inversely related to one another. Decommodification should reduce the dispersion in incomes as well as lessen reliance on the market for economic well-being. However, to the degree that decommodified social welfare practices reflect the broader balance of power between the polity and the economy, as suggested by institutional-anomie theory, decommodification is expected to have an effect on the level of crime independent of its relationship with inequality.

FIGURE 1: Scatterplot of Homicide Rates and Decommodification Scores for Esping Andersen's 18 Nation Sample

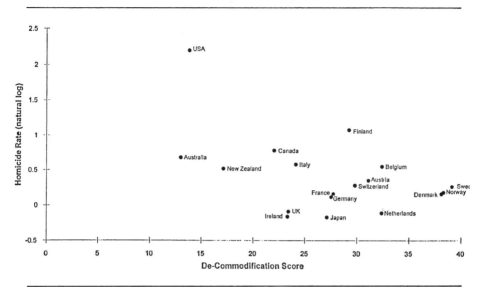

We include two measures of economic inequality. One is the commonly used Gini coefficient of household income distribution. The primary data source for this measure is Hoover (1989), supplemented in a few cases with data from Krahn, Hartnagel & Gartrell (1986). Unfortunately, the available data for the Gini coefficient of income inequality refer to the period "circa 1969" (Hoover 1989), which is earlier than our time period of interest (1980-90). Although income distribution is a reasonably stable feature of societies (Muller 1988), the measurement error associated with this time lag could attenuate the effects of income inequality in our analyses.

The second measure reflects an ascriptive form of economic inequality: economic discrimination against social groups. The specific measure is an ordinal rating scale based on expert judgments about the extent to which groups experience objective economic disadvantages that are attributable to deliberate discrimination. A nation's score represents the most extreme level of economic discrimination experienced by any minority group in that nation. The economic discrimination index is based on information contained in the "Minorities at Risk" data file compiled by Gurr (Gurr & Scarritt 1989).

Data for all variables except the Gini coefficient and economic discrimination are available for the maximum sample of 45 nations (see Appendix A). In the analysis of this sample, mean substitution is applied to cases with missing data on the two measures of economic inequality. We also conduct parallel analyses on the subsample of nations with complete data across all variables to assess the sensitivity of the results to mean substitution.

1404 / *Social Forces* 75:4, June 1997

TABLE 1: OLS Regressions of the Average Homicide Rate, 1980-90, on the Proxy Decommodification Index and Controls

Independent variable	Equation			
	1	2	3	4
Development index	-.104*	-.017	-.097*	-.097*
	[-.342]	[-.057]	[-.355]	[-.363]
Gini coefficient of	3.802	3.274	1.474	1.432
income inequality	[.246]	[.212]	[.108]	[.108]
Economic discrimination	.213*	.172	.151*	.146
index	[.226]	[.182]	[.180]	[.176]
Sex ratio (ln)	-5.709*	-5.754*	-5.509*	-5.551
	[-.248]	[-.250]	[-.268]	[-.157]
Decommodification index	—	-.209*	-.161*	-.161*
		[-.386]	[-.334]	[-.337]
R^2	.357	.402	.547	.548
Adjusted R^2	.293	.326	.487	.480
N	45	45	44	39

[a] Standardized regression coefficients are reported in brackets. Homicide rates are log (ln) transformed.
* Unstandardized regression coefficient is at least 1.5 times its standard error.

Results

Before turning to the multivariate analysis of homicide rates for the full sample of nations, it is instructive to examine the bivariate relationship between levels of homicide and Esping-Andersen's original decommodification index for the 18 advanced capitalist nations with available data. As expected, the Pearson correlation coefficient is inverse and statistically significant at the .05 level despite the small sample: $r = -.48$.[13] Nations with greater decommodification scores thus tend to have lower homicide rates.

Figure 1 presents the scatterplot for these two variables. A striking feature of the scatterplot is the distinctiveness of the U.S. Even with homicide rates expressed in natural logarithms, the rate for the U.S. is unusually high. The U.S. also has a very low decommodification score (the second from the bottom), suggesting that this case plays a major role in producing the observed inverse association.[14] It is thus important to determine whether decommodification exhibits the predicted association with homicide rates in a larger sample of nations not as sensitive to the influence of any single case.

Institutional-Anomie Theory / 1405

The bivariate relationship between the decommodification proxy measure and homicide rates for the sample of 45 nations is highly similar to that observed with the original measure in the smaller 18-nation sample: $r = -.52$ (see Appendix B). Of course, the nations in this larger sample are quite heterogeneous, raising the possibility that at least some of the simple association between decommodification and homicide is confounded with the effects of other structural characteristics of nations.

To assess this possibility, we turn to the multivariate analyses. Table 1 reports the estimates from four multiple regressions. The first column of the table provides a baseline model that includes only the control variables. Consistent with past research (Krahn, Hartnagel & Gartrell 1986; Messner 1989), the two indicators of economic inequality — the Gini coefficient of income dispersion and the index of economic discrimination against social groups — yield moderate positive effects on homicide rates, although the coefficient for the Gini coefficient does not quite reach statistical significance. Both the development index and the sex ratio are negatively related to homicide rates. The negative coefficient for development is consistent with the "modernization thesis" on crime, which predicts a decline in rates of violent crime with greater urbanization and industrialization (Gurr 1989; Shelley 1981). This finding is similarly compatible with arguments that development is associated with reduced opportunities for the kinds of interpersonal contacts that lead to homicide (LaFree & Kick 1986). In addition, the negative effect of development probably reflects demographic factors captured by the composite index (an elderly population and low population- growth rates).

The negative association observed for the sex ratio is counter-intuitive. It indicates that low homicide rates tend to be found in nations with large numbers of males relative to females. This association is contrary to individual-level research on criminal violence, which shows higher levels of victimization and offending for males, but it is compatible with arguments by Messner & Sampson (1991). They suggest that low sex ratios may promote family arrangements that are conducive to crime and that counterbalance the crime-reducing compositional effect at the macro-level of relatively small male populations.

In equation 2, the decommodification proxy index is added to the baseline model. The results are consistent with theoretical predictions. Decommodification exhibits a significant, negative relationship with homicide rates net of the control variables. The standardized coefficient ($B = -.386$) is moderately strong and is the largest for any of the predictors in this model.[15] Comparing across equations 1 and 2, including the decommodification measure in the model reduces slightly the effect of the Gini coefficient and the economic discrimination index, while the coefficient for the sex ratio remains virtually unchanged. The most dramatic change is observed for the development index, the effects of which become trivial in equation 2.

Equation 3 estimates the same model as equation 2 for the subsample of 44 nations without Syria, an outlier on homicide. Excluding this case raises

1406 / *Social Forces* 75:4, June 1997

TABLE 2: Effects of the Proxy Decommodification Index on the Average
Homicide Rate, 1980-90, across Alternative Specifications

	Sample[a]		
Model	A	B	C
1. Excluding the development index	-.227* [-.419]	-.258* [-.535]	-.232* [-.487]
2. Excluding the Gini coefficient	-.225* [-.414]	-.166* [-.345]	-.159* [-.333]
3. Excluding the economic discrimination index	-.240* [-.443]	-.187* [-.387]	-.187* [-.392]
4. Excluding the sex ratio (ln)	-.208* [-.383]	-.160* [-.331]	-.175* [-.367]
N	45	44	39

[a] Standardized regression coefficients are reported in brackets. Homicide rates are log (ln) transformed.

[b] Sample A is the maximum sample yielded with mean substitution for income inequality and economic discrimination; sample B excludes Syria; sample C is the sample yielded with listwise deletion of cases with missing values.

* Unstandardized regression coefficient is at least 1.5 times its standard error.

the explanatory power of the model appreciably (compare the adjusted R^2s) and increases the observed effect of the development index in comparison with the previous model. The effect for the decommodification index is lessened slightly in equation 3 in comparison with equation 2, but it remains significant and moderately strong.

In the final equation (equation 4), the analysis is repeated without mean substitution, which is required in the analysis of the larger samples for cases with missing values on the Gini coefficient and the economic discrimination index. The results for the theoretically strategic measure prove to be very similar to those in the previous equations. Nations with high scores on the decommodification index tend to have low homicide rates, net of the effects of the other variables in the models.[16]

To assess further the sensitivity of the effects of the decommodification proxy to alternative specifications, we re-estimate the regressions deleting each of the control variables, one at a time. These analyses are performed on the full sample of nations, the subsample without Syria, and the subsample without mean substitution. Table 2 reports the regression coefficients for the decommodification proxy across these alternative specifications for the respective samples. The results reveal a highly robust pattern. Consistent with our theoretical argument, the coefficients for decommodification are negative, significant, and moderately strong in all specifications.

Our findings for other predictors of homicide are less stable, as shown in Table 1, although the overall patterns of relationships are theoretically meaningful. The instability in the estimates for the development index may reflect problems of multicollinearity. Despite our efforts to simplify the covariance structure of predictors through principal components indexing, a troublesome degree of multicollinearity remains for this variable.[17] We also suspect that the rather unimpressive effects of income inequality are attributable, at least in part, to measurement error (noted earlier) resulting from the time lag between the measurement of inequality and homicide rates.

Finally, we consider the possibility that the observed effect of decommodification applies only to the nations originally studied by Esping-Andersen and not to other nations in the sample. We do so by creating a dummy variable coded 1 for nations in Esping-Andersen's sample and 0 for the other nations, and by constructing a product term for this dummy variable and the decommodification proxy. The product term is then added to the regression models for each of the three samples reported in Table 1, along with the constituent terms. In all cases, the coefficients for the product term fail to attain statistical significance. This finding suggests that the net effect of decommodification on homicide rates for the nations originally studied by Esping-Andersen is comparable to the effect observed for the other nations in the analysis.

SUMMARY AND CONCLUSIONS

In this article, we have addressed the consequences of political restraints on the market for societal levels of lethal violence. Drawing upon recent work on the nature of welfare state regimes, the institutional-anomie theory of crime, and previous cross-national analyses of homicide, we have derived a specific hypothesis that overall levels of homicide will be lower in capitalist societies that have decommodified labor by reducing dependence on the market for personal well-being. This hypothesis has been tested in cross-national regression analyses using a theoretically grounded measure of decommodification, along with relevant controls.

The results support our basic hypothesis. Controlling for a wide range of other structural characteristics of nations, the decommodification measure exhibits a significant negative effect on homicide rates. This effect is moderately strong and is robust across alternative specifications and varying subsamples. Our analyses thus replicate the findings of previous cross-national studies of homicide that have incorporated measures of social welfare spending, and they indicate that these earlier findings are generalizable to larger samples of nations and to more inclusive measures of homicide.

Our research also lends credibility to the theoretical perspective informing the analysis — the institutional-anomie theory of crime — and helps to empirically distinguish this perspective from more conventional stratification-based accounts of variation across societies in the level of homicide. Although these perspectives are in many respects complementary, there are two important distinctions between them.

First, institutional-anomie theory broadens the *structural* focus of traditional economic stress or deprivation perspectives by directing attention to aspects of the economic organization of market societies beyond the stratification system, and to the interplay of the economy and other social institutions. In this article, we have restricted our attention to restraints imposed on market economies by the political system. Additional research is needed on the role of other institutions, such as the kinship, religious, and educational systems, in fostering or curbing crime in market societies. Such an expanded institutional focus might help to account for nations such as Japan and Ireland, which have exceptionally low levels of homicide among the developed countries, and yet only moderate scores on the decommodification index (see Figure 1). In the case of Japan, we would attribute the low rate of homicide to the prominent role of the family and its restraining influence on the anomic forces emanating from the market (cf. Adler 1983). It would seem promising to pursue in further research the corresponding role of organized religion in a nation such as Ireland.

A second difference between institutional-anomie theory and more traditional economic perspectives on societal levels of crime involves the significance assigned by institutional-anomie theory to *cultural* orientations, which ostensibly operate in tandem with features of economic stratification. It is not possible to document any such cultural effects with the existing data because valid and reliable measures of culture are not available for cross-national analysis, but it is interesting to note that our development index captures to some extent levels of economically induced deprivation via the indicators of overall economic resources (GDP/capita) and life chances (infant mortality and life expectancy). The effects of decommodification on homicide rates net of the development index are thus at least suggestive of the kinds of cultural dynamics postulated by institutional-anomie theory.[18] Nevertheless, further research is clearly needed to clarify the precise nature of the social mechanisms linking the welfare state, institutional balance, and levels of crime and violence in market societies.

We close with a final comment on the practical implications of our analysis. It is hardly an exaggeration to claim that the current era is one of profound social change in the history of capitalism. With the fall of the Soviet empire and with the economic reforms taking place in the People's Republic of China, a much larger segment of the world's population is exposed to market arrangements. Moreover, in the U.S. and other advanced capitalist societies, there have been growing concerns about the scope, cost, and even the very logic of the welfare state (e.g., Stevenson 1995; Whitney 1995). If the findings reported here are sustained in subsequent research, then proposals to substantially reduce social welfare spending and deregulate market

Institutional-Anomie Theory / 1409

economies should be considered with due regard for unintended social consequences, including possibly higher rates of criminal violence.

Notes

1. See, for example, Archer & Gartner (1984); Avison & Loring (1986); Braithwaite & Braithwaite (1980); Conklin & Simpson (1985); Fiala & LaFree (1988); Gartner (1990); Groves, McCleary & Newman (1985); Kick & LaFree (1985); Krahn, Hartnagel & Gartrell (1986); Krohn (1976); LaFree & Kick (1986); Messner (1980, 1982, 1989); and Wellford (1974).

2. From a more critical perspective, the function of the welfare state is to stabilize the capitalist economic order and legitimate class rule (Habermas 1989; O'Connor 1973). See Esping-Andersen (1990:12-14) for a discussion of the similarities between structural functionalist and Marxist approaches to the modernization process.

3. Esping-Andersen (1990) defines the market replacement value of social entitlements as the difference between benefit levels and "normal earnings or the standard of living considered adequate and acceptable in the society" (47).

4. Merton directs attention to the contemporary U.S. in his discussion of the nature and sources of anomie, as do Messner and Rosenfeld (1997) in their discussion. However, as Gouldner (1970) suggests, Merton's arguments (and by extension Messner and Rosenfeld's) can be applied more generally to societies dominated by a market economy, i.e., to "bourgeois utilitarian societies." In Gouldner's words: "The 'almost exclusive concern with outcomes' to which Merton refers is a distinctive characteristic of utilitarian culture; it is not an aberration of utilitarian society but its normal cultural emphasis" (1970:68; see also Rosenfeld & Messner 1997).

5. Messner and Rosenfeld's discussion of economic dominance in the institutional balance of power raises themes similar to those contained in Currie's analysis of a "market society" as distinct from a "market economy." According to Currie (1991:255), a market society refers to "one in which the pursuit of private gain becomes the organizing principle of all areas of social life — not simply a mechanism that we may use to accomplish certain circumscribed economic ends."

6. John Gagnon comments on the general tendency in market societies for the logic of the economy to permeate discourse over an ever widening range of social phenomena, both inside and outside academic social science: "Within the social sciences there has been a 100-year struggle to extend the reach of economic metaphors and analyses to include all aspects of mental and social life. Outside the social sciences, in practical society, a parallel attempt to subject all forms of conduct to the discipline of commodification and pricing has become part of the normal order" (Gagnon 1994:1078).

7. The categories for the origin of social security receipts are: contributions from insured persons, contributions from employers, special taxes, state participation, other public participation, income from capital, and "other" receipts. The categories for the distribution of benefits are: sickness-maternity, employment injuries, pensions, unemployment, and family allowances.

8. The factor loadings for the decommodification index, average annual benefits per household, expenditures as a percent of GDP, and the percent of benefit expenditures allocated to employment injuries are .90, .86, .82, and -.82 respectively. Although these loadings are reasonably high, some unshared variance obviously remains. This probably reflects the limitations of expenditure data as indicators of the "theoretical substance of

the welfare state," as well as random measurement error. See Esping-Andersen (1990:18-21).

9. In the construction of the index, we reverse the polarity of the item on the distribution of benefits by using the percentage of benefits distributed to categories other than employment injuries (i.e., 100 — "the percent distributed to employment injuries"). This ensures that all items are scored in a consistent direction.

10. See Bennett and Lynch (1990), Huang (1993), Kalish (1988), and Messner (1992) for discussions of the quality and comparability of international crime statistics.

11. We plotted the residuals from an OLS regression of the untransformed homicide rate against predicted Y values. The scatterplot conforms to a classic heteroskedastic "fan" pattern, with greater variance in residuals for higher predicted Y values (Hamilton 1992:117). The plot for residuals with the transformed homicide rates reveals a more homoskedastic distribution. The transformation of homicide rates implies that the modeled relationship between homicide and other variables is curvilinear with respect to the original metrics. For a discussion of the interpretation of regression coefficients under different transformations, see Hamilton (1992:145-82).

12. Three additional controls were considered in preliminary analyses but were excluded because they consistently failed to yield appreciable net associations with homicide rates: population size, population density, and Gurr's institutionalized democracy index (ICPSR 1990).

13. Although tests of statistical significance are not technically applicable given the nonrandom nature of the sample, we nevertheless follow the common practice of reporting significance as a rule-of-thumb to identify nontrivial relationships. The criterion for significance in the regression analysis is a t ratio of 1.5, which corresponds approximately to the .05 level (one-tailed test).

14. With the U.S. removed from the sample, the correlation between the homicide rate and decommodification score drops to $r = -.25$. Although still in the expected direction and moderately strong, this correlation is not statistically significant for the remaining 17 nation sample. The outlier status of the U.S. in the homicide distribution depicted in Figure 1 is consistent with the hypothesis derived from institutional-anomie theory that a society characterized by economic dominance will have unusually high levels of serious crime. See Messner and Rosenfeld (1997). More generally, the proposition that the U.S. is distinctive on a number of social and cultural dimensions when compared with other advanced industrial nations is part of the thesis of "American exceptionalism." See Lipset (1996) for a recent statement.

15. In this larger sample of nations, removing the U.S. has a minor impact on the observed relationship between the decommodification proxy and homicide rates. The association is still moderately inverse and statistically significant. The unstandardized regression coefficient without the U.S. is -.200; the B coefficient is -.361.

16. We computed values of Cook's D for each of the three subsamples in Table 1 to search for influential cases in the estimation of regression parameters. No case reaches the generally accepted critical value of "1" on this diagnostic statistic. As a further check for a disproportionate impact of a single case or a small number of cases on the parameter estimates, we performed a robust regression on the full sample using the Huber iteratively reweighted least squares technique (Hamilton 1992:183-216). The robust WLS results for the decommodification index are virtually identical to those obtained through OLS: the unstandardized coefficients are -.217 and -.209, respectively.

Institutional-Anomie Theory / 1411

17. Appendix C reports variance inflation factors (VIF) for the independent variables in the analyses of the respective samples. The values for the development index in all instances exceed the conventional threshold for high multicollinearity of 4.0. This problem is particularly severe in the analysis of the 39 nation sample without mean substitution. The VIFs for the decommodification proxy, however, are always below the conventional criterion.

18. Similarly, in her analysis of the relationships between family structure, welfare expenditures, and child homicide, Gartner (1991) proposes a broader interpretation of indicators of welfare practices, suggesting that "perhaps spending on social programs should be thought of as an indicator of a cultural orientation or social ideology inhibiting personal violence" (238).

References

Adler, Freda. 1983. *Nations Not Obsessed with Crime*. Rothman.

Archer, Dane, and Rosemary Gartner. 1984. *Violence and Crime in Cross-National Perspective*. Yale University Press.

Avison, William R. and Pamela L. Loring. 1986. "Population Diversity and Cross-National Homicide: The Effects of Inequality and Heterogeneity." *Criminology* 24:733-49.

Beirne, Piers. 1993. *Inventing Criminology*. SUNY Press.

Bellah, Robert N., Richard Madsen, William M. Sullivan, Ann Swidler, and Steven M. Tipton. 1992. *The Good Society*. Knopf.

Bennett, Richard R. and James P. Lynch. 1990. "Does Difference Make a Difference? Comparing Cross-National Crime Indicators." *Criminology* 28:153-81.

Braithwaite, John and V. Braithwaite. 1980. "The Effect of Income Inequality and Social Democracy on Homicide." *British Journal of Criminology* 20:45-53.

Chamlin, Mitchell B. and John K. Cochran. 1995. "Assessing Messner and Rosenfeld's Institutional Anomie Theory: A Partial Test." *Criminology* 33:411-29.

Conklin, George H. and Miles E. Simpson. 1985. "A Demographic Approach to the Cross-National Study of Homicide." *Comparative Social Research* 8:171-85.

Currie, Elliot. 1991. "Crime in the Market Society." *Dissent* (Spring):254-59.

Esping-Andersen, Gosta. 1990. *The Three Worlds of Welfare Capitalism*. Princeton University Press.

Fiala, Robert and Gary LaFree. 1988. "Cross-National Determinants of Child Homicide." *American Sociological Review* 53:432-45.

Gagnon, John H. 1994. "Review Essay: The Dismal Science and Sex." *American Journal of Sociology* 99:1078-82.

Gartner, Rosemary. 1990. "The Victims of Homicide: A Temporal and Cross-National Comparison." *American Sociological Review* 55:92-106.

____. 1991. "Family Structure, Welfare Spending, and Child Homicide in Developed Democracies." *Journal of Marriage and the Family* 53:231-40.

Gouldner, Alvin W. 1970. *The Coming Crisis of Western Sociology*. Basic Books.

Groves, W. Byron, Richard McCleary, and Graeme R. Newman. 1985. "Religion, Modernization, and World Crime." *Comparative Social Research* 8:59-78.

Gurr, Ted Robert. 1989. "Historical Trends in Violent Crime: Europe and the United States." Pp. 21-54 in *Violence in America*. Vol. 1, edited by T.R. Gurr. Sage.

Gurr, Ted Robert, and James R. Scarritt. 1989. "Minorities at Risk: A Global Study." *Human Rights Quarterly* 11:375-405.

1412 / *Social Forces* 75:4, June 1997

Habermas, Jurgen. 1989. "The Crisis of the Welfare State and the Exhaustion of Utopian Energies." Pp. 284-99 in *Jurgen Habermas On Society and Politics: A Reader*, edited by Steven Seidman. Beacon Press.

Hamilton, Lawrence C. 1992. *Regression with Graphics: A Second Course in Statistics*. Duxbury Press.

Hirschman, Albert O. 1992. *Rival Views of Market Society and Other Recent Essays*. Harvard University Press.

Hoover, Gary A. 1989. "International Inequality: A Cross-National Data Set." *Social Forces* 67:1008-26.

Huang, W.S. Wilson. 1993. "Are International Murder Data Valid and Reliable? Some Evidence to Support the Use of Interpol Data." *International Journal of Comparative and Applied Criminal Justice* 17:77-89.

ICPSR. 1990. "Polity II: Political Structure and Regime Change, 1800-1986: Summary." *Inter-University Consortium for Political and Social Research*, Machine-Readable Datafile (Study #9263; Principal Investigator: Ted Robert Gurr).

ILO (International Labour Office). 1992. *The Cost of Social Security*. International Labour Office.

Kalish, Carol B. 1988. *International Crime Rates*. U.S. Department of Justice.

Kick, Edward L., and Gary D. LaFree. 1985. "Development and the Social Context of Murder." *Comparative Social Research* 8:37-58.

Krahn, Harvey, Timothy F. Hartnagel, and John W. Gartrell. 1986. "Income Inequality and Homicide Rates: Cross-National Data and Criminological Theories." *Criminology* 24:269-95.

Krohn, Marvin D. 1976. "Inequality, Unemployment, and Crime: A Cross-National Analysis." *Sociological Quarterly* 17:303-313.

LaFree, Gary D., and Edward L. Kick. 1986. "Cross-National Effects of Developmental, Distributional, and Demographic Variables on Crime: A Review and Analysis." *International Annals of Criminology* 24:213-35.

Land, Kenneth C., Patricia L. McCall, and Lawrence E. Cohen. 1990. "Structural Covariates of Homicide Rates: Are There Any Invariances Across Time and Social Space?" *American Journal of Sociology* 95:922-63.

Lipset, Seymour Martin. 1996. *American Exceptionalism: A Double-Edged Sword*. Norton.

Marshall, T.H. 1950. *Citizenship and Social Class*. Cambridge University Press.

Marx, Karl. 1859. "Europe: Population, Crime, and Pauperism." *New York Daily Tribune* (16 Sept.).

Merton, Robert K. 1964. "Anomie, Anomia, and Social Interation." Pp. 213-42 in Anomie and Deviant Behavior, edited by Marshall Clinard. Free Press.

_____. 1968. *Social Theory and Social Structure*. Free Press.

Messner, Steven F. 1980. "Income Inequality and Murder Rates: Some Cross-National Findings." *Comparative Social Research* 3:185-98.

_____. 1982. "Societal Development, Social Equality, and Homicide: A Cross-National Test of a Durkheimian Model." *Social Forces* 61:225-40.

_____. 1989. "Economic Discrimination and Societal Homicide Rates: Further Evidence on the Cost of Inequality." *American Sociological Review* 54:597-611.

_____. 1992. "Exploring the Consequences of Erratic Data Reporting for Cross-National Research on Homicide." *Journal of Quantitative Criminology* 8:155-73.

Institutional-Anomie Theory / 1413

Messner, Steven F., and Robert J. Sampson. 1991. "The Sex Ratio, Family Disruption, and Rates of Violent Crime: The Paradox of Demographic Structure." *Social Forces* 69:693-713.

Messner, Steven F., and Richard Rosenfeld. 1997. *Crime and the American Dream*. 2d ed. Wadsworth.

Muller, Edward N. 1988. "Democracy, Economic Development, and Income Inequality." *American Sociological Review* 53:50-68.

Neuman, W. Lawrence, and Ronald J. Berger. 1988. "Competing Perspectives on Cross-National Crime: An Evaluation of Theory and Evidence." *Sociological Quarterly* 29:281-313.

O'Connor, James. 1973. *The Fiscal Crisis of the State*. St. Martin's Press.

Pampel, Fred, and Rosemary Gartner. 1995. "Age Structure, Socio-political Institutions, and National Homicide Rates." *European Sociological Review* 11:243-60.

Pampel, Fred, John B. Williamson, and Robin Stryker. 1990. "Class Context and Pension Response to Demographic Structure in Advanced Industrial Democracies." *Social Problems* 37:535-50.

Parsons, Talcott. 1966. *Societies: Evolutionary and Comparative Perspectives*. Prentice-Hall.

Polanyi, Karl. 1944. *The Great Transformation*. Rinehart.

Population Reference Bureau. Various years. *World Population Data Sheet*. Population Reference Bureau.

Rosenfeld, Richard, and Steven F. Messner. 1994. "Crime and the American Dream: An Institutional Analysis." *Advances in Criminological Theory* 6:81-103.

____. 1997. "Markets, Morality, and an Institutional-Anomie Theory of Crime." In *The Future of Anomie Theory*, edited by Nikkos Passas and Robert Agnew. Northeastern University Press.

Shelley, Louise I. 1981. *Crime and Modernization*. Southern Illinois University Press.

Stevenson, Richard W. 1995. "A Deficit Reins in Sweden's Welfare State." *New York Times* (2 Feb.), A1, A5.

Tawney, R.H. 1920. *The Acquisitive Society*. Harcourt Brace.

United Nations. Various years. *Demographic Yearbook*. United Nations Publishing Service.

Wellford, Charles F. 1974. "Crime and the Dimensions of Nations." *International Journal of Criminology and Penology* 2:1-10.

Whitney, Craig R. 1995. "In Europe, Touches of Leanness and Meanness." *New York Times* (1 January), p. E5.

Wilensky, Harold L. 1975. *The Welfare State and Equality: Structural and Ideological Roots of Public Expenditures*. University of California Press.

World Bank. 1987. *World Development Report*. Oxford University Press.

World Health Organization. 1980-90. *World Health Statistics Annual*. World Health Organization.

APPENDIX A: Sample of Nations

Argentina
Australia
Austria
Belgium
Brazil
Canada
Chile
Colombia
Costa Rica
Denmark
Dominican Republic
Ecuador
Egypt
El Salvador
Finland
France
Germany, Federal Republic
Greece
Guatemala
Ireland
Israel
Italy
Jamaica
Japan
Kuwait

Mauritius
Mexico
Netherlands
New Zealand
Norway
Panama
Peru
Portugal
Singapore
Spain
Sri Lanka
Sweden
Switzerland
Syria
Thailand
Trinidad
United Kingdom
United States
Uruguay
Venezuela

APPENDIX B: Correlations and Univariate Statistics

I. Correlation Matrix

	Y	X1	X2	X3	X4	X5
(Y) Average homicide rate (ln)	1.00	-.52	-.44	.51	.34	-.02
(X1) Decommodification index		1.00	.82	-.63	-.28	-.38
(X2) Development index			1.00	-.68	-.19	-.46
(X3) Gini coefficient				1.00	.34	.17
(X4) Economic discrimination index					1.00	.13
(X5) Sex ratio (ln)						1.00

(N = 45)

II. Univariate Statistics

	Mean	Standard Deviation
Average homicide rate (ln)	.97	1.29
Decommodification index	.00	2.38
Development index	.00	4.24
Gini coefficient	.40	.08
Economic discrimination index	1.63	1.37
Sex ratio (ln)	4.59	.06

(N = 45)

1416 / *Social Forces* **75:4, June 1997**

APPENDIX C: Variance Inflation Factors for Fully Specified Models across Different Samples of Nations

	Sample		
	Maximum	Excluding Syria	No Mean Substitution
Predictors			
Development index	4.2	4.3	7.6
Gini coefficient	2.2	2.3	2.9
Economic discrimination index	1.2	1.2	1.3
Sex ratio (ln)	1.4	1.3	2.6
Decommodification index	3.3	3.3	3.4
N	45	44	39

[18]

SOCIAL ORGANIZATION AND INSTRUMENTAL CRIME: ASSESSING THE EMPIRICAL VALIDITY OF CLASSIC AND CONTEMPORARY ANOMIE THEORIES*

ERIC P. BAUMER
REGAN GUSTAFSON
Department of Criminology and Criminal Justice
University of Missouri—St. Louis

KEYWORDS: anomie, Institutional Anomie Theory, Merton, crime rates

This research assesses the empirical validity of the classic anomie theory articulated by Robert Merton and the important contemporary extension of his work encompassed in Messner and Rosenfeld's institutional anomie theory. Using a unique aggregate-level data set, our empirical investigation reveals that, consistent with theoretical expectations, instrumental crime rates are significantly higher in areas where both a strong commitment to monetary success goals and a weak commitment to legitimate means exist. The tendency for this "goals/means" value complex to translate into higher rates of instrumental crime is reduced in the context of higher levels of welfare assistance and more frequent socializing among families. We also find that low levels of educational and economic attainment and high levels of inequality enhance the degree to which commitment to monetary success translates into instrumental crime. Overall, the findings are supportive of some claims by classic and contemporary anomie theories, but also they point to the need for further refinement of these perspectives and additional assessments of their empirical validity.

Do social collectivities in which there is an especially strong commitment to monetary success goals and a weak commitment to legitimate means for pursing such goals exhibit the highest prevalence of money-generating crime? Is this particularly apt to be true in places where legitimate opportunities for pursuing monetary success goals are insufficient and

---

*   We thank Richard Rosenfeld and Steven Messner for constructive comments on an earlier draft. Direct correspondence to Eric P. Baumer, University of Missouri—St. Louis, 8001 Natural Bridge Road, St. Louis, MO 63121 (e-mail: baumer@umsl.edu).

where levels of economic attainment are low and unequally distributed? These questions were at the heart of the puzzle that Robert Merton addressed in his seminal essay, "Social structure and anomie" (1938). Merton presented persuasive arguments in the affirmative to these questions in that essay and in subsequent contributions that expanded on and clarified his position (Merton, 1949, 1957, 1964, 1968).

The theory of deviance Merton articulated in this work has been highly influential in sociology and other disciplines (Cole, 1975; Garfield, 2006; Orru, 1987): It solidified anomie as a distinctly sociological concept relevant to explaining various forms of deviance, and it stimulated several theoretical elaborations and extensions of his arguments (e.g., Agnew, 1992; Cloward and Ohlin, 1960; Cohen, 1955; Messner and Rosenfeld, 1994). Yet, despite the importance of Merton's anomie theory in the social sciences, we still know very little about the empirical validity of its core claims. Scores of studies over the past several decades have evaluated the empirical connection between goal blockage and deviance among individuals (for reviews, see Agnew, Cullen, and Burton, 1996; Bernard, 1984; Burton and Cullen, 1992; Burton et al., 1994; Cole, 1975; Farnworth and Leiber, 1989; Kornhauser, 1978; Liska, 1971). These studies have produced valuable knowledge about propositions implied in Merton's anomie theory, but none directly addresses his arguments about the link between social organization and social deviance (see also Bernard, 1987; Messner, 1988; Messner and Rosenfeld, 2001). Nearly 70 years have passed since the publication of "Social structure and anomie" (Merton, 1938), and yet we still do not know whether places with a high level of commitment to monetary success goals and a low level of commitment to legitimate means for pursing monetary success goals exhibit higher levels of crime and whether this is especially likely to be the case when legitimate opportunities for pursuing monetary success goals are insufficient.

During the past two decades, a significant revival of interest in and attention to Merton's work has occurred, mostly because of the important extension of his work by Messner and Rosenfeld (1994, 2007) in what has been labeled "institutional anomie theory" (IAT). Messner and Rosenfeld (2007) elaborate significantly on Merton's discussion of the sources of cultural disjuncture that are central to his explanation of deviance, and more importantly, they redirect his social structural focus on the stratification system to other key dimensions, namely noneconomic social institutions. Messner and Rosenfeld's IAT has reinvigorated the anomie perspective as a major sociological explanation of crime and deviance, and it has stimulated a flurry of macrolevel research during the past decade (Chamlin and Cochran, 1995; Maume and Lee, 2003; Messner and Rosenfeld, 1997; Piquero and Piquero, 1998; Pratt and Godsey, 2003; Savolainen, 2000;

VALIDITY OF ANOMIE THEORIES 619

Stucky, 2003; for reviews, see Messner and Rosenfeld, 2006; Pratt and Cullen, 2005). Again, however, although these studies have generated important empirical insights about macrolevel variation in crime rates, they do not directly evaluate the most central propositions of IAT. In particular, it remains unknown whether the instrumental crime-generating tendencies of a high commitment to monetary success goals and a low commitment to legitimate means for pursing such goals are lessened where a high commitment to and involvement in noneconomic social institutions exists.

The primary objective of the current study is to go beyond previous work in this area by evaluating the empirical validity of some core predictions contained in the anomie theories presented by Merton (1938, 1949, 1957, 1964, 1968) and Messner and Rosenfeld (1994, 2007) as they apply to cultural and social structural arrangements relevant to the pursuit of monetary success goals and variation in rates of instrumental crime across social collectivities. Our analysis is based on a macrolevel data set that combines survey data from the General Social Survey (GSS) on levels of commitment to monetary success goals and on levels of commitment to institutionalized means with data from a variety of sources regarding the availability of legitimate economic opportunities, levels of economic attainment and inequality, participation in and commitment to noneconomic social institutions, and levels of instrumental crime.

THEORETICAL BACKGROUND

Given the uncertainty that exists about the precise causal linkages implied in the classic and contemporary perspectives examined in the current study (Agnew, 1987; Bernard, 1987; Chamlin and Cochran, 1995; Maume and Lee, 2003), we begin by describing in some detail our interpretation of the types of concepts that should be measured and the relationships that should be evaluated in a comprehensive assessment of their empirical validity. To aid in this effort, we translate our interpretation of the two theories into causal models, which we display in figure 1. We first discuss Merton's anomie theory (displayed in panel A) and then explicate Messner and Rosenfeld's IAT (displayed in panel B).

MERTON'S ANOMIE THEORY

Disagreement on basic theoretical and methodological issues exists with respect to the theoretical model of deviance outlined by Merton, including the most relevant units of analysis; the distinct concepts that are represented; how those concepts are linked; and the types of measures and model specifications required to evaluate adequately the core predictions

Figure 1. Models of Instrumental Crime Implied in Classic and Contemporary Anomie Theories

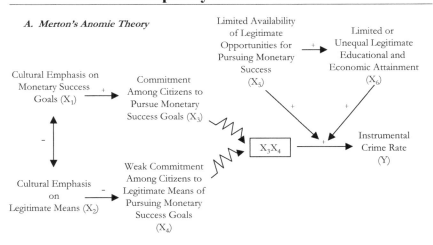

A. Merton's Anomie Theory

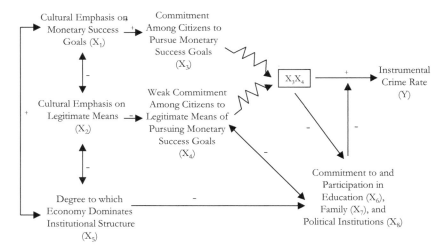

B. Messner and Rosenfeld's Institutional Anomie Theory

(Messner, 1988). Pinning down Merton precisely on how or why the features of social organization upon which he focused translate into differences in rates of instrumental crime across social collectivities is a challenge, but such efforts are critical for specifying appropriate tests of the empirical validity of his theoretical account, for assessing the relevance

VALIDITY OF ANOMIE THEORIES   621

of the extant empirical literature, and more generally for building a knowledge base on the perspective that is theoretically and empirically reflective. In that spirit, we present in panel A of figure 1 a causal model that conveys in precise terms our interpretation of the theoretical account by Merton of differences across social collectivities in levels of instrumental crime.[1]

As others have noted, Merton's theory emphasizes the potential deviance-generating role of two dimensions of cultural structure and one dimension of social structure (Messner, 1988). With respect to cultural structure, Merton highlights as particularly important both the degree of emphasis placed on monetary success and the degree of emphasis placed on pursuing monetary success through *legitimate* means (X_1 and X_2 in figure 1, panel A). With regard to social structure, Merton emphasizes the potential importance of the degree to which available legitimate opportunities (or means) are insufficient to permit most members of the population to pursue monetary success goals (X_5). Merton's writings suggest that the primary role of the cultural structure is to shape the value commitments of the populations exposed to them, which are expressed as $X_1 \rightarrow X_3$ and $X_2 \rightarrow X_4$ in the figure; the corresponding estimates for the paths connecting these variables would reflect a socialization process, in particular the degree to which cultural values have been assimilated. Somewhat similarly, Merton's discussion of the opportunity structure suggests that it is integral mainly for shaping the degree to which all, or at least most, members of the population are able to employ legitimate means to pursue monetary success goals, or at least perceive that this is a viable option (i.e., $X_5 \rightarrow X_6$).

Given this interpretation, differences in instrumental crime across social collectivities in Merton's theoretical model are primarily a function of the degree to which populations across different areas are committed to pursuing monetary success goals (X_3), are weakly committed to doing so through legitimate means (X_4), and are confronted by limited access to, and low levels of, attainment in the legitimate opportunity structure (X_5 and X_6).[2] Importantly, Merton's argument suggests that higher values on

---

1.   Here we focus on only the core elements of Merton's theoretical model for explaining variation in instrumental crime across social collectivities. See Baumer (2007) for a more detailed discussion of issues underlying the translation of Merton's discursive formulation into a formal causal model, including a description of several implied links excluded from figure 1 that are not central to the current investigation.

2.   We use the terms "social collectivities," "societies," and "communities" interchangeably throughout this article. Although Merton and Messner and Rosenfeld highlight America as a good example of a social collectivity that scores at the extreme on the key cultural and social structural variables they emphasize, in our

any one of these key variables alone would not yield significantly higher levels of instrumental crime. This suggestion implies that none of these variables is expected to have a significant main effect on instrumental crime and that if they do, then such effects should be relatively weak. But, as several other scholars have noted (e.g., Bernard, 1987; Cullen, 1984; Messner, 1988), Merton suggested that these variables should exhibit relatively strong multiplicative effects. He emphasized two interaction effects, in particular.

First, as highlighted in Merton's discussion of the "modes of adaptation," the pressure toward innovative behaviors, such as instrumental crime, stems from a discrepancy between the degree to which community members are committed to pursuing monetary success goals and the degree to which they are committed to pursuing these goals through legitimate means, which is an imbalance that is indicative of high levels of anomie (e.g., Featherstone and Deflem, 2003; Messner and Rosenfeld, 2007; Orru, 1987). This component of Merton's argument is represented as a multiplicative effect in panel A of figure 1 by way of sawtoothed arrows emanating from the two indicators of value commitments in order to form the specified two-way interaction effect on instrumental crime ($X_3X_4 \rightarrow$ Y).[3] A literal reading of Merton's discussion of the possible modes of adaptation to the prevailing cultural structure reveals that this two-way interaction effect is necessary for explaining community differences in instrumental crime, but it may not be sufficient. Merton suggests the effects of the two-way interaction should be amplified when considered in the context of other relevant contingency or moderator variables.

Particularly important in this regard, and implicated in the second key multiplicative relationship developed in Merton's theoretical model, is the distribution of legitimate means that can facilitate the pursuit of monetary success goals. Merton's (1938: 678–81) conceptualization of "legitimate opportunities" in this regard is open to multiple interpretations, but his elaborated discussions of insufficient and unequal "access" to legitimate means/opportunities seem to emphasize not only the degree to which the

---

view their theoretical arguments are not limited to explaining "American exceptionalism" in crime and deviance or variation in deviance across a particular type of social collectivity.

3. Given the centrality of higher order interactions in the theoretical models outlined by Merton (1938) and by Messner and Rosenfeld (2001), we adopt the method of using sawtoothed arrows to represent key two-way interactions as distinct variables, such as X_3X_4 in figure 1 (see Bollen, 1998; Bollen and Paxton, 1998). To convey how other factors moderate this two-way interaction effect, as implied in the two theoretical models (i.e., to form the implied three-way interactions), we then use the more common approach of drawing an arrow from the specified moderator to the causal path that represents the two-way interaction effect.

VALIDITY OF ANOMIE THEORIES   623

social structure provides a sufficient stock of opportunities suitable for members of the population to pursue monetary success goals (e.g., the sheer number of jobs available) but also the degree to which available opportunities actually yield, or are at least perceived to provide the possibility of yielding, the achievement of monetary success (e.g., the level and equality of educational and economic attainment) for all or most members of a given social collectivity (Rosenfeld, 1989). These two dimensions of the social structure parallel at the macrolevel what some social scientists refer to as equality of opportunities and equality of outcomes, respectively (see, e.g., Breen and Jonsson, 2005).

In essence, Merton suggests that an insufficient supply of legitimate opportunities constrains the range of options people have, in theory, for pursuing valued monetary success goals and also reduces the likelihood that using legitimate opportunities, in practice, will enable them to satisfy culturally valued goals. All else equal, this insufficiency increases the possibility that people will turn to illegitimate means to attempt to achieve the culturally extolled goal of accumulating money and monetary success (see also Bernburg, 2002; Maume and Lee, 2003). The logic of Merton's theory is that when people are strongly encouraged and committed to pursue monetary success goals but weakly encouraged and committed to pursue them via institutionalized norms, the tendency to use illegitimate means (e.g., instrumental crime) to attempt to satisfy monetary goals, will be greater in the context of particular structural realities. Specifically, this tendency will be heightened where fewer legitimate opportunities exist that can facilitate the accumulation of money and wealth (e.g., places where jobs are relatively scarce and access to higher education is relatively limited), where the social structure does not yield a high level of economic attainment for most people (e.g., places with high levels of poverty and unemployment, low levels of educational attainment, and relatively few people in high earning jobs), and where high levels of economic and educational inequality ensue. According to Merton, this is likely to be the case because illegitimate means are perceived as more expedient under such circumstances or because people in such situations experience stress or become frustrated (e.g., Agnew, 1987; Bernard, 1987; Messner, 1988).[4] In

---

4. The validity of the proposed moderating role of "legitimate opportunities" may depend on the reasons behind the evident failings of the social structure, something Merton does not appear to address systematically. Although Merton referred in his writings to the potential downside of relatively large segments of a population being "denied effective opportunities" or experiencing "blocked opportunities" or "differential access to the approved opportunities," he did not discuss at length the various and complex ways in which these conditions can arise (see Rosenfeld, 1989). For instance, variation across places in the degree to which people are able to pursue monetary success goals through legitimate means could arise because of variation across places in the number of legitimate

624   BAUMER & GUSTAFSON

either case, our view of Merton's discussion of the role of opportunity structure in constraining the ways in which individuals can legitimately satisfy monetary success goals translates into three-way statistical interactions involving, on the one hand, variables that reflect differences across social collectivities in value commitments (i.e., a relatively high level of commitment to pursuing monetary success goals and a relatively weak commitment to legitimate means of pursuing monetary success) and, on the other hand, variables that capture differences in access to and success in pursuing legitimate opportunities. We express this in figure 1 with moderating effects of the degree to which an insufficient stock of legitimate opportunities (X_5) exists and the degree to which levels of attainment are relatively low and unequally distributed (X_6) on the causal path that represents the multiplicative effect on instrumental crime of a strong commitment to monetary success goals and a weak commitment to institutionalized means (X_3X_4). Statistically, this amounts to the following three-way interaction effects on instrumental crime ($X_3X_4X_5 \rightarrow Y$ and $X_3X_4X_6 \rightarrow Y$).

MESSNER AND ROSENFELD'S INSTITUTIONAL ANOMIE THEORY

In *Crime and the American Dream*, Messner and Rosenfeld (1994, 2007) provide an account of American exceptionalism in levels of criminal violence, especially instrumental violence, that draws heavily from Merton's anomie theory. Although Messner and Rosenfeld did not set out to propose a formal theory or to critique Merton's theory causal-path by causal-path, the model that we extract from their work is compatible in many ways with the central focus of Merton's theory. Messner and Rosenfeld (2007) also incorporate into their theoretical model, however, insights from the sociological literature on social control and on the nature and functioning of noneconomic social institutions, which are issues that Merton alludes to in his writings but does not fully develop in his theoretical explanation. In panel B of figure 1, we illustrate our interpretation of the causal model implicit in Messner and Rosenfeld's explanation of differences in instrumental crime across social collectivities, which is now widely referred to in the literature as IAT.[5]

As the figure shows, the anomic cultural arrangement that is central to

---

opportunities available; the suitability of available opportunities; the motivation, skills, and ability of persons eligible to consider available opportunities; the ways in which opportunities are allocated; or some combination of these elements. Presumably, some of these contributing factors to insufficient opportunities, low attainment, and/or high inequality might be more "frustrating" than others or be more apt to make illegitimate opportunities look particularly expedient.

5.   As in our description of Merton's theoretical model, here we focus on only the elements of IAT that are central to the issues investigated in the current study.

VALIDITY OF ANOMIE THEORIES 625

Merton's anomie theory—a strong cultural emphasis on monetary success goals and a weak cultural emphasis on pursuing monetary success goals through institutionalized or legitimate means—also is prominent in Messner and Rosenfeld's explanation. Although not shown in the figure, Messner and Rosenfeld go much further than Merton by specifying the distinctive value complex upon which this cultural imbalance rests and by offering a vivid description of the historical and contemporary forces that gave rise to and continue to sustain it (see also Bernburg, 2002). More central to the issues addressed in our research, however, the underlying logic of their description of how this cultural imbalance translates into relatively high levels of instrumental violence seems identical to the logic in Merton's description. That is, Messner and Rosenfeld imply a process wherein the cultural values of a society are transmitted to individuals who then pursue actions that make sense given the value commitments they have internalized, conditional on other factors that moderate this process. As noted, the implication of this argument is that the key proximate predictor of spatial variation in instrumental crime rates is the interaction between the extent to which populations across different areas are committed to pursuing monetary success goals and the extent to which they are weakly committed to doing so through legitimate means, as displayed in panel B of figure 1 (i.e., $X_3 X_4 \rightarrow Y$). Like Merton, Messner and Rosenfeld (1994, 2007) argue that this association is likely to be a highly conditional one, moderated by several elements of the social structure.

Significant overlap exists between Messner and Rosenfeld's IAT and Merton's theoretical model, but these perspectives differ in the way that they conceptualize social structure. In many ways, Messner and Rosenfeld provide a much more detailed explication of the social structure than Merton, but they also largely omit from early articulations of their arguments a discussion of the dimension of social structure that is central to Merton's thesis: the stratification system. As Bernburg (2002: 738) aptly points out, "Messner and Rosenfeld ignore Merton's insight on the role of the unequal distribution of people's objective conditions in translating the anomic ethic into crime and deviant behavior." Messner and Rosenfeld (2006, 2007) have recently acknowledged this omission, and they suggest that integrating it into their model would provide a more complete explanation of geographic differences in levels of instrumental crime.

Despite the limited attention they give to the legitimate opportunity

---

See Messner and Rosenfeld (2007) for a more detailed treatment of other pertinent casual links, including those that reference the sources of variation in cultural arrangements, the degree to which the economy dominates institutional structures, and the factors associated with levels of participation and investment in noneconomic institutions.

structure, Messner and Rosenfeld (1994, 2007) greatly expand the conceptualization of social structure found in Merton's work by highlighting the potential importance of several key social institutions. Specifically, they emphasize the relative strength of economic, political, educational, and familial institutions in the United States and suggest that the balance of power between these institutions is both a consequence of and a contributor to the prevailing cultural structure. Messner and Rosenfeld's explanation for the exceptional levels of instrumental violence in the United States highlights the dominance of the economy and an associated weakness of familial, educational, and political institutions. According to their argument, this is an institutional imbalance that, coupled with existing cultural arrangements, has produced a population that is more likely than other populations to pursue monetary success goals "by any means necessary."

Messner and Rosenfeld (1994, 2007) do not provide explicit guidance about the causal mechanisms that link the institutional balance of power to variation in instrumental crime, but as we show in the bottom half of figure 1, they seem to suggest a process whereby the dominance of the economy in the institutional structure (X_5) reinforces the cultural emphasis on monetarily defined success (i.e., X_1) and dampens the cultural emphasis on using only legitimate means to pursue monetary success goals (i.e., X_2), which in turn increases the degree to which people are highly committed to pursing monetary success goals and weakly committed to pursing such goals through legitimate means (i.e., X_3X_4). Furthermore, the dominance of the economy in the institutional structure and the joint occurrence of a high degree of commitment to monetary success goals and a high degree of weak commitment to legitimate means (i.e., X_5 and X_3X_4) diminish participation and investment in key noneconomic social institutions, namely familial, educational, and political institutions, which are designated as X_6, X_7, and X_8, respectively, in panel B of figure 1.[6]

Messner and Rosenfeld suggest that the devaluation of noneconomic social institutions enhances the likelihood that members of the population will prioritize the pursuit of monetary success goals at the expense of other goals. More central to the current research, they argue that weakened

---

6.   It is unclear whether Messner and Rosenfeld meant for the concepts we label as "degree to which economy dominates institutional structure" and the "degree of commitment to and participation in education, family, and political institutions" to be distinct. We treat them as such in our presentation given that the former might refer to the public's perceived value of different institutional roles and various government policies and programs that advantage particular institutions in broad terms (e.g., deregulation of the economy or limits on family leave), whereas the latter might capture potential outcomes of such valuations and policies (e.g., time spent with family or various profamily employment benefits).

commitment to and investment in noneconomic social institutions also increase the likelihood of illegitimate responses to culturally induced pressures for achieving monetary success (e.g., instrumental crime) indirectly by disrupting the transmission of prosocial norms about the virtues of pursuing monetary success goals only through legitimate means and more directly by reducing exposure to external social controls and social support (Messner and Rosenfeld, 2007). Although the precise meaning of these links is open to debate (Maume and Lee, 2003), based on our reading, the primary causal role of noneconomic social institutions in IAT is a moderating one. Specifically, the capacity of noneconomic social institutions to temper the ways in which people pursue monetary success goals in the context of weakened commitment to legitimate means is compromised when participation in and commitment to such institutional arrangements is low (for a similar interpretation, see Chamlin and Cochran, 1995; Piquero and Piquero, 1998; Savolainen, 2000).[7] We capture this process in figure 1 with an arrow drawn from commitment to and participation in educational, familial, and political institutions (i.e., X_6, X_7, and X_8) to the causal path that reflects the interactive effect on instrumental crime of strong commitments to culturally valued monetary success goals and weak commitments to legitimate means of pursuing those goals (i.e., $X_3X_4 \rightarrow Y$). Thus, our interpretation is that the key arguments contained in Messner and Rosenfeld's theory are captured by a series of three-way interaction effects (e.g., $X_3X_4X_6 \rightarrow Y$, $X_3X_4X_7 \rightarrow Y$, and $X_3X_4X_8 \rightarrow Y$).

THE CURRENT STUDY

A complete evaluation of the numerous research puzzles displayed in the two panels of figure 1 would require multiple waves of data on social collectivities (potentially defined in various ways, ranging from neighborhoods to nation–states) that exhibit variation in levels of instrumental crime and in the explanatory variables emphasized in the two perspectives. A full test also would require direct indicators of global cultural features

---

7. Maume and Lee (2003) interpret Messner and Rosenfeld's (1994, 2007) theoretical discussion as also implying that noneconomic social institutions also mediate the effects of anomic conditions on levels of instrumental crime. In our view this specification is inconsistent with the underlying logic of IAT, which implies that the social control and social support functions of noneconomic social institutions would not be necessary for regulating levels of instrumental crime *unless* a strong commitment to monetary success goals and a weakened commitment to legitimate means existed. This logic implies moderation rather than mediation. Nevertheless, Maume and Lee's interpretation yields an interesting empirical prediction to which our data can partially speak, so we return to this issue in the results section.

(i.e., the degree of cultural emphasis on monetary success goals and legitimate means of pursuing such goals) and of structural arrangements (e.g., the structure of the economic system and indicators of institutional functioning) reflected across a reasonably large sample of places. Because these societal features are emergent properties of social systems (see Lazarsfeld and Menzel, 1965; Liska, 1990)—not merely aggregations of individual relationships, attitudes, and behaviors—they would need to be measured through an assessment of government policies and the customs, rituals, manners, and practices in specified communities, as reflected in "cultural artifacts" such as books, newspapers, magazines, film, speeches, and other such sources (Messner and Rosenfeld, 2006). Finally, a complete test would require data on the extent to which the populations of the social collectivities under study have assimilated cultural values, have access (or perceive that they have access) to opportunities to pursue monetary success goals through legitimate means, are committed to or value noneconomic social institutions, and are involved in instrumental criminal activities.

A comprehensive empirical test of the anomie theories under review is well beyond the reach of existing sources. However, the data used for our study allow us to assess some relationships that are central to these theoretical arguments and that have not received a great deal of previous empirical scrutiny. The empirical predictions we evaluate are summarized in figure 2, which integrates insights from Merton's anomie theory and Messner and Rosenfeld's IAT on the proximate predictors of instrumental crime.

As illustrated, we examine whether geographic differences in levels of instrumental crime are a function of the interaction between the degree of commitment among citizens to pursue monetary success goals and the degree of weak commitment among citizens to pursue monetary success goals via legitimate means ($X_1X_2 \rightarrow Y$). Furthermore, we examine whether any observed multiplicative effect of these conditions is moderated by differences across places in 1) the degree to which legitimate opportunities for pursing monetary goals are limited (X_3) and the degree to which educational and economic attainment is limited or unequally distributed (X_4), as emphasized by Merton (i.e., $X_1X_2X_3 \rightarrow Y$ and $X_1X_2X_4 \rightarrow Y$); and 2) the degree of commitment to and participation in noneconomic social institutions ($X_5 ... X_9$), as emphasized by Messner and Rosenfeld (i.e., $X_1X_2X_5 \rightarrow Y$, $X_1X_2X_6 \rightarrow Y$, $X_1X_2X_7 \rightarrow Y$, $X_1X_2X_8 \rightarrow Y$, and $X_1X_2X_9 \rightarrow Y$). With respect to the latter, we consider the potential moderating role of indicators of commitment to and investment in each of the institutions highlighted by Messner and Rosenfeld (familial, educational, and political

Figure 2. Integrated Anomie Causal Model

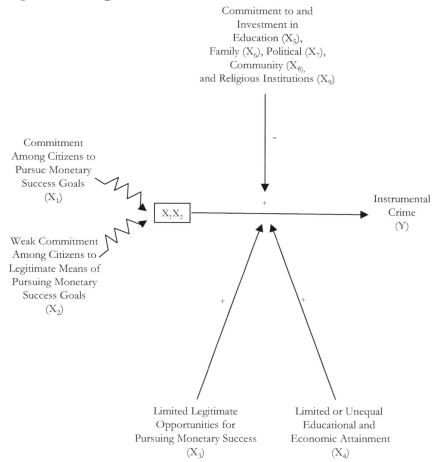

institutions) along with indicators of community social capital and religious institutional strength, both of which have been featured in recent theoretical discussions and empirical research on aggregate crime rates (e.g., Messner, Baumer, and Rosenfeld, 2004; Putnam, 2000).

Although well short of a full test of IAT or Merton's anomie theory, our study goes significantly beyond previous efforts to assess the empirical validity of these perspectives. Most studies examine important implications of these theories rather than directly assess the implied causal links (Chamlin and Cochran, 1995; Hannon and DeFronzo, 1998; Krahn, Hartnagel, and Gartrell, 1986; Maume and Lee, 2003; Messner, 1983;

Messner and Rosenfeld, 1997; Piquero and Piquero, 1998; Pratt and God-sey, 2003; Savolainen, 2000). These studies contribute much to our under-standing of spatial variation in crime and deviance, but they do not speak directly to the core questions of whether instrumental crime rates are higher in places where a stronger commitment to monetary success goals and a weaker commitment to legitimate means exist and of whether any observed effect of this goals/means imbalance is moderated by adverse economic conditions or levels of participation in and commitment to noneconomic social institutions.

Three recent studies have examined more directly some cultural argu-ments contained in classic and contemporary anomie theories (Cao, 2004; Cullen, Parboteeah, and Hoegl, 2004; Jensen, 2002). Cao (2004) and Jen-sen (2002) evaluate whether America exhibits the type of exceptional cul-tural features emphasized by Merton and by Messner and Rosenfeld. Using the World Values Survey (WVS), the results of these studies chal-lenge claims that Americans are exceptional in their commitment to mon-etary success or in their willingness to justify deviant means of pursuing such success. However, these studies do not fully consider the main causal processes implied by Merton or by Messner and Rosenfeld, and a recent critique of their findings reveals that conclusions drawn from the WVS on these issues are highly sensitive to the specific items used to measure the core concepts (Messner and Rosenfeld, 2006).

Cullen, Parboteeah, and Hoegl (2004) use individual- and aggregate-level data from the WVS for 3,450 managers from 28 nations to assess the main effects of several dimensions of national culture that Messner and Rosenfeld (2007) identify as foundations of the American dream (e.g., achievement, individualism, universalism, and pecuniary materialism) and of several indicators of the strength of social institutions on the degree to which managers report that it is justifiable to engage in various deviant business practices. Although they do not examine the interactive effects that are central to Messner and Rosenfeld's theory (i.e., interactions between the indicators of culture and the indicators of institutional strength) nor do they consider actual involvement in instrumental crime, their analysis reveals evidence consistent with some basic tenets of Merton's theory and IAT. In particular, Cullen, Parboteeah, and Hoegl (2004) find that exposure to the cultural values of universalism and pecu-niary materialism increases the degree to which managers are willing to justify deviant business practices. Overall, however, their results provide mixed support for predictions derived from IAT.

In sum, previous research rarely has considered key variables in classic and contemporary anomie theoretical models, such as the extent to which members of different populations are strongly committed to monetary suc-cess goals and weakly committed to legitimate means. Thus, past research has not addressed whether these variables exert main effects on crime rates, interact with one another, or interact with other variables, including the distribution of educational and economic opportunities and attainments as well as the strength of noneconomic institutions, in such a way as to affect crime rates as specified theoretically. Our analyses are directed at answering these key theoretical questions.

DATA AND METHODS

DATA

We evaluate the links shown in figure 2 with data on instrumental crime rates from the Uniform Crime Reports (UCR); indicators of the level of commitment to pursuing monetary success goals, the level of commitment to using legitimate means to pursue monetary success goals, and other conditions from an aggregate-level version of the GSS; measures of socio-economic and demographic conditions from the U.S. Census Bureau; and other relevant variables drawn from a variety of additional sources for 77 geographic areas in the United States for the mid-to-late 1970s. The crime and census data used in the analysis are standard for most aggregate-level crime studies (see, e.g., Kposowa, Breault, and Harrison, 1995; Land, McCall, and Cohen, 1990), but the aggregated GSS data and the units of analysis employed are less common and therefore warrant some elaboration.

Although the GSS has been used extensively for individual-level analyses of various topics, a distinctive feature of the GSS data used for our research is that they contain geographic codes that identify the primary sampling units (PSUs)—metropolitan areas and non-metropolitan counties—from which respondents were selected. The GSS sampling units are chosen with the purpose of generating a nationally representative sample of households in the continental United States. They therefore reflect a broad selection of geographic areas across the nation, and samples drawn within these units are "self-representing" so that aggregated individual responses are representative of the area from which they are drawn (for a more detailed discussion of GSS sampling methods, see Davis and Smith, 1998: Appendix A). Previous studies have used the geocoded GSS to link aggregate-level data from external sources to the household respondents (e.g., Baumer, Messner, and Rosenfeld, 2003; Taylor, 1998) and to aggregate survey household-level data from the GSS to describe levels of social capital, gun prevalence, and other attributes of the geographic areas sampled in the survey (e.g., Kleck, 2004; Moody and Marvell, 2005; Rosenfeld, Messner, and Baumer, 2001). We use the procedure applied in the latter studies for the purposes of our research and aggregate GSS individual responses within sample units to construct aggregate-level measures of concepts that are central to evaluating the empirical validity of the predictions derived above from Merton's theory and IAT.

Relying on the GSS for key measures means that our analysis is based on a somewhat novel sample, at least compared with most conventional aggregate-level samples, and that we must employ data from the 1970s, the only period for which the relevant GSS measures are available. The units of analysis for our study represent 77 of the 87 geographic units that composed the sampling frame for the GSS during the 1970s; 52 of the units included represent metropolitan areas, and the other 25 represent individual non-metropolitan counties.[8] Past research on crime and social control has shown that the GSS sample of counties and metro areas generates findings that are very similar to analyses based on more conventional samples of cities, counties, and metropolitan areas (e.g., Rosenfeld, Messner, and Baumer, 2001; Stults and Baumer, 2007). With respect to the time frame covered in our study, to preserve the implied temporal order as best we can, we assess the effects of measures from the GSS and other sources estimated approximately for 1975–1976 on levels of instrumental crime rates estimated for 1977. Although it is usually preferable to evaluate research issues with more recent, and ideally the most recent data available, a strong theoretical rationale does not seem to exist against using data from the 1970s to evaluate the predictions outlined in the theories developed by Merton and by Messner and Rosenfeld, nor have we found arguments suggesting that the predictions found in these theories have changed over time so that they would be more or less relevant within a given historical era. Furthermore, using data from the 1970s allows us to go beyond most previous studies, which have been restricted to standard census-derived explanatory variables that may have limited relevance for the theoretical frameworks under review.

MEASURES

DEPENDENT VARIABLE

As noted, we limit our attention to the implications of Merton's and Messner and Rosenfeld's arguments for explaining community differences in *instrumental crime rates*. Accordingly, we focus our empirical analysis on a composite dependent variable that captures differences across places in the relative frequency of crime geared primarily toward the acquisition of money or goods that could be converted to cash. Specifically, using county-level data from the UCR program (U.S. Department of Justice,

---

8.   We exclude 10 of the original 87 GSS sample units (5 metropolitan areas and 5 non-metropolitan counties) because of insufficient data for several key variables included in the analysis. The biggest source of missing data that led to exclusion was incomplete or nonexistent data on levels of instrumental crime.

VALIDITY OF ANOMIE THEORIES 633

1998), we construct a measure of instrumental crime that reflects the number of robberies, burglaries, larcenies, and auto thefts per 100,000 residents in our sample units for 1977.[9]

KEY EXPLANATORY VARIABLES

Two of our key explanatory variables are 1) the degree of commitment to pursuing monetary success and 2) the degree of commitment to legitimate means of pursuing monetary success goals among members of the communities in our study. We combined GSS data from 1973 to 1976 and aggregated survey responses within our sample units to construct estimates of the prevalence of these value commitments.[10] The degree of *commitment to monetary success goals* is measured with an item from the GSS that taps whether residents of the sample communities agreed with the statement that "next to health, money is the most important thing." The measure used in our study represents the percentage of community respondents who indicated that they agree with that statement. We interpret higher values on this variable to reflect a stronger commitment by community members to pursue activities directed at maximizing monetary success.

The degree of *weak commitment to legitimate means* for pursuing monetary success goals is measured by aggregating, within sample units, responses to a GSS item that assesses whether respondents agree with the statement that "there are no right or wrong ways to make money, only hard and easy ways." The measure used in our analysis reflects the percentage of persons who agree with this statement, and we interpret higher scores on this measure as being reflective of a weaker commitment by community members to pursue monetary success through legitimate means.

As noted, Merton emphasizes as potential moderator variables not only the degree to which the social structure provides a sufficient stock of opportunities suitable for members of the population to pursue monetary success goals but also the degree to which available opportunities actually yield or are at least perceived to yield the achievement of monetary success for all. This broad conceptualization of "limited legitimate opportunities" calls for analyzing indicators of the relative number of economic opportunities available in a given area, along with indicators of the level of

---

9. For this measure and several others used in our study, to obtain estimates for the metropolitan areas represented in our study, we then aggregated the county-level data.

10. We pool data across multiple years of GSS data to maximize sample sizes within sample units. Sample sizes range from 75 to 350 across the 77 units included in the study.

economic attainment and inequality (see also Rosenfeld, 1989). We include measures of each in our analysis.

We gauge the extent of legitimate employment opportunities in 1976 with a ratio of the total number of persons aged 16 years and older in our sample units who were employed or who were seeking employment (i.e., the labor or work force) to the number of jobs available within the labor market areas that encompass our sample units, a ratio we label as *limited job availability*. The size of the labor force in 1976 was estimated by interpolating from 1970 and 1980 county census estimates. Estimates of the number of existing jobs in 1976 in the labor market areas that cover our sample units are based on annual county-level information obtained from the Regional Economic Information System (REIS) maintained by the Bureau of Economic Analysis (BEA), which we aggregated to characterize labor market areas. This source provides the most reliable estimates of the number of jobs in a given area and is preferred over other sources such as the decennial census, which counts people (employed and unemployed) rather than the number of jobs (see Bureau of Economic Analysis, 2007; Scorsone and Zimmerman, 2003). As constructed, higher scores on the ratio used in our study indicate a surplus of current and would-be workers relative to the number of jobs for our sample units or, alternatively, a scarcity of job opportunities available relative to the number of persons who are working or looking for such opportunities.[11]

We use two measures to capture variation across places in the degree to which available opportunities yield outcomes that are indicative of a social structure that yields insufficient and unequal chances of achieving monetary success and accumulating wealth. On their face, these measures are conceptually distinct from the measure of legitimate opportunities just described and may be particularly germane to shaping perceptions about whether achieving monetary success goals through legitimate means is realistic for all individuals, independent of the available stock of legitimate opportunities.

The first measure, which we label as *low educational and economic attainment*, combines six items that indicate differences across our sample

---

11.   For the metropolitan areas in our sample we simply used the sum of jobs within the geographic boundaries covered by these areas as the equivalent labor market area. For single county units in our sample, the labor market areas reflect economically defined commuting zones (using 1980 definitions), which are designed to reflect the full geographic area in which county residents might work or seek jobs, irrespective of county population size (Tolbert and Sizer, 1996). In supplementary analyses, we experimented with an alternatively defined measure that captures people not currently in the labor market, the ratio of all persons aged 16–64 years to the number of jobs. The findings for this measure were very similar to those reported below.

VALIDITY OF ANOMIE THEORIES 635

units in absolute attainment levels (alpha = .86). Specifically, we standard-ized and summed the following six items to construct a scale capturing differences across areas in low levels of attainment: 1) the percentage of persons aged 16 to 19 years who are not high-school graduates or currently in school (i.e., school dropouts), 2) the percentage of persons aged 25 years and older who did not finish high school, 3) the percentage of per-sons in the civilian labor force who are unemployed, 4) the percentage of persons in the labor force who are employed in nonmanagement and non-professional jobs, 5) the percentage of families with incomes below the poverty line, and 6) the community average self-reported social class standing. The first five items were estimated for 1976 by interpolating from 1970 and 1980 county census data and aggregating to the GSS PSUs, and the last item was created from the GSS by aggregating within PSUs data from 1973 to 1976 on a question that asks respondents to self-report their social class (i.e., 4 = lower class. . .1 = upper class).

Our second measure of economic attainment captures variation across places in the distributional equality of outcomes for legitimate economic and educational pursuits. Specifically, we constructed a multi-item scale that combines the Gini index of income inequality and the Gini index of educational inequality, both of which have been linked to crime in previ-ous macrolevel studies (e.g., Galea and Ahern, 2005; Maume and Lee, 2003). We first estimated the two indices of inequality for 1976 by interpo-lating from decennial census data for 1970 and 1980, and then we stan-dardized the measures and summed them to create a scale that we label *educational and income inequality* (alpha = .92).

To assess claims relevant to Messner and Rosenfeld's IAT, we include several indicators of the degree of commitment to or value placed on noneconomic social institutions. The measures developed are constrained somewhat by the available data and the time period under review, but each seems to have sufficient face validity to assess in a preliminary way the mechanisms emphasized by Messner and Rosenfeld (2007). The *per-centage of government expenditures on education* in 1976 and the number of *pupils per teacher* in the schools in our sample communities during the 1975/1976 academic year serve as indicators of the commitment to educa-tional institutions. The former was created by interpolating from estimates of government spending on education and other functions in 1972 and 1977 taken from County and City Data Books (U.S. Department of Com-merce, 1999, 2000). The latter was obtained from the Elementary and Sec-ondary General Information System (ELSEGIS) data (U.S. Department of Education, 2001). We also use two measures to gauge levels of commit-ment to family. The first measure reflects differences across places in the amount of time people spend socializing with family members (*time spent with family*). This variable was constructed by aggregating responses to three items from the 1974–1977 GSS to measure the percentage of persons who socialized several times a month with siblings, parents, and other relatives, respectively, and summing standardized values for these items (alpha = .79). The second indicator of family institutional strength captures community differences in *commitment to marriage*. This index combines two items that were constructed by aggregating responses to GSS questions from 1974 to 1977 about current marital status and views on divorce laws: the percentage of respondents currently married and the percentage who indicated support for laws making it more difficult to divorce (alpha = .62). Consistent with previous research (e.g., Maume and Lee, 2003), we use data on voting and welfare assistance as indicators of the degree to which the polity is organized in ways that might regulate how people respond to culturally induced pressures to pursue economic success goals. Specifically, we include an index of *voter participation* (alpha = .90), which combines the percentage of persons aged 18 years and older registered to vote in 1976 and the percentage of registered voters who voted in the 1976 Presidential election (Inter-University Consortium for Political and Social Research (ICPSR), 1991, 1995), as well as an index of *welfare assistance* (alpha = .64) that combines the percentage of poor families receiving welfare and the average monthly welfare payment per poor person, adjusted for local cost of living (see Hannon and DeFronzo, 1998). The two welfare items used in this index were estimated for 1976 by interpolating county census data from 1970 and 1980.

Finally, we incorporate measures of the strength of two additional institutional spheres not emphasized in IAT but highlighted in several recent empirical investigations (e.g., Maume and Lee, 2003; Messner, Baumer, and Rosenfeld, 2004; Rosenfeld, Messner, and Baumer, 2001). Specifically, we use data from the 1970 and 1980 Census of Churches to interpolate the 1976 *civically engaged church adherence rate* for our sample units (Glenmary Research Center, 1973, 1981). And, consistent with past research, we measure levels of *social capital* for our sample units by combining indicators of community participation with indicators of social trust (Messner, Baumer, and Rosenfeld, 2004; Paxton, 1999; Putnam, 2000; Rosenfeld, Messner, and Baumer, 2001). We combined four measures from the GSS for the period covering 1973–1977 and aggregated them within sample units to construct an index of social capital that combines the percentage of respondents who indicate that most people can be trusted, the percentage who say that most people try to be fair, the percentage who say that most people try to be helpful, and the per capita number of groups and associations to which respondents belong (alpha = .84).

VALIDITY OF ANOMIE THEORIES   637

CONTROL VARIABLES

We also consider several other potentially important variables in our analysis. Although we could not find any statements in the original articulations of Merton's theory or IAT that claim that the causal processes implied are *net of other factors*, these anomie perspectives obviously should be tested against plausible alternative models; therefore the models we estimate incorporate measures directed at capturing key concepts that are emphasized in some of the most prominent alternative aggregate-level theoretical perspectives (e.g., routine activities theory and social disorganization theory) as well as other known correlates of crime (e.g., Kposowa, Breault, and Harrison, 1995; Land, McCall, and Cohen, 1990). The controls include the mean number of hours that residents spend watching television in a typical day, population structure (an index that combines logged population size and logged population density), the number of police officers per 100,000 residents, structural disadvantage (an index that combines the percentage of residents who are black and the percentage of families with children headed by a female), the percentage of individuals aged 16 to 34 years, and a dummy variable that distinguishes sample units located in the south from those located elsewhere. The inclusion of these variables provides a conservative test of the hypothesized links outlined in figure 2.[12]

ANALYTICAL STRATEGY

We use ordinary least squares to examine the effects of the explanatory and control variables on instrumental crime rates. Our analysis proceeds in the following manner. We begin by briefly describing descriptive statistics and bivariate correlations for the sample and measures employed in the study. We then estimate a series of regression models that examine the empirical predictions outlined in figure 2. As the figure illustrates, the key empirical predictions of interest in the regression models are multiplicative relationships, specifically two-way and three-way statistical interactions. To minimize concerns about multicollinearity and to enhance the interpretability of the interactions estimated in our regression models, each predictor variable hypothesized to form multiplicative relationships was mean centered (Aiken and West, 1991; Jaccard and Turrisi, 2003). Our initial focus in the multivariate analysis is on testing for the hypothesized two-way interaction between the level of commitment to monetary goals

---

12.   The measure of television viewing was created by aggregating GSS data for 1975–1977 within sample units, and the indicator of police strength was constructed by aggregating agency-level data from the 1975 Census of Law Enforcement Agencies. The other control variables (save for region) were estimated for 1976 by interpolating from 1970 and 1980 decennial census data.

and the level of weak commitment to using legitimate means for pursuing monetary success. The empirical expectation here is for a statistically significant positive coefficient for the interaction term, which signifies that the effect of each component of the interaction is enhanced given higher levels of the other. Subsequent models are directed at testing for the three-way interactions specified in figure 2. Specifically, we evaluate whether factors such as limited access to legitimate opportunities, indicators of low and unequal levels of educational and economic attainment, and measures of noneconomic institutional strength condition the potential crime-elevating interactive effects of a high degree of commitment to monetary goals and a weak commitment to using legitimate means to do so. Based on our interpretation of the classic and contemporary anomie theories under review, we expect significant positive coefficients for the three-way interactions involving the availability of legitimate opportunities and the indicators of low achievement and high inequality, as well as significant negative coefficients for three-way interactions involving the indicators of noneconomic institutional strength.

RESULTS

Before turning to the regression results, it is instructive to consider the descriptive statistics for the key variables represented in our hypotheses, which are presented here in table 1.[13] The average rate of instrumental crime (robberies, burglaries, larcenies, and auto thefts) for the 77 areas represented in our sample is 5,348 per 100,000 residents, which is very similar to the national rate for this period (U.S. Department of Justice, 1978). Considerable geographic variation exists in instrumental crime rates, however, with some areas experiencing just over 200 instrumental crimes per 100,000 and others more than 9,500 per 100,000. The geographic areas in our sample also exhibit variation on key explanatory variables examined in the study. For instance, more than a quarter (29.6 percent) of persons across these areas agreed that "next to health, money is the most important thing," which we use as an indicator of relative commitment to monetary success, but this sentiment varied across places from about 15 percent to 49 percent. Similarly, in the average area, nearly one quarter (23.3 percent) of persons expressed a weak commitment to using legitimate means to pursue monetary success as indicated by their agreement that "there are no right or wrong ways to make money, only hard and easy ways," but agreement with this statement ranged from under 5 percent to more than 41 percent across our sample areas. The indicators of the availability of

---

13.   To conserve space, we do not present results for the control variables in any of the tables (results available on request).

Table 1. Descriptive Statistics for Dependent Variable and Explanatory Variables (N = 77)

	Mean	SD	Minimum	Maximum
Dependent Variable				
Instrumental Crime Rate (per 100,000)	5,347.84	2,071.51	209.81	9,592.92
Explanatory Variables				
Value Commitments				
Commitment to monetary success				
% agreeing that next to health, money is most important	29.60	8.04	15.22	48.84
Weak commitment to legitimate means				
% agreeing there are no right or wrong ways to make money	23.33	7.83	4.55	41.30
Structural Realities				
Limited job availability				
Work force to jobs ratio	.96	.10	.66	1.37
Low educational and economic attainment[a]	.00	4.32	-8.79	13.88
% of persons 16–19 not in school or a high-school graduate	13.86	4.64	4.77	29.58
% who did not graduate from high school	39.71	9.88	24.31	68.86
% of civilian labor force unemployed	5.73	2.07	3.06	14.00
% employed in nonmanagement/nonprofessional jobs	76.95	4.73	63.36	85.86
% of families with incomes below the poverty line	13.10	6.13	6.02	43.76
Mean self-reported social class (4 = lower class, 1 = upper class)	2.54	.12	2.15	2.98
Educational and income inequality[a]	.00	1.80	-3.09	7.25
Income Gini	.35	.03	.30	.47
Education Gini	.25	.03	.21	.33
Strength of Noneconomic Social Institutions				
Educational				
% government expenditures on education	50.45	7.70	37.19	75.83
Pupils per teacher	21.00	5.30	15.23	56.08

Table 1 (cont.)

	Mean	SD	Minimum	Maximum
Familial				
Time spent with family[a]	.00	2.52	-5.82	6.93
% who spend several evenings a month with parents	47.47	22.49	.00	100.00
% who spend several evenings a month with siblings	34.15	15.23	.00	75.00
% who spend several evenings a month with other relatives	55.30	9.46	34.43	80.00
Commitment to marriage[a]	.00	1.70	-3.69	4.64
% currently married	68.08	9.04	51.79	89.47
% who support laws making it more difficult to divorce	48.95	10.72	26.67	75.00
Political				
Voter participation[a]	.00	1.90	-5.74	4.54
% 18 and older registered to vote	70.08	12.06	33.79	99.01
% of registered voters who voted in 1976 Presidential election	53.67	8.95	29.23	77.68
Welfare assistance[a]	.00	1.73	-2.67	5.65
% of poor families receiving welfare	6.80	2.47	3.24	15.01
Average monthly welfare payment per poor person	134.70	24.84	96.28	196.60
Religious				
Civically engaged church adherence rate	19.19	9.14	6.00	56.32
Community				
Social capital[a]	.00	3.30	-8.39	7.14
% who say most people can be trusted	43.05	11.38	21.82	69.64
% who say most people try to be fair	62.03	10.77	32.69	88.89
% who say most people try to be helpful	52.56	10.31	24.56	73.02
Mean self-reported number of group memberships	1.86	.38	1.03	2.92

[a]Multi-item standardized additive scale that combines the indicators listed directly below it.

VALIDITY OF ANOMIE THEORIES 641

employment opportunities, economic attainment and inequality, and commitment to and participation in noneconomic institutions exhibit substantial variability across places as well. It remains to be seen, however, whether these factors affect instrumental crime in the manner posited by Merton and by Messner and Rosenfeld.

The bivariate correlations displayed in table 2 indicate a significant positive, albeit relatively weak, linear relationship between levels of commitment to monetary success and weak commitment to legitimate means ($r = .279$, $p < .05$). Neither of these variables exhibits a significant bivariate linear association with instrumental crime rates, which is perhaps not surprising in light of the strong theoretical emphasis on their presumed interactive effects. The indicator of job availability, which has not been used in past crime research as far as we know, is not related significantly to levels of instrumental crime or the other economic indicators, low economic attainment and economic inequality. The latter measures are strongly correlated as expected, and they yield significant inverse relationships with instrumental crime rates, presumably because such conditions reflect limited opportunities for instrumental crime.[14] An additional noteworthy feature of the bivariate associations shown in table 2 is that many indicators of noneconomic institutional strength yield significant negative relationships with instrumental crime rates. Below, we examine whether these indicators also condition any observed interactive effect of commitment to monetary success and weak commitment to legitimate means, as implied by Messner and Rosenfeld (2007).

Tables 3 and 4 present the multivariate regression results that are most central to the theoretical predictions examined in our research. Table 3 displays nonstandardized coefficients and standard errors for five regression models relevant to Merton's anomie theory. Model 1 presents results for the main effects of the explanatory variables, whereas the other models test for the significant interaction effects implied in Merton's theory, beginning with the two-way interaction between commitment to monetary success goals and weak commitment to legitimate means (model 2), followed by models that evaluate hypothesized three-way interaction effects between value commitments and the three indicators of economic conditions highlighted in his work (models 3–5).

Model 1 reveals two noteworthy findings.[15] First, several explanatory

14. Kposowa, Breault, and Harrison (1995) report similar findings for property crime in their comprehensive analysis of county-level crime correlates. We find the more typical positive relationships between these indicators and crime when we substitute homicide rates for instrumental crime rates (results not shown).

15. We tested for homogeneity of error variance using the Breusch–Pagan test (e.g., Greene, 1993); no significant heteroskedasticity was observed. Visual inspection of model residuals showed no indications of significant non-normality. Some

Table 2. Bivariate Correlations for Dependent and Explanatory Variables (N = 77)

Variable	(1)	(2)	(3)	(4)	(5)	(6)	(7)	(8)	(9)	(10)	(11)	(12)	(13)	(14)
(1) Instrumental crime rate	—	.158	.058	-.065	-.482*	-.297*	-.527*	.035	-.508*	-.621*	-.234*	-.364*	-.465*	-.016
(2) Commitment to monetary success		—	.279*	.211	.034	.133	.015	.013	.044	-.061	-.134	.012	-.149	-.143
(3) Weak commitment to legitimate means			—	.187	-.136	.017	-.008	-.075	-.035	.016	-.020	-.201	.010	.004
(4) Limited job availability				—	.178	.130	.202	-.011	.161	-.040	-.038	.057	-.276*	-.204
(5) Low educational and economic attainment					—	.730*	.463*	-.024	.539*	.483*	-.090	.659*	-.084	-.426*
(6) Educational and income inequality						—	.371*	-.065	.414*	.274*	-.183	.477*	-.161	-.473*
(7) % govt. expenditures on education							—	-.240*	.424*	.358*	.143	.148	.125	-.063
(8) Pupils per teacher								—	.073	.080	-.089	-.084	-.060	-.082
(9) Time spent with family									—	.329*	-.019	.364*	.128	-.230*
(10) Commitment to marriage										—	.226*	.226*	.459*	.136
(11) Voter participation											—	.110	.280*	.433*
(12) Welfare assistance												—	-.146	-.109
(13) Civically engaged church adherence rate													—	.431*
(14) Social capital														—

*$p < .05$, two-tailed test.

Table 3. Regression of Instrumental Crime Rates on Value Commitments and Structural Realities (N =77)

Independent Variables	(1)	(2)	(3)	(4)	(5)
Commitment to monetary success	39.08	32.64	30.68	24.74	44.63*
	(22.14)	(20.94)	(21.69)	(19.23)	(20.47)
Weak commitment to legitimate means	3.07	35.11	46.55	36.60	39.08
	(21.80)	(23.27)	(25.55)	(21.55)	(23.21)
Limited job availability	608.31	-580.75	-1091.75	-649.43	-116.87
	(2061.67)	(1981.30)	(2659.05)	(1882.26)	(1951.22)
Low educational and economic attainment	.02	15.01	15.18	-27.58	-32.84
	(94.57)	(89.08)	(92.58)	(85.11)	(84.14)
Educational and income inequality	50.41	-76.97	-108.01	-269.98	-160.74
	(172.89)	(168.37)	(174.44)	(162.80)	(160.48)
% govt. expenditures on education	-83.46*	-90.41*	-90.39*	-80.88*	-102.12*
	(26.59)	(25.12)	(27.92)	(23.47)	(25.04)
Pupils per teacher	-14.66	-7.10	3.67	-12.44	-19.54
	(31.03)	(29.29)	(30.69)	(26.83)	(27.34)
Time spent with family	-149.13*	-151.65	-205.26*	-176.96*	-187.12*
	(74.08)	(79.07)	(89.63)	(74.10)	(73.97)
Commitment to marriage	-363.65*	-302.80*	-323.98*	-236.60	-185.74
	(138.46)	(131.87)	(133.83)	(123.57)	(129.21)
Voter participation	69.51	77.86	47.67	47.88	85.68
	(103.03)	(96.93)	(101.63)	(89.02)	(91.18)
Welfare assistance	-257.30	-177.47	-71.19	12.60	-38.24
	(166.92)	(159.34)	(183.66)	(163.18)	(158.63)
Civically engaged church adherence rate	-63.37*	-60.50*	-51.21*	-57.32*	-53.71*
	(25.45)	(23.96)	(25.91)	(22.46)	(22.48)
Social capital	136.74	121.92	146.12	30.72	58.40
	(74.89)	(70.61)	(75.53)	(73.28)	(69.88)

Table 3 (cont.)

Independent Variables	(1)	(2)	(3)	(4)	(5)
Commitment to monetary success X Weak commitment to legitimate means		7.92* (2.72)	9.08* (3.28)	9.52* (2.55)	9.11* (2.87)
Commitment to monetary success X Limited job availability			−38.31 (302.68)		
Weak commitment to legitimate means X Limited job availability			407.29 (306.80)		
Commitment to monetary success X Weak commitment to legitimate means X Limited job availability			−17.06 (28.47)		
Commitment to monetary success X Low educational and economic attainment				16.33* (6.13)	
Weak commitment to legitimate means X Low educational and economic attainment				−1.68 (6.00)	
Commitment to monetary success X Weak commitment to legitimate means X Low educational and economic attainment				−1.26 (.76)	
Commitment to monetary success X Limited legitimate opportunities					26.67* (12.51)
Weak commitment to legitimate means X Limited legitimate opportunities					2.13 (13.66)
Commitment to monetary success X Weak commitment to legitimate means X Economic inequality					−4.11 (2.78)
R^2	.714	.752	.762	.805	.799

*$p < .05$, two-tailed test.

NOTE: Estimates shown are unstandardized regression coefficients with standard errors in parentheses. The control variables also were included in the estimation of the models shown.

variables—some of which have not been considered in previous macrolevel crime research—exert significant main effects. Net of other factors, instrumental crime rates were lower in the late 1970s in geographic areas where education comprised a larger share of overall spending, families spent more time together, there was a stronger commitment to marriage, and the rate of adherence to civically engaged religious denominations was higher. Second, and more important for the focus of our research, neither levels of commitment to monetary success nor weak commitment to legitimate means exerts a significant main effect on instrumental crime rates. This finding is not unexpected because, as noted, neither Merton's theory nor IAT predicts main effects for these variables. But they do predict that these variables interact to generate higher levels of instrumental crime, an issue to which we now turn.

We tested for the hypothesized interaction between commitment to pursue monetary success and weak commitment to legitimate means by adding a variable that represents the product of these measures. As model 2 shows, this estimation reveals a statistically significant interaction effect ($b = 7.92$, $p < .05$) that is in the theoretically expected direction, net of a comprehensive set of other variables.

To illustrate the nature and magnitude of this interaction effect, we used the coefficients in model 2 to compute the relevant simple slopes implied by the interaction (see, e.g., Aiken and West, 1991). Since the theories under review here do not favor either of the two explanatory variables involved in the interaction as a focus or moderator variable, we first computed the simple slopes for the regression of instrumental crime on commitment to monetary success goals at different levels of weak commitment to legitimate means (ranging 1 standard deviation above and below the mean), and then we repeated these steps for computing simple slopes for the regression of instrumental crime on weak commitment to legitimate means at different levels of commitment to monetary success goals. The resulting regression lines are displayed in panels A and B of figure 3. As figure 3 reveals, the effect of each variable on instrumental crime rates is greater at higher levels of the other and, in fact, only the slopes reflected

---

independent variables included in our regression models yield moderate-to-strong correlations, particularly associations between some indicators of economic conditions (e.g., levels of low attainment, high inequality, and the welfare index) and some control variables (e.g., population density and structural disadvantage). An assessment of model variance inflation factors (VIFs) and conditioning indices suggested that these variables could be a significant source of multicollinearity. However, the estimation of several alternative specifications revealed that the conclusions drawn about the effects of the explanatory variables, and most importantly about the two-way and three-way interactions considered in the study, are not at all sensitive to the simultaneous inclusion of these variables.

Figure 3. Predicted Instrumental Crime Rates at Different Levels of Commitment to Monetary Success and Commitment to Legitimate Means

A. Effect of Commitment to Monetary Success on Instrumental Crime

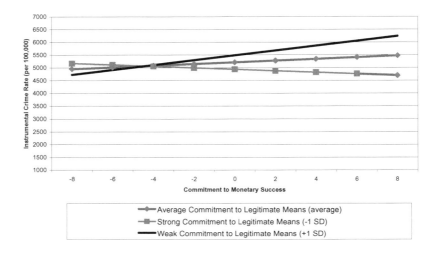

B. Effect of Commitment to Legitimate Means on Instrumental Crime

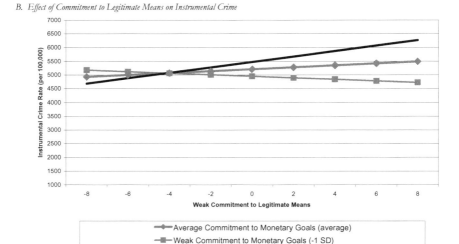

in the top lines in each figure (when the moderator is set to 1 standard deviation above the mean, which is denoted with the solid black lines) are statistically significant. This interaction indicates that instrumental crime rates were highest in the late 1970s in areas where there was both a strong

VALIDITY OF ANOMIE THEORIES 647

commitment to monetary success and a weak commitment to legitimate means, which is consistent with theoretical expectations derived from the classic and contemporary anomie theories considered in this study.[16]

The results presented in the remainder of table 3 (models 3–5) address the question of whether the observed interaction between commitment to monetary success and weak commitment to legitimate means is conditioned by the elements of social structure emphasized by Merton. Empirically, these models test for possible three-way interactions among commitment to monetary success, weak commitment to legitimate means, and the indicators of job availability (model 3), levels of attainment (model 4), and inequality (model 5). As the results show, we find no support for the idea that the instrumental crime pressures emanating from a strong commitment to monetary success and a weak commitment to legitimate means are amplified in the contexts of limited job availability, low levels of educational and economic attainment, and high levels of inequality, as suggested by Merton's anomie theory. It is noteworthy, however, that we find statistically significant two-way interactions involving the indicator of commitment to monetary success goals and both the measure of low levels of educational and economic attainment (model 4, $b = 16.33$, $p < .05$) and the measure of economic inequality (model 5, $b = 26.67$, $p < .05$). We find similar results after dropping the nonsignificant three-way interaction terms in these models. These results suggest that the effect on instrumental crime of strong commitments to monetary success goals is amplified when accompanied by particularly low levels of economic attainment and conditions of high economic inequality. Although not consistent with the predictions we derived above from Merton's writings, as we elaborate in the discussion these findings are on par with other explications of his theory and they affirm some of Merton's comments about the conditional link between crime and adverse economic conditions.[17]

---

16. It is also interesting to note that the estimated effect of this interaction effect without the indicators of noneconomic institutional strength (not shown in tabular form) is 17 percent larger than shown in model 3 ($b = 9.59$), which includes these indicators. This is consistent with Maume and Lee's (2003) suggestion that stronger noneconomic social institutions mediate a nontrivial portion of the effect of anomic conditions on levels of instrumental crime.

17. Merton (1938) also implies that factors such as perceptions of formal punishment risk and the level of subjective financial satisfaction also may serve as moderators of the degree to which a commitment to monetary success goals in a context of weakened commitment to institutionalized means is translated into instrumental crime. In supplementary analyses (not shown), we used police force size and the arrest-to-crime ratio as indicators of the degree of objective risk of detection (e.g., Yu and Liska, 1993) and an indicator of the percentage who claim to be satisfied with their financial circumstances and tested whether these factors moderated the two-way interaction effect central to Merton's theory. These analyses do not support the three-way interactions implied by Merton, but they do reveal

Table 4. Regression of Instrumental Crime Rates on Value Commitments and Participation in and Commitment to Noneconomic Social Institutions (N = 77)

Independent Variables	(1)	(2)	(3)	(4)	(5)	(6)	(7)	(8)
Commitment to monetary success	30.22 (24.21)	31.20 (21.16)	13.26 (19.82)	33.32 (22.01)	40.63 (22.11)	19.30 (19.79)	25.32 (22.12)	35.70 (21.83)
Weak commitment to legitimate means	38.32 (23.78)	32.27 (23.62)	46.59* (21.47)	36.15 (23.83)	29.43 (23.94)	36.52 (21.98)	32.00 (24.86)	36.40 (24.68)
Commitment to monetary success X Commitment to legitimate means	8.68* (3.09)	8.62* (2.87)	12.12* (2.76)	7.82* (2.84)	9.59* (2.89)	9.01* (2.64)	6.84* (2.93)	8.02* (3.42)
Commitment to monetary success X Commitment to legitimate means X *Pupils per teacher*	.03 (1.17)							
Commitment to monetary success X Commitment to legitimate means X *% of government spending devoted to education*		-.31 (.38)						
Commitment to monetary success X Commitment to legitimate means X *Time spent with family*			-3.23* (1.11)					
Commitment to monetary success X Commitment to legitimate means X *Commitment to marriage*				-1.50 (1.64)				
Commitment to monetary success X Commitment to legitimate means X *Voter participation*					-.88 (1.92)			
Commitment to monetary success X Commitment to legitimate means X *Welfare assistance*						-5.08* (1.72)		
Commitment to monetary success X Commitment to legitimate means X *Civically engaged church adherence rate*							-.07 (.39)	
Commitment to monetary success X Commitment to legitimate means X *Social Capital*								.43 (.99)
R^2	.760	.776	.806	.758	.766	.800	.759	.759

*$p < .05$, two-tailed test.
NOTE: Estimates are unstandardized regression coefficients with standard errors in parentheses. The parameter estimates shown are from equations that also include main effects of all explanatory and control variables as well as the relevant two-way interaction for each three-way interaction.

VALIDITY OF ANOMIE THEORIES   649

We now turn to an assessment of whether indicators of commitment to and participation in various noneconomic social institutions lessen the criminogenic pressures associated with a strong commitment to monetary success and a weak commitment to legitimate means, as suggested by Messner and Rosenfeld's IAT. To explore this issue, we estimated regression models that test for three-way interaction effects involving the two indicators of value commitments and each of the eight indicators of noneconomic institutional strength outlined earlier. To conserve space, we limit our tabular presentation to the key parameters of interest and summarize the results for these estimations in table 4, which includes for each model the main effects of the two value commitment variables, the two-way interaction term that represents the product of these two variables, and the relevant three-way interaction term (the estimations summarized in the table also included the relevant lower order two-way interaction terms and the main effects for all explanatory and control variables).

Table 4 shows that although all but one of the indicators of noneconomic institutional strength yield the expected pattern (i.e., a negative coefficient for the three-way interaction term), only two emerge as statistically significant moderators in our analysis: welfare assistance and time spent socializing with family members. In both cases, the results are consistent with Messner and Rosenfeld's (2007) theoretical arguments for how relatively strong noneconomic institutions can temper the degree to which the combination of high levels of commitment to pursue monetary success and low levels of commitment to legitimate means translate into higher levels of instrumental crime.[18]

To illustrate more concretely the nature of these findings, we computed the theoretically relevant simple slopes generated by the three-way interactions involving the indicators of time spent with family (model 3) and levels of welfare assistance (model 6). Given the logic of IAT we focus on demonstrating how these two measures of noneconomic institutional strength condition the slopes of the indicators of commitment to monetary success goals and weak commitment to legitimate means when the latter are relatively high (i.e., +1 and +2 standard deviations above their means) or, in other words, under conditions that are most conducive to high instrumental crime rates according to the results presented above (e.g., figure 3). The estimated simple slopes are displayed in two panels in table 5. Panel A presents the simple slopes for the effects of commitment to monetary success at different levels of weak commitment to legitimate

---

that police force size reduces the degree to which higher levels of commitment to monetary success translate into higher instrumental crime rates, which is consistent with the spirit of Merton's arguments.

18. None of the two-way interactions involving the indicators of commitment to noneconomic institutions was statistically significant.

means and welfare assistance, and the effects of weak commitment to legitimate means at different levels of commitment to monetary success goals and welfare assistance. Panel B is structured similarly but with the indicator of time spent socializing with family as the higher order moderator variable.

Table 5. Simple Slopes for Three-Way Interaction Among Commitment to Monetary Success Goals, Weak Commitment to Legitimate Means, and Selected Indicators of Noneconomic Strength ($N = 77$)

A.   Simple Slopes for Three-Way Interaction Among Commitment to Monetary Success Goals, Weak Commitment to Legitimate Means, and Welfare Assistance

Effect of Commitment to Monetary Success Goals on Instrumental Crime

Weak Commitment to Legitimate Means	Welfare Assistance				
	−2 SD	−1 SD	Mean	+1 SD	+2 SD
+1 SD	186.64*	138.24*	89.83*	41.43	−6.97
+2 SD	394.44*	277.41*	160.37*	43.34	−73.70

Effect of Weak Commitment to Legitimate Means on Instrumental Crime

Commitment to Monetary Success	Welfare Assistance				
	−2 SD	−1 SD	Mean	+1 SD	+2 SD
+1 SD	209.61*	159.31*	109.01*	58.71	8.41
+2 SD	423.15*	302.32*	181.50*	60.67	−60.16

B.   Simple Slopes for Three-Way Interaction Among Commitment to Monetary Success Goals, Weak Commitment to Legitimate Means, and Time Socializing with Family

Effect of Commitment to Monetary Success Goals on Instrumental Crime

Weak Commitment to Legitimate Means	Time Spent with Family				
	−2 SD	−1 SD	Mean	+1 SD	+2 SD
+1 SD	187.30*	147.72*	108.14*	68.57	28.99
+2 SD	409.28*	306.15*	203.03*	99.90	−3.22

Effect of Weak Commitment to Legitimate Means on Instrumental Crime

Commitment to Monetary Success	Time Spent with Family				
	−2 SD	−1 SD	Mean	+1 SD	+2 SD
+1 SD	226.77*	185.43*	144.10*	102.76	61.43
+2 SD	454.88*	348.24*	241.60*	134.96	28.322

*$p < .05$, two-tailed test.

The two panels in table 5 tell a consistent story. The effects of commitment to monetary success goals when weak commitment to legitimate means is prevalent (1 and 2 standard deviations above its mean), and the effects of weak commitment to legitimate means when commitment to monetary success goals is strong (1 and 2 standard deviations above its

VALIDITY OF ANOMIE THEORIES   651

mean), dampen significantly as the two higher order moderators (welfare assistance and time spent with family) take on larger values.[19] In other words, higher levels of welfare assistance and more time socializing with family significantly reduce the crime-generating tendencies of a high level of commitment to monetary success and a low level of commitment to legitimate means, which are findings that are consistent with the predictions derived from Messner and Rosenfeld's IAT. In fact, the results reveal that, collectively, a high level of commitment to monetary success goals and a particularly weak commitment to legitimate means (denoted in the table with higher values on the "weak commitment" variable) significantly increase instrumental crime when the indicators of welfare assistance and time with family are average or relatively low, but they have no significant effect on crime when these indicators are above average.

DISCUSSION

We derived and examined several empirical predictions about spatial variation in instrumental crime rates contained in the anomie theories presented by Merton (1938, 1949, 1957, 1964, 1968) and Messner and Rosenfeld (1994, 2007). Our interpretation of these perspectives highlighted the crime-generating effect of a high level of commitment to monetary success goals combined with a low level of commitment to legitimate means for pursuing such goals, and we outlined various factors that have been theorized to condition this effect. Using a unique aggregate-level dataset, our analyses revealed empirical support for a central prediction of classic and contemporary anomie perspectives: Instrumental crime rates are significantly higher when both a relatively high level of commitment to monetary success and a low level of commitment to legitimate means exists. This two-way interaction effect persisted after considering simultaneously several other explanatory variables and controls, and its effect was nontrivial in magnitude. The evidence was mixed regarding whether this effect is moderated by features of the social structure. As predicted, the data indicated that higher levels of welfare assistance and more frequent socializing among families reduce the tendency for this "goals/means" value complex to translate into higher rates of instrumental crime. But several other factors widely believed to play a similar moderating role did not do so as tested in this work.

The key dimensions of social structure emphasized by Merton—limited

---

19. We compared the simple slopes for high and low values (e.g., +1 and −1 standard deviation from the mean) of the higher order moderators shown in table 5 using a significance test of slope differences for three-way interactions (Dawson and Richter, 2006). In each case, the resulting *t* test indicated that the estimated simple slopes were significantly different ($p < .05$).

and unequally distributed legitimate opportunities—were not found to exhibit the significant moderating role we anticipated from a careful reading of his theoretical writings, at least as measured by limited job availability, low levels of educational and economic attainment, and high levels of educational and economic inequality. For reasons noted above, we expected these indicators of economic conditions to amplify the degree to which a high level of commitment to pursue monetary success goals *and* a weakened commitment to legitimate means translate into higher levels of instrumental crime. We found no support for this implied three-way statistical interaction, instead we found that low levels of educational and economic attainment and high levels economic inequality amplify the degree to which commitment to monetary success goals translates into instrumental crime, regardless of the degree to which members of the population exhibit a weakened commitment to legitimate means.

The discrepancy between our empirical findings and our interpretation of Merton's theoretical argument could be a function of several factors, including the general difficulties in detecting higher order statistical interactions and specific aspects of our study design that add to this challenge (e.g., the relatively small sample size or measurement error). But it is also possible that either Merton overestimated the necessity or importance of weakened commitment to legitimate means under conditions of economic insufficiency or that we overestimated the importance he attributed to this element. As others have noted (Messner, 1988), Merton does at times suggest that instrumental crime will likely be particularly high where there is a strong commitment to pursue monetary success goals and insufficient legitimate opportunities to do so effectively, irrespective of the level of commitment the population may have in using only legitimate means. This position is perhaps best reflected in the initial statement of the theory, where Merton states that, "It is only when a system of cultural values extols, virtually above all else, certain common symbols of success for the population at large while its social structure rigorously restricts or completely eliminates access to approved modes of acquiring these symbols for a considerable part of the same population, that antisocial behavior ensues on a considerable scale" (1938: 680). Merton (1968: 203) later qualifies such statements by explicitly stating that the potential deviance-generating effect of a discrepancy between commitment to monetary success goals and blocked access to legitimate means *presupposes* that individuals have imperfectly assimilated institutionalized means, and as we noted, the basic logic of his modes of adaptation signals a significant and necessary causal role for commitment to legitimate means (our emphasis). Whatever his intentions, though, our empirical findings are consistent with the idea that certain objective economic conditions amplify the "pressures" toward instrumental crime created by a strong commitment to pursue monetary

VALIDITY OF ANOMIE THEORIES 653

success goals. Furthermore, the economic conditions that seem to matter most are actual (absolute and relative) levels of attainment rather than the mere availability of employment opportunities, although perhaps a finer measure of the latter, such as the availability of jobs for low-skilled workers, which could not be constructed from available data, would yield a different pattern.

The significant two-way interactions we observed between the indicator of high levels of commitment to monetary success goals and the measures of low levels of attainment and high levels of inequality, respectively, also have relevance for Merton's specific comments on the expected association among crime rates, poverty, and other indicators of economic disadvantage. There is a long tradition of research on the link between economic disadvantage and crime rates, and the findings have been somewhat inconsistent. There are a variety of potential reasons for this inconsistency, including estimation issues (e.g., Land, McCall, and Cohen, 1990), but one possibility foretold by Merton (1938) long ago is that the effects on crime of poverty and other indicators of limited opportunity, such as inequality, may be conditioned by the value commitments of a population. In particular, writing shortly after the Great Depression, Merton (1938: 681) noted that "Poverty as such, and consequent limitation of opportunity, are not sufficient to induce a conspicuously high rate of criminal behavior. Even the often mentioned 'poverty in the midst of plenty' will not necessarily lead to this result." Rather, Merton goes on to argue that the conditions of economic disadvantage yield higher levels of crime mainly when they are accompanied by a high level of commitment to monetary success goals. The two-way interaction effects revealed in models 4 and 5 of table 3 are consistent with this prediction. This finding is relevant for our understanding of the role of economic disadvantage in generating higher levels of crime, and it also suggests a possible reason why the effects of economic disadvantage on crime may be contingent on the sample or era in which they are estimated.

Our findings for the moderating role of some noneconomic social institutions are in-line with empirical expectations derived from institutional anomie theory. Drawing on the insights of Esping-Andersen (1990), Messner and Rosenfeld (1997) suggest that more generous social welfare programs limit total dependence on the market for material well-being and tend to provide some insulation from criminogenic pressures generated by cultural prescriptions to pursue monetary success by any means necessary. Presumably this result is because welfare assistance represents a legal mechanism through which to satisfy culturally valued goals of acquiring money, which may lessen the need to pursue illegal avenues to do so (Hannon and Defronzo, 1998). Although our research cannot evaluate precisely why greater levels of welfare assistance play the observed moderating role, the results do add to a growing body of evidence that more generous welfare policies can mitigate the potentially criminogenic consequences of heightened economic pressures (e.g., Hannon and Defronzo, 1998; Maume and Lee, 2003; Messner and Rosenfeld, 1997; Savolainen, 2000). This pattern of findings presents an intriguing policy dilemma given recent research showing that escalations in the prevailing crime-reduction strategy in the United States—imprisonment—are associated with reductions in the nation's social welfare program (Beckett and Western, 2001; Stucky, Heimer, and Lang, 2005). The evidence is mounting that both of these public policy strategies may yield crime reduction, but given the growing appreciation for the collateral costs of mass imprisonment, perhaps it is time to reconsider the current policy balance, particularly in light of contemporary trends of escalating imprisonment rates (Harrison and Beck, 2005) and declining welfare benefit rates (Somers and Block, 2005).

Our findings for the moderating role of more frequent socializing with family members also are consistent with the central arguments of IAT. Messner and Rosenfeld (2006: 86–87) suggest that a strong commitment to, or high value placed on, noneconomic social institutions such as the family reduces the likelihood of illegitimate responses to culturally induced pressures for achieving monetary success by promoting the transmission of prosocial norms about the virtues of pursuing monetary success goals only through legitimate means and by increasing exposure to external social controls and social support (see also Cullen and Wright, 1997; LaFree, 1998). The results presented here are supportive of this reasoning, although we cannot rule out plausible alternative interpretations. Specifically, from a routine activities/opportunity theoretical perspective, more frequent socialization with family members is likely to increase guardianship of potential residential crime targets and to reduce personal exposure to situations conducive to property crimes such as robbery and larceny (e.g., Cohen and Felson, 1979). It is also possible that more frequent socializing with family members in an area impedes the development of subcultures organized to support illegitimate enterprises (e.g., Cloward and Ohlin, 1960). Whatever the process implied, one implication of our results is that efforts to facilitate more frequent contact between families that are increasingly separated geographically and by the day-to-day demands of a complex society may help to reduce levels of instrumental crime significantly. Messner and Rosenfeld (2006: 112) advocate a substantial expansion of family-friendly policies and benefits (e.g., paid family leave, flexible work schedules, or employer-provided child care) that reduce the degree to which the family is subjugated by the economy and that provide "opportunities to devote more time and energy to exclusively family concerns." The results of our research support the idea that such

VALIDITY OF ANOMIE THEORIES   655

policies would contribute significantly to a comprehensive crime control policy.

None of the other indicators of noneconomic institutional strength considered (i.e., educational spending, pupils per teacher, commitment to marriage, voter participation, civically engaged church adherence, and social capital) was found to perform the hypothesized moderating role outlined by Messner and Rosenfeld. Again, this result could be a function of the data used for our study, and we caution against drawing definitive conclusions until additional research weighs in. But it is plausible that these other institutions may not be as important for regulating culturally induced pressures to engage in illegitimate activity as IAT suggests. Whereas higher levels of welfare support provide a direct means to bolster one's efforts to accumulate financial resources and the family is a particularly vital social institution that is well suited to provide the kinds of internal and external social control and social support needed to regulate behavior, the other institutions highlighted by Messner and Rosenfeld provide more temporary attachments for individuals, are arguably less central to their day-to-day lives, and are probably far less influential in shaping how people respond to culturally induced pressures.

It would be useful for future research to address in more detail these and other intricacies of classic and contemporary anomie theories. Several basic questions remain unanswered about concepts, measurements, and implied causal linkages in these perspectives that might be resolved by additional efforts to explicate the models in precise terms and by discussions about how best to evaluate the models. The meaning of some concepts, for example, seems to be taken for granted when, in actuality, their meaning is fairly elusive (e.g., What does "access" to legitimate opportunities really mean?). And although almost everybody in the field probably would be able to recite the basic stories of Merton's anomie theory and IAT, there seems to be little by way of formal efforts in the literature to translate these stories into precise causal models that can be digested, modified, and agreed on in theory so that we will know when a given study design is appropriate and how to assess the relevance of empirical results. More clarification of the complex arguments and additional work on translating the largely discursive statements into precise and testable causal models would be useful. So would additional empirical work that evaluates some of the other research puzzles contained in Merton's and Messner and Rosenfeld's anomie theories, which could not be explored with the data used for our study (e.g., the factors that shape the assimilation of cultural values and how this process varies by key demographic attributes), as well as research that reconsiders the linkages examined in our study with alternative measures, data sources, and samples. Although we feel that the aggregate data used here were suitable for a preliminary assessment of some core predictions contained in Merton's theory and IAT, the key data source (the aggregate-level version of the GSS) was not specifically designed for this purpose, the units of analysis are relatively large and heterogeneous, and the relevant data were available only for the mid-to-late 1970s. Thus, efforts to replicate our results with alternative data sources that contain multiple measures of key concepts would be highly useful for advancing our understanding of how social organization is linked to crime rates.

Overall, our study provides support for some aspects of the macrolevel anomie theories developed by Merton and Messner and Rosenfeld, but it also points to the need for refinements to these perspectives. In particular, given our interpretations of the two theoretical models and our findings, it seems that a fuller integration of these models would be profitable. Messner and Rosenfeld (2007) make a significant contribution to the theoretical literature by broadening Merton's conceptualization of social structure to include relevant noneconomic social institutions, and our findings hint that these additions are meaningful empirically. But our results also affirm the importance of bringing back in the stratification system in a meaningful way if we are to fully understand the anomic tendencies of our society that make the vitality of noneconomic institutions so important. A model that integrates insights from Merton and Messner and Rosenfeld would better capture the motivational element of anomie theories by incorporating economic circumstances that amplify the degree to which culturally assimilated values are more apt to translate into criminal behavior, while also attending to the many social forces that can regulate these motivational pushes. A model that integrated these two anomie perspectives would therefore be more "sociologically" complete than either one is alone.

REFERENCES

Agnew, Robert. 1987. On testing structural strain theories. *Journal of Research in Crime and Delinquency* 24:281–86.

Agnew, Robert. 1992. Foundation for a general strain theory of crime and delinquency. *Criminology* 30:47–87.

Agnew, Robert, Francis T. Cullen, and Velmer S. Burton. 1996. A new test of classic strain theory. *Justice Quarterly* 13:681–704.

Aiken, Leona S., and Stephen G. West. 1991. *Multiple Regression: Testing and Interpreting Interactions.* Thousand Oaks, CA: Sage.

Baumer, Eric P. 2007. Untangling research puzzles in Merton's multilevel anomie theory. *Theoretical Criminology* 11:63–93.

VALIDITY OF ANOMIE THEORIES 657

Baumer, Eric P., Steven F. Messner, and Richard Rosenfeld. 2003. Explaining spatial variation in support for capital punishment: A multilevel analysis. *American Journal of Sociology* 108:844–75.

Beckett, Katherine, and Bruce Western. 2001. Governing social marginality: Welfare, incarceration, and the transformation of state policy. *Punishment & Society* 3:43–59.

Bernard, Thomas J. 1984. Control criticisms of strain theories: An assessment of theoretical and empirical adequacy. *Journal of Research in Crime and Delinquency* 21:353–72.

Bernard, Thomas J. 1987. Testing structural strain theories. *Journal of Research in Crime and Delinquency* 24:262–80.

Bernburg, Jon G. 2002. Anomie, social change, and crime: A theoretical examination of Institutional-Anomie Theory. *British Journal of Criminology* 42:729–42.

Bollen, Kenneth. 1998. Path analysis. In *Encyclopedia of Biostatistics,* eds. Peter Armitage and Theodore Colton. Sussex, U.K.: Wiley.

Bollen, Kenneth, and Pamela Paxton. 1998. Interactions of latent variables in structural equation models. *Structural Equation Modeling* 5:267–93.

Breen, Richard, and Jan O. Jonsson. 2005. Inequality of opportunity in comparative perspective: Recent research on educational attainment and social mobility. *Annual Review of Sociology* 31:223–44.

Bureau of Economic Analysis. 2007. http://bea.gov/bea/regional/articles/lapi2004/employment.pdf.

Burton, Velmer S., and Francis T. Cullen. 1992. The empirical status of strain theory. *Journal of Crime and Justice* 15:1–30.

Burton, Velmer S., Francis T. Cullen, David T. Evans, and Gregory Dunaway. 1994. Reconsidering strain theory: Operationalization, rival theories, and adult criminality. *Journal of Quantitative Criminology* 10:213–39.

Cao, Linqun. 2004. Is American society more anomic? A test of Merton's theory with cross-national data. *International Journal of Comparative and Applied Criminal Justice* 28:17–31.

Chamlin, Mitchell B., and John K. Cochran. 1995. Assessing Messner and Rosenfeld's Institutional Anomie Theory: A partial test. *Criminology* 33:411–9.

658   BAUMER & GUSTAFSON

Cloward, Richard A., and Lloyd E. Ohlin. 1960. *Delinquency and Opportunity.* New York: The Free Press of Glencoe.

Cohen, Albert K. 1955. *The Delinquent Boys.* New York: The Free Press.

Cohen, Lawrence, and Marcus Felson. 1979. Social change and crime rate trends: A routine activities approach. *American Sociological Review* 44:588–607.

Cole, Stephen. 1975. The growth of scientific knowledge: Theories of deviance as a case study. In *The Idea of Social Structure: Papers in Honor of Robert K. Merton,* ed. Lewis A. Coser. New York: Harcourt Brace Jovanovich.

Cullen, Francis T. 1984. *Rethinking Crime and Deviance Theory: The Emergence of a Structuring Tradition.* Totowa, NJ: Rowman and Allenheld Publishers.

Cullen, Francis T., and John Paul Wright. 1997. Liberating the anomie-strain paradigm: Implications from social support theory. In *The Future of Anomie Theory*, eds. Nikos Passas and Robert Agnew. Boston: Northeastern University Press.

Cullen, John B., K. Praveen Parboteeah, and Martin Hoegl. 2004. Cross-national differences in managers' willingness to justify ethically suspect behaviors: A test of Institutional Anomie Theory. *Academy of Management Journal* 47:411–21.

Davis, James Allen, and Tom W. Smith. 1998. *General Social Surveys, 1972-1998: Cumulative Codebook.* Chicago, IL: National Opinion Research Center.

Dawson, Jeremy F., and Andreas W. Richter. 2006. Probing three-way interactions: The development and application of a slope difference test. *Journal of Applied Psychology* 91:917–26.

Esping-Andersen, Gosta. 1990. *The Three Worlds of Welfare Capitalism.* Princeton, NJ: Princeton University Press.

Farnworth, Margaret, and Michael J. Leiber. 1989. Strain theory revisited: Economic goals, educational means, and delinquency. *American Sociological Review* 54:263–74.

Featherstone, Richard, and Mathieu Deflem. 2003. Anomie and strain: Context and consequences of Merton's two theories. *Sociological Inquiry* 73:471–89.

VALIDITY OF ANOMIE THEORIES 659

Galea, Sandro, and Jennifer Ahern. 2005. Distribution of education and population health: An ecological analysis of New York City neighborhoods. *American Journal of Public Health* 95:2198–205.

Garfield, Eugene. 2006. HISTCITE Bibliographic Analysis and Visualization Software. http://garfield.library.upenn.edu/histcomp/index-merton.html.

Glenmary Research Center. 1973. Churches and Church Membership in the United States, 1971 (Counties). Mars Hill, NC: Glenmary Research Center.

Glenmary Research Center. 1981. Churches and Church Membership in the United States, 1980 (Counties). Mars Hill, NC: Glenmary Research Center.

Greene, William H. 1993. *Econometric Analysis*. Upper Saddle, NJ: Prentice Hall, Inc.

Hannon, Lance, and James DeFronzo. 1998. The truly disadvantaged, public assistance, and crime. *Social Problems* 45:383–92.

Harrison, Paige M., and Allen J. Beck. 2005. Prisoners in 2004. Bureau of Justice Statistic Bulletin, October 2005. Washington, DC: U.S. Department of Justice, Office of Justice Programs. http://www.ojp.usdoj.gov/bjs/pub/pdf/p04.pdf.

Inter-university Consortium for Political and Social Research (ICPSR). 1991. Voter Registration in the United States, 1968-1988 [Computer file]. Ann Arbor, MI: Inter-university Consortium for Political and Social Research [producer and distributor], ICPSR 9405.

Inter-university Consortium for Political and Social Research (ICPSR). 1995. General Election Data for the United States, 1950-1990 [Computer file]. ICPSR ed. Ann Arbor, MI: Inter-university Consortium for Political and Social Research [producer and distributor], ICPSR 0013.

Jaccard, James, and Robert Turrisi. 2003. *Interaction Effects in Multiple Regression*. 2nd ed. Thousand Oaks, CA: Sage.

Jensen, Gary. 2002. Institutional anomie and societal variations in crime: A critical appraisal. *International Journal of Sociology and Social Policy* 22:45–74.

Kleck, Gary. 2004. Measures of gun ownership levels for macrolevel crime and violence research. *Journal of Research in Crime and Delinquency* 41:3–36.

660   BAUMER & GUSTAFSON

Kornhauser, Ruth. 1978. *Social Sources of Delinquency.* Chicago, IL: University of Chicago Press.

Kposowa, Augustine J., Kevin D. Breault, and Beatrice M. Harrison. 1995. Reassessing the structural covariates of violent and property crimes in the USA: A county level analysis. *British Journal of Sociology* 46:79–105.

Krahn, Harvey, Timothy Hartnagel, and John Gartrell. 1986. Income inequality and homicide rates: Cross-national data and criminological theories. *Criminology* 24:269–95.

LaFree, Gary. 1998. *Losing Legitimacy: Street Crime and the Decline of Social Institutions in America.* New York: Westview Press.

Land, Kenneth C., Patricia L. McCall, and Lawrence E. Cohen. 1990. Structural covariates of homicides rates: Are there any invariances across time and social space? *American Journal of Sociology* 95:922–63.

Lazarsfeld, Paul F., and Herbert Menzel. 1965. On the relations between individual and collective properties. In *Reader on Complex Organizations,* ed. Amitai Etzioni. New York: Holt, Rinehart and Winston.

Liska, Allen E. 1971. Aspirations, expectations, and delinquency: Stress and additive models. *Sociological Quarterly* 12:99–107.

Liska, Allen E. 1990. The significance of aggregate dependent variables and contextual independent variables for linking macro and micro theories. *Social Psychology Quarterly* 53:292–301.

Maume, Michael O., and Matthew R. Lee. 2003. Social institutions and violence: A sub-national test of Institutional Anomie Theory. *Criminology* 41:1137–72.

Merton, Robert K. 1938. Social structure and anomie. *American Sociological Review* 3:672–82.

Merton, Robert K. 1949. Social structure and anomie: Revisions and extensions. In *The Family: Its Functions and Destiny,* ed. Ruth N. Anshen. New York: Harper & Brothers.

Merton, Robert K. 1957. *Social Theory and Social Structure.* Revised and enlarged ed. New York: The Free Press.

Merton, Robert K. 1964. Anomie, anomia, and social interaction: Contexts of deviant behavior. In *Anomie and Deviant Behavior,* ed. Marshall Clinard. New York: The Free Press.

VALIDITY OF ANOMIE THEORIES 661

Merton, Robert K. 1968. *Social Theory and Social Structure.* Enlarged ed. New York: The Free Press.

Messner, Steven F. 1983. Regional and racial effects on the urban homicide rate: The subculture of violence revisited. *American Journal of Sociology* 88:997–1007.

Messner, Steven F. 1988. Merton's social structure and anomie: The road not taken. *Deviant Behavior* 9:33–53.

Messner, Steven F., and Richard Rosenfeld. 1994. *Crime and the American Dream.* Belmont, CA: Wadsworth.

Messner, Steven F., and Richard Rosenfeld. 1997. Political restraint of the market and levels of homicide: A cross-national application of Institutional-Anomie Theory. *Social Forces* 75:1393–416.

Messner, Steven F., and Richard Rosenfeld. 2001. *Crime and the American Dream,* 3rd ed. Belmont, CA: Wadsworth.

Messner, Steven F., and Richard Rosenfeld. 2006. The present and future of Institutional Anomie Theory. In *Taking Stock: The Status of Criminological Theory. Advances in Criminological Theory,* vol. 15., ed. Francis T. Cullen. Piscataway, NY: Transaction Books.

Messner, Steven F., and Richard Rosenfeld. 2007. *Crime and the American Dream,* 4th ed. Belmont, CA: Wadsworth.

Messner, Steven F., Eric Baumer, and Richard Rosenfeld. 2004. Dimensions of social capital and rates of criminal homicide. *American Sociological Review* 69:882–903.

Moody, Carlisle E., and Thomas B. Marvell. 2005. Guns and crime. *Southern Economic Journal* 71:720–36.

Orru, Marco. 1987. *Anomie: History and Meanings.* Boston, MA: Allen & Unwin.

Paxton, Pamela. 1999. Is social capital declining in the United States? A multiple indicator assessment. *American Journal of Sociology* 105:88–127.

Piquero, Alex, and Nicole Leeper Piquero. 1998. On testing Institutional Anomie Theory with varying specifications. *Studies on Crime and Crime Prevention* 7:61–84.

Pratt, Travis C., and Francis T. Cullen. 2005. Assessing macro-level predictors and theories of crime: A meta-analysis. In *Crime and Justice:*

662   BAUMER & GUSTAFSON

A Review of Research, vol. 32., ed. Michael H. Tonry. Chicago, IL: University of Chicago Press.

Pratt, Travis C., and Timothy W. Godsey. 2003. Social support, inequality, and homicide: A cross-national test of an integrated theoretical model. *Criminology* 41:101–33.

Putnam, Robert D. 2000. *Bowling Alone: The Collapse and Revival of American Community.* New York: Touchstone.

Rosenfeld, Richard. 1989. Robert Merton's contributions to the sociology of deviance. *Sociological Inquiry* 59:453–66.

Rosenfeld, Richard, Steven F. Messner, and Eric P. Baumer. 2001. Social capital and homicide. *Social Forces* 80:283–309.

Savolainen, Jukka. 2000. Inequality, welfare state, and homicide: Further support for the Institutional Anomie Theory. *Criminology* 38:1021–42.

Scorsone, Eric A., and Julie N. Zimmerman. 2003. What counts? Measuring jobs, income, and unemployment. University of Kentucky: Social and Economic Education for Development.

Somers, Margaret R., and Fred Block. 2005. From poverty to perversity: Ideas, markets, and institutions over 200 years of welfare debate. *American Sociological Review* 70:260–87.

Stucky, Thomas D. 2003. Local politics and violent crime in U.S. cities. *Criminology* 41:1101–35.

Stucky, Thomas D., Karen Heimer, and Joseph B. Lang. 2005. Partisan politics, electoral competition and imprisonment: An analysis of states over time. *Criminology* 43:211–47.

Stults, Brian J., and Eric P. Baumer. 2007. Racial context and police force size: Modeling intervening processes. *American Journal of Sociology.* In press.

Taylor, Marylee C. 1998. How white attitudes vary with the racial composition of local populations: Numbers count. *American Sociological Review* 63:512–35.

Tolbert, Charles M., and Molly Sizer. 1996. *U.S. Commuting Zones and Labor Market Areas: A 1990 Update.* Staff Paper No. AGES 9614. Rural Economy Division, Economic Research Service, U.S. Department of Agriculture.

U.S. Department of Commerce, Bureau of the Census. 1999. *County and City Data Book [United States], 1983* (ICPSR 8256).

VALIDITY OF ANOMIE THEORIES 663

U.S. Department of Commerce, Bureau of the Census. 2000. *County and City Data Book [United States], 1977* (ICPSR 7697).

U.S. Department of Education, National Center for Education Statistics. 2001. Elementary and Secondary General Information System (ELSEGIS): Elementary-Secondary Staff Information, 1975-1976 [Computer file]. ICPSR version. Washington, DC: U.S. Department of Education, National Center for Education Statistics [producer]. Ann Arbor, MI: Interuniversity Consortium for Political and Social Research [distributor], 2001. (ICPSR 2241).

U.S. Department of Justice, Federal Bureau of Investigation. 1978. *Crime in the United States, 1977.* Washington, DC: U.S. Department of Justice, Federal Bureau of Investigation.

U.S. Department of Justice, Federal Bureau of Investigation. 1998. Uniform Crime Reporting Program Data [United States]: County Level Arrest and Offenses Data, 1977-1983 [Computer file]. Washington, DC: U.S. Department of Justice, Federal Bureau of Investigation [producer], 1984. Ann Arbor, MI: Inter-University Consortium for Political and Social Research [distributor].

Yu, Jiang, and Allen E. Liska. 1993. The certainty of punishment: A reference group effect and its functional form. *Criminology* 31:447–64.

Eric Baumer received his PhD degree in sociology from the University at Albany, State University of New York, in 1998 and is currently an associate professor in the Department of Criminology and Criminal Justice at the University of Missouri—St. Louis. His research is concerned primarily with how social structural and cultural features of communities affect individual behavior. He has examined this issue empirically in multilevel studies of the influence of neighborhood characteristics on individual-level outcomes, in macrolevel studies of urban crime levels and trends, and in case studies of crime and social control in Iceland, Malta, and Ireland.

Regan Gustafson is a doctoral candidate in the Department of Criminology and Criminal Justice at the University of Missouri—St. Louis. Her primary research interests include communities and crime, with an emphasis on rural communities, criminological theory, and collateral consequences.

[19]

Institutions, Anomie, and Violent Crime: Clarifying and Elaborating Institutional-Anomie Theory

Steven F. Messner, University at Albany, State University of New York, United States
Helmut Thome, Martin-Luther-University, Halle-Wittenberg, Germany
Richard Rosenfeld, Department of Criminology and Criminal Justice, University of Missouri – St. Louis, United States

A limited but accumulating body of research and theoretical commentary offers support for core claims of the "institutional-anomie theory" of crime (IAT) and points to areas needing further development. In this paper, which focuses on violent crime, we clarify the concept of social institutions, elaborate the cultural component of IAT, derive implications for individual behavior, summarize empirical applications, and propose directions for future research. Drawing on Talcott Parsons, we distinguish the "subjective" and "objective" dimensions of institutional dynamics and discuss their interrelationship. We elaborate on the theory's cultural component with reference to Durkheim's distinction between "moral" and "egoistic" individualism and propose that a version of the egoistic type characterizes societies in which the economy dominates the institutional structure, anomie is rampant, and levels of violent crime are high. We also offer a heuristic model of IAT that integrates macro- and individual levels of analysis. Finally, we discuss briefly issues for the further theoretical elaboration of this macro-social perspective on violent crime. Specifically, we call attention to the important tasks of explaining the emergence of economic dominance in the institutional balance of power and of formulating an institutional account for distinctive punishment practices, such as the advent of mass incarceration in the United States.

1. Introduction

The influence of the anomie perspective in criminology has risen and fallen over the past seven decades or so. Merton's well known formulation, which was originally published in 1938, dominated sociological inquiry into crime during the 1950s and 1960s, only to be relegated by some to the dustbin of criminological history (Hirschi 1969; Kornhauser 1978; see also Messner and Rosenfeld 2007, 12–14). However, researchers have subsequently responded to critiques of earlier formulations of anomie theory, crafted expanded versions of the theory, and applied the theory in novel ways. To paraphrase Mark Twain, developments in the discipline in the latter years of the twentieth century and the beginning of the twenty-first century suggest that the earlier reports of the death of anomie theory had been greatly exaggerated.

One effort to revive and revitalize the anomie perspective in criminology has been the formulation of "institutional-anomie" theory (hereafter IAT). The core arguments of this approach were initially presented as part of an explanation of the comparatively high rates of serious crime in the United States (Messner and Rosenfeld 2007). Over time, these arguments have evolved into a theoretical framework with more general applicability. The distinguishing feature of IAT is its principal focus on culture and social structure as manifested in social institutions. Following in the spirit

This research was supported by the Center for Interdisciplinary Research at Bielefeld University, Germany, which organized a research group on "Control of Violence," directed by Wilhelm Heitmeyer and Heinz-Gerhard Haupt. We are grateful to the members of the research group for their feedback on a presentation based on this research, and to Susanne Karstedt and an anonymous reviewer for helpful comments on earlier drafts of the manuscript.

of Durkheimian sociology, IAT is built upon the underlying premise that the "normal" levels and forms of criminal activity in any society reflect the fundamental features of social organization.

In this paper, we seek to further advance the IAT research program by clarifying key concepts, elaborating the arguments about the impact of social organization on levels of violent crime, and extending the scope of the theory. We begin with a formal treatment of the core concept of "institutions," explaining how it has been derived from and expands upon the classic conceptualization employed by Talcott Parsons (1990 [1934]).[1] This exercise in conceptual clarification is fruitful for two reasons. One, it highlights the central role of cultural values in understanding institutional dynamics. We take this important insight as a point of departure for explicating in greater detail than in previous statements of the theory the kinds of fundamental value orientations that are theorized to be conducive to pervasive criminal violence in the advanced societies. Two, our explication of the concept of "institutions" draws attention to some of the individual-level processes upon which IAT implicitly rests. Concrete human actors ultimately produce and reproduce the institutional dynamics that operate at the macro level. A comprehensive statement of IAT thus requires identification of the linkages between the level of social systems and the level of individual action. By elaborating cultural processes and identifying the multilevel linkages implicit in IAT, we can uncover new "puzzles" that might stimulate research on violent crime in the future.[2]

2. The Concept of "Social Institutions"

As noted, IAT adopts a conceptualization of "institutions" that is derived from Parsons' work on general sociological theory (see also Bellah et al. 1991, 287–306) and is compatible with more recent applications in other social science disciplines. Parsons explains that two valid approaches to the study of institutions can be differentiated: the "subjective" and the "objective" (Parsons 1990 [1934], 319). The

former adopts the viewpoint of the actor and is essential for understanding individual-level behavior. The latter refers to the perspective of the sociological observer and is particularly relevant to the characterization of the institutional order in society at large.

From the subjective point of view, institutions play an influential role in guiding "action," which generally involves some kind of "means-ends" relationship.[3] Actors formulate goals (ends), and they choose "suitable" means (or ways) of obtaining these goals. The "suitability" of the means can be determined with reference to a specified standard of rationality. The precise standard of rationality invoked differs depending on the nature of the ends. For example, the appropriate standards for assessing the rationality of empirical ends (e.g., securing resources) differ from those that pertain to transcendental ends (e.g., attaining salvation).

Individual actors have multiple ends and multiple sets of means that involve "complex 'chains' of means-ends relationships, so constituted that the 'end' of one sector of the chain is a means to some further end" (Parsons 1990 [1934], 322). Moreover, for social order to exist, different individuals must coordinate their actions. Parsons assumes that this can only occur if there is an appreciable degree of integration of ultimate ends among those in a social system. In other words, he assumes that a concrete, on-going society presupposes a value system that is to some meaningful degree shared or common to the members of that society. Of course, not all people embrace every single value, and even those who accept the values do not always act in ways compatible with them. Nevertheless, Parsons maintains that a situation lacking any agreement on ultimate values would be highly unstable and would likely lead to chaos, i.e., the Hobbessian state of nature, the war of all against all.

The common value system is, therefore, the foundation on which social institutions rest for Parsons. The members of society collectively formulate or accept rules, or regulatory

---

1 A preliminary effort along these lines can be found in Messner and Rosenfeld (2004).
2 See Cole (1975) for a discussion of problem-generation as a key latent function of theories.

3 Parsons has often been accused of overextending the means-ends conceptualization of action, blurring, for example, the distinctive features of habitual or expressive behaviour and

glossing over the human potential for creativity (see, e.g., Joas 1997). In the context of our present discussion we let this matter rest.

166

norms, that govern the means that are judged to be acceptable in the pursuit of ends. These norms are accompanied by sanctions, and they have an obligatory quality surrounding them; they are in an important sense "coercive" to use Durkheim's language (1964b [1895]). There are of course a multitude of norms that pertain to different forms of behavior, and it is accordingly useful to conceptualize systems of regulatory norms that pertain to particular kinds of tasks and performances that are commonly differentiated on the basis of functional considerations. These systems of rules or regulatory norms constitute the major social institutions in a society (e.g., the economy, the family, etc.).

Parsons has been legitimately criticized for exaggerating the degree of value consensus in concrete societies and for largely neglecting the role of factors other than institutional norms that can coordinate action and create social order, such as the exercise of raw or "charismatic" power, and considerations of self-interest. Similarly, although he acknowledges a role for "implicit" rules in constraining behavior (1990 [1934], 329), he does not display much appreciation for the extent to which social interactions are infused with taken-for-granted presumptions that have little direct relationship to any ultimate value system. Nevertheless, his analytic framework introduces some highly useful conceptual distinctions for institutional analysis. For example, a common approach to institutions is to equate them with observed patterns of behavior. From this perspective, behaviors that occur with a high degree of regularity are "institutionalized" behaviors. Parsons, in contrast, restricts his conceptualization of institutions to the rules that contribute to the emergence of these regular patterns of behavior. A very similar approach appears in the "new institutionalism" that has emerged in economics, political science, and economic sociology in recent decades. As Douglass North puts it: "Institutions are the rules of the game in a society or, more formally, are the humanly devised constraints that shape human interaction" (1990, 3).

The analytic distinction between the "rules of the game" or institutional norms and concrete forms of behavior is critically important because it allows for an empirical assessment of the role of institutional controls in contrast with the role of other factors. Parsons recognizes that concrete

behaviors are determined by many factors, including the physical environment, biological heredity, and psychological traits (1990 [1934], 320). If institutions are equated with behavioral regularities themselves, it is impossible to isolate the distinctive contribution of institutional factors in the explanation of these behaviors.

Parsons also distinguishes between moral and utilitarian sources of compliance with institutional norms. He theorizes that the primary motive for obeying an institutional norm "lies in the moral authority it exercises over the individual" (1990 [1934], 326). When a norm is imbued with such authority, the actor complies with the norm because the prescribed behavior is "good for its own sake" and is not merely a means to some other end. The moral authority of institutional norms, however, is never perfect. A secondary, utilitarian type of control invariably accompanies the moral type in ongoing societies. This involves a "calculation of advantage" rooted in an appeal to interest, which may take the form of positive advantages on the one hand or disadvantageous consequences on the other.

Shifting from the "subjective" to the "objective" view of institutions, Parsons goes on to argue that institutions themselves can be thought of as constituting a collective system. Each institution has implications for others. In his words, the institutions are inter-related with respect to their mutual "requiredness" (1990 [1934], 332). The norms of a given institution are not compatible with just any kinds of norms in other institutions. Only some kinds of norms would "fit" with others. The degree of fit between institutions can be understood as constituting the degree of "structural integration" of the institutional order. Parsons cites the medieval relations between church and state as an instance of weak structural integration. Each of these institutions "claimed an allegiance which inevitably encroached on the requirements of the other" (1990 [1934], 332).

Parsons identifies an additional feature of the institutional order—its "regulatory integration" (1990 [1934], 332). This refers to the degree to which and the means by which institutional norms govern behavior in practice. In a hypothetical society with perfect regulatory integration, conformity with the norms would be universal and would be brought about entirely by the moral authority of the norms. Such a hypothetical concept is not intended as a "descriptive category" but as an "ideal type," a "polar concept" (1990 [1934], 332). Such a society will not exist in the empirical world. At the opposite end of the continuum is a hypothetical society wherein the moral authority of the norms has dissolved. Initially, considerations of self-interest might produce conformity with social norms in such a society, although Parsons anticipates that such a situation would eventually result in a "loss of control even by that means" (1990 [1934], 333). Following Durkheim (1966 [1897]), Parsons uses the term "anomie" to refer to the situation in which the moral authority of the institutional norms has broken down (see also Merton 1964). In essence, a high degree of anomie implies that concrete behavior is no longer "institutionalized" in the sense of being governed by the moral authority of social norms.

In sum, Parsons has put forth a useful, albeit highly abstract, analytic framework for institutional analysis that potentially has wide applicability for understanding social phenomena. Institutions refer to systems of rules intended to control behavior that have the distinctive quality of being "moral," i.e., rooted in some overarching value system.[4] Furthermore, processes of institutional control can be understood as operating at dual levels. At the individual level, institutional rules constitute part of the environment confronting actors as they select the means to realize their ends. At the macro-level, institutions form different configurations exerting constraining but also orienting and enabling influences upon the members of society. Though these configurations ultimately arise from and are maintained by individual and collective actions their emergent properties (that need to be theoretically reconstructed) cannot be (fully) "designed" by specific actors.

3. Institutional-Anomie Theory

IAT builds on and adapts this general framework for institutional analysis to explain the specific phenomenon

of crime. In so doing it also draws liberally on Merton's variant of the anomie perspective (1968:189), incorporating in particular his keen insights about the tendency of considerations of technical expediency to override moral concerns under conditions of extreme anomie. However, whereas Merton places primary emphasis on the stratification system when considering the social structural determinants of anomie, IAT broadens the focus to include other primary institutions of society.[5]

3.1. Bringing Institutions into Criminological Theory

Social institutions are to some extent distinct with respect to the primary activities around which they are organized, which is the basis of conventional classifications of institutions. To illustrate, the system of institutional norms that relates to activities pertaining to the subsistence requirements of human organisms—food, clothing, shelter—is typically labeled the "economy," though today the economy goes far beyond these minimal requirements. The system of institutional norms that governs behaviors related to the biological reproduction of the species is referred to as the family, and so on (Messner and Rosenfeld 2007; see also Turner 2003).

The functions associated with the institutional norms are necessarily overlapping and interdependent in the sense that the functioning of a given institution has consequences for the functioning of the others. For example, the performance of the economy is dependent on the quality of the "human capital" cultivated in the schools. The capacity of the schools to develop human capital is circumscribed by the individual backgrounds that students bring with them from their families. The effective functioning of all three of these institutions—the economy, education, and the family—presupposes an environment with at least a modicum of social order, for which the polity has formal responsibility. Finally, the effectiveness of the polity in promoting the collective good (at least as perceived by those who wield political power) depends on the nature and quality of

---

4 It is important to distinguish this usage of the term "moral" from a conceptualization that invokes a transcendental standard of morality. A concrete society might secure compliance with institutional norms by virtue of the moral authority that they exercise over societal members, but the prescribed behaviors might be judged to be immoral according to some "ultimate" standard of morality.

5 See Messner (2003a) for an extended discussion of poits of overlap and divergence between Merton's theory of social structure and anomie and IAT.

168

economic resources and human capabilities supplied by the other institutions.

The interdependence of major social institutions implies that, for the society to "work" at all, there must be some coordination among institutions, just as there must be some coordination among the ultimate ends of individual actors. The requirements for the effective functioning of any given institution, however, may conflict with the requirements of another. This potential for conflict is manifested in two important ways. One source of conflict involves competing demands associated with role performance. Given the fact that time is a finite resource, performing a given institutional role (e.g., working overtime) may preclude performing another role (e.g., taking one's daughter to soccer practice). In addition, the kinds of orientations towards action that are appropriate differ in certain important respects depending on the institutional domain.

An especially stark contrast can be seen between the orientations for interactions embodied in the institutions of a market economy and the family. Family relationships are expected to be regulated by the norms of particularism, affective engagement, and diffuseness, whereas transactions in the marketplace are governed by universalism, affective neutrality, and specificity (Parsons 1951). Concrete actors are thus required to shift their basic orientations towards interactions as they negotiate the different institutional demands that they face.

Any given society will therefore be characterized by a distinctive arrangement of social institutions that reflects a balancing of the sometimes competing claims and requisites of the different institutions, yielding a distinctive "institutional balance of power."[6] Indeed, a very useful way of classifying whole societies is according to the prevailing form of institutional balance. In some societies, such as the former Soviet Union, the political system dominates the institutional order. In others, the so-called primordial insti-

tutions (family, clan, ethnic group) are dominant. The core claim of IAT is that the type of institutional configuration that is conducive to high levels of crime in the advanced societies is one in which the rules of the economy are awarded highest priority in the system of institutions. In such a society, the economy tends to dominate the institutional balance of power, thereby creating institutional imbalance.

Economic dominance is manifested in three principal ways. One is devaluation. Non-economic institutional roles tend to be devalued relative to economic roles. Non-economic roles carry less prestige than economic roles and their occupants receive fewer rewards for effective role performance. A second manifestation of economic dominance is accommodation. Individuals feel pressures to sacrifice other roles to economic roles when conflicts emerge, as when a family abandons collective meals because they conflict with members' work schedules. The third manifestation of economic dominance is penetration. The logic of the marketplace intrudes into other realms of social life. Paying students for their educational accomplishments is a particularly stark example (Messner and Rosenfeld 2007, 82–83). On a larger scale, the increasing commercialization of sports and the arts and the "privatization" of public institutions and functions provide countless examples of such intrusions.

Economic dominance in the institutional balance of power can be linked specifically with criminal behavior via both internalized normative controls and informal social controls. With respect to the former, economic norms in market capitalist economies are predicated on a calculative orientation towards action. Economic thinking, economizing, intrinsically involves cost/benefit assessments to determine how to allocate scarce resources among alternative uses. In their performance of economic roles, actors are thus encouraged to apply "efficiency" norms in the selection of the means to achieve their ends, and to accumulate as much as possible the prime medium of exchange used in economic transactions: money.

---

6 We use the term "power" in the phrase "institutional balance of power" in the sense of functional primacy and not in the sense of political struggles. When an institution domi- nates the institutional balance of power, the claims and requisites of that institution take precedence over those of other institutions.

IAT predicts that under conditions of economic dominance in the institutional balance of power, the orientation toward action associated with the performance of economic roles "spills over" into social action more generally. Concrete actors are prone to use whatever means are technically expedient to realize their ends, regardless of the normative status of these means. To return to the language introduced above, institutional norms have little moral authority when the economy dominates the institutional balance of power. The means of social action have been literally de-moralized, resulting in anomie.[7] Under conditions of extreme anomie, the internalized restraints against crime are expected to be quite weak. Compliance with institutional norms, including legal norms, is thus dependent on the "secondary type of control," i.e., the "calculation of advantage."

Yet economic dominance tends to undermine this alternative type of control as well. Economic dominance implies that non-economic institutions are enfeebled. The roles of these institutions become less attractive; people fail to develop strong attachments to them; and the enactment of these roles is subservient to the enactment of economic roles. The incentives and disincentives associated with non-economic role performance are thus rendered less salient to actors as they orient their behaviors away from such roles. Accordingly, the two principal motives for compliance with institutional norms explicated above—their moral authority and the potency of the incentive/disincentive structures associated with them—are likely to be weak under conditions of economic dominance. It follows that behaviors contrary to the norms, including behaviors that violate norms that

have been codified in criminal law, will be relatively frequent and commonplace.

3.2. The Value Foundations of Economic Dominance in the Institutional Balance of Power and the Explanation of Criminal Violence

IAT thus describes how a specific configuration of social institutions and the accompanying normative order it represents create a social environment that is more or less conducive to criminal behavior by virtue of the operation of internalized moral controls and external social controls. The original formulation of the theory does not fully explain, however, the interconnections between institutional structure and fundamental cultural values. If institutions reflect values that are in some meaningful sense shared and "basic" to a society, as argued persuasively by Parsons, then any institutional structure that endures for an appreciable amount of time, even one that exhibits "imbalance" among the constituent institutions, must be grounded in a distinctive set of values.[8]

Moreover, the applicability of IAT specifically to violent criminal offending—the focus of the present inquiry—requires explicit consideration. The erosion of the moral authority of institutional norms and the weakening of external social controls are in principle relevant to the explanation of all forms of criminal conduct and of deviant behavior more generally. Research by Karstedt and Farrell (2006) indicates that insights from IAT can in fact be applied to explain the so-called "crimes of everyday life," i.e., morally dubious acts, not all of which are technically illegal. In addition, a paradox emerges when the applicability of

---

7 The "demoralization" of the means of action as a result of the penetration of the logic of a market economy is not the only possible source of anomie. Anomie may reflect features of the normative order itself, such as internal inconsistencies among norms or lack of clarity in the norms. See Thome (2003; 2007) for an extended discussion of the different subtypes of anomie in Durkheim's work and, in particular, the distinction between "developmental" or "process induced" anomie and "chronic" or "structural" anomie. The former is a temporary condition that emerges during periods of rapid change; the latter refers to a stable feature of the institutional order. IAT focuses primarily on "chronic" or "structural" anomie, although it has potential applicability for other forms of anomie as well.

8 Although we adopt Parsons' general approach to the conceptualization of social institutions, we depart here from the spirit of much Parsonian sociology in one important respect. Parsons emphasizes the smooth functioning of social systems, and he thus might have conceived of "economic dominance" as a temporary form of structural malintegration, one that would be rectified through equilibrating mechanisms. We leave open the possibility that a social system characterized by economic dominance in the institutional balance of power is viable and durable, although we expect that such a social system will exhibit high rates of criminal violence as part of its "normal" functioning (see Rosenfeld and Messner forthcoming).

170

IAT to violence is considered in historical context. Historical studies reveal that levels of interpersonal violence, and in particular homicide, have declined substantially over the course of the past several centuries, at least in Europe, where rich historical data are available (Eisner 2003a, 2003b). How can the institutional dynamics depicted in IAT, which pertain to highly developed market societies, be reconciled with these documented trends in violence? A comprehensive account of the impact of social organization on levels of criminal violence requires that the cultural underpinnings of economic dominance in the institutional balance of power be explicated clearly and fully, and that the hypothesized institutional and cultural processes be situated within the larger historical context.

We can advance such an account by drawing upon Durkheim's insights about the morality of traditional versus advanced, highly differentiated societies.[9] In his classic formulation of the processes of societal evolution, Durkheim (1964a [1893]) explains the transition from primitive or segmentally divided to modern societies with reference to a fundamental shift in forms of social solidarity—from the "mechanical" type to the "organic" type. Durkheim also identifies a concomitant erosion of "collectivism" and rise in "individualism." This latter distinction is directly relevant to understanding patterns in violence. Specifically, Durkheim suggests that "with the progress of civilization homicide decreases" (1958 [1950], 113). The reason for this trend lies in the demystification of the collectivity and its devaluation relative to the "worshipping" of the individual. Durkheim construes "collectivism" as an integrative pattern in which the group—the family, the clan, a professionally defined group, a religious or ethnic community—is valued much more than the individual and his or her well-being.

Premised on this foundational value pattern, Durkheim identifies two major, closely intertwined organizing prin-ciples which, in his view, shaped the institutional order of pre-modern European societies and made such an order prone to interpersonal violence: honor and a rigidly defined social hierarchy, within a society divided into estates. The importance of honor and its counterpart, "defamation," in stimulating violent conflict has been widely recognized in a variety of contexts and need not be elaborated here (see, for example, Nisbett and Cohen 1996; Spierenburg 1998). With respect to hierarchy (Roth 2001, 47), we note in particular the following aspect. If the group counts more than the individual, particular persons are typically regarded as closer to the gods than the masses; there are leaders and followers, masters and servants, insiders and outsiders. In other words, members of the various strata differ in the amount of honor, respect, and general human worth granted them. These differences are likely to be criminogenic on their own, as indicated in various historical studies (e.g., Ruggiero 1980; Lehti 2004, with reference to Ylikangas 2001) and also in experimental research (Zimbardo et al. 1974).[10] The potential for hierarchy and processes of social marginalization to contribute to violence is likely to be relevant to the (post-) modern societies as well as to the traditional, collectivistic societies.

Durkheim argues that traditional collectivism had to break down in the course of an increasingly advanced division of labor and the transformation from a segmentally divided, rigidly stratified society to a functionally differentiated society. In the latter type of society, the individual is no longer tied into a closely knit mesh of norms, symbols, and rituals that define his or her own identity primarily in terms of belonging to a collectivity. The fusion of personal and collective identities dissolves. The individual's social standing and reputation are no longer defined by a group-specific code of honor that, for example, makes blood revenge obligatory.[11] Violence that injures, mutilates, or kills another person becomes increasingly repugnant, abominable.

9 The following discussion is based on Thome (2007). Advances in historical knowledge and sociological theory have corrected and modified many of Durkheim's ideas (Fenton 1984, Turner 1993). Nevertheless, some of his insights are still valid and quite helpful in explaining the long-term developments in violent crime.

10 Baumeister et al. (1996) review some of the psychological literature confirming the violent implications arising from claims of superiority. For the connection between sharpened economic competition and the "renaturalization" of inequality resulting in differential claims of moral worth, i.e. superiority, see Bauman (1990) and Young (1958).

11 The code of honor is still relevant in certain situations involving group relationships, such as adolescent street life in inner city ghettoes (Anderson 1999).

Although traditional collectivism erodes as societies evolve, Durkheim by no means posits a total disappearance of collective sentiments (Bellah 1973, xli). There is a "collective conscience" even in individualized societies, but the highest-ranking value is the individual "in general"; not just the individual "self" but also the individual "other." This "moral" or "cooperative" individualism respects the individual as the carrier of universal rights and obligations. As a social praxis, moral individualism is based on mutual sympathy and respect for others—any other person. It seeks to increase social inclusion, and it postulates the right of self-actualization for all. It runs counter to "free-riding" practices, promotes adherence to the principles of reciprocity (solidarity based on fairness), and occasionally calls for (bearable) sacrifices to help those in need. Cooperative individualism thus implies a principled readiness to invest in collective goods (like having a democratic government or preserving the natural environment) even without calculable individual payoffs or losses.

Moving from culture and social praxis (forms of interaction) to the social structural and the political plane, we note that cooperative individualism seeks to secure justice and to balance personal freedom and equality, mainly by combining social welfare provisions and parliamentary democracy. Durkheim insists on the functional primacy of the state over the economy, because the latter is immanently amoral. The state serves as "the organ of moral discipline" (1958 [1950], 72), and at the same time it is the champion of individualism (1958 [1950], 69). Without the state, the individual could not have been set free from primordial bonds; without the state, there would be no power to protect the individual against the tyrannical claims of the group. Durkheim, on the basis of his reading of history, is led to the conclusion that "except for the abnormal cases . . . the

stronger the state, the more the individual is respected" (1958 [1950], 57). [12] On the other hand, Durkheim also stresses the necessity of counterbalancing the power of the state with strong secondary social groups—what political scientists and sociologists have later conceptualized as various forms of "corporatism" (e.g., Siaroff 1999; Hall and Gingerich 2004).

In Durkheim's view, then, it was mainly the erosion of collectivism that brought about the long-term decline in levels of interpersonal violence. [13] In his earlier, more optimistic, writings he also assumed that the emerging individualism would predominantly take on the cooperative form just described: the presumably "normal" type of modern society that would stabilize the low level of interpersonal violence. The new value system implies, among other things, a lower level of passion and stronger control of emotions. The reason why passions, in particular the impulse to retaliate and punish violently, are lower or more constrained in individualist cultures seems to be that the person who violates the norms (and is to be punished for that) is, so to speak, an incarnation of the very object which is now being worshipped, i.e., the individual in general (Durkheim 1978 [1895]).

Durkheim's account of the large-scale pacification associated with the growth of individualism is similar in some respects to Elias's views on the "civilizing" process (1982 [1939]), but with an important distinction. For Elias, the disciplinary forces of the advanced societies hold down individual impulses; for Durkheim, individuals are freed from the closely knit bonds that tied them to the collectivity. Durkheim also theorizes, however, that the restructured agents of social control and moral guidance, particularly the nuclear family, the school, professional organizations,

---

12 Durkheim's faith in the capacity of the state to serve as "the guardian, promoter and enforcer of civic morality" can certainly be challenged given subsequent historical developments, as noted by Varga (2006, 463). See also Wolfe (1989) for an extended discussion of how expansion in the authority of the state can threaten the vitality of civil society.

13 This thesis has been supported by a statistical analysis of crime data available for Germany at the end of the nineteenth century (Thome 2002). Karstedt (2006) also reports evidence consistent with Durkheim's claim about the effect of the movement from collectivistic to individualistic values on levels of violence. In her analysis of cross-national variation in homicide rates in the latter decades of

the twentieth century, she finds that an indicator of individualism is negatively associated with levels of homicide. See also Karstedt (2001, 2004).

172

and most importantly, the authority of a democratically legitimized state, play a critical role in providing the moral underpinnings of the new social order.

Thus far we have recounted Durkheim's thesis of the "normal" evolution of cultural values. He also identifies an important "pathological" departure from cooperative individualism, which he refers to as "egoistic" or "excessive" individualism.[14] The defining characteristics of this form of individualism are hedonistic self-fulfillment instead of social solidarity; ruthless pursuit of one's own interests while using others as a mere "means" in strategic interactions. In the tradition of the Frankfurt School of social thought, it is the triumph of "instrumentalism" or, in Habermas' terms (1984), the dominance of strategic interaction over communicative action seeking mutual understanding and recognition. Durkheim is skeptical about the long term viability of this type of cultural value system, explaining that such orientations are ultimately self-delusive: a meaningful life can be found only within solidary social relationships. Tocqueville had already warned that materialism and egoism triggered by too much competition would threaten the moral base for political democracy.[15]

We suggest that what Durkheim depicted as a pathological but possibly temporary cultural condition is in fact compatible with an ongoing institutional order. As noted above, the emergence of the new forms of social solidarity predicated upon a moral individualism presupposes the effective operation of the restructured agents of social control and moral guidance—the family, the schools, the democratic state, and other entities associated with civil society. However, as described by IAT, economic dominance in the institutional balance of power implies that these sources of effective social control and moral guidance are rendered relatively impotent. The type of individualism that emerges along with the erosion of collectivism as societies become more highly differentiated is thus likely to give increasing weight to the "egoistic" form rather than the "moral" or "cooperative" form. Moreover, under these conditions, egoistic individualism at the level of cultural values is likely to go hand in hand with anomie at the level of normative regulation. The values of this type of individualism do not promote social integration; quite the contrary, they interfere with effective integration and are distinctly disintegrative (Thome 2007). In short, we propose that egoistic or disintegrative individualism provides the cultural foundation for economic dominance in the institutional balance of power and widespread anomie.[16]

A heuristic model of our elaborated formulation of IAT is presented in Table 1. This model highlights the core features of an institutional order that is theorized to be conducive to high levels of violent crime in advanced industrial/post-industrial societies.

---

14 At this point we somewhat expand Durkheim's concept of egoistic individualism so as to bridge the conceptual gap implied in his original distinction between egoistic and anomic suicide. One might refer to this modified concept under the title of "disintegrative individualism" (Thome 2007). Durkheim himself, in several passages of Suicide, constructed tenuous bridges of this kind. See also footnote 16 below.
15 On the causal connections between a culture of competition, social and economic inequality, and violence see also Hagan et al. (1998), Jacobs and Carmichael (2002), Messner (2003b), and Pescosolido and Rubin (2000). An interesting approach to studying the anomic consequences of highly

marketized societies is also offered by Burkatzki (2007); see also the Burkatzki paper in this issue. Studying data from European surveys conducted in 1969 and repeated in 1990, David Halpern (2001) finds evidence for increasing importance attached to "self-interest." He also finds a rather strong positive relationship between aggregated self-interest and national victimization rates, particularly when combined with relatively high level of social inequality. It fits into this picture that of all the various types of criminal violence robbery rates exhibit the largest increase since the 1960s.

16 Durkheim himself, in his book on suicide, does not interpret egoistic individualism as a force that would promote violence; he views it only as an aggravating condition with respect to suicide. Thome (2004) has argued that Durkheim's reasoning is not convincing on this point. Dicristina (2004) notes that Durkheim concentrates on unpremeditated murder which he could more easily line up with his notion of "passions" presumably preeminent in collectivistic societies. Premeditated murder, instrumental killings, and other forms of intentional assault, however, should be clearly within the reach of egoistic individualism, particularly so if it is joined with anomie in the form of disintegrative individualism.

Table 1: Predicted rates of homicide under varying economic conditions.

Characterization of the institutional order		Predicted aggregate behavioral outcome	
Value foundations:	Type of structural integration:	Degree of regulatory integration:	High levels of criminal violence
Disintegrative (egoistic) individualism	Economic dominance in the institutional balance of power	Tenuous moral authority (anomie) and weak institutional control	

4. Integrating Levels of Analysis

IAT was originally advanced as a distinctively macro-level perspective on the social determinants of crime. The key concepts and processes that constitute the theory pertain to objective properties of large-scale social systems. It is important to recognize, however, that institutions can also be approached from the subjective view of concrete actors, as stressed by Parsons. The institutional dynamics depicted in the heuristic model in Table 1 are ultimately grounded in individual-level processes. Institutions emerge from human agency, and the level of violent crime in a society is ultimately comprised of the aggregated volume of discrete acts of criminal violence. From the vantage point of individual actors, violence might be appealing for a variety of reasons. It might serve the expressive purpose of inflicting harm on others in response to grievances or humiliations, or it might be used for the instrumental purpose of securing compliance from others against their will (Tedeschi and Felson 1994) or eliminating them to obtain some type of external "good." Accordingly, in the absence of salient normative considerations and moral obligations, the likelihood that violence enters into social interaction increases.

IAT implies that the probability of selecting violent means that are proscribed by the criminal law will be related to actors' orientations towards the institutional norms, their valuation of economic roles and goals relative to non-economic roles and goals, and their "performance repertoires" of economic and non-economic roles and the resources available to them. With respect to orientations towards norms, the distinctive prediction to be derived from IAT is

that the likelihood of criminal violence will be high when actors are not particularly sensitive to the moral status of the means of action in general. Such actors will lack strong internal controls against the use of whatever means are expedient in pursuit of their goals, including violent means.

We emphasize the reference to the means of action in general in the formulation of our hypothesis. The prediction that the strength of allegiance to a specific legal norm is related to the probability of violating that norm is certainly plausible but is not particularly original. This prediction could be readily translated into the "belief" element of conventional social bonding theory (Hirschi 1969). Moreover, the connection between beliefs and violent crime becomes tautological if the committing of the crime is regarded as definitive evidence of the lack of allegiance to the corresponding criminal law. Persons commit acts of criminal violence when they have little respect for the laws prohibiting such violence; the lack of such respect is manifested in the violation of the criminal laws. The novel and testable prediction to be derived from IAT, in contrast, pertains to the "spillover" effect hypothesized as characteristic of a situation of high anomie. The theory implies that the tendency for actors to adopt a calculative orientation to the selection of means in non-economic but legal realms of life will predict the degree of involvement in criminal violence.

With respect to the relative valuation of institutional roles, the prediction from IAT is that actors who perceive economic roles to be more attractive and more highly valued than non-economic roles are expected to be at comparatively high risk of criminal behavior, including violent crime. Such individuals will not be strongly bonded to conventional society through the diverse array of institutional attachments and will thus be exposed to weak external controls (Hirschi 1969). These perceptions of the relative attractiveness and valuation of institutional roles are likely to be empirically related to, but analytically distinct from, behavioral repertoires. The performances of various types of institutional roles depend not only on subjective evaluations but also the opportunity structures and role demands confronting actors. Accordingly, an additional prediction follows from the vantage point of IAT: actors who tend to privilege economic roles over non-economic roles in their

174

actual role performance, especially under conditions of role conflict, will be more likely to engage in violent crime.

The hypotheses about individual action considered thus far pertain to the balancing and prioritizing of the respective roles considered across distinct institutional domains. We also suggest that the macro-level condition of economic dominance in the institutional balance of power is reflected in the nature of the performance of roles within the institutional complex of the economy itself. Here it is important to recall Parsons' distinction between concrete forms of behavior and the institutional element contained in such behaviors. The performance of economic roles by definition contains a paramount economic element. However, concrete interactions, such as transactions in the marketplace, can and usually do incorporate to varying degrees social elements in addition to the purely economic element.

Fred Block (1990) has proposed the very useful concept of "marketness" to capture variation in the social content of economic activity. Marketness refers to a continuum that essentially reflects the extent to which market transactions are "embedded" in more general social relationships.[17] At one end of the continuum, that of high "marketness," actors are primarily responsive to price signals, and their motivations for the transactions are purely instrumental (1990, 51–54). Actors engage in exchanges that are most rational in terms of an economizing cost/benefit assessment, and the character of these exchanges reflects the orientations of homo economicus. The participants are regarded universalistically; there is little affect involved; and the activity is highly specific to the task at hand. At the other end of the continuum, market transactions are not exclusively economic in character. Considerations other than price come into play, and instrumental motives are blended with expressive motives.

To illustrate, consider the customer of a convenience store who develops an acquaintanceship with the owner and

patronizes that particular establishment despite higher costs of products because the interactions are enjoyable. The "marketness" of the ensuing transactions—the purchase of commodities on the market—has been lessened, although economic institutional roles are nevertheless being enacted. In principle, the nature of involvement of a given member of a society in economic transactions could be characterized with respect to the overall degree of their "marketness" (Block 1990, 56). The associated prediction to be derived from IAT is that persons who exhibit a high degree of "marketness" in their economic transactions will tend to exhibit anomic orientations towards social norms and be at relatively high risk of involvement in criminal violence.

These arguments about the underpinnings of institutional processes in the behaviors of concrete actors suggest an individual-level counterpart to the system-level arguments of IAT elaborated above. The two sets of arguments can be merged into an integrated multi-level model, which is presented schematically in Figure 1. The inner circles represent the realm of individual action, while the outer circles depict the associated properties of the social system. At the level of individual action, our arguments imply that the risks of committing violent crimes will be high for actors: (1) who prioritize economic roles over non-economic roles (perceptually and behaviorally); (2) who are insensitive to the moral status of the means of action; and (3) whose enactment of economic roles is high on the "marketness" continuum. The specific intervening mechanisms are individual-level analogues to the postulated macro-level processes and are the well established proximate causes of crime as enumerated in much conventional criminological theory. Specifically, individuals with the designated orientations to institutional roles and goals, and the designated behavioral repertoires, are expected to have weak internal (moral) controls and weak external institutional controls.

---

17 Block's arguments are informed by the classic work of Karl Polanyi (1957 [1944], 1968 [1947]) on the "disembedding" of economic activity from social relationships as part of the emergence of market capitalist societies. For a discussion of the affinities between Polanyi's ideas and IAT, see Messner and Rosenfeld (2000).

Figure 1: Multi-level model of institutional-anomie theory

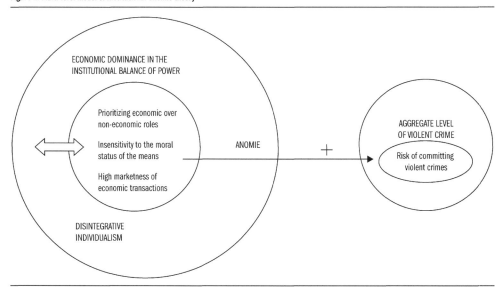

Individual action, of course, is nested within a larger institutional environment. The type of institutional order that is hypothesized to generate the criminogenic individual-level properties in the model is one in which the economy dominates the institutional balance of power, anomie is pervasive, and fundamental cultural values emphasize a disintegrative form of individualism. The institutional environment and action in the form of the enactment of institutional roles and expressions of institutional orientations are themselves mutually constitutive, as reflected in the wide two-headed arrow. Institutions are created collectively by concrete actors, but these creations are in important respects external to any single actor. Finally, the level of violent crime in any society is in the final analysis the simple aggregation of discrete acts of criminal violence.

5. Empirical Applications of IAT at the Macro- and Individual Levels of Analysis

An accumulating body of research offers some support for key claims of IAT. The most common empirical applications of the theory involve efforts to assess the impact of indicators of institutional dynamics on crime at the macro-level. For example, several studies have operationalized "economic dominance" with reference to indicators of social welfare policies and considered how these indicators act in concert with measures of the vitality of non-economic institutions such as family, polity, and school to affect levels of crime. The general conclusion to be drawn from these studies is that the expansiveness and generosity of the welfare state seem to be associated with reduced levels of crime, especially lethal criminal violence, either directly or by mitigating the effects of other criminogenic conditions, such as economic inequality or economic insecurity (Antonaccio and Tittle 2007; Messner and Rosenfeld 1997, 2006; Pratt and Cullen 2005; Savolainen 2000). However, the evidence is mixed, and given the inconsistencies across studies, further efforts along these lines are clearly warranted to generate greater confidence in the utility of IAT as a macro-level sociological explanation of crime.

176

Less attention has been devoted to the cultural dynamics implied by IAT than to the institutional dynamics in the macro-level research. This is not entirely surprising given that cultural phenomena tend not to be recorded and published in standard administrative data sources. Efforts to circumvent these limitations by using the World Values Survey (WVS) to assess claims in IAT have not yielded much support for the theory, although the interpretation of the findings is open to question (Cao 2004; Jensen 2002; Messner and Rosenfeld 2006).

More encouraging results concerning the impact of cultural factors have been reported by Baumer and Gustafson (2007). In a highly innovative analysis, these authors assess key propositions from both IAT and Merton's classic anomie theory (1938) using data on individual value commitments taken from the General Social Survey (GSS) in the United States aggregated to counties and county clusters. By aggregating individual survey responses to the area level, they are able to characterize populations according to theoretically strategic cultural constructs such as the strength of commitment to monetary success goals and the degree of respect for the legitimate means of attaining monetary success. They also include several measures of non-economic institutional strength (e.g., time spent with family, marriage rates, attitudes toward divorce, school expenditures, voter participation, welfare assistance) and examine both main effects and theoretically derived interaction effects. As with most of the research in this field, their analyses yield a complex picture, with some hypotheses receiving support (e.g., a criminogenic effect of a strong commitment to monetary success and a weak commitment to the legitimate means for pursuing success) and others not receiving support (e.g., higher level interactions between cultural orientations and indicators of the vitality of non-economic institutions). Nevertheless, Baumer and Gustafson's research illustrates quite nicely the potential for combining survey-based data with records from administrative sources to assess propositions about both cultural and institutional dynamics derived from IAT.

Efforts to apply IAT at the individual level are quite rare. One notable exception is a study of a minor form of deviance—student cheating—by Muftic (2006). Muftic explicitly sets out to assess the "robustness" of IAT by operationalizing key cultural and institutional variables at the individual level. Her research is based on survey data for a sample of 114 U.S. and 48 foreign-born undergraduates. Muftic creates scales to measure cultural values associated with the American Dream such as individualism, universalism, achievement orientation, and "monetary fetishism." She also constructs indicators of commitment to the family, the educational system, the economy, and the polity.

The results of her analyses provide partial support for hypotheses derived from IAT. "[S]tudents with higher adherence to the cultural values of universalism and the fetishism of money had a higher likelihood of cheating" (2006, 648).[18] In addition, the indicators of commitment to the family and the polity were negatively associated with the probability of cheating, as expected. Hypotheses about interactions between cultural and institutional variables, however, were not supported. The most powerful predictor of self-reported cheating by far was place of birth. The U.S. students were much more likely to report cheating than the foreign-born students.

The most ambitious and sophisticated attempt to apply insights derived from IAT at the individual level is the research by Karstedt and Farrell (2006). They focus on relatively common "morally dubious" acts, which they characterize as the "crimes of everyday life" (2006, 1011). These include behaviors such as avoiding taxes, not paying fees, and claiming benefits, subsidies, and refunds one is not entitled to. Karstedt and Farrell develop an elaborate, integrated analytic framework that combines E. P. Thompson's

---

18 As explicated above, "universalism" also characterizes moral individualism. In our view, it should therefore not be treated as an isolated variable but rather as an element in a broader interactive constellation of values and cognitive orientations.

concept of the "moral economy" with claims from IAT. On the basis of this framework, they theorize that a key determinant of the level of involvement in the crimes of everyday life is the "syndrome of market anomie." This syndrome is conceptualized as a constellation of normative orientations comprised of three dimensions: a lack of trust of others in the marketplace, fears of becoming a victim of disreputable practices of others, and legal cynicism.

Karstedt and Farrell test their hypotheses with survey data collected from random samples of households in England and Wales and the former East and West Germany. They estimate structural equation models to assess the impact of the syndrome of anomie, treated as a multidimensional latent construct, on measures of intentions to engage in the crimes of everyday life. Their results in all three regions are consistent with theoretical expectations. The syndrome of anomie is positively associated with intentions to offend, and this syndrome mediates the effects of other relevant predictors of offending.

6. Directions for Future Research

The research applying IAT has thus been encouraging, but the evidence is obviously quite limited. In particular, applications of the theory to understand individual-level behavior, such as those by Muftic and by Karstedt and Farrell, are rare. We accordingly encourage further efforts along these lines.

We can also propose some new lines of inquiry at the individual level that are suggested by our explication of multilevel linkages above. The prior applications of IAT at the individual level have focused on minor forms of offending—student cheating and morally dubious but common misbehaviors in the marketplace. Our theoretical arguments, however, imply that insensitivity to the moral status of the means is likely to be a generalized phenomenon. It is likely to extend beyond the realm of norms governing instrumental behaviors and culturally prescribed success goals. We therefore predict that indicators of anomie at the individual level, such as Karstedt and Farrell's measures of the syndrome of market anomie, should be capable of explaining involvement in serious forms of non-normative behavior, including (but not limited to) criminal violence.

We also note that prior individual-level research on the institutional determinants of criminal involvement has focused primarily on perceptual and attitudinal measures (see, for example, Muftic 2006, 642). These are intended to capture survey respondents' subjective evaluations of the worth and importance of non-economic institutional roles. While such measures are useful and quite relevant to IAT, it would also be instructive to develop further and incorporate into statistical models indicators of "performance repertoires." Such indicators could be based on accounts of the actual allocation of time devoted to the enactment of roles in the respective institutional domains. In addition, reports of how role conflicts have been resolved in practice would shed light on the extent to which, at the level of individual actors, the economy tends to dominate the institutional balance of power.

It would be quite interesting as well to pursue the line of inquiry suggested by Block (1990) and to attempt to operationalize the "marketness" of economic transactions. Our elaboration of multilevel linkages in IAT stipulates that economic dominance pertains not only to the balancing of roles across institutional domains but also to the manner in which economic roles themselves are enacted. Individual actors can embed their transactions in the marketplace with greater or lesser social content. In principle, it should be possible to measure the extent to which the economic activity of individuals is in practice more or less socially embedded. Our explication of IAT implies that the marketness of transactions should be positively related to anomie, and through anomie, positively related to criminal involvement, including involvement in violent crime.

In carrying out individual- and multi-level research on IAT it will be necessary to include indicators from other theoretical perspectives, some of which are theoretical "close cousins," such as Agnew's general strain theory (1992, 2006), and others seemingly at odds with IAT, such as Gottfredson and Hirschi's general theory of crime (1990). We do not view insensitivity to the moral status of the means of social action, the marketness of social interactions, and the other individual-level attributes and processes we have described as the sole source of individual criminality or

178

necessarily as competing alternatives to indicators derived from other perspectives. They may also interact with indicators from other perspectives such that their effect on criminal behavior depends on the distribution of other factors, for example, suitable criminal opportunities and targets (Cohen and Felson 1979).

The individual-level dimension of IAT, however, does differ from other individual- or micro-level theories in two important and related respects: First, from the perspective of IAT, the individual attributes and repertoires that lead toward or away from criminal behavior arise in and, in turn, reinforce the defining cultural and structural features of whole societies. As such, they should be understood and investigated in multilevel context. Second, the characteristics that distinguish criminals from others in IAT should not be interpreted as signs or symptoms of abnormality, pathology, or other individual deficiencies or defects. On the contrary, they are the normal, expected outcomes of socialization in contexts in which anomie is rampant, non-economic institutions are weak, and disintegrative individualism prevails.

We acknowledge that further theoretical questions remain unanswered in current formulations of IAT. Perhaps one of the most basic questions pertains to the origins of economic dominance or other forms of imbalance in the institutional balance of power. One approach to this issue is to direct attention to the decreasing power of the nation-state and other political institutions to regulate economic processes or to compensate for certain dysfunctional consequences they produce in other spheres of social life.[19] These processes have often been summarized under the heading of "globalization", i.e., the worldwide expansion of markets which has been proceeding during the last three decades at a much greater pace than the internationalization of political decision making (with the development of globally effective democratic control structures lagging even further behind) (Messner and Rosenfeld 2000). Major dimensions and consequences of these processes are: the increase of inequality in income and economic wealth in most societies worldwide (since the late 1970s); increasing poverty rates and social marginalization of growing segments of the population in many of the economically advanced nations; the rearrangement of social welfare regulations moving the social-democratic and the conservative type towards the "liberal" type, with less generous support and an emphasis on rigorous means testing (Esping-Anderson 1990); the increase of antagonistic forms of competition between states (indicated by falling tax rates on capital and business profits) and within states (indicated by increasing rates of insolvencies among businesses and private households as well as an expansion of advertising and marketing strategies); a concomitant decrease in the level of corporatist structures and employment protection; and a decreasing level of trust in government, political parties and parliament. All these developments are likely to be potentially criminogenic (Thome and Birkel 2007).[20]

A final issue that should be addressed by any criminological theory with claims to comprehensiveness is the problem of punishment. Recent scholarship on imprisonment and the "mass incarceration" program in the United States and, to a

---

19 Of course, there is a wide spectrum of ideological positions regarding the desirable degree of the regulatory power of the state. But independent of one's personal ideological position there are clear indications that during the last three decades the state has generally suffered from a loss of (democratic) political control over the economy. This is partly due to technological advancements (particularly in the means of communication) but also by political decision making like the dismantling of the Bretton Woods agreement and the liberalization of the financial markets (pioneered and pushed through mainly by the United States and Great Britain). For an analysis of these developments from a neo-Marxist perspective, see Harvey (2005).

20 Modern versions of systems theory take a completely different approach to the questions that we are addressing. The answers offered (for example, in the work of Niklas Luhmann [1990, 1998]) rest on the assumption that there is an evolutionary process by which social systems become increasingly functionally (rather than segmentally) differentiated thereby forming sub-systems which tend to reach beyond national borders. Though "structurally coupled" they operate autonomously on the basis of "symbolically generalized media of communication" (or "exchange"), each subsystem defined by the use of a dominant medium which it specifically, and in contrast to other subsystems, applies. These are, for example, money in the economic subsystem, power in the political realm, or proven truth in the realm of science. In each subsystem actors seek to maximize their own share of the dominant currency in order to secure or widen their range of future options. Morality "falls behind" in societal evolution because it is not supported by or rooted in a specific social subsystem (Luhmann 1990; 1998, 1036–45); it even tends to disturb smooth operations within these subsystems. Such a system-theoretic framework shares thematic concerns with core claims of IAT about institutional imbalances, and it would be instructive to derive and test formally complementary and competing hypotheses from the respective approaches.

lesser degree, England directs attention to the institutional underpinnings of the punishment process in advanced societies, but does not integrate theories of punishment with theories of crime (Garland 1990; Garland 2001; Sutton 2004). The heavy reliance on formal social control, and specifically imprisonment, as a response to crime is explicable from the perspective of IAT, particularly in its elaborated form presented in this paper. Societies in which "soft" behavioural controls have been vitiated by the institutional dominance of the economy can be expected to rely on imprisonment as a means of final resort to control high levels of violent crime. We can also expect such societies to exhibit an anomic insensitivity to the means by which the collective goal of crime control is attained and, therefore, to pursue punishment policies such as mass incarceration without scruples about the economic, social, and moral costs of escalating rates of imprisonment. At the same time, crime control through mass incarceration is incompatible with a strong cultural emphasis on the moral worth of the individual. In short, the resort to formal social control generally and the adoption of a policy of mass incarceration in particular are consistent with some of the core claims of IAT. One of the most promising aspects of the theory is the possibility of integrating explanations of crime and punishment within a single conceptual framework.

To sum up, IAT remains a work in progress. It emphasizes the importance of the larger institutional and cultural context for understanding crime and violence, and in that sense it seeks to stimulate a thoroughly "sociological" criminology. We argue that it is applicable at multiple levels of analysis, ranging from that of individual action to the dynamics of social systems. However, many core empirical claims have yet to be verified, and key mechanisms associated with the development of forms of social organization that are likely to be more or less criminogenic have yet to be adequately theorized. Nevertheless, we are hopeful that even in its evolving form, IAT will continue to generate fruitful puzzles for criminological theorizing and research.

References

Agnew, Robert. 1992. Foundations for a General Strain Theory of Crime and Delinquency. *Criminology* 30:47–87.

Agnew, Robert. 2006. General Strain Theory: Recent Developments and Directions for Further Research. In *Advances in Criminological Theory, Taking Stock: The Status of Criminological Theory*, volume 15, ed. Francis T. Cullen, John Wright, and Michelle Coleman. New Brunswick: Transaction

Anderson, Elijah. 1999. *Code of the Street: Decency, Violence, and the Moral Life of the Inner City*. New York: Norton.

Antonaccio, Olena, and Charles R. Tittle. 2007. A Cross-National Test of Bonger's Theory of Criminality and Economic Conditions. *Criminology* 45:925–58.

Bauman, Zygmunt. 1990. *Thinking Sociologically*. Oxford: Basil Blackwell.

Baumeister, Roy F., Laura Smart, and Joseph M. Boden. 1996. Relation of Threatened Egotism to Violence and Aggression: The Dark Side of High Self-Esteem. *Psychological Review* 103:5–33.

Baumer, Eric P., and Regan Gustafson. 2007. Social Organization and Instrumental Crime: Assessing the Empirical Validity of Classic and Contemporary Anomie Theories. *Criminology* 45:617–63.

Bellah, Robert N., ed. 1973. *Emile Durkheim on Morality and Society: Selected Writings*. Chicago: University of Chicago Press.

Bellah, Robert N., Richard Marsden, William M. Sullivan, Ann Swidler, and Steven M. Tipton. 1991. *The Good Society*. New York: Knopf.

Block, Fred. 1990. *Postindustrial Possibilities: A Critique of Economic Discourse*. Berkeley: University of California Press.

Burkatzki, Eckhard. 2007. *Verdrängt der Homo oeconomicus den Homo communis? Normbezogene Orientierungsmuster bei Akteuren mit unterschiedlicher Markteinbindung*. Wiesbaden: Deutscher Universitätsverlag.

Cao, Liqun. 2004. Is American Society More Anomic? A Test of Merton's Theory with Cross-National Data. *International Journal of Comparative and Applied Criminal Justice* 28:17–31.

Cohen, Lawrence E., and Marcus Felson. 1979. Social Change and Crime Rate Trends: A Routine Activity Approach. *American Sociological Review* 44:588–607.

Cole, Stephen. 1975. The Growth of Scientific Knowledge: Theories of Deviance as a Case Study. In *The Idea of Social Structure: Papers in Honor of Robert K. Merton*, ed. Lewis A. Coser, 175–220. New York: Harcourt Brace Jovanovich.

Dicristina, Bruce. 2004. Durkheim's Theory of Homicide and the Confusion of the Empirical Literature. *Theoretical Criminology* 8:57–91.

Durkheim, Emile. 1958 [1950]. *Professional Ethics and Civic Morals*. Glencoe, IL: Free Press.

Durkheim, Emile. 1964a [1893]. *The Division of Labor in Society*. New York: Free Press.

Durkheim, Emile. 1964b [1895]. *The Rules of Sociological Method*. New York: Free Press.

Durkheim, Emile. 1966 [1897]. *Suicide: A Study in Sociology*. New York: Free Press.

Durkheim, Emile. 1978 [1895]. Crime and Social Health. In *Emile Durkheim on Institutional Analysis*, ed. Mark Traugott. Chicago: University of Chicago Press.

Eisner, Manuel. 2003a. Long-term Historical Trends in Violent Crime. In *Crime and Justice: A Review of Research*, vol. 30, ed. Michael Tonry, 84–142. Chicago and London: University of Chicago Press.

Eisner, Manuel. 2003b. The Long-term Development of Violence: Empirical Findings and Theoretical Approaches to Interpretation. In *International Handbook of Violence Research*, ed. Wilhelm Heitmeyer and John Hagan, 41–59. Dordrecht, Boston, and London: Kluwer Academic.

Elias, Norbert. 1982 [1939]. *The Civilizing Process*, 2 volumes. Oxford: Basil Blackwell.

Esping-Andersen, Gosta. 1990. *The Three Worlds of Welfare Capitalism*. Princeton: Princeton University Press.

Fenton, Stephen, ed. 1984. *Durkheim and Modern Sociology*. Cambridge: Cambridge University Press.

Garland, David. 1990. *Punishment and Modern Society: A Study in Social Theory*. Chicago: University of Chicago Press.

180

Garland, David. 2001. *The Culture of Control: Crime and Social Order in Contemporary Society.* Chicago: University of Chicago Press.

Gottfredson, Michael and Travis Hirschi. 1990. *A General Theory of Crime.* Stanford: Stanford University Press.

Habermas, Jurgen. 1984. *The Theory of Communicative Action,* translated by Thomas McCarthy. Boston: Beacon.

Hagan, John, Gerd Hefler, Gabriele Classen, Klaus Boehnke, and Hans Merkens. 1998. Subterranean Sources of Subcultural Delinquency: Beyond the American Dream. *Criminology* 36:309–41.

Hall, Peter A., and Daniel W. Gingerich. 2004. *Varieties of Capitalism and Institutional Complementarities in the Macroeconomy: An Empirical Analysis,* Discussion Paper 04/5, ISSN 0944-2073. Cologne: Max-Planck-Institut für Gesellschaftsforschung.

Halpern, David. 2001. Moral Values, Social Trust and Inequality. *British Journal of Criminology* 41:236–51.

Harvey, David. 2005. *A Brief History of Neoliberalism.* Oxford: Oxford University Press.

Hirschi, Travis. 1969. *Causes of Delinquency.* Berkeley: University of California Press.

Jacobs, David, and Jason T. Carmichael. 2002. The Political Sociology of the Death Penalty: A Pooled Time-series Analysis. *American Sociological Review* 67:109–31.

Jensen, Gary. 2002. Institutional Anomie and Societal Variations in Crime: A Critical Appraisal. *International Journal of Sociology and Social Policy* 22:45–74.

Joas, Hans. 1997. *The Creativity of Action,* translated by Jeremy Gaines and Paul Keast. Chicago: University of Chicago Press, co-published with Polity Press.

Karstedt, Susanne. 2001. Individualismus und Gewalt: Extreme Modernisierung oder Re-Traditionalisierung der Gesellschaft? Ein interkultureller Vergleich. In *Gewaltkriminalität zwischen Mythos und Realität,* ed. Günter Albrecht, Otto Backes, and Wolfgang Kühnel, 236–55. Frankfurt am Main: Suhrkamp.

Karstedt, Susanne. 2004. Typen der Sozialintegration und Gewalt: Kollektivismus, Individualismus und Sozialkapital. In *Gewalt: Entwicklungen, Strukturen, Analyseprobleme,* ed. Wilhelm Heitmeyer and Hans-Georg Soeffner, 269–92. Frankfurt am Main: Suhrkamp.

Karstedt, Susanne. 2006. Democracy, Values, and Violence: Paradoxes, Tensions, and Comparative Advantages of Liberal Inclusion. *Annals of the American Academy of Political and Social Science* 605:6–23.

Karstedt, Susanne, and Stephen Farrell. 2006. The Moral Economy of Everyday Crime: Markets, Consumers, and Citizens. *British Journal of Criminology* 46:1011–36.

Lehti, Martti. 2004. Long-Term Trends in Homicidal Crime in Finland 1750–2000. Paper presented at the 3rd GERN Seminar on "Interpersonal Violence." Brussels, December.

Luhmann, Niklas. 1990. *Paradigm Lost: Über die ethische Reflexion der Moral.* Frankfurt am Main: Suhrkamp.

Luhmann, Niklas. 1998. *Die Gesellschaft der Gesellschaft.* Frankfurt am Main: Suhrkamp.

Merton, Robert K. 1938. Social Structure and Anomie. *American Sociological Review* 3:672–82.

Merton, Robert K. 1964. Anomie, Anomia, and Social Interaction. In *Anomie and Deviant Behavior,* ed. Marshall Clinard, 213–42. New York: Free Press.

Merton, Robert K. 1968. *Social Theory and Social Structure.* New York: Free Press.

Messner, Steven F. 2003a. An Institutional-Anomie Theory of Crime: Continuities and Elaborations in the Study of Social Structure and Anomie. *Cologne Journal of Sociology and Social Psychology* 43:93–109.

Messner, Steven F. 2003b. Understanding Cross-National Variation in Criminal Violence. *International Handbook of Violence Research,* ed. Wilhelm Heitmeyer and John Hagan, 701–16. Dordrecht, Boston, and London: Kluwer Academic.

Messner, Steven F., and Richard Rosenfeld. 1997. Political Restraint of the Market and Levels of Criminal Homicide: A Cross-National Application of Institutional-Anomie Theory. *Social Forces* 75:1393–1416.

Messner, Steven F., and Richard Rosenfeld. 2000. Market Dominance, Crime, and Globalization. In *Social Dynamics of Crime and Control: New Theories for a World in Transition,* ed. Susanne Karstedt and Kai-D Bussman, 13–23. Portland: Hart Publishing.

Messner, Steven F., and Richard Rosenfeld. 2004. Institutionalizing Criminological Theory. In *Beyond Empiricism: Institutions and Intentions in the Study of Crime,* vol. 13 of Advances in Criminological Theory, ed. Joan McCord, 83–105. Piscataway, NJ: Transaction.

Messner, Steven F., and Richard Rosenfeld. 2006. The Present and Future of Institutional Anomie Theory. In *Taking Stock: The Status of Criminological Theory,* vol. 15 of Advances in Criminological Theory, ed. Francis T. Cullen, John Paul Wright, and Kristie R. Blevins, 127–148. New Brunswick: Transaction.

Messner, Steven F., and Richard Rosenfeld. 2007. *Crime and the American Dream,* 4th ed. Belmont: Wadsworth.

Muftic, Lisa R. 2006. Advancing Institutional Anomie Theory: A Microlevel Examination Connecting Culture, Institutions, and Deviance. *International Journal of Offender Therapy and Comparative Criminology* 50:630–53.

Nisbett, Richard E., and Dov Cohen. 1996. *Culture of Honor: The Psychology of Violence in the South.* Boulder: Westview.

North, Douglass C. 1990. *Institutions, Institutional Change and Economic Performance.* Cambridge: Cambridge University Press.

Parsons, Talcott. 1951. *The Social System.* New York: Free Press.

Parsons, Talcott. 1990 [1934]. "Prolegomena to a Theory of Social Institutions." *American Sociological Review* 55:319–33.

Pescosolido, Bernice A., and Beth A. Rubin. 2000. The Web of Group Affiliations Revisited: Social Life, Postmodernism, and Sociology. *American Sociological Review* 65:52–76.

Polanyi, Karl. 1957 [1944]. *The Great Transformation: The Political and Economic Origins of Our Time.* Boston: Beacon.

Polanyi, Karl. 1968 [1947]. Our Obsolete Market Mentality. In *Primitive, Archaic, and Modern Economics: Essays of Karl Polanyi,* 59–77. Garden City: Anchor.

Pratt, Travis C., and Francis T. Cullen. 2005. Assessing Macro-Level Predictors and Theories of Crime: A Meta-Analysis. In *Crime and Justice: A Review of Research,* vol. 32, ed. Michael H. Tonry, 373–450. Chicago: University of Chicago Press.

Rosenfeld, Richard, and Steven F. Messner. Forthcoming. The Normal Crime Rate, the Economy, and Mass Incarceration: An Institutional-Anomie Perspective on Crime-Control Policy. In *Criminology and Public Policy: Putting Theory to Work,* ed. Scott H. Decker and Hugh Barlow. Philadelphia: Temple University Press.

Roth, Randolph. 2001. Homicide in Early Modern England, 1549–1800: The Need for a Quantitative Synthesis. *Crime, Histoire & Sociétiés / Crime, History & Societies* 5:33–67.

Ruggiero, Guido. 1980. *Violence in Early Renaissance Venice.* New Brunswick: Rutgers University Press.

Savolainen, Jukka. 2000. Inequality, Welfare State, and Homicide: Further Support for the Institutional Anomie Theory. *Criminology* 38:1021–42.

Siaroff, Alan. 1999. Corporatism in 24 Industrial Democracies: Meaning and Measurement. *European Journal of Political Research* 36: 175–205.

Spierenburg, Pieter, ed. 1998. *Men and Violence: Gender, Honor, and Rituals in Modern Europe and America.* Columbus: Ohio State University Press.

Sutton, John R. 2004. The Political Economy of Imprisonment in Affluent Western Democracies, 1960–1990. *American Sociological Review* 69:170–89.

Tedeschi, James T., and Richard B. Felson. 1994. *Violence, Aggression, and Coercive Actions.* Washington, DC: American Psychological Association.

Thome, Helmut. 2002. Kriminalität im Deutschen Kaiserreich, 1883–1902. Eine sozialökologische Analyse. *Geschichte und Gesellschaft* 28:519–53.

Thome, Helmut. 2003. Das Konzept sozialer Anomie als Analy-
    seinstrument. In *Diktatur, Demokratisierung und soziale
    Anomie*, ed. P. Waldmann, 37–59. Munich: Vögel.
Thome, Helmut. 2004. Theoretische Ansätze zur Erklärung langfris-
    tiger Gewaltkriminalität seit Beginn der Neuzeit. In *Gewalt: Ent-
    wicklungen, Strukturen, Analyseprobleme*, ed. W. Heitmeyer and
    H.-G. Soeffner, 315–45. Frankfurt am Main: Suhrkamp.
Thome, Helmut. 2007. Explaining the Long-Term Trend in Violent
    Crime: A Heuristic Scheme and Some Methodological Consider-
    ations. *International Journal of Conflict and Violence* 1:185–202.
Thome, Helmut, and Christoph Birkel. 2007. *Sozialer Wandel und Ge-
    waltkriminalität: Deutschland, England und Schweden im Vergleich,
    1950 bis 2000*. Wiesbaden: VS Verlag für Sozialwissenschaften.
Turner, Jonathan. 2003. *Human Institutions: A Theory of Soci-
    etal Evolution*. Landham, MD: Rowman & Littlefield.
Turner, Stephen P., ed. 1993. *Émile Durkheim: Sociolo-
    gist and Moralist*. London: Routledge.
Varga, Ivan. 2006. Social Morals, the Sacred and State Regula-
    tion in Durkheim's Sociology. *Social Compass* 54 (4): 457–66.
Wolfe, Alan. 1989. *Whose Keeper? Social Science and Moral Ob-
    ligation*. Berkeley: University of California Press.
Ylikangas, Heikki. 2001. What Happened to Violence? In *Five Centuries of
    Violence in Finland and the Baltic Area*, History of Crime and Crimi-
    nal Justice Series, 1–84. Columbus: Ohio State University Press.
Young, Michael. 1958. *The Rise of Meritocracy: 1870–2033: An Es-
    say on Education and Equality*. London: Thames and Hudson.
Zimbardo, Phillip G., Craig Haney, W. Curtis Banks, and David Jaffe.
    1974. The Psychology of Imprisonment: Privation, Power and Pa-
    thology. In *Doing Unto Others: Explorations in Social Behavior*,
    ed. Z. Rubin, 61–73. Englewood Cliffs, NJ: Prentice-Hall.

Steven F. Messner
sfm96@albany.edu

Helmut Thome
helmut.thome@soziologie.uni-halle.de

Richard Rosenfeld
Richard_Rosenfeld@umsl.edu

Name Index